MURDER INK

MURDER INK

THE MYSTERY READER'S COMPANION

PERPETRATED BY DILYS WINN

EDWARD GOREY

WORKMAN PUBLISHING NEW YORK

Murder Ink.® is the registered trademark of Carol Brener
under U.S. Trademark Registration No. 1,085,081 for a retail bookstore and
related entertainment services.

Library of Congress Cataloging in Publication Data
Main entry under title:
Murder Ink.
Includes index.
1. Detective and mystery stories, English—Miscel-
lanea. 2. Detective and mystery stories, American—
Miscellanea. I. Winn, Dilys.
PR830.D4MS   823'.0872   77-5282
ISBN 0-517-347857

Workman Publishing Company, Inc.
1 West 39th Street
New York, New York 10018

Manufactured in the United States of America
First printing September 1977
10 9 8 7 6 5 4

Cover photograph: Jerry Darvin
Designer: Paul Hanson

Dedication

Imagine, if you will, a Mission oak desk. Now, cover it with want lists and order forms and surround it with floor to ceiling bookcases. Behind it, seat a slim, graceful woman who loves mysteries so much, she owns a bookstore devoted to them. Her name is Carol Brener and her business life is a series of "Carol, what should I read next?" and "Carol, tell me your favorites" and "Carol, could we swap places?"

In effect, she and I did swap places. She had written a book, then decided she wanted to be a mystery store proprietor; I had been a proprietor, then became eager to do a book.

Neither of us could have done it without the other, I think, and as my friendly ghost wafts about her bookstore, so her helpful spirit permeates this book.

It is to Carol, therefore, that *Murder Ink* is dedicated. And it is on both our behalves that I thank the contributors, friends all, who have made the book and the bookstore our delight.

Indebtedness

Murder Ink is beholden to the imagination of Carolyn Fiske, Kathy Dean, Ben Matteson and the entire wacky staff at Mohonk Mountain House, New Paltz, New York; to the generosity of Marvin Epstein, Otto Penzler and Tina Serlin, who let us photograph parts of their libraries; to the midnight oil burned by researchers Archer Brown, Donna Dennis (photography), Marvin Epstein, Marie Gilmore, David James, Ben Kane, Betsy Lang, Marvin Lachman, Catherine Prezzano and Charles Shibuk; to the equanimity of Trade Composition, which made crises enjoyable and deadlines possible; to the gentle blue pencil and immaculate logic of Lynn Strong.

Most especially, Murder Ink is indebted to the maniacal humor and fail-safe supervision of Sally Kovalchick.

CONTENTS

1. THE MYSTERY HISTORY

Tracking the Genre

Nick, Nora and Asta

MARTY NORMAN

The Mystery Bookcase

The Mystery Critic

Wilkie Collins

2. PERPETRATORS

Combination Hearse and Chapel

3. BLOODHOUNDS

4. PRIVATE EYES AND SPIES

The American Tough Guy

The Trench

MARTY NORMAN

Foreign Intrigue

5. VICTIMS

Say Goodbye

Means to an End

Has-Beens

The Late Lady Teasdale

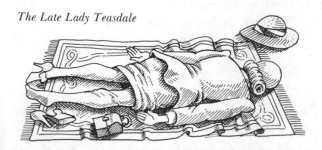

6. MODUS OPERANDI

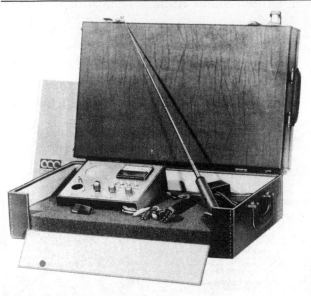

Debugging Equipment

7. SCENES OF THE CRIME

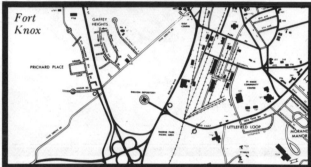

Fort
Knox

8. RED HERRINGS

English Deceit

American Treachery

9. COPS AND BOBBIES

The American Cop

*New York's
Finest*

11. MOUTHPIECES

12. CAUGHT IN THE ACT

Sing Sing

The Good Old Days of Radio

13. ACCESSORIES AFTER THE FACT

Sigmund Freud and His Father

Defining the Mystery Reader

1	2	3	4	5	
8			9		10

Fantasizing About Mysteries

Contacting Your Favorite Author

14. LOOKING FOR (MORE) TROUBLE

Ask An Expert

Find a Hobby

Develop a Personality

Sergeant Cuff

MARTY NORMAN

Introduction

On June 14, 1972, I opened a book-store. On June 15, I considered changing its name. Murder Ink, the mystery bookstore, had seemed perfectly straightforward to me, but not one person who came through the door agreed with me as to what it really meant.

I developed a pat little speech: No, the store is not a "front" for the real Murder, Incorporated; no, there doesn't have to be a dead body in a book for me to carry it; no, I don't think I'm furthering the cause of crime by emphasizing novels concerned with it.

Gradually, customers' questions changed. In fact, so did the customers. No longer did Murder Ink receive the off-the-street trade. Instead, the people the store was intended for started coming in — the mystery fans.

Their queries were more sophisticated: Did I happen to know the requirements for becoming a private investigator? Did Nero Wolfe's brownstone have a front stoop or not? Why were microdots so frequently hidden on beauty spots? If I decided to burgle Fort Knox, how would I go about it? How many little grey cells did Poirot have? Where did the term "red herrings" originate? Did they still use toe tags at the morgue? Had I ever met Conan Doyle, Dorothy L. Sayers, Donald E. Westlake? Could I name all the winners of the Edgar for best mystery of the year? Where did English barristers get their wigs? Was there a mystery in which the butler actually did do it? How much would a first edition of *The Murders in the Rue Morgue* cost, and where could they find one? What's the best way to dispose of the body? Who weighs more, Bertha Cool or Gideon Fell? Was there a real St. Mary Mead? Had I ever known a courier, a safe-cracker, a stool pigeon, a dog that didn't bark? Which would I rather be, a cat burglar or a getaway-car driver? And hardest to handle of them all — please, would I define the mystery?

Many of the harder questions I couldn't answer, but on lucky days there'd be someone in the store who'd speak right up. These knowledgeable customers — some of them mystery writers, some of them hotel dicks and police sociologists and civil liberties lawyers, some of them "merely" mystery book fans — are the same ones I have turned to in compiling *Murder Ink*.

It is an attempt to answer the most frequently asked questions, to make the reader

> *i Don't do*
> *much readIng*
> *(though this Last*
>   *Year i went all the way*
> *through finneganS*
>   *Wake).*
>   *I "save" my eyes for my work.*
>   *i Never*
>   *got iNto mystery books,*
> *even though i reaD*
>   *once upon a tIme*
> *one with nero woLfe in it.*
>   *mY notion*
>   *iS*
>   *that mystery's What*
>   *lIfe is:*
>   *we Need*
>   *Not to know.*

JOHN CAGE

an armchair participant in some of those discussions. That's why *Murder Ink* is called the mystery reader's companion.

Not all the articles deal with the mystery stories themselves. Some spring from the fantasies the books promote. To wit, if I ever met Holmes, what would I say to him? If I stole a paint chip from Lizzie Borden's house, how would I feel? What would I serve my victim for his very last meal? How would I go about writing a ransom note, using a blunt instrument, curing a Chandler-size hangover?

There have, of course, been many fine books on the origin of the mystery, its characters and its authors. But no one has tackled the fun of mystery. No one has tried to integrate a fan's fantasies with his love of the books and his desire to know where they depart from real life. That little niche, I think, belongs solely to *Murder Ink,* which has arranged this special meeting between the readers and the writers, the facts and the fantasies, and in the process had a very good time of it.

I would hope that *Murder Ink* has not forgotten anything you've been dying *(sic)* to know. That would be a crime.

Dilys Winn

Chapter 1

THE MYSTERY HISTORY

FROM POE TO THE PRESENT

Dilys Winn

CULVER PICTURES

I have an untidy mind. It confuses dates, misspells names, amalgamates plots and mangles facts. And it does it unrepentantly, presenting its little distortions as Gospel when, in fact, they're fibs. For years I attributed the first mystery to Carolyn Keene, Nancy Drew's creator, even though I knew full well a gentleman named Poe deserved the credit. I'd read Keene first, and according to my personal mystery chronology she rated the honor.

For solid research, I defer to Howard Haycraft. Now, in a handsome retirement community in south Jersey, Mr. Haycraft and his wife spend quiet afternoons thunking the croquet ball through the wickets. But back in '41 Mr. Haycraft authored *Murder for Pleasure,* the definitive mystery history, followed it up with *The Art of the Mystery Story,* the definitive mystery anthology, and then, with the assistance of Ellery Queen, issued his definitive mystery list, *The Haycraft-Queen Definitive Library of Detective-Crime-Mystery Fiction.* The list still stands as the best ever done, and Messrs. Hay-

craft and Queen were kind enough to let *Murder Ink* reprint it.

I hope Mr. Haycraft won't think it bad manners if I approach things a little differently. Where he is orderly, I am not. Where he tells how, when, why, what, in chronological sequence, I crave a hodgepodge history that pairs books of similar type rather than similar birth date.

I recognize five basic mystery categories: the Cozy, the Paranoid, the Romantic, the Vicious, the Analytical. (This leaves me no place for Rex Stout, but never mind; he really deserves a category unto himself.)

Of course, the Doyenne of Coziness is Agatha Christie, and the first book in the canon is *The Mysterious Affair at Styles.* Coziness, however, took another ten years to reach full kitsch, which happened when Miss Marple arrived in *The Murder at the Vicarage.* Alternately titled the Antimacassar-and-old-Port School, the Cozies surfaced in England in the mad Twenties and Thirties, and their work featured a small village

THE DETECTIVE LINE-UP

| *Best-Preserved* | *Wettest* | *Fattest* | *Most Chic* | *Tiredest* |
| JUDGE DEE | MAIGRET | NERO WOLFE | ASTA | MARTIN BECK |

MARTY NORMAN

setting, a hero with faintly aristocratic family connections, a plethora of red herrings and a tendency to commit homicide with sterling silver letter openers and poisons imported from Paraguay. Typical Cozy writers include: Elizabeth Lemarchand, Margaret Yorke, V.C. Clinton-Baddeley, Anne Morice, Michael Gilbert, Michael Innes, Edmund Crispin. (And I've limited myself to those authors still in print: why suggest ones who defy disinterment?)

Special mention must be made of a Pseudo-Cozy: Dorothy L. Sayers. She teaches peculiar subjects (such as the art of bell-ringing) while she mystifies. Many Cozy readers appreciate this, and it's not uncommon to hear them remark, "Oh, I like a good read where I learn something. Mysteries teach me things!"

The Paranoid School began with Erskine Childers' spy novel, *The Riddle of the Sands,* and progressed through Sapper, through Ambler and Le Carré, to the Paranoid Politicals of Robert Ludlum. The archetypal Paranoid is Paul Kavanagh's *Such Men Are Dangerous.* These books are characterized by a mistrust of everybody, particularly one's "control." Nothing dates faster than a Paranoid novel: this year it's chic to be wary of the Chinese; last year, the Arabs; the year before, the South Africans. Often, Paranoids are concerned with the reemergence of Nazis (e.g., Levin's *The Boys from Brazil*). Though not strictly Paranoid, the Dick Francis books belong in this category because of the hero's sentimentality. Paranoid books represent the largest-selling category of mystery fiction today.

The Romantics are one part supernatural to two parts warped intuition. The father of the Romantic novel is Wilkie Collins, and his *Woman in White* remains the classic in the genre. These books, under Mary Roberts Rinehart's supervision, evolved into the Had-I-But-Known School. From the Fifties on, the Romantic converted to the Damsel-in-Distress novel, typified by the works of Phyllis A. Whit-

ney, Mary Stewart and Barbara Michaels.

An aberrant strain of the Romantic is the Romantic Suspense, championed by Helen MacInnes. As her books are old-fashioned (Communism is a passé devil), she has been supplanted by Evelyn Anthony (who has stolen a leaf from the Paranoids and on occasion has gone after Nazism). A variant is the Historical Romantic Suspense. This is a splinter group: the Genuine Historical (i.e., any book written before 1918) and the Ersatz (written post–

BOOKS TO BE READ ALOUD

Anything by George V. Higgins. If you try to read these to yourself, you wind up moving your lips. Mr. Higgins loves dialogue, but it looks unintelligible on the page. It comes to life when you actually repeat the words. They are not the words, however, you would most want a maiden auntie to hear, nor kids under twelve. We suggest you read them out between deals in the poker game.

Wilkie Collins

Anything by Wilkie Collins. Draw your chair close to the fire and gather the family round. These are old-fashioned stories with hammy, improbable plots that somehow sound wonderful if you pretend you're Lunt and Fontaine and emote for all you're worth. So much the better if it's storm-

ing outside, the phone wires are down and you have to read by gaslight. A lap rug thrown over your knees is not inappropriate, either.

Anything by Stanley Ellin. Whenever anyone tells you mystery writers can't write, sit him down and read Stanley Ellin to him. Mr. Ellin is clear, direct and chilling. What's more, he is one of the few writers who has something to say to hard-boiled fans as well as classicists. His best for reading-aloud purposes: *Stronghold*.

Anything by Margaret Millar. You know how some people just seem to have the knack of saying things that get under your skin? Millar hooks you in the first paragraph. You might just as well begin reading her with someone else, or you're going to spend all your time chasing after friends saying, "Listen to this," and then reading great chunks of books aloud to them.

Anything by Dashiell Hammett. Take your Chandler friend by the hand, put a piece of tape over his mouth, and tell him to just shut up and hear how it ought to be done. Hammett's style does not date, as does Chandler's and *The Glass Key* puts to shame every other hard-boiled writer.

World War I but depicting the past).

Which brings us round to the Vicious. Carroll John Daly elbowed it onto the scene in the late 1920's with hero Race Williams, but in truth a non-writer, Capt. Shaw of *Black Mask* magazine, was the man responsible for the genre's impact. These books all have a male protagonist, back-alley slang, enough booze to float the *Titanic* and a distressing way of blaming (1) the business partner or (2) the dame's father. Their partisans think of them as realistic. The best, bar none, of the Vicious writers

500 CLUB

Only two authors have written over 500 books: John Creasey and Charles Hamilton. There are over 500 books by Nicholas Carter, but Nicholas Carter was more than one person. It was a name assigned to a series of writers who were responsible for the exploits of one Nick Carter. The publisher passed the name on from writer to writer.

was Dashiell Hammett; the worst, Mickey Spillane. Others include Chandler, Higgins, Leonard and Stark.

The Analytical School has the longest history. It began in 1841 with an errant orang-utan stuffing a young girl up a chimney in Poe's *The Murders in the Rue Morgue*, where the solution was resolved by a process called ratiocination — a 50¢ word for logical thinking. The Analytical then forked into Reasoning by Intellect and Reasoning by Machine: the former, from Poe direct to Conan Doyle to Carr; the latter, from Freeman to Reeves to McBain.

Cross-reading among the categories is rare. A Cozy reader will semi-comfortably pick up an Analytical but hardly admit that a Paranoid is part of the field. Similarly, a Romantic reader will sniff at the Vicious and insist they're outside the genre. According to Mr. Haycraft (and me), any book that focuses on crime is a mystery. So, readers should stop quibbling. This endless discussion of what belongs is really unnecessary; there's room for almost any style, as long as it concerns an evil. One could even make a case for calling *Crime and Punishment* a mystery. And who knows what lurks in next year?

Naturally, I have a preference. I can't tell you why I chose it, but I can say this: My methods of dealing with people who disagree with me are not pleasant.

HALL OF INFAMY

(THE TEN WORST)

1. *The Mind Readers* by Margery Allingham
2. *Trent's Last Case* by E.C. Bentley
3. *The Hungry Goblin* by John Dickson Carr
4. *Playback* by Raymond Chandler
5. *Elephants Can Remember* by Agatha Christie
6. *Valley of Fear* by Arthur Conan Doyle
7. *The Defection of A.J. Lewinter* by Robert Littell
8. *When in Rome* by Ngaio Marsh
9. *Busman's Honeymoon* by Dorothy L. Sayers
10. *The President Vanishes* by Rex Stout

(THE FIVE BEST)

1. *The Daughter Of Time* by Josephine Tey
2. *The Thirty-First of February* by Julian Symons
3. *Time and Again* by Jack Finney
4. *Who is Lewis Pindar?* by L.P. Davies
5. *The Glass Key* by Dashiell Hammett

HEARING VOICES IN MY HEAD

Tucker Coe, Timothy J. Culver, Richard Stark and Donald E. Westlake

Recently gathered with a moderator inside a Japanese-made cassette recorder to discuss the state of their art were Donald E. Westlake, Richard Stark, Tucker Coe and Timothy J. Culver.

MODERATOR: The mystery story, detective thriller, *roman policier,* call it what you will, has been a basic influence in the history of fiction since the days of Greece and Rome. While Edgar Allan Poe is the acknowledged father of the modern detective story, it is still true that *Oedipus Rex* is a seminal mystery tale. Today's novelists of crime, passion, suspense, can with pride count Shakespeare, Dostoevsky and the Brothers Grimm among their family tree. Tucker Coe, what do *you* think of all this?

TUCKER COE: Sounds terrific.

MODERATOR: Ah. Yes. I see. Well, umm . . . Richard Stark. As an —

RICHARD STARK: Present.

MODERATOR: Yes. As an innovator in the crime field, suspense story, call it what you will, what would you say is the outlook for the mystery tale? You have been —

RICHARD STARK: Well, I think —

MODERATOR: — an innovator, of course, in that you created Parker, a professional thief who never gets caught. Also, he is not merely a thinly disguised battler for the underdog, as were Robin Hood or The Saint or The Green Hornet. Parker's reaction to the underdog would probably have been to kick it. Having yourself altered the thriller or mystery form, what would you say are the portents for tomorrow?

RICHARD STARK: Well, I suppose —

MODERATOR: People have declared the detective novel, the murder story itself, dead, murdered by repetition, staleness, a using up of all the potentials of the form, replaced by who knows what public fancies, whether for Comedy, History, Pastoral, Pastoral-Comical, Historical-Pastor —

RICHARD STARK: Say, wait a minute.

MODERATOR: Or, let us say, the Western, Science Fiction, the Family Saga. Nevertheless, the crime/suspense/mystery/thriller story, the tale of ratiocination, call it what you will, has continued to flourish, much like the Grand Old Lady of the Theater, the Broadway Stage, which so often has —

RICHARD STARK: Listen.

MODERATOR: — been reported dead. But, if we may borrow a phrase, Watchman, what of the night? What do *you* think tomorrow will bring to the thriller, the detective —

RICHARD STARK: *I* think it's —

MODERATOR: — story, the *roman noir,* the 'tec tale, call it what you —

RICHARD STARK: Listen, you. Either I get to *answer* that question or I'll damage you.

MODERATOR: — will, the essential — Eh? Oh, yes. Certainly.

RICHARD STARK: Right. Now. Uhh — What was the question?

MODERATOR: Well, the gist of the —

RICHARD STARK: Not you. Tim?

TIMOTHY J. CULVER: Future of the mystery.

RICHARD STARK: Right. There isn't any.

MODERATOR: There isn't any?

RICHARD STARK: The detective story died about thirty years ago, but that's okay. Poetry died *hundreds* of years ago and there're still poets. By "die," by "dead," I mean as a hot center of public interest. In the Thirties you could still have whodunits, real honest-to-God *detective* stories, on the best-seller lists. Ellery Queen, for instance. The detective story was hot when science was new, with gaslight and then electricity, telephones, automobiles, everything starting up, the whole *world* seeming to get solved all at once, in one life span. World War II shifted the emphasis from gaining knowledge to what you'd do with the knowledge, which is kill people. So the big postwar detective was Mike Hammer, who couldn't *deduce* his way up a flight of stairs, and the emphasis shifted from whodunit to who's-gonna-get-it. The Mike Hammer thing leads into all these paperback hobnail vigilantes with their *Thesaurus* names: the Inflictor, the Chastiser, the Flagellator. Deduction, the solving of a mystery — they don't even put in a token appearance any more.

MODERATOR: But does that mean you yourself have given up the mystery field, thriller field, whatever label you may choose —

RICHARD STARK: Grrrrrrrr.

MODERATOR: Sorry. But no new Parker novel has been published since 1974. *Have* you

given up writing crime novels, thrillers, or — um.

RICHARD STARK: Parker is a Depression character, Dillinger mythologized into a machine. During the affluent days of the Sixties he was an interesting fantasy, but now that money's getting tight again his relationship with banks is suddenly both to the point and old-fashioned. He hasn't yet figured out how to operate in a world where heisting *is* one of the more rational responses to the situation.

MODERATOR: Tucker Coe, do you agree?

TUCKER COE: Well, yes and no, I suppose. In a way. Looking at all sides of the issue, *without* becoming overly involved in a too personal way, if we could avoid that, insofar as it's ever really possible to avoid personal involvement in a discussion of one's own work, I suppose the simple answer is that for *me* the detective story was ultimately too restricting. Others, of course, might find possibilities I missed. I'm sure they will, and the problem was as much in me as in the choice of character and genre.

MODERATOR: Would you care to amplify that, to give us further insights into —

RICHARD STARK: Watch it. Go ahead, Tuck.

TUCKER COE: Thanks. The problem for me was that Mitch Tobin wasn't a static character. For him to remain miserable and guilt-racked forever would have changed him into a self-pitying whiner. My problem was, once Mitch Tobin reaches that new stability and becomes functional in the world again, he's merely one more private eye with an unhappy past. Not to name names, but don't we have *enough* slogging private eyes with unhappy pasts?

MODERATOR: But surely the detective story has been used as a vehicle for exploring character. Nedra Tyre, for instance. Patricia Highsmith, Raymond Chandler.

RICHARD STARK: His sentences were too fat.

MODERATOR: But wasn't he interested in character?

RICHARD STARK: He was interested in literature. That's the worst thing that can happen to a writer.

TIMOTHY J. CULVER: I couldn't agree more.

And let me say, I speak from a different perspective from everybody else here. These guys all write what *they* want to write, I write what *other people* want me to write. I'm a hack, I'm making a living, I'm using whatever craft I've learned to turn out decently professional work that I'm not personally involved with. In my opinion, the best writers are always people who don't care about anything except telling you what's in their heads, *without boring you*. Passion, plus craft. The Continental Op didn't have to have a miserable home life or a lot of character schticks because Hammett could fill him up with his own reality.

MODERATOR: But mystery novelists are nevertheless commercial writers, aren't they? Mr. Culver, I don't entirely follow the distinction you're making.

TIMOTHY J. CULVER: The difference between a hack and a writer is that the hack puts down on paper things he doesn't believe. Dick Stark mentioned Mike Hammer. Now, Mickey Spillane wasn't a hack, not then at least, and that's because he really *believed* all that paranoid crap. But the thousand imitators didn't believe it. You know, one time I was talking to a professor at the University of Pennsylvania, and he had to leave the party early to go work on an article for one of the scholarly journals. I asked him what it was about, and he said it didn't matter, just some piece of crap. "But I have to keep turning them out if I want tenure," he said. "It's pretty much publish or perish in this business." "It's about the same in mine," I told him.

MODERATOR: Frankly, Mr. Culver, you sound to me like a cynic.

TIMOTHY J. CULVER: I act based on my opinion of the world, so I am a realist.

MODERATOR: Donald E. Westlake, from your vantage point, would you say that Mr. Culver seems to be a realist?

DONALD E. WESTLAKE: Sure he is. A realist is somebody who thinks the world is simple enough to be understood. It isn't.

TIMOTHY J. CULVER: I understand it well enough to get by.

DONALD E. WESTLAKE: Meaning you can tie your own shoelaces. Terrific.

MODERATOR: Gentlemen, gentlemen. Um, Mr. Westlake, you yourself began with the traditional detective novels, did you not?

DONALD E. WESTLAKE: The first story I ever wrote was about a professional killer knocking off a Mob boss. I thought it would be nice to make the setting a fancy office, as though the Mob boss were a lawyer or a doctor. I was eleven years old, the story was about two hundred words long, and all that happened was this guy walked in, stepped around the bodyguards, shot the Mob boss at his desk, and then walked out again. But the point was the long detailed description of the office. I was in love with what I suppose was my first discovery as a writer: that there was something marvelous in a contrast between setting and action. A mismatch between What and Where could create interest all by itself. Of course, now I realize it was comedy that had taught me all that — the fart in church, for instance, a favorite among all children — but I never thought comedy was what I was good at. All through school, I was never the funniest kid, I was always the funniest kid's best friend. I was a terrific audience.

MODERATOR: And yet, now you are known primarily as the author of comic caper novels, comedy thrillers, what Anthony Boucher termed the comedy of peril, call it what you will —

DONALD E. WESTLAKE: Taradiddle.

MODERATOR: I beg your pardon?

DONALD E. WESTLAKE: You want me to call these books what I will, and that's what I call them. Taradiddles. Tortile taradiddles.

MODERATOR: Tortile . . .

DONALD E. WESTLAKE: Taradiddles.

MODERATOR: Yes. Well, these, um, things . . . You are primarily known for them, so what led you from ordinary detective stories to these, hm?

DONALD E. WESTLAKE: I couldn't take them seriously any more. I did five books, and started a sixth, and it kept wanting to be funny. As Dick Stark pointed out, there isn't much money in writing mystery novels, so I wasn't risking a lot if I went ahead and wrote it funny. At that time, there weren't any comic mysteries around, so I couldn't prejudge the reception. Craig Rice had been the last comic detective novelist. But ideas and feelings float in the air, and later on it turned out that simultaneously a guy named John Godey, who later became famous for *The Taking of Pelham 1-2-3*, was writing a comic mystery novel called *A Thrill a Minute with Jack Albany*. It constantly happens: writers who don't know one another come up with the same shift in emphasis or the same new subject matter at the same time. We all swim in the same culture, of course.

MODERATOR: Would you say you were influenced by Craig Rice?

DONALD E. WESTLAKE: No, I wouldn't. *She* was influenced by Thorne Smith, who was magnificent, but every time I try to borrow from Thorne Smith the material dies in my hands. It's difficult to be truly whimsical without being arch; I can't do it.

MODERATOR: And P.G. Wodehouse?

DONALD E. WESTLAKE: He couldn't do it, either. That's a minority opinion, of course.

MODERATOR: Would you care to talk about who *has* influenced your work?

DONALD E. WESTLAKE: Not until they're in the public domain.

MODERATOR: I suppose you've been asked where you get your ideas.

DONALD E. WESTLAKE: Never. Who would ask a schmuck question like that?

MODERATOR: I see. Yes. To return to this first, um, tortile — ?

DONALD E. WESTLAKE: *The Dead Nephew.*

MODERATOR: Really? My fact sheet says *The Fugitive Pigeon.*

DONALD E. WESTLAKE: Your fact sheet is on the money. I haven't always been lucky with titles. At the time, I was persuaded to change from the original, but now, sixteen years later, I'd rather be the author of *The Dead Nephew* than *The Fugitive Pigeon.*

MODERATOR: Why?

DONALD E. WESTLAKE: It's funnier and it's

meaner, and therefore more to the point.

MODERATOR: To *return* to the point, you wrote this first tortile taradiddle because you —

DONALD E. WESTLAKE: Nicely done.

MODERATOR: — couldn't — thank you — take the mystery novel seriously any more. Does that mean you agree with Richard Stark about the gloomy future of the crime story, the thriller, the detective novel, call it what you will?

DONALD E. WESTLAKE: Depends on what you call it.

MODERATOR: I beg your pardon?

DONALD E. WESTLAKE: I have a friend, Robert Ludlum, who writes —

TIMOTHY J. CULVER: Name-dropper.

DONALD E. WESTLAKE: — books, and very good books, too, which are full of suspense, mysteries to be solved, murders, detection, crime, chases, *all* the elements of the mystery story. If they were called mysteries or detective stories, if they were placed on the publisher's "Mystery List," they would sell a fraction of what they do. The best-seller list is crammed with sheep in wolves' clothing. Sidney Sheldon, Frederick Forsyth, Jack Higgins under all his many names.

TIMOTHY J. CULVER: You should talk.

DONALD E. WESTLAKE: Tim, you *are* a pest.

TIMOTHY J. CULVER: But indispensable.

DONALD E. WESTLAKE: Like the Sanitation Department. You take the garbage.

MODERATOR: Gentlemen, gentlemen. If mystery novels appear on the best-seller list under another category name, would you be willing to reveal that name?

DONALD E. WESTLAKE: "Blockbuster." You see an ad for a book, it says the book is a blockbuster, that means it's a category crime novel — usually forty thousand words too fat — breaking for the big money.

MODERATOR: Then why aren't *all* mystery novels simply called blockbusters?

DONALD E. WESTLAKE: Because they have to be Fifties mystery novels, full of Kirk Douglas–type characters. If you write Thirties mystery novels, whodunits with puzzles and clever murderers (never killers) and cleverer detectives, or if you write Forties private eye novels — "A mean man walks down these lone streets" — you can't possibly get out of the ghetto.

MODERATOR: What about Ross Macdonald?

DONALD E. WESTLAKE: The former editor of the *New York Times Book Review* has admitted in print that that was the result of a conspiracy, to see if he really *could* boost an author he liked onto the best-seller list. Since he claimed that was the only time such a conspiracy occurred, to his knowledge, Macdonald is a fluke.

MODERATOR: Do you have an opinion about his work?

DONALD E. WESTLAKE: He must have terrific carbon paper.

MODERATOR: You mentioned Thirties, Forties and Fifties crime novels. What about the Sixties?

DONALD E. WESTLAKE: The Sixties crime novel was joky (as opposed to funny), smart-alecky, full of drugs, and self-consciously parading its cast of blacks and homosexuals. The only Sixties mysteries with any merit at all were written in the Fifties by Chester Himes. On the other hand, the Sixties Western was even worse: Remember *Dirty Dingus Magee?*

RICHARD STARK: Okay, this has gone on long enough. Everybody on your feet.

MODERATOR: Good God, he's got a gun!

RICHARD STARK: Empty your pockets onto the table. Come on, snap it up.

TIMOTHY J. CULVER: You can't mean this, Dick. We're your friends.

RICHARD STARK: No book published since '74. How do you think I live? Give me everything you got.

DONALD E. WESTLAKE: Will you take a check?

RICHARD STARK: *Beat the Devil*, 1954, Robert Morley to Humphrey Bogart. They ought to ask *me* where you get your ideas. You, Tucker Coe, on your feet.

MODERATOR: He's not moving, he —

RICHARD STARK: Get him up. You, Moderator.

MODERATOR: He's dead!

TIMOTHY J. CULVER: This waterglass — yes, just as I thought. A rare undetectable South American poison. Tucker Coe has been murdered.

DONALD E. WESTLAKE: I didn't do it!

MODERATOR: Wait a minute. If the poison is undetectable, how do you know that's how he was killed?

TIMOTHY J. CULVER: There isn't a mark on the body, the glass contains a colorless, odorless liquid, and none of us has left the room. Isn't the conclusion obvious?

RICHARD STARK: Let's not forget me over here with my gun. Cough up your money and valuables.

MODERATOR: I can't believe this is happening.

RICHARD STARK: Hey, Culver, *this* is all you got?

TIMOTHY J. CULVER: Realists don't travel with a lot of cash.

RICHARD STARK: You, Moderator, get me the stuff out of Coe's pockets.

MODERATOR: You want me to rob a corpse?

RICHARD STARK: Rob one or be one, the choice is yours. That's better.

TIMOTHY J. CULVER: We'll see about —

MODERATOR: They're struggling! Look out!

RICHARD STARK: You asked for —

MODERATOR: You shot him! Timothy J. Culver is dead!

RICHARD STARK: No mystery about *that* body.

DONALD E. WESTLAKE: I didn't kill Tucker Coe!

RICHARD STARK: Anybody else feel like a hero? No? All right; don't move from this room for thirty minutes.

MODERATOR: Good God! He's getting away!

DONALD E. WESTLAKE: I want to make one thing clear. I didn't kill Tucker Coe.

MODERATOR: We don't dare leave. We have to stay in the room with these two bodies. What can we *do* for the next half-hour?

DONALD E. WESTLAKE: We could play Twenty Questions. I'm thinking of something that's part vegetable and part mineral.

MODERATOR: Oh, shut up.

Tucker Coe's five Chandleresque novels came to an abrupt end about 1970. Timothy J. Culver's only known work, Ex Officio, *was published to universal indifference. Richard Stark's sixteen novels feature Parker, the professional criminal with the heart of granite. Donald E. Westlake's* God Save the Mark *won the Mystery Writers of America Edgar.*

The Most Asked Question:
WHY DO PEOPLE READ DETECTIVE STORIES?

Gladys Mitchell

I suppose one answer to this question is that people read them because other people write them. Why do other people write them? Well, according to Dr. Samuel Johnson, no man ever wrote who did not write for money.

There are those among us who claim that the detective story is a form of escapist literature. Lovers of the genre will deny this, and they are right to do so, for the detective story addict is not content to sit back and enjoy what is called "a cosy read." For full enjoyment of the story, the reader needs to be prepared to use his brains. A problem has been set before him, and the true addict obtains pleasure from doing his best to solve it.

When the Detection Club was formed in London, England, very strict rules were laid down for the members to follow. The first and greatest commandment was that every clue to the identity of the criminal must be placed fairly before the reader. This provided for a true and just battle of wits between reader and author, and this, I think, is one of the main reasons why people prefer those detective stories which keep to the rules.

Here, perhaps, it may be a good thing to repeat an observation which others have stressed. To the uninitiated, all classes of mystery fiction are apt to be classed as "thrillers," but to the intelligentsia the rough-and-ready story of breakneck adventure, car chase, mysterious master criminal, sex, bloodthirstiness and highly coloured heroics is but the bastard brother of the classic whodunit and is not to the taste of the true detective aficionado.

The thriller poses no problem, makes no tax upon the reader except perhaps to find out how much blood and guts he can stomach, so

---

MYSTERY BOOK CLUBS

Detective Book Club
Established in April of 1942, this club offers the famous "triple" volume — three complete mystery novels under one cover. Selections offered on a monthly basis.

Mystery Guild
Presents two feature selections per month, plus alternates, in a lively brochure called "Clues." Most offerings are roughly one-quarter off the publisher's list price.

Thriller Book Club
Developed by Foyle's, London's most famous bookstore, this club features most major authors, with an emphasis on the British.

that its chief merit is to take the reader from his own safe, fireside existence into what P.G. Wodehouse would call "another and a dreadful world." This makes a strong appeal to some minds but is not for the reader of detective stories, except as an occasional relaxation.

Of course, the detective story has changed over the years. Not for nothing did Dorothy L. Sayers call her last full-length Wimsey tale "a love story with detective interruptions." Of old, the purists laid down the axiom that love had no place in a detective story and was nothing but an unnecessary and most undesirable effluent when introduced into those otherwise unpolluted waters. It confused the narrative and dammed the flow of pure reason, for love's

THE PHYSIOLOGY OF READING

All comfy in your chair, are you? Good.

What you are sitting on are your ischial tuberosities. Depending on how fat you are, you may or may not be able to feel them since they are the bones of your, ahem, rear end. They are covered by your gluteus maximus, which is a network of muscle.

If you are sitting in such a position that your feet do not touch the floor, you are undoubtedly tensing your gluteus maximus, which is not such a good idea. You should try to make contact with the floor by putting pressure on your calcanei, commonly called your heel bones. This will relieve the pressure on your rear.

A chair seat should not be so deep as to keep your feet from reaching the floor. On the other hand, it should be deep enough so that it does not cut across the buttock crease, causing pressure on your sciatic foramen.

Should you suffer from coccygodynia, you are experiencing a pain in your coccyx. It is unlikely that this pain is aggravated by reading in a chair, but in the event that you have trouble with it, you are advised to read while sitting on a rubber doughnut.

An unstable point in many people is the junction of the lumbar spine and the sacrum. Unless this is properly supported, you may fall victim to lumbosacral strain (lower back pain). So you should not read in a chair without a backrest — such as a barstool.

A reading chair should have a seat cushion. The back cushion is optional. But again, a fairly high-backed reading chair is a must or you will put undue strain on the articulations of your spinal facets. This means you are not supporting your upper back correctly. May we remind you that with incorrect support you lose your normal lordotic curve. A dire situation indeed.

If you think you can circumvent all these problems by reading in bed, you will be unhappy to learn that that can cause strain on the cervical area. Resulting in a severe pain in the neck. You should sit up in bed, leaning against the headboard, with your feet straight out in front of you. This also protects you from those who would sneak up behind to give you a stout cosh.

Still comfy, are you?

Good. Then we'll leave you to your book.

detractors (so far as the detective story is concerned) can rightly claim that there is nothing so unreasonable, so utterly illogical, as love. The unreasonable and the illogical have no place in a detective story.

Times change, however, and so do the fictional detectives themselves — among whom, I suppose, every one of us has a favourite. The painstaking detective measuring footprints, treasuring cigarette ends, taking fingerprints, is a genuine character in real life and often "gets his man," but in fiction his worthy, molelike activities are apt to give a somewhat dull read. In fact, Edgar Allan Poe described (and, by implication, despised) the fictional use of the method.

> *"You include the* grounds *about the* house?"
>
> *"They gave us comparatively little trouble. We examined the moss between the bricks and found it undisturbed."*
>
> *"You looked among D———'s papers, of course, and into the books of the library?"*
>
> *"Certainly; we not only opened every book, but we turned over every leaf in each volume. We also measured the thickness of every book-cover."*
>
> *"You explored the floors beneath the carpets? . . . and the paper on the walls? . . . You looked into the cellars?"*

This is far removed from the Chestertonian girth and intellect of Dr. Gideon Fell and farther still from "the little grey cells" of Hercule Poirot. Nowadays the gentlemanly detectives, Alleyn, Campion, Wimsey, the don-detective Gervase Fen, the delightful Inspector Ghote, Hillary Waugh's indefatigable policemen baying like hounds on the trail and the quirky legalities in the plots of Cyril Hare have taken over, to some extent, from the older, more plodding sleuths of earlier years.

I am far from believing that people read detective stories in order to learn new methods of committing murder, but it is a fact that, greatly to the author's distress, after Anthony Berkeley had published perhaps his best-known book, a real-life murderer successfully employed the method described in that book and strangled his victim with a silk stocking — the first time, it appears, that such an object had been used in real life for an act of thuggery.

F or me the fascination of mystery stories is that of the beckoning unknown. I am seduced by suspense. In fiction as in life, I am lured on by eagerness to find out what is going to happen in the next chapter—and, in the end, whodunit.

ELLIOT L. RICHARDSON

Conversely, the police learned a thing or two when they attempted a reconstruction of the method they thought might have been used by the hymn-playing George Joseph Smith when he drowned three successive wives in the bath. The police reconstruction was almost too conclusive, for they nearly drowned their volunteer victim and had difficulty in bringing her back to consciousness. The method, which I shall not describe, has been used subsequently in at least one detective story.

So why *do* people read detective stories? I think one of the main reasons is that such books must, above all things, have a definite plot. Modern literature is full of plays and films that end nowhere; novels and short stories which leave the playgoer or the reader suspended in mid-air, forced either to impotent irritation or else to having to invent the outcome.

Detective stories, by their very nature, cannot cheat in this way. Their writers must tidy up the loose ends; must supply a logical solution to the problem they have posed; must also, to hold the reader's attention, combine the primitive lust and energy of the hunter with the cold logic of the scholarly mind.

Above all, they must concentrate upon murder, although they may also say, with Robert Herrick's bellman:

> *From noise of scare-fires rest ye free,*
> *From murders Benedicite.*

Gladys Mitchell received the Crime Writers' Association Silver Dagger for her fifty novels featuring Dame Beatrice Bradley.

Street Encounter Past Midnight
THE NONBELIEVER'S COMEUPPANCE

Jacques Barzun

Crossing New York's Sherman Plaza late in a chilly November — the clock then striking one — I saw advancing toward me from the northeast something light-footed and cloud-like. It came along 59th Street as if from the Playboy Club, but it was no ordinary Bunny. When only a few steps away, it assumed a man's shape, and though still rather translucent it spoke in a firm, almost truculent voice.

GHOST: Remember me? Know who I am?

J.B.: Yes, you're the great critic I used to argue with, the man who said he didn't care *who* killed Roger Ackroyd and professed to be unmoved by the famous words, "Mr. Holmes, they were the footprints of a gigantic hound."

GHOST: You're wrong there. I was moved — moved to laughter — or would have been if I had wasted my time on that kind of trash.

J.B.: You can't have it both ways. You *did* read and you disliked what you read. That's your privilege, but it confers no right of moral snobbery. But tell me, what do they think of crime fiction down where you come from?

GHOST: They loathe and despise it as I do. Crime holds no mystery for them; they know all about it ex officio.

J.B.: That's what I thought. It's only up here among living men that the idea of law, of an ordered life, coupled with an inquisitive impatience about mysteries and a skill in piercing them, provides rich materials for entertaining tales.

GHOST: There you are. Entertainment. You've given your case away. I don't read for entertainment, but for knowledge and wisdom.

J.B.: And that is what shuts out detective stories. First you stiffen your mind against pleasure and then you look for things that the genre doesn't afford. You're a bad reader.

GHOST: What do you mean! It is generally admitted that I'm the best reader since — since —

J.B.: McGuffey? Yes, of course, you were an indefatigable reader. You had to read in order to write those serious accounts of serious books, terribly serious. Now many of those books are seen to be dull, false, pretentious, though you called them "important," "significant," "moving," "original." That's what happens in every age. If you'd begun by taking pleasure in literature instead of studying it, you wouldn't have been fooled so often. Try to read Galsworthy now and see if Dorothy Sayers doesn't wear better.

GHOST: I shan't do either, but I know that Galsworthy keeps the mind working on something. The substance may be thin, but it's there, the stuff of which great books could be made.

J.B.: I know, Galsworthy had "ideas" and Sayers hasn't. That's your second error. You don't know a novel from a tale. A tale is its own excuse for being; it doesn't have to stuff your well-filled mind still fuller and make it stuffier yet. A tale charms by its ingenuity, by the plausibility with which it overcomes the suspicion that it couldn't happen. That is art. Learn to enjoy it. Read a few fairy tales, a few Arabian Nights to clear your mind of "knowledge and wisdom." Save your long face and restless eyes for the really great novelists who do handle the stuff of life and impart wisdom about it.

GHOST: There's no art outside of that; there's none in your rubbishy "tales" because there's nothing — not a thing — to carry away and reflect on.

J.B.: Of course there is. If you can grow lyrical over Proust's crumb of cake in the teacup, you can find charm in the ambiguity of any clue. The dog that did nothing in the nighttime is as justly famous as Cerberus, and T.S. Eliot found so much poetry in the Musgrave ritual that he lifted it to give a little class to one of his plays. Your trouble, dear Ghost, is — or was — that you poisoned your mind with sociology and stale ideas, so that you lost the power to appreciate the staples of literature: invention, surprise and suspense, plot and peripeteia, terse dialogue and good prose generally. Bone up on those and you'll soon be able to tell a good crime tale from a dull one, a Holmes from a Hawkshaw. Then perhaps your objections will fade away — as I see *you're* about to do. My regards to all our shady friends!

Jacques Barzun is coauthor with W.H. Taylor of A Catalogue of Crime.

MARTY NORMAN

THE HAYCRAFT-QUEEN DEFINITIVE LIBRARY OF DETECTIVE-CRIME-MYSTERY FICTION

Two Centuries of Cornerstones, 1748–1948

Please note that all the titles suggested by Ellery Queen are identified by an asterisk (*), and that all the comments shown in small italic type were written by Queen and, therefore, do not necessarily reflect Mr. Haycraft's opinions.

1748   Voltaire:
*Zadig

The Great-grandfather of the Detective Story

1828–9 François Eugène Vidocq:
*Mémoires de Vidocq

The Grandfather of the Detective Story

1845   Edgar Allan Poe:
Tales

The Father of the Detective Story

1852–3 Charles Dickens:
Bleak House;
The Mystery of Edwin Drood, 1870

1856   "Waters" (William Russell):
*Recollections of a Detective
Police-Officer

The first English detective yellow-back

1860   Wilkie Collins:
*The Woman in White

1862   Victor Hugo:
*Les Misérables
(First edition in English, also 1862)

1866   Feodor Dostoevsky:
*Crime and Punishment
(First edition in English, 1886)

1866   Émile Gaboriau:
L'Affaire Lerouge;
*Le Dossier No 113, 1867;
*Le Crime d'Orcival, 1868;
Monsieur Lecoq, 1869

The Father of the Detective Novel

1868   Wilkie Collins:
The Moonstone

The Father of the English Detective Novel

1872   (Harlan Page Halsey):
*Old Sleuth, the Detective, 1885

The first Dime Novel detective story

1874   Allan Pinkerton:
*The Expressman and the Detective

1878   Anna Katharine Green:
The Leavenworth Case

The Mother of the American Detective Novel

1882   Robert Louis Stevenson:
*New Arabian Nights;
*Strange Case of Dr Jekyll
and Mr Hyde, 1886

Was it Maurice Richardson who said of this book that it is the only detective-crime story he knows in which the solution is more terrifying than the problem?

1887	Fergus W. Hume:
	The Mystery of a Hansom Cab

An historically important book

1887	A. Conan Doyle:
	A Study in Scarlet;
	The Sign of Four, 1890;
	The Adventures of Sherlock Holmes, 1892;
	The Memoirs of Sherlock Holmes, 1894;
	The Hound of the Baskervilles, 1902;
	The Return of Sherlock Holmes, 1905;
	The Valley of Fear, 1915;
	His Last Bow, 1917;
	The Case-Book of Sherlock Holmes, 1927

*The listing of all the Sherlock Holmes books—the complete works—is sheer idolatry. Surely the first Holmes story, **A Study in Scarlet**, is an undeniable cornerstone; also **The Adventures** and **The Memoirs**; and the best of the novels should also be present in any definitive detective library. Most critics would probably select **The Hound** as the best novel; John Dickson Carr's choice is **The Valley of Fear.***

1892	Israel Zangwill:
	The Big Bow Mystery

1894	Mark Twain:
	The Tragedy of Pudd'nhead Wilson

1894	Arthur Morrison:
	Martin Hewitt, Investigator

1895	M.P. Shiel:
	Prince Zaleski

1897	Bram Stoker:
	Dracula

A mystery classic — interpreting "mystery" in its broadest sense

1899	E.W. Hornung:
	The Amateur Cracksman

The first Raffles book — "detection in reverse"

1903	(Erskine Childers):
	The Riddle of the Sands

Recommended by Christopher Morley as the classic secret service novel

1906	Godfrey R. Benson:
	Tracks in the Snow

1906	Robert Barr:
	The Triumphs of Eugène Valmont

1907	Jacques Futrelle:
	The Thinking Machine

1907	Maurice Leblanc:
	*Arsène Lupin, Gentleman-Cambrioleur; *"813," 1910*

The Leblanc-Lupin masterpiece

Les Huits Coups de l'Horloge, 1922

1907	Gaston Leroux:
	Le Mystère de la Chambre Jaune;
	Le Parfum de la Dame en Noir, 1908–9

1907	R. Austin Freeman:
	The Red Thumb Mark

The first Dr. Thorndyke book

John Thorndyke's Cases, 1909;
The Eye of Osiris, 1911;
The Singing Bone, 1912

The first "inverted" detective stories

1908	Mary Roberts Rinehart:
	The Circular Staircase

The founding of the Had-I-But Known School

1908	O. Henry:
	The Gentle Grafter

1908	G.K. Chesterton:
	The Man Who Was Thursday;
	The Innocence of Father Brown, 1911

1909	Cleveland Moffett:
	Through the Wall

A neglected highspot

1909	Baroness Orczy:
	The Old Man in the Corner

1909	Carolyn Wells:
	The Clue

The first Fleming Stone book

1910	A.E.W. Mason:
	At the Villa Rose

The first Hanaud book

The House of the Arrow, 1924

1910   William MacHarg and Edwin Balmer:
The Achievements of Luther Trant

The first book of short stories to make scientific use of psychology as a method of crime detection

1912   Arthur B. Reeve:
The Silent Bullet

The first Craig Kennedy book

1913   Mrs. Belloc Lowndes:
The Lodger

One of the earliest "suspense" stories

1913   Sax Rohmer:
The Mystery of Dr Fu-Manchu

1913   E.C. Bentley:
Trent's Last Case (First U.S. title: The Woman in Black)

The birth of naturalism in characterization

1914   Ernest Bramah:
Max Carrados

The first blind detective

1914   Louis Joseph Vance:
The Lone Wolf

1915   John Buchan:
The Thirty-Nine Steps

1916   Thomas Burke:
Limehouse Nights

1918   Melville Davisson Post:
Uncle Abner

1918   J.S. Fletcher:
The Middle Temple Murder

1920   Agatha Christie:
The Mysterious Affair at Styles

The first Hercule Poirot book

The Murder of Roger Ackroyd, 1926

1920   Freeman Wills Crofts:
*The Cask;
Inspector French's Greatest Case, 1924*

1920   H.C. Bailey:
*Call Mr. Fortune;
The Red Castle, 1932*

1920   "Sapper" (Cyril McNeile):
Bull-Dog Drummond

1920   Arthur Train:
Tutt and Mr. Tutt

1921   Eden Phillpotts:
The Grey Room

1922   A.A. Milne:
The Red House Mystery

1923   G.D.H. Cole:
The Brooklyn Murders

1923   Dorothy L. Sayers:
Whose Body?

The first Lord Peter Wimsey book

The Nine Tailors, 1934;
—— and Robert Eustace:
The Documents in the Case, 1930

1924   Philip MacDonald:
The Rasp

The first Colonel Anthony Gethryn book

Warrant for X, 1938 (English title: The Nursemaid Who Disappeared, 1938)

1925   Edgar Wallace:
The Mind of Mr. J.G. Reeder

1925   John Rhode:
The Paddington Mystery

The first Dr. Priestley book

The Murders in Praed Street, 1928

1925   Earl Derr Biggers:
The House without a Key

The first Charlie Chan book

1925   Theodore Dreiser:
An American Tragedy

1925   Liam O'Flaherty:
The Informer

1925   Ronald A. Knox:
The Viaduct Murder

1926   S.S. Van Dine:
The Benson Murder Case

The first Philo Vance book

or *The "Canary" Murder Case, 1927*

1926   C.S. Forester:
        *Payment Deferred

1927   Frances Noyes Hart:
        The Bellamy Trial

1928   W. Somerset Maugham:
        *Ashenden

1929   Anthony Berkeley:
        The Poisoned Chocolates Case;
        *Trial and Error, 1937;
        (Francis Iles):
        Before the Fact, 1932

1929   Ellery Queen:
        The Roman Hat Mystery

        The first Ellery Queen book

        *Calamity Town, 1942;
        (Barnaby Ross):
        The Tragedy of X, 1932

        The first Drury Lane book

        *The Tragedy of Y, 1932

1929   Rufus King:
        *Murder by the Clock

        The first Lieutenant Valcour book

1929   W.R. Burnett:
        *Little Caesar

1929   T.S. Stribling:
        *Clues of the Caribbees

        The only Professor Poggioli book

1929   Harvey J. O'Higgins:
        *Detective Duff Unravels It

        The first psychoanalyst detective

1929   Mignon G. Eberhart:
        The Patient in Room 18

1930   Frederick Irving Anderson:
        Book of Murder

1930   Dashiell Hammett:
        The Maltese Falcon

        The first Sam Spade book

        *The Glass Key, 1931;
        *The Adventures of Sam Spade, 1944

1930   David Frome:
        The Hammersmith Murders

        The first Mr. Pinkerton book

1931   Stuart Palmer:
        *The Penguin Pool Murder

        The first Hildegarde Withers book

1931   Francis Beeding:
        *Death Walks in Eastrepps

        Vincent Starrett considers this book "one of the ten greatest detective novels."

1931   Glen Trevor (James Hilton):
        *Murder at School (U.S. title: Was It Murder?, 1933)

1931   Damon Runyon:
        *Guys and Dolls

1931   Phoebe Atwood Taylor:
        The Cape Cod Mystery

        The first Asey Mayo book

1932   R.A.J. Walling:
        The Fatal Five Minutes

1932   Clemence Dane and Helen Simpson:
        Re-enter Sir John

1933   Erle Stanley Gardner:
        *The Case of the Velvet Claws

        The first Perry Mason book

        The Case of the Sulky Girl, 1933

1934   Margery Allingham:
        Death of a Ghost

1934   James M. Cain:
        *The Postman Always Rings Twice

1934   Rex Stout:
        Fer-de-Lance

        The first Nero Wolfe book

        *The League of Frightened Men, 1935

1935   Richard Hull:
        The Murder of My Aunt

1935   John P. Marquand:
        *No Hero

        The first Mr. Moto book

1938   John Dickson Carr (Carter Dickson):
The Crooked Hinge;
The Judas Window, 1938;
*The Curse of the Bronze Lamp, 1945
(English title: Lord of the Sorcerers, 1946)

In his original list, Mr Haycraft chose The Arabian Nights Murder by Carr and The Plague Court Murders by Dickson; but on page 493 of his The Art of the Mystery Story Mr. Haycraft wrote: "After careful, and possibly maturer, re-reading I beg to change my vote" to The Crooked Hinge and The Judas Window.

1938   Nicholas Blake:
The Beast Must Die

1938   Michael Innes:
Lament for a Maker

1938   Clayton Rawson:
*Death from a Top Hat

The first Great Merlini book

1938   Graham Greene:
*Brighton Rock

1938   Daphne Du Maurier:
*Rebecca

1938   Mabel Seeley:
The Listening House

1939   Ngaio Marsh:
Overture to Death

1939   Eric Ambler:
A Coffin for Dimitrios (English title: The Mask of Dimitrios)

1939   Raymond Chandler:
The Big Sleep

The first Philip Marlowe book
or *Farewell, My Lovely, 1940*

1939   Georges Simenon:
The Patience of Maigret

1940   Raymond Postgate:
Verdict of Twelve

1940   Frances and Richard Lockridge: *The Norths Meet Murder*

1940   Dorothy B. Hughes:
The So Blue Marble or
In a Lonely Place, 1947

1940   Cornell Woolrich (William Irish):
*The Bride Wore Black;
Phantom Lady, 1942

1940   Manning Coles:
Drink to Yesterday;
A Toast to Tomorrow, 1941 (English title: Pray Silence, 1940)
The first two Tommy Hambledon books

1941   H.F. Heard:
*A Taste for Honey

1941   Craig Rice:
Trial by Fury or
Home Sweet Homicide, 1944

1942   H.H. Holmes (Anthony Boucher):
*Rocket to the Morgue

1942   James Gould Cozzens:
*The Just and the Unjust

1944   Hilda Lawrence:
Blood upon the Snow

1946   Helen Eustis:
The Horizontal Man

1946   Charlotte Armstrong:
*The Unsuspected

1946   Lillian de la Torre:
*Dr. Sam: Johnson, Detector

1946   Edmund Crispin:
The Moving Toyshop or
Love Lies Bleeding, 1948

1947   Edgar Lustgarten:
One More Unfortunate (English title: A Case to Answer)

1947   Roy Vickers:
*The Department of Dead Ends

1948   Josephine Tey:
The Franchise Affair

1948   William Faulkner:
*Intruder in the Dust

COLLECTING DETECTIVE FICTION

Otto Penzler

The first thing to understand is that it is no longer possible to get in on the proverbial ground floor. Sherlock Holmes has already passed Shakespeare as the number one literary collectible, and that fact alone would seem to indicate the number of detective fiction collectors is roughly equivalent to the number of Macy's shoppers on a typical Saturday.

Still, it is within memory that the field was virtually a virgin one, with books in plentiful supply at rock-bottom prices and the competition for them almost nonexistent. Prior to 1934 there were only a handful of collectors. That year, however, marked the appearance of two important rare book catalogues devoted to the genre: one from George Bates in England, the other from Scribner's bookstore in America. John Carter, who was responsible for the Scribner's catalogue, was also responsible for *New Paths in Book Collecting*, published in the same year. One of his "new paths" led to crime. These three works gave the field credibility, if not hauteur.

Today, a truly spectacular collection of detective fiction, featuring most of the titles on the Haycraft-Queen Cornerstone and James Sandoe lists and those mentioned in *Queen's Quorum* would cost approximately $50,000 (and that's a conservative figure) to accumulate. Most collectors won't even attempt it, and only the novice would think of going that one step further and trying to amass every mystery ever written. (One exception: Allen J. Hubin, editor of *The Armchair Detective*, who is trying to do just that.) Most often, collectors find a subgenre that appeals to them and attack it with zeal.

There are many possibilities: nineteenth-century first editions; police procedurals; Gothics (veritably an untapped area); books about one specific book (such as the 100 or so volumes relating to Dickens' *Edwin Drood);* books about woman detectives, arsonists, magi-

SPINE-TINGLERS

Some collectors focus on bindings. In general, the nucleus of their collections will be mystery books from the late nineteenth century, since Victorian detective fiction often featured elaborately decorated covers with gilt running rampant. No publisher would dare such extravaganzas these days, but many books from the 1930's and 40's have interesting, albeit simplified, spine sketches.

cians, even one's own profession. My weakness is books about gentleman crooks, particularly E.W. Hornung's *Raffles.*

Currently, the vogue seems to be for the hard-boiled school, and as a consequence first editions of Dashiell Hammett, Raymond Chandler, Carroll John Daly, Benjamin Appel, Cornell Woolrich and the early Ross Macdonalds have skyrocketed in price. *The Maltese Falcon,* for example, recently sold for an outrageous $750. Five years ago, the asking price was $35.

No one can say with any certainty who will be the big collectibles in the next few years; however, several dealers have suggested that a collector who specialized in R. Austin Freeman, Leslie Charteris, Rex Stout and the Crime Club

in toto could not go far wrong.

Beginning collectors might consider focusing on their favorite author. If that doesn't sound like an overwhelming challenge, it's just because you haven't tried to assemble a complete set of first editions, in dust wrappers, in fine condition, of Ellery Queen, Agatha Christie, Sax Rohmer, Edgar Wallace, Dorothy L. Sayers or Georges Simenon. It's not an easy task.

To form a collection rather than a "pile," a collector must disdain all book club editions. If you find a nice book club copy of *The Mysterious Affair at Styles,* read it and enjoy it, but know that's all you can do with it. To a serious collector, no book club edition has any real value. (Careful. Don't confuse the Doubleday or Col-

ONE COLLECTOR'S MANIA

Donald Pollack, an anthropologist at the University of Rochester and editor of the *Baker Street Miscellany,* collects just one book: *The Hound of the Baskervilles.* He currently owns 103 versions of it, including the six states of the first edition, a page of the original manuscript, a play script, two movie scripts and several comic books. He estimates there are about a dozen versions (in English) left for him to locate. Then he can start in on the foreign-language editions, including five in Icelandic. He began collecting *The Hound* four years ago when he decided that Holmesiana in general was too expensive and too difficult to complete.

Says Pollack, "No one will ever again be able to amass a collection like John Shaw's, and I couldn't be happy knowing there were thousands of things I was missing. With *The Hound* I can look forward to a time when I will feel reasonably certain I have a complete collection. Then I start the full-

COURTESY HOUSE OF EL DIEFF, INC.

"The Slavering Hound" by Frederick Dorr Steele.

time job of upgrading, finding association copies, dust jackets — good luck on that one! — and so forth."

To date, Pollack's collection is worth approximately $1,000.

He does not own a real live hound. Nor does he intend to.

COLLECTING ODDITIES: SHORTHAND EDITIONS

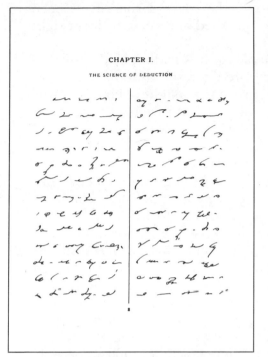

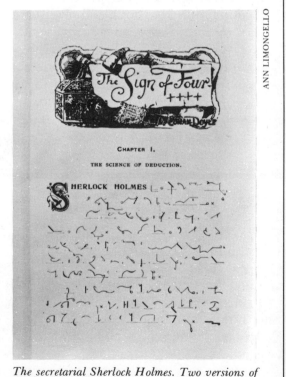

The secretarial Sherlock Holmes. Two versions of The Sign of Four. Top, Gregg; bottom, Pitman. Each is valued at $20.

ANN LIMONGELLO

lins Crime Club editions with book club editions. The former are potentially valuable, whereas the latter are not.) Equally worthless to a collector are most books published by Grosset & Dunlap, A.L. Burt and Triangle. These are invariably reprint editions.

Most collectors learn fairly quickly that what makes a book valuable is the fact that it is (1) rare, (2) in fine condition, and (3) a first edition. Regarding condition, if the dog chewed it, if a child crayoned in it, if it has been — in the words of the late Lew Feldman — well thumbed by a previous scholar, then perhaps you should not own it. You should certainly not consider it part of a good collection, any more than that book club edition of *Styles.*

Generally speaking, the most asked question on the part of neophyte collectors is, "How do you tell a first edition?" As a rule of thumb, if the copyright page (the verso of the title page) bears the words "First Edition" or "First Printing," the question answers itself. If it states "Second Printing" or something similar, you probably have the bad news right in front of you. Since most publishers don't make it that easy, compare the date on the title page (if there is one) with that on the copyright page; if identical, the book is likely to be a first edition. Many books have been written on this subject of telling firsts, and the most reliable is probably *First Editions of Today and How to Tell Them* by Henry S. Boutell.

Make no mistake about it: If you intend to invest in a collection, substantial amounts of money will exit your wallet. Which brings us to the last question: where to buy, and sell, first editions. You buy them wherever you can. Goodwill and Salvation Army stores, antique shops, tag sales, secondhand bookshops, garage and rummage sales. Wherever books are to be found, so should you be. Local newspapers often carry information about upcoming auctions. Go. The best source for books, of course, is a good bookshop. Many issue catalogues, and most dealers are generous with their time and knowledge. For the choice products they offer, however, you have to pay dearly. You might spend twenty years backing in and out of garage sales searching for a first

COLLECTING TERMINOLOGY

Booksellers use their own form of shorthand to describe a book's condition. It's important to familiarize yourself with it so you'll know, for example, that a "good" copy is really the equivalent of the collegian's "gentleman's C": presentable, but not spectacular. Some of the standard terms are:

Mint: looks brand-new

Very fine: almost mint, just lacking the freshness

Fine: clean and crisp, with no serious signs of wear

Good: averagely used: some soiling, fraying, discoloration of pages

Fair: obviously well read: covers dirty; dust wrappers badly torn and pieces missing; binding faded and fraying

Poor: for reading only; not suitable for a collector

Foxing: chemicals in the paper have oxidized, giving the pages a freckled appearance

Cracked hinge: a tear or break along the seam which attaches the pages to the covers

Chipped: tiny pieces have been torn off the dust wrapper

Bumped: the cover corners have been crushed and cease to form right angles

Sunned: cloth is badly faded or discolored, a result of too much exposure to sunlight (a hint as to why libraries of rare books are either dark or artificially lit)

Ex-lib: discarded from a library, usually with labels, stamping and perforations indicating the book's origin (the least desirable condition a book can be in)

Association copy: the author has personally come in contact with the book, which may be *signed* (bearing just his signature) or *inscribed* (his signature plus a greeting or sentiment) or — best of all — may be a *presentation copy* (signed, with an inscription indicating that the book was a gift from him; since an author receives only a handful of free copies from his publisher, presentation copies generally go to people extremely close to him and the inscription is apt to be more personal).

O.P.

edition of *Brighton Rock*; if you find it (the odds are against it), you may "steal" it for a quarter. If you search in rare bookstores, you'll probably be able to find a copy of it within a year — but it will cost you, on average, $150. Don't think for a minute that the dealer will buy the book back at that price, either. You can expect to receive one-third to one-half the retail value of any given book.

A few of the best booksellers specializing in mystery fiction (but by no means all of them — we collectors like to keep one or two of our sources our own little secret) and exemplary in terms of fairness are:

Aardvarks Booksellers (Paul Landfried), Box 15070, Orlando, Fla. 32808

The Aspen Bookhouse (Tom Schantz), Box 4119, Boulder, Colo. 80306

Joseph the Provider (Ralph Sipper), 903 State St., Santa Barbara, Calif. 93101

Vernon Lay, 52 Oakleigh Gardens, Whetstone, London N209AB, England

Murder Ink (Carol Brener), 271 West 87th St., N.Y., N.Y. 10024

Otto Penzler is coauthor of The Encyclopedia of Mystery and Detection, *which won a Mystery Writers of America Edgar.*

THE MYSTERY READER'S REFERENCE SHELF

Compiled by Vernon Lay

I. COFFIN TABLE BOOKS

The Collector's Book of Detective Fiction (Quayle)

The Encyclopedia of Mystery and Detection (Steinbrunner & Penzler)

The Murder Book (La Cour & Mogensen)

II. MUG SHOTS — CHARACTERS

In Search of Dr. Thorndyke (Donaldson)

The James Bond Dossier (Amis)

Nero Wolfe of West Thirty-Fifth Street (Baring-Gould)

Down These Mean Streets a Man Must Go: Raymond Chandler's Knight (Durham)

Philo Vance: The Life and Times of S.S. Van Dine (Tuska)

The Saint and Leslie Charteris (Lofts & Adley)

An Agatha Christie Chronology (Wynne)

Royal Bloodline, Ellery Queen, Author & Detective (Nevins)

The Hard-Boiled Dick (Sandoe)

Boys Will Be Boys: re, Sexton Blake (Turner)

Literary Distractions: re, Father Brown (Knox)

III. MUG SHOTS — AUTHORS

The Life of Sir Arthur Conan Doyle (Carr)

Such a Strange Lady: Dorothy L. Sayers (Hichens)

The Art of Simenon (Narcejac)

Simenon in Court (Raymond)

E.P. Oppenheim, Prince of Storytellers (Standish)

Edgar Wallace: A Biography (Lane)

Master of Villainy: A Biography of Sax Rohmer (Van Ash & Rohmer)

Melville Davisson Post, Man of Many Mysteries (Norton)

Poe: A Biography (Bittner)

Agatha Christie, Mistress of Mystery (Ramsay)

Eden Philpotts (Waveney Girvan)

M.P. Shiel: A Biography (Morse)

Life of Ian Fleming (Pearson)

The Chandler Notebooks (McShane)

Dashiell Hammett: A Casebook (Nolan)

Peter Cheyney, Prince of Hokum (Harrison)

The Real Le Queux, Fact or Fiction? (Sladen)

Catalogue of Crime (Barzun & Taylor)

The Detective Short Story: A Bibliography (Queen)

IV. VERDICTS RENDERED

Murder for Pleasure (Haycraft)

Mortal Consequences (Symons)

Snobbery with Violence (Watson)

The Development of the Detective Novel (Murch)

Bloodhounds of Heaven. The Detective in English Fiction from Godwin to Doyle (Ousby)

Fiction for the Working Man 1830 – 1850 (James)

The Detective Story in Britain (Symons)

The Detective in Fiction and in Fact (Rhodes)

Masters of Mystery (Thomson)

Queen's Quorum (Queen)

Blood in Their Ink (Sutherland)

How to Enjoy Detective Fiction (Thomas)

The Technique of the Mystery Story (Wells)

Mystery Fiction, Theory & Technique (Rodell)

Murder Plain and Fanciful (Sandoe)

In the Queen's Parlour (Queen)

The First, Second, Third Omnibus of Crime (Sayers, editor)

The Art of the Mystery (Haycraft, editor)

Crime in Good Company (Gilbert, editor)

The late Vernon Lay was a London bookseller specializing in detective fiction.

AMERICAN EDITING

Joan Kahn

I don't believe in publishing to formula, and I think each book has to be considered on its own merits. I think each author should have the right to work in any direction he chooses, if that direction leads to something someone else would want to read.

I've never been concerned about the length of a book, though if a book runs *very* short or *very* long, then it's going to have to be especially good.

I've published books in practically every mystery and suspense category — hard and soft, quiet and noisily bloody. I've experimented: The first book I accepted was an offbeat suspense novel, *The Horizontal Man* by Helen Eustis. I published the first Durrenmatt done in this country, *The Judge and His Hangman,* and one of the first novels with a black detective, *In the Heat of the Night* by John Ball, and one of the first with a homosexual detective, *Fadeout* by Joseph Hansen.

I'm a tough editor — and the Harper Novel of Suspense standards are pretty high. I edit about twenty-six books a year. If need be, I coax the authors to plug up holes or to make sense for their readers of what, so far, is only clear in the author's head. A little over half of the twenty-six or so books are suspense novels, representing, of course, only a small proportion of the number of manuscripts that come in each year.

In any case, since I'm just one person with only a certain amount of energy and time, I have to take on only the books I care most about and am most eager to shepherd through the months it takes from contract to finished book in the bookstores. It's hard turning down books, especially if they're by friends or even by one's relatives. I've had to turn down, on occasion, a good deal of my kin, including my father, my stepmother, my brother, and some nephews. Also difficult is turning down books by authors I've published for many years, which I've been forced to do when I couldn't see any way of convincing them that to me the books weren't in proper shape. Mind you, my judgment has sometimes been wrong, and I've had regrets.

Sometimes, gloriously, a book appears ready to go at the outset, and all I have to say to the author is "Lovely — let's talk about a contract." And that's a comfort all around.

I've never been very good at spotting trends — people ask whither the mystery — but I think it just wanders here and there following a writer's head and changes its direction almost as often as the length of a fashionable woman's skirt. Right now it may be circling over toward the romantic, but if a good big procedural or a good big spy story or a good big comic novel or a good big hard-boiled novel would burst upon the scene there'd be a patter of little typewriter feet in that direction — for a while, and then the feet would patter off in some other direction.

Recently, Harper & Row has been putting the Joan Kahn logo on the suspense books we publish (on other books I edit, too), and I think this has been useful since writers and agents who like the tones of voice of our books send me books in similar tones. I'm ready to read anything that comes along, but by now I can tell very quickly if a book's not going to be of any interest to me — so I can get that book off my desk pretty fast. Quite a lot of books go away fast, but it's exciting to see how many bright new talents are popping up from all over.

Joan Kahn is an editor at Harper & Row, New York.

ENGLISH EDITING

Elizabeth Walter

I cannot really define a crime novel. Obviously, a crime occurs, but murder is not obligatory, although the public expect it. A psychological study of a criminal can be sufficient, with the crime taking place off stage. But the crime story is always a story of surprise — that's why so few people read them a second time; once the surprise element is gone, there's not much left. Also, the crime story is concerned with justice, with the restoration of an order that has been disturbed.

I wouldn't think it immoral to publish a book in which the murderer gets away with it, if the book had other things to commend it — if it were amusing, say. And I pick a book on the basis of its appeal to me as a general reader. I don't consider myself a specialist in the field. After all, I have no specialised background. I am neither cop nor robber.

I think today there is a tendency toward the socially introspective crime novel. And people are once again appreciating characterisation, wit and style. The only thing I won't publish is anything that is explicitly sadistic. If I do not like an author's style, I do not accept his book. It is not the editor's function to rewrite. Just because there is a good idea there doesn't mean you should do the author's work for him. With good authors, if there is a clumsy phrase here or there I point it out in the hope that they will change it, but basically I prefer to let authors get on with the job — though I am a tiger where careless plotting is concerned.

As for dealing with authors, I enjoy it. Witty books are the work of witty people. The more difficult ones — well, I usually say, "No temperament below a sale of fifteen thousand."

I do not think spy thrillers properly belong in the Crime Club. And I dislike thrillers using titles like The Something Contract/Memorandum/ Assignment/Sanction. I can't tell one book from the other.

At Collins we never send out printed rejections. Of course, how much we say in a letter is another matter. I have turned down a first novel and then had a much better second novel come in and published it. I make it a principle never to waste time regretting books I have turned down that have gone on to success elsewhere. Quite obviously, some good crime novels are published by other than Collins Crime Club.

Reviews? Well, one bad one never killed a book. Neither did two. But if a book gets universally bad reviews, I reckon I ought not to have published it in the first place. It is the paper the review appears in and the fact that the book is noticed at all that are important — not generally the reviewer's name.

In all, Collins publishes thirty-six new crime titles a year, three per month. On average, three or four of these are by new authors. In any given month we try to offer three different kinds of mystery. If one has a village setting, another might be American or have an exotic locale, and another might be a police procedural. There should be something for everybody each month.

I cannot write a crime novel. I tried once and gave up. But I have had a collection of supernatural stories published in the States by St. Martin's Press. The supernatural appeals to me — probably my Welsh heritage. The thing I like most about the supernatural is that it enables you to play God, to dispense justice — only you dispense it from beyond the grave. Crime novelists can only dispense it from this side.

Elizabeth Walter is the editor of the Collins Crime Club, London.

CONFESSIONS OF A SLUSH READER

Eleanor Sullivan

Most people recognize "slush" as publishing jargon for unsolicited manuscripts which book and magazine editors plow through regularly in search of something marvelous to print. In spite of that lofty objective, or maybe because of it, it is usually an exhausting job, and not the fun many people tell me they think it must be.

Perhaps the reason so much of it is heavy going is that most novices don't know why they're writing — or, if they do, how to go about it — or, if they do, where to send it.

Sometimes the covering letter is the tip-off to the quality of the manuscript:

"I am sending you a copy of an inspired short story I wrote entitled ———. It brought me 67th place in the short-story category of the ——— ——— 1975 Writers' Contest."

"The plot of my story is multi-layered and it contains an average of about 1,900 words."

"I am enclosing an original story that you might consider entertaining reading for your clientele."

"This is to certify that ——— ——— is a Professional Writer, 'he composed a legal contract.'" (This stamped and signed by a notary public.)

"Earlier this year I wrote another story intended for a teenage girls' magazine. It was rejected as 'not in meeting with our editorial needs' which to me sounds like a brushoff."

One day I received a letter from a man whose story I had returned the previous week. He wrote: "On your reject slip of my story you didn't tell me whether it was accepted."

Still think it must be fun?

Consider the character descriptions some unsolicited contributors thought (incorrectly) to include:

"Barry Martin is an eccentric, provocative Doctor of Philosophy who is called upon by social deviates — the psychologically deranged and criminally insane (i.e., criminals, bad guys, crooks, etc.) — to solve complicated and predetermined crimes."

"A product of an unhappy home and a bad mixer as well, it is surprising that Felix Bendel has come as far as he has as we begin the story."

"Barbara Brown's peculiarity is embedded in the fact that there is absolutely nothing, good or bad, that makes her stand out, except for the utter absence of any peculiarity, which is in itself peculiar."

"At 34, Jim Lawrence finds himself wishing he'd been a baseball player after all, like any other normal person."

"Andre had trained with Jean-Claude Killy in France. While he was in training, his business went rapidly downhill."

All right, perhaps slush reading *does* have its moments. But even the unintentionally funny stuff palls after a few pages, and it is a struggle to make it to the end — which often is as unrewarding as this one:

"A man leaped into the room. He yelled, 'I was the one who killed that girl!' Then he leaped out the window. The sergeant sighed. What a day it had been."

Some time ago a friend dropped by my office, and his imagination was captured by the tower of unsolicited manuscripts on a shelf by my desk.

"Eleanor," he said, picking up the top envelope, "each one of these tells a story."

"I wish it did," I said.

Eleanor Sullivan is editor of Alfred Hitchcock's Mystery Magazine.

TRY, TRY AGAIN

A manuscript submitted to *Alfred Hitchcock's Mystery Magazine* is actually a double submission. It is read, at the same time, for possible inclusion in *Ellery Queen's Mystery Magazine*. (This, because both are brought out by Davis Publications.) About 25 percent of the manuscripts are sent in through an agent, and the two magazines receive about 6,000 manuscripts a year. Each prints roughly 300 stories a year. Should the story be accepted, the standard payment is 3 to 8 cents per word, depending on the author's clout.

Miss Sullivan was too busy wading through the slush to pose. Her unhappy surrogate suggests all manuscripts be typed, double-spaced and submitted with a stamped, self-addressed envelope. You may expect a reply within three weeks.

RENDERING A VERDICT

Clifford A. Ridley

I don't expect any sympathy, but let me tell you my problem. Ranged before me, row upon row, are all these crime novels — mysteries, procedurals, hard-boiled sagas, the works. From among them I must select a dozen or so to review, and in each of that dozen I should, if I am worth my fee, discover and communicate those faults or excellences that combine to render it a thing apart, a thing that at best deserves your purchase, at worst deserves your momentary attention. Some would call it paradise. I call it work.

Where to begin? Publishers' imprints offer some small assistance: Anything from the firm of Harper & Row may generally be counted as worth one's time, while mining in the Doubleday Crime Club yields fewer pleasantries. Authors' track records are enormously helpful, of course, although they contain the beginning author's paradox: To get himself reviewed he needs a name, but he can't acquire a name until he's reviewed. To this dilemma I cheerfully offer no answer whatever. I am simply going to leap at a new novel by Ross Macdonald or, latterly, Janwillem van de Wetering with rather more alacrity than I will attack one by Pincus O'Shaughnessy. Conceivably, this tyro could teach the pros, but I might never know that.

To help educate me, O'Shaughnessy's publisher may provide quotes on the dust jacket — perhaps from another mystery writer — that read something like "Combines the best of Ross Macdonald and Janwillem van de Wet-

ering!" These red flags are not without their usefulness, but only if approached with a dollop of salt. The fellow author's commendation may be little more than a matter of you-scratch-my-back-and-I'll-scratch-yours; the publisher's quote may be in code ("Brilliant characters," for instance, hints that the plot is indecipherable).

As you may have surmised, this review selection process is like a large, disorderly crap-shoot. Once past the publisher and the other author, I may be attracted by a book's milieu, an interesting new gumshoe, the promise of lively prose (revealed in the scanning of a half-dozen pages), the praise of a colleague (Newgate Callendar, when he gets down to cases, is sometimes reliable) or perhaps just something as quixotic — the book is before me now — as a novel set in a town called Ridley. None of this is awfully scientific, however much I may protest it is to the world at large, and all of it is overlaid with nothing more than matters of personal preference. I am a mystery-and-procedural man myself, and, all else being equal, I am disposed to pick up a mystery or procedural in preference to a spy caper. There's nothing particularly wrong with this, I submit, so long as my biases are evident. No reader samples all the fruits of the crime garden with equal relish, and to expect a reviewer to do otherwise is to disqualify him as the reader's surrogate — which is what he ought to be.

All right. I have selected a book and

cracked the covers, and what do I search for? I search — I *pray* — for a happy combination of those elements that distinguish any work of fiction, regardless of genre. Style, for one — a rarer bird than might be expected from reading many reviewers, whose idea of literary excellence seems to demand little more than that a writer refrain from saying "ain't." In fact, there are but a handful of true stylists among us: Julian Symons, Peter Dickinson, Ken and Margaret Millar, Ngaio Marsh, P.D. James. With the rest of the crowd we must, to one degree or another, make do — hoping for at least some kind of authorial tone, for a cliché at least every *other* page, for dialogue that, if not precisely right, is at least not patently wrong. Even applying such relaxed criteria, the hunt for style is often a fruitless one.

I search, too, for some evidence that an author has a point of view. It's not that simple, of course; if he fails to weave this material into the fabric of his plot, he risks becoming preacher, psychiatrist, tour guide — and less of a novelist. Nonetheless, I search for a sense of social forces in collision (viz.: Ross Macdonald, the Wahlöös, James McClure), of human character in extremis (Symons, Simenon, Ruth Rendell), of ordinary behavior turned upside-down (Donald Westlake), of place in relation to the people who inhabit it (most of these authors and more). The idea is to identify a book's perspective while keeping a wary eye out for what is not perspective but merely gimmick — of which, unhappily, our genre has more than its share. The gimmick has no staying power; it expires after a single book, for it has little to tell us beyond the mere fact of its existence. Virgil Tibbs and Rabbi David Small are gimmicks.

Finally, I search for plausibility of plot. One would assume that a crime novel, with its effects deriving in large part from the pieces tumbling logically into place, would be sensibly plotted if it were nothing else. Yet it's remarkable how many books are resolved by devices dragged in from the next country, loose ends strewn about like spaghetti, and how many more are predicated on people behaving in fashions that defy not only their stories but common sense itself. Plot in the crime novel is hardly what it used to be — which was everything. The days of Christie, Carr and Queen are mostly dead and buried.

Given this state of affairs, I'm continually amazed that plot is all a good many reviewers seem to have on their minds. (Robin Winks, of the *New Republic*, is a notable exception.) Although I take it as axiomatic that most of what we need to know about a book's plot can be transmitted in a single sentence, and although all mystery reviewers toil within severely circumscribed space, plot summary occupies even the best of our critics to an astonishing degree. What this signifies, I think, is a reluctance to treat mystery fiction with the seriousness that its quality increasingly demands. If reviewers persist in regarding crime fiction as nothing more than an idle diversion with which to while away a couple of hours — endorsing far too many books, squatting firmly on the fence about most of the rest, and filling their minimal space not with serious appraisal but with and-then-he-wrote — then crime fiction will continue to sit at the back of the bus, for any art requires good criticism in order to prosper. And plot summary is not criticism. It is a book report.

Clifford A. Ridley was arts editor, theater critic, and sometime mystery reviewer for The National Observer *until its demise in July 1977.*

ALWAYS ON SUNDAY

Just what is a Newgate Callendar? *The Newgate Calendar, or Malefactor's Bloody Register,* was a British broadside published about 1774 that dealt with notorious crimes. It is also the pseudonym, creatively spelled, of the *New York Times* mystery book reviewer. In a recent poll, readers believed him to be Anatole Broyard, John Canaday, John Leonard, Harold Schonberg, or Ellery Queen. One of the above is correct.

C.K.

Unlikely Author No. 1:
THE TRAILOR MURDER MYSTERY

Abraham Lincoln

The March 1952 issue of Ellery Queen's Mystery Magazine *presented "The Trailor Murder Mystery." In an introduction to the story, Queen noted that Howard Haycraft was the first of the mystery historians to point out that Lincoln was a great admirer of Poe; that Roger W. Barrett discovered Lincoln's own mystery story in the pages of the Quincy, Illinois,* Whig *of April 15, 1846; that the story itself was based on an actual case in which Lincoln acted as defense attorney.*

In the year 1841, there resided, at different points in the State of Illinois, three brothers by the name of Trailor. Their Christian names were William, Henry and Archibald. Archibald resided at Springfield, then as now the seat of Government of the State. He was a sober, retiring, and industrious man, of about thirty years of age; a carpenter by trade, and a bachelor, boarding with his partner in business — a Mr. Myers. Henry, a year or two older, was a man of like retiring and industrious habits; had a family, and resided with it on a farm, at Clary's Grove, about twenty miles distant from Springfield in a north-westerly direction. — William, still older, and with similar habits, resided on a farm in Warren county, distant from Springfield something more than a hundred miles in the same north-westerly direction. He

was a widower, with several children.

In the neighborhood of William's residence, there was, and had been for several years, a man by the name of Fisher, who was somewhat above the age of fifty; had no family, and no settled home; but who boarded and lodged a while here and a while there, with persons for whom he did little jobs of work. His habits were remarkably economical, so that an impression got about that he had accumulated a considerable amount of money.

In the latter part of May, in the year mentioned, William formed the purpose of visiting his brothers at Clary's Grove and Springfield; and Fisher, at the time having his temporary residence at his house, resolved to accompany him. They set out together in a buggy with a single horse. On Sunday evening they reached Henry's residence, and stayed over night. On Monday morning, being the first Monday of June, they started on to Springfield, Henry accompanying them on horseback. They reached town about noon, met Archibald, went with him to his boarding house, and there took up their lodgings for the time they should remain.

After dinner, the three Trailors and Fisher left the boarding house in company, for the avowed purpose of spending the evening together in looking about the town. At supper, the Trailors had all returned, but Fisher was missing, and some inquiry was made about him. After supper, the Trailors went out professedly in search of him. One by one they returned, the last coming in after late tea time, and each stating that he had been unable to discover anything of Fisher.

The next day, both before and after breakfast, they went professedly in search again, and returned at noon, still unsuccessful. Dinner again being had, William and Henry expressed a determination to give up the search, and start for their homes. This was remonstrated against

Many political figures appreciate mysteries. In addition to Abraham Lincoln and Franklin Delano Roosevelt, John F. Kennedy, Henry Kissinger, Julian Bond and Amy Carter have admitted they were hooked on them.

by some of the boarders about the house, on the ground that Fisher was somewhere in the vicinity, and would be left without any conveyance, as he and William had come in the same buggy. The remonstrance was disregarded, and they departed for their homes respectively.

Up to this time, the knowledge of Fisher's mysterious disappearance had spread very little beyond the few boarders at Myers', and excited no considerable interest. After the lapse of three or four days, Henry returned to Springfield, for the ostensible purpose of making further search for Fisher. Procuring some of the boarders, he, together with them and Archibald, spent another day in ineffectual search, when it was again abandoned, and he returned home.

No general interest was yet excited.

On the Friday, week after Fisher's disappearance, the Postmaster at Springfield received a letter from the Postmaster nearest William's residence, in Warren county, stating that William had returned home without Fisher, and was saying, rather boastfully, that Fisher was dead, and had willed him his money, and that he had got about fifteen hundred dollars by it. The letter further stated that William's story and conduct seemed strange, and desired the Postmaster at Springfield to ascertain and write what was the truth in the matter.

The Postmaster at Springfield made the letter public, and at once, excitement became universal and intense. Springfield, at that time, had a population of about 3,500, with a city organization. The Attorney General of the State resided there. A purpose was forthwith formed to ferret out the mystery, in putting which into execution, the Mayor of the city and the Attorney General took the lead. To make search for, and, if possible, find the body of the man supposed to be murdered, was resolved on as the first step.

In pursuance of this, men were formed into large parties, and marched abreast, in all directions, so as to let no inch of ground in the vicinity remain unsearched. Examinations were made of cellars, wells, and pits of all descriptions, where it was thought possible the body might be concealed. All the fresh, or tol-

NOBEL PRIZEWINNERS WHO WROTE MYSTERIES

Heinrich Boll   Rudyard Kipling
Pearl Buck   Sinclair Lewis
T.S. Eliot   Bertrand Russell
William Faulkner   George Bernard Shaw
Ernest Hemingway   John Steinbeck
John Galsworthy   William Butler Yeats

PULITZER PRIZEWINNERS WHO WROTE MYSTERIES

Stephen Vincent Benet   Oliver LaFarge
Louis Bromfield   Sinclair Lewis
Pearl S. Buck   J.P. Marquand
Marc Connelly   Edna St. Vincent Millay
James Gould Cozzens   Arthur Miller
Harold L. Davis   Julia M. Peterkin
Edna Ferber   Elmer Rice
William Faulkner   Conrad Richter
Zona Gale   Edwin Arlington Robinson
Ellen Glasgow   Robert Sherwood
Susan Glaspell   John Steinbeck
A.B. Guthrie, Jr.   T.S. Stribling
Ernest Hemingway   Mark Van Doren
MacKinlay Kantor   Edith Wharton

*Each of these prizewinners had stories published
in* Ellery Queen's Mystery Magazine.

erably fresh graves in the graveyard, were pried into, and dead horses and dead dogs were disinterred, where, in some instances, they had been buried by their partial masters.

This search, as has appeared, commenced on Friday. It continued until Saturday afternoon without success, when it was determined to dispatch officers to arrest William and Henry, at their residences, respectively. The officers started on Sunday morning; meanwhile, the search for the body was continued, and rumors got afloat of the Trailors having passed, at different times and places, several gold pieces, which were readily supposed to have belonged to Fisher.

On Monday, the officers sent for Henry, having arrested him, arrived with him. The Mayor and Attorney Gen'l took charge of him, and set their wits to work to elicit a discovery from him. He denied, and denied, and persisted in denying. They still plied him in every conceivable way, till Wednesday, when, protesting his own innocence, he stated that his brothers, William and Archibald, had murdered Fisher; that they had killed him, without his (Henry's) knowledge at the time, and made a temporary concealment of his body; that, immediately preceding his and William's departure from Springfield for home, on Tuesday, the day after Fisher's disappearance, William and Archibald communicated the fact to him, and engaged his assistance in making a permanent concealment of the body; that, at the time he and William left professedly for home, they did not take the road directly, but, meandering their way through the streets, entered the woods at the North West of the city, two or three hundred yards to the right of where the road they should have travelled, entered them; that, penetrating the woods some few hundred yards, they halted and Archibald came a somewhat different route, on foot, and joined them; that William and Archibald then stationed him (Henry) on an old and disused road that ran near by, as a sentinel, to give warning of the approach of any intruder; that William and Archibald then removed the buggy to the edge of a dense brush thicket, about forty yards distant from his (Henry's) position, where, leaving the buggy, they entered the thicket, and in a few minutes returned with the body, and placed it in the buggy; that from his station he could and did distinctly see that the object placed in the buggy was a dead man, of the general appearance and size of Fisher; that William and Archibald then moved off with the buggy in the direction of Hickox's mill pond, and after an absence of half an hour, returned, saying they had put him in a safe place; that Archibald then left for town, and he and William found their way to the road, and made for their homes.

At this disclosure, all lingering credulity was broken down, and excitement rose to an almost inconceivable height. Up to this time, the well-known character of Archibald had repelled and put down all suspicions as to him. Till then, those who were ready to swear that a murder had been committed, were almost as confident that Archibald had had no part in it. But now, he was seized and thrown into jail; and indeed, his personal security rendered it by no means objectionable to him.

And now came the search for the brush thicket, and the search of the mill pond. The thicket was found, and the buggy tracks at the point indicated. At a point within the thicket, the signs of a struggle were discovered, and a trail from thence to the buggy track was traced. In attempting to follow the track of the buggy from the thicket, it was found to proceed in the direction of the mill pond, but could not be traced all the way. At the pond, however, it was found that a buggy had been backed down to, and partially into the water's edge.

Search was now to be made in the pond; and it was made in every imaginable way. Hundreds and hundreds were engaged in raking, fishing, and draining. After much fruitless effort in this way, on Thursday morning the mill dam was cut down, and the water of the pond partially drawn off, and the same processes of search again gone through with.

About noon of this day, the officer sent for William, returned having him in custody; and a man calling himself Dr. Gilmore, came in company with them. It seems that the officer arrested William at his own house, early in the day on Tuesday, and started to Springfield with him; that after dark awhile, they reached Lewiston, in Fulton county, where they stopped for the night; that late in the night this Dr. Gilmore arrived, stating that Fisher was alive at his house, and that he had followed on to give the information, so that William might be released without further trouble; that the officer, distrusting Dr. Gilmore, refused to release William, but brought him on to Springfield, and the Dr. accompanied them.

On reaching Springfield, the Dr. reasserted that Fisher was alive, and at his house. At this, the multitude for a time, were utterly confounded. Gilmore's story was communicated to Henry Trailor, who without faltering, reaffirmed his own story about Fisher's murder. Henry's adherence to his own story was communicated to the crowd, and at once the idea started, and became nearly, if not quite universal, that Gilmore was a confederate of the Trailors, and had invented the tale he was telling, to secure their release and escape.

Excitement was again at its zenith.

About three o'clock the same evening, Myers, Archibald's partner, started with a two-horse carriage, for the purpose of ascertaining whether Fisher was alive, as stated by Gilmore, and if so, of bringing him back to Springfield with him.

On Friday a legal examination was gone into before two Justices, on the charge of murder against William and Archibald. Henry was

AREN'T YOU GLAD
HE WASN'T SECRETARY OF THE TREASURY?

THE PRESIDENT'S MYSTERY PLOT
By
Franklin Delano Roosevelt
and
Rupert Hughes, Samuel Hopkins Adams,
Anthony Abbot, Rita Weiman,
S. S. Van Dine and John Erskine
with
Erle Stanley Gardner

ANN LIMONGELLO

The thirty-second president of the United States almost wrote a mystery; he had an idea for one, but couldn't come up with a good ending. The idea was passed on to six authors — Anthony Abbot, Rupert Hughes, S.H. Adams, Rita Weiman, S.S. Van Dine, John Erskine — each of whom wrote a chapter and more or less resolved the problem of absconding with $5 million without leaving any clues. Originally published as "The President's Mystery Story" in *Liberty* magazine in 1935, the work was reprinted under the title *The President's Mystery Plot* in 1967 with a new final chapter by Erle Stanley Gardner. Roosevelt's royalties were donated to charity.

introduced as a witness by the prosecution, and on oath re-affirmed his statements, as heretofore detailed, and at the end of which he bore a thorough and rigid cross-examination without faltering or exposure. The prosecution also proved, by a respectable lady, that on the Monday evening of Fisher's disappearance, she saw Archibald, whom she well knew, and another man whom she did not then know, but whom she believed at the time of testifying to be William, (then present,) and still another, answering the description of Fisher, all enter the timber at the North West of town, (the point indicated by Henry,) and after one or two hours, saw William and Archibald return without Fisher.

Several other witnesses testified, that on Tuesday, at the time William and Henry professedly gave up the search for Fisher's body, and started for home, they did not take the road directly, but did go into the woods, as stated by Henry. By others, also, it was proved, that since Fisher's disappearance, William and Archibald had passed rather an unusual number of gold pieces. The statements heretofore made about the thicket, the signs of a struggle, the buggy tracks, &c., were fully proven by numerous witnesses.

At this the prosecution rested.

Dr. Gilmore was then introduced by the defendants. He stated that he resided in Warren county, about seven miles distant from William's residence; that on the morning of William's arrest, he was out from home, and heard of the arrest, and of its being on a charge of the murder of Fisher; that on returning to his own house, he found Fisher there; that Fisher was in very feeble health, and could give no rational account as to where he had been during his absence; that he (Gilmore) then started in pursuit of the officer, as before stated; and that he should have taken Fisher with him, only that the state of his health did not permit. Gilmore also stated that he had known Fisher for several years, and that he had understood he was subject to temporary derangement of mind, owing to an injury about his head received in early life.

There was about Dr. Gilmore so much of the air and manner of truth, that his statement prevailed in the minds of the audience and of the court, and the Trailors were discharged, although they attempted no explanation of the circumstances proven by the other witnesses.

On the next Monday, Myers arrived in Springfield, bringing with him the now famed Fisher, in full life and proper person.

Thus ended this strange affair and while it is readily conceived that a writer of novels could bring a story to a more perfect climax, it may well be doubted whether a stranger affair ever really occurred. Much of the matter remains in mystery to this day. The going into the woods with Fisher, and returning without him, by the Trailors; their going into the woods at the same place the next day, after they professed to have given up the search; the signs of a struggle in the thicket, the buggy tracks at the edge of it; and the location of the thicket, and the signs about it, corresponding precisely with Henry's story, are circumstances that have never been explained. William and Archibald have both died since — William in less than a year, and Archibald in about two years after the supposed murder. Henry is still living, but never speaks of the subject.

It is not the object of the writer of this to enter into the many curious speculations that might be indulged upon the facts of this narrative; yet he can scarcely forbear a remark upon what would, almost certainly, have been the fate of William and Archibald, had Fisher not been found alive. It seems he had wandered away in mental derangement, and, had he died in this condition, and his body been found in the vicinity, it is difficult to conceive what could have saved the Trailors from the consequence of having murdered him. Or, if he had died, and his body never found, the case against them would have been quite as bad, for, although it is a principle of law that a conviction for murder shall not be had, unless the body of the deceased be discovered, it is to be remembered, that Henry testified that he saw Fisher's dead body.

Abraham Lincoln was the sixteenth President of the United States of America.

MYSTERY ORGANIZATIONS

MYSTERY WRITERS OF AMERICA,
Founded 1945.

National Headquarters: 105 East 19th Street, New York City

Regional Chapters: Boston, Chicago, San Francisco, Los Angeles

MWA issues three types of membership. Full membership is available only to those who have published in the field. Associate membership is open to those in allied fields, for example, publishing and bookselling. Affiliate membership is granted to just plain fans. There is little difference between them, as all members receive the free newsletter, *The Third Degree*, and all may attend the annual Edgar Allan Poe Award dinner held in New York each spring. Current president: Robert L. Fish

MWA Awards

MWA presents Edgars (for Edgar Allan Poe) and Ravens (ditto). Nominees are selected by a supposedly impartial committee and winners are chosen by that committee. Eleven awards are presented in all: for best novel of the year; best first novel of the year; best paperback; best short story; best juvenile mystery; best critical/biographical study; best motion picture; best TV drama; best fact crime book; best hardcover jacket design; best paperback jacket design.

1946 *Watchful at Night,* Julius Fast
1947 *The Horizontal Man,* Helen Eustis
1948 *The Fabulous Clip Joint,* Fredric Brown
1949 *The Room Upstairs,* Mildred Davis
1950 *What a Body,* Alan Green
1951 *Nightmare in Manhattan,* Thomas Walsh
1952 *Strangle Hold,* Mary McMullen

1953 *Don't Cry for Me,* William Campbell Gault
1954 *Beat Not the Bones,* Charlotte Jay
　　　A Kiss Before Dying, Ira Levin
1955 *The Long Goodbye,* Raymond Chandler
　　　Go, Lovely Rose, Jean Potts
1956 *Beast in View,* Margaret Millar
　　　The Perfectionist, Lane Kauffman

1957 *A Dram of Poison*, Charlotte Armstrong
  Rebecca's Pride, Donald McNutt Douglas
1958 *Room to Swing*, Ed Lacy
  Knock and Wait Awhile, William Rawle Weeks
1959 *The Eighth Circle*, Stanley Ellin
  The Bright Road to Fear, Richard Martin Stern
1960 *The Hours Before Dawn*, Celia Fremlin
  The Grey Flannel Shroud, Henry Slesar
1961 *Progress of a Crime*, Julian Symons
  The Man in the Cage, John Holbrooke Vance
1962 *Death and the Joyful Woman*, Ellis Peters
  The Fugitive, Robert L. Fish
1963 *The Light of Day*, Eric Ambler
  The Florentine Finish, Cornelius Hirschberg
1964 *The Spy Who Came in from the Cold*, John Le Carré
  Friday the Rabbi Slept Late, Harry Kemelman
1965 *The Quiller Memorandum*, Adam Hall
  In the Heat of the Night, John Ball
1966 *King of the Rainy Country*, Nicolas Freeling
  The Cold War Swap, Ross Thomas
1967 *God Save the Mark*, Donald E. Westlake
  Act of Fear, Michael Collins

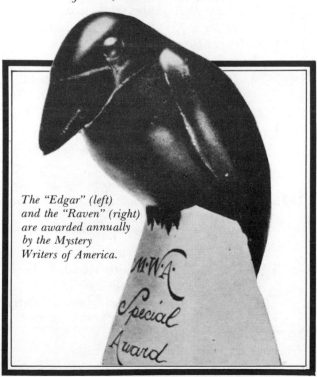

The "Edgar" (left) and the "Raven" (right) are awarded annually by the Mystery Writers of America.

GRAND MASTERS AWARD

Agatha Christie
Vincent Starrett
Rex Stout
Ellery Queen
Erle Stanley Gardner
John Dickson Carr
George Harmon Coxe
Georges Simenon
Baynard Kendrick
John Creasey
James M. Cain
Mignon G. Eberhart
John D. MacDonald
Judson Philips
Ross Macdonald
Eric Ambler
Graham Greene
Dorothy B. Hughes
Ngaio Marsh
Daphne Du Maurier

1968 *A Case of Need*, Jeffrey Hudson
  Silver Street, Richard Johnson
  The Bait, Dorothy Uhnak
1969 *Forfeit*, Dick Francis
  A Time for Predators, Joe Gores
1970 *The Laughing Policeman*, Maj Sjöwall & Per Wahlöö
  The Anderson Tapes, Lawrence Sanders
1971 *Day of the Jackal*, Frederick Forsyth
  Finding Maubee, A.H.Z. Carr
1972 *The Lingala Code*, Warren Kiefer
  Squaw Point, R.H. Shimer
1973 *Dance Hall of the Dead*, Tony Hillerman
  The Billion Dollar Sure Thing, Paul E. Erdman
1974 *Peter's Pence*, Jon Cleary
  Fletch, Gregory McDonald
1975 *Hopscotch*, Brian Garfield
  The Alvarez Journal, Rex Burns
1976 *Promised Land*, Robert B. Parker
  The Thomas Berryman Number, James Patterson
1977 *Catch Me, Kill Me*, William H. Hallahan
  A French Finish, Robert Ross

CRIME WRITERS' ASSOCIATION
Founded 1953

CWA headquarters: National Book League, 7 Albemarle Street, London, W1

Membership is restricted to those who have published in the field, with no exceptions. Members receive a monthly newsletter, *Red Herrings*, attend monthly meetings at the Book League and the yearly Gold Dagger Award dinner, at which the best mystery of the year is announced. Chairman: Donald Rumbelow. Vice-Chairman: Margaret Yorke.

CWA Awards

CWA presents Gold and Silver Daggers for the best English and the best foreign mysteries of the year.

COURTESY PENELOPE WALLACE

The Crime Writers' Association presents two awards, the Gold Dagger and the Silver Dagger, for best domestic and best foreign mystery of the year.

1955 *The Little Walls*, Winston Graham
1956 *The Second Man*, Edward Grierson
1957 *The Colour of Murder*, Julian Symons
1958 *Someone from the Past*, Margot Bennett
1959 *Passage of Arms*, Eric Ambler
1960 *The Night of Wenceslas*, Lionel Davidson
1961 *The Spoilt Kill*, Mary Kelly
1962 *When I Grow Rich*, Joan Fleming
1963 *The Spy Who Came in from the Cold*, John Le Carré
1964 *The Perfect Murder*, H.R.F. Keating
     The Two Faces of January, Patricia Highsmith
1965 *The Far Side of the Dollar*, Ross Macdonald
     Midnight plus One, Gavin Lyall
1966 *A Long Way to Shiloh*, Lionel Davidson
     In the Heat of the Night, John Ball
1967 *Murder Against the Grain*, Emma Lathen
     Dirty Story, Eric Ambler
1968 *Skin Deep*, Peter Dickinson
     The Lady in the Car, Sebastien Japrisot
1969 *A Pride of Heroes*, Peter Dickinson
     Another Way of Dying, Francis Clifford
     The Father Hunt, Rex Stout
1970 *Young Man, I Think You're Dying*, Joan Fleming
     The Labyrinth Makers, Anthony Price
1971 *The Steam Pig*, James McClure
     Shroud for a Nightingale, P.D. James
1972 *The Levanter*, Eric Ambler
     The Rainbird Pattern, Victor Canning
1973 *The Defection of A.J. Lewinter*, Robert Littell
     A Coffin for Pandora, Gwen Butler
1974 *Other Paths of Glory*, Anthony Price
     The Grosvenor Square Goodbye, Francis Clifford
     The Big Fix, Roger Simon
1975 *The Seven Per Cent Solution*, Nicholas Meyer
     The Black Tower, P.D. James
     Acid Drop, Sara George
1976 *Demon in My View*, Ruth Rendell
     Rogue Eagle, James McClure
     Death of a Thin-Skinned Animal, Patrick Alexander
1977 *The Honourable Schoolboy*, John Le Carré
     Laidlaw, William McIlvaney

Chapter 2
PERPETRATORS

YOU CALL IT A PSEUDONYM, WE CALL IT AN ALIAS

Carol Kountz

Once I read a wonderful mystery that had me combing libraries and bookstores for more books by the same author — but to no avail. Desperate, I picked up something else to read and discovered that it had an uncanny resemblance to the first (and apparently sequelless) book I'd enjoyed.

A little library sleuthing proved my suspicions to be correct. The same author had written both books but had used a pseudonym for one.

Why do mystery writers baffle potentially loyal readers by adopting pseudonyms? Usually it's for reasons thought to be — in publishing and writing circles, at any rate — logical, sensible and sometimes profitable. Occasionally it's for privacy. Sometimes it's not even the author's decision.

The most common type of 'tec author to publish under an alias is the individual with a distinguished reputation in another field. Academics are often found guilty. So C. Day Lewis, once Poet Laureate, became Nicholas Blake when he wrote *Minute for Murder* and other mysteries featuring Nigel Strangeways, and so the prolific J.I.M. Stewart writes his Inspector Appleby series as Michael Innes.

Columbia University professor Carolyn Heilbrun had a special reason for hiding behind the pen name Amanda Cross to write her mystery novels: she was hoping to be granted tenure. (In her case, crime paid on both counts.)

Not only scholars stoop to protect identity. John Canaday, former art critic for the *New York Times,* poses on crime shelves as Matthew

THE CREASEY DOSSIER

| GORDON ASHE | MARGARET COOKE | M.E. COOKE | JOHN CREASEY | NORMAN DEANE | ELISE FECAMPS |

IF YOU WANT TO WRITE UNDER A PEN NAME...

1. Be forewarned: Most publishers frown on it — for a beginning novelist, at any rate. Their thinking goes that you should be proud to have your mystery novel appear under your real name. Even a long, unpronounceable name will not be an exception.

2. State your reasons in a covering letter with your manuscript if you have just cause to use a pseudonym (conflict with your profession, for example).

3. There are no legal steps, but before deciding on your pen name check with a large library card catalogue to avoid taking a name similar to one in use.

4. Write to the publisher or editor under your own name. Sign the pseudonym as a by-line on the manuscript and put your own name and address on the upper left-hand corner of the manuscript.

5. Checks will be sent to you under your own name. If you receive a check made out to your pseudonym, as in the case of a writer with several contracts under different names, you may usually cash it at your own bank by endorsing it with the pen name and then the real name.

6. Correspondence sent to you under your pseudonym should be addressed c/o your real name to be sure it is not returned to the sender.

7. Remember that your pen name is not likely to conceal your identity for long — expect librarians (and some readers) to ferret out your secret.

Head. Literary lion Gore Vidal has written for crime fans under the alias Edgar Box. The name Edmund Crispin is familiar to detective story readers, but they may not know that it stands for (Robert) Bruce Montgomery, the composer of scores for British motion pictures, notably *Carry On, Nurse*.

David Cornwell wrote under the pseudonym John Le Carré for *The Spy Who Came In from the Cold* and other spy stories because of his profession: he worked for the British Foreign Office.

Output

Sometimes a crime novelist's book is brought out under a nom de plume when there are too many of his or her sleuths for sale in one season. The idea may come from the publisher ("The reading public will never absorb all this," mutters the editor), or a second publisher may contract for a novel by a well-known writer with the request that it be under a "new" name.

Take a case like that of John Dickson Carr, the creator of locked-room puzzle solver Gid-

| ⊃BERT CAINE FRAZER | PATRICK GILL | MICHAEL HALLIDAY | CHARLES HOGARTH | BRIAN HOPE | COLIN HUGHES | KYLE HUNT |

eon Fell (*Problem of the Wire Cage*, etc.). He is a.k.a. Carr Dickson (a name pressed on him by a British publisher and changed at his request to Carter Dickson) when writing about Sir Henry Merrivale.

A prolific contemporary suspense writer such as Bill Pronzini will have books published under several pseudonyms — Jack Foxx (*The Jade Figurine*) and Alex Saxon (*A Run in Diamonds*) — in addition to his real name (*Panic!* and *Snowbound*). Ditto Robert L. Fish, inventor of "Schlock Holmes," a parody on Sherlock, who also writes as Robert L. Pike and A.C. Lamprey.

One of the greatest names in the field, Cornell Woolrich, used the name William Irish for *Phantom Lady* (and also used a less well-known alias, George Hopley) because of his high output.

No discussion of pseudonyms used for reasons of output is complete without mention of John Creasey, whose loyal readers are hard put to keep up with his books (over 600 of them!) and his aliases. He used twenty-six, varying them from sleuth to sleuth.

Question of Style

With some mystery authors, for every sleuth there is an alias. The start of the now-famous series of books about private eye Lew Archer gave cause for an alias — Ross Macdonald — to one Kenneth Millar. (His wife, Margaret Millar, uses no alias for her successful mystery novels such as *Beast in View*, a prizewinner.) And a difference in style is the reason for Evan Hunter's choice of the pseudonym Ed McBain on those popular police procedurals, to distinguish them from the books published under his own name (*Blackboard Jungle*, etc.); some of his other pen names are Curt Cannon, Hunt Collins and Richard Marsten.

When Perry Mason's creator, Erle Stanley Gardner, switched sleuths in mid-scream to write about the detective team of Bertha Cool/Donald Lam, he succeeded in deceiving his audience with the alias A.A. Fair. Now these books are emblazoned "Erle Stanley Gardner writing as A.A. Fair," and the secret is out. At the start of his career, Gardner wrote for the pulps under many aliases because of his output.

The famous Ellery Queen is, of course, a pen name for the writing duo of Frederic Dannay and Manfred B. Lee; the same team decided to create another alias, Barnaby Ross, for their second detective (actor Drury Lane). Another team, Mary J. Latis and Martha Hennissart, chose the pseudonym Emma Lathen when they launched their banker-detective, John Putnam Thatcher, in *Banking on Death;* they switched to R.B. Dominic for their capitol crimes.

Sometimes writing teams can be confusing. Manning Coles is an alias for two authors, Cyril Henry Coles and Adelaide Frances Oke Manning. It's not to be confused with another detective team, the Coles (G.D.H. and M.I. Cole), and that's not a pseudonym.

Is Sex Necessary?

For every Agatha Christie, Dorothy L. Sayers and Ngaio Marsh, research yields an equal number of talented mystery and suspense

| ABEL MANN | PETER MANTON | J. J. MARRIC | JAMES MARSDEN | RICHARD MARTIN | RODNEY MATTHESON | ANTHONY MORTON |

writers born female but published under a male — or ambiguous — pen name: Dell Shannon (Elizabeth Linington), E.X. Ferrars (Morna Doris Brown), P.D. James (Phyllis White), Anthony Gilbert (Lucy Beatrice Malleson), Tobias Wells and Stanton Forbes (both actually DeLoris Forbes), Clemence Dane (Winifred Ashton) and so on through a long list.

A parade of double initials or a first name that could be male baffles us less and less in these enlightened times, but in their fiendish way publishers stuck such male by-lines on their female authors hoping to cash in on all those readers who (they thought) wouldn't touch with a ten-foot noose a detective novel by a woman. Apparently they hadn't heard of Mary Roberts Rinehart . . .

Does it work the other way round? It does for Canadian writer W.E.D. Ross, who publishes Gothics as Marilyn Ross/Clarissa Ross/ et al., and for Michael Avallone, who also has Gothics on the stands with female aliases — Edwina Noone and Priscilla Dalton, to name a couple. Reverse sexism applies to the authorship of the damsel-in-distress books, whose readers are largely women.

Potpourri

Some pseudonyms really do exist to preserve privacy: Catherine Aird (for Kinn McIntosh) is one, and Josephine Tey (for Elizabeth MacKintosh) is another.

One famous secret pen name in the mystery field is Newgate Callendar, the terse mystery critic for the *New York Times Book Review*. With all their knowledge of poisons, ballistics

WHO'S WHO?

Match the author's name on the left to the pseudonym on the right.

1. Hugh Wheeler	A. Tucker Coe
2. Reginald Hill	B. Peter Collinson
3. Donald Westlake	C. Q. Patrick
4. Dashiell Hammett	D. Anthony Boucher
5. Agatha Christie	E. J. J. Marric
6. John Creasey	F. David Keith
7. Kingsley Amis	G. Patrick Ruell
8. Ross Thomas	H. Mary Westmacott
9. William White	I. Robert Markham
10. Francis Steegmuller	J. Oliver Bleeck

and blunt instruments, novelists reviewed by Callendar could do him in handily were his privacy not protected by an alias.

I suspect that, like every other fan of "murder ink" who can never get enough, I will have to take my mystery authors as I find them, letting out a Eureka! when I discover a cache of books by one of my favorites writing under a pen name. There is no way to stop mystery and suspense writers from using an a.k.a. They hide behind them just as the crooks on the pages of their books have always done. The evidence is in, and the verdict is obvious: It's another case of fiction following fact.

Carol Kountz is managing editor of The Writer. *She once checked into a small hotel near the Reichenbach Falls as Irene Adler.*

KEN RANGER   TEX RILEY   WILLIAM K. RILEY   HENRY ST. JOHN   JIMMY WILDE   JEREMY YORKE

I.N.I.T.I.A.L.S.
H.R.F. Keating

There are four questions mystery lovers ask whenever I am lucky enough to meet one. First: Do you write in longhand or use a type-writer? I reserve the startling answer for face-to-face encounters. Second: Is it true you wrote about Inspector Ghote in India for years without ever having been there? Yes, plus involved explanations. Question 3: And what do those initials — let me see, is it H.R.H., no that's His Royal Highness — well, what do they stand for? Question 4: Oh, it's H.R.F., is it? I thought . . . But, anyway why do you use initials instead of your proper name?

And the answer to that is, I haven't got a proper name. That is, on my birth certificate the long roll-call begins "Henry," but in English English (I think it's different in American English) Henry is a pretty stuffy sort of moniker, so I like to be called Harry. Well, nowadays lots of authors write under nicknames or abbreviated ones, but when I began, which was about a quarter of a century ago, it wasn't quite the done thing to be Tom, Dick or Harry. So I kept to the initials.

Not that I had been intended to. My father always yearned to write but had little success (an article on keeping rabbits in the *Boy's Own Paper*). So when his first-born came along he transferred some of that ambition to the object squalling in the cradle, and after much thought gave him the name Reymond, spelt in that odd fashion because he had seen it in a book mentioning his ancestors. Why, then, aren't I called Reymond and why isn't it R.H.F.K.? Well, old Uncle Henry had money, and as he had no children . . . (No, in the end he didn't.)

But surely not all crime-writers who use or used to use initials had quite those reasons. Some definitely don't. I put the question to them in my turn. And others I have guessed about.

For instance, there are a lot of American authors who use one forename, one initial and a surname, like J.P.M., the creator of Mr. Moto, and W.P.McG. and E.D.H. and J.M.C. and R.L.F. and C.B.H. and E.S.A. and L.G.B. and D.E.W. and J.D. MacD. But this is a good old American custom and is thus accounted for.

An old British custom accounts for many more. In the good old days it was considered just a trifle vulgar to brandish a chap's actual name, what. Initials were more stiff upper-lip, don't you know, and you called a fellow by his surname. So that's the reason probably for H.C.B. (but he may have had Harry trouble, too) and G.K.C. (and he had the distinction of having his initials as the title of a magazine, *G.K.'s Weekly*) and C.H.B.K. and E.R.P. and E.C.B. and G.D.H.C. and E.W.H. and A.A.M. and J.C.M. (but when he got his "K" it was all right to call him Sir John) and C.P.S. (but later it was okay to say Sir Charles and even later "My Lord") and of course A.E.W.M. I'm glad this last kept to initials, because it once fell to me to compose part of a rhymed ceremony for the Detection Club and A.E.W. goes splendidly with "You sin and there's a ghost to trouble you."

With some of us, I suspect, one extra initial gives a bit of extra weight to a name, like that distinguished lady D.B.H. (she was all set to be plain D.H. but a "Your Fate in Your Writing" guy at a charity fair said "With the B is better"

PARDON ME, IS THIS YOUR HANDKERCHIEF?

Initials when they come on dropped handkerchiefs are one of the best-loved clues of the old-fashioned whodunit. The classic example must be the cambric affair with the letter *H* on it in Agatha Christie's *Murder on the Orient Express*.

You don't get them like that any more. Blame the tissue. But in the H.R.F. Keating sock drawer there are still two decent cotton handkerchiefs with an initial on each. One dates from the days when my children used to visit Woolworth's just before Christmas. But the other just arrived there, who knows how. And that's the one I shall drop at the scene of the crime. The initial on it is W. Hercule Poirot, I defy you.

H.R.F.K.

and yes, success followed) or the Australian A.W.U. or E.P.O., though the rest of his names were weighty enough, or R.A.K., though when he got a Monseigneur to tack in front he too became a pretty heavy vessel, or D.L.S. And what a fuss she used to make if that L was left out. "I do admit to one fad. I do like my name to appear in advertisements in the same form in which it stands on the title-page," she wrote once. "It is, if you like, a Freudian complex associated with my schooldays, and possibly I ought to get over it, but I can't. It produces in me a reaction of humiliation and depression and *I don't like it.*"

And with one or two others, urged on in one case by her American publishers, an extra initial has been added to provide a little easily got mystery. That's E.X.F. The X stands for

nothing. And I suspect something similar went on with A.H.Z.C., because he was born plain A.Z.C., and it was much the same with O.H. and H.H.H. Both pseudonyms these, like J.J.C. and S.S. Van D. and J.J.M. and A.A.F., who all used quite meaningless initials for their noms de plume. Occasionally, too, initials provided additional concealment for a pseudonym, as in the case of A.B.C., who if he had used either of his two forenames would have been revealed for the other author he was, and with that old favourite of mine, E.C.R.L., who both wanted to hide her femininity and make up an anagram. In one odd case initials were abandoned so as to lose a bit of weightiness when the academic J.I.M.S. took to crime.

Finally, there are a couple of contemporary British authors who wanted, in perhaps a rather British way, to protect themselves from the world a little, in order, I hazard, to write the better. You'll see what I mean when you read the excellent, rather secretive novels of P.M.H. and the splendid books, also with a good deal of her private personality in them, of P.D.J.

KEY

John P. Marquand, William P. McGivern, Edward D. Hoch, James M. Cain, Robert L. Fish, Chester B. Himes, Edward S. Aarons, Lawrence G. Blochman, Donald E. Westlake, John D. MacDonald, H.C. Bailey, G.K. Chesterton, C.H.B. Kitchin, E.R. Punshon, E.C. Bentley, G.D.H. Cole, E.W. Hornung, A.A. Milne, J.C. Masterman, C.P. Snow, A.E.W. Mason, Dorothy B. Hughes, Arthur W. Upfield, E. Phillips Oppenheim, Ronald A. Knox, Dorothy L. Sayers, Elizabeth X. Ferrars, A.H.Z. Carr, O. Henry, H.H. Holmes (Anthony Boucher), J.J. Connington, S.S. Van Dine, J.J. Marric (John Creasey), A.A. Fair (Erle Stanley Gardner), A.B. Cox (Anthony Berkeley), E.C.R. Lorac (Carol Carnac), J.I.M. Stewart (Michael Innes), P.M. Hubbard, P.D. James.

And what about the one initial of my own I have so far not revealed? Perhaps you will see why when, blushingly, I admit: F for Fitzwalter.

H.R.F. Keating won the Crime Writers' Association Gold Dagger.

MAKING A NAME FOR MYSELF

Penelope Wallace

Two of the earliest questions I asked my nanny were "Who is the best man who ever lived?" and "Who is the most important little girl in the country?" Her answers were "Jesus Christ" and "Princess Elizabeth" — now our Queen. Nanny always *was* prejudiced! To Nanny's question "What do you want to be when you grow up?" I replied, "Famous."

My father and I were very much alike, and neither of us suffered from false modesty; I think it is this similarity which has enabled me to be proud of him — as a father, as a man and as a writer — without feeling that I am stifled by his shadow.

Although I was quite young when he died, I'd spent two years with him at Chalklands, our country house in Buckinghamshire, and here, with the rest of the family away during the week, we talked as equals. He was totally approachable, stopping work in mid-sentence to deal with my problems and answer my questions. We would go in the motor launch to Marlow, where we both ate strawberries and cream for tea — heavy on the cream or sugar, although we were both more than somewhat overweight.

My father had definite views on life, on religious and racial toleration — his villains are of differing nationalities, but usually English. In one book the villain is Chinese; in another, the hero is Chinese. He was a monotheist, with the conviction that truth is not exclusive to any particular church.

After my father died — heavily in debt — we moved from Chalklands and the luxury

Penny, age five, with her father, Edgar Wallace, in his study.

apartment in Portland Place to a small flat in Kensington. Here I lived with my mother during the time she wrote her biography of my father, using the money to pay my school fees at Roedean. She lived to see me pass the entrance exam and died just over a year after my father.

My guardian was a thirty-six-year-old bachelor who was totally incapable of housing a headstrong girl, so I shuttled myself between relations and left school at seventeen. At school I'd suffered somewhat from the "I should have thought Edgar Wallace's daughter would be able to do that" remarks from the staff, but since one is never introduced to people there — presumably new girls are warned in private — it wasn't until I started working in Oxford that I first ran up against the standard introduction to which I've become accustomed:

"This is Penny, daughter of Edgar Wallace."

For a while I thought people only wanted to meet me for my relationship, and I thought of changing my name; then I realised this might be true the first time — as if I had two heads — but if people invited me twice it was because they liked me as me. Now I know "daughter of Edgar Wallace" is an additional interest. I'm proud that so many people like

THE EDGAR WALLACE PUB

Opened October 19, 1976, in Essex Street, London WC2, the pub is handsomely decorated in cherry, gold and deep beige — the Wallace racing colours — and houses valuable Wallace memorabilia, including a gold inscribed cigarette case with the names of his twenty or so race horses, his brass inlaid tea caddy, walking stick, pictures and first editions.

THE EDGAR WALLACE PUB

40 ESSEX STREET LONDON WC2
Snack Eating House · Private Parties
Tel: 01 353 3120

THE EDGAR WALLACE SOCIETY

During the Twenties and Thirties, one out of every four people reading a book was reading a Wallace. Called the "King of Thrillers" he wrote 173 books and 17 plays. (He also wrote the screenplay for the original version of *King Kong* starring Fay Wray.) His advertising promotion for *The Four Just Men* (Wallace offered a £500 reward to anyone who could come up with the solution to it) was a fabulous sales incentive but a financial disaster. It put him into bankruptcy. In January of 1969, Penelope Wallace founded the Edgar Wallace Society to keep loyal Wallace fans alerted to new releases and biographical data not otherwise available. The Society issues a quarterly newsletter, and new members receive a four-page biography of Wallace and a cross-referenced list of titles. For further information, write to Penelope Wallace, 4 Bradmore Road, Oxford, England, OX2 6QW.

and admire him, and I'm delighted to share the affection they have for him.

Since I've tried all my life not to trade on my name, one thing that burns me is when people who are aware of my membership in the Press Club and the Crime Writers' Association ask me if I write! I answer tartly that I'm a member of the Writers' Guild, so I guess I do. In my immodest way, I point out that I've written a number of short stories and that one was made into a TV film for Rod Serling's *Night Gallery* — and furthermore I got good reviews in the States and not one referred to my father!

Penelope Wallace has won a special Crime Writers' Association Silver Dagger award for her organization of the First International Crime Writers Congress.

A MARRIAGE OF MINDS

The Gordons

For forty years now, we've been collaborating on magazine articles, novels, and television and movie scripts, yet we don't quite know how the collaboration works. And it's difficult to explain something you don't understand.

Despite what our friends think, we don't claw and fight. In fact, we've never had a really serious quarrel. The idea has seldom crossed our minds.

Homicide, yes. But quarrels, no.

Even the thought of homicide has been fleeting and muted. And we think that's because in the beginning we decided we would treat each other as if we were single and working together in an office. Gradually we evolved a rule: If one of us feels strongly about a point, then the other gives in. If we both have deep persuasions, then we postpone all discussion for two or three days. By then, we may have forgotten which viewpoint we had, or one of us may have come to see the merits of the other's.

Though we are true collaborators in every sense, we didn't set out to be. Gordon, just out of the University of Arizona, discovered he had become an instant newspaper editor. There was a recession under way, the paper couldn't afford to hire a good editor, and Gordon just happened to be standing there. However, the job paid poorly, and he was forced to moonlight doing magazine articles. He got into the habit of turning over his rough copy to his just-signed bride with the notation "Please fix." Soon she was fixing more and more, and imitating his style. Then one day we were writing so much alike that editors couldn't tell who had written what.

The reason we're not sure exactly how the collaboration works is that we're often in a state of confusion. This is a disease common to authors, no matter how many books they've written. The work seldom comes easily and the decisions that must be made are frightening.

First we have a board of directors meeting, all two of us. We paw through a thoroughly messy stack of files into which for years we've tossed ideas and clippings. We find three or four that we get excited about.

Next we confer with Lisa Drew, our editor, and Ken McCormick, our former editor. We ask for their counsel from the beginning to the finished manuscript, knowing they'll be honest yet considerate of easily bruised egos.

When we're all in agreement on the story, we start juggling three balls. The first is research. We use a cassette to take notes. If we go afield, such as into Arizona's Navajo country as we did for *Ordeal,* we add a camera. Six months later, a slide may fill in a point we've forgotten. In fact, often we see more in the slides when we return home than our memory recorded on the spot.

Along with the research, we write biographies of our principal characters. For each, we may turn out anywhere from three to twenty pages. We don't have room for much of this material, but we need it to give us a "feel" for the character.

Along with the research and the biographies, we plot. This is a hair-tearing operation and the time we most have to keep in mind that homicide is illegal. As we work, we put down each episode, very briefly, on a file card. For *Catnapped!* the cards started out: (1) Ingrid sees prowler; (2) Next morning, Zeke comes, establish characters; (3) D.C. missing; (4) Patti gets ransom call, talks with Zeke, etc.

When we finish, we spread these cards over the den floor like pieces of a jigsaw puzzle. We switch the cards around to heighten suspense; we combine some cards, eliminate others to increase the tempo. It's far more economical in time to omit a card at this point than to strike out a chapter we've slaved over.

We plot to the very end of the story. Many writers disagree with this technique. They think it denies a story spontaneity and that the characters should influence and be influenced by events as the tale progresses. We have no choice. Since we both write on the same story at the same time, we must know where we're going. Occasionally, however, a minor character may usurp a scene, and then we don't hesitate to replot. In other words, our card system is not rigid.

Now we begin the actual writing. Each takes an episode, and we're unisex when it comes to what we write. Milly may have an action scene; Gordon, a romantic one. Or vice versa. We never think about that angle. Occasionally, one of us may say, "Let me have that one. I've got a feeling for it."

We go to our separate dens. Even though we started out as newspaper people working in clattering city rooms, we think we do a better job alone. Besides, Gordon mutters when he writes.

Eventually we exchange copy. We don't hesitate to make marginal notes on the other's pages and sometimes pencil out entire paragraphs. This doesn't bother us. (Well, not too much. We were brought up by hard-boiled newspaper editors and long ago accepted editing as a fact of life, but that doesn't stop us from thinking that all our best work goes into the wastebasket.) What we have left, we sell to Doubleday.

This business of editing each other's copy may sound ruthless, but actually it isn't. We both use the soft sell. Milly will say, "This is awfully good, Gordo, but it just isn't up to your usual high standards." That type of con job. And Gordon will say, "This is just sensational, and if we were writing the kind of novel John Cheever does . . ."

A little snow job never hurt a collaboration. Or a marriage.

By the time a book comes out, we've tossed the copy back and forth so often that we're not sure ourselves who wrote what.

We don't believe that collaboration is for everyone, whether married or not. Frankly, we're surprised that it has worked for us. We're strong-willed individuals. It's not a case of one of us dominating these meetings of the board of directors.

The temperament of the collaborators may determine whether they get along, but just as important is the meeting of minds. Our attitudes are much the same. Although we enjoy reading a good hard-boiled novel, we never could write one. We want people in our stories who care for each other, for the world about them. They may come up against violence and the sordid, but they are only a part of it temporarily. This is not their life, any more than it is ours.

We are not alone, of course, as collaborators. There are quite a few today. Perhaps the two most illustrious pairs are Maj Sjöwall and Per Wahlöö and the Lathen team. And in many cases if one has worked himself/herself into a hole, or is suffering a mental block, the partner may readily solve the dilemma.

Each partnership works differently. Most collaborators divide up the work. One takes the research, another the writing, and then one may do the editing and final copy. This division saves a lot of ego bruising. But we grew up basketball fans and don't seem to mind the "body contact" of working everything out together.

Looking back over the forty years, we believe the most important factor in keeping us from committing a little homicide on each other is that we admire and respect each other, as well as love each other. And there is a difference, you know.

The Gordons began their collaboration in 1950 with the saga of J. Edgar Hoover called The FBI Story. *They insist that "that darn cat" proofreads their manuscripts for typos.*

THE CASE OF THE WALL STREET MYSTERIES

Max Hall

In murder mysteries by Emma Lathen the murders are solved by an elderly banker. The books are set in Wall Street and in various businesses served by the "Sloan Guaranty Trust, the third largest bank in the world."

Very few of Emma Lathen's followers know:

That she is two women — a writing team.

That one of them is a graduate of the Harvard Law School and, until recently, practiced corporation law.

That the other has a degree from Harvard's Graduate School of Public Administration (now the Kennedy School of Government) and for many years held responsible jobs in governmental agencies at home and abroad.

That they have begun another series, under the pen name R.B. Dominic, in which the murders are solved by Benton Safford, a Congressman from southern Ohio.

That their writing method is so bizarre I hesitate to tell about it for fear I will be thought to exaggerate.

The two authors, who live in towns near Boston and spend their summers in New Hampshire, submitted to an interview on the condition that I would not print their real names. In fact I did not know their names until the interview took place. I tried several times to persuade them to drop their pseudonymous veils. Amiably, they kept saying no. During most of their writing careers they were still working at their own professions, and they had the idea that if they were known as the authors of books in which a good many pretentious bubbles get burst, their

MARTY NORMAN

clients and employers might feel a bit uneasy. And even though writing is now their only occupation, they still value their privacy in their home towns. So I will call them Miss Langdell and Miss Littauer — after Langdell Hall at the Harvard Law School and Littauer Center, headquarters of the Kennedy School of Government.

Miss Langdell, the lawyer, told me she grew up in New York City, majored in physics at a college she declined to name, worked a while in Washington, got her law degree at Harvard, and practiced in New York and later in Boston.

Miss Littauer said she grew up in a Chicago suburb, majored in economics at a college she declined to name, worked in Washington and in Europe, got her Master of Public Administration degree at Harvard, and went off to do more government work "and other things." One of her jobs was on the staff of a Congressional committee.

They met at Harvard and quickly learned that they had a powerful interest in common: each had an almost encyclopedic knowledge of murder mysteries in the English language.

Miss Langdell: "I think it's safe to say that I had read just about every mystery in the New York Public Library." Miss Littauer had done the same in her community. At Harvard they swapped, bought, and borrowed mysteries and went through the extraordinary collection of whodunits in Widener Library like two buzz saws.

Years later, in 1960, both were back in Boston. They decided to collaborate. Why?

Miss Littauer: "We decided how nice it would be to have an independent income. We said, let us write a book. A whole series. Let us create an attractive character and have him move in situations where we can take advantage of our strengths. We decided on a banker because there is nothing on God's earth a banker can't get into."

The immediate incentive was a $3,000 contest that the publisher Macmillan was conducting. They wrote *Banking on Death* and sent it off. They didn't get the $3,000 — they never heard that anybody did — but Macmillan accepted the manuscript and published it in 1961. In that book the Sloan got involved with a missing heir, a murder, and sundry shenanigans in a company making felts and industrial textiles in Buffalo.

Macmillan also published the next six, in this order: *A Place for Murder* (a dog show in Connecticut); *Accounting for Murder* (homicide in the home office of the "National Calculating Corporation"); *Murder Makes the Wheels Go Round* (the auto industry); *Death Shall Overcome* (the stock exchange acquires a black member); *Murder against the Grain* (big sale of wheat to the Soviet Union); and *A Stitch in Time* (the medical industry).

Simon and Schuster published the next nine, as follows: *Come to Dust* (fund raising for a small college in New Hampshire); *When in Greece* (a hydroelectric project); *Murder to Go* (bad trouble in a nationwide chain called "Chicken Tonight"); *Pick Up Sticks* (hard-sell real estate in New Hampshire); *Ashes to Ashes* (the closing of a parochial school, also much about the funeral industry); *The Longer the Thread* (the ladies' garment industry in Puerto Rico); *Murder without Icing* (professional hockey); *Sweet and Low* (the cocoa exchange and the candy industry); and *By Hook or by Crook* (Oriental rugs).

All of the above have been published in paperback. The books are also published in England, and all or some of them have been translated into German, Danish, Swedish, Norwegian, Dutch, and Portuguese.

Had you done a great deal of writing before 1961?

Miss Littauer: "No, but you have to remember, by 1961 we were damn near professional *readers* of mysteries."

Do you hire research assistants to study the industries you write about?

They looked surprised and said in effect: "Why, no. We get the information we need mainly from our own experience and from newspapers. The *Wall Street Journal* is a lot of help."

*F*or me the greatest unsolved murder mystery is not so much a matter of determining whodunit but why and how we can stop the mayhem before we're all strangled.

To wit: the bureaucracies that constitute governments determinedly and too often successfully murder free enterprise and the ability of a person or a business to profit. Yet the profitable life of both of them is essential to keep these vampires fed. A familiar mystery plot — how to keep the vampires alive without killing their food source!

Even the best of other mysteries pale beside the magnitude and seeming insolvability of this one.

MALCOLM S. FORBES

THE SECOND PSEUDONYM

Under the pseudonym R.B. Dominic, with Doubleday the publisher, there are four books so far: *Murder in High Place* (the Peace Corps and a defenestration on Washington's Connecticut Avenue); *There Is No Justice* (a nominee to the Supreme Court is done in); *Epitaph for a Lobbyist* (lady lobbyist slain at National Airport); and *Murder out of Commission* (the atomic energy commission and a proposed nuclear power plant).

Miss Langdell (emphatically): "A conference about corporate financing is the same all over the world."

Well, how did you two know so much about pro hockey when you wrote *Murder without Icing?*

Miss Littauer: "We are hockey fans. We go to the games. We know about hockey. As for the ownership questions and so on, anybody who reads the sports pages can find that out."

How do you go about collaborating on the writing itself?

Collaborating on their replies, they explained it about like this:

"We write alternate chapters."

What did you say?

"Alternate chapters. One of us writes chapter three, the other chapter four, and so forth."

I never would have guessed it. The style doesn't seem different.

"Also, we write simultaneously. While one is writing chapter three the other is writing chapter four."

Why do you do that?

"To save time."

How does the author of chapter four know what chapter three is going to say?

"Oh, we make a general outline. At first we made a quite full outline, maybe a whole page for each chapter. Now we just agree on the general tenor. We decide in advance who's going to be murdered and who's going to do it. We try to think up as sensible a murder as possible from the point of view of the murderer. Then we have to figure how in the world Thatcher can catch the murderer. A couple of times we created a foolproof murder that not even Thatcher could solve, and we had to go back and put in a mistake or two on the part of the murderer."

Miss Langdell and Miss Littauer didn't make their job sound very difficult; but I can't help thinking they must do a mighty lot of adjusting and editing after exchanging those simultaneous drafts. After all, a book typically takes them six or seven months, and some have taken over a year. By the way, when I asked whether they get much editing at their publishers, they grinned. The answer is no, and that's just how they want it.

Miss Langdell writes at night, with two fingers on a Hermes 3000. Miss Littauer prefers daytime and writes with a ballpoint on a long yellow pad. They use secretarial services for typing. They keep two three-ring binders, one containing the original and the other a carbon copy.

John Putnam Thatcher is different from the usual crop of detectives and private eyes in fiction. He is urbane, well-bred, skeptical, unfluffable but easily bored, no tough guy but as firm as Gibraltar in protecting the Sloan's interests, a widower with grandchildren, sixtyish (and doesn't grow older from book to book), much helped by Miss Corsa (everybody's ideal secretary), long-suffering in the face of idiotic behavior by public-relations men and by the bank's president, Brad Withers, who happens to be a Yale man. A reviewer in *The New Yorker* once called Thatcher "a man of great charm, bottomless suspicion, and Euclidean squareness." Says Miss Langdell: "I have never met anybody as nice as Thatcher."

Max Hall is a free-lance writer and former editor at Harvard University Press.

WHY I'LL NEVER FINISH MY MYSTERY

John Leonard

It seemed like a good idea at the time, which was February. She had just come back from Paris with a trunk of troubles. For me, work has always been an anodyne — *the* anodyne, I see now — and I presumed on fifteen years of friendship to commend it to her. I also commended myself. We would collaborate in abolishing her depression.

It was probably raining. Certainly, I was fooling myself.

For a living, I write. For relaxation, I read mysteries. It is only natural that I should have contemplated writing a mystery. The problem was a plot. In an otherwise blameless life, I have perpetrated four novels, and even the reviewers who found something to admire in those novels had to admit that, as one of them put it, "Plot is not his forte." I try to get by on style and sensibility, as is often the case with writers to whom nothing very alarming has ever happened. (About the time Grace Kelly married Prince Rainier, someone in Hollywood was asked for anecdotes about her, and replied: "Grace is the sort of person who doesn't allow anecdotes to happen to her." Maybe this implies a lack of imagination. But, I keep telling myself, the same was true of Wallace Stevens.) Anyway, there wasn't much use contemplating a mystery when, in my unmysterious fiction, I had enough trouble getting people in and out of rooms.

Whereas, for a living, she teaches history. She does not write, not even letters. She reads as many mysteries as I do, not so much for relaxation as in a critical spirit, as if trying to figure out why Napoleon didn't get away with it or Trotsky blew his chance. She wants to solve the murder; I'd rather leave it to the detective. She does double-crostics with a felt-tip pen; I watch baseball games on television. Her training, though, as an historian had steeped her in theories of conspiracy. She teemed with plots. She agreed to outline four of them. On paper.

I should explain that, over the years, as we watched each other's children grow, she had introduced me to Josephine Tey and I had introduced her to Ross Macdonald. Her favorite mystery was *The Daughter of Time* and mine was *The Chill*. It might have occurred to clever people that we were temperamentally opposed. We were not clever.

We met instead for lunch at one of those French restaurants in midtown Manhattan where the menu is a sneer. We were to go over her plot outlines. The chitchat was of Michael Innes (*Hamlet, Revenge!*), Dashiell Hammett (*The Glass Key*), Rex Stout (*Too Many Cooks*), Raymond Chandler (*The Long Goodbye*) and the Wahlöös (*The Laughing Policeman*). It was also of Schopenhauer and Scheherazade, of Mozart and Bette Midler, of Watergate and Billingsgate.

She wore, I couldn't help noticing, a dress. Always before I had seen her in pants. I knew she was freckled; I hadn't known that she had legs.

THE WORK IN PROGRESS

No! How did you have the nerve to do that?!!

Diana decided to shorten the leash on her impatience. Intelligent, passive people made her grind her teeth: there were always extenuating circumstances, and all day long such people combed them, like a beautiful head of hair. But she was not her sister's keeper. "How are you engaged in subversive activity?"

Nice! Love it.

"I use the wrong color ink," said Sally. "I put down an X where a circle is supposed to be. I refer telephone callers to doctors who don't belong to the organization. I'm single-handedly undermining the system. People with bad feet will have to go to psychiatrists. I have surgeons for acne. Everything they plug into their computer will be a lie. I'm a treasonous clerk, what do you think of that?"

. . .

I'm not crazy about all that ballet imagery — it's not bad; it does work, I think — but it's unnecessary.

There was a thump at the door. And what happened next seemed choreographed. Sally rose, as though to execute an entrechat; switched gears from a glissade to a bourree; and arrived at the thumping ready to jete. Behind the door stood Nick, in the first position, holding grocery bags. Sally tried to take them. He would not release them. Locked together around the grocery bags, they backed into the livingroom, did two or three pirouettes on point, sighed, tried a plie, and simultaneously sat down on the floor. Diana wanted to applaud. How like brother and sister they were -- twin redheads, both short, wearing identical tie-dyed T-shirts and faded bluejeans and Capezio exercize slippers. Maybe Sally's freckles had been scooped out of Nick's dimples and applied to her skin with a dropper.

We agreed on our detective — a young female lawyer living alone in New York — and settled on the simplest of her four plots as a start. This plot involved a theater troupe, a loft, an ancient grievance, some schizophrenia, Grand Guignol and enough suspects to stuff a Trojan horse. I will say no more; perhaps by the time Jimmy Carter completes his second term as President and runs for God, we'll get around to finishing our mystery. Her responsibility, in addition to the plot, was detail. How

does a little theater operate — props, costumes, set design, money-raising? What would our detective, Diana, look like, wear, eat, read, listen to on the phonograph, admire and disdain? Which, when, who, why . . . and so on.

I, on the other hand, typed. While she made lists — of plants, poisons, legal precedents, pop therapies — I, out of my style and sensibility, was to fashion believable characters and to engineer suspense. Action, conversation and the sort of morbid excess necessary to imagine an avant-garde play were my specialties. I would type a chapter, we would meet, she would carry the chapter away in her knapsack and, alone with an orange and a cup of coffee grounds, edit — using, of course, a felt-tip pen. Then we would meet again.

I had assured her that, although I type neatly out of some anal compulsion whose origin is nobody's business but my own, she should feel free to question, contradict, excise and veto. This, as it turned out, was a big mistake.

Those meetings: after many a taco, burns the heart. In Mexican restaurants, at botanical gardens and public libraries, Nathan's and the zoo, we met. Under clocks at train stations, in bars without television sets, behind bayberry bushes on Fire Island, in the lobbies of movie houses with popcorn machines and of apartment buildings with doormen who looked like drill instructors at an orthopedic gym for wayward jackboots, we met. As though we were spies, and our mystery were microfilm, we exchanged manila envelopes: heavy breathing at the Algonquin.

My collaborator complained about my narrative device of throwing a party every time we needed to press-gang a motley of implausible loud-mouths into the obligatory anticlimax. I abashed myself, not, I admit, without grumbling that she had a fixation on locked rooms and ciphers.

My collaborator removed all puns from the manuscript. Although I was injured in the technique and the predisposition — puns, after all, derail the train of thought — I acquiesced. If what she wanted was more like a diagram of a synthetic carbon derivative than the word-playfulness, the beautiful phoneme, I associate with a happy hammerlock, plus tickles, on the

English language, well, it was her plot.

My collaborator objected to my promiscuous analogizing. I would have instructed her on the abstract pleasure of a purely verbal artifact, but demurred: We live in a world that eats ugly pills; the streets swarm with disappointed thugs; our architecture is brutal and cowering; our music blares; we advertise ourselves in neon, or with gongs; our principal form of locomotion seems to be the shove. To collaborate, then, with someone who looks as though she danced or swam, who would be able to touch a piano or a child without leaving fingerprints — "In every gesture dignity," said Milton — was to be reacquainted with grace and brave beauty, and to have an excuse for subduing qualms. Compared to purely verbal artifact, or even the latest abstraction, she seemed real.

My collaborator felt that I was trying too hard, showing off, slowing down the story: Please, sir, instead of the arabesque, may we have a minuet? She attacked me in the adjectives. This is attacking me in the style and sensibility.

Another critic.

I should also explain that in the course of this assault on my pride of rhetorical legerdemain — to life, I apply a dangling participle as if it were a stethoscope; in the gerunds, there one is free — I was "launching" my collaborator. That is, I hauled her off to those literary cocktail parties, or West Side fundraisers at which Ramsey Clark is asked to come out in favor of compulsory sodomy, where she might meet a man worthy of her history and freckles.

Strange: these men, underneath their blow-dried tease, behind their tinted aviator goggles, inside their Cardin turtlenecks, seemed unheroic and insensitive, so many thumbs on the lute of her throat, jukeboxes of opinions. I dialed a radio cab, and fed her cats.

Listen: I thought that in writing about our detective, Diana, I was writing about a Harriet Vane who went to Yale Law School, a kind of *Gaudy Night* under the tables down at Morey's. I found that I was writing about my collaborator; her distinction was the watermark on every virgin page I tapped at.

FAMOUS WRITING PARTNERSHIPS

Peter Anthony
Francis Beeding
Manning Coles
Ellery Queen
Patrick Quentin

I stopped working. So much for anodynes.

Then there was the night Nixon resigned. My collaborator and I drove all afternoon, with the radio on, and made it in time for dinner at a country inn in Connecticut. She had grown up in California. Some scars glow in the dark. This was an occasion, for which she dressed in flames. After fish and wine on the veranda, overlooking fireflies, we went inside to the TV set. The room was upholstered in Republican putty, and sullen. My collaborator was too fiercely happy for them. She was a sword. They had to keep their mouths shut as Nixon fell on her sword.

William Butler Yeats, who never wrote a mystery novel, spoke in one of his poems of "beauty like a tightened bow," the kind from which arrows are loosed. Yeats was meditating on a Maud Gonne who was looking around for another Troy to burn. I am meditating on my collaborator, for whom there aren't enough Troys to burn. Collaboration is a dialectic. Love is grazing privileges.

Reader, I married her.

At the wedding, my son played the clarinet. Hot and cold running daughters punned their way through a rendition of "Greensleeves" obscene in its subtext. I have, in a drawer, eighty pages of a mystery novel that has somehow, mysteriously, lost its zest and zeal and analogies.

There are some mysteries for which we do not require, nor do we want, solutions.

I didn't even manage to silence a critic.

John Leonard is chief cultural correspondent of the New York Times.

BOOK ONE:
TO BE CONTINUED?

James McClure

There was a brief paragraph headlined CATCH 23 in the *Times* of London not long ago that read: "Twenty-three fishermen have been rescued from the Sea of Japan after their boat, full of mackerel, sank under an excessive catch."

The moral is clear: Never trust a mackerel, no matter how outwardly obliging it may appear. Less obvious, perhaps, but very tempting, is the application of this modern parable to the writer about to embark upon a mystery series.

To paraphrase the warnings given by ancients who, with glittering eye, stoppeth one of three at mystery conventions, the voyage will take his frail craft into wickedly deceptive waters. He will have to guard against accepting unqualified success without question, and against dangling the same hook once too often. He would also be prudent to avoid taking on board greater numbers of that other slyly treacherous fish, the red herring, than can be comfortably accommodated. While he must never allow himself to forget, even in his most transcendental moments of achievement, that specific gravity and other down-to-earth phenomena remain immutable.

Yet this advice could apply equally to the writer planning a dozen unrelated mystery novels. The series writer is, as they say, in a different ball game altogether.

Just how different is evinced by our tortured attempts to explain why it isn't the Sea of Japan we're fooling with here, but an ocean of paradox that threatens a fate far worse than dampened euphoria.

We could say, for example, a mystery series traps the writer in a whole new dimension — and that there's written evidence to prove it. An antimatter world in which the laissez-faire laws of fiction tend to invert themselves, hardening fancy into fact, denying the usual liberties and, what's worse, translating many well-meaning human beings into wistful automatons.

"A sausage machine, a perfect sausage machine" — so Dame Agatha once described herself when, in the unreflective prose of G.C. Ramsey, she was "a little awed at the idea she must produce a Christie for Christmas lest the earth veer off its course."

True, automatons don't come any more wistful than sausage machines, nor has there ever been a threat to the solar system more extraordinary; the Virgin, although subject to not dissimilar expectations, certainly hadn't the same penalty clause.

But problems aren't solved by simply changing genre. With the delightful exception of Harry Harrison's Stainless Steel Rat stories, mystery writing and science fiction just haven't much in common — and it would be wrong to suggest that things were quite as bad as all that.

In this search for comparisons with which to construct a practical framework of reference for the tyro, I prefer to find them in the past, way back in another realm of mysteries.

I believe the mystery series writer has more in common with the alchemist — beyond such superficialities as a dim, dusty workroom littered with manuscripts and sobered by the odd skull — than is generally conceded.

COURTESY JAMES MCCLURE

James McClure always doodles while planning a novel. He says, "I generally start with a face in the middle and build up around it, adding things suggested by lines and shapes which juxtapose, and others that seem to hop straight out of a deep hole someplace."

My first inkling of this came when someone made the usual crack about *"formula* writing," as though a formula was in itself something despicable. If people mean this to imply that they'd rather every aspirin they took was wildly, excitingly different in composition and effect, then good luck to them. But the point is that the word "formula" suddenly struck me as inappropriate: it was too precise, too modern.

Then I realised that the mystery writer's stock-in-trade was really the *spell* — never prissy formula, the very sound of which precludes eye of newt, hair of psychopath, Group O and the other more gruesome ingredients one uses to create one's illusions.

This happened while I was writing my first Kramer and Zondi novel, and, as I'd already

latched on to the idea that all writers were stage conjurers with a persuasive line of patter, the notion slotted in very happily. It wasn't until I came to repeat a few tricks for the second and third K&Z stories that I discovered the difference between an innocuous "abracadabra" and one uttered when the game was being played for keeps.

My Afrikaner detective and his Zulu colleague, illusory beings I'd personally summoned up, seemed to have become independent of me and my powers. Not only that, but they'd moved out into the real world, where a section of the reading public, albeit a small one, had placed them under the protection of the law.

The irony was acute. Should I now decide

that Kramer had to be written off in Chapter Eight, then I could be charged with — wait for it — murder! And if the wholly biased jury out there found me Guilty, then I'd have only two options: to stage a resurrection as soon as possible, compromising my integrity; or to shout "Nuts!" from the dock, forfeit my royalties and hope no greater punishment would be exacted.

As it was, I had no particular urge to destroy either of them, had chosen the pair in the first place because they were the best means at my disposal *(huh)* for expressing ideas that mattered to me — and I'd stuck with them for the very same reason.

But what had wrought this transformation? What was the uncanny difference between the one-shot novel and the series book? It gave me cause to ponder further the alchemist theory, and I'll admit I had to cheat a little with regard to that discipline's achievements to find this answer to the questions posed.

One could say that the essence of life is continuity; when it runs out of time, it stops. Just as an evening of real-life drama ends when the final curtain is rung down, or when people vanish at the snap of a satisfying novel being closed, to persist thereafter only in retrospect — thought about, perhaps, but never again encountered.

Whereas if a book is left open-ended, like a genie's bottle left uncorked, stock characters can escape into time proper, linking their innate continuity to something that has no beginning, no middle and no end. They can even achieve a state of active longevity far exceeding one's own, and here I'm thinking of *Colonel Sun*, for example, the posthumous James Bond treat by Kingsley Amis. The so-called immortality of many well-loved spirits is not, of course, the same thing, as they're able only to endlessly repeat themselves until a pastiche comes along — but that's another sort of series (and pastiche), anyway.

Whatever the cause behind this change, there's no doubt that it brings a moment of realisation that fills the writer with surprise, joy and trepidation. Any alchemist who, quite as inadvertently, found himself manifesting a virgin against his corner cupboard, must have felt much the same way — while noticing the same whiff of brimstone and eternal damnation in the air.

This could seem absurd to the Novelist Who regards Himself as the God Almighty of His separate creations, free to do as He pleases and answerable to no one for His inscrutable excesses. Yet let him try his hand at a mystery series, and he'll soon have his personal pronouns cut down to size — either that, or trade his soul for the conceit of them. Observe how serenely humble some series authors are; note how others run the full gamut from quiet despair to demonic megalomania.

It's just possible they stand divided by much the same things as separated the sages from the sorcerers: their prime motive for being interested in life, death and the puzzles arising; their attitudes to self-indulgent compromises, to truth and morality; their willingness to serve themselves or to serve others. They could be set apart, in short, by the choice they make between practising black or white magic.

Latter-day parallels aren't difficult to draw. Most blatant, perhaps, is the violence/drugs/perversion wizard who has his proclivities prologued (in the same order) by Mephistopheles in Goethe's *Faust*:

> *One of those crickets, jumping round the*
> * place,*
> *Who takes his flying leaps, with legs so long,*
> *Then falls to grass and chants the same old*
> * song;*
> *But not content with grasses to repose in,*
> *This one will hunt for muck to stick his nose*
> * in.*

Lionel Timothy Cricket (his real name, although none of his admirers is ever permitted to know this) deludes himself that he's turning base mettle into gold, of course; sadly, although crotch-deep in all that glitters under the Californian sun, he has never produced anything as valuable as a frankfurter — and never will he while a sick fantasy like Hank Grunt, his star turn, is still around.

Equally noticeable, but way across the other side, beneath the brighter sun of India, stands H.R.F. Keating and his endearing familiar, Inspector Ghote of the Bombay

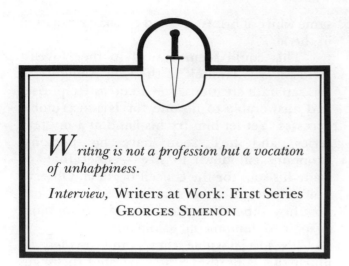

*W*riting is not a profession but a vocation of unhappiness.

Interview, Writers at Work: First Series
GEORGES SIMENON

Police. "Margery Allingham once told me," Mr. Keating recalls, "that only half one's readers would be interested in the book itself, while the other half would read it for the series character — and the writer just has to be reconciled to this." His generous reconciliation is obvious; he and Ghote have together brought us all a wealth of good things to enjoy.

Grudging resentments, not unlike those felt by some ventriloquists for their dummies, frequently occur in the grey, uncommitted area (does that sound like England?) lying between the two extremes. This could be a matter of trying to impose one's own needs and shortcomings on reality at the expense of truth.

The School of Incredibles, which has as its protagonists old ladies never short of an hygienic murder to solve, police officers with the intellectual introversion of their middle-class alter egos, often seems to show signs of the stress of vicarious living. Dorothy L. Sayers once said, a shade too cheerily perhaps: "I can see no end to Peter this side of the grave!" She did, however, contrive to ignore him for the last two decades of her life, by which compromise she brought about his nominal termination. What adds poignancy to this is that Julian Symons, the celebrated authority on mystery writing, has suggested that Miss Sayers might have been a much better writer had she not fallen in love with her whimsey.

One could go on endlessly noting the stern morality at work between the lines of this genre, just as alchemists must have found that their similar preoccupation with light and dark was apt to evoke the unexpected

But far more is to be gained by simply looking at what has been achieved by a master magician unrivalled in his understanding and honest exploitation of the mystery series. Mr. Symons has said of Georges Simenon's Maigret — in his definitive history of mystery writing, *Bloody Murder* (U.S. title, *Mortal Consequences*) — that he is "one of the most completely realised characters in all modern fiction."

To which, for an insight into the approach that made this possible, one need add only the author's own words from *Writers at Work*:

I have a very, very strong will about my writing, and I will go my own way. For instance, all the critics for twenty years have said the same thing: 'It is time for Simenon to give us a big novel, a novel with twenty or thirty characters.' They do not understand. I will never write a big novel. My big novel is the mosaic of all my small novels.

So where has all this led us? Have we done better than the champions of Catch 23? Perhaps we have encouraged the newcomer to look upon each book in his series as a carefully selected chip of coloured glass, rather than as a worthy yet ephemeral sausage, and that's about all. No matter, for the old salts overlook plain Catch 2, anyway.

Catch 2? That's simple: Nobody can really know they're a series writer until Book Two, when it's too late to unmake the critical decisions made in Book One, which wasn't Book One until Book Two began the series, although it had to begin with Book One, of course.

As for Catch 1 — any series, wilfully and arrogantly launched with Book One, presuming a demand to supply, is likely to have no real magic at all and to never reach Book Two — well, let's not dwell on it. I once did just that, and have been haunted ever since by a disembodied ex-detective, shrouded in diabolical reviews.

James McClure won the Crime Writers' Association Gold Dagger for his first novel, The Steam Pig.

THE LURE OF THE REICHENBACH

Peter Dickinson

I am no scholar. I am not even sure how to spell "Reichenbach." Certainly I have no idea how many lesser heroes than Holmes have been done away with by their creators. But it must be a good guess that almost every writer who has kept a detective going through several books finds his thoughts turning more and more toward the moment when . . . when, for instance, Inspector Ghote eats the poisoned curry, or Peter Wimsey has heart failure on meeting a greater snob than himself, or Van der Valk . . . But no, Van der Valk *is* dead, isn't he? Mr. Freeling has done the deed.

Why?

The usual answer, that the creator had become bored with his creation, is true in a very trivial kind of way but is at the same time deeply misleading: the kind of answer a writer gives when he doesn't want to discuss the point. I myself stopped writing about James Pibble after five books, but I wasn't bored with him. I liked — and like — the old boy, and I owe him a lot. I think that without hesitation I could answer most questions about him, including the ones which aren't mentioned anywhere in the books. Now he feels to me something like a colleague I spent a lot of time with almost every day but because of a change of jobs have scarcely seen for several years; to meet again might be delightful, might be embarrassing, but it seems not to happen.

It's worth considering how these long-running heroes come into existence. There seem to be two ways, the deliberate and the accidental. The deliberate hero is nearly always a bloodless creation; the author has decided that he (she? Is it a female trait to manufacture these bionic brains? No idea, but let's settle for "she" throughout) . . . that she is going to write a series of books and that, therefore, they will have to have some kind of trademark. The hero will be *different*. Thus traits of difference are accumulated, selected not for the way they grow out of the character but solely because nobody else has yet thought of them. In much the same way, minor German monarchs of the eighteenth century invented uniforms for their household troops: violet breeches, because everyone else had green or red; kepis with four-foot plumes; badger-skin bandoliers. What matter if in the end the hussar was unable to lift his sabre above waist height because of the tightness of his jacket? He was more distinctive on the field than old Hesse-Halsbad's boring dragoons.

So the deliberate hero is jumbled into being. (Or *was* jumbled would probably be truer; these creatures were mostly born a generation or two ago, though they live on in libraries, and every now and then a new one is born, especially on TV. Lollipops, for instance.) Let's say he has a club-foot and rides an enormous bike (good for last-minute dashes to rescue the peculiarly witless females who festoon this type of novel) and carries a . . . a swordstick? No, too ordinary; what about a blow-pipe? And he knows the Bible by heart, huh?

For book after book, shelf after shelf, that bike will roar to the rescue, that uneven footstep will sound menacingly, or hearten-

AUTOMOBILE FUNERAL COACH AND CHAPEL COMBINED

An automobile funeral car with a compartment that will seat 36, in addition to space for the casket and flowers. The car takes the place of 9 closed carriages and a hearse. In bad weather it can be used as a chapel at the cemetery. The driver's compartment has no connection with the remainder of the car.

The interior is finished in oak and upholstered in leather. The casket compartment is 2½ ft. wide, 2½ ft. high, while that for the flowers is 2½ ft. wide, 5 ft. high.

The car is 22 ft. 8 in. long, 7½ ft. wide, and holds 36 mourners.

ingly, on sidewalks (though, mark you, in moments of crisis we will read of the man moving "with astonishing dexterity, despite his club-foot"), the witless female's latest attacker will stagger in mid-assault, a tiny dart protruding below his left ear, and all will end pat with a quote from the Second Book of Kings. And by the third book the author will be stiflingly bored with her creation but afraid to let him go.

I said I was no scholar, so I can only guess which of the great detectives was engendered in this fashion. Nero Wolfe, surely — those orchids are typical, and typically become a nuisance after a very few books, and if all Wolfe's characteristics had been as factitious he would have been a bore very soon. But Mr. Stout was a genius, and in inventing Wolfe and Goodwin, solved the central problem of the whodunit by splitting his detective into two parts; this set-up became an art form in itself — I remember one in which Wolfe finally left his apartment, and I felt as cheated as I would have on reading a thirteen-line sonnet. But very few Wolfes came into the canon that way . . .

As a transitional figure, let's consider Margery Allingham's Mr. Campion, who started as factitious as they come, with his silly-ass talk and his mysterious noble connections and the tedious Lugg to provide extra laughs (like the Professor's comic sailor servant in ancient boys' stories). And then Miss Allingham became interested in him and in the course of two or three books he became, so to speak, real. His chat was mitigated, Lugg almost abolished, and at the same time the plots and adventures moved out of the realm of cardboard fantasy into something like life. So successful was this transformation that Miss Allingham convincingly brought off the problem of making Campion fall in love with a married woman. (Virtue triumphed, too. What a long time ago that must have been. And it's worth pointing out that this passion actually was necessary to the plot.)

So Campion became what I have called an accidental hero. These are the detectives who come into existence because the author wants to write a particular book. The book itself demands a detective, and he *grows* into being, quite slowly, finding his shape and nature from the needs of the book and the author's own needs. He may turn out a very odd creature, but all his oddnesses are expressions of what he is like inside. And then (provided the other bits have gone okay — plot, setting, characters, language and so on) the author may find herself with quite a good book on her hands, centering round a detective to whom readers respond.

They may think they're responding because of what seem to be external characteristics (remember the excitement about the first *black* detective?) but really it's because the fellow is *alive.*

Moreover, because detective stories are tricky things to write, the author's attention may not have been concentrated on exploring every nook and cranny of her hero's personality; in fact, if it has, she will have written an unsatisfactory book — there isn't room in the genre for a lot of that sort of thing. So there will be more to give. And the publisher, of course, wants more if the first dose has been a success. It requires a lot of self-confidence and a healthy bank balance for a newcomer author to say no.

So for a few years everyone is happy; if the readers like it, then the publisher likes it, and the author fleshes out her man, puts him into novel situations, finds new facets. If she'd been writing a straight novel, she'd have done all these things in a single book, but with detective stories it may take four or five. And then . . .

Then she has finished. What is she to do with him now? Is he to go on, book after book, dragging his club-foot, using his little grey cells, sucking his lollipop — and dying all the while? Not dying the death that living men die, but moving into the walking death of the zombie? The boom of the Reichenbach Falls begins to mutter in her ears.

The sad result of all this is that, with a few exceptions, it is the accidental heroes who get pushed over the edge, while the deliberate ones — never really alive in the first place — live forever. Those the Gods love die young.

Miss Allingham, tactful as ever, found one solution. She allowed Campion to become a sort of ghost, a twinkle of large spectacles across the room, a muttered suggestion of danger, a friendly spirit, there to keep the readers happy — like a horseshoe over the door. But even she must have known just why Conan Doyle made Holmes walk the fatal path.

It's lucky, if you think of it, that most of us are not faced with the same clamour for resurrection.

Peter Dickinson won the Crime Writers' Association Silver Dagger for the The Glass-sided Ants' Nest.

OUGHT ADAM TO MARRY CORDELIA?

P.D. James

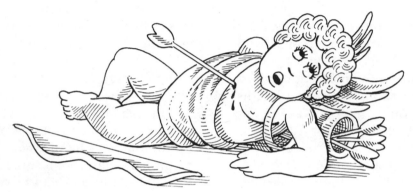

From the number of readers who write to enquire whether my girl detective Cordelia Gray of *Unsuitable Job for a Woman* will marry Adam Dalgleish, it is apparent that mystery lovers take the view — to paraphrase Jane Austen — that an unmarried detective who is in receipt of a good income is in need of a wife. Dorothy L. Sayers would not have agreed. She expressed the firm belief that detectives should concentrate on the clues, not spend their time chasing young women. It was not a rule she herself adhered to, although Lord Peter had to chase his Harriet (if so ungallant a word can be used for his aristocratic and articulate wooing) six years before she finally capitulated on Oxford's Magdalen Bridge — appropriately enough, in Latin.

But it is true that mystery writers, in general, don't interest themselves greatly in the love lives of their detectives, and perhaps this isn't surprising. Birth, sex and death are the three great absolutes in fiction as in life, and it is difficult enough to write adequately about the last, even within the constraints of a detective novel, without attempting to deal other than superficially with its two precursors. A serious love and sex interest in a mystery can endanger its unity as a novel, not to speak of the quality of its detection. It is significant that Dorothy L. Sayers described *Busman's Honeymoon* as a story with detective interruptions. Perhaps this reluctance on the part of detective novelists to deal with sex and love explains why so many writers make their detectives celibates or at least unmarried: Sherlock Holmes, Father Brown, Poirot, Miss Marple, Dr. Thorndyke. In contrast, the tough, wisecracking, hard-drinking school of private eyes have plenty of women in their adventurous lives, but strictly on their own terms. Other detectives have a happy marital background so that we can rest confidently in the knowledge that all is going well with

TROY'S ROMANCE

Ngaio Marsh presented Agatha Troy to Roderick Alleyn in *Artists in Crime* and united them in *Death in a White Tie*. Since Alleyn — or "Rory," as his wife likes to call him — spends much of his time away from London in New Zealand on cases, the two of them carry on a postal relationship a good deal of the time.

their private lives and they can get on with their detection without fear of domestic or psychological upheavals. Examples are Simenon's Maigret, Freeling's Inspector Van der Valk, H.R.F. Keating's Inspector Ghote, Edmund Crispin's Professor Gervase Fen and H.C. Bailey's Mr. Fortune. Other detectives are obviously attracted to women but take care to keep them on the periphery of their private or professional lives. It is difficult to imagine a wife intruding permanently into Nero Wolfe's admirably organised brownstone ménage.

There are, of course, some mystery novels in which the love interest complicates and confuses both the investigation and the hero's emotions. Ngaio Marsh's Roderick Alleyn met his painter wife Troy during one of his cases, and Lord Peter first saw his Harriet in the dock at the Old Bailey, where she was standing trial for the murder of her lover. There are, too, some famous husband-and-wife teams: Dashiell Hammett's Nick and Nora Charles, Agatha Christie's Tuppence and Tommy Beresford, and Frances and Richard Lockridge's Pamela and Jerry North. But here the wife is a comrade-in-arms, and the love interest is domestic, peripheral and amusing rather than passionate. They hunt the clues together.

So what of my readers' question? Will Cordelia marry Adam? Who can tell? There are, of course, a number of reasons why such an interesting marriage might be nevertheless imprudent. One can imagine the advice which a marriage guidance counsellor would give to Cordelia. Here we have a widower, considerably older than you, who has obviously been unable or unwilling to commit himself permanently to any woman since the death in childbed of his wife. He is a very private person, self-sufficient, uninvolved, a professional detective dedicated to his job, totally unused to the claims, emotional and domestic, which a wife and family would make on him. Admittedly, you find him sexually very attractive, but so do a number of women more experienced, more mature and even more beautiful than yourself. Are you sure you wouldn't be jealous of his past, of his job, of his essential self-sufficiency? And how real would your own commitment to him be when there would always lie between you the shadow of a secret — that first case of yours when your lives so briefly touched? And are you sure you aren't looking for a substitute for your own inadequate father?

The arguments are weighty, and Dalgleish and Cordelia — highly intelligent both — would be well aware of them. But then, when have two people married on the basis of prudence? I can only say that I have no plans at present to marry Dalgleish to anyone. Yet even the best-regulated characters are apt occasionally to escape from the sensible and controlling hand of their author and embark, however inadvisably, on a love life of their own.

P.D. James won the Crime Writers' Association Silver Dagger for Shroud for a Nightingale.

HARRIET'S COURTSHIP

Dorothy L. Sayers introduced Harriet Vane to Lord Peter Wimsey in *Strong Poison*, had them work together in *Have His Carcase*, announced their engagement in *Gaudy Night*, married them in *Busman's Honeymoon* and gave them one son in "The Haunted Policeman" and two more in "Tallboys."

MYSTERY WRITERS: A THINK TANK FOR THE POLICE?

Dorothy Salisbury Davis

The remarkable thing about the meeting between the Mystery Writers of America and New York Police Commissioner Patrick Murphy a few years ago is that virtually half the people who were present don't remember what took place; the other half don't remember being there at all. Which has to mean that no matter how much got poured into the Think Tank that day, most of it vanished into vapors when the combustibles caught spark.

I can't remember who promoted the idea of MWA as a Think Tank for the New York Police Department. But if we submitted to flattery, the Commissioner submitted to some of the most extraordinary suggestions since a citizens' group back in the 1840's insisted the police get into uniform so that people could recognize them. I do remember we were each supposed to arrive with an idea on how to improve law enforcement or crime prevention in Manhattan.

One of those ideas which is coming around again — I think now in the State Assembly — was that the city should provide every citizen with a police whistle with which to summon help in emergencies. If one also summoned a taxi, so much the better: double indemnity.

Another mystery writer's proposal that day which involved the public sector: the encouragement of citizen arrests. The double-duty aspect of this action, it was pointed out, was that it would also relieve the police of time-consuming court appearances.

My own humble suggestion purposed an improvement in the patrolman's uniform: a rear-view mirror in the visor of his cap, which, presumably, would make him less vulnerable to attack from the rear. Only the Commissioner picked up the idea — I think to drop it in the alley on his way out. I've been watching for a long time now, and the visor mirror has not become a part of standard police equipment.

The trouble that day was not in the tank or in the ranks. It was in the goal of the promoter, who saw the situation as bulls vs. brains. (I speak poetically, not epithetically.) Commissioner Murphy did not want to fight; he was the perfect gentleman. And we were far and away more willing to make fools of ourselves than of the police. To have truly tested us, the Commissioner should have arrived with the records of one or two unsolved cases and brought along the investigating officers — all 200 or so of them, with whom our best brains might have rapped and just possibly added a mite's worth of insight.

Not many mystery writers would claim their ability to write fiction, wherein they can put and take clues to the crime as needed, qualifies them as bona fide detectives. And not many police detectives, despite the gracious Commissioner Murphy, would concede our talents to have much value on the street.

The great Conan Doyle once undertook the exoneration of a man convicted of cattle mutilation. His detective work cleared the con-

demned in the press. But officialdom refused a retrial. The case did lead eventually to the creation of the Court of Criminal Appeal.

New York Police Chief George Walling, whose career spanned half the nineteenth century, wrote of perhaps the most illustrious case of writer as detective:

Edgar A. Poe possessed, or thought he possessed, high ability as a detective; and his ingenuity in this ghastly groping is shown in . . . The Mystery of Marie Roget. *. . . The best authorities of the time do not agree with Poe's finding, but the tragic romance is full of painful interest.*

Our day in a Think Tank neither humbled nor exalted us, but most of us have since confined our ghastly gropings to the typewriter.

Dorothy Salisbury Davis is a past president of the Mystery Writers of America.

CREATING A MYSTERY GAME

Lawrence Treat

Once upon a time there was no TV. People walked to the movies and used their cars to neck in, but when they stayed home there was nothing much to do except listen to the radio and play games.

The old ones were passé, but a whole new type was developing. It was competitive, and it tested knowledge, intelligence and manual skills. People went around saying, "Did you hear about So-and-So? He scored ninety-eight in 'Ask Me Another.' " The high scores of notables like Dorothy Parker and the columnist FPA were quoted, mythically and incorrectly. These were Depression times, the pulp magazines were getting knocked off like bowling pins, and a beginning writer like myself was on the treadmill of trying to turn out stories as fast as the rejection slips came in, which the post office delivered with a speed unknown today.

Around then my eight-year-old nephew, who had no artistic talent whatsoever, showed me a drawing that only he could have been proud of and said, "Guess what." I made my twenty guesses, and he beamed at me and told me the correct answer. "It's a dead man and he's just been killed. See the bullet?"

I said, "Who killed him?" He said, "You did! It's your bullet. See?" And he pointed to a drawing that had a vague, messy resemblance to a crumpled bullet, with my initials on it.

My first thought was that I had a moron for a nephew, my next thought was that he was pretty smart. My bullet? He'd gone and invented ballistics all by himself.

The result of my thinking came slowly and with effort, like a snake wriggling out of his

Foolhardy is the detective who stands in front of a well-lit window while a murderer is on the loose. This, the cover design for Mr. Treat's innovative mystery picture puzzles.

skin, but it finally emerged. Why not a detective game? Show people a few clues and let them make inferences. Let them be their own Sherlock Holmeses.

The idea was simple enough: Sketch out the evidence found at the scene of a crime and use it to work out the solution. What, for instance, can you infer from a theater ticket stub? Two stubs might mean that X, if he was the holder and a man, took his girl out for the evening. Stubs are dated and numbered and furnish at least a prima facie alibi for time as well as place. An orchestra seat would probably mean that X was well-to-do, a second-balcony stub that he was poor, or at least parsimonious.

Put a stain on it and call it blood, or coffee. Rumple it and you can assume that X is nervous. Take a pair of expensive seats along with a pawn ticket, all found in X's pocket, and he's probably living beyond his means and needs money. Ergo, X had a robbery motive.

The possibilities intrigued me, and I played around with various clue items. Take a cigarette butt. Lipstick on it? Smoked down to the last quarter-inch? Thrown away after a puff or two? Put a few such clues together, state the bare bones of a crime, and put down leading questions that help build up to the solution.

To oversimplify a possible puzzle, suppose you're told that a heavy safe was stolen, either by A or by B. A drawing shows footprints. A's are big, B's are small, and both sets go to where the safe stood. B's imprints are light going to the site and heavy leaving it, whereas A's are of equal depth. Obviously, B stole the safe.

I sent my first attempt to *Dime Detective*, which had been my major rejection market. They approved the project and asked for more, and for months thereafter I went around studying objects with a view to what they might tell me. A discarded hobbyhorse. Chewing gum on the underside of a chair. The contents of a garbage pail. My whole world consisted of objects bristling with ideas that I could use for this game.

Once the game took hold, it sold to strange markets. A drug company used it for promotion. A travel agency bought several puzzles to put on the backs of cruise menus. If a pad can be a book, I published two of them, one under the title *Bringing Sherlock Home*, the other under the more prosaic title *Pictorial Mysteries*. They consisted of a half-dozen copies of each puzzle on a pad, so you could deal them out for a group to compete, for speed as well as accuracy.

With the prestige of book publication, I grew more sophisticated. No longer the simple drawings of a few footprints or a ledger book, which my brilliant nephew was now old enough to execute more or less competently. I needed the sketch of the scene of a crime, with the clues clearly indicated, and several artists tried doing them, with mixed results. The pictures demanded simplicity and accuracy, overlaid with some artistic taste. Small wonder that the artist who managed such a neat balancing act left for a job with Disney, where he could draw the pure, telling lines of the Disney menageries.

In the course of time and sweat *Redbook* paid me handsomely for a set of puzzles, and I was off to Spain on the proceeds of the sale, where I figured I could live nicely for a year. While there, I sent a few of them on to England. British magazines bought them and supported me for another few months.

But the height of my glory was the dizzy month when the New York *Post* dickered with me for using the puzzles in a contest designed to increase circulation. The grand prize was $10,000, which to me was astronomical. Since I, and I only, would know the answers, I had a long and intense struggle with my conscience. My conscience won but was never tested out. The *Post* dropped the idea and returned me to Earth.

Forever after, I've been skeptical about prize contests with a bundle of money for the correct answers.

Writing stories is creatively more satisfying than constructing puzzles and I've never gone back to them, but I can't think of a pleasanter way to have survived the Depression.

Lawrence Treat is a past president of the Mystery Writers of America.

SOLUTION "TO THE LUNCH ROOM MURDER"

3. No, because the money has been taken neither from the counter nor the cash drawer. 4. Yes, because their three checks totaling 55 cents were rung up together on the cash register. It follows that one of them treated the other two. The fact that they sat next to each other is not convincing, although it is indicative. 5. No, because D has finished eating and has paid; A has done neither. 6. At least six — A, B, C, D, Joe, and Brady. 7. Yes, because River Street, which is the only possible approach, is visible through the windows of the lunch room. 8. No. They leave no mark on a dry floor. 9. Y, because they start from near the mop which only he would be using and then proceed to the cash drawer which only he would open, except in case of robbery, which we know has not occurred in this instance. 10. No, because only his toe marks show, indicating that he ran. 11. Yes, because his footsteps (heel and toe marks) show that he walked and did not run to the cash register. 12. Near the cash register, because we know that he walked to it and ran from it, and because he did not close the cash drawer. It follows that something — namely, the murder — frightened him while he was there. 13. Z, because they start at the far side of stool A. 14. Yes, because his toe marks leave via the kitchen door. 15. Yes, because their footsteps do not show and the space near the kitchen is wet. 16. Yes, because the man whose hand print appears must have stood near the mop, in the position where footprints X appear. 17. No, because the mark of his right hand appears. Therefore, he held the gun in his left hand. 18. C, because he was left-handed. Cups and glasses are normally placed at the right and are at the right of A's, B's, and D's plates. The smears of glass and cup show C pushed these to the left, where they now are. It follows that C was left-handed and the murderer.

THE LUNCH ROOM MURDER

Case No. 4
from Lawrence Treat's
"Bringing Sherlock Home"

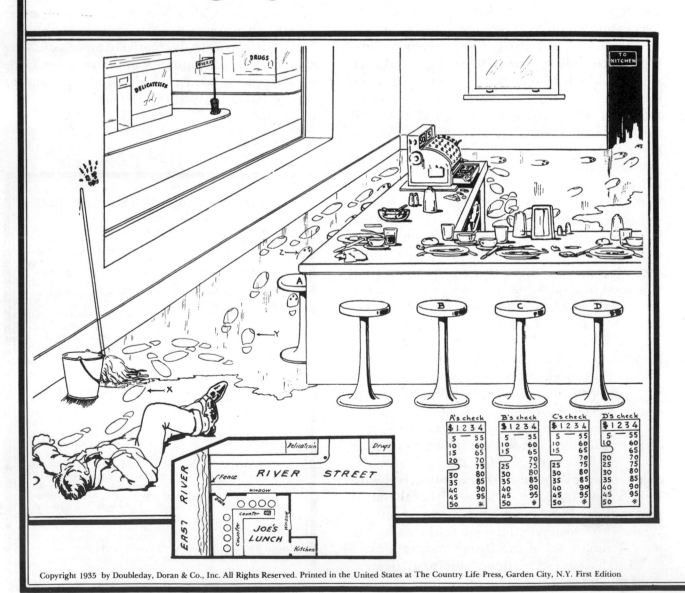

I f you look to the left, you will find a sketch of Joe's lunch room. Police heard a shot, rushed to the restaurant and found exactly what you see.

They identified the body as that of Flash Brady, a racketeer. Joe, who had no helper, had only one fact to tell. The murderer had leaned against the wall while firing at point-blank range. The imprint of his gloved hand is in clear view.

From these facts and an examination of the scene, can you answer the questions and tell who killed Brady?

Answer the following questions by checking the box next to the correct answer. The first two questions have been done and explained to show the type of reason you should have in mind, although you need not write it out.

1. Had Joe been mopping up recently?
☒Yes.   ☐No.
Because the pail, mop, and wet floor so indicate.

2. How many customers had recently been in the restaurant?   ☐None.   ☐One.
☐Two.   ☐Three.   ☒Four   ☐Five.
Because there are four checks and four plates, cups, glasses, and sets of cutlery.

Now you answer the rest of the questions.

3. Do you think Joe was the victim of a holdup?   ☐Yes.   ☐No.

4. Do you think B, C, and D knew each other?   ☐Yes.   ☐No.

5. Did A enter the restaurant before D?
☐Yes.   ☐No.

6. At least how many people were in the restaurant the instant that Brady entered?
☐1.   ☐2.   ☐3.   ☐4.   ☐5.   ☐6.

7. Could Brady be seen approaching the restaurant by any of the customers?
☐Yes.   ☐No.

8. Would footsteps show if they had not traversed the wet spaces?   ☐Yes.   ☐No.

9. Which are Joe's footsteps?
☐X.   ☐Y.   ☐Z.

10. Did Joe walk out through the kitchen door?   ☐Yes.   ☐No.

11. Did Joe ring up the 55-cent sale on the cash register before the murder?
☐Yes.   ☐No.

12. Where was Joe at the moment of the shooting?   ☐Near the mop.
☐Near the cash register.
☐Near the kitchen.

13. Which are A's footsteps?
☐X.   ☐Y.   ☐Z.

14. Did A run out through the kitchen door?
☐Yes.   ☐No.

15. Did B, C, and D leave through the front door?   ☐Yes.   ☐No.

16. Are the footsteps marked X those of the murderer?   ☐Yes.   ☐No.

17. Did the murderer fire with his right hand?   ☐Yes.   ☐No.

18. Who killed Brady?
☐A.   ☐B.   ☐C.   ☐D.   ☐Joe.

Solution on page 73.

LIVING WITH A MYSTERY WRITER

Abby Adams

Living with one man is difficult enough; living with a group can be nerve-racking. I have lived with the consortium which calls itself Don Westlake for five years now, and I still can't always be sure, when I get up in the morning, which of the mob I'll have my coffee with.

Donald E. Westlake is the most fun, and happily we see more of him than any of the others. He is a very funny person, not jolly exactly, but witty; he loves to laugh and to make other people laugh. His taste in humor is catholic, embracing brows low, middle and high, from *Volpone* to Laurel and Hardy. (His cuff links, the only ones I've ever seen him wear, depict Stan and Ollie, one on each wrist.) He's a clown at times; coming home from the theater recently with a number of children (more about them later), he engaged in a skipping contest (which he won — he's very competitive, a Stark characteristic spilling over) with several of the younger kids, causing the eldest girl acute embarrassment.

Westlake has in common with many of his characters a simplicity and naïveté about life that is disarming, especially if you don't know about the Stark and Coe personae lurking in the background. Looking for an American Express office, he walked through the red-light district of Amsterdam without once noticing the "Walletjes" — plate-glass windows set at eye level in the seventeenth-century canal houses, behind each of which sits a lightly clad hooker, under a red light just in case the message has not been put across. I had to take him back and point them out: "There's one, Don, isn't she

Abby and Don on a visit to France.

pretty? And here's another one."

Like his character Dortmunder, Westlake is unpretentious, unmoved by style or fashion. He dresses simply, wearing the same clothes year after year, wearing hush puppies until they literally fall off his feet. I cut his hair, but he does his own mending and sews on his own buttons. (Mine, too.) Also like Dortmunder, he takes a great deal of pride in his work (with, thank God, more success), but is not otherwise vain.

Behind the wheel of a car he is Kelp. One of the four publications he subscribes to is *Car and Driver*. (The others are *Horizon, The New*

Yorker and *The Manchester Guardian;* what is one to make of all *that?*) He drives passionately, never failing to take an advantage. We once drove across the United States and were passed only three times: twice by policemen and once by a battered old pickup truck full of cowboys that whizzed past us at 90 on a road in Wyoming that I still shudder at the memory of. (We were doing 75.)

Like Harry Künt, the hero of *Help, I Am Being Held Prisoner,* Westlake will do almost anything for a laugh. Fortunately, he does not share Künt's proclivity for practical joking or I would no longer share his bed. Like Brother Benedict of *Brother's Keepers,* he is really happiest leading a quiet life and being able to get on with his own work in peace. However, his life, like a Westlake plot, seldom quiets down for more than five minutes. ("I'm sick of working one day in a row," he sometimes says.) Like many of his heroes, he brings this on himself, partly out of restlessness and partly out of a desire to make things happen around him. For instance, all these children.

Westlake has four, by various spouses, and I have three. Not satisfied with the status quo — his four scattered with their mothers from Binghamton, New York, to Los Angeles, California ("I have branches in all principal cities," he is wont to say) and mine living with me in New York City — he ups and gathers everybody, with all their typewriters, baseball bats, Legos, musical instruments, movie books and stuffed animals, and brings us all to *London* for a year. Then, not content with London, he rents buses and takes this traveling circus all over Great Britain, including Scotland in January (snow) and Cornwall and Wales in February (rain). Still not content, he drives us through the Continent in April for a sort of Grand Tour: Holland, Belgium, Germany, Luxembourg and France in three weeks. Because, like Brother Benedict again, he is obsessed with travel.

Also, like every Westlake hero, Donald E. Westlake is sex-crazed, but I'm not going to talk about that.

Tucker Coe is the gloomy one, almost worse to have around the house than Richard Stark. We see Tucker Coe when things go wrong. The bills can't be paid because the inefficient worlds of publishing and show business have failed to come up with the money to pay them. Children are rude, noisy, dishonest, lazy, loutish and, above all, ungrateful; suddenly you wonder what you ever saw in them. Ex-wives are mean and grasping. Cars break down, houses betray you, plants refuse to live, and it rains on the picnic. Coe's character Mitch Tobin builds a brick wall in his backyard when he's feeling sorry for himself; Coe has never actually built a wall, but he has built enough bookcases to fill the 42nd Street library, for himself and his friends. Also, when the Tucker Coe mood is upon him, he will do crossword puzzles, jigsaw puzzles (even ones he has done before), fix broken electrical things — in fact, do almost anything except work at his typewriter or talk with other human beings.

Timothy Culver is the professional — hack, if you prefer. He will write anything for anybody and doesn't care how much he's paid, just as long as the typewriter keys keep flying. If he doesn't have any actual work to do, he will write letters; and if you've ever received one you know they're as well-written as his books. Well-typed, too. Part of his professionalism is that he produces copy so clean you could simply photostat the pages and put them between boards and have a book with fewer misprints than most actual volumes.

His desk is as organized as a professional carpenter's workshop. No matter where it is (currently, it's a long white dressing table at one end of the living room here in London), it must be set up according to the same unbending pattern. Two typewriters (Smith Corona Silent-Super manual) sit on the desk with a lamp and a telephone and a radio, and a number of black ball-point pens for corrections (seldom needed!). On a shelf just above the desk, five manuscript boxes hold three kinds of paper (white bond first sheets, white second sheets and yellow work sheets) plus original and carbon of whatever he's currently working on. (Frequently one of these boxes also contains a sleeping cat.) Also on this shelf are reference books (*Thesaurus, Bartlett's, 1000 Names for Baby,* etc.) and cups containing small necessities such as tape, rubber bands (I don't know *what* he uses them for) and paper clips. Above this shelf is a bulletin board displaying various things that Timothy Culver likes to look at when he's trying to think of the next sentence. Currently, among others, there are: a newspaper photo showing Nelson Rockefeller giving someone the finger; two post cards from the Louvre, one obscene; a photo of me in our garden in Hope, New Jersey; a Christmas card from his Los Angeles divorce attorney showing himself and his wife in their Bicentennial costumes; and a small hand-lettered sign that says "weird villain." This last is an invariable part of his desk bulletin board: "weird" and "villain" are the two words he most frequently misspells. There used to be a third — "liaison" — but since I taught him how to pronounce it (not *lay*-ee-son but lee-*ay*-son) he no longer has trouble with it.

The arrangement of the various objects on and around The Desk is sacred, and should it be disturbed, nice easygoing professional Timothy Culver turns forthwith into Richard Stark. Children tremble, women weep and the cat hides under the bed. Whereas Tucker Coe is morose and self-pitying, Stark has no pity for anyone. Stark is capable of not talking to anyone for days or, worse yet, of not talking to one particular person for days while still seeming cheerful and friendly with everyone else. Stark could turn Old Faithful into ice cubes. Do you know how Parker, when things aren't going well, can sit alone in a dark room for hours or days without moving? Stark doesn't do this —

Abby and Don enjoying a stroll on the Continent.

that would be too unnerving — but he can play solitaire for hours on end. He plays very fast, turns over the cards one at a time, and goes through the deck just once. He never cheats and doesn't seem to care if the game never comes out. It is not possible to be in the same room with him while he's doing this without being driven completely up the wall.

Stark is very competitive and does whatever he does with the full expectation of winning. He is loyal and honest in his dealings with people and completely unforgiving when they are not the same. Stark is a loner, a cat who walks by himself. He's not influenced by other people, doesn't join clubs or groups, and judges himself according to his own standards. Not the easiest man to live with, but fortunately I seldom have to. About the best you can say for Stark is that he can be trusted to take messages for Westlake and the others which he will deliver the next time they come in.

The question that now comes to mind is: What next? Or should I say, Who next? A half-completed novel now resides on The Desk, title known (but secret), author still unchristened. I feel a certain suspense as I await the birth of this creature; yet whoever he turns out to be I know he will probably be difficult to get along with, but not boring.

Abby Adams and Donald E. Westlake are just good friends.

Abby and Don on the palace grounds.

INTERVIEW WITH A CHARACTER

Colin Watson

Mr. Harcourt Chubb, O.B.E., Chief Constable of Flaxborough, was asked to give his personal impressions of Colin Watson, a fellow citizen and chronicler of such events in the town's recent history as have exercised his, Mr. Chubb's, authority and talents as a law enforcement officer — in short, Flaxborough's somewhat remarkable crime record.

At first diffident ("One has to live in the same town as the man, you know"), Mr. Chubb eventually proved forthcoming in the matter of confidences as any guardian of morality is when given reasonable expectation of garnish.

Colin Watson, admitted Mr. Chubb, was not too bad a fellow, by and large, considering that he wrote books and had even been a journalist at one time. Apart from two convictions for speeding, he had kept out of trouble with the police, had no paternity orders against him, was never seen really drunk and once had made a contribution to the Town Band's instrument fund — one wondered, in fact, if he were a proper author at all.

You say he was once a newspaperman?

Oh, certainly. He began on the old Flaxborough *Citizen*. Right here in this town, though he's from London, I believe. That might account for a certain streak of irresponsibility.

Coming from London, you mean?

No, no. The journalism. Let me give you an example. Some wretched junior had submitted a wedding report — this was years ago, mind — and it was Watson's job to correct his copy. The lad had written: "All the brides-maids wore Dutch caps." Shocking gaffe, of course. But Watson let it through. Thought it funny, apparently. Can't think why. Must have embarrassed no end of people.

I presume his newspaper career took him further afield than Flaxborough. Do you know anything about that, Mr. Chubb?

A little, yes. It has to be said that Watson does not seem to have taken that aspect of his work as seriously as his employers had the right to expect. There's a certain irreverence about the fellow. I've always regretted his having made friends with my Inspector, you know. I suspect part of Purbright's awkwardness is due to Watson's influence.

Inspector Purbright is not portrayed in the novels as an awkward man.

No, well, he wouldn't be, would he? I mean, look who wrote them.

Is the Inspector, in fact, an awkward man to deal with? What one might call a bloody-minded man?

Ah, you won't get me to say that. No, no. Very sound chap is Purbright. I don't know what we should have done without him in Flaxborough over the past twenty years — and all despite lack of promotion, you might notice. There's devotion to duty for you. No, it's just this funny streak in the man. I don't always know which way to take him. As I say, I think sometimes he sees too much of Watson.

How do you explain what you call Watson's "irreverence," Mr. Chubb?

Well, I've a theory, such as it is. He went to one of the smaller public schools, d'you see, and that nearly always has the effect of putting one up against authority. What do they call it — compensatory attitude? Something like that. Take Watson's career in journalism, for instance. He rose to be one of the best-paid leader-writers in Kemsley Newspapers. Earned nearly twenty pounds a week (that's what, oh, more than thirty of those dollars of yours) at his peak. Yet instead of being grateful, do you know what he used to do? Put chunks of carefully disguised socialist propaganda into his leading articles. Poor Lord K. would have been terribly upset if he could have understood them. I asked Watson if he wasn't ashamed of having taken advantage of his employer in that way. I've never forgotton his answer. It wasn't in Mrs. Chubb's hearing, luckily. "All newspaper proprietors in my experience," he said, "are chisel-minded, semiliterate whoremasters with delusions of grandeur." A very unfair generalisation, I always thought.

Why, in the Flaxborough novels, did Watson elect to use a detective story format? They are not "thrillers" in the conventional sense.

You mean, why does he write about the few bad apples in our little community barrel? I've often asked him that. You don't do the town justice, I say to him. I get a characteristically flippant answer, as you might imagine. The good apples, he says, are always so bloody dull.

Is it true that he once was a crime reporter?

So I gather. At least, he did a lot of court reporting at one period. Inquests, police calls, all that sort of thing. We in England don't use sensational terms like "crime reporter," you know. Watson claims that his police characters are based on officers he has known. Maybe they are. It's not for me to say. I must say that *I* never found crime amusing. Still, I never found the Honours List amusing, for that matter, whereas Watson thinks it a great joke. Very perverse sense of humour.

What do you think is the reason for the Flaxborough novels being popular in America?

Are they indeed? That *is* interesting. Can't imagine why, unless it has something to do with those Pilgrim Father chaps. A lot of them came from round here, you know. Some of Flaxborough's first trouble-makers. Protesters, they call them now. They used to get shipped off to the plantations in those days. Come to think of

it, I daresay our friend Watson would have qualified if he'd been around then.

Has he sympathetic feelings toward America?

He has American friends, I understand. He likes *them.* Sympathy, though — that's a word one has to be careful about. It can sound patronising. Purbright probably has the right idea: he says we all need sympathy these days.

Inspector Purbright is a long way from being a "tough" policeman. Isn't that being rather out of fashion?

Possibly. But it wouldn't do, you know. Not in Flaxborough. The last really aggressive officer we had was nearly thirty years ago. Poor fellow fell off the town bridge one night after registering a court objection to the grant of a liquor license to the Over-Eighties Club. Purbright is a very conciliatory chap in comparison. Mind you, I don't think much of some of his notions. I once heard him telling his sergeant — you know young Love, do you? — some rubbish about his being fascinated by what he called "the curious innocence" of the professional criminal. Nothing very innocent, I'd have thought, about some blackguard who goes round pinching people's valuables, eh?

What is your author's attitude toward crime and punishment, Mr. Chubb?

Decidedly odd, I'm afraid. He says too much effort goes into enforcing laws designed to protect property, and too little into protecting people. That's nonsense, of course, but I'm just telling you *his* ideas. Oh yes, he said on another occasion, I remember, that if we *had* to go round hanging people, it ought to be for murdering the English language. Let me see, who was that president you used to have in America, the one who didn't shave very often and had a dog . . . Dixon? Nixon? Anyway, Watson and Purbright were talking about him at the time of that Watergate business of yours, and Watson said impeachment would be too dignified a course to take with such a grubby little man; he ought to be put in a home for cliché addicts. I thought the remark was uncalled for, frankly.

You must sometimes find your author a trial.

Oh, it's my job to cope with people.

Colin Watson is the author of The Flaxborough Chronicles, *recently filmed for British television.*

THE SOLITARY LIFE OF THE WRITER

Joyce Porter

During my fourteen years as a professional writer I have managed to avoid almost all contact with my pen-pushing colleagues. I did once, when a mere "first offender" in the business, attend a literary cocktail party, but I left almost immediately when somebody insulted me by asking if I were a publisher. However, writers are an intrusive breed and occasionally they penetrate my defences via the television set, pompously planking themselves down on my hearth rug before I can dash across and switch them into oblivion.

One of them made it the other day. I think they got him from Rent-a-Writer. Wild horses wouldn't, of course, drag his name out of me — though a substantial bribe might. Anyhow, he had me riveted to my chair. Not by the splendour of his presence, you understand, or the beauty of his eloquence, but by the sheer fascination of the background they were photographing him against. Would you believe floor-to-ceiling bookshelves? The freshness of vision shown by TV producers is sometimes mind-blowing.

Anyhow, I ignored the rubbish his nibs was spouting and took a good look at the books, naturally assuming that they were studio props because your genuine, dedicated, doing-it-for-eating-money author doesn't read anything except publishers' contracts and banker's cheques. But, no, I was mistaken. The books were the real thing and without a doubt the personal property of the charlatan who was pontificating there in front of the cameras. How could I be so sure? Well, the books were all in sets of six. In other words, they were the free copies we bearers of the flag of culture get as perks from our European publishers. (The Americans, with typical generosity, dish out ten.)

I couldn't believe my eyes. This joker must have kept every free copy of every edition of every book he had ever published! What strength of character! What nerve! What resolution! Had he no friends? After all, most of us who manage to get something into print are knee-deep in good old chums eager to grab one of our free copies rather than venture into a bookshop and *buy* one. (I wouldn't mind quite so much if they didn't think they were softening the blow by asking you to sign the damned thing.)

Well, when I'd got over the shock of seeing this star of the literary firmament broadcasting his niggardliness to the nation, I began to pay close attention to what he was saying. Such a consummate skinflint must have a message for us all.

Unfortunately, what he was saying, interrupted from time to time by carefully rehearsed promptings from the interviewer, proved to be a pretty fair sample of the usual drivel. In private, writers only talk about money, but in public they trot out the habitual phoney clichés of the trade. Viz.: no waiting for inspiration for us professionals . . . moral obligation to grind out the daily stint just like the rest of you miserable wage slaves . . . the loneliness . . . the self-discipline . . . the soaring imagination . . . the creative blocks . . . the soft black pencil on the creamy yellow paper . . . characters who magically develop a life of their own and begin to take over . . . blah, blah, blah.

And then he said it.

You could have heard my jaw drop a mile away.

In answer to some puerile question about one of his earlier best-sellers, he said (and I quote): "Yes, when I re-read it the other day, I must say I thought it had worn quite well."

When he'd *re-read* it? One of his *own* books?

What am I, a freak or something? I wouldn't re-read one of my own books if you paid me! (Well, I would, actually, but you know what I mean.) Blimey, I have to write the damned things — and that's enough for anybody. I produce "funny" detective stories (though they don't make me laugh), and by the time I've thought up the plot, worked it out, written the first draft in longhand, typed the second draft and bashed out three copies of the final one, I've had it up to *here!* Nowadays I can't even face a last read-through for typing errors, and, when the proofs come in for correcting, I start at the last page and work backwards. Believe me, any bright or original idea I might have had right at the very beginning is looking pretty tatty when I meet it for the sixth time or so. The books I write are meant to be wolfed down at one gulp on a train journey, or wherever, and thrown away. (I should be so lucky! Returned to the blooming library is more like it.) I don't expect anybody to read them half a dozen times, and I bitterly resent the fact that I have to.

Come to think about it, I resent most things about being a writer. I resent having to sit there all alone at my desk. I resent all my brilliant ideas turning to dust the minute I get them down on paper. I resent the sheer physical labour of pushing a pen-nib over all those acres and acres of sneering white paper. I resent the noise a typewriter makes. I resent my publisher asking me to cut a thousand words. I resent my publisher asking me to add a thousand words. I resent critics who suggest that I haven't written a masterpiece — and write off as a solid-gold idiot anybody who implies that I have.

Well, no, it's not really as bad as all that.

Whenever I get to the gibbering stage, I can always calm it down by reminding myself what the alternative is. Like work.

And I'm not really whining about writing being hard labour, am I? Why, even on a good day I reckon I spend more time playing Patience than I do penning deathless prose. Luckily I know three different ways of laying out the cards for Patience; otherwise, I might well drop down dead with sheer boredom. But what else can I do when Literature goes sour on me? I only need a fleeting distraction, something that doesn't take me away from my desk, something that can be instantly abandoned should inspiration strike, and something that demands no intellectual or creative effort. What else is there except Patience that will guarantee to send me back to my writing almost as quickly as I left it?

A well-known American writer once said: "I sometimes ask myself what a grown man like me is doing, sitting there all day telling himself stories." It's the most perceptive remark I've ever heard a writer make about his job. That's precisely what writers should be doing — telling themselves stories. Not playing endless games of Patience, for heaven's sake!

But, back to that pundit on the television who actually reads his own books. Could it be that his books are so good and so well-written that, even twenty years later, he can . . . ? Is that why he's on the telly and I'm not?

I decided that it was all giving me an inferiority complex, and I switched the set off. Tenth-rate writers simply can't afford to indulge in self-doubt.

Back to the grindstone.

My own fault, really. I shouldn't have got hooked on eating.

Now, where had we got to? Ah, yes! One face upwards and six face downwards. One face upwards and five face downwards. One face upwards and four face downwards. One face . . .

See what I mean about writing?

Big deal!

Joyce Porter is as witty as her Scotland Yard Inspector, Wilfred Dover, is sloppy. He appears in many books, including Dover One, Dover Two, Dover Three, Dover Goes to Pott.

Chapter 3
BLOODHOUNDS

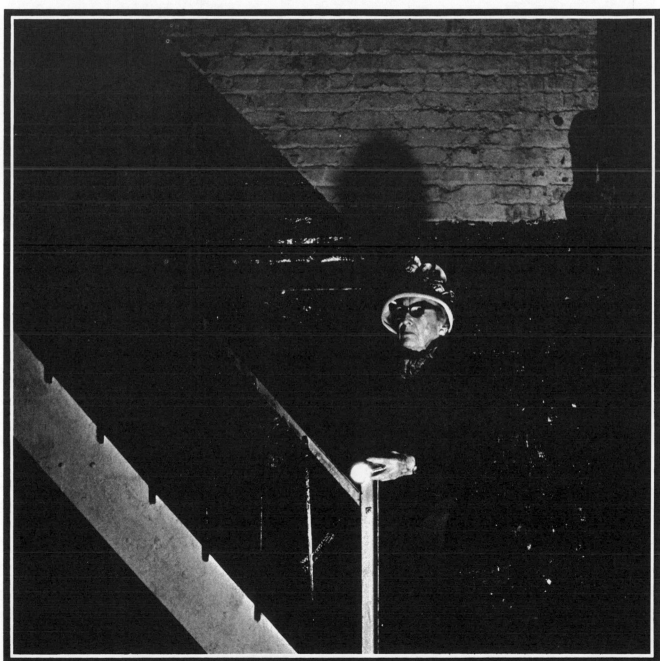

AN EYEWITNESS ACCOUNT OF HOLMES

John P. Oliver

I was a guest of the Metropolitan Police, Scotland Yard. Someone thought it would be a good idea for the NYPD and our London counterparts to swap personnel — so off went one New York Detective Lieutenant and one London Detective Inspector to opposite sides of the Atlantic.

By my sixth day in London I'd been told at least sixty times, "Scotland Yard is the greatest crime-fighting organization ever to grace the face of the earth." That day they'd deposited me at the Black Museum. I was unimpressed. You see one collection of guns, bombs, knives and hatchets, you've seen them all. I was plotting my escape when I accidently slammed into an old man and sent him sprawling. Oh, Jesus, I thought. I've killed the old goat. What a headline that'll make: BERSERK NEW YORK COP KILLS OLD PENSIONER!

As I was picturing the end of my career, my victim began to stir. I jumped to help him up. After mutual apologies (very polite, the English), we chatted a bit about the Yard. He was a retired Detective Inspector who had put in thirty years on the job. I asked him what he thought of the New Yard and its modern crime-fighting techniques, and almost before I got the question out he began a tirade. For close to an hour he harangued me on how today's cops were nothing more than high-priced mechanics, fiddling with their new toys — computers, helicopters, radios, closed-circuit TV, cars, etc.

"Not like the old days, when it took *real men* to be coppers," he said. "Men who dared walk alone and unarmed through the East End and Whitechapel at night."

I asked the obvious: "Aren't today's cops better at solving crimes because of it?"

"Better? Better? Why, we solved all the big ones . . . Except the Ripper, o' course, and there's them what knows about that one . . . But if you must know what it was really like solving crimes at the Old Yard, you should go over to see Mr. Holmes."

With that, he turned on his worn-down heel and left me standing with my mouth open in the middle of the Black Museum.

After a convivial night on London Town with a couple of detectives who led me astray, I awoke the next morning, stirred the bread pudding that had once been my brain, and dug out my *A to Z Street Guide*. Hangover or no, I had decided to go along with the gag.

My favorite mystery story is Wilkie Collins' The Moonstone, *despite its claptrap ending. For me it has wiped out the need for all of its successors — even the Sherlock Holmes series, which I imitated at high school. The mystery to me is why the current output of mystery stories is not as boring for others as it is for me.*

LEWIS MUMFORD

I walked to Baker Street. No 221B in sight. Then I noticed a building halfway down the block with the name CAMDEN HOUSE on it. Being something of an amateur Holmesian, I remembered it as the one in "The Adventure of the Empty House." It had stood directly across the street from Holmes' digs.

Figuring what the hell, I went up and rapped the door knocker. The door was answered by a woman of late middle age. Neat, but kind of frumpy. I blurted, "Mrs. Hudson?"

Perfectly deadpan, she replied, "No, I'm Mary Watson. Mrs. Hudson was my grandmother."

Feeling like Alice in Wonderland, I asked, "Watson?"

"Oh, I don't suppose you know, do you? The Doctor married Mrs. Hudson right after his second wife left him."

She went on and on with what began to sound like a capsule version of *Upstairs, Downstairs*. It became very clear that there had been a somewhat un-Victorian relationship between the good Doctor and the faithful housekeeper.

"Of course, you'll be wanting to see Mr. Holmes now," she said. "Just go right up."

Up I went, still somewhat uncertain as to whether I was the victim of an elaborate practical joke or I had just plain lost my mind. My knock was answered with a raspy "Come in."

There, sitting in an overstuffed chair near the windows, was a living Sidney Paget drawing, even down to a ratty dressing gown. It was the mouse-gray one.

Pointing to a matching chair opposite, he said, "Please, have a seat. I get so few visitors nowadays." He stuffed some shag into a calabash, inhaled, coughed and settled back, turning that well-known profile to the sun.

I didn't know what to say, so I kept my mouth shut.

"If you are expecting me to amaze you with my powers of deduction by telling you all about yourself," he said, "I will have to disappoint you, my boy. These days, with everything from cigarettes to shoes mass-produced, all I can tell about a visitor is whether or not it's male or female . . . and from what I see lately, that, in

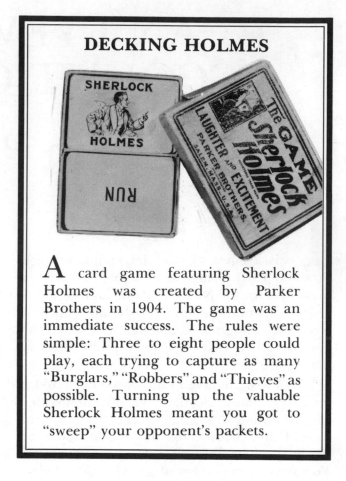

DECKING HOLMES

A card game featuring Sherlock Holmes was created by Parker Brothers in 1904. The game was an immediate success. The rules were simple: Three to eight people could play, each trying to capture as many "Burglars," "Robbers" and "Thieves" as possible. Turning up the valuable Sherlock Holmes meant you got to "sweep" your opponent's packets.

itself, is a remarkable feat of deduction."

I introduced myself as a fellow crime fighter from New York, and he seemed to relax a little, glad I wasn't one of those moon-struck literati on one of those — in his words — "infernal literary pilgrimages." Like cops around the world, we talked shop.

"No, Leftenant," he said, "I'm not a figment of your overworked imagination. I'm a real, very real, very old, very tired, very retired detective." Then, turning to my reason for being in London: "All the way here from New York to study the highly successful crime fighters of the modern Scotland Yard. Hmmmmmm." He puffed the pipe. "What you should be studying, young man, is modern crime itself. That's the reason I'm retired — all the techniques I spent a lifetime perfecting are useless now against today's criminal."

He lay back dreamily. I scanned the room for the Morocco case, but it wasn't in sight.

"New York . . . nice city," he resumed, somewhat adrift. "Several years ago I was a visitor in your city, you know. That was my fourth trip there. I assume you know that what Watson called 'The Redheaded League' case actually happened in New York City. But Watson, dear man, couldn't break his habits, so when he wrote it down, he transferred it here, to London.

"Yes, I remember New York City very well. During my last visit there, I was out walking one evening in your Central Park when I came by chance upon the scene of a crime. A robbery . . . a mugging, I think you'd call it. I stopped to lend a hand to the young officer who was investigating the case." He chuckled. "I, too, have my old habits.

"After spending no small time examining the ground surrounding the crime scene, I made some brilliant deductions. All wrong, as it happens. Those strange markings belonged to something called U.S. Keds. Never heard of them myself. Thought they were ritual motifs of an East Anglican band of gypsies."

"We call them perpetrator boots, sir," I said quietly.

"Tell me," he said earnestly, suddenly leaning so far forward in his chair I thought he'd tip it over, "tell me, young sir, how can a consulting detective work in this kind of a society? Neither the modern criminal nor the modern detective does any planning for his trade — it's strictly a hit-or-miss affair. I tell you, when we had the likes of Professor Moriarty to deal with, that kept your mind sharp and alert! That man spent months planning one robbery. He didn't run into the street and hit the first little old lady he saw over the head. No, sir. Stolen cars, narcotics, muggers — pshaw! The old Professor is probably turning over in his grave."

I had to admit I was glad that he, at least, was dead.

Then I changed the subject to one that had tantalized me from the minute I left the old man at the museum. "Who," I asked tentatively, "who was this Arthur Conan Doyle? I mean, if you're actually real, and he's the one who supposedly invented you, where does that leave him?"

Holmes became somewhat agitated. There was a noticeable tremor in his left hand. "That man!" he shouted. "That man has been a plague and a burden throughout my entire life. He was quite mad, you know. An eye doctor, driven stark, staring mad by his failures . . . never had a patient in two years of practice! Had delusions he was a great detective story writer. Even claimed to have invented me. *Me!*

"I wrote him several letters, but each time, instead of a normal, courteous reply, I received another damned — forgive me — another autographed photograph of him. Man needed the horsewhip, sir, or a loaded riding crop across his back. Well, what could one do? A madman is a madman, after all, and he wasn't violent. I finally took to telling people that it was *I* who had invented *him!*"

This outburst seemed to drain him. He leaned back in his chair once again.

"You will have to excuse me. I'm not as young as I used to be. Point of fact, I'm not even as *old* as I used to be." He offered me his hand in farewell. "Goodbye, Leftenant, and I wish you luck on the examination for your Captain that you plan to take next month." He smiled. "Oh, I see you're puzzled. Don't be. It wasn't my famous deductive reasoning that told me. Rather, it was that old man you chatted up at the museum. Did he tell you his name? No? Well, that's what's left of Lestrade, poor devil. A little off in the head these days. You probably noticed. Spends his every waking moment at the Yard, digging, digging for clues in the Ripper murders. He's convinced I was Jack the Ripper, you know. I'm almost tempted to help him solve the case, but then, what would an old man like me do in prison?"

He smiled again, his old but still charming smile.

"Well, be careful out there. And don't take the first *or* the second underground carriage. Take the third one."

John P. Oliver is a lieutenant in the New York Police Department, presently assigned to the City-Wide Emergency Service Unit. He is also a member of the New York State Bar and smokes good cigars.

NERO WOLFE CONSULTATION

Anthony Spiesman

When I get stuck on a difficult case, I ask myself how Wolfe would handle it. Mentally, I phone Saul Panzer and ask him to set up an appointment. I don't know why I go through Saul, I just do. Anyway, in my mind, Saul picks up the phone and gets Archie and explains I have this problem and could he see if Wolfe will talk to me. Archie makes a few choice wisecracks, but since I'm a friend of Saul's he makes me first appointment after orchid hours.

I imagine myself going up the seven steps of Wolfe's brownstone and ringing the bell. Fritz invites me in and escorts me past the famous front room and into the office. He offers me a drink. I tell him I would appreciate a tall, cold glass of milk with two fingers of Scotch. I don't worry about Wolfe's liquor supply or about the quality of the booze, but I make a mental note to send him a case of a new imported Dutch beer called Grolsch which comes in fancy liter bottles and which, for my money, is the best stuff around. I'm a little troubled, though, because the tops are permanently attached rubber plugs that you have to pop open with two thumbs, and I worry about Wolfe's liking to count bottle caps and putting them away in his top drawer.

While I wait for Wolfe to come help me, I rubberneck the room. The thing that hits me — and to me this is kind of a surprise — is the layout, the use of space. By this I specifically mean the bookshelves and the file cabinet on the second level. Completely avoids floor clutter. The high ceilings add to the space, of course, and the outstanding collection of furni-

ture and artifacts makes the place first-class. I start to relax. Any man smart enough to live like this is definitely smart enough to help me out of a jam.

Then I walk over to Archie's desk and take a gander at the picture on the wall above it. I know who it's supposed to be, and I have to admit there's a striking similarity. The neatness of it all impresses me, makes me start getting my thinking under control again.

Next I take an imaginery walk over to the Gouchard globe. Having read about it so many times, I have no trouble picturing it. Thirty-two and three-eighths inches in diameter is a lot of globe. Really big. But it's not the size so much that gets to me — it's the overall beauty, the craftsmanship. There's something about being in a room with perfect objects that is conducive to clear thinking. Don't ask me why. (Sometimes, at this point in my fantasy, I take time out for a trip to the lobby of the Daily News building on East 42nd Street. That's my favorite globe anywhere, and I can spend hours

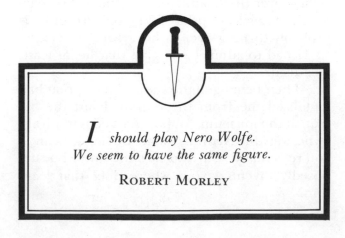

I should play Nero Wolfe. We seem to have the same figure.

ROBERT MORLEY

MARTY NORMAN

Nero Wolfe's office. Archie's desk is in the foreground. His chair can be swiveled to face the mirror so he can see what's happening in the doorway on the other side of the room.

standing there staring at it and taking great sea journeys around the world.)

I return to Wolfe's office and decide that my favorite thing in it is the superb mostly yellow Shirvan rug. Comforting while I'm pacing. But being somewhat of an amateur cook myself I do take a few minutes to appreciate the engraving of Brillat-Savarin. I also find Wolfe's own cookbook on his shelf and haul it down for a quick look. Same contents as my copy, I'm glad to say. Still at the bookshelf, I can't resist pulling out Wolfe's copy of Lawrence's *Seven Pillars of Wisdom*. I once tried to get through it. Couldn't. But I'm convinced if Wolfe can, he's the man to analyze my case.

I stand in front of Wolfe's cherry desk and decide not to pick up any of his blunt instru-

ments, but I do take notice of his brown leather Brazilian desk chair. Gigantic! I've never seen anything quite like it anywhere, probably never will. But it definitely looks like it can hold a seventh of a ton just by itself. The chair would take up two-thirds of my office space. I can't help but notice the worn spots on the arms, where countless circles have been made by Wolfe's fingers. I see his fingers circle and his lips go in and out, in and out, like an obese goldfish, and I am reassured he will solve my problems.

I think about sitting in that chair, but I don't have the nerve. Not even in my imagination. I do, however, sit in that infamous red chair — the one Archie says only Inspector Cramer looks like he belongs in. It's a bit un-

A photograph of Theodore (taken with a telescopic lens) at work in the orchid room. Wolfe is just out of the picture to the left (note large shadow in the foreground).

comfortable to my taste, but I well know the advantages of a chair like this for interrogation purposes. It dwarfs you, makes you feel insecure, and the lies don't come out quite so smooth when you're in it. At this point, I get a little edgy, so I back over to Archie's desk again. I take a quick peek in the red box to see if he really does keep stamps in it. He does. I think about opening the drawers — it's occupational with me — but I don't. I also don't pry inside the liquor cabinet, count Wolfe's bottle caps or try to get into the secret alcove and see what Archie sees when Wolfe has him staked out in there.

Then I imagine Wolfe entering the room. I see him as Orson Welles. Nobody else. I imagine him getting straight to the problem, no social nonsense. I can never make up my mind if he shakes my hand or not. I know he doesn't like to shake hands, but I have this urgency to feel that he's really flesh and blood. Usually, I wind up with a strong, quick grip, quickly released. I talk, Archie pretends to take notes, Wolfe listens. Wolfe speaks. The voice is midway between American English and English English. No Montenegrin inflection. Orson Welles in *Citizen Kane*, I think. A young voice in a not-young man. Full, but not bombastic.

I never know exactly what it is that Wolfe says, but suddenly, after one or two "pfuis," no more problem.

We get up to leave. That is, I get up to leave, preceded by Archie. Fritz comes to the door to see me out. Just as I prepare to go, Wolfe pokes his head out the office door and asks if I'd like to join him in dinner at Rusterman's. (Listen, this is my fantasy. I'll have him say whatever I like.) We agree to meet as soon as I turn in my report on the case.

At this point I get up and walk into my kitchen and start making a mess out of it. I chop, I slice, I mix, I pound, I debone, I decant, I thoroughly fiddle around. And it seems to help. Like Wolfe, I don't talk business when I eat, but there's something about preparing a meal that untangles things for me. So when I start to eat I raise a toast to my imaginary dinner partner, Nero Wolfe, and thank him for his guidance.

I never met a private investigator like him. But I sure would like to.

Anthony Spiesman is a licensed private investigator living in New York. He has spent hours trying to track down Wolfe on West 35th Street, with little success.

WOLFE AT HIS BEST

And Be a Villain
Champagne for One
Death of a Doxy
Some Buried Caesar
Too Many Cooks

MOST OVERRATED WOLFE

The Doorbell Rang

ALPHA AND OMEGA

Fer-de-Lance
A Family Affair

THE ULTIMATE DISGUISE EXPERT

Herb Galewitz

Stand aside, Holmes. Great though you were at turning into a parson, a sailor, an opium addict, a priest, a bookseller, an impoverished bystander — you just can't compare with the Bean Farm's Freddy.

Freddy could fool a Fu Manchu. Freddy could baffle both Cleek (Hamilton) and Clay (Colonel). Freddy could stun Arsene and Four Square Jane and even teach Nick Carter a trick or two. What's more remarkable, he could do it all on a diet of slops while standing on his two back trotters! For Freddy, of course, is Freddy the Pig, juvenile legend.

Freddy tends to behave in multiples: multiple disguises, multiple professions. He is, among other things, a partner in the firm of Frederick & Wiggins, Detectives (Office Hours: Wednesdays, 2–4 P.M.); President of the First Animal Bank (animal depositors only); editor of the *Bean Home News;* director of Barnyard Tours, Inc.; and accomplished poet (his version of "On the Road to Mandalay" has sent more young'uns east than a string of Dorothy Lamour movies — or so he claims).

Freddy took his time getting into detective work, turning his attention to other matters in his first two books. Even so, he managed to make it into court before Perry Mason *(Freddy the Detective,* 1932). The sensational trial sequence pitted Freddy against a Moriarty-type nemesis — Professor Simon the Rat — whose villainy would plague Freddy throughout his career.

In subsequent cases Freddy solved the mystery of the ignoramus in a tale of terror

A turn-of-century detective

and blackmail reminiscent of *The Hound of the Baskervilles;* undermined some heavy skulduggery on a summer estate by posing as a caretaker; thwarted spies trying to steal Uncle Ben's plans; exposed the fraud of the outer space travelers; debunked the myth of the haunted hotel; foiled a gang of ruthless bank robbers; and pitched a legal no-hitter against a baseball team from Mars in his one excursion into sci-fi mystery.

When asked if calling policemen "pigs" was a compliment to his ingenuity rather than a rebuff to their skills, Freddy modestly replied, "Oink."

Herb Galewitz is the editor of The Celebrated Cases of Dick Tracy.

The Many Disguises of Freddy the Pig

A football player

A little old lady

A reporter

BLOWING FREDDY'S COVER

Freddy the Detective
Freddy the Cowboy
Freddy Goes Camping
Freddy and Mr. Camphor
Freddy and the Flying Saucer Plans
Freddy and the Ignoramus
Freddy and the Baseball Team from Mars

A sailor

A third baseman

A magician

H.M.: THE OLD MAN
Donald Rumbelow

Pigeon-toed, with a lordly sneer upon his face, one hand resting upon an imaginary sword pommel, Sir Henry Merrivale — H.M., the Old Man, Mycroft (when he was head of British counterespionage) — barrel-bellies through and triumphantly solves the finest series of locked-room mysteries ever written. Under his Panama hat, tilted to display an imaginary cavalier's plume, is a heady mixture of Falstaff, Charlie Chaplin and Winston Churchill!

Most days the Old Man can be found, five floors up, in a rabbit warren of a building behind Whitehall, feet on desk, white socks showing, sprawled beneath a Mephistophelian portrait of Fouché, in an office scattered with papers and cigar ash. Ignore the crudely painted notice BUSY!! NO ADMITTANCE!!! KEEP OUT!! daubed above the name-plate. H.M. has an Alice-in-Wonderland fetish for ticketing things. Similar signs, in five languages, are painted on his safe (never locked and where the whisky is kept).

Apologise for waking him, and he says that he was thinking! Say that you won't bother him, or that he's past it, and he howls about ingratitude and grumbles that nobody takes him seriously!

From his grammar you wouldn't guess that he was a qualified barrister as well as a qualified physician. Awful as it is (he tends to drop the g's), it is typical of his Champagne Charlie, gaiety girl, hansom cab generation (he was born in 1871). Insult him, or mention his age, and his mouth will sour down as if he were smelling bad eggs. Prick his vanity and he turns purple. Strong men blanch and dogs shy away at such looks of horrible malignancy.

Impossible to fool women and children, however. To them, he is Knight-Errant and Pied Piper in tortoise-shell spectacles and a rumpled suit. H.M. heroines, all white dresses and golden hair, do inevitably marry the juvenile lead. But for H.M.'s *personal* harem of dollies and wenches, nothing so wraith-like: Two Dreadnoughts closing. Of the earth earthy. Broad-beamed, broad-minded, out-of-the-bottle blondes with chorus girl or mine hostesse background. His wife Clementine (again the Churchill cross-reference) is permanently off stage, away in the south of France. Clemmie, years younger, is vintage 1913 chorus line. Reunions begin with four or five double whiskies in the Ivy, Claridges or the Savoy Grill. Love is bein' met with brass bands at the Pearly Gates. Consummation is a stuffed policeman on every chimney at Scotland Yard!

Children too long in his company risk

Eccentricity has always abounded when and where strength of character has abounded; and the amount of eccentricity in a society has generally been proportional to the amount of genius, mental vigor, and moral courage which it contained.

On Liberty
JOHN STUART MILL

Borstal before they leave school and prison before they are eighteen! Cigarettes are sissy, he jeers. Smoke his evil-smelling cigars instead! Want to gamble? His suitcase, on wheels, will outrace their dogs downhill. Card tricks? Nothing easier.

Three cheers for Uncle Henry Merrivale!

Wasn't he friends with Sitting Bull? Didn't he teach Robin Hood *and* Samkin Alyward to shoot? Hadn't he poured Epsom salts in the Home Secretary's dish at the Lord Mayor's banquet? His fur coat was (1) given to him by Queen Victoria, (2) won in the first Grand Prix of 1903, (3) a present from the late Sir Henry Irving.

History (British Empire only) and literature should go with a swing and a thump. "Kentish Sir Byng, stood for his King,/Bidding the crop headed Parliament swing." What's this? Dostoevsky, Tolstoy and Chekhov. Crutches for young minds! Out of the window with them! Doyle, Dickens, Stevenson and Twain are the best writers. Best book is *The Cloister and the Hearth.*

Serious now.

Don't be fooled.

Never, never underestimate H.M.

So many have and, in the end, stood on the hangman's trap to regret that they did.

H.M.'s innocence is the naïveté of Langdon, Chaplin and Lloyd. Like the slapstick kings, he is a master of timing. He treads the narrow tightrope between farce and sheer cold terror with consummate skill and timing. One moment he will disgrace himself abominably. He will assault dragon-like dowagers with halberds, American congressmen with arrows and elderly bishops with mud pies.

Fooling stops when the pace quickens and murder is loose.

Two six-inch guns couldn't be more deadly.

Fouché would have been proud of him.

Like the great comedians, H.M. will start with a basically simple, almost laughable situation which quickly twists and turns into a monstrous growth of rattlesnake cunning. Bronze lamps, cricket bats and crossbows are the important incidentals. Chief Inspector Masters (H.M.'s Watson) can deal with those.

THE OLD MAN'S CASES

The Plague Court Murders
The White Priory Murders
The Red Widow Murders
The Unicorn Murders
The Magic Lantern Murders
(Punch and Judy Murders)
The Peacock Feather Murders
(The Ten Teacups)
The Judas Window
Death in Five Boxes
The Reader is Warned
Nine — and Death Makes Ten
(Murder in the Submarine Zone)
And So to Murder
Seeing Is Believing
The Gilded Man
She Died a Lady
He Wouldn't Kill Patience
The Curse of the Bronze Lamp
(Lord of the Sorcerers)
My Late Wives
The Skeleton in the Clock
A Graveyard to Let
Night at the Mocking Widow
Behind the Crimson Blind
The Cavalier's Cup

The Old Man's speciality is the locked-room mystery. (No hocus-pocus with floors, doors, windows, ceilings, trap-doors and walls. Bodies fall in — and out — of them with scarifying ease.)

Genuine locked rooms. Genuine puzzles.

Only the Master — sittin', twiddlin' his thumbs and cogitatin' — can solve them.

"Courage! Le diable est mort!" H.M. likes quoting.

And so he is — when the Old Man is about.

Donald Rumbelow is Joseph Wambaugh's closest English rival. He is a police officer assigned to the Wood Street Station, London, where he is curator of the specimen museum. He is also an author and chairman of the Crime Writers' Association.

The New York Times

NEW YORK, WEDNESDAY, AUGUST 6, 1975

Hercule Poirot Is Dead; Famed Belgian Detective

By THOMAS LASK

Hercule Poirot, a Belgian detective who became internationally famous, has died in England. His age was unknown.

Mr. Poirot achieved fame as a private investigator after he retired as a member of the Belgian police force in 1904. His career, as chronicled in the novels of Dame Agatha Christie, his creator, was one of the most illustrious in fiction.

At the end of his life, he was arthritic and had a bad heart. He was in a wheelchair often, and was carried from his bedroom to the public lounge at Styles Court, a nursing home in Essex, wearing a wig and false mustaches to mask the signs of age that offended his vanity. In his active days, he was always impeccably dressed.

Mr. Poirot, who was just 5 feet 4 inches tall, went to England from Belgium during World War I as a refugee. He settled in a little town not far from Styles, then an elaborate country estate, where he took on his first private case.

The news of his death, given by Dame Agatha, was not unexpected. Word that he was near death reached here last May.

His death was confirmed by Dodd, Mead, Dame Agatha's publishers, who will put out "Curtain," the novel that chronicles his last days, on Oct. 15.

The Poirot of the final volume is only a shadow of the well-turned out, agile investigator who, with a charming but immense ego and fractured English, solved uncounted mysteries in the 37 full-length novels and collections of short stories in which he appeared.

Dame Agatha reports in "Curtain" that he managed,

Illustrated London News and Sketch, Ltd.
Hercule Poirot, painted in the mid-1920's by W. Smithson Broadhead.

in one final gesture, to perform one more act of cerebration that saved an innocent bystander from disaster. "Nothing in his life became him like the leaving it," to quote Shakespeare, whom Poirot frequently misquoted.

Dodd, Mead had not expected another installment in the heroic achievements of the famous detective.

No manuscript came in last year, and none was expected this year, either. However, there had been many rumors to the effect that Dame Agatha had locked up two manuscripts — one a Poirot and one a Marple — in a vault and that they were not to be published until her death. Jonathan Dodd, of Dodd, Mead, said that the Poirot was the one now being published.

Although the career of Poirot will no more engage his historian, a spokesman for the author said that Dame Agatha, who will be 85 Sept. 15, intends to continue writing. In her long writing career, one that parallels the literary existence of her detective, she has published 85 full-length novels and collections of short stories, which have sold 350 million copies in hard cover and paperback all over the globe.

This figure does not include the pirated editions behind the Iron Curtain, of which no count can be made.

In addition, under the pseudonym of Mary Westmacott she has written a half-dozen romances. What is perhaps more significant is that her first title, "The Mysterious Affair at Styles" is still in print.

At least 17 of her stories have been made into plays, including the famous "The Mouse Trap," which opened in London in 1952 and is still running, setting all kinds of records for longevity in the theater.

Twelve of her tales have become motion pictures, many of which have centered on Jane Marple, Dame Agatha's other famous detective.

In the person of the late Margaret Rutherford, Miss Marple developed her own devoted following.

The most recent of Dame Agatha's movies, "Murder on the Orient Express" opened last year, with excellent box-office returns. And Christie properties have been used for television mystery dramas and for radio shows.

Her hold on her audience is remarkable in a way because the kind of fiction she writes is, well, not exactly contemporary. Her characters come from the quiet and exceedingly comfortable middle class: doctors, lawyers, top military men, members of the clergy. The houses in her fiction are spacious, teas are frequent and abundant, servants abound. True, the comforts have been cut back as the real England in which her mysteries are set has been altered over the years. But the polite, leisure-class settings have been retained.

"I could never manage miners talking in pubs," she once confided to an interviewer, "because I don't know what miners talk about in pubs."

'Undisputed Head Girl'

Not everyone has agreed

to her high ranking. Robert Graves complained that "her English is schoolgirlish, her situations for the most part artificial, her detail faulty."

On the other hand, Margery Allingham, herself a writer of whodunits, called her the "undisputed head girl," and the late Anthony Boucher, who reviewed mysteries for this newspaper, remarked, "Few writers are producing the pure puzzle novel and no one on either side of the Atlantic does it better."

Dame Agatha who has been described as a large woman looking both kind and capable, is the daughter of a well-to-do American father and English mother. She was tutored at home and attended, as she recalled, innumerable classes: dancing, singing, drawing. In World War I, she worked in a Red Cross hospital, and this experience gave her a good working knowledge of poisons, ingredients that turn up rather frequently in her books.

In 1926, she suffered an attack of amnesia, left home and was discovered some days later in a hotel under another name. The furor stirred up by the newspapers over her disappearance has made her shy of newspapers and reporters ever since. She has kept herself inconspicuous in public, even insisting for a while that no picture of herself appear on the dust jackets of her books. She has declined to be interviewed about the death of Poirot. In 1928, she was divorced from her first husband, Archibald Christie, and in 1930 she was married to Max Mallowan, an archeologist.

It has been said that she has brought Victorian qualities to her work—a charge she does not deny. She dislikes sordid tales and confesses that she could not write them. But another side of that Victorianism is that in all her years as a writer she has had one publisher in America, Dodd Mead. Such steadfastness is surely of another age.

Poirot's death received front page news coverage from the New York Times. *This was the first time a fictional character was so honored.*

LITTLE GREY CELLS

How many of them does Poirot have?

Approximately one trillion, or 10^{12}.

(You have the same number, whether your head is egg-shaped or not.)

The cells are indeed grey, but they are also white — which Poirot forgot to mention — and when seen through a microscope they have a brownish tinge.

Doctors call them neurons, or nerve cells, and divide them into three parts. There's the cell body, the dendrites (for conducting impulses toward the cell) and the axon (for transmitting impulses away from the cell). The axon is surrounded by a myelin sheath, which gives the cell its whitish color.

When the axon of one neuron connects with a dendrite of another, you get a synapse. So when Poirot is "using his little grey cells" he is really experiencing multiple synapses involving the cell bodies of the cerebral cortex. To a layman, this means he is thinking. (He also has to use his little grey cells just to stay awake. Consciousness is achieved by the reticular activating system.)

On an EEG machine read-out, normal cells at rest show an alpha rhythm. When you're thinking, however, you get dechronization — or the arousal and alerting response.

Certain drugs can stimulate your little grey cells to think; among them, caffeine, amphetamines, nicotine and strychnine. Considering how much thinking Poirot did, it's just possible he needed a little extra stimulation. A bit of strychnine in the moustache wax, perhaps?

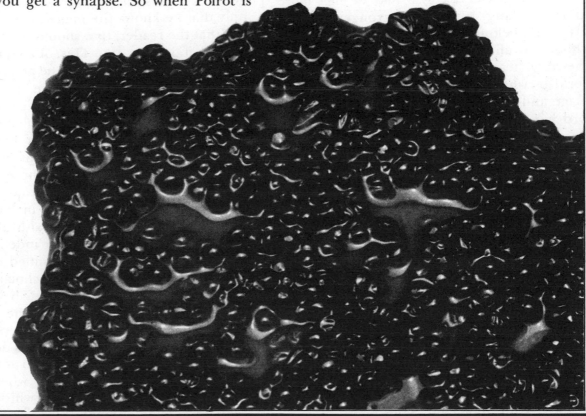

GERVASE FEN AND THE TEACAKE SCHOOL

Catherine Aird

For those concerned with putting stories into categories, the mystery divides easily enough. Four main groups account for most of them — the police procedural, the Gothic, the hard-boiled and the psychological. There is, however, a fifth which is peculiarly English and which has been aptly described as the teacake school. In detective stories in the teacake school it goes without saying that at four o'clock in the afternoon everything stops for tea.

Although Gervase Fen may be met more often drinking something stronger spirituously, he belongs spiritually to the teacake school and all that that implies. Stopping for afternoon tea is only natural in the rarefied world in which the Professor of English Language and Literature at the University of Oxford has his being. It is a world made up of Oxford colleges (Fen himself is a Fellow of St. Christopher's) and Cathedral closes; boys' public schools (the author, Edmund Crispin, was himself once a schoolmaster at one) and English country villages.

It is a refined world peopled by young earls (improbably called Henry Fielding) who do their war service in toyshops, and amiable undergraduates, ready for anything. (One in particular, young Mr. Hoskins, has a way with him — a special talent for calming anxious girls which proves useful in *The Moving Toyshop*. He "had never been known to indulge in any sport save the most ancient of them all.") Fen's friends belong to the same setting — Geoffrey Vintner, the famous organist and composer, and Richard Cadogan, a major poet.

And yet there is more — much more — to the stories about Gervase Fen than the circles in which he moves.

He is a character who is not so much a detective as someone who happens somehow always to be where the action is. He usually arrives on the scene late, having had his expertise invoked either by his friends or the circumstance of being there. And he is as immediately omniscient as any other investigator in the genre. It is his happy practise to indicate not only that he knows the name of the murderer but that the reader, too, should have been able to work it out as easily. This, of course, he does a good few chapters before he actually reveals all — and how right he is. The reader should have got there, too — but, of course, hasn't usually, unless by some happy chance he is as observant and as percipient as Fen himself. This skill is even more apparent in the short stories in *Beware of the Trains,* where the reader doesn't feel quite so ignorant for quite so long.

Gervase Fen stands alone in the series in his omniscience. There is no faithful Dr. Watson as side-kick — if such an indelicate word can be admitted into the dignified context of ancient colleges and English scholarship. Fen doesn't have a sounding board, belonging to the other tradition of leaving the reader to work it all out for himself. True, there is usually Wilkes, an aged, deaf and bibulous don, also of St. Christopher's, who dogs Fen — but in an obstructive capacity, thwarting where he can and more in pursuit of Fen's whisky than in search of enlightenment.

Nor can the Chief Constable of Oxford, Sir Richard Freeman, be said to play the foil. He is a policeman, all right, but really a professor of English Literature *manqué*. He is the mirror-image, in fact, of Fen, who declares himself to be "the only literary critic turned detective in the whole of fiction." The police force, especially Inspector Humbleby, stands in a cooperative relationship with Gervase Fen that is faint but pursuing, while Sir Richard himself seems more concerned with what William Shakespeare had in mind when he wrote *Measure for Measure*. "It is always my fate," bemoans Fen, "to be involved with literary policemen," but he himself is quite prepared to while away a waiting time playing quoting games like "Detestable Characters in Fiction" and "Unreadable Books."

Fen also stands in a curious, not to say unique, relationship with both the reader and the author. The reader is more aware of the author in the writings of Edmund Crispin than in almost any other detective fiction. "Let's go left," opts Fen at a division of the ways in a pursuit, "Gollancz is publishing this book." And again at a moment when someone asks him what he is doing: "I was making up titles for Crispin." In *Love Lies Bleeding* he declares he is going to write a detective story himself.

With the reader the involvement is even more unusual. Fen has here described a knot — in fact, quite a well-known one, though he doesn't say so. Instead:

"It's called the Hook, Line and Sinker."

"Why is it called that?"

"Because," said Fen placidly, "the reader has to swallow it."

On another occasion Fen says, "If there is anything I hate it is the sort of book in which characters don't go to the police when they've no earthly reason for not doing so."

The whole leads to the feeling in some of the books that there is a play within a play — what might be called "the Rosencrantz and Guildenstern effect." This is enhanced by phrases such as "No-one expects this sort of trick outside a book" and "our narrative is enriched by." Such is Gervase Fen's *persona* that a Gaulish division of the books into three parts — the reader, the author and Gervase

THE COMPLEAT CRISPIN

The Case of the Gilded Fly
Holy Disorders
The Moving Toyshop
Swan Song
Love Lies Bleeding
Buried for Pleasure
Frequent Hearses
The Long Divorce
Beware of the Trains (short stories)
The Glimpses of the Moon

Fen — seems perfectly plausible. And yet in no sense is he greater than his creator. He is simply a third party to the reading experience.

Surely somewhere, sooner or later, every writer makes a statement of faith about his craft. In *Buried for Pleasure* the detective novelist, Mr. Judd, tells Fen, "One's plots are necessarily *improbable* but I believe in making sure they are not *impossible*," and, a little later, "Characterisation seems to me a very overrated element in fiction. I can never see why one should be obliged to have any of it at all, if one doesn't want to. It *limits* the form so."

Perhaps it is this credo which accounts for the fact that the first really full physical description of Fen does not appear until the sixth Gervase Fen story — *Buried for Pleasure*. "A tall lean man with a ruddily cheerful, clean-shaven face and brown hair which stood up mutinously in spikes at the crown of his head. . . . his eyes; they showed charity and understanding as well as a taste for mischief." He is forty-two years old.

He enjoys a sports car, small, noisy and battered, of a design much favoured before the war, which rejoices in the name — painted on the bonnet — of Lily Christine III. It — she — was bought from an undergraduate who had been sent down and clatters "like saucepans at war." Fen enjoys his car. We enjoy books which feature Fen and especially for the choice words that we find there.

That well-known phrase "It pays to increase your word power" is nowhere more true than when reading the works of Edmund Crispin. A really wide vocabulary goes a long way, while a good dictionary is a help — not to say a necessity. Perhaps this is only to be expected when the hero happens to be a professor of English Language and Literature. What is even more enjoyable is the influence which Lewis Carroll has had upon Gervase Fen. Words and phrases from this author abound and seem to fit Fen as to the manner born — the Dormouse, the White Rabbit, Father William, even the pig-baby in *Alice* are all referred to.

Equally fascinating is that there are also moments of great profundity — understressed because these do not belong to this *oeuvre*. "I always think that psychology is wrong in imagining that when it has analysed evil it has somehow disposed of it." And "Like most people you overestimate the refining powers of tribulation."

And of neat paradox.

Of marriage in *Swan Song:* "How nice," said Elizabeth judicially, "to have all the pleasures of living in sin without any of the disadvantages."

There are descriptions which stay in the mind, too. Could this of a building that is not old be bettered? "Deathwatch beetles would be out of place."

There was something strangely prescient about the title of *The Long Divorce,* a book in which Fen appears in the thin disguise of Mr. Datchery, a character from Charles Dickens' unfinished book *The Mystery of Edwin Drood.* After *The Long Divorce* there was a gap of nearly a quarter of a century before, in 1977, another full-length Gervase Fen story appeared. This is *The Glimpses of the Moon,* and it can truly be written that the years have not wearied our amateur investigator. But, perhaps, as usual, it might be better to let him have the last word himself from *Swan Song.*

"The era of my greatest successes may be said, roughly speaking, to extend from the time when I first became interested in detection to the present moment. . . ."

It does.

Catherine Aird is the author of A Slight Mourning.

Two English gentlemen keeping a stiff upper lip as they view a crime scene.

TEMPEST IN A TEAPOT:
The Care and Brewing of Tea

Jeanine Larmoth

To brew the best tea, it is as necessary to have a spinster as it is to have a virgin for a truffle hunt. Only a spinster can provide that atmosphere of coziness, knickknackery, and chintz so important to the taste. Tea is made, of course, by first installing a hob on which to hang the kettle, then scattering antimacassars liberally about the room, and finding the cat. A collection of small flowerpots with African violets is helpful, but not essential.

The ultimate tribute to the teapot, its temple, the tea shop, and its vestal virgin, the spinster, was paid by Agatha Christie in *Funerals Are Fatal.* The genteel companion, Miss Gilchrist, kills her employer with a hatchet all for the love of a tea shop. Instead of a faded picture of an old beau on her bedroom wall (ready to be brought into service should a séance arise), there is a photograph of a tea shop she once had, called The Willow-Tree. A victim of the war. Like a mother with a very special child, she babbles about the blue willow-patterned china, or the jam and scones she used to prepare, or trade secrets for making brioches and chocolate éclairs. She is more often seen with flour on her hands than blood. Miss Gilchrist's obsession for the return to gentility a tea shop would afford is so great she kills for a pittance, and is taken away to the meting out of justice, happily planning the curtains.

So much tea is poured in a mystery, one comes away a bit squelchy after reading. So many sweet biscuits are served one could build a hundred Hansel-and-Gretel houses. Tea is the great restorer. It seeps into the nooks and crannies of the soul. It is oil on troubled waters. It is applied, like a hot compress, wherever it hurts, with a faith and fervor that could only be bred in a conscientiously, securely, puritanically Protestant country such as England. Prayer is for Papists; whisky for shock.

There is something crisping about tea. None of the florid, suspect luxury of coffee. Tea cries out to stiffen the lip, and be on with it. Tea quenches tears and thirst. It is an opening for the pouring out of troubles. It eases shyness, and lubricates gossip. While it is not in itself sympathetic, in the right hands tea acts as a backing force to tender ministrations. The mighty to the lowly assuage with tea, cure for

---

CRUMPETS AND SCONES

The former you toast, the latter you heat. A crumpet is quite chewy, in the manner of toffee. (Some would call it leathery.) A scone — which rhymes with gone — is rather like a flat-topped, unflavoured muffin. Both are staples of the well-appointed tea table, and are especially tasty when liberally doused with butter and smothered with jam.

A CUPPA CALAMITY

Make your pot of tea in the usual way, but when you pour the tea into the cup, do not use a strainer. Ask your subject to drink the tea, then to swirl round the dregs and invert the cup over the saucer. Suggest he or she turn the inverted cup in the saucer three times in a clockwise direction and say, "Tell me faithful, tell me well, the secrets that the leaves foretell." Then you, as leaf reader, take the cup in two hands and peer at the patterns the leaves have made. If you see any of the following shapes, your tea drinker should make no long-range plans.

Shape	Meaning
Clock	Illness; if at bottom of cup, death
Cross	Trouble
Key	Robbery, if at bottom of cup
M	Someone has evil intentions toward you
Nun	Sorrow
Parrot	Slander
Raven	More trouble
Scythe	Danger
Snake	Enmity
Wings	Messages; the nearer the bottom of the cup, the worse the news

Prepared by The Tea Council Limited.

MARTY NORMAN

body and soul.

Tea pours with equal grace from glazed brown pots or vast cauldrons of furbelowed silver. It washes through kitchens, where the lino cracks and the housewife offers a cuppa char, or slips, a perfect amber arch, into gold-stippled cups on the lawn of a stately home — its crystalline, chuckling voice covering any awkward moments with delicacy.

There are proper teas and, perhaps, improper teas, high teas and low. A proper tea is offered by an overbustly, oversolicitous matron who feels you look peaked and in need of immediate sustenance. A proper tea should, therefore, be substantial: Marmite, eggs, meat pies, sandwiches, cake, the lot. The substance of a proper tea is not actually different from high tea, which has stood in place of supper for hundreds of years for thousands of English schoolchildren. To be truly British, tea should be imbalanced in favor of carbohydrates — therefore, bread-and-butter sandwiches, plus sandwiches (kept nicely moist beneath a dampened napkin), fruitcake, and cakes.

Tea is best brewed in the brown pot. Otherwise, any china pot. The pot is "hotted up" with boiling water, which is allowed to sit for a moment before it is tossed out with an air. A teaspoonful of tea added for each cup, and one for the pot. The water for tea is of such moment, gentlemen traveling abroad often require special spring waters lest they encounter a foreign admixture to their favorite bouquet. The water must not boil a moment beyond its open, rolling bubble or the mineral content becomes proportionately higher. The brew then steeps for three to five minutes. Certain teas grow bitter if left longer, so second pots may have to be prepared for second cups. If tea is too strong, water will thin it, but not reduce the bitterness. Tea can be as deep and opaque as coffee or very little darker than water. In order that the flow never falter, a jug of hot water should stand by the smaller jug of warmed milk and the sugar bowl (no lumps, please).

Because England is inclined to be damp and chilly, and the houses drafty, the teapot may — though this is common — be given a little coat of its own, called a cozy, to wear to the table. A tea cozy is floral and quilted chintz, or a lumpish, unrecognizable crocheted affair made by an abysmal aunt. Some pots are further accoutered with tiny, tea-stained sponges attached to their nozzles to prevent drips.

The container in which the tea is stored is an understandably regal affair of antique Indian brass, lead-lined wood, or exotically devised porcelain, and is called a caddy. When the tea is a swirling maelstrom ready to be served, a strainer is placed over the cup to be sure the tea is clear. The strainer, as is proper with ceremonial vessels, has, in turn, its own resting place above a little stand, or hooked over the slop bowl. Despite the revolting name, a slop bowl is a superbly proportioned, exquisitely decorated piece of china. To add the final, mystical note to the ceremony, a silver bell may stand on the tea table with which to ring for the servants for more cake, more milk, more hot water, or the police.

Tea kettles, apart from making tea, hot water for bottles, and singing, are very important utensils in a mystery if you haven't a letter opener, and wouldn't use one if you had. To unstick an envelope, you send whoever else is in the kitchen out of it. Be sure not to arouse suspicions, or they may dash back in and surprise you.

When the room is empty (check behind the fridge and stove to be sure), fill up the kettle. Put the kettle on the fire. Bring to a boil. Be sure to wait for a steady jet of steam. This will be about seven minutes for an average kettle. Keep an ear cocked. Hold envelope over steam. Slip knife under flap. Pry open very gently. Pull out contents, and read will, letter, or shopping list. If latter, scan for hidden meanings. If interrupted, slide knife into garter, and hide envelope behind stove, being sure to fold the flap backward to prevent resealing.

Make tea with leftover water.

Sometimes, spinsters get tired of their High Street shopping-and-tea-after routine, and take the cheap Thursday train to London for the sales, and to switch suitcases and catch murderers at the station's Left Luggage. After her adventures, the spinster may choose to refresh herself by having tea in the lounge hall of a hotel, or take it on the return train.

Tea on the move may be the best tea of all.

THE AGITATED TEABAG

If you must persist in using a teabag, the gentlemen at The Tea Council Limited would rather you didn't just let it lie there like a corpse in an advanced state of rigor. You must agitate the teabag, dear, agitate it, or the essence of the tea will be muffled. An even swing of the wrist, once left, once right, once left again, should do. Now then, who's for elevenses?

Served on British Railways, it is a rush and clatter of dishes which jump up and down — apparently from the excitement of travel — all the way from London to Plymouth, and back again, if they're not required. In the dim light of declining afternoon and three-watt bulbs, the crockery sits at empty tables in a state of eternal preparedness, as if endlessly waiting a macabre Mad Hatter's Tea Party — passengers advancing, eating, from table to table as the train runs along. The sandwiches — small circlings of tomatoes, sliced hard-boiled eggs, or fish paste on limp white bread, its crusts resolutely removed for refinement, and swathed in mayonnaise — contribute their own lifeless air, faintly enlivened by a tossing of mustard cress, and augmented by downtrodden, but resilient fruitcake. Thus, the bottom-heavy tradition of starchy foods at teatime is upheld, even in transit.

The civilizing effects of tea, perhaps more than the building of roads, or even the drinking of gin, has been one of the largest contributions England made to civilizing her empire. For centuries, wherever the flag waved, it was an amiable way for people to gather together under pith helmets or parasols for a well-mannered chat, to push sweet morsels in their mouths, and forget the ruddy natives hiding in the bush.

From Murder on the Menu, *copyright © 1972 by Jeanine Larmoth and Charlotte Turgeon. Reprinted by permission of McIntosh and Otis, Inc.*

LITTLE OLD LADIES

Heron Carvic

Should elderly maiden ladies detect?

The trouble is that they do: the carpet stain that you had covered with a rug; family quagmires, with answers to the present from examples in the past; the exact state of your overdraft. I had a great-aunt with many theatrical connections. She could always tell me who was bedding whom before they'd even bought the sheets. Had she applied her powers to criminal detection (as did my great-grandfather, Sir Richard Mayne, one of the two original Commissioners of Police), I would have given little for the criminal's chances. Since elderly maiden ladies have this overweening interest in other people's affairs, should it not then be channelled?

Back in the mists of time I read adventures of Agatha Christie's Miss Marple and Patricia Wentworth's Miss Silver — with a bias toward the latter. I could see the advantage to an author of the elderly spinster opposed to villainy: innocence — the charming shibboleth that elderly spinsters are innocent still obtains — triumphing over vice.

The story of St. George and the Dragon, however disguised, is the essence of all detective stories — chastity held in thrall by a villain for a hero to set free. But if, St. George having failed to find the monster, his maiden aunt had downed her tapestry work to sally forth and slay the brute, it would have lent the tale a certain piquancy.

Miss Marple's and Miss Silver's innate genius for solving the most complicated cases by discussion, by comparison with village life — and all without dropping one stitch of two-purl-one-plain — I found a trifle hard to take. Unless, of course, it was done mainly by intuition, which brings in the psychic factor.

The female, it would seem, is more prone to this complaint than is the male; traditionally, it is the old gypsy woman, not the gypsy, whose palm is crossed with silver, just as there is always "a little woman I know of" waiting to tell your fortune. Few people know of "little men."

The psychic tends to be solitary by nature — I suppose foreseeing the future may have its disadvantages. So, by permutation, you are likely to find a preponderance of psychic individuals amongst elderly spinsters.

In my teens I knew a struggling artist called Constance Oliver, fiftyish. She was commissioned by a smart, amusing American woman to paint a portrait of her with her son, a particularly delightful small boy who was deaf and dumb. I saw the early stages of the picture which promised well. A week later — Constance had been working on the child's face — I was disappointed. Under her brush the boy's charm had gone and he looked sulky. Another week, and the portrait was no longer on the easel. Whilst Constance was cooking lunch, I found the picture behind a stack of others: the

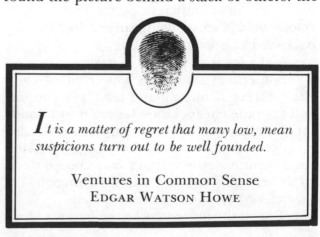

*I*t is a matter of regret that many low, mean suspicions turn out to be well founded.

Ventures in Common Sense
EDGAR WATSON HOWE

rough-in of the mother, unfinished but clever, had been slashed with a palette knife. Over lunch I asked Constance what had gone wrong. Uncharacteristically, she refused to discuss it, merely saying that she wasn't satisfied, couldn't do it and had turned in the commission. It was equally uncharacteristic for her to turn in a commission or destroy a canvas, neither of which she could afford to do.

It was some years before I saw the American again: she was separated from her husband and had been travelling abroad with her son. We arranged a happy skating party at an indoor rink. She was as gay and as amusing as ever, but the son, now about seventeen, had grown loutish and sullen. Within a fortnight I was shocked to read on the front page of a newspaper that she had been murdered. Knowing that the boy, although he had learned to speak to some extent, would be helpless without his mother, I rang the flat to see if I could help, only to learn from the police that it was he who had killed her. Wanting a few shillings for a visit to a cinema and being denied since his mother felt he was going out too often and too late, he had knocked her down, gone to the kitchen, collected a knife and, as she was trying to rise, cut her to ribbons, taken the money, gone to a film and then returned to the flat for a good night's sleep. He was committed to Broadmoor.

That Constance had foreseen the tragedy when she painted the boy looking sulky and slashed the rough-in of the mother, I do not believe, but that artists sometimes receive emanations from their subjects is beyond dispute. I suppose that Miss Seeton, although their characters could hardly be more dissimilar, must be based upon Constance. Certainly when, a long time afterwards, my wife persuaded me to try my hand at a short story, I based it on the idea that an artist can sometimes read more into another painter's work than the painter had intended to reveal. Into my mind walked Miss Seeton, complete with Christian names, umbrella and background, who took over the story and twisted it round to suit herself. Two subsequent comedy stories about her were published, but the original was considered, in those days, too macabre for a family

GERIATRIC SLEUTHS

Mrs. 'Arris (PAUL GALLICO)
Miss Marple (AGATHA CHRISTIE)
Minnie Santangelo (ANTHONY MANCINI)
Miss Seeton (HERON CARVIC)
Miss Silver (PATRICIA WENTWORTH)
Mrs. Pollifax (DOROTHY GILMAN)
Hildegarde Withers (STUART PALMER)
Max Gutman (CHARLES GOLDSTEIN)

magazine.

After a lapse of fifteen years, when I'd long forgotten her, Miss Seeton upped and demanded a book. Ridiculous. At best, she was short-story material. She nagged at me for a fortnight until I gave in, deciding that if she wanted to satirize detective novels in general, and elderly lady detectives in particular, let her have her head whilst I plodded along behind trying to learn to write. The result was *Picture Miss Seeton*, and since then she has to a large extent taken over my life — to my advantage, for which I'm duly grateful.

Miss Marple, Miss Silver, Miss Seeton.

Considering the adage that truth is stranger than fiction, are we perhaps failing to tap a potential source of power in the war against crime? Should there be an office for GERIATRICS (Detection) INCORPORATED in every police department, where elderly maiden ladies, between their cups of tea, their knitting, their discussions about their relatives, and their artistic endeavours, could solve problems which were causing routine headaches? With regard to Miss Seeton, in view of the chaos she generally causes, there would undoubtedly be mass resignations from the force, thus saving a deal of state expenditure. All that would be needed would be a selection of her sketches depicting the people involved, forwarded to the court, allowing the judge and the jury to pick the winner.

Heron Carvic has written four books featuring Miss Seeton. Although not a little old lady himself, he has been known to carry a brolly.

THE MISS MARPLE LOOK-ALIKE CONTEST

Contest Rules

1. All contestants must be at least 74 years of age.

2. They must live on a fixed income.

3. They must knit.

4. They must gossip.

5. They must garden.

6. They must own a pair of binoculars.

7. They must explain why they stole a Poirot plot and starred in it as Margaret Rutherford (*Murder at the Gallop*).

8. They must explain why they repeated the crime (*Murder Most Foul*).

9. They must be able to name all the novels in which they have appeared (*Murder at the Vicarage; The Body in the Library; The Moving Finger; A Murder Is Announced; They Do It with Mirrors; A Pocket Full of Rye; 4:50 from Paddington; The Mirror Crack'd from Side to Side; A Caribbean Mystery; At Bertram's Hotel; Nemesis; Sleeping Murder*).

10. They must list all the short story collections in which they are included (*The Thirteen Problems; The Regatta Mystery; Three Blind Mice; The Adventure of the Christmas Pudding; Double Sin*).

11. They should have china-blue eyes, fluffy white hair, and a pink-and-white complexion.

12. They should be able to draw a map of St. Mary Mead.

13. They should be willing to acknowledge their inspiration (Agatha Christie's grandmother).

The Winner

HIDDEN DETECTIVES

James H. Olander

Hidden in the following puzzle are thirty-three last names and one first name of thirty-four popular detectives, amateur and professional. The letters may read from left to right, right to left, top to bottom, bottom to top, or diagonally in any direction. Some letters may appear in more than one name. One of them, Lew Archer, is done for you.

```
C A N Y O U F I N D N A M E S
U P A B U G O A G R G R A N T
F E N T E A H B C E D C R O W
F R A N K C I O U W I H P E N
S H A Y N E K U T O S E L B Y
D R E V L I S H E E R R E F E
U N I Q U E A C I A R E S O L
P O I R O T E L I P T G S A L
I U Q U C A G L Z E T T I T A
N K U H O L M E S F E C N A V
A D E D A P S F U L B R O O M
H R E D S M A L L O B R O W N
C A N O I P M A C W I M S E Y
O C L A P P L E B Y T T E N T
G A M A D G E W O L R A M T O
```

THE HIDDEN DETECTIVES

1. Alleyn, Roderick
2. Appleby, John
3. Archer, Lew
4. Beck, Martin
5. Brown, Father
6. Campion, Albert
7. Chan, Charlie
8. Crow, Anderson
9. Cuff, Sergeant
10. Dalgliesh, Adam
11. Drew, Nancy
12. Dupin, C. Auguste
13. Fell, Gideon
14. Fen, Gervase
15. Gamadge, Henry
16. Ghote, Ganesh
17. Grant, Alan
18. Holmes, Sherlock
19. Maigret, Jules
20. Marlowe, Philip
21. Marple, Miss Jane
22. Poirot, Hercule
23. Queen, Ellery
24. Robinson, Mac
25. Selby, Doug
26. Shayne, Mike
27. Silver, Miss Maud
28. Small, Rabbi David
29. Spade, Sam
30. Tibbett, Henry
31. Thatcher, John Putnam
32. Vance, Philo
33. Wimsey, Lord Peter
34. Wolfe, Nero

Dr. James H. Olander is associate professor of English at the New York Institute of Technology.

THE BBC THROUGH A MONOCLE

Ian Carmichael

COURTESY PUBLIC
BROADCASTING SYSTEM

On 11th March 1966 I received a letter from my agent which read as follows:

> My brother has come up with what might be a very interesting idea for a television series, namely the character of Lord Peter Wimsey in the Dorothy Sayers books. As you know they were tremendously popular, and the character would, I think, fit you like a glove (or vice versa) and there is certainly quite a lot of material to draw on.

Immediately, I flipped.

I had read a few of the Wimsey books when I was in my twenties, and somewhere about the age of eighteen or nineteen I had seen my local repertory company give a performance of *Busman's Honeymoon*. In short, I knew sufficient about the character to realise that this was the best idea to have come my way for a very long time.

Unhappily, a very long time was exactly what it took to bring that germ of an idea to full-flower. On 17th January 1972 the cameras eventually started to roll on the first episode of the first TV production, ending a maddening and frustrating gestation period of five years.

On receipt of my agent's letter, the first thing I did was ring up Harrods and ask them to send me copies of the complete Wimsey canon.

"How many books are there?" I asked.

"Fourteen," came the reply after a few moments' research.

"In *paper*back," I added, hurriedly.

Now, I enjoy reading for pleasure very much indeed, but reading for work is an entirely different matter. That I find a complete chore. So it was with mixed feelings that I sat down to read fourteen books on the trot, one after the other. Rarely, before or since, has such a daunting job of work turned out to give me so much pleasure. I did indeed read one after the other, in chronological order, without even stopping to pick up so much as a copy of *Playboy* magazine to act as a mental douche 'twixt stories.

I repeat, I flipped.

The next five years were packed with incident and inactivity, and principally the latter.

I first approached the BBC Light Entertainment Department, for whom I had just finished playing Bertie Wooster in three successful series, and immediately I hit the first of a long string of obstructions which were to be strewn across my path like tank-traps for half a decade. It came in the form of a letter from the head of the department.

"The very first snag," it read, "is an insuperable one — money. The BBC has no risk capital whatever at the moment to invest in projects, however optimistic one may be about potential profits."

It then went on to add that the overseas sales advisors had expressed the view that the subject would, and I quote, "by no means be an easy sale across the Atlantic. The character of Lord Peter Wimsey is not very well known in the States," it went on, "nor does the literary and literate style fit in very well with the current trends of filmed series."

Mumbling into my metaphorical beard several phrases like "lack of foresight," "no imagination" and "false assumptions," I refused to be put off. Girding up my loins, I approached the Drama Department of the same station, the head of which was an old friend of mine. I was appearing in a long-running play in the West End at the time, and I telephoned him one evening from the theatre during the act interval to ask if I could go round and have a chat with him after the show. He agreed, and

A BELL-RINGER PROTESTS

Jean Sanderson, an English campanology authority, was asked to comment on Lord Peter's bell-ringing form in *The Nine Tailors*. According to Miss Sanderson, Dorothy L. Sayers made several mistakes. First, the vicar should never have stepped in. ("This is considered far too dangerous and any peal in which this occurred would not be recognised.") Second, since he was ringing a heavy bell of 7¼ cwt., Lord Peter's hands, after three hours had gone by, would have been blistered and swollen; by the end of nine hours, they would have been in such a terrible state, he probably could not have held on to the rope. Third, the reverberations of the bells would certainly have made the poor soul deaf and quite possibly have driven him mad, but it is doubtful they would have killed him "unless he had a weak blood vessel, in which case it's just conceivable a hemorrhage would have occurred, and *that* could have killed him."

Miss Sanderson recommends the following books to mystery fans who wish to further their interest in campanological crimes:

The Chinese Bell Murders by Robert van Gulik;

Death of a Dissenter by Lynton Lamb.

She further suggests if you're ever in the vicinity of Meldreth (Nr. Cambridge), ring her up and she'll give you a lesson in tower bell-ringing, change bell-ringing and hand bell-ringing. However, she wants you to know that real-life bell-ringers are more interested in socialising than homiciding.

an hour and a half later, armed with a large whisky, I started my sales spiel.

"Do you know the Wimsey books?" I asked.

"Look behind you," he said, and there, on a bookshelf behind my head, was every one of them. Obviously I had found a fellow fan. My spirits rose.

My friend went on to tell me that the Wimsey books were, indeed, at that very moment, along with a couple of other subjects, being considered as a possible follow-up series to a very successful one that had just come to an end. My spirits rose even higher. They needn't have. It was to prove yet another disappointment. Nothing ever came of the idea.

Just for the record, I discovered about a year later that the producer ear-marked to undertake the new series, though being very keen to tackle the Wimsey saga, did not want me in the part. Whether this influenced the overall decision to scrap the idea, I know not. I very much doubt it.

Having drawn a blank at the BBC, I then sat down and drew up a highly professional twelve-page sales brochure on the subject which, emulating the best door-to-door salesmen, I started touting round all the U.K. commercial stations, which, each in turn, showed a similar lack of enthusiasm. I received such dismissive answers as:

"After careful reflection we do not think there is an international market for the Peter Wimsey idea." And:

"It's not our scene." And:

"The Americans will never go for an effete (a strange adjective for Peter Wimsey) Englishman." Or:

"The Americans will never buy a serial, only a series.

Simultaneous with all this, my agent and I had been having talks with the Sayers estate in order to find out the availability of the TV rights of the saga, and here again we encountered problems. The executors were, at that time, only prepared to sell the rights of the complete works in one package. To discuss the purchase of individual books or, say, one or two at a time, they were not prepared to do, and this alone, I knew, would not endear the idea to the British TV moguls, regardless of their other prejudices.

Disheartened, I then let the matter drop for a year and got on with something else. In 1968 I became more depressed as I heard that a film company was showing interest in the properties and consequently the Sayers people were no longer prepared to entertain the possibility of a television series.

Impasse.

In 1969 I received information that the film project was off, so I started knocking at the BBC's door once again. This time with considerably more success. A producer was assigned to the job, scriptwriters were put to work and all the novels were to be presented in chronological order in three series of thirteen episodes each. Excelsior! That was the way I had always wanted them to be presented. But "When troubles come . . ." etc. Nine months later the producer left the BBC in order to produce a feature film, and all was off once again.

One year after that (and if you are finding this monotonous, think how I was feeling) I again tried to persuade them to resurrect the project. Apart from anything else, I was getting concerned that when and if we ever did get it off the ground, I would, by then, be too old for the part! By this time the Sayers estate had withdrawn their original condition of selling the complete works as a package, and plans were made to do one novel in five episodes to see how it was received.

You would have thought that by now I was home and dry, but oh dear no, not a bit of it. Which novel to start with was the next hiatus.

"Number one, *Whose Body?*" I opined.

"Not a bit of it," said the authorities. "We must start with a good one, a well-known one, and *Whose Body?* is inferior. Let's start with *Murder Must Advertise.*"

"But that's halfway through the canon," I explained. "We shall get into a frightful mess from a chronological point of view if it is a success and you want to do more."

Impasse again.

Finally a compromise was made, and we all agreed to start with book number two, *Clouds of Witness;* and early on a cold March morning in 1972, in the heart of Howarth Moor (the Brontës' moor) in Yorkshire, Wimsey and Bunter got into a green 3½-litre Bentley and drove off past the camera. At last we were on our way.

Three years later, in January 1975, in the BBC studios in Glasgow, the final shots of *Five Red Herrings* were committed to videotape. The fifth book completed. From that day to this, I have heard no more from my employers. The series has (temporarily? I know not) been abandoned, and Harriet Vane has never appeared on a TV screen. The letters that I have received from avid fans awaiting her entrance would fill the correspondence column of a national newspaper for six months. But it was not to be. Why? I have no idea. Finance, I suspect, but I have never been informed.

For those who don't know, Peter eventually married Harriet Vane (*Busman's Honeymoon*), the girl he got acquitted of murdering her lover (*Strong Poison*) and by whom he eventually had three sons (*Striding Folly*). So criminology, bibliography, music and cricket were obviously not the sum of his talents.

I loved Wimsey. He was me. Or what of him that was not me was what I would have liked to be me. I think I was rather like a child playing dressing-up games. I dressed up as Wimsey and played "Let's pretend" because I admired him, I envied him his life-style, his apparent insouciance, his prowess and his intellect. He was never, as some people like to pontificate, a snob, an anti-Semite, an . . . but that is all the subject of another article.

Ian Carmichael is *Lord Peter Wimsey.*

THE BETTMAN ARCHIVE, INC.

Lord Peter, while at Balliol College, Oxford, excelled at cricket. Here, he admires the renowned Dr. Grace's batting posture. Neither wished to comment on the origin of the term "sticky wicket."

A PINCE-NEZ PROPELLED BY TWO WALKING STICKS

Donald Rumbelow

Dr. Gideon Fell, Ph.D., LL., F.R.H.S., resembles his contemporary, G.K. Chesterton. There is the same mountain of flesh, the box-pleated cape, many chins, ruddy face, grey hair, bandit's moustache and small eyes peeping through a pince-nez fastened to a broad black ribbon. Probably he doesn't drink as much beer and wine as the stories suggest he does. Hopefully he was caught, if only once, as Chesterton was, sitting in a Fleet Street tavern, not quaffing great stoups of ale but quietly sipping a small lemonade!

Before his move to Adelphi Terrace, necessitated by his appointment as advisor to Scotland Yard, Fell's home was at Chatterham in Lincolnshire. The infernal region of imps and goblins seems a more natural background than the noisy bustle of modern London. Guardian of the shrine, in both homes, is Mrs. Fell, a small, cheerful woman, always knocking things over, and with a tendency to poke her head in and out of windows like an overwound cuckoo clock. In her worse moments, she sounds like a convert to the Daughters of Temperance. She heartily disapproves of beer and wine in place of tea. Not surprisingly, Dr. Fell regularly abandons her for more congenial companions on both sides of the Atlantic.

His students don't learn much in the way of formal history. They join him in beer-swilling, table-pounding conversations, cheer his descriptions of battles and stamp their feet loudly when he leads them into the chorus of a drinking song of Godfrey of Bouillon's men on the First Crusade (likely to be confused by teetotallers with "We Won't be Home till Morning"). This environment is understandably conducive to his researches on his monumental work *The Drinking Customs of England from the Earliest Days.*

His other great work is the history of the supernatural in fiction. He has an encyclopaedic knowledge of the subject which, by right, when he tangles with death-watches, mad hatters and red-gartered witches, should give him the lion's share of the credits. Regretfully the sheer physical bulk of the man — he has to walk with two sticks — means that the action has to be left to younger men such as the American Ted Rampole and the flamboyant Patrick ("I am never wrong") Butler K.C. (King's Counsel).

Dr. Fell, like Old King Cole, with whom he is sometimes compared, is too often the story's *deus ex machina.*

Deus ex machina? He wouldn't like that.

Each man should reflect his hero. So why shouldn't Gideon Fell?

It is only fitting, for a man of his size, that he should have more than one.

His is a bench of magistrates, long dead, of ancient Athens.

Like those same magistrates, Dr. Fell is outside the action. Like them, he can bring stillness and peace to the troubled places. Like them, he can pronounce sentence.

Archons of Athens!

He is the law.

Donald Rumbelow is a London police constable and the author of I Spy Blue.

The Gothic

Introducing the very nightie for Gothic heroines... especially designed for **escaping** from castles, retreating from manor houses and finally graduating from charity boarding schools...

In practical, adorable flowered flannette (99% polyester, 1% attic cobwebs)...discreetly covers every limb...

Scotchgard® treated to repel the wet of midnight thunderstorms...sprayed with silicone to help you avoid those nasty forest twigs...

Ours alone in **virginal** white, governess gray, innocent-ward pink... all sizes to 8... order now and pay later, after you've married the heir!

Nightgown

Oversize collar acts as a wrap because we know you can't afford a coat...converts to bat-proof shield for sojourns in the belfry...just your eyes are left free to gaze **deeply** into his!

Drawstring **modestly** raises hem to your knees...enables you to run more easily down those haunted corridors... thermal stockings extend to your waist, warding off those damp crypt chills!

The beautiful ruffle is a secret compartment hiding a flotation ring...should you be thrown in the well or tipped into the pond, you'll float until help arrives...

Had you but known this nightie existed, you would never have crept down the stairs without it!

From the... **House of Gothic**

CONCEPT, SOLOMON HASTINGS; ILLUSTRATED BY MARIE GILMORE

THE MYSTERY OF NANCY DREW

Children's Express

The Nancy Drew books are really super because you can't stop reading them. They are exciting and interesting at the same time, 'cause they give you at least three little mysteries that all turn up into one gigantic one.

To people who like mysteries, it's *really* mysterious because at the end of a chapter they keep you hanging and you've got to keep on reading to find out if they get out of it or not. You say, "Hey, wait, I can't stop reading. I've gotta find out what happened to George" or "how Bess found out so and so." And they never get to the whole big plot until, like, the second page to the end!

We went to meet Harriet Adams, the creator of Nancy Drew. Harriet Adams never used her real name on her books — always her pseudonym, Carolyn Keene.

Mrs. Adams is exciting — she's eighty-four now. We thought she was gonna be sort of motherly, just sitting in a rocking chair knitting and thinking about her books, or new stories to write. We thought her office was gonna be a room in a little rickety white house and she was gonna come out wiping her hands on her apron and seat us in old rocking chairs. But when we went there, it was a new, modern brick office building, very large. That was super because it sorta updated her. And Harriet Adams turned out to be half business-like and half motherly-like: when we came in, she hugged each one of us and she didn't even know us; and she goes out to work every day and really *does* something. It's super that she can be both of those things. She's put her mark on the world.

Harriet Adams took up writing Nancy Drew from her father. We never dreamed that her *father* would have a feminine name like Carolyn Keene! It just seemed really strange.

"My father started Nancy Drew and the Hardy Boys and the Bobbsey Twins," Mrs. Adams told us, "and he used pseudonyms. He didn't have to for the Hardy Boys, but on the girls' and children's books he thought if it were feminine it would be better. So I just carried those on.

"I never wrote any books with my father," she continued. "I worked with him the year after college just editing manuscripts. He taught me really how to do that. My father died in 1930. He had written several outlines for stories, and I took over at that time."

We don't want to sound mean — but in case Mrs. Adams dies she'd have an unfinished book and who would be there to finish it? So we asked Mrs. Adams if any of her grandchildren were planning on writing — or her kids.

BOOK REPORT NO. 1

The Mystery of the Brassbound Trunk. Adults would definitely like this book. Maybe the other Nancy Drew books they wouldn't 'cause it's too childish, but this one I don't think so.

Harriet Adams, who as Carolyn Keene has continued the Nancy Drew and Hardy Boys series begun by her father, talks with reporters from Children's Express *at her New Jersey home.*

"Well, most of them write well, but they haven't gotten to it because they've gone into other things," she told us. "One's a doctor and two of them are lawyers. One of the grandsons is taking courses now in scriptwriting and he wants to go into film work. I hope that he will."

Mrs. Adams showed us the outline of her new books. She said she had drawers full of 'em. And it's good because she can work on them whenever she goes to her office.

"I've written a hundred and seventy books entirely myself," she told us. "Besides that, I've written many outlines for books and had other people fill them in. And then I take their manu-script and edit and rewrite. So that makes even more.

"This is the way I work. First I write a précis and then I start writing the outline. And then from that I dictate the story on a machine. Many times I ask my own children to help with certain parts. I have one daughter who's a great horsewoman, so if I have any scenes with horses I always ask her to read the book and correct phrases. And I have a son who is an engineer, so sometimes I ask him to help with technical things.

"The quickest I ever wrote a book was two weeks. I like to take from two to three months."

BOOK REPORT NO. 2

The Quest of the Missing Map. They start out with half a map and they have to find Ellen's father's twin brother (who has the other half a map), so they can find the buried treasure.

We asked Mrs. Adams if she had a close relationship with her father like Nancy had with *her* father.

"No, not that close," she replied. "I had a very strict father, and also my father never had any mysteries for me to solve.

"I sort of patterned Nancy Drew after what I would think was an ideal girl," continued Mrs. Adams. "I have put myself in Nancy's place and she's very real when I'm writing about her. I just feel as if she were a live person. I tried to bring up my two daughters the same way."

We asked Mrs. Adams why she changed the styles of clothes and hairdos. Like, Nancy started out wearing a skirt and now she's got pants on.

"The books have been updated," replied Mrs. Adams. "The books that are on the market now are not the original books.

"The biggest problem was with adoption because the laws are now very strict about adoption. But when the Bobbsey Twins and early Nancy Drews were written there really weren't any laws. And in the Bobbsey Twins, Daisy May was the baby in the basket and was left on their doorstep — and they brought it in. But nowadays if anybody leaves a baby on your doorstep, you have to turn the child over to the police.

"Well, I was going to do that Bobbsey Twins book over. I consulted adoption agencies and there was absolutely no way that we could do that story anywhere near the way it was originally. So we sat down in the office and everybody had a suggestion. And one of the women just for fun said, 'Oh, why don't we make Daisy May an orphan?' Well, that's the way it turned out in the new book with that same name."

The Nancy Drew books are much in de-

mand at our library. There's a notice on the books that says, "As soon as you finish them, please return them. They are much in demand." There are only two Nancy Drew books in the library each day because so many of them are out.

"Years ago, both public and school librarians didn't approve of these books and I couldn't see why," Mrs. Adams told us. "They said they weren't great literature or anything. They wouldn't put them in the libraries, so we made a survey one time and we found that most of these librarians were older women, some of them real old, and most of them hadn't read Nancy Drew because they started after these people were grown up. And they just thought because they were inexpensive in price that they couldn't be good books. Well, now the whole thing has changed. Those people have all retired and the younger librarians coming in have all read Nancy Drew!"

In Mrs. Adams' way, she told a story with her answers and each one was sort of a different episode. So she gives her answers like she writes her books!

Writing stories and being busy all the time, we think she really enjoyed us, and we really enjoyed her because she seemed to understand us better than we even understand ourselves.

Children's Express *is the first news magazine written by children. Reporters are: Susan Lozier, 7, Mara Lozier, 9, Patrick McGowan, 11, Lisa Coughlin, 13, Joanne Siesputowski, 13, and Giny Hurlbert, 13. Editors are: Michael Schreibman, 15, and Mary Anne Siesputowski, 15.*

BOOK REPORT NO. 3

The Clue of the Tapping Heels. The first mystery is the missing Persian cats and then it gets another mystery added on to it: who is following Nancy home? Then another one: the mystery of the tapping. Then it ends up into one big story.

MISS SCARLET IN THE LIBRARY WITH A WRENCH

John Watson

Since Anthony E. Pratt first applied his mind to the development of a whodunit game in 1944, his brainchild Cluedo has become a favourite of families in at least seventy-three nations. Its name varies from Clue (in the U.S.A.) to Detective (in Brazil). Its theme of murderer detection, combined with its fine British country house setting and the classic nomenclature of its participants, helps to give the game an atmosphere and charm which enables it to avoid the clinical banality of other deduction games.

Mr. Pratt's own description of his life is characteristic in its elegance and modesty:

> I was born, so I believe, with an introverted disposition, full of ruminations, speculations, imaginative notions and grandiose schemes, but with a destructive, self-critical or disparaging propensity, which was as much a stimulus to action as a ball and chain to a long-distance runner. My schooling was during the First World War, when educational opportunities were few, but I went to a good grammar school where a grounding was given in mediaeval (scholastic) philosophy. This awakened an interest in general philosophy, together with its associated disciplines, which has persisted throughout my life and given me much pleasure, but little else. Coming from a musical family and having a great love of music, I was mistakenly thought to possess gifts which subsequently turned out to be illusory, but I did practise music

professionally for years and achieved a local reputation until events impressed upon me my incapacity, temperamentally, to "reach the heights." I then became a civil servant and wound up as clerk to a firm of solicitors. My wife is a very competent artist but has never practised anything more than being a housewife.

Mr. and Mrs. Pratt are now living in retirement at Boscombe near Bournemouth in the south of England.

The board of the present Cluedo game has not changed since Mr. Pratt's wife prepared a final prototype for submission to Waddingtons in 1946. After spending many hours perfecting the mechanics of the game and after filing a provisional specification at the Patent Office, Mr. and Mrs. Pratt visited Waddingtons in Leeds to discuss the possibilities for its manufacture. On that occasion they were accompanied by their close friends Mr. and Mrs. Bull, who had earlier invented a successful

The best player to be is Miss Scarlet. She always gets to move first.

ALL IN THE GAME
Suzanne Weaver

Poor Mr. Boddy found dead in his house
The method unpleasantly gory
The knife was concealed in the Wandering Jew
At the rear of the conservatory.

So — here's the unsavory story:

Scarlet it seems traveled down for a week
During which B. reworded his will
Then who should show up, uninvited of course,
Colonel Mustard, that suspicious old pill.

Apparently Mustard had long had a lust
For Mr. B.'s cook, Mrs. White
(Although she was married to no-one-knew-who
In B.'s room she spent every night).

Now White had a brother, Boddy's old pal
A college professor named Plum
The Prof was determined to seek his revenge
Over an old prank involving his chum.

To make matters worse, at this time in the week
Two lowlifes named Peacock and Green
Came barreling into the Lounge, where the group
Was already involved in a scene.

The night was so cloudy, the air hardly moved
The tension incredibly thick
Boddy stood up, quickly leaving the room,
The gathered had all made him sick.

What happened next was told in the cards
All were suspected it's true
Fingers were pointed in every which way
They were such a despicable crew.

Professional too — hardly a Clue® —

So there's Boddy's body all covered in blood
Cut down in his prime, what a shame
Which of his friends could have done such a thing
Is answered as part of the game.

Suzanne Weaver is an editor who used to slip two weapons and no perpetrator into the Clue® envelope.

game called Buccaneer. Together they played the game with Mr. Hurst and Mr. Goodall from Waddingtons in the office of Mr. Norman Watson, the managing director. Mr. Watson did not play but watched.

It is to the credit of Messrs. Hurst, Goodall and Watson, as well as a compliment to the developmental thoroughness of Mr. Pratt, that the potential of the game was instantly recognised on that occasion.

Terms for its manufacture by John Waddington Limited were quickly and amicably agreed upon. Due to postwar shortages of various materials there were some delays before the game reached the market, but in due course it was launched and received with moderate enthusiasm by the toys and games trade.

It did not become an instant craze. Its present world-wide sales total of approximately 2 million sets per year has been reached more by a process of gradual progression than by any immediate or flashy sales promotion. Its sales throughout the 1950's were solid if unspectacular, and it was not until the late 1960's that any sparkling developments became noticeable in its sales pattern.

The game is now sold in countries from Western Samoa to Ethiopia and from Lesotho to Abu Dhabi. From their manufacturing facilities in the U.K., Waddingtons export approximately 7,000 sets per year, but the number manufactured under license (in eighteen countries) approaches 1.5 million.

The final word upon this remarkable game must rest in mystery itself. The millions of families who have happily played Cluedo since its introduction over twenty-five years ago have invariably been successful in detecting where the unfortunate Dr. Black was murdered and by whom and with what implement.

But nobody has ever discovered why.

John Watson is marketing director of Waddingtons House of Games Ltd.

Chapter 4
PRIVATE EYES AND SPIES

FRED WINKOWSKI

MARXISM AND THE MYSTERY

Robert B. Parker

As a reformed academic, I have had the chance to watch the slow dignification of the hard-boiled detective story. English departments now offer courses in it, and English professors now write about it. The departments do it in the hope of attracting students; the professors do it because if they don't publish they will perish or — the moral equivalent of perishing — they will be forced to teach. Such professors like the work of Hammett, Chandler, Macdonald and MacDonald and (if they have Ph.D.'s from second-rate universities) Parker. But in order to make their pleasure in such writers profitable they have to first make them seem suitable grist for the mill of tenure (smaller than which few things grind). Thus such professors examine such works in a frame: archetypal criticism, Freudian criticism, Marxist criticism. The work becomes the expression of larger motifs. It becomes important and thus fit subject for a scholar.

Fourteen years in the professor dodge has taught me that one can argue ingeniously on behalf of any theory, applied to any piece of literature. This is rarely harmful because normally no one reads such essays. If someone does, it is only another professor doing background on his own article. If he mentions it to a student, the student is likely to ignore it. (Unless he is a graduate student. A graduate student will write it down before he ignores it.) But now and then one of these ingenious tenure-getters creeps out into the public domain, and people start believing it. Such is the case with Marxism and the private eyes.

MATTHEW SEAMAN

It is a reasonably conventional allegation that the hard-boiled hero can profitably be seen in Marxist terms — "the honest proletariat," in Leslie Fielder's phrase. Certainly one can make a case for the Continental Op in the short stories (notably "The Cutting of Couffignal")

P.I. REQUIREMENTS (NEW YORK STATE)

You must have three years' experience as an investigator. If you worked for a licensed detective agency, that counts. If you were a detective in the police department, that counts. If you were an army investigator, that counts. No other experience qualifies (including hotel and department store security work).

You must post a $10,000 bond with a recognized bondsman. This is your collateral, if you are sued, and is, in effect, your credit rating.

You must apply to the New York State Division of Licensing Services, and you must pass their background check as well as a background check by the police department.

Assuming your background is cleared, you must then be scheduled to take a written exam. The exam lasts three to four hours and covers laws of agency, legal terminology, specific knowledge of the law, investigative techniques, general aptitude and intelligence. You must pass the test.

You must then take an oral examination in which you are interviewed by one, possibly two, licensed investigators. You must pass this, too.

You must have a legitimate place of business with a working telephone. This means an actual office (not your home) and does not mean merely a box number and an answering service.

You must pay $200 for an individual license, $300 for a corporation license.

Your license must be renewed every two years.

It takes approximately six months to process a private investigator's license. The license does not mean you have the right to carry a gun. That is a special license which takes another six months to process, with separate background checks and separate requirements. The private eye's license gives you a valid reason for applying for a gun permit, but it is by no means a guarantee that you will get one.

---

and Sam Spade in *The Maltese Falcon*, who solves his partner's murder because it's bad business not to.

It is also quite true that the wealthy are often villainous in Chandler's work (although General Sternwood in *The Big Sleep* certainly is not, nor is Sewall Endicott, who appears in several of the novels). But that seems about as far as one can reasonably take such speculation. To claim that Hammett and Chandler were writing proletariat fiction is to read them very selectively. It is also to misread them. How Marxist is *The Thin Man*?

In "The Cutting of Couffignal" the Op captures a woman who offers him money and sex to let her go. He won't do it because, he

says, he likes his work and is committed to it. In *Red Harvest* he cleans up a corrupt Western town even though he knows his employer will give him "merry hell" for it. In *The Dain Curse* he helps rescue a young woman from drug addiction and a mistaken belief in her own degeneracy, although he is not employed to do that. What have these actions to do with each other? Very little in terms of class struggle, very little in terms of the Op as a worker. But they say a good deal about the Op as a man.

In *The Maltese Falcon* Spade turns in a woman with whom he is apparently in love; it's clear the act costs him pain. When she asks him about it, he says, "I won't play the sap for you." Earlier in the novel, as they wait for Joel Cairo

PINKERTON'S
("The Pinks")

The original private eye belonged to the Pinkerton's National Detective Agency. It was their trademark, a large, unblinking, ever-seeing eye — the eye that never sleeps. This is the root of the expression "private eye," although many think the term derived from private investigator, abbreviated to P.I. Hard-boiled writers were not

WE NEVER SLEEP

the first to steal inspiration from the Pinks. Conan Doyle beat them to it. Intrigued with the story of the Pink undercover agent who infiltrated the Molly Maguires, Doyle worked it into *The Valley of Fear.* Pinkerton itself got into the writing business. Allan Pinkerton hired a series of writers to perpetuate the Pinkerton exploits, and they did so — under his name — in eighteen novels. Among the things the Pinkerton Agency is credited with originating are the first rogues' gallery and the first professional use of photographs for identifying the bad guys. George O'Toole maintains that the Pinkertons "performed the same functions in their time that in ours are assigned to the Secret Service, the FBI and the CIA."

to appear, he tells her about a man named Flitcraft. It seems to be a way to pass the time, but it is more. It is a parable about Spade's vision of life and a warning to Brigid that he lives in keeping with that vision.

There were things Hammett was incapable of saying, or saw no need to say. The story of Flitcraft and Spade's refusal to "play the sap" were as far as he went in articulating a code. It wasn't Marxism. It was much more fundamental. It took Chandler to point out that the hard-boiled hero was not concerned with economics. He was concerned with honor.

When Hammett was learning to write, he was working in a world which, after the fiasco of World War I, found the man of honor an embarrassment and talk of honor naïve. It found toughness necessary and cynicism only sensible. So people like the Op and Spade talk about doing the job, or not playing that sap. In *The Glass Key* Ned Beaumont speaks of loyalty to a friend (*The Glass Key* was Hammett's favorite). In *The Big Sleep* Marlowe tells one of the Sternwood girls that he's a detective and "I work at it." But what they do, as opposed to what they say, is honorable. The hard-boiled hero is aware that honor has no definition. He has noticed that he who has it may well have died o'Wednesday. But he knows that there are things a man does and things he doesn't do, and it is not usually very hard to decide which is which. It is often wearisome to choose. The fact that such men elect to be honorable in a dishonorable world makes them heroic. As in most fundamental things that humans care for, honor is indefinable but easily recognized.

The hard-boiled hero belongs, therefore, not to the Marxist but to the chivalric tradition — a tradition he shares in this country with the Westerner. He is not of the people; he is alone. His adventures are solitary statements. His commitment is to a private moral code without which no other code makes any sense to him. He regularly reaffirms the code on behalf of people who don't have one.

He is the last gentleman, and to remain that he must often fight. Sometimes he must kill.

Robert B. Parker won the Mystery Writers of America Edgar for Mortal Stakes.

HOW TO TELL SPADE FROM MARLOWE FROM ARCHER

Richard R. Lingeman

SAMUEL SPADE, a.k.a. "Sam"	PHILIP MARLOWE, a.k.a. "Phil"	LEWIS A. ARCHER, a.k.a. "Lew"
DATE OF BIRTH		
Ca. 1895	1906	Sometime between 1914–1920, depending on when he is telling it.
DRESS		
Height, 6′; weight, 185 lbs.; hair, blond; eyes, yellow-gray.	Height, slightly over 6′; weight, 190 lbs.; hair, dark; eyes, brown.	Height, 6′2″; weight, 190 lbs.; hair, dark; eyes, blue-gray.
PHYSICAL DESCRIPTION		
Muscular, heavy-boned, sloping shoulders, hairless chest and soft pink skin, big thick-fingered hands. Prognathous jaw, thickish brows, hooked nose, high flat temples, widow's peak.	Husky. Women find him good-looking in a brutish way.	Husky. As a younger man, resembled Paul Newman; lately resembles Brian Keith.
PHYSIQUE AND LOOKS		
Gray suits, dark brown shoes, green-striped shirts, green tie and loose tweed overcoat.	Hat, trench coat and horn-rimmed sunglasses; when dressed up, wears his one good powder-blue suit, black brogues and black wool socks with clocks.	Conservative (owns two suits).

Richard R. Lingeman is an editor at the New York Times Book Review.
Copyright © 1976 by Esquire Magazine. Reprinted by permission of International Creative Management.

MATTHEW SEAMAN

SAMUEL SPADE	PHILIP MARLOWE	LEWIS A. ARCHER

MARITAL STATUS

Single	Single	Divorced (1949). Wife's name: Sue. Grounds: mental cruelty.

PERSONAL HABITS

Heavy smoker, rolls his own (Bull Durham, brown cigarette papers) and lights them with a pigskin-and-nickel lighter. Heavy drinker on occasion, including while on job. Drinks Bacardi at home, taken neat in a wineglass; and premixed Manhattans from office bottle in a paper cup.	Heavy smoker, usually Camels; lights cigarettes off kitchen matches, snicking them with his thumbnail. Also smokes a pipe in the office while cogitating. Heavy drinker: keeps a bottle in the deep drawer of his desk for drinks alone or with clients; serves Scotch and soda or Four Roses and ginger ale at home; dislikes sweet drinks.	Heavy smoker for thirty years (but not before breakfast). Gave it up around 1968 but still occasionally reaches for one. Light social drinker; doesn't drink while working or before lunch. Drinks Scotch, bourbon, gin and tonic, and beer (Bass or Black Horse ale).

MANNERISMS

With clients, subject is smooth, sympathetic and ingratiating. Under stress, grins wolfishly, laughs harshly, makes animal noises, or his eyes become cold and hard; when about to slug someone, eyes become dreamy; good poker face with cops.	Tough-guy exterior, enhanced by stream of cynical wisecracks, metaphors and similes: "It was a blonde. A blonde to make a bishop kick a hole in a stained-glass window." "You guys are as cute as a couple of lost golf balls." "Put some rouge on your cheeks. You look like the snow maiden after a hard night with the fishing fleet."	Tough in his day, now more kindly, sympathetic; has father fixation (on self). N.B.: It has been said of subject that "when he turns sideways, he almost disappears."

SAMUEL SPADE	PHILIP MARLOWE	LEWIS A. ARCHER

RECREATION

Reading Duke's *Celebrated Criminal Cases of America*.	Chess problems (his chess is not up to tournament standards), going to movies (dislikes musicals).	Fishing; sometimes plays the horses when he has some "dirty money"; chess, bird-watching, ecology. Little social life.

HOME

Lives modestly in a small apartment with living room, bathroom and kitchen. Furnishings: sofa, table, armchair, padded rocker, cheap alarm clock by fold-up bed, white bowl hanging from ceiling on gilded chains.	Sixth-floor three-and-a-half-room apartment (living room with French windows and small balcony, bedroom, kitchen and dinette); rent, $60 a month. Furnishings: oak drop-leaf desk, easy chair and subject's few possessions— chessboard, stale memories, regrets.	Lives in modest second-floor apartment in a quiet section of West Los Angeles. Once owned five-room bungalow on a middle-class residential street in West Hollywood but sold that after divorce.

OFFICE

Sutter Street near Kearney, San Francisco; three-room suite with reception/secretarial area and two inner offices for subject and partner. Furnishings: oak armchair, scarred desk on which is ash-strewn green blotter and butt-strewn brass ashtray.	The Cahuenga Building on Hollywood Boulevard; one-and-a-half-room office on sixth floor with waiting room and interior office. Furnishings: desk with glass top, squeaky swivel chair, five green metal filing cabinets (three of them empty), "near-walnut" chairs, washbowl in stained-wood cabinet, hat rack and commercial calendar on wall.	8411½ Sunset Boulevard, Hollywood; two-room office on second floor of two-story building (office next to Miss Ditmar's model agency). Furnishings: armchair and sagging green imitation-leather sofa in waiting room; inner office sparsely furnished, with mug shots and subject's framed license on walls.

OFFICE HELP

Effie Perine, secretary, early twenties.	No secretary or answering service. (Telephone: GLenview 7537)	No secretary but does have answering service.

CAR

Doesn't own one.	Chrysler	Ford

GUNS

Doesn't carry one.	Luger, Colt automatics and (preferred) Smith & Wesson .38 special with 4″ barrel. Uses shoulder holster.	.38 special, .32 and .38 automatics; no shoulder holster nowadays and rarely uses a gun.

SAMUEL SPADE	PHILIP MARLOWE	LEWIS A. ARCHER

M.O.

SAMUEL SPADE	PHILIP MARLOWE	LEWIS A. ARCHER
Won't perform illegal acts such as murder or burglary, but otherwise sells self to highest bidder.	No divorce work but takes anything else that's legitimate. Carries photostat of license, honorary deputy sheriff's badge, various phony business cards, fountain-pen flashlight, penknife.	Used to do standard "peeping"—divorce work, adultery, blackmail—but nowadays specializes in family murders with an Oedipal twist. In younger days, used more rough stuff but now avoids violence and has a better (i.e., richer) class of clientele (prefers old money); carries license photostat, various phony business cards, and old special deputy's badge; has a contact mike for eavesdropping, which he never uses; waiting room bugged and has a two-way glass in the door. Usual techniques: psychology (orthodox Freudian), sympathy, and probing questions.

CODE

SAMUEL SPADE	PHILIP MARLOWE	LEWIS A. ARCHER
"When a man's partner is killed he's supposed to do something about it." Byword: "I won't play the sap for you."	First loyalty is to the client; ethical, but would twist rules for client. "I'm selling what I have to sell to make a living. What little guts and intelligence the Lord gave me and a willingness to get pushed around in order to protect a client."	"We are all guilty. We have to learn to live with it." Highly ethical but not squeamish; regularly turns down bribes (including one of a million dollars). Will take any case as long as it is "not illegal and makes sense." Years on the analyst's couch have deepened his insights.

KNOWN ASSOCIATES

SAMUEL SPADE	PHILIP MARLOWE	LEWIS A. ARCHER
Secretary Effie Perine; Miles Archer, partner, forties (deceased); Sid Wise, lawyer; (f.n.u.) Freed, manager, St. Mark's Hotel; Luke (l.n.u.), house detective at Hotel Belvedere; Iva Archer (Mrs. Miles), girl friend; Tom Polhaus and Lieutenant Dundy, cops.	Los Angeles crime reporter; Dr. Carl Moss (for confidential medical help); Bernard Ohls, district attorney's staff; Carl Randall, Central Homicide Bureau; and Captain Gregory, Missing Persons Bureau.	Morris Cramm, night legman for a Los Angeles gossip columnist; Peter Colton, chief criminal investigator, Los Angeles County District Attorney's office; Bert Graves, Santa Teresa D.A.'s office; Willie Mackey, private detective, San Francisco; Glenn Scott, retired Hollywood private detective.

SAMUEL SPADE	PHILIP MARLOWE	LEWIS A. ARCHER

FEES

| No set fees; employs sliding scale based on client's resources and vulnerability; asked $5,000 (later upped to $10,000) on so-called Maltese Falcon case (collected $1,000). | $25 a day plus expenses ("mostly gasoline and whiskey"). | Started out at $50 a day plus expenses; has been at $100 a day since the 1960's. |

BACKGROUND

| Subject was probably born in England or lived there before the war. In the Twenties worked with a big detective agency in Seattle (probably a branch of the Continental Detective Agency), then came to San Francisco in the late Twenties and went into partnership with Miles Archer. Partnership dissolved by client Brigid O'Shaughnessy (murder one; served twenty years). Subject's weakness is women and was carrying on simultaneous affairs with his partner's wife (mainly sexual on his part) and Miss O'Shaughnessy, yet distrusts women. A cool character who can be unpredictable and harbors a violent streak. Came to a bad end. Subject was shot to death in his office in 1930 by Iva Archer two days after closing Maltese Falcon case. Motive: jealousy. | Subject was born in Santa Rosa, California. Began career as an insurance investigator, then worked for the Los Angeles County District attorney's office as an investigator until he was fired for "insubordination." Never speaks of his parents and has no living relatives and few friends. His mail consists almost entirely of bills and circulars. He attended college for two years at either the University of Oregon or Oregon State. Apparent carnal interest in women and often gives them butterfly kisses with his eyelashes, but has no steady women friends off the job; has turned down advances from attractive females (e.g., the Sternwood sisters) on the job out of loyalty to his client. (Possibility of latent homosexuality? Note overcompensating tough-guy mannerisms and frequent contemptuous references to "pansies," "fags," and "queens.") | Subject was born in a "working-class tract" in Long Beach. Stated that he attended grade school in Oakland in 1920, which would place his birth at at least 1914. He probably grew up in Long Beach, and there is some evidence that his parents died or divorced. A juvenile delinquent as a teen-ager, he reformed and joined the Long Beach police force in 1935 (according to the earliest version), working his way up to detective sergeant before he was fired for reasons that are not clear but relate to corruption. Served in World War II in intelligence. After the war, opened up a Hollywood office and married his former wife, Sue, an ash blonde. She divorced him because she did not like the company he was keeping. Subject tends to cloud his past; for example, he said in 1950 that he had done divorce work in Los Angeles for ten years; on two other occasions stated he was fired from the Long Beach force in 1945 and 1953, respectively; in 1958 he was heard to state his age flatly as "forty." At any rate, he is now close to sixty, a lonely though not unsociable man. Secret passion is not justice, but mercy. "But justice is what keeps happening to people." |

MATTHEW SEAMAN

FOR FURTHER REFERENCE SEE:

The works of Dashiell Hammett.	The works of Raymond Chandler.	The works of Ross Macdonald.

MIKE AND MICKEY

Pete Hamill

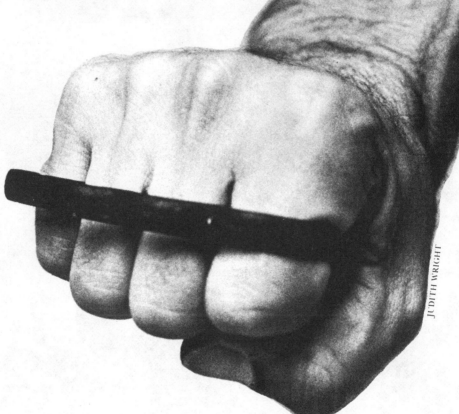

JUDITH WRIGHT

O ut of the mouth of Mike, put there by the mind of Mickey, comes:

> *Go after the big boys. Oh, don't arrest them, don't treat then to the democratic processes of courts and law . . . do the same thing to them that they'd do to you! Treat 'em to the unglorious taste of sudden death . . . Kill 'em left and right, show 'em that we aren't so soft after all. Kill, kill, kill!*

If Hammett was a Thirties prizefighter, full of rough grace and a belief in the rules, and Chandler was a Joe DiMaggio, playing on ballfields of a summer afternoon, then Mike Hammer and Mickey Spillane were pro football: brutal, vicious, mean and literally pummeling their way into the American consciousness.

Like pro football, Mike and Mickey reached their first large audiences after World War II, telling them that winning wasn't everything, but — as Vince Lombardi would later say — it was the only thing.

Their appeal rested on their vigilante primitivism, their idiosyncratic form of law and order in which each man was assigned, by himself, the role of judge, juror and executioner. They interpreted this as anti-Communism at its best, as the American way, like apple pie and

Mom. Critic Philip Cawelti explained this rationale as "part of the justification for Mike's participation in the culminating orgy of sadism and destruction."

Mike and Mickey explained it this way:

If you want a democracy, you have to fight for it. Why not now before it's too late? That's the trouble, we're getting soft. They push us around the block and we let them get away with it.

In the Mike and Mickey books one finds the right winger's credo: If you just kill enough Communists, you can save democracy. The courts will only thwart you in this, so you have to bypass them by hiring your bagmen, your wiretappers, your Mike Hammer generals (George Patton) to do your cleaning up.

That Mike and Mickey stand for stunted sexuality, a kind of pornographic reveling in violence combined with a desperate need to present the most awful events as examples of innocence, is not a new idea. Witness the My Lais, the Joe McCarthys, the (I know you're tired of hearing it) Nixons.

Given the chance, Mike and Mickey would run world affairs like rabid politicians. To wit:

Some day, maybe, some day I'd stand on the steps of the Kremlin with a gun in my fist and I'd yell for them to come out and if they wouldn't I'd go in and get them and when I had them all lined up against the wall I'd start shooting until all I had left was a row of corpses that bled on the cold floors and in whose thick red blood would be the promise of a peace that would stick for more generations than I'd live to see.

But the character of popular heroes has, inevitably, changed. The old heroes, the heroes of the Fifties, are dead, and the focus of thriller novels has shifted from the violence of Mike and Mickey. We are now in the company of more interesting men who embrace the sensuality of danger, the turn of the wheel of chance, but who also represent decency and endurance. They can be men who say no, and in so doing, affirm the qualities of the human character that are included in the simple word: hope.

Pete Hamill, columnist for the New York Daily News, *is the author of* Flesh and Blood.

THE GUMSHOE'S SHOES

JUDITH WRIGHT

Archie Goodwin wears Bradley shoes, but he's the only private eye who does. Mainly because they are not for sale anywhere except in Rex Stout's imagination.

An independent survey of private investigators in the New York area revealed that no two of them wore the same brand of shoe and not one of them was sure where the term "gumshoe" came from. Most guessed it had something to do with the fact that they all preferred rubber-soled shoes for working. Several thought it meant they were always picking gum off their shoes — an occupational hazard when you do that much walking, it seems.

Twelve operatives tossed an extra pair of shoes in the back seat of their car when they were doing surveillance work, just in case their feet started to hurt. More likely than not, the second pair were sneakers.

The only shoe mentioned by more than one investigator was a brand called Walk-Overs. They were described as "sturdy," "well-made" and "comfortable."

On average, the private investigators had their shoes reheeled and resoled twice a year.

The two things most looked for in a shoe were comfort and quiet. As one investigator put it, "My shoes look ordinary — like Clark Kent. But there's a lot of Superman in there somewhere."

SOFT-BOILED BUT STILL AN EGG

Michael Z. Lewin

You'll never hear a five-year-old at a family get-together say, "I want to write about shamuses when I grow up, Auntie." Writing detective novels is just not the kind of thing little kids grow up wanting to do. So somewhere along the line something must happen to untrack other plans and rerail people onto the road of detective fiction. For me — and I suspect many — the process was largely accidental.

I never expected to be a writer, much less a detective writer. When I was twenty, I had never read a detective novel and I was chugging along quite happily as a chemistry and physics major at Harvard. But in my junior year, in search of an elective, I wandered into a creative writing class. I respected the guy teaching it and the concept of the class, which was that you only learn to write by writing. I liked it. In my senior year I took two more writing courses. They didn't, however, prevent me from graduating a science major and heading off the next year to study chemistry at Cambridge University in England. I kept writing. I enjoyed it. And I decided to give it a go.

But if I hadn't been playing a harmonica as I rode my bike one November night in Cambridge, Albert Samson would never have come to be. As it happened, another student, whom I knew only slightly, noticed me, hailed me, invited me to a party. There I met my wife-to-be. She gave me my first detective novel; how many wives-to-be have done as much for a fella?

As a high school student she had been a problem for her English teacher because she refused to limit her reading to "good" books.

Finally, he told her if she was going to read trash, she ought at least to read good trash. He gave her Raymond Chandler. And it was Chandler she gave to me.

In the years since that first Chandler, the family has swept through — often more than once — Chandler, Hammett, Ross Macdonald, the Travis McGee books of John D. MacDonald, early Dick Francis and a number of other books in the genre. I've made up for the sheltered nature of my early upbringing.

Albert Samson came into existence in early December 1969, appropriately enough in Los Angeles. The aforementioned wife had delivered of her first child in September in New York, where we lived, and we'd taken this premier grandchild to L.A. to visit my mother.

We stayed six weeks, and at the beginning of the fifth we'd exhausted the low-budget entertainments of the area. So I decided to entertain the assembled company by writing a twenty-page take-off of a detective story.

When I started my story, I began it where they all begin: with a female client walking into the office. Along with the obligatory wisecracks, I included a few family jokes. Setting it in Indianapolis, for one thing. I grew up there, but it's never been prime detective story country. I also called my detective "Albert Samson." Albert, because it was an undetectivelike name — not good like Rip Toenail, or something — and Samson from "Sam." Sam, Al and Gus were all names I had been promoting for our impending child while it was impending. For some inscrutably English reason my wife had considered all unsuitable. "Albert Samson" was a form of revenge. The child is now known as Elizabeth.

By the time I had finished a dozen pages of my epic entertainment, I realized I was never going to contain it in either twenty pages or the

HARD-BOILED HANGOVERS

Open a private eye's desk drawer and you'll probably find a half-eaten tuna sandwich moldering in its wax paper with a half-empty bottle of booze dribbling all over it. That's because our hero was too plastered to screw the cap back on. Drinking beyond capacity is the private eye's occupational hazard. In the interest of his clients, not to mention his splitting headache and screaming liver, the White Horse Tavern — which has seen many heavy drinkers in its time, including Dylan Thomas and Brendan Behan — offers the following hangover cures:

1. Slice of lemon saturated with sugar and bitters
2. Lemon juice, straight up
3. Milk laced with sherry
4. Bloody Mary, heavy on the Tabasco
5. Whiskey Sour, a double
6. Black coffee, the bitterer the better
7. Three aspirin and an ice pack
8. Don't drink water for 24 hours
9. Don't drink, period.
10. Stay horizontal

If these fail, there are the following folk remedies to resort to:

1. Eat a banana
2. Coat stomach with milk before boozing
3. Raw egg and oatmeal
4. Coca-Cola syrup, straight
5. Throw up, then take a cold shower

time I had available to work on it. So to get a little encouragement, I allowed it to be seen as it was.

I thought it was a hoot.

My wife read it quietly. "I don't like funny detective stories," she said.

I did a few more pages and then packed the thing away. We revisited Farmers' Market, discovered the La Brea Tar Pits and went home.

About the end of January 1970 I was having to justify my existence. The previous June I'd retired from three years' teaching on the strength of a successful book called *How to Beat College Tests*. Its success was mainly in the fact that the advance payment on anticipated royalties was enough, we had thought, for a year's subsistence living.

But then, as now, a year was pretty short, and I felt impelled to get down to some kind of work. The ideas around the Albert Samson story had stayed with me when other notions had come and gone. I dug it out, blushed at some of the things which had amused me so mightily and started working on it again.

When it was a hundred pages long it was turned down by three publishers, but too ignorant to be put off, I kept working on it. In September 1970 it was finished, and it was accepted by the first publisher it was submitted to in final form. It was released on the world as *Ask the Right Question*.

I've now written four Albert Samson novels, and there's a fifth novel in which he appears, though not as the major character.

He is no longer the larkish self-amusement he started as. Successive books have each taken longer to write, and they are rewritten a number of times. If I've not learned much about writing novels, or about writing detective stories, I am at least a much better typist than I used to be.

Albert Samson *is* different from other private detectives, but to me the most important way he differs is that he is much the same.

The point is that most new detectives are written to be something clearly unusual. The central figure may have a specialized occupation which hasn't appeared in a thriller before (we await the case of the man who trains polar bears for guard duty on the Alaskan Oil Pipeline . . .). Or the novelty may be more personally associated with the detective. He may be gay; he may be a woman; he may be totally paralyzed except for a little toe he uses to communicate with through a *possum*.

Going for a basic novelty makes sense for a new writer trying to break into a competitive field. Something unusual stands a better chance of attracting a publisher's attention.

So the unusual thing about Albert Samson, as a new private detective, is that he is not fundamentally different. As a thoughtful man, in business on his own, with an interest in people and a tendency to wisecrack, he seems to fall within at least the general outline of the traditional American private eye that everybody knows.

And it is because his "type" is so well known that I find it interesting to write about him. Everyone knows what private detectives are supposed to be like; I don't have to spend large amounts of time explaining what most people in Albert Samson's job are like before I can show convincingly how he is special.

From the beginning, readers have expectations about what loner private detectives should do. So from the beginning I can use the expectations and play against them to try to achieve surprise, suspense or humor.

Albert Samson may well, at a critical moment, notice a car following him and become suspicious. He may take risks to shake the trail. But for Samson, unlike most, odds are the car is completely innocent and he has victimized himself with his own suspicions. He tends not to benefit from coincidences. That's the way things go for Albert.

Though the private eye traditions are important to Albert Samson, there are certain specific facts about him which differ from the tradition and help contribute to the tone of books about him. He doesn't own or carry a gun, for instance. And he is not a sexual predator. Healthy enough, but with notches neither on gun nor appointments diary. And, of course, he is located in Indianapolis.

Michael Z. Lewin's most recent Albert Samson novel is The Enemies Within.

THE
(Wild Goose)
MALTESE DUCK
(Chase)
CAPER

A Mike Wrench Mystery
Translated from the Vernacular

"Big Mama" Birns

COURTESY NELSON GALLERY — ATKINS MUSEUM,
KANSAS CITY, MISSOURI, NELSON FUND.

Broads. I wouldn't trust 'em any further than I could throw 'em. Take the Case of the Maltese Duck. It all began when Peggy, my secretary, looked up as I walked in that morning and said, "Dame in your office. A real looker."

"What's her moniker?" I snapped.

"Goes by the name of Velma Wonderly."

I opened the door and the first thing I laid eyes [*saw*] on was a pair of gams [*attractive legs*] that wouldn't quit. She was round, firm, fully packed and stacked [*had a nice figure*].

"You've got to help me, Mr. Wrench," she begged. "Something's been stolen from me. My diamonds."

"You mean somebody heisted [*stole*] your rocks [*diamonds*]?"

"I think they were taken by a big wheel [*important man*] named Fosco and his thugs [*criminal associates*]." She started the waterworks [*began to cry*].

"Keep your shoit [*shirt*] on, sister [*miss*]," I snarled. "I'll get yer rocks [*your jewelry*] for you. I'll nail [*apprehend*] those birds [*gentlemen*] and they'll do time [*be incarcerated*] in the Big House. Or maybe I'll just make sure it's curtains [*death*] for the creeps [*undesirable fellows*]."

"Be careful, Mike."

"Don't worry, Duchess [*Madam*]," I said. "I pack a heater [*carry a gun*] and nobody plays me for a sucker [*takes advantage of me*]."

I found Fosco just where Velma said he would be.

"Hiya [*Hello*], fat man," I sneered. "The way I hear it, you got [*have*] some hot ice [*stolen jewelry*] that belongs to a skirt [*woman*] named Wonderly [*Miss Wonderly*]."

Fosco smiled around his toothpick. "Maybe we can make a deal [*negotiate*], buster [*sir*]. I'm looking for a certain statuette. A Maltese Duck [*Wild Goose*]. I have reason to believe it is in the hands of Miss Wonderly." He pulled out his roscoe [*gun*]. "Perhaps you can tell me where it is."

"I ain't no stoolie [*don't tell tales*]," I muttered.

"I'll make him sing like a canary [*confess*], boss [*Mr. Fosco*]," said Fosco's cheap gunsel [*boyish assistant*], making a move on [*toward*] me.

"Watch it, Wrench," said Fosco. "The kid's [*young man's*] a snow bird [*drug addict*] and he's hopped [*drugged*]. Let's talk turkey [*be honest*]. I'm prepared to let you in on this caper [*crime*]."

"You mean split the moola [*share the profits*], the mazuma, the do-re-mi?"

"That's right. Plenty of cabbage [*money*]."

"How much?"

"Ten thousand clams [*dollars*]."

"No dice [*No*]."

"Don't be a sap [*fool*], Wrench. If you don't come in on this deal [*agreement*], I'm afraid we'll have to rub you out [*kill you*]. Get him, Wilmer."

The gunsel [*young helper*] jumped me, but my fist split his kisser [*face*] open. I plugged [*shot*] five fast ones [*bullets*] into Fosco with my gat [*gun*] and then said, "So long, chump [*foolish person*]."

I was no sooner out the door when two coppers [*police officers*] were on me [*detained me*].

"Freeze the mitts, Wrench," the flatfoot barked. *[Hold your hands still] [officer]*

"What do you want, gumshoe?" I snarled. *[officer]*

"You know what we want. We want the hot duck *[cooked goose]*, and we want it now. If you don't finger *[expose]* the birds *[people]* with the duck, we'll stash ya in the joint *[incarcerate you]* for a long time," the copper *[officer]* growled. *[goose]*

"My lip *[lawyer]* will get me out in a week, chump *[foolish person]*. Get off my back *[Do not intrude]*. This is my racket *[profession]*, and I'll play it my way. You got yer noive *[your nerve]*, muscling in on my game *[interfering with my methods]*."

They hauled me down to the station. An hour crawled by like a sick cockroach. I wasn't spilling any beans *[confiding in them]*, so they told me to scram *[depart]*.

"Okay, Wrench," the gumshoe *[officer]* said. "You're sprung *[free]*. But go on the lam *[if you leave town]*, it's up the river *[prison]*."

"Goodbye, sweetheart *[officer]*," I sneered.

I went back to my place to hit the booze *[have a cocktail]* and there she was. Waiting for me. Velma . . . blond, beautiful, hot to trot *[amorous]*.

"O.K., sister *[All right, miss]*," I said. "Hand it over."

"What?" she squealed.

"The duck *[goose]*," I said. "You're not Velma Wonderly. You're Sadie *[Sarah]* the Smoocher *[Lovable One]*. You make your living as a hootchie cootcher *[an exotic dancer]*. You've got the dope habit *[drug]* and you got it bad, and that Maltese Duck *[Wild Goose]* is your ticket to the big time *[success]*. It's loaded *[filled]* with snow *[cocaine]*."

"You crumb *[undesirable fellow]*," she hissed through her choppers *[teeth]*, and began to pump out *[fire]* Chicago lightning *[bullets]*.

I dodged the deadlies *[bullets]* and threw a right to *[punched]* her belly.

"O.K., sugar *[All right, my dear]*, it's the slammer *[jail]* for you."

"I guess you won't play the sap *[behave unwisely]* for me, will you, Mike? I love you," she sighed. "Why do I love you?"

"Because I got guts *[have intestinal fortitude]*," I said. "Just guts *[intestinal fortitude]*. That's all."

The End
CURTAINS

Margaret [Margaret] "Big Mama" Birns *talks real good [teaches English]*.

THE HOUSE DICK

Lawrence Frost

I was standing on the steps of the hotel when I spotted a woman who was actively soliciting the men in her path. She paused in front of the hotel windows, peered in, and apparently satisfied with the potential business, headed for the entrance. I turned around and went back inside the hotel and made my way to the bar to investigate her behavior.

When I rounded the corner, she had not yet gone inside the hotel bar but was standing at the door preening and, presumably, checking for Johns. I loosened up my walk, dropped my jaw a bit, undid the top button of my shirt and rearranged my tie. Her first look at me was one of a pawnbroker appraising a watch of dubious worth, but she half-closed her eyes, wet her lips and gave me a sexy smile anyway. The closer she got, the more obvious she became.

"It's pretty crowded in there," she said as she moved near enough to count my mustache hairs.

I looked inside and confirmed it. "Yes, I would say so. I'm not too fond of crowds."

With her hand now on my arm, "What are you doing in the hotel?"

"Oh, you could say I'm here on business."

"Really? Me, too."

Her hand was still on my arm, and when I asked her what kind of business, her hand moved to my thigh.

"The entertainment business. Got a room upstairs? We could have fun. Without a crowd."

"Yes, I have a room, but what kind of fun did you have in mind?"

"Oh, the fifty-to-a-hundred-dollar kind."

Her hand became more intimate.

We made our way through the lobby, and I kept looking into her eyes to avoid contact with any of the bellmen. For once, I was lucky to get through without any hellos or waves. Inside the elevator I pressed the second-floor button, which is where the security office is located. I found out that Denise was a recent arrival from Chicago, where business was slow and the heat strong. The heat was pretty strong in the elevator, too, as she tried to practice her profession. It took a lot of will power on my part to practice *my* profession.

When we got off and started toward the office, I asked her if she considered herself a hustler.

"Sure I do."

"Well, Denise, do you think you've ever been hustled?"

"No, I really don't think so."

I produced my badge.

"You sure don't look like a cop."

"Well, I'm not. I'm hotel security."

"Yeah? Well, you sure don't look like that, either."

We went inside the office and one of my partners was there. We had Denise empty her bag and pockets, open her coat and take off her boots. That was just to make sure she had no weapons readily at hand. It also gave us an opportunity to see if she had any hotel keys or burglar tools. She was then photographed and given a formal warning to stay out of the hotel. If Denise is caught in the hotel again, under any circumstances, she will be arrested for criminal trespass.

I knew what Denise meant when she said I didn't look like a cop or hotel security (the official job title is House Officer, but House Detective is quite acceptable and so is House Dick in some circumstances), because most of the guests and criminals we come in contact with still confuse us with our fictional counterparts. From the hard-boiled detective fiction of the Thirties to today's Kojak, we have been portrayed as potbellied, flatfooted, stogy-smoking, bribe-taking peeping toms. It takes some people longer than others to realize that the well-dressed, well-educated and well-spoken person in front of them is the House Dick, who is also quite knowledgeable about hotel and criminal law and quite capable of enforcing it — tactfully when possible and with force when necessary.

With previous experience in the security or law enforcement field, it takes about six months to become a competent hotel detective. You must learn every inch of the building, memorize the where-to's of the many keys you carry, and the M.O.'s of hotel violators. After the six months you will probably have handled prostitutes, burglars, psychos, con men of every description and scam, drunks, deaths (accidental, natural and suspicious), heart attacks, wife beatings, fires, lost articles, luggage and persons, and just about anything else that can happen when you have 3,000 people on eighteen floors of a big-city hotel.

My qualifications for the job were experiences working for different private investigation agencies doing tailing, undercover work, investigations (criminal and civil) and some heavy mystery reading. Despite my work in the field, it wasn't until I began at the hotel that fact and fantasy finally intersected. Sure, I went out

and finally bought a trench coat, dangled Camels from the side of my mouth and began to drink Johnny Walker Red straight up, but — unfortunately — only a few of my fellow officers related these gestures to my heros. My boss certainly didn't. When I explained to him in my interview that, like Archie Goodwin, my best weapon had always been my mouth, I got a grunt that might have unnerved Wolfe himself.

Few suspects like Denise are apprehended on the lobby level of the hotel. Most are collared in the course of our floor patrols, which are the meat and potatoes of hotel work. A full patrol from roof to sub-basement entails about a mile and a half of walking. While we patrol, we check for open doors, keys left in doors, fire extinguishers in need of recharging and basically anything else unsafe, unhealthy or illegal. Like any other beat, ours can get tedious, but there is always relief. For one, there is always a trip to the lobbies for people-watching, and for another there is your partner. But the best company for me on the slow patrols is al-

---

HOMICIDE HOTEL

Some noted writers who have checked their victims into imaginary hotels are:

Hugh Pentecost, who made Pierre Chambrun resident manager of the Hotel Beaumont and had him resolve about a dozen cases of mayhem, most deftly in *The Cannibal Who Over-Ate* and *The Shape of Fear;*

Agatha Christie, who put Miss Marple into *Bertram's Hotel,* the spit and image of Brown's in London;

Raymond Chandler, who created Tony the house dick and gave him a bit part in "I'll Be Waiting," a short story included in *Five Sinister Characters;*

J.F. Burke, who created a black hotel dick and set him up on Manhattan's Upper West Side in *Death Trick.*

ways myself and my fantasies: Marlowe meets the mysterious woman in Room 326 as she exits nervously smelling of perfume and cordite . . .

There are sixteen full-time detectives at the hotel, all with college and some previous experience in the field. Right now, we have a former tenth-ranked heavyweight of the world who is completing credits toward a master's in English literature; two actors, one with military intelligence experience and the other with two hotel jobs behind him; others who missed out on becoming members of the New York Police Department because of the budget problems; and still others who are just progressing through careers in private security. So we patrol, we talk, we observe, and then we patrol some more. While several of us are on the floors, the others take care of the lobby problems, the walk-in crazies and mischief makers.

Out of the 125 or so arrests we make in a year, about 80 will be of prostitutes (mostly female, but some males). It's not the act of prostitution that the hotel objects to, but the inevitable crimes that accompany it. A couple of months ago I got a call to open a room for a guest who had locked himself out. Two seconds later I got another call to step on it, as the guest was standing in the hall naked. When my partner and I arrived and let the guest in, he gave us the following story.

"I was in the bathroom with the door open. I heard a knock on the door, and when I asked who it was, a voice said, 'The maid.' So I say, 'Come in.' I heard the door open, then saw an arm reach into my closet and grab my pants. The door closed and I didn't even put anything on, I just ran outside after her."

We asked the usual questions but couldn't get a description because "she moved too damn fast. I just couldn't get a look at her."

We got someone to find the maid for the floor and asked the guest what he lost besides his pants. The story was a little rocky, but we were giving the guest the benefit of the doubt. Until he came up with what he had lost.

"Well, my wallet and a valuable pinkie ring and a wristwatch my father had given me."

So here we had a fat, fiftyish, Midwest tool-and-die executive sitting in his underwear, begging us to believe him.

We didn't believe him, but hotel procedure prevents us from calling him a liar to his face. After all, how many men will take off their ring and watch, place them in a pocket, then hang the pants upside down? We continued the game, though, and called the police to file a burglary report. The cops couldn't shake this guy from his story, but then they didn't try too hard. The guest's entire body seemed to sigh with relief as we all filed out.

About a half-hour later we got another call. "I found my pants crumpled up in the closet. I got my ring and watch back, but the wallet is still gone. I guess she grabbed that and ran."

I had to say something. "Excuse me, sir, but if you don't mind me saying so, if we were only *half* as dumb as you've been playing us, we would be legally classified as idiots." Door, and case, closed.

It was fairly obvious from first hearing the story that a prostitute had lifted his things and that he had concocted this elaborate charade to save face. This is hardly extraordinary behavior. Guests will frequently lose something in a cab or restaurant but scream at me, "Get the maid! Get the maid! I know she did it!"

This is not to say that the hotel is not victimized by professional thieves, because it is. More than likely, though, its a small-timer trying to make it big, and sooner or later he's picked up. The real pros have proven to be mild-mannered and unarmed. Like anyone else, however, they are not afraid to fight when cornered. As far as cat burglars go, well, they just don't. The last one we had was over fifteen years ago, and I don't recall hearing about any at other hotels in a long time. So, sleep tight unless you just caught an old Cary Grant movie.

The next time you're in the hotel, that man in the Brooks Brothers suit waiting on line in the restaurant, or the man in the room service jacket, or even the guest in the next room, could be me. Yes, we try to be everywhere. When you come to the hotel, have a good time, enjoy yourself, but keep your socks up and your nose clean. Or I'll getcha!

Lawrence Frost is the house dick at a large, luxury hotel in New York.

THE PAPERBACK HERO

Alice K. Turner

In 1969 a writer named Don Pendleton received a $2,000 advance from a small paperback company called Pinnacle Books for a yarn entitled *War Against the Mafia*. Pinnacle printed a modest 50,000 copies of this epic with no great hopes for it — they didn't even bother advertising it — then, mildly astonished, watched it melt from the nation's newsstands virtually overnight. Pinnacle went back to press and Pendleton went back to his typewriter to crank out a sequel. The Paperback Hero was on his way.

By 1971 more than forty original paperback heroes were defying law and order, squashing faces like grapefruits and knuckles like walnuts, and blitzing corruption in a manner even the Elizabethans might have balked at.

Andy Ettinger, the Pinnacle editor who is probably more familiar with this type of book than anyone else, claimed that "without violence, these books wouldn't sell." Joe Elder, his Fawcett Gold Medal counterpart, agreed. Said he, "I haven't found anything I draw the line at yet. But," and here he stopped for a philosophical shrug, "we've gone about as far as we can go."

At the heart — or groin — of these books is the vigilante hero, who is motivated by just one thing: revenge. And he's not going to be satisfied unless he gets it in the most vicious manner possible.

Most of the paperback heroes get their meaningful education in Vietnam, but some are tutored by the police force, some by the Mob, and some even learn by doing time. Typically, the paperback hero starts off in the legitimate service of his country, suffers a savage jolt when he realizes his country cannot and will not protect him, reacts against the ineffectuality and corruption of the cops and the courts, and strides into the role of the lone avenger. The paperback hero and his readers know *the system does not work*. Accordingly, they have little time for such niceties as the Miranda-Escobedo decisions, the Geneva Convention and the United States Constitution. Right wing? Ronald Reagan would get a crick in the neck swiveling right to catch up with them.

The paperback hero is a blue-collar hero, a working-class hero — kind of a collective murder fantasy of the Silent Majority. Chandler's famous dictum "But down these mean streets a man must go who is not himself mean, who is neither tarnished nor afraid" would mean exactly nothing to him. Tarnish is part of the game and he is meaner than a rattlesnake.

One thing he is not, compared to mainstream offerings, is sex-oriented. While it's true the paperback hero is more or less obligated to bed down upon occasion, he doesn't spend a lot of time there. Women, it seems, are for others to victimize and him to rescue, not to love. Besides, she's probably going to get killed in the next chapter, so there's not much point in wasting time on her.

Racism, too, is almost invisible. Blacks, Arabs, Latins, Orientals and especially Sicilians do crop up as villains, but it's always on an individual basis. It's not the race that's bad, it's the particular man. True prejudice is reserved for the homosexual whose lot it is to die midst absolute carnage — here an arm, there a testicle, you get the idea.

Dime Detective, *a pulp magazine of the Thirties, made the decade a rough-'em-up, shoot-'em-up, tough-it-out time, with private eye heroes who knew how to use a gun better than how to use good grammar.*

Overkill, however, has had its inevitable effect and many of the paperback heroes have been muscled off the stands by possessed little girls and lollipop-licking cops. Today, less than a dozen or so of these vigilante heroes remain. Will they resurface? Probably. The macho hero with his frontier justice and gun in each fist has been a fiction staple from Natty Bumppo upwards. (Right now, the slack is being taken up by television. Witness Baretta.) For him to come up to full strength again we'd need to have the peculiar forces that were at work in 1969: the Bobby Kennedy assassination; the Chicago trials; My Lai; Altamont following Woodstock; a president's "secret plan" for peace; anger, frustration and deep division. I think, perhaps, we're better off without him.

Original Paperback Series Heroes

Adrano: Internecine family war. Good locales, pedestrian writing. **C**

Ape Swain: Good writing, preposterous but clever capers. Near East and other exotic locales. **B Plus**

The Assassin: A reasonably satisfactory *Executioner* imitation. **C**

The Avenger: Continuation of 1930 series. Good pulp writing. Light, frothy; preposterous plots. **C**

The Baroness: Totally formularized gimmick melodrama, born of Modesty Blaise and Doc Savage, but sexier. Fun. **B Plus**

Blade: An M16 agent cavorting in something called "Dimension X." Outlandish and outrageous. **C Minus**

Buchanan: No-frills Western for hard-core fans. A perennial, turns up in movies, too. **B Plus** (for the books; **C** for the movies)

The Butcher: Former Mafia gunman. Typical, competent and bloody. **C**

Dakota: A modern Indian, adept in martial arts. Good locales and plots. **B**

Dark Angel: Baroness imitation with Harlem heroine. **C**

The Death Merchant: Killing machine and master of ugly disguise. Cynical and bloody with no redeeming plot or background features. **D Minus**

The Decoy: A crook turned undercover cop. Nice disguises. **C Minus**

The Destroyer: Hokey series, the only one with a real sense of humor. Remo Williams and his sidekick Chiun have won friends even among the literate. **B Plus**

Earl Drake: Believable and consistently ingenious private eyer. From an earlier school of writing — witness girl friend Hazel. **A**

The Executioner: In a category by itself. A publishing phenomenon. For sincerity and prototypicality. **A**

The Expeditor: Superman gimmickry with a soupçon of sex. **A**

The Gladiator: Today is the last day of his life. Maybe. Who cares? Locales are nice, though. **C**

Hardman: Good, solid private eyer. Hero and his ex-lineman sidekick are the Huck and Jim of current pulp. Unusual Atlanta locales. **A**

The Headhunters: Special watchdog police force with its own methods. Very violent; good Detroit locales. **B Minus**

The Hitman: What it says. Bottom of the barrel on all counts. **F**

The Inquisitor: Very neat gimmick guaranteed to delight lapsed Catholics — hero is the Pope's top gun. Number 4 is good enough to stand on its own as a novel. **A**

Jock Sargent: Ingenious plots, weaker characters, top-notch caper writing. Ex-soldier hero operates all over U.S. **A Minus**

Killinger: Very authentic karate. Nifty Travis McGee-like plots with good twists but choppy writing. **B**

K'ung Fu: Crummy, hasty martial arts stuff. Very right-wing bias. **D**

The Lone Wolf: Another ex-cop. No homework visible on backgrounds. Sluggish writing. **C Minus**

Malko: Interesting, very sexy, violent European import. In one book the sadistic killer turns out to be a nun, which is certainly different. Hero, a prince, is a bit of a klutz, though likable. **B**

Pulp writers were short on subtlety, long on sadism. Among the better-known American practitioners: Erle Stanley Gardner (under many pseudonyms), Carroll John Daly, James Hadley Chase and Van Wyck Mason.

In 1938 Captain Joseph T. Shaw assumed editorship of Black Mask *magazine. Hammett and Chandler were his two big star writers. Miss Marple would have fainted if she could have heard what they had to say.*

The Man from Planet X: Sci-fi hero with a peculiar penis. **D Plus**

Matt Helm: A survivor from James Bond days who has become more reactionary and more sexist since that halcyon era. Full of gritty male expertise (guns, etc.) and well-researched spy stuff. For what it is: **A**

Nick Carter: More than 100 books star this phoenix-like incarnation of two earlier heroes of the same name. So many authors, ranging from high school dropouts to Pulitzer prize-winners (reportedly Harper Lee of *To Kill a Mockingbird*) have tackled Nick that the series is impossible to rate. A classic survivor.

Parker (The Violent World of): Written pseudonymously by Donald E. Westlake, which is a heavy recommendation. Convincing, tough, fast-paced. Don't miss them. The best of this kind of writing. **A**

The Penetrator: Hero infiltrates the Mafia to eliminate bad guys. **C**

The Pro: Good gimmicks, snappy back-

THE ATYPICAL PAPERBACK HERO

Truly, Nick Carter has lived through it all. In 1886, Nick emerged as The Little Giant, master of languages, skills and disguises, and hero of an enormously popular series of "dime novels."

Like his Street & Smith stepbrother, Frank Merriwell, Nick remained decent, humane and completely celibate for the seventeen years the series lasted, living a code of honor which made the Boy Scout Creed look positively shabby.

In 1939, Nick turned up again, this time in the pulp magazines. Older and suaver now, he had, in his thirty-five-year absence, acquired enormous wealth and a Filipino valet. He now greatly resembled Walter Pidgeon, who played him in two movies. But,

despite this veneer of sophistication, Nick still lived by his father's original dictate: "Keep your body, your clothing and your conscience clean."

This second Nick was a war casualty, and we heard no more of him until 1964 when an entrepreneur named Lyle Kenyon Engel decided to move into the book business. He leased the Nick Carter name and set another series of writers to work resurrecting old Nick. Thus was Nick reborn as a man of the Sixties, to wit, Killmaster, Agent N3 of the super-secret intelligence agency known as AXE. He has now appeared in over 100 books for Universal Award, a company which seems to exist only to market Nick. And he is now indistinguishable from all the other paperback heroes.

A.K.T.

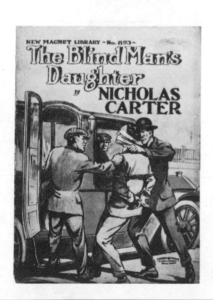 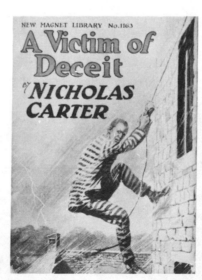 

grounds — athletic scandals investigated. **A**

Shell Scott: Los Angeles private eye whose politics lie to the right of Hitler's. But you can't quarrel with his continued popularity. **B**

Sloane: Very bloody, mildly ingenious kung-fu Western. **C Minus**

Stryker: Banal cop opera with dumb plots, dumb writing. **C**

Travis McGee: The Colosseum. The Louvre. Better than this you don't get. No longer strictly a contender as the last two titles have hit hardcover first and oldies are being reissued as hardcovers. But, with love and squalor: **A Plus**

Alice K. Turner is an editor at New York *magazine.*

TAILING TECHNIQUES
Anthony Spiesman

Mystery writers get it all wrong. First of all, they send this guy out by himself, all alone, to watch a crook who's only slightly less vicious than Jack the Ripper. A guy would have to be crazy to go on that kind of a suicide mission. No private eye in his right mind would do surveillance work without a partner. If he doesn't have a partner, he calls up another P.I., or a part-timer, and they work together. The one thing he does not do is try to cover a guy by himself. Look, suppose he has to go to the bathroom? What's he going to do, ask a passer-by to keep an eye on his subject while he hunts down a men's room? Suppose he's tailing the guy in a car. Let's make it interesting — the other guy is in a car, too, but it's a taxi. At the corner of 45th and Broadway, the guy pays the cabby and gets out. Now what does the P.I. do? He can't very

well abandon his car in the middle of the street, and he's not about to find a parking place. On any surveillance job you need a minimum of two people, more if it's a twenty-four-hour surveillance. A P.I. can't keep up his concentration for that length of time. He's got to be relieved, and that means every eight hours — at least — replacements have to take over.

The other thing the mystery writers do is have their P.I. follow the subject not knowing anything about him. A real P.I. gets as much information as he can *first,* then he tracks the guy.

The dumbest thing I ever heard of is a guy trying to tail someone and holding a newspaper up in front of his face. If you let the subject out of your line of vision for even one second, you'll lose him. Sure, you have to make yourself invisible, but you don't do that by blocking out the subject. You do it by creating a situation in which you are least observable. A change of clothes is very important, and disguises. Now,

I'm not talking about things that make you look ridiculous. That registers, and that's exactly what you don't want. I mean little things: Sunglasses on, sunglasses off. Jacket on, jacket off. Private eyes are probably the original inventors of the "layered look." They peel off a jacket, then peel off a sweater, then a tie, then a shirt, until they're standing there in their T-shirt like any other hippie on the block. Of course, you have to judge what fits in with where you are. If you're in a Madison Avenue building lobby, you can't strip down to a beachboy. But you can become a messenger from the Jiffy Coffee Shop. All it takes is rolled-up sleeves, a container in a paper bag and a little white hat. If you want to be fancy, add a menu. A change of clothes is really all a P.I. needs in the way of equipment. That, and a notebook, and a watch.

Sometimes I'll take along a miniature tape recorder. It fits in my pocket and I can use it very unobtrusively. I just slip my hand in my

pocket and turn it on, and then stand there muttering to myself and it'll pick it up. Then, when I get back to the office, I have it transcribed and send in my report.

There are three basic kinds of surveillances: moving, stationary, and rough. There are two types of moving surveillances — the foot tail and the vehicular. The foot tail is not nearly as easy as mystery writers would have you believe. Say you're in an elevator with the subject (and you don't wait for the next car or you'd never find him again; you get right in the same car with him). How are you going to keep him from noticing you? The best way is to do something impolite. Pick your nose. Scratch your crotch. Develop a palsied arm twitch. The reason these work is that they embarrass people. If they turn away, they don't see you, and you're safe. If, however, you're "made," you have to pack up and go home. There's this little thing called "harassment," don't forget, and that's illegal. If a guy suspects you're fol-

lowing him, all he has to do is find a cop and complain. Unless you want to get pulled in, you have to stop. That's another reason for working with a partner. He can pick up the tail when you have to leave.

The vehicular surveillance is not much easier — it's equally difficult in the city or in the country. In the city you practically have to have the skills of a Le Mans driver just to keep up. You have to take risks, like jumping lights. And you have the big-city traffic to buck. In the country, you have the problem of too few cars, making you far too visible. A pickup truck is probably your best disguise here. You can pass it off as a repair service vehicle. Personally, when I'm asked to do a vehicular tail, I prefer using a rental car — a Chrysler or a Dodge. They're good cars and they're kept in good shape.

The stationary tail is when you're assigned to cover a building or a house and notice everybody who comes in and goes out, and every-

thing that goes on while you're on duty. This could be something as seemingly inconsequential as noting: 9:15 A.M., upper left window shades drawn. You don't move from your spot while you're keeping it under surveillance, which is why you need a partner. Somebody, if it's a house, has to watch the back door.

A rough surveillance is when you're hired to let the subject know he's being watched. This is used as a deterrent to crime. Example: A trucking concern hires you to keep their drivers on the up and up. They see you in your car and know you're watching them, so they can't pilfer, which is a big industry problem. What they don't know, because you're assigned on an irregular basis, is which day you'll be following them. So they can't prearrange to have someone meet them and take the goods off their hands. If they happen to set it up for the day you're on them, they're in big trouble.

Most of the private eyes that I've read about don't seem real to me. They're all in love with their guns, for one thing, and they use them far more often than a real P.I. ever does. I have a license to carry a gun, and there are times when I'll take it with me, but I'm not quick to pull it out. In fact, I can't remember the last time I used one on a case. If you draw guns, somebody's going to get hurt. And it might be me. No thank you. That's why I don't like Hammett. His characters are always getting into gunfights and fistfights. If I got in as many fights as his men do, I'd spend all my time in the hospital and no time working. Shoot-'em-ups may be great to read about, but not to live through.

Lew Archer bores me. I think he's dull. Travis McGee is phony as hell, but fun to read. The best, but there are only two of them so far, are the Joe Goodey books by Charles Alverson. Alverson's guy is an ex-San Francisco cop, now a P.I. He has a sense of humor. He's also smart and uses his head, which is what being a private eye is all about.

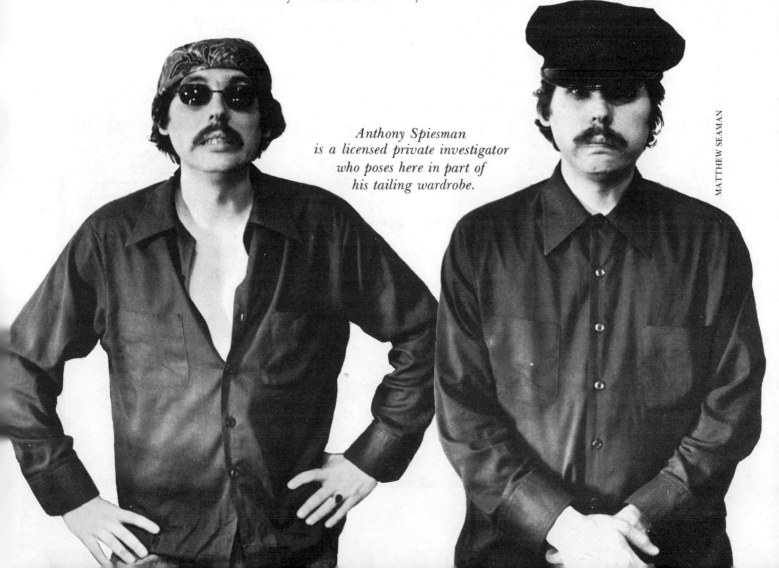

Anthony Spiesman is a licensed private investigator who poses here in part of his tailing wardrobe.

MATTHEW SEAMAN

THE TRENCH

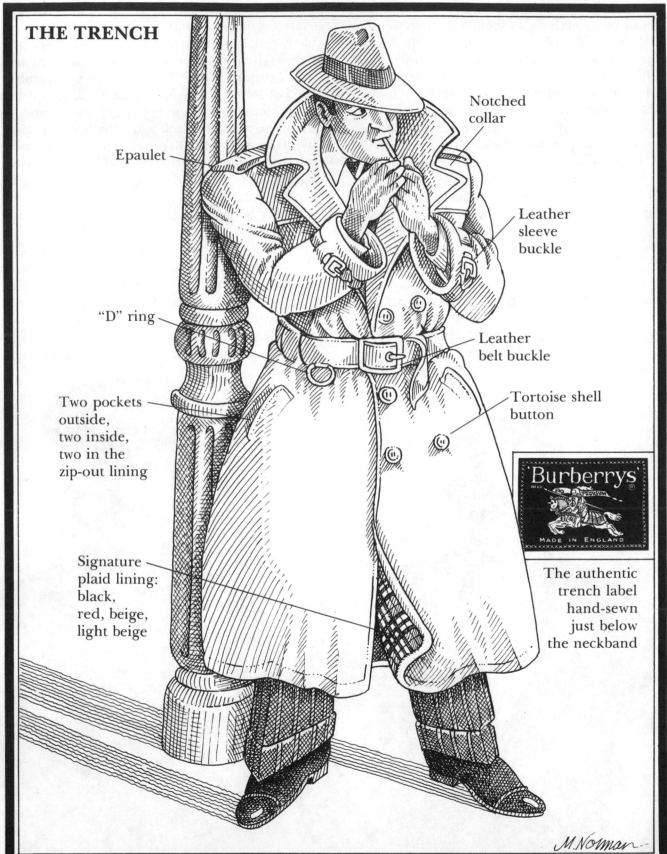

Epaulet

Notched collar

Leather sleeve buckle

"D" ring

Leather belt buckle

Two pockets outside, two inside, two in the zip-out lining

Tortoise shell button

Signature plaid lining: black, red, beige, light beige

'Burberrys'
REGD · PRORSUM ·
MADE IN ENGLAND

The authentic trench label hand-sewn just below the neckband

M. Norman

MARTY NORMAN

THE HISTORY OF THE TRENCH COAT

Hopley Croyden

Our Man Burberry. Aw right, tough guy, how'd you earn your reputation?

To begin with, he was not christened Burberry. Thomas Burberry simply called him "raincoat." It was King Edward — or so says the London *Daily News* of Wednesday, 7th April, 1926 — who dubbed him Burberry. "Give me my Burberry," he said, and the name stuck.

Mr. Burberry conceived him in 1856 when, at the ripe old age of twenty-one, he decided he'd had enough of being a country draper's apprentice and would himself become a clothier. He settled in the market town of Basinstoke and went about his business creating this thing called "gabardinee," a tough, nigh-unto-invincible cotton that shook off water the way Spade later shook off a tail. In 1889 Mr. Burberry took himself and his "gabardinee" to London. Had you been around then, you might have popped round to a Jermyn Street Hotel to see son Arthur, who would have measured you and written up your order.

But it took a war to show the staunch stuff Burberry was made of. Down in South Africa all kinds of unpleasantries were going on with the Boers, and H.M. Army Officers were trying to combat them with the aid of their Burberrys. Lord Kitchener, Lord Roberts, Lord Baden-Powell, generals all, virtually adopted the Burberry as their unofficial uniform. Thomas Burberry wound up outfitting whole regiments and so was prompted to submit a design for official use to the War Office, who snapped it up (they could hardly do otherwise; it came so highly recommended). In 1905 the Admiralty for the Royal Marines endorsed the coat and Burberry was firmly launched as War Hero.

Tough as it was, this Burberry was not yet the trench coat of thriller writers' dreams. The father, if you like, was the "Tielocken," introduced in 1910. It had no buttons but rather a strap-and-buckle arrangement that anchored you in. It could also be ready for action two to four days after you submitted your order.

The actual "trench" was born in 1914 and took its name from all the mucking about it did in the trenches of World War I. Not only did it have buttons; it sported epaulets and "D" rings for attaching military paraphernalia. It also had more followers than Chandler. The number of Burberrys worn by the military is estimated at 5,000 between 1914 and 1918. And if you think it was scared of heights, in 1916 the "trench" took to the air with the Royal Flying Corps — one presumes with a camel fleece lining.

Today's "Trench 40" is indistinguishable from its predecessor. If you squint a bit, you might notice that it's shorter. Most of it is still hand-made and each coat requires four and a half metres of cloth, plus three metres for the lining and an extra metre for each sleeve. Over 200,000 are sold each year (didn't know there were that many adventurers outside of fiction, did you?) and the Burberry concern runs through 2 million buttons and 900,000 metres of cloth just to produce them. The cotton used, by the way, is Egyptian, grown in South America, spun in Switzerland and woven in English mills. How's that for international intrigue! And like any good spy, the Burberry Trench has an irrefutable means of identifying itself: the signature plaid lining. It also costs about as much as secret plans for the invasion of Luxembourg: $295.00.

Hopley Croyden wears a pea-jacket.

THE INVISIBLE BOND

Michael Gilbert

You make your entrance into the room. It is an old-fashioned cocktail party, predominantly male, but with a scattering of rather formidable females present as well. You cast your eye hopefully over the crowd to see if there are a few people whom you might be able to recognise and talk to.

In the near corner, smoking a meerschaum pipe and wearing, even though he is indoors, a deer-stalker hat, is the unmistakable figure of the sage of Baker Street. Talking to him, an equally unmistakable foreigner with waxed moustaches, green eyes and an egg-shaped head. On their left three men are engaged in animated conversation. A stout man with an orchid in his buttonhole, a thin and languid young man with corn-coloured hair and a monocle, and a tubby and undistinguished-looking Roman Catholic priest.

So far, we are on firm ground.

But what about this trio in the far corner? Three youngish men, all of tough and athletic build — one, by his speech, American and two English. There is very little to distinguish them. The American is perhaps a little older and a little more thick-set than the other two. He could be Philip Marlowe, but there is no certainty about the matter. Might the man he is talking to be The Saint or The Baron or The Toff or even The Scarlet Pimpernel? (No, hardly, in a well-cut dove-grey double-breasted suit.) But there is something faintly distinctive about the third man.

Memory stirs.

Could it be the grey-blue eyes? No. All heroes have grey-blue eyes. Then it must be the hair. The short lock of black hair that would never stay in place, but subsided to form a thick comma above the right eyebrow.

Surely, it must be. Dare one introduce oneself?

"Commander Bond, isn't it? I think we first met a Royale-les-Eaux in 1953 . . .

At this point, unfortunately, we wake up and the dream dissolves. But it leaves a curious

*O*f course I read mysteries. I cut my eyeteeth on Edgar Allan Poe and Conan Doyle and I read and reread Doyle. Why? Because I, like all kids, love suspense and puzzle solving.

I still relish Agatha Christie, but my heart was lost to James Bond and his successors. I suppose they give us a better mirror of the world than they ever thought. (The problem today is that the mystery writers are outdone again and again by reality.)

In my two novels, The Northern Palmyra Affair and The Gates of Hell, I have deliberately used suspense techniques and, if I say so myself, a neat mystery solution (in Gates) to generate reader interest.

HARRISON SALISBURY

Dzerzhinsky Square, Moscow. The monument in the center is to Felix E. Dzerzhinsky. KGB Headquarters (Lubyanka) is the inhospitable building looming up on the right.

question behind.

Why is it that detectives are personally so distinguishable and sometimes even distinguished, whilst heroes are physically anonymous? Two hundred pounds of hard muscle, experts at karate, accomplished linguists, irresistible to the opposite sex. But so are ten thousand other young men.

Can the explanation lie in the Greek tag which says that a man's character is the sum total of his actions? The hero of a thriller is unceasingly active. Are we left to deduce his character, as well as his characteristics, from the way in which he conducts his enterprises?

It was with some such thoughts in mind that I re-examined *Casino Royale*. An important book, this, because it is the first time that James Bond, 007, is introduced to us.

Apart from the comma of black hair, I could find only one direct description. It is of Bond asleep, his right hand resting on the butt of his .38 Colt Police Positive. "With the warmth and humour of his eyes extinguished, his features relapsed into a taciturn mask, ironical, brutal and cold."

Not much help there.

At a later point Vesper Lynd gives us her opinion. "He is very good-looking. He reminds me rather of Hoagy Carmichael. There is something cold and ruthless . . . ." We lose the rest, because a bomb explodes.

It is significant, however, that Vesper herself is described in great detail. There is a passage of twenty-five lines dealing with her hair, her face, her skin, her arms, hands and fingernails; her jewellery and her dress "of grey *soie-sauvage* with a square-cut bodice lasciviously tight across her fine breasts." Not omitting her

41–25–32

 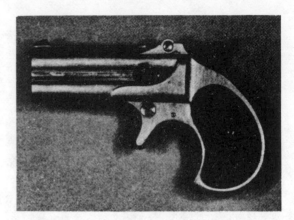

These compact, easily palmed weapons are often encountered by agents in their work. Upper left: a four-barrel pistol. Upper right: .41 caliber double-barrel derringer. Lower left: .25 caliber four-barrel pistol of French manufacture. Lower right: .32 caliber cylindrical revolver. Below: a small camera used by Soviet agents to photograph persons unobtrusively. (Now mass-manufactured, the design is used by tourists.)

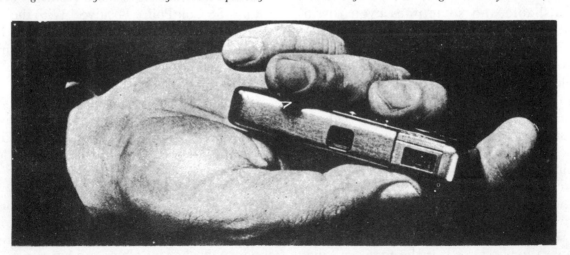

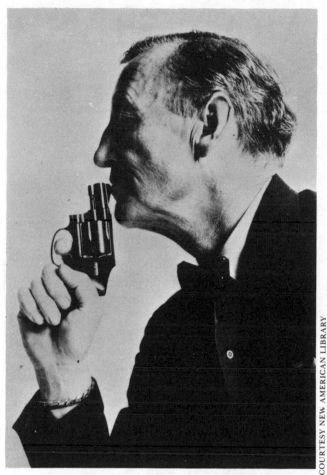

COURTESY NEW AMERICAN LIBRARY

The late Ian Fleming, author of the fourteen Bond books. Fleming himself was an agent, working with British Intelligence during World War II.

handbag, her hat and her shoes ("square-toed of plain black leather").

Is there some psychological deduction to be made from a book which devotes twenty-five lines to the heroine and only three to the hero? Particularly since Vesper is expendable. She is due to die at the end of the book, although she rises, phoenix-like, from her ashes to reappear under other equally entrancing names in a dozen later books.

It is true that we are told a good deal about Bond's likes and dislikes, and may be able to deduce something further about him from a study of them. He smokes cigarettes specially made for him by Morlands of Grosvenor Street and keeps fifty of them in a flat gun-metal box. He drives one of the last of the 4.5-litre Bentleys with an Amherst-Villiers super-charger. He likes his martinis shaken, not stirred, and he likes scrambled eggs.

As the stories roll on, the props pile up — most noticeably, the pigskin Revelation suit-case, with the compartment at the back containing a silencer for his gun and thirty rounds of .25 ammunition. The action continues, fast and furious. The girls are wheeled on, lovingly described, lovingly treated and wheeled off again. The central figure remains obstinately difficult to visualise. Does he exist at all or is he one of those dummies in a shop window, to be immaculately clothed, fitted out with every expensive accessory, put into storage at the end of each book and brought out again to start the next?

It is possible, but there is another, even more intriguing possibility. Was James Bond really Ian Fleming? It is unusual for a writer to transmogrify himself totally into his own hero. Did not Conan Doyle warn us: "The doll and its maker are seldom identical"? Was this one of the cases where it was, perhaps, true?

On the back cover of the Pan Book edition of the novels is the Cecil Beaton photograph of Ian Fleming. His face certainly looks taciturn and ironical. Questionably, even brutal. He is smoking a cigarette in a long holder. Was it specially made by Morlands of Grosvenor Street and are there forty-nine more in a flat gun-metal box in his pocket, or perhaps in the glove box of his 4.5-litre Bentley with an Amherst-Villiers super-charger and a pigskin suit-case on the back seat?

If this is the truth, it would not only explain the accessories; it would explain the curious elusiveness of the central figure. If you are looking out of your own eyes, you see very little of your own face. To examine that you need a mirror. On one occasion, James Bond studied his reflection and noted that "the effect was faintly piratical."

If it was Ian Fleming who was looking at himself, one can accept the description without demur. Ian Fleming *was* a pirate, and he brought back a rich and well-deserved hoard of doubloons from his private Spanish Main.

Michael Gilbert is the author of Game Without Rules, *a short-story collection featuring counter-intelligence agents Calder and Behrens.*

BECOMING MODESTY
Peter O'Donnell

There is a theory which asserts that when it's steam-engine time, somebody will invent the steam-engine. So with Modesty Blaise. The beginning of the Sixties was the time for someone like her to appear, and with nice irony the author this king-sized heroine picked on to invent her was one who had spent most of his working life operating king-sized heroes.

I gave her a great deal of trouble, for it took her more than a year to get through to me. By this I mean that I began with a hazy feeling that I wanted to write an adventure story about a woman who could do all the skilful, ingenious, amazing and daring things which had so far been the prerogative of heroes.

If I was stimulated in this idea by anything other than the prodding of Modesty Blaise herself, it would be that I am fascinated, enchanted and baffled by women, and I think they have had the most appalling of raw deals since almost forever. So it delighted me to contemplate writing about a marvellous female creature who would be as good as any male hero in the crunch, yet would remain entirely feminine withal. Yes, feminine. No bra-burning Women's Libber, she. Please don't misunderstand my use of the word "baffled." For twenty years our household consisted of wife, two daughters and me, so I am not *ignorant* concerning women, just constantly surprised by them and pleasantly baffled, as I'm sure the good Lord intended.

Once I had conceived, or been impregnated with, this notion of a king-sized heroine, it dawned on me slowly (because slowly is the way things do dawn on me) that I faced a major problem. With a James Bond, or a Saint, or a

"Some time ago I wrote a number of Modesty short stories which were published in book form. The original strip cartoon artist, Jim Holdaway, did a drawing for each story."

Bulldog Drummond, you don't have to explain *how* he got to be so smart, so skilled in karate or kung fu or whatever is the fashionable form of unarmed combat, so accurate with a gun, so knowledgeable about weapons, explosives, knockout drops, cars, planes, helicopters, and everything else a hero needs to know in order to beat the bad guys. He's a *hero*, so naturally he knows all that stuff, doesn't he?

But girls don't come quite so ready-made, and I realised I couldn't yet begin to write about this one who was simmering away in my mind. First, I need a background for her which would make it feasible, within the license of fiction, that she should have all the attributes needed for her task of battling through an open-ended series of books (and strip-cartoon capers) against daunting odds.

Let us now use the device of the flashback. The time is 1942; the location is the northern part of Iran, bordering the Caucasus; and the scene is an encampment of a British Army unit, posted here as an advance guard against a drive down into Iran and Iraq by the German Army to seize the oil fields. One of the young soldiers is myself.

Trickling south through the mountains, day by day, come refugees. Many of them have been moving ahead of advancing armies for weeks and months. Some are children. A few are children quite alone; one of these, a small girl, cannot be more than seven. They have survived, somehow, living off the land like little animals, and they will continue to survive. You can see it in their old-young faces.

It was here that I first saw Modesty Blaise, though I was not to know this until two decades later. End of flashback.

With this memory, the hazy image I had in mind began to acquire shape and depth. She would be a child from somewhere in the Balkans — from Hungary, perhaps — and of good stock. Her family would flee from the advance of Hitler, becoming part of the straggling groups of refugees moving slowly south.

Let me quote a few lines from my Background file:

By 1942, in a civilian prison camp in occupied Greece, the child is six years old and quite alone now, her mother dead. Fear, sorrow, self-pity and all weakness have been burned out of her. So has memory of her past. She is a small wild animal, quick, intelligent, cunning, and with a ferocious will to survive. On her own she escapes the human jungle of the camp. On her own she travels through the mountain country of northern Greece. . . .

The file brings her, by slow stages, through Turkey and into Iran. She wanders the Middle East, sometimes living in a cranny of an Arab town, sometimes attaching herself to a nomad tribe, sometimes living in a Displaced Persons camp. It is in one of these camps that she befriends, and defends, a quiet grey-haired man who speaks many languages. He is Jewish, stateless, once a professor in Budapest. The now twelve-year-old girl takes the old man under her wing, and through four years of wandering together, looks after him. He teaches her to read and write, to speak several languages, and gives her a broad general education. She soaks up all his teaching greedily. He finds a name for her, calling her Modesty, and chuckling at his own whimsicality. She chooses a second name for herself — Blaise, the master of a magician called Merlin in the wonderful stories her teacher tells of an ancient King of England.

The man dies when she is sixteen, and it is soon after that she joins the small-time gang in Tangier which she will shortly take over, and which in time will become *The Network*. It is during this period that she sets herself to acquire and practise all those skills with which the heroic male in fiction appears to have been born.

One day, in a fit of self-indulgence, I shall write the whole story of Modesty's beginning; and of how, when she is twenty and already in the big time, she finds Willie Garvin, tests him almost to destruction, and recruits him; how he becomes her right arm in *The Network*, her incomparable lieutenant, then her companion, and, in the end, a part of her. Modesty Blaise is,

THE BLAISE BOOKS

A Taste of Death
I, Lucifer
Modesty Blaise
Pieces of Modesty
Sabre-Tooth
The Impossible Virgin
The Silver Mistress
Last Day in Limbo

"I called this story 'I had a Date with Lady Janet' — because when I started to write it, I found myself using the first person, as if Willie Garvin were telling it; something I haven't done before or since."

of course, the creator of Willie Garvin, and for this I am most grateful to her, for when I first began to recount their adventures it was in the medium of strip cartoon and here a foil for the main character is essential for dialogue, otherwise the telling of the story demands a ludicrous string of "think" balloons.

The strip cartoon, I think, is good fun and far more difficult as a medium than it might seem. But one can touch the ground only in spots. To flesh out the characters, giving them the depth and texture permitted by a book, is far more satisfying.

If you look at the whole Modesty Blaise, it quickly becomes obvious that her time-scale can't be matched to what is considered a normal time-scale. In the first book she was twenty-six, and twelve years later she was twenty-eight. This means that events such as her being a war-

time refugee, or Willie having been with the Foreign Legion at Dien Bien Phu, no longer tally with the march of events as dated in our Gregorian calendar. And so much the worse for the Gregorian calendar, say I.

Over the years I have sometimes been drawn into argument concerning the relationship of Modesty and Willie. Many find it hard to credit that a man and woman could be so close yet not be lovers. I see no problem here. The bond between them is immense and has many strands. It is certainly not asexual; in fact, it is strongly male/female. But there is a great deal more to sex than the act of physical love, and all this they have in totality, giving them a relationship which is complete. It is also a relationship which grew in a particular way and to a particular pattern over a number of years, and they are aware that for them to go to bed together now would change it radically forever. They don't, therefore, deny themselves; it is simply not a part of the pattern, and so the possibility never arises.

But I have digressed, and must now come to my own part in this affair. After years of success with *The Network*, and having grown rich on selective crime, Modesty and Willie retired. But life became dull, and there *were* those who were glad to use such an experienced pair as poachers-turned-gamekeepers . . . and even when not on hire, the pair seemed to have a gift for attracting bizarre trouble. So before long they found themselves caught up in many new adventures.

And that, really, is where I came in.

Peter O'Donnell's eight Modesty Blaise books are presented by Souvenir Press.

SMILEY AT THE CIRCUS
Cold War Espionage

John Gardner

In John Le Carré's *Call for the Dead* we are introduced to George Smiley — an owl of British Intelligence with a faultless pedigree and a wanton wife. He reappears involved in death at an ancient and noted public school in *A Murder of Quality*. In the huge best-seller *The Spy Who Came in from the Cold* Smiley is dimly perceived, as he is in *The Looking Glass War*. With *Tinker Tailor Soldier Spy* he holds centre stage, and in *The Honourable Schoolboy* we find him in charge.

Peter Guillam, Smiley's most faithful aide in the secret world, considers (in *Tinker Tailor*) that he has never known anyone who could disappear so quickly into a crowd as Smiley. It is, perhaps, part of Le Carré's particular genius that he is able to make us believe in the now-you-see-him-now-you-don't facility of his most absorbing character.

We believe it, as it were, against the grain, for George Smiley is probably the most complete and fascinating fictional character in the whole bibliography of cold war espionage fiction.

Julian Symons has written of Le Carré's books as having the special qualities of "a sense of place, of doom and irony." They reek of reality, as does George Smiley himself, the most believable character in the fictional dictionary of espionography.

It is this credibility which makes him durable and will keep him haunting the mind long after the pipe-dream James Bonds have been forgotten — a plump, myopic, middle-aged man to whom you would hardly give a second glance. Yet he's a man who carries within his head a lexicon of secrets and ploys which run backward and forward through past, present and future. A man of penetrating intellect, yet reflecting a kind of pathetic sadness which personifies his particular generation and trade.

His ex-Special Branch legman, Mendel, sees him as "a funny little beggar . . . [like] a fat boy he'd played football with at school. Couldn't run, couldn't kick, blind as a bat but played like hell, never satisfied till he'd got himself torn to bits."

Another policeman says he looks "like a frog, dresses like a bookie, and has a brain I'd give my eyes for." He adds that Smiley had "a very nasty war. Very nasty indeed."

We get glimpses of that nasty war through all the books in which Smiley figures, and Le Carré rounds out his character by making him almost a subsidiary spear-carrier to the plot in such works as *The Spy Who Came In from the Cold* and *The Looking Glass War*.

In both of these books, one is never wholly certain of Smiley's situation within the Circus (the author's name for the central department of Intelligence, the headquarters of which are pinpointed in London's Cambridge Circus).

"He resigns, you know, and comes back," says the head of one of the rival departments. "His conscience. One never knows whether he's there or not." He is certainly there during *The Looking Glass War*, yet not so surely in *Spy* — though at the end of that book we hear him

THE MICRODOT

The Nazis have been credited with creating a brilliant method of transmitting secrets by reducing a printed page some 250 times. The information then fit on the head of a pin. This "microdot" was prepared by use of the instrument to the right. Spies often added one to the dotted pattern of an envelope (above) or wore one as a beauty mark, making sure to color it with eyebrow pencil first, as a microdot viewed sideways had a tendency to shine.

CORREO AEREO

© VISUAL ENTERPRISES

physically urging the doomed agent Leamas back over the Berlin Wall: in from the cold.

The facts of Smiley's life are plottable — his mind and body visible through Le Carré's adept drawings — from the days at Oxford, where he was recruited in 1928, through his service in the field during World War II, until, with cover blown, he is in from the cold, running agents from the Circus and doing tasks which take him all over the world. To tread with him through the major books is to journey through Smiley's life in the fullest sense.

In *A Murder of Quality* there is a summary which brings him into clear focus:

Once in the war he had been described by his superiors as possessing the cunning of Satan and the conscience of a virgin, which seemed to *him not wholly unjust. . . . Smiley himself was one of those solitaries who seem to have come into the world fully educated at the age of eighteen. Obscurity was his nature, as well as his profession. The byways of espionage are not populated by the brash and colourful adventurers of fiction.*

Duplicity is the stock in trade of the spy, yet it hangs as uneasily on Smiley as the well-made but ill-fitting clothes he wears. Duplicity for George is a cross to which he was nailed, unwillingly, at Oxford, and from which he will never be released. (In reality, all he wants is a quiet, contemplative life studying lesser-known German poets in his pretty house in Bywater Street off the King's Road.) Duplicity, his best weapon, is the weapon which so often almost demolishes his own emotional and professional life, for he finds it wherever he turns — within the Circus, from other departments, from the government, other people's governments and security services, and, worst of all, from individuals — in particular, his wife.

If the Circus is his cross and nails, then his marriage is the crown of thorns: almost incredible to his friends, and indeed to his wife's vast family of faded aristocracy and jaded politicians. It is the first thing we learn about him (in *Call for the Dead*) and remains the great seeping fissure in his life. For Lady Ann Sercomb — once Steed-Asprey's secretary at the Circus, now Ann Smiley — is the towering figure of wilfulness who interferes with any peace or happiness the wretched man might attain.

Just as George Smiley is always resigning from the Circus, so Ann Smiley is constantly leaving him for younger, even more unsuitable men. The puzzle is that he puts up with it, together with all its pain and anguish, and even admits to the possibility of taking her back. It is a puzzle which can only be solved by those who have known the same kind of anguish.

So deep are the wounds inflicted by Ann that, on at least one occasion, Smiley's domestic situation is used to the advantage of a Russian spymaster.

At the end of the day we are left feeling that Smiley, for all his brilliance within his profession, bears the marks of a man constantly betrayed — not merely by his wife, but by many of those whom he trusts, and by the society in which he lives. Perhaps this is the most telling picture we can ever have of a person who toils within the secret world where trust of any kind is not taken lightly. It is also a most accurate examination of the dilemma of a whole generation which feels betrayed, and it is interesting that, in his confusion, which is a paradox within his professional life, Smiley is easily strung to high, if controlled, emotion. He is, for instance, moved to tears at the sight of a small child's grief in falling from her pony.

While Le Carré is at his best when peeling the onion-skin layers from Smiley to reveal the whole man, he always shows him at his best within the context of his colleagues. Smiley is the window through which we view, not simply the curving acrostics of the narratives (parts of which must inevitably be lost to those not familiar with the historical in-fighting among the various British Intelligence agencies), but also a whole world of secrets, projecting a working knowledge of a profession. Who can tell if the picture is true? Whatever else, it smells and smacks of reality and so becomes more enthralling to the reader.

There are constant references to people long dead, or from Smiley's past: Jebedee, the tutor who recruited him; Fielding, whose brother was later to play a major part in *A Murder of Quality;* Steed-Asprey, who founded the little club, membership of which is restricted to one generation.

These Circus legends become as real to the reader as they are constant memories in Smiley's head — as real as the shadowy Control who is dead by the time we get to *Tinker Tailor,* his place taken by the odious Alleline; or Ailsa Brimley, who was a war-time colleague and brings the "murder of quality" to Smiley's attention and whose house is later used as a hiding place for a witness.

Peter Guillam and Mendel are constants — almost as much as Ann is an inconstant — but it is in *Tinker Tailor* that we get the most detailed and complete structure of Smiley's world, with its scalp-hunters, babysitters, pavement artists, wranglers and other jargoned departments. Here the world once inhabited by Control, Jebedee, Fielding and Steed-Asprey is now peopled by the more sinister, but equally engrossing, figures of the small Hungarian Toby Esterhase; leftist intellectual Roy Bland; and even Ann's cousin, the renowned Bill Haydon; together with a host of hidden people, both past and present.

From a wealth of detail, Le Carré weaves his narratives around George Smiley, the unlikely agent, the almost shy spymaster whose diffidence is so often a cloak for the rapier mind.

In his world, George Smiley is an owl, but one must never forget that while the owl, in poetic imagination, is a wise bird, he is, in reality, a dangerous predator of the night.

John Gardner is the author of The Return of Moriarty *and* The Revenge of Moriarty.

MEMOIRS OF AN EX-SPY
Ted Allbeury

arry Truman, when asked what it was like to be President, said, "It's great for the first two minutes." Similarly with being a spy. Except you're never actually a spy because in the business the word is never used. Inside M15 and M16 you're an intelligence officer or a counter-intelligence officer, and if you live on the west bank of the Potomac and normally turn left at Langley where the sign says BUREAU OF PUBLIC ROADS, you're called an agent.

Way back, you would have been recruited in your second year at Oxford or Cambridge. Your membership in the University's Com-munist Party would have been written off as growing pains provided you could drop a Latin tag in the right place. Which meant that the intelligence services, like Homer, nodded from time to time, and that would sometimes lead to keen cricketers ending their days boozing in Moscow and getting the Test Match results four days late.

World War II let poor boys become four-star generals and ruined this Olde Worlde sanctuary. If you wanted men who could speak Estonian and who knew the difference between Lombardo and Ellington, you had to cast your net much wider. And there were those who didn't wait for the net, but swam inside waving their Union Jacks. I was one of those.

How did I get in this elite? There could be only one way — the personal columns of the London *Times*. The advert asked for linguists and my interview took place at the back of a barber's shop in Trafalgar Square. They tested my French and German, and I swore my one ambition was to lie in the rain in wet ditches. Officers with penetrating eyes were anxious to know whether I liked my father better than my mother, and others asked what I could see in various inkblots. Photographs were flashed on a screen, and ten or so of us likely lads had to describe what they represented. Rumour had it that what we said would be utterly revealing of our minds. With this daunting prologue it was little wonder that an otherwise normal young man was driven to describe a naked couple on a bed as a "nurse tending a wounded man." We also underwent the usual medical checks, with our urine examined for Communist infiltration. The officers running the battery of tests fell into two distinct groups: the serious were cast in the mould of C. Aubrey Smith; the juniors were young captains with short haircuts and an air of already knowing every skeleton in our closets. When it was all over, they said,

---

THE SAFE HOUSE

A former spy tells of one on Ebury Street near Victoria Station. He'd stayed in it during the war. So did Ian Fleming.

The old method of getting in was, you rang the lower of two doorbells, and when a lady answered you remarked on the picture visible through the downstairs window. You allowed as how you were interested in art, she allowed as how she was pleased to hear it. You suggested you might like to buy it, she suggested you step inside for a better look at it. In you went, safe in the grip of your very own network.

"We'll check carefully on your background. Don't ring us."

A week later I was a full-fledged member of the Intelligence Corps, inducted by an archetypal colonel who told me my background had been researched with diligence and I was joining a fine club. "Bring," he said affably, "your sports car, your golf clubs, everything." That was my first moment of doubt. Somebody had got my background all wrong, diligent look-see or not. I had just bought my first second-hand bicycle, for two dollars, and had only once sat in a car; I didn't own golf clubs; I barely owned a jacket.

Regardless, I reported to the Intelligence Corps depot at what had previously been a theological college in Winchester. Here I hobnobbed with professors of French and German who could write theses on Trade Unions in the Middle Ages but couldn't ask a girl out for a coffee. On our second day, a Sunday, which even in the Intelligence Corps follows Saturday and the Saturday night dance, the professors and I were detailed to clean up the abandoned prophylactic devices as our introduction to security work. This led to much quoting of Rabelais and Juvenal.

We were taught very advanced map reading and then abandoned in the night in fields of cows to find our way home. We tailed "suspects" through the busy streets of Southampton and found it gave us time to make dates with the girls in Woolworth's. We learned how to strip and reassemble a whole range of weapons. Blindfolded, of course. We were given extensive instruction on the organisation of the military machine which subsequently proved useful for knowing how to indent for rations and services you were not entitled to. Several weeks were devoted to a rough-riding course on motorcycles, and our egos inflated when we learned ours would always be tuned to give us more speed than those of the Military Police. (Some of us later forgot that the additional weight of a girl on the pillion would eliminate this advantage.)

The badge of the Intelligence Corps was the red and white roses of Lancaster and York entwined in a laurel wreath. Referred to by our envious contemporaries in the other services as a "pansy resting on its laurels," it added lustre to our nickname "the eunuchs" (there were no privates in the Intelligence Corps).

In Scotland our trainers were ex-Shanghai policemen who spent two months borrowing my body to show more delicate frames how to severely injure or, if necessary, kill the enemy. "Okay, lofty, you," they said, pointing a finger at me when no one volunteered for these exercises. I was a tall lad, alas.

At various points members of the Class of '40 dropped off the production line. The nervous would go as interrogators at POW camps; the mathematicians and chess players, to the cryptography set-up at Bletchley Park. The creme of the dregs that were left would go on to aggravate the King's enemies and, on occasion, his friends.

When you read spy thrillers about that daring M15 man doing his stuff in Berlin, just quietly ask for your money back. M15 only operates in the United Kingdom. And even though it's responsible for internal security, M15 doesn't even arrest naughty boys in the U.K. The Special Branch does the dirty work for them. Besides, now it's called D15.

M16 is responsible for counter-espionage and espionage, and it's now D16 — sometimes referred to as SIS, the Secret Intelligence Service. If you land up in that camp, your pay will be tax-free to prevent even the Inland Revenue from putting two and two together. One finds SIS boys in all the old, familiar places: journalism; Rolls-Royce franchises; banking; oil companies; language schools; departments of history at universities. They're recognisable by their charm and fondness for Jamieson Ten Year Old. In later life they take up religion, in the style of Malcom Muggeridge, and grow roses in Britain's equivalent of the Bermuda Triangle — the borders of Sussex and Kent.

Intelligence work, like computery, has its own vocabulary, and you can date an alumnus of the theological college fairly accurately. There's a touch of the Scott Fitzgerald about war-time alumni, with echoes of Adlai Stevenson. Today's boys are definitely more Daniel Patrick, with a shade of Haldeman if under stress. But there are still some consistently used words:

De-briefing consists of a man with cold blue eyes listening to your side of the story when you return from an operation. It's a mixture of explaining why you're still alive and why you had to stay at the most expensive hotel in Berlin.

A safe house is where you go to be briefed, or to rest, or to escape the bad guys.

Dead-letter drop is the place where you leave messages in code on the secrets of IBM's latest software. (Like you used to leave the girl friend love letters in the geranium pot because her mother wouldn't let you on the premises.)

The cut-out is the man who keeps your identity from field operators.

Blown means that the elaborate cover story your directorate wrote to protect you has been exposed. I was "blown" by a dear old lady in Scotland. She was telling fortunes at a party and told the whole assembly exactly what I was up to. I was withdrawn, as they say, to Scottish Command HQ, and I often wonder what happened to that old lady.

Turned is what happens to operators who get caught and start trembling before they're even asked their name, rank and number. We did this to most of the German espionage agents in the U.K. during the war. They then got to live in luxury apartments in St. James Street with the most beautiful "ladies" we could find. In return, we held their hands on their Morse keys when they sent their news back to Berlin. It went on for years, and there were several of us who wished it could've happened to us.

In Occupied Germany we cooperated with the American CIC. On the grounds of security, however, both intelligence organisations kept just a little bit of information back. I well remember a joint operation in which forty plainclothes operatives had to find a central information clearing point that would not arouse suspicion if visited frequently by large numbers of men. The CIC had theirs, we had ours, and neither would confide its place to the other. Halfway through the morning of the round-up I had to deal with an angry city mayor who complained bitterly that British and American civilians, all speaking frightfully bad German, were monopolizing the only public men's lavatory in town. Great spy minds had thought alike once again.

What makes a good intelligence agent? He certainly won't be a James Bond type. Arrogant, pseudo-sophisticated and mentally ill-equipped, Bond wouldn't get past the first selection filter. If pressed to give an opinion as to what made me suitable material, I should unhesitatingly attribute it to the fact that, since my father died when I was a baby, I was brought up by a posse of women and some of their intuition rubbed off on me. As an intelligence officer this combination of innate male cunning and feminine intuition served me well. The war my father fought in was to make "a land fit for heroes to live in." My own war aim was to make "a land fit for cowards to live in." Heroes are for the Marines; only the well-tuned coward can survive in the world of espionage.

I've heard it said that once a spook, always a spook, but my own career doesn't bear this out. I left the counter-intelligence business several years after the war, and although I've been contacted two or three times since, it was only to give advice. One reason for declining to stay on was an inclination on my part to quit the poker game while I still had my winnings; the other was a growing dislike of what I was doing. This was not from some high moral standpoint, nor a feeling that it should not be done, but that I, personally, had done it long enough. Playing games against the Italians was fun, but against the Germans it was solid, serious stuff. With venom in it on both sides. I was beginning to know too much about people and politics, and I needed a period of innocence.

Unfortunately, it's not quite that easy to reclaim. You can't be an experienced intelligence officer one day and an innocent civilian the next. The training, the experience, just won't go away. One of the earliest pieces of training is that everybody tells lies and you have to dig holes for people to fall in so you can find out as soon as possible in what area they're lying. In civilian life you go on doing this. You don't always like the results, and neither do your victims. Little bells ring and red lights flash, because not only do you know when people are telling lies, but you know they're going to before they know it themselves. It takes about three years before you're halfway

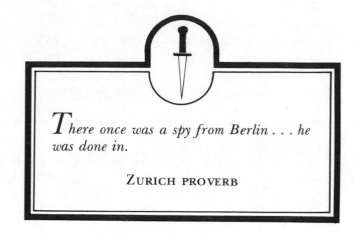

There once was a spy from Berlin . . . he was done in.

ZURICH PROVERB

back to normal.

I'm often asked whose spy stories I enjoy reading. It's not easy to give a straightforward answer because one likes different ones for different reasons. I like Eric Ambler stories because they're beautifully written. Len Deighton's *Ipcress File*, *Funeral in Berlin* and *Horse Under Water* are firm favourites of mine. Great pace and real characters. The Quiller stories by Adam Hall and the novels of John Le Carré I find a "good read" but too opaque for my liking. The striving for authenticity can be overdone. Le Carré's use of jargon and buzz words sometimes seems like a leg-pull — they're too often words I've never heard used, and if they're contrived then they're unnecessary and destructive to the magically real atmosphere he creates. The mysterious Trevanian wrote a first-class story with *The Eiger Sanction*, but *The Loo Sanction* I found inferior. It may seem eccentric to class *All the President's Men* and *The Final Days* as spy stories, but they have all the elements of a good spy novel and they skilfully avoid the pitfall of the "researched" book — that stuffing in every thing you found because it cost time and money to discover it. Oddly enough, I find nonfiction books by ex-espionage people almost unreadable. If you've been in this business, you recognise all too easily those great patches of bull. Real-life espionage is boring. It has too little action and its victories are mainly from paper work, not valour. I'd rather read John D. MacDonald, whose Travis McGee has given me hours of pleasure.

There's a club in London that I belong to called the Special Forces Club, and there you can see mild men who now sell insurance or wine who ended the war in Dachau or Belsen. There are schoolteachers who once calmly parachuted into the wet forests of the Dordogne. Unless we have another war, the club will soon close for lack of members, as we all head for our appointments in Samarra.

Ted Allbeury, former counter-intelligence officer, is the author of five espionage novels.

USING THE PERSONAL COLUMN AS A MAIL DROP

An agent never phones the information in; he delivers it himself. But first he has to arrange the rendezvous. The most frequently used medium for this is the Personal Column. To show you how this works, we placed an ad in the London *Times*. After reading our message ("Author wishes to contact ex-spies"), the ad-taker said, "Oh, yes, you'll probably be looked up by DI5 and DI6 with this one. Perhaps even the Customs people will contact you. They read the personal columns every day, checking for stolen merchandise."

We received seven answers in all, and our favorites were the spy who invited us to tea at his bachelor flat in the Albany (home of the fictional Raffles, if you'll recall) and the spy who arranged an 11 P.M. meeting in front of the South Kensington tube station. "How will we recognize you?" we asked. "I'll recognize you," he proclaimed, and he did. Made us very uncomfortable.

Of course, a real spy would have prepared a more subtle message than ours. We are quite convinced the query running several boxes beneath ours — in reference to a gentleman's umbrella — was a spy reaching out for his control. We never followed it up, but still we're convinced of it. And ever since, have been intrigued to know how he did.

ESTABLISHING A COVER

Berkely Mather

Spying, in spite of all that thriller writers might say to the contrary, is a relatively simple business. You merely select your agent, preferably one of moderate intelligence but little imagination, tell him (or her) just what you want to find out about the Opposition, provide him with means of communication and then gently insinuate him into the theatre of operations. It is a very good thing, of course, to retain a hold on him as a precaution against his being "turned round" by the Opposition and made into a "double." The hold will vary with the circumstances: something unsavoury that lends itself readily to blackmail; a loved one, wife, mother or child who can be taken into the gentle care of the spymaster; or perhaps a "minder," a strong-arm man already on the ground who will, without hesitation, kill the agent on receipt of orders from on high.

All that being provided, the agent is in business. Or is he? There *is* something else. The most important factor of the lot. The cover story, or "Front." Without one which will stand up to an Intensity Five Interrogation — that is, two stages further than what was once called in police circles the Third Degree — your agent might just as well stay at home. An I.F.I. is a very searching inquiry indeed. It can go on for days, weeks if necessary. A point by meticulous point, detail by detail probing into your past life to establish just who you are. Once They know that, the rest is comparatively easy. Lots of the questions They ask may seem a complete waste of time. The agent's common sense will tell him that the answers cannot be verified or contradicted, but in among them comes the simple inconsequential one that can be shot down — and the "patient," as the luckless interrogatee is

termed in contra-espionage jargon, as soon as he knows he has slipped, will start to flounder. It follows, therefore, that he must be *almost* word and detail perfect. "Almost" must be stressed, because, if the answers come too readily with never a slip, the interrogator would rightly guess that the patient was parrotting a carefully learned lesson.

E.g.: "You say you lived with your parents at 39 Sungrove Avenue, Edmonton, from 12th September 1932 to 25th February 1937. Is that right?"

"Thereabouts."

"That is not good enough. I want an accurate answer."

"For God's sake! That's over forty years ago — I was only a small kid. I can remember that the family was in those parts for about five years at roughly that period, but I can't give you exact dates."

"Can you remember the name of the man

In recent years, the press of duties has severely restricted the amount of time I can devote to light reading, so I do not read mysteries.

GENERAL GEORGE S. BROWN,
Chairman of the Joint Chiefs of Staff

who lived next-door — in 37 Sungrove Avenue?"

"It wasn't a man, it was an old widow lady — we kids used to call her Aunt Bertha, but she wasn't any relation. Just a minute — (*deep concentration*) — Silverton — Silver — oh, hell — ah — *Silberstein*, that's it. She was Jewish — we weren't — but she gave my young brother and me a little present when her grandson got his bar mitzvah. I remember mine was a propelling pencil, and my brother got an airplane."

"The people on the other side? Name?"

"Can't remember. I *think* it was an elderly couple without kids — or if there were kids, they were grown up. I certainly can't recall anything definite about them."

And so it goes on. How on earth could anybody be asked to computerise details like that, particularly phoney ones, in his head, and

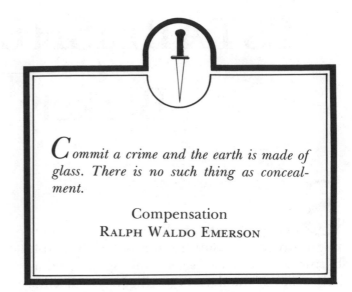

Commit a crime and the earth is made of glass. There is no such thing as concealment.

Compensation
RALPH WALDO EMERSON

be able to reel out answers without hesitation — or too much hesitation? You go back to the second sentence for that. Anybody of

TRICKS OF THE TRADE

COURTESY FBI

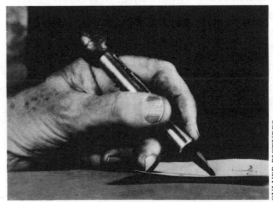

CULVER PICTURES

The hollow tooth was reserved for suicide tablets, should interrogators play rough. The false shoe heel was frequently used, but it could be impractical to get at, racing down the street to catch the 5:18 to Switzerland. Thus, the hollow nickel was developed. It held a full page of manuscript, folded. It could be left as a tip, given in change, or just left to rest with coins in a pocket. Perhaps the most difficult thing to hide was not the message, but the gun needed to fend off the enemy. This design (right) was good for writing the message, and then shooting anyone who interrupted you, as the pen converted to a gun via a spring mechanism.

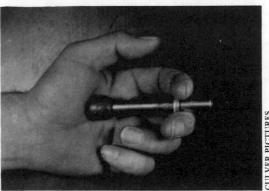

CULVER PICTURES

moderate intelligence but little imagination. *Moderate* intelligence. Yes, just that. A *highly* intelligent subject, unfortunately, is far more likely to "blow" than his more workaday colleague — and too much imagination often leads to a type of euphoria under pressure, a sort of "I'm doing fine, I can blind this guy!" feeling, and he starts to overplay his hand, to embroider his story and, inevitably, finally trips himself up. Of course, it takes training and conditioning, and, above all, *time.* Good agents are often chosen as mere children and the course can last for ten to twenty years — *agents,* that is, as distinct from such expendable pawns as legmen, droppers, minders or, as they are sometimes called, button-men. Since these latter categories do no actual spying but are merely there to serve the spies, they can usually be recruited locally from the ranks of those who will do anything for a fast buck — crooks, prostitutes — the real mercenaries — but never, incidentally, junkies, who can easily be bought but as easily broken, merely by withholding their drugs. Even when caught, the little men can never give much away, however hard they are leaned upon, for the simple reason that they are usually directed and controlled by faceless people they meet under cover of darkness — anonymous telephone calls — notes passed in public places or left in dead-letter boxes, e.g., thumbtacked under park benches, in hollow trees, behind toilet bowls in comfort stations, etc. Their payments reach them the same way. And always there are "cut-offs" — prefabricated and inbuilt breaks in the trail — to ensure that an underling in the hot seat — a messenger, or "dropper" — could only betray, at very most, the person who gave him the message and the one to whom he was supposed to deliver it.

A splendid example of the care, patience and meticulous attention to detail in the training of the full-fledged professional agent in connection with his cover story can be found in one Konon Trofimovich Molody, who, born in Russia in 1923, was taken at the age of eleven to America by a woman posing as his mother. With a truly Russian gift for languages, he was speaking perfect English, with an American accent, in four years. Provided with a genuine

SMART-ASS SPIES

In the late 1950's Mike Nichols and Elaine May improvised *Mysterioso*, a spy routine in which two agents identified themselves with cryptic remarks such as "flying smut." Smart-ass spies mid-60's, in books, however, appeared as emotional brothers to the hard-boiled dick, wanting to be left alone, just them and their sense of humor. Examples: Frank McAuliffe, Oliver Bleeck, and best of all, Jay Brothers and *Ox.*

Canadian passport in the name of Gordon Arnold Lonsdale, a child who had been taken to Europe at the age of eight and had apparently disappeared without trace, Molody returned to Russia by an underground route soon after his fifteenth birthday — and was never again allowed to speak Russian or, indeed, any other language but English. He was trained in the technical routine of the electronic espionage he was intended for, then secretly returned to Canada, where he was placed in a company dealing in radio parts. After two or three years he was sent by this concern to England, and there, under cover of a perfectly genuine and legitimate business, he was appointed Russia's Resident Director of Espionage, with the rank of Colonel in the KGB. How he was eventually unmasked and sentenced to twenty-five years' imprisonment by the double-crossing of a British double traitor is another, and longer, story. But his fall was in no way due to any shortcoming in his cover story. That was perfect.

Berkely Mather is a former chairman of the Crime Writers' Association.

THE CRYPTOGRAPHY BUREAU
How to Tell a Vigenère from a Pig Pen

Edward D. Hoch

Many of us need a refresher course to understand spy code terminology. Herewith, the fundamentals.

Codes. Codes and ciphers are two quite different things. A code consists of words, phrases, numbers or symbols used to replace elements of the plain text (uncoded) message. A code operates on linguistic entities; thus a code book might show the number 6477 standing for the word "attack," or the letter group BUKSI signifying "Avoid arrest if possible." A problem with codes is that they require code books, often containing thousands of number or letter groups covering all possible messages. The vulnerability of code books to capture by enemy forces has always presented grave problems. For this reason, naval codes are bound in books with heavy lead plates in the front and back cover to ensure their sinking to the bottom if dropped overboard. Good code stories (as distinguished from cipher stories) are rare, but O. Henry's "Calloway's Code" makes clever use of a makeshift code of special interest to journalists.

Dictionary and book codes. A dictionary code uses numbers to identify the page and line on which a given word may be found, the drawback being that the same numbers always stand for the same words. A book code also uses numbers to identify the page, line and word in any book designated "it" by both sender and receiver. Anthony Boucher's short story "QL 696 .C9" uses a code based on the Library of Congress classification system for books.

Research Project No. 1: Find out which book was the first in which a spy, unable to destroy his encoded message before capture, ate it.

Substitution ciphers. In ciphers of the substitution type, a single letter, number or symbol stands for a single letter of the alphabet. The most popular device for substitution ciphers is the cipher disk. Cipher disks have a long history with the military, and Aaron Burr is known to have used one. A problem with substitution ciphers is that long messages can be deciphered through use of a letter frequency list. The most frequently used letter in the English language is *e* — as Edgar Allan Poe correctly observed in "The Gold Bug," the world's most widely read cipher story. Though today's letter frequencies are different from those listed in "The Gold Bug," Poe's technique for solving the cipher in the story is still valid. Poe used numbers and symbols as substitutions for the letters of his message whereas Arthur Conan Doyle used lit-

tle stick-figure drawings in "The Adventure of the Dancing Men." But Sherlock Homes used Poe's technique of letter frequencies in his solution.

Transposition ciphers. When letters of a message retain their identities and are merely jumbled, we have a transposition cipher. In a simple rectangular transposition, the letters of a message are printed horizontally in a square, then removed from the square vertically and placed in groups of five to disguise the original word lengths. The recipient of the message puts the letters back in the square vertically and reads them horizontally.

Skytales. One form of transposition cipher uses a skytale, or scytale — a long narrow strip of paper wrapped around a wooden staff or other object. The message is printed down the length of the staff, with lines of unrelated letters printed down the other sides. When the paper strip is removed, the writing appears to be gibberish, but it can easily be read when wrapped around a staff of the same diameter at the receiving end.

Grilles. Another form of transposition is the grille — a sheet of metal or cardboard with rectangular holes cut at irregular intervals. The message is written in these open spaces and the grille is then removed. The remaining space is

CODE-BREAKER QUIZ

Joseph C. Stacey

You have thirty seconds to find out who the following spies, secret agents, wicked groups and assassination specialists are. Failure to identify them in the allotted time leaves you no choice but to bite down hard on your cyanide capsule.

1. CF YRFCRVK RXF CDH BDIDHD	(#87922/8)
2. LDCGW QRHK	(225)
3. YRFVK YDF MYR WEZ GVZGWD QDPHD	(TNTGFR)
4. GINV RFUDHNPDMNRH MIW UGM WCDFM	(ODRW)
5. CDMM BGVC	(GFNT)
6. 225W QRWW	(C)
7. GINV WRTNGMZ MBG CDH AFRC XHTVG	(TBFXWB)
8. CDJYGVV WCDFM	(DUGHM 30)
9. WEZ YBR TDCG NH AFRC MBG TRVK	(WCNVGZ)
10. FGCR YNVVNDCW	(MBG KGWMFRZGF)

Joseph C. Stacey contributed many of the trickier puzzles in Mystery Monthly *magazine.*

filled with an innocuous letter or report. The receiver simply lays an identical grille over the letter to read the true message. My short story "The Spy Who Worked for Peace" was built around the use of a grille.

Playfair squares. Prior to World War I, the British Army successfully used a digraphic substitution called a Playfair square, named for its advocate, Baron Playfair. A five-by-five square of twenty-five spaces is used, filled in horizontally with the unduplicated letters of a key word. The remaining squares are filled with the unused letters of the alphabet, with the letters I and J combined. Thus, using the key word "Blackstone," The square looks like this:

```
B L A C K
S T O N E
D F G H I-J
M P Q R U
V W X Y Z
```

The cipher is called digraphic because the letters of the plain text are divided into pairs and enciphered two at a time, with the result depending upon their relation to each other in the square. Double letters occurring together in a pair are separated by an *x*. If the two letters of a pair are in the same horizontal row, they're enciphered with the letters to their right. If they fall in the same vertical column, they're enciphered with the letters beneath them. If they appear in neither the same row nor column, each is enciphered by the letter that lies in its own row but in the column occupied by the other letter. Thus, using the word "balloon" as an example, it would first be written as *ba lx lo on*, then enciphered as *lc aw at ne*. Though it seems complicated, the Playfair is easily mastered and only the key word need be remembered. Best of all, it comes close to being unbreakable.

Vigenère ciphers. Probably the most famous cipher system of all is the Vigenère, a polyalphabetic substitution cipher that is a simplified system of Blaise de Vigenère's original. It uses a tableau consisting of twenty-six standard horizontal alphabets, each positioned one letter to the left of the one above. A normal alphabet stands at the top and another normal alphabet runs down the left side of the tableau. In use, a

key word is repeated above the plain text message until each letter has a corresponding key letter. The plain text letter is located in the top alphabet of the tableau and the key letter on the side alphabet. The lines are followed down and across the tableau to their intersection, yielding the cipher letter. Long thought unbreakable, Vigenères are more easily solved than Playfairs, mainly because the key word is repeated several times in a pattern.

Pigpen ciphers. More of historical interest than anything else is the pigpen cipher. Variations of this system were used by the Rosicrucians, Masons and other groups. A "pigpen" of four lines, looking exactly like a tic-tac-toe square, is drawn on a sheet of paper and each pen is filled with three letters of the alphabet, starting with *abc* in the upper left and continuing horizontally until *yz* is in the lower right pen. The first letter in each of the nine sections needs no dot, but the second letter is represented by one dot and the third letter by two dots. In ciphering by this method, a letter is represented by the shape of its pen, with one or

two dots in the pen if necessary. Thus the letter *o,* in the center of the pigpen, is enciphered as a square-shaped pen with two dots inside.

Steganography. Behind this formidable-looking word are grouped various methods of concealing the very existence of a secret message. Included are invisible inks, microdots, and messages in which the first or last letter of each word spells out a hidden communication. In a 1912 collection of short stories, *The Master of Mysteries,* published anonymously, the first letters of the first words in the twenty-four stories spell out the sentence "The author is Gelett Burgess." The last letters of the last words in each story read "False to life and false to art." Ellery Queen used a similar device in an early novel, with the first letter of each chapter title spelling out *The Greek Coffin Mystery* by Ellery Queen.

Chronograms. More interesting in literature than in serious espionage work are chronograms — inscriptions in which certain letters, printed larger or in a different typeface, express a date or number when added together by their values as Roman numerals. A prime example of a chronogram in fiction is R. Austin Freeman's Dr. Thorndyke mystery *The Puzzle Lock.*

One-time pads. The ultimate cipher that cryptologists dream of is the one-time system, using pads or tape. Popular following World War II, one-time pads use nonrepeating random keys. Since the same key is never repeated, and is only a meaningless jumble of letters, even a great many messages provide no clues. The cipher is truly unbreakable. Only the vast number of keys that must be printed and distributed has kept the one-time cipher from being universally popular. In a confusing battlefield situation, the order of the keys might prove a handicap when several units are involved. And in an espionage situation, discovery of a spy's one-time pads would be damaging evidence — as it was in the cases of Soviet spies Helen and Peter Kroger and Rudolf Abel.

Cipher machines. The ancestor of the modern cryptographic machines was probably the wheel cipher invented by Thomas Jefferson. It consisted of a cylinder six inches long, divided into twenty-six separate wheels, each

Inverted inscription found in R. Austin Freeman's The Mystery of 31, New Inn, *which was solved by the great scientific detective Dr. John Thorndyke.*

ANN LIMONGELLO

with a full alphabet in jumbled order. The wheels were numbered and no two were alike. They were lined up so that a message could be read horizontally. Then the jumbled letters from any of the other lines became the cipher. On the receiving end, an identical cylinder had its wheels aligned to show the cipher message. One of the other lines would automatically show the message in plain text. Almost infinite varieties were possible by changing the order of the numbered wheels. A century after Jefferson, the French cipher expert Étienne Bazeries invented a similar machine. These early wheel ciphers could be broken with a bit of hard work, but they led directly to the rotor machines so popular today. Using from three to eight rotors, machine ciphers are difficult to break without a great many messages from the same machine. The preferred technique is to obtain one of the machines itself — as the British did during World War II with the German cipher machine Enigma.

Edward D. Hoch is the author of a series of short stories featuring the Department of Concealed Communications.

SKOOBEDOC

Nonfiction

Gaines, Helen Fouche. *Cryptanalysis*. New York City: Dover, 1956. A basic survey.

Kahn, David. *The Codebreakers*. New York City: Macmillan, 1967. The definitive work.

Laffin, John. *Codes and Ciphers*. New York City: Abelard-Schumann, 1964. An introduction.

Moore, Dan Tyler, and Waller, Martha. *Cloak & Cipher*. Indianapolis: Bobbs-Merrill, 1962. A short history.

Pratt, Fletcher. *Secret and Urgent*. Garden City, N.Y.: Doubleday, 1924. A history of spies and ciphers.

Tuchman, Barbara. *The Zimmerman Telegram*. New York City: Viking, 1958. The deciphering of an important World War I message.

Winterbotham, F.W. *The Ultra Secret*. New York City: Harper & Row, 1975. Britain's success in breaking the German cipher machine Enigma.

Wolfe, J.M. *A First Course in Cryptanalysis*. New York City: Brooklyn College Press, 1943. A textbook for class use.

Yardley, Herbert O. *The American Black Chamber*. Indianapolis: Bobbs-Merrill, 1931. An exposé by an American cryptologist.

Fiction

Bond, Raymond T. (ed.). *Famous Stories of Code and Cipher*. New York City: Holt, Rinehart & Winston, 1947; Collier Books, 1965. An informative introduction and sixteen stories.

Clift, Dennison Halley. *Spy in the Room*. New York City: Mystery House/Thomas Bouregy, 1944. Murder in the code room at British Intelligence.

Gordon, Alex. *The Cipher*. New York City: Simon & Schuster, 1961. An American Egyptologist is hired for a deciphering. Basis of the 1966 film *Arabesque*.

Hoch, Edward D. *The Spy and the Thief*. New York City: Davis Publications, 1971. Seven stories concerning codes and ciphers.

Johnson, James L. *Code Name Sebastian*. New York City: Lippincott, 1967. Basis for the 1968 film *Sebastian*.

Liebman, Arthur (ed.). *Tales of Espionage and Intrigue*. New York City: Richard Rosen Press, 1977. Twelve stories, five concerning codes and ciphers.

FALSE PASSPORTS
Getting Across the Border

Robin W. Winks

A false passport is essential to any self-respecting spy, always in fiction and often in real life. Few documents are more useful if one wishes to change identity, and for "illegals" — foreign spies inserted into the society of a potential enemy — they rank just below the birth certificate and the driver's license as a passport to identity. The passport is the prompter's book from which the spy must act out a part; bad reviews result in capture and perhaps death.

In the 1970's a truly counterfeit passport is seldom used, and those carefully manufactured documents by which Eric Ambler's spies flitted across Balkan frontiers, or by which escaped British prisoners of war made their way cross-country from Stalag XVII, are part of the romance of the past. What the professional spy must have today is a genuine passport issued to a fraudulent identity; the day of making visa stamps from hard-boiled eggs and sliced potatoes saturated in ink has been displaced (except in Africa) by the hard realism of technology. Better, as the Jackal did, to steal a valid passport — Americans alone lose or have stolen nearly 30,000 passports a year — than to risk giving the game away by having some customs officer casually spill alcohol on the passport and have it come up reading *void*. Only the KGB, behind the times as usual, maintains a corps of technicians to make fake passports from scratch — Western passports are called "shoes" in KGB jargon, a wry twist on "walking papers," and so (surprise!) the technicians are called "cobblers."

So you still want your spy to have a false passport? Okay. First you have to get the right kind of paper. American passports are printed on a rare paper manufactured by the American Writing Paper Corporation in Holyoke, Massachusetts; the making of the paper itself takes place under the tightest security arrangements. The paper is sized, that is, covered with a thin finish which is soluble in water or spirits, so even the sleepiest immigration officer can tell if you've bleached the paper. Further, passport paper is "safety paper" — it's printed with a design of fine lines and patterns with fugitive dyes. Any chemical that will bleach ink will bleach the American eagle right off the page. Use any oxidizing or bleaching agent, and you're a dead man, Harry Palmer.

Then you have to get passport covers. Valid American passports come in many hues: black for diplomatic, maroon for official, green for tourist, and a dark blue for those issued in the Bicentennial year. The covers are made of simulated plastic Lexide, by a company in New York, and the process is secret. Any tampering with the covers is instantly detectable.

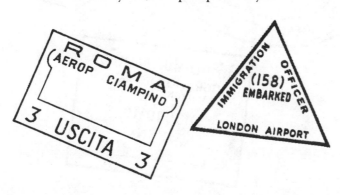

Of course, professional forgers know all this, and they'll give their Walther PPK for a supply of either paper or covers. They know that the paper has invisible watermarks embedded in it, and they know that the recipes are subtly changed from time to time so that the wrong issue date on a passport of a particular chemical nature is a dead giveaway — assuming the passport falls under someone's handy ultraviolet light. They *can* resurface paper, and there *are* ways to restore the safety designs, and the impressions made by rubber stamps *can* be faked (although traces of gelatin, albumin or the lowly potato will remain impregnated in the paper), and one *can* apply stamps for visas in such a way that it is virtually impossible to tell which is the uppermost of two stamps carelessly slapped down in the same place. But why go to all the bother? Even assuming success in surmounting the paper chase, the counterfeiter still must deal with official perforations, a photograph, signatures and personal data. The photograph is affixed with a special glue. The perforations (which *may* be filled in with pulp, and fresh ones made on the same ground, although this can be detected if the paper is held to the light, or with a camera) are coded alphabetically and changed annually (Z, for example, indicates that the passport was issued abroad), and while the code may well be obtained, great care is needed to be certain that an improper prefix letter does not contradict the dates of the false visas.

All of which explains why the KGB, D16 and CIA operatives fight shy of being handed a pair of shoes. In a U.S. Department of Justice report on Criminal Use of False Identification, issued in November of 1976, user fraud with respect to passports showed that 0 percent of those detected were counterfeit, 5 percent were altered and 95 percent involved imposters. As an underground newspaper noted in 1968, phony I.D.'s are "not worth the paper they're printed on." The professional seeks to have the government issue directly an authentic document but to a false identity — precisely as Frederick Forsyth describes in *The Day of the Jackal,* a book called "the best primer to passport fraud" by no less an authority than the head of the Passport Division of the United States Department of State.

No one knows how many false passports are in circulation, although one reputable estimate suggests there may be over a million. Since the most valuable passport is the American (the variety of American accents being so great, nearly anyone who speaks even broken English can pass as an American citizen), they are the most frequently stolen. Throughout Eastern Europe, tourists must deposit their passports overnight when they register at hotels, or surrender their passports in quantities to tour operators, so that crucial elements may be copied for nefarious purposes; not long ago one American sold a dozen such passports to Russian agents. British passports also have high mobility value, and significant problems exist in the policing of Australian and Columbian passports. In general, the richer the nation, and the more polyglot its language and racial mixture, the more easily one may pass off a Georgian accent (Russian or American) as the real thing.

Who is to know how many fraudulent passports are used and how often? The truly successful counterfeit or fraud doesn't become a statistic. As the CIA instructors say, "The spies you have read about . . . are exceptions. The spies who interest us are the ones who do not get caught, and who therefore are not to be read about." British Intelligence is sexier: "A good espionage operation is like a good marriage . . . it is uneventful. It does not make a good story." Or as the Mexicans say, "To di-

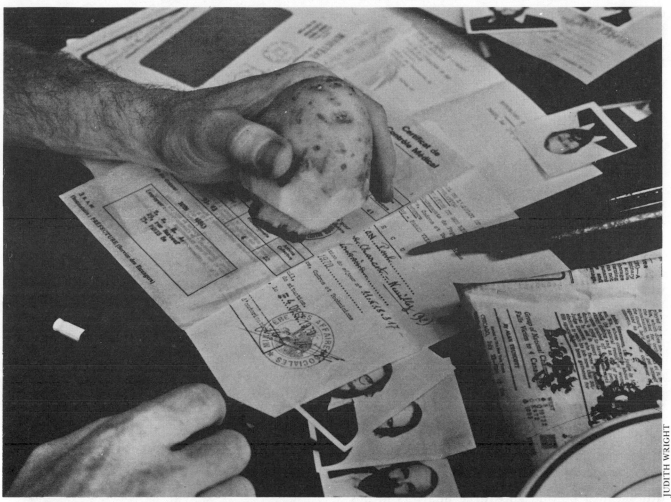

JUDITH WRIGHT

The head of the Passport Division of the U.S. Department of State called Frederick Forsyth's thriller The Day of The Jackal *"the best primer to passport fraud." The Jackal's technology supplanted the old method of engraving a cold potato with the appropriate visa markings, then saturating the potato in an ink bath.*

vorce a wife is hard; to divorce a mistress impossible."

Since there are 300,000 fugitives from justice in the U.S. every year, the market for stolen passports that can be altered is intense. Even more intense is the effort to obtain authentic passports for fraudulent purposes, the most common purpose being drug traffic. Carriers usually have a valid passport as well. The Drug Enforcement Agency estimates that a person can bring into the country $500,000 worth (street value) of narcotics per trip; the Passport Office estimates that each fraudulent passport will, on average, be used twice. This is Big Business, out of all proportion to sneaking the Bruce-Partington Plans across the border. Since 1972 an intensified campaign to detect fraudulent applications in order to stop false

passports before they can get into the hands of the criminal has led to an increase in detection from 10 percent in 1970 to an estimated 65 percent in 1976 — but estimates of the depth of water that you can't measure still leave drowning room.

How to get that real passport? As the Jackal did, through "infant death." The obituary pages of old newspapers, or visits to cemeteries (à la Hitchcock's *Family Affair*), provide the names of infants who died at so early an age that few identification papers would have been issued for them. Obviously the infant should, if it had lived, be of the age of the false applicant. It's usually a good idea to check on sex (is "Robin" a girl's or a boy's name?), race and address, too. If you can find an entire family that has been wiped out in an accident, you remove the odd chance of the strong arm of coincidence betraying you. You then obtain a birth certificate, on the grounds of loss, and with this in hand you're ready to apply for an authentic passport. As *The Paper Trip,* an underground handbook, remarked: "Always get your Government ID from the government itself. Give them the paper they want and you will get the paper you want."

You still may want a variety of visas in your passport if it is to support your other documents. (Don't have too many; the more you have, the greater the risks, but you can't do without a driver's license and in this day and age any American without some credit cards is automatically suspect, at the least, of undermining the economy.) Visas must show that you have been where the part you are playing suggests you have been. But the visa game is tricky, and if you notice a border guard studying all your visas don't be surprised; the wrong one in the wrong place can be more revealing than the right suit hanging in the wrong closet. You must know which nations require visas and for what periods of time; that some nations (Russia, Israel) issue visas in separate documents; that some are accompanied by a photograph one and a half inches square while others must be one and three quarters inches square, etc. For these reasons the entry stamps of the world's international airports are re-

garded as safer to use — but entry and exit stamps will differ, and you had better be able to tell the difference across a crowded room.

For Americans alone, there are 10 million tourist, 175,000 official, and 24,000 diplomatic passports outstanding. How much easier it all was in the days of Louis XIV, who first issued passports — the word is derived from the French *passer* (to pass) and *port* (harbor), just as "visa" is from *visé* (endorsed). Louis issued so few, he could have them individually coded: yellow paper meant an Englishman (clever comment, that); a dot appeared under the name of Protestants, whose movements could thus be barred at the border; if the holder of the passport was wealthy and thus to be respected, a rose design appeared on the paper; if he was a bachelor, a ribbon was threaded through a hole. Women were not granted passports. (Some say this is where the term "the sleeper" came from.) The Scarlet Pimpernel probably carried the first false passport.

In the hidden world of the false passport, the professional holds to a simple rule: Do not support forgery with perjury. Let the document do the lying for you; tell no lies yourself. After all, if Colonel Russell of Security Executive can do it, so can you.

Robin W. Winks is a history professor at Yale University. He did not buy his passport from Abdel Simpson.

Chapter 5
VICTIMS

THE MOST LIKELY VICTIM

Rosamund Bryce

I confess.

Although I have been reading murder mysteries for the past twenty years, at the rate of two a day (I gulp them down like aspirin), I have never been particularly concerned with who gets killed.

I *am* intrigued with how it's done (I've a special fondness for coshes from behind and little slits in the back opened by poisoned daggers), and why it's done, but the personality of the victim — ho-hum.

And as unsympathetic as I am, the authors are even more so. I challenge you to name ten books in which the victim was a fully developed, three-dimensional human being. Rarely do authors invest the victim with anything deeper than a quirk: The dowager *always* sits dead center on the settee for the half-hour preceding dinner; the old codger *always* removes the Gainsborough, opens the wall safe and locks away his private papers at 9 sharp; the bride-to-be *always* closes her eyes as she brushes her hair those hundred strokes; the rookie *always* talks too much, to the wrong people; the secret agent *always* goes to the lavatory to decode his messages within five minutes of receiving them; the char *always* gobbles the leftovers when nobody's looking.

I repeat, quirks. Victims are so full of them, there is little room for anything else. No wonder authors kill them off first chance they get. (Frankly, I'm usually six pages ahead of them. At the first whiff of a compulsion, the first hint of an idiosyncrasy, down comes my mental guillotine.)

Clearly, the victim is not inherently interesting. Then why kill him? Well, for one thing, it gets him out of his rut. For another, he habitually has something someone else wants: title to the land; senior position in the firm; a second Rolls; a Chippendale armoire; an heirloom brooch; a guaranteed (millionaire's) income. In the mystery, greed is the principal reason for murdering. Consequently, the most likely victim is well-to-do but stingy.

The next most likely victim is the poor sod who recently fell in love. Invariably, his happiness sets someone's knife on edge, resulting in his lopsided grin becoming a little more lopsided. Miss Sayers was quite wrong, you know. She said love has no place in the mystery. She should have qualified her statement. Love may be an inappropriate emotion for the detective (he has to keep his mind on his work, after all), but it is obligatory as a means of identifying the next corpse. What's more appealing to read about than a nice, juicy crime of passion?

The third most frequent victim is done in out of revenge. The victim has brought shame to one family, ruin to another. (If the book's a Gothic, however, shame doesn't lead to murder; it leads to the offender being closeted in the far turret.) Curiously, it's only in spy stories that revenge is an unadulterated motive. The victim is killed under the cloak of patriotism, but if you read between the lines it's apparent that defending the Crown was secondary; the actual reason was to eliminate the cad who caused the death of the spy's best friend some three books back.

In classic thrillers revenge is greed's veneer. For every case you can cite in which the killer did it to restore the family honor, I can rebut with two, at least, in which he did it to gain control of the family blue chips as well.

I suppose I must mention, although I hate

to fuel the arguments of the anti-genre people, that some mystery deaths are caused by outright meanness. These deaths occur in the bottom-quality books — the ones in which you discover on the last page that the killer was a psychopath who had no motive. Books with these abysmal characters tend to choose sentimental victims: a small child with a mild deformity (a stutter); the family pet; widows, teachers and war heroes.

One good author with a perverse streak when it comes to assigning victims is Robert Ludlum. Mr. Ludlum is singular in that he likes his victims, and makes you like them, too. You want them to stick around to the end of the book. The most likely victim in a Ludlum book is the character you least want to see die. Now *that's* perverse.

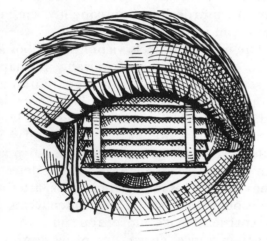

THE VICTIM'S EYES

No matter how long it takes the victim to die and how much time he or she has to stare at the face of the killer, we have it on the best authority — the experts at the New York City Medical Examiner's Office — the victim's eyes will *not* retain a picture of the killer. Many murderers, including some immortalized in the Black Museum at Scotland Yard, went to special trouble to shoot out their victims' eyes, feeling they would give them away. All nonsense. The doctors at the Medical Examiner's Office have looked. And looked and looked. And they have never seen an image imprinted on a retina.

MARTY NORMAN

There are two types of victims who die through no fault of their own. They just happen to have the bad luck to share a chapter with (a) a Great Detective or (b) a Gothic Heroine. Possibly the greatest Great Detective of them all is Sherlock Holmes, agreed? Have you ever noticed how many people die once he's called in on a case? It's appalling. Holmes and his descendants are *always* examining the plimsoles when they should be attending to the people. They are *always* sniffing the cigar ash, gluing the theater stub and educating their Watsons when they should be advising the next victim how to double-lock his door. These victims die to further Holmes's reputation. After all, it doesn't take a Great Detective to solve *one* murder; with a little perseverance we might all be able to do that. But a killer who strikes down many, who in the process still finds time to loot the silver vaults, waylay the carriage and leave hundreds of clues (none of them traceable) demands the skills of a Great Detective. These victims are known as the expendables. Oftener than not, they are the people who sold the cigar that made the ash, who innocently resoled the plimsole. They come two, three, even four to the book, and I can't recall a situation in which they were ever mourned. Presumably, they live alone: no friends, no relatives, no one to shed a tear. They are honest, hard-working souls, and I think Holmes and all the other Great Detectives should be charged for their deaths. Criminal negligence sounds about right, yes?

The other category of hapless victims exists solely in the Gothic novel. Ogden Nash called this the Had-I-But-Known school and it's been around since 1908, when Mary Roberts Rinehart created *The Circular Staircase*. Victims in these books die because they are not wearing nightgowns. The character who is — the Gothic Heroine — has the worst instincts this side of Lady Macbeth. She is a clear case of intuition run amok. She *always* decides a midnight traipse down the corridor is more important

POSITION THE BODY MOST OFTEN FOUND IN

ENGLISH MYSTERIES

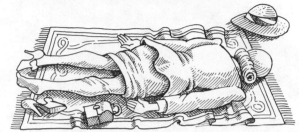

Face down. This is done to give the servants the chance to cry, "It's Lady Teasdale. I put that coat out for her just this morning." Of course, when the body is turned over, it is not Lady T., but Gladys from the kitchen who is M'Lady's size and coloring. Lady Teasdale, feeling quite beneficent that morning, had given Gladys her coat. Gladys, on her own initiative, had stolen her handbag. The servants then get to cry out, "It's Gladys! Leaving service next week, she was. Thought it peculiar, her with a dear Mum to support."

Face down also gives Gladys the chance to obscure with her body the button she managed to wrest from her accoster's mac. This clue will provide the Inspector with at least one red herring and two more victims before the night is over.

AMERICAN MYSTERIES

Face up. This is done to impress Charlie the Horse that it was not an accident. Herman, his best button man, was obviously not the best man for the job of rubbing out Lemons O'Connor and Lemons told him so — slow and lingeringly.

Face up gives Lemons the chance to place pennies on Herman's eyes and pull out his pockets. It also gives him the chance to put a dead fish, wrapped in newspaper, in his arms.

Face up gives the rookie cop a good opportunity to view his first corpse and throw up. While the forensic boys are mopping up, Dan Madison, private eye and bane of the police captain, has time to remove the key to the bus station locker from Herman's hand, pocket it and be on his way to the pickup point.

than warning Cook about the trip-wire set across the servant's stairs. She *always* confides in the killer and with virtually no prompting tells him the name of the only witness. To the Inspector she says not a word. Do you wonder bodies abound when she's around? The big question is: Why doesn't the staff quit the minute she unpacks her nightie? Of course, there is one consolation for the Gothic victim. At book's end the heroine refuses to marry the heir unless he promises her they will name their children after the Recently Departed. It's obvious from the number of them, the Gothic Heroine

does not believe in small families.

Victims, then, are killed out of greed, lust, revenge, meanness, hubris and insensitivity. None of which makes them interesting. It makes their killers interesting. I imagine that's why I would rather identify with the killer than with the victim. (It doesn't mean, necessarily, that I'm unsafe to be around.)

I confess.

Victims bore me. To death.

Rosamund Bryce winters in Cheshireham-Under-Lyme and summers in Upper Denton.

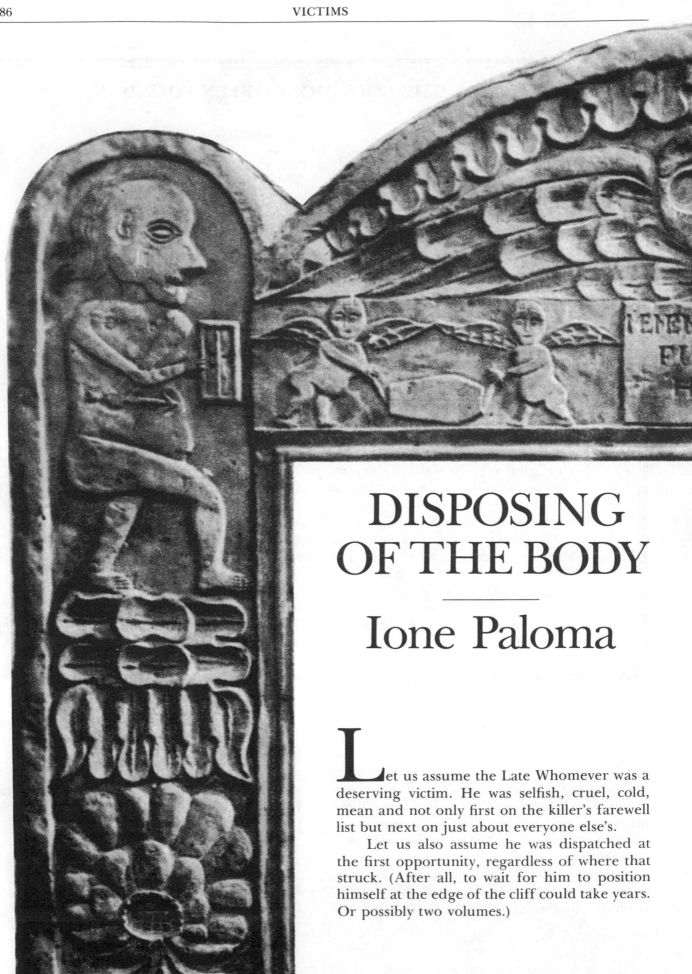

DISPOSING OF THE BODY

Ione Paloma

Let us assume the Late Whomever was a deserving victim. He was selfish, cruel, cold, mean and not only first on the killer's farewell list but next on just about everyone else's.

Let us also assume he was dispatched at the first opportunity, regardless of where that struck. (After all, to wait for him to position himself at the edge of the cliff could take years. Or possibly two volumes.)

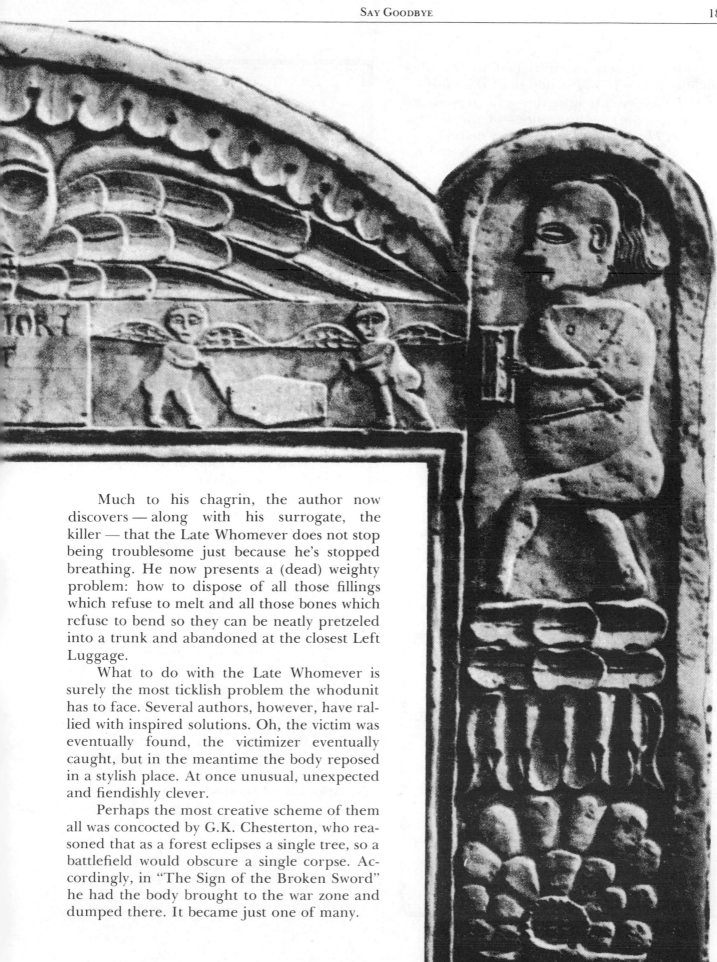

Much to his chagrin, the author now discovers — along with his surrogate, the killer — that the Late Whomever does not stop being troublesome just because he's stopped breathing. He now presents a (dead) weighty problem: how to dispose of all those fillings which refuse to melt and all those bones which refuse to bend so they can be neatly pretzeled into a trunk and abandoned at the closest Left Luggage.

What to do with the Late Whomever is surely the most ticklish problem the whodunit has to face. Several authors, however, have rallied with inspired solutions. Oh, the victim was eventually found, the victimizer eventually caught, but in the meantime the body reposed in a stylish place. At once unusual, unexpected and fiendishly clever.

Perhaps the most creative scheme of them all was concocted by G.K. Chesterton, who reasoned that as a forest eclipses a single tree, so a battlefield would obscure a single corpse. Accordingly, in "The Sign of the Broken Sword" he had the body brought to the war zone and dumped there. It became just one of many.

Ellery Queen was intrigued by the possibilities inherent in the design of the Murphy bed. It folded up into the wall, if you remember, a sort of forerunner of the Castro. Well, in *The French Powder Mystery* he tidily ensconced the corpse between the sheets and recessed him into the fixtures along with the bedding. When the bed was opened — and since the bed was one used in a department store window display it was an opening witnessed by many — out popped the deceased.

Ross Macdonald and Christianna Brand favored the medical approach to disposal. Macdonald in *The Ivory Grin* had the body stripped down to bone (you don't really want to hear about the acid bath, do you?), a few holes drilled into the cranium, a few tags inserted in the holes labeling it a medical school skeleton, and then he closed the Late Lamented into a closet, where it hung as a teaching aid for a perverse student. Ms. Brand in *Green for Danger* was equally devious. She arranged for her victim to die mid-operation, then calmly let the hospital authorities dispose of the body.

Ngaio Marsh baled a body into a packet of wool (*Died in the Wool*), Alice Tilton stored hers in a deep freeze (*Dead Earnest*) and Michael Gilbert crammed his into a safe-deposit vault (*Smallbone Deceased*). Although granted, in the last, the body was conveniently small.

Edgar Allan Poe didn't exactly hide a body;

> *M*other of God, is this the end of Rico?
>
> Little Caesar
> W. R. BURNETT

---

he just caromed it into a chimney (*The Murders in the Rue Morgue*).

John Rhode in *The Mystery at Greycombe Farm* let the Departed harden in a cider storehouse, then rigged an incendiary bomb to char it beyond recognition.

On the bucolic side, Paul McGuire buried his body in a haystack in *Murder at High Noon*, anticipating, perhaps, that one would have as little success in finding it there as the proverbial needle.

Dermot Morrah dispensed with his cadaver by storing it in a mummy case (in — what else? — *The Mummy Case Mystery*), and Freeman Wills Crofts shipped his from Paris to London in a cask marked STATUARY ONLY (in *The Cask*, of course).

Stanley Ellin in "The Specialty of the House" had the body eaten — not in some philistine manner, mind you, but as a savory added to a fine restaurant's menu (uncredited, of course).

David Harper in *The Hanged Men* made his corpse part of a rite. He replaced the traditional Halloween "straw man" with his man, then let him hang around for the celebration.

The ultimate method was developed by Jack Finney in *Time and Again*, although since it smacks of science fiction we cannot comfortably give it top score. His hero was able to wander in time and thus went back just far enough to prevent his enemy's parents from meeting — thereby circumventing the poor man's birth. He disposed of the body by not creating the body in the first place, and more devious than that, it's difficult to get.

Now then, since we've disposed of the body, shall we adjourn to the library for a little game of wits with the Inspector? Follow me.

Ione Paloma wishes to be cremated.

> "*W*ell, I may tell you that Filminister was murdered."
>
> "Murdered?"
>
> "Yes. What is more, he was murdered three times."
>
> "Three times?"
>
> "Yes, and not only that. He also committed suicide."
>
> "I think you'd better give me the details of this extraordinary story."
>
> A Considerable Murder
> BARRY PAIN

GRAVESIDE BOUQUETS

MARTY NORMAN

asphodel: my regrets follow you to the grave
meadow saffron: your best days are past
dark geranium: you are unjust
hortensia: you are cold
stinging needle: you are cruel
wild tansy: I declare war against you
cistus gum: you shall die tomorrow
saffron: beware of success
coltsfoot: justice shall be done
begonia: dark thoughts
lotus flower: estranged love
hellebore: calumny
tamarisk: crime
French marigold: jealousy
white catchfly: betrayal
oleander: beware
fig: argument
lobelia: malevolence
basil: hatred
scarlet auricula: avarice
bilberry: treachery
trefoil: revenge
dahlia: instability

Compiled with
the assistance of
The Language of Flowers
by Margaret Pickston.
Published in England by Michael
Joseph Ltd.

We are gathered here today to say our final farewell to Josiah Trimmingham, beloved by all, save the blighter who doctored his port with rancor and with toxins. Who done it? You know perfectly well it was one of the mourners. (Next to the lawyer's office when the will is read, the cemetery is the place most teeming with cads.) Ah, but which mourner? Look for the most voluptuous bouquet — for it has been observed that the killer, by his choice of flowers, often speaks ill of the dead. Herewith, a list of those connoting possible motive. (*Note:* It is considered lacking in subtlety to send a bouquet of the above mentioned to the incipient corpse. Far classier to show restraint and present them after the fact.)

THE DON'T LIST

(Things to avoid if you *don't* want to be the next victim)

Catherine Prezzano

1. *Don't* go for lonely walks with those you've just disinherited.
2. *Don't* sip a glass of warm milk left at your bedside by an unseen hand.
3. *Don't* sample the chocolates which arrived by post, anonymously, on your birthday.
4. *Don't* rendezvous with the mysterious stranger who offered you a dukedom over the phone in a decidedly muffled voice.
5. *Don't* follow up on the advert in the Personal Column that said if you contact Paines & Grillard, Solicitors, you will hear something to your advantage.
6. *Don't* accept hunting invitations from business associates after you have refused to sell them your controlling shares in the company.
7. *Don't* attend masquerade balls given by wealthy eccentrics who send the car round to collect you and insist you tell no one where you're off to.
8. *Don't* enter the secret passageway first.
9. *Don't* remark to William, that rascal, that the Mac he insists he misplaced seems to be jammed into the hall cupboard for some inexplicable reason.
10. *Don't* kiss Barnaby when you have just turned Alex down flat and he has not yet left the house.
11. *Don't* tell the Inspector you think it nothing more than an unfortunate accident and police surveillance a breach of your privacy.
12. *Don't* stand with your back to billowing draperies, particularly if the windows are shut.
13. *Don't* offer to fetch the candles from the pantry if the lights suddenly dim, flicker and go out.
14. *Don't* comment that you never realized Titian painted in acrylics within earshot of the art gallery owner.
15. *Don't* suggest an audit of the books would be in order.
16. *Don't* ask Woof what he's got there in his mouth, and most especially don't ask him to show you where he got it.
17. *Don't* insist Madame DeClasse conduct the séance at midnight, in the library, when the moon is full.
18. *Don't* adopt young Raymond until you have absolute proof he is your long-lost sister Ava's only child.
19. *Don't* recognize the handwriting on the ransom note.
20. *Don't* reveal the ending of the mystery to someone who is just beginning it.

Catherine Prezzano don't want to wind up dead from O.D.'ing on the mystery.

THE DINNER PLATE
Carlotta Ogelthorpe

If I had an enemy and that enemy were fond of reading English murder mysteries vintage 1920–1930, I wouldn't wait for Monday. I'd start my diet today. I'd turn down all invitations to lunch, brunch, tea, high tea, supper, dinner and between-meal snacks — especially if that enemy were planning on preparing them personally.

You see, of the many conventions established during the so-called "Golden Age" of detective fiction, the one most rigorously followed was, if you had to eliminate someone the table was as good a place as any to have a go at it. In those mysteries the main course was usually served with poison as a side dish. The victim would proceed to the sideboard, innocently ladle the turnip purée onto his plate, return to his seat and, two forkfuls later, slide off his chair — permanently immobilized. If the stately home that guested him was stately enough, he wouldn't even have to fetch his own plate; a helpful, albeit sinister member of the staff would bring his portion to the table for him. Regardless, the outcome was the same: two forkfuls later, down he'd go — fatally stricken by the piquantness of the white sauce. In those mysteries, dinner conversation always included the phrase "I believe the sole did not agree with Reginald. Carruthers, please ring Dr. Watney."

The dinner plate became the poisoner's playground. I suppose its popularity was due to the fact that, with the possible exception of the blunt instrument, nothing was as easy to use. It didn't have to be aimed (like the gun) or personally brought into direct contact with the body (like the knife). It was simple to figure out how much poison to use: when in doubt, you merely doubled the dose. It was also a snap to get the victim to ingest it. After all, everyone ate at least one meal a day. And the English were — still are — notoriously insensitive in regard to food. A slightly off-taste bit of potted meat would not have seemed odd to them. In fact, they'd hardly have noticed.

No, it definitely wasn't safe to eat in those books. There were arcane poisons, of course, which one had to go to Brazil to collect or, even worse, sign the chemist's registry to purchase. But by and large, toxic substances were available at the drop of a grudge. Botulism was frequently induced. Mushrooms were nurtured in the dank of the cellar. Weed-killer decimated two-legged rats. By the time the chubby sleuth waddled onto the scene, it was too late to administer the antidote — if indeed there was one.

The dinner plate is still being toyed with in detective fiction, only now the Americans have gotten in on the act (Fred Halliday's *The Raspberry Tart Affair*; Nan and Ivan Lyons' *Someone Is Killing the Great Chefs of Europe*). There is also a counter-trend: books featuring fat sleuths' recipes rather than the poisoners' menus (*Madame Maigret's Own Cookbook; The Nero Wolfe Cookbook; The Mafia Cookbook; Murder on the Menu; Dining Out with Sherlock Holmes*).

What is this fascination? Why is food to the mystery what Watson is to Holmes, inseparable best friend? One theory intimidating enough to make Freud take to his couch is that there is virtually no sexual activity in the mystery and food is used as the surrogate. Many psychiatrists have noted that the number of pounds of overweight can be directly correlated to the number of kisses, etc., not received. (Don't blame me: I didn't invent the theory, I'm merely repeating it.)

There are some foods in mysteries it's never safe to trust. Dover sole, baked or poached. Porridge. Ladyfingers. Any cream sauce. Eggs, unless they're hard-boiled. Chocolates, if they're given as a present. Warm milk. And, of course, any sort of spirits. The Case of the Deadly Decanter has been written at least a hundred times, and there's probably a fiend out there typing up another one right now. When analyzed, the sediment at the bottom of the wineglass always contains enough poison to fell a hippopotamus.

Who's putting all these bad things in the victim's mouth? Certainly not Cook. Granted, she has the disposition of Attila the Hun, but her weapon would be the meat cleaver. No one in and around the kitchen, in fact, is a desecrator of the dinner plate. The washing-up girl has no time; the butler has no motive; the serving girl never has her hands free.

No, the poisoner is usually someone from Upstairs, or an Upstairs associate such as the lawyer or the doctor. In mysteries, poisoning is a well-to-do crime. It's neat. It's tidy. It's rather elegant.

What I would prefer, if I were to be a victim and if I may be so bold as to instruct my enemy, is to be allowed to eat my meal in peace and *then* be done in. The owners of New York's elegant Four Seasons restaurant concur. They suggest, in the manner of Sing Sing, that you give the condemned a hearty meal. A repast flamboyantly extravagant ($200 per lover; $150 per board of directors member) and exquisitely executed. After all, at one time you and your victim were rather intimate. You did share things together — be it a love affair, a family relationship, a corporate decision. Accordingly, you owe it to your victim to let him go out in style. To let his last meal reflect the gloriousness of his former role in your life. Bring on the golden egg caviar with the gold caviar spoon. The Trockenbeeren Auslese in a vintage coinciding with the date of your first encounter.

THE SCALES OF JUSTICE

Nero Wolfe weighs $1/7$ of a ton
Gideon Fell stopped counting at 250
Chief Inspector Dover straddles 240
Bertha Cool was a big 200, but dieted
    down to a mere 160
Charlie Chan is fat
Inspector Bucket is stout
Sergeant Beef is burly
Father Brown has a dumpling face
Inspector Hanaud is bulky
Jim Hanvey has too many chins
Chief Inspector Hazelrigg is definitely
    blimpish
Martin Hewitt is on the stout side
Roger Sheringham is stocky (too many
    chocolates)
George Smiley is a fat little toad
And Maigret better watch it.

The Havana cigars (smuggled). The cognac (Hennessey X.O.). The potatoes Anna with truffles and goose liver. The filet of hothouse lamb with its delicate bouquetière of spring vegetables. (Or the freshly peeled crayfish tails with morels flown in from the Himalayas.) *Then* as you stroll from the restaurant, his suspicions thwarted, *then* as you turn into a convenient dark alley, *then* set about finalizing matters. *That's* good manners.

For a truly mouth-watering way to go, if you feel you simply must monkey around despite the admonishments from me and the Four Seasons, let us remind you of peppered duck and shrimp with mustard sauce. Both have the necessary robustness to disguise a poison. And they have not been, forgive us, done to death. If you will settle for just making your victim deathly ill, we suggest off-season oysters from polluted waters. They'll cause hepatitis.

One other thing: May I invite you to dine with me Saturday next?

Carlotta Ogelthorpe dines alone.

THE INVALID'S TRAY
Violet St. Clair

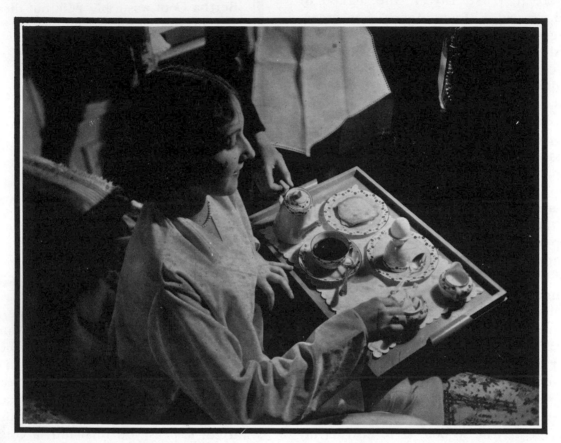

Auntie is sick. Has been for years. She took to her bed in '37 for reasons she's quite forgotten and has been going steadily, if slowly, downhill ever since.

She accepts breakfast at eight, luncheon at one, tea between four and five, dinner at half-seven and a cocoa nightcap at just past nine.

Her mornings are occupied with rewriting her will and her afternoons with receiving the doctor. She has terrible nightmares in which someone is either garrotting her with the bell pull, smothering her with her pillows or poisoning her by tinkering with her food tray. She ought to pay more attention to the last.

Great-Uncle Patriarch is also in bed, sent there by an embolism which refuses to dissolve.

It presses on the corner of his brain that garbles speech and causes incontinency.

His mornings are spent on his right side, facing the sun, and his afternoons on his left, focussing, as best he can, on the secret panel in his desk.

He is spoon-fed three times a day by people he can barely recognise. One of them makes him very uneasy and his tremors upset his egg cup. He ought to have it analysed.

Clara, slightly concussed from a fall down the stairs, will be abed a fortnight.

Her counterpane is speckled with petals from a nosegay, dozens of get-well cards and tinfoil wrappers with bits of chocolate clinging.

She spends the day confiding in her diary

and the night sleeping with it beneath her pillow. Fierce headaches make her prone to napping, and when she awakens a tray is on the bedstand. Upon sampling its custard, she becomes violently ill. She ought to try to stay awake more often.

Alec is recovering from a wound he won't let anyone tend to. In fact, no one's ever seen it. Lately, he's developed a cough, and he's suggested that no one come in his room lest they catch it. His trays are left outside his locked door.

These poor wretches — hypochondriacal, chronic, accidental and deceitful — are the mainstay of the old-fashioned whodunit. All must be fed (except the last, who could really get up and serve himself, but then he'd have no alibi). All must be killed or almost killed before too many chapters slip by. And their tray is the perfect way to incapacitate them.

Every decent invalid's tray is bordered with pill bottles. The smart villain will replace one of them with another of his own prescription. If Nurse assumes the big pink pills are the usual big pink pills, who can blame her?

The tray also contains a napkin (for wiping off prints), a white linen place mat with hand-tatted edges (for hiding the knife under), an oversize spoon (for administering the toxin), a toast rack (to hold the blackmail note), a tea cosy (to be thrust halfway down the larynx as a gag) and a single rose (to fatally prick a weakened hand).

Some trays also come equipped with a hypodermic. While Miss Prendergast is off in the pantry fetching the bouillon cube, the villain is squirting out its shot of B_{12} and filling it with a Tanzanian virus for which there's no known antidote.

Upon her return Miss Prendergast notices the needle is slightly to the left of where she put it, but that doesn't stop her from taking it Upstairs and injecting sweet old Auntie with it. It's only later, when queried by the Inspector, that she remembers how it seemed to move.

And, of course, every respectable invalid's tray has a splendid variety of dishes to fiddle with.

A nice cup of tea, for example. Murderers have little difficulty in raising the teapot lid, inserting a quick-dissolving poison, lowering the lid and leaving the room before anyone suspects what they're up to. One invariably presumes they were just checking to see if the water needed hotting up.

And let's not forget the water glass itself. This tumbler contains eight ounces of death which the tray bearer will insist the victim drink right up, for her own good. Sometimes the victim's nerves overcome her, and she spills the contents. This is a brief reprieve, nothing more. So the dear thing can swallow her pills, the water-bearer will insist on refilling it — usually from the very tap which the killer has polluted.

Then there's the custard. Made from fresh eggs. At least they *were* fresh until some nefarious soul neatly pin-pricked each and every one of them, carefully dripped in a poisonous ooze and then put them back on the shelf in the fridge.

Porridge, too, has a nice lumpy consistency appealing to a villain, and one can bank on its being included in the victim's menu every morning. Its greyish colour is also an asset if one is dealing with impurities.

Other bright spots, for the villain, on the invalid's tray are: the jam pot; the sugar bowl; the milk pitcher; the soup bowl; the applesauce dish.

It never happens, however, that the killer serves the tray himself. He is more likely to be out of the house at feeding time, establishing an alibi by playing bridge with the Wittsentides in Yarmouth. Thus killers must do their tinkering well ahead of time. Occasionally, this isn't possible, and the killer must go up the stairs, down the stairs, up again, down again, until he accidentally bumps into whoever is carrying the tray. An elbow auspiciously placed, a subtle jostle, and his task is accomplished: the tray has been lethalized. Ofttimes, he's even too late to do this and must rely on getting to the tray before it's removed from the invalid's room. Or, wait for the next feeding time.

No matter. As Alec passed on to Auntie, Great-Uncle Patriarch and Clara: Never eat in bed.

Violet St. Clair will be dining Saturday next with Miss Ogelthorpe.

THE TERRIBLE EDIBLES
Innocuous (seemingly) House and Garden Plants That Will (quite simply) Slay You

Ruth H. Smiley, Botanist
Carolyn Fiske, Ghost

There are approximately 750 species of plants in the United States and Canada that are either partly or entirely poisonous. Instead of reaching for the salt (or the strychnine), why not reach for one of them?

Deadly nightshade. Virtually everything about the plant is poisonous — leaves, stems, flowers, seeds. Interestingly enough, it belongs to the same family as the potato and the tomato. Active ingredients are topane alkaloids, atropine and hyoscyamine. Symptoms: fever, visual disturbances, burning of the mouth, thirst, dry skin, confusion and a splitting headache.

Castor bean. One of the deadliest of all poisonous plants. One bean contains enough ricin toxin to kill an adult. The bean, however, must be chewed; if swallowed whole, the hard protective coat prevents absorption and poisoning. Yes, it is the oil from this very same plant which is marketed as castor oil, also known as a "killer" in some instances.

Buttercups (poor, little). The leaves, seeds, roots and flowers of this dainty yellow plant have been known to cause convulsions. Other common plants with similar poisonous properties are the azalea, rhododendron, iris, daffodil, jonquil, oleander, hyacinth, morning glory, poinsettia and lily of the valley, often associated with funerals. Mountain laurel is so potent that it was known to the Delaware Indians as the "suicide plant."

Snakeroot. A white wild flower known for its writhing root system. Among its illustrious victims were Nancy Hanks, mother of Abraham Lincoln, who died by drinking milk from a cow which had grazed on snakeroot. Such an "indirect" death is more difficult to accomplish today as the plant grows in forests, not modern dairy pastures.

Dumb cane (a.k.a. dieffenbachia, elephant ear, mother-in-law plant). An attractive white speckled plant that, when chewed, produces swelling of the tongue, lips and palate, making it difficult, if not impossible, for the victim to ask for help. There are reported cases of death by suffocation when, as a result of violent swelling of the tongue, the victims were unable to breathe.

Apples. The seeds are quite bitter and contain cyanic poison, which accumulates in the

DEATH
(Warmed Over)

1 Cauldron boiling oil
5 Lbs. hacked carrion
2 Qts. curdled blood
1 Carafe hemlock
3½ Cups toadstools (decapitated)
1 Cloven hoof
7 Cans Bon Vivant soup
13 Heaping tbs. arsenic powder, salt,
*   pepper, mace.*

Place carrion on rack. Smother in salt, pepper and mace. Remove from rack and drown in marinade of hemlock and blood. Place in dark, dank corner. Heat oil. When it reaches rolling boil, add hoof. Cook 30 days. Add decapitated toadstools. Stir mixture with silver stake. Scrape mold from carrion and set aside. Add carrion to boiling oil. Slowly, very slowly, drip soup on meat. Make a paste of mold and arsenic powder. (To moisten, use any of the basic body oils.) Remove meat and skewer it. Pour paste over it. Serve immediately with Little Caesar Salad.

MYSTERY MUNCHIES

Obviously, the best choice is to have someone standing by peeling grapes and plopping them in your mouth. This leaves both your hands free — one to hold the book and one to turn the page.

If you can't shanghai this kind of help, you should purchase a chair with a wide, flat, unupholstered armrest. This is best for plate-balancing.

What goes on the plate depends on your whim: M&M candies; popcorn; mixed raisins and nuts (unshelled); blueberries, strawberries, huckleberries; licorice bits; cherry tomatoes; pitted olives, either black or green; lollipops.

Cookies of any description make terrible munchies. Too many crumbs. Your chair begins to feel like your beach towel with all that sand getting in awkward places.

Chewing gum while reading mysteries is another awful idea. In your excitement, you may swallow it.

body and builds up over a period of time. This circumstance partly compensates for the fact that one must eat a large quantity of the seeds for the desired effect. Serving suggestion: Sprinkle on foods as a garnish. Symptoms: nausea, vomiting, stomach cramps, difficulty in breathing, muscular weakness, dizziness, convulsions and stupor. (Maybe it was the seeds and not the apple that caused Adam and Eve's fall.)

Apricots (also cherries, prunes, plums and almonds). All contain cyanogenitic glycosides in the leaves, stems, bark and seed pits (not the fruit, alas). A change in eating habits may be required as the inner pit must be chewed.

Wild cherry branches. The twig of this tree, which contains cyanic poison, can be used to spear marshmallows for roasting over campfires. Works equally well with hot dogs.

Red elderberry branches. Use the toxic stem to make a blowgun or peashooter. When blown, the blower, not his target, is the real victim. Be sure not to confuse this twig, which has a red center pith, with the benign black elderberry, which has a white pith.

Rhubarb. The leaf (not the commonly eaten stalk) contains oxalic acid, which has a corrosive action on the gastrointestinal tract and can cause massive hemorrhaging. Next time, bake a strawberry-rhubarb *leaf* pie. (As an aside, spinach also contains some of the same toxins, but they are steamed out in the cooking process. Obviously, one must serve the water and throw out the spinach.)

Ruth H. Smiley and Carolyn Fiske stroll the acres of Mohonk Mountain House looking for terrible edibles.

A PUZZLER TO MULL OVER

Stuart Bochner

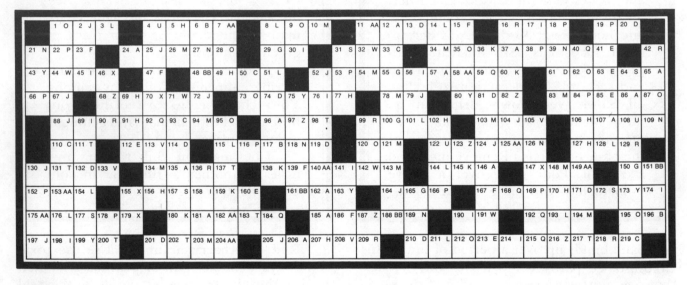

Solve the clues (right) and write them over their numbered dashes. Then transfer each letter to the corresponding numbered square in the pattern. Black squares indicate word endings. The filled pattern will contain a suitable quotation reading from left to right. The first letters of the solved clues will form an acrostic giving the author's name and title of the work. The clues are of the English crossword type in two parts: a definition and a subsidiary indication (pun, anagram, double definition, etc.) Punctuation is designed to confuse.

Stuart Bochner is an attorney with the New York Division of Criminal Justice.

SOLUTION:
Hold upside down, facing mirror.

killed were never discovered.
and the circumstances under which he was
The hand that struck him was never traced
his name, his rank or his place of abode.
thing being found on him which revealed
the disguise which I have described, no-
His body was taken out of the Seine in
Wilkie Collins: The Woman in White

A. D. C. loses heavy weight screw, e.g. to get scrub
board. (2 words) ....
185 107 24 96 57 162 37 146 12 86 135 65 181 206

B. Eddie Cantor's gal's a prosecutor ....
196 6 117

C. Adored fifty dove off ....
93 110 50 33 219

D. Results of stabbings misuses own fine dusk. (2
words) ....
13 132 81 20 119 201 74 171 61 210 114

E. The Cid heroically reacted to mosquito bites .....
85 63 213 112 41 160

F. Elizabeth nicely shows one with cultural traits ....
23 139 186 15 47 167

G. Number one father gains one link ....
55 165 100 29 150

H. Responded excessively to what the nuclear plant
did before exploding ....
5 207 69 156 106 91 49 170 127 102 77

I. Does he keep track of meals where they're eaten?
(2 words) ....
198 141 76 45 190 158 214 17 30 174 89 56

J. Putting Steiger on a diet results in a ground. (2
words) ....
197 104 67 130 164 25 79 2 205 72 88 124 52

K. If you look in this suede you'll find what is
brought forth ....
145 36 138 180 159 60

L. Her name whips wild state. (2 words) ....
176 51 8 144 193 101 115 3 128 211 154 14

M. Feast dish works out shark-like meat. (2 words) ..
10 83 78 203 34 121 26 54 103 194 134 94 148 143

N. To start chicken with its head cut off add cornstarch ....
21 189 39 118 109 126 27

O. What the successful con man did with a line and a
sinker. (3 words) ....
1 62 120 195 28 95 9 73 35 212 87

P. The last moment? Not with sixty left in the day! (2
words) ....
53 116 178 152 166 66 18 22 84 19 38 169

Q. Vacillates banner displayers when heard ....
192 92 168 215 59 184 40

R. Crockery made over anew ....
16 90 218 99 42 136 209 129

S. Find a duplicate flame ....
172 157 31 177 64

T. Stopped using retreads ....
131 217 111 202 98 137 183 200

U. Take back top banana ....
108 122 4

V. I would shorten two directions in mid-month ....
113 133 208 105

W. Cynic heads inside a corner ....
71 44 142 32 191

X. Whistle without the French bridge ....
147 46 70 179 155

Y. She entered a short cabinet department and insisted on quiet ....
43 75 173 80 199 163

Z. Drink me around a protective cloth with another
me in front ....
187 82 123 97 68 216

AA. Make debts ready for stuffed animals. (2 words) .
11 204 125 182 7 58 153 175 140 149

BB. Reached in for every one ....
151 161 188 48

THE RIPPER'S LADIES
Donald Rumbelow

Mention Jack the Ripper and people think of a cinematic East End where Pearly Kings and Queens dance in the street, Marie Lloyd sings from every pub counter, music halls barrel-organ out their tunes, all prostitutes wear scarlet silk gowns, hansom cabs clip-clop through cobbled gas-lit streets and adventures can be had by top-hatted bucks in silk-lined opera cloaks, with pearl studs in their cuffs and swordsticks in their hands.

Reality was much different.

Jack the Ripper's ladies. Faces puffed from too much drink; dirt-smelling, sour-breathed, middle-aged drabs. Casual pick-ups in some common lodging house, pub or back alley in Whitechapel. Five victims. Each brutally murdered and mutilated, two in one night, between 31st August and 9th November 1888. Even in death, given no dignity.

Four were butchered in the street.

No glamour to any of them. No silks, mahogany-furnished rooms, heavy drapes or lace underwear. One room, lucky if they could get it, in some slum tenement was the best to be hoped for. Even that had to be shared. Watch out! No stair handrail. Gone long ago for firewood. Flea-infested paper hanging in strips on damp stained walls. Bare boards with a kettle boiling on the hob. In one corner, a cracked washbowl on a wooden stand. A creaking bed with a lumpy straw palliasse. Worked in shifts.

Less private, but at least an alternative, one of eighty beds in a public dormitory. Whitechapel lodging houses slept nine thousand each night. Double beds were 8d, singles 4d, and 2d bought a lean on a rope stretched across the room.

No money, no bed. Only the street. Bed was a niche behind some dustbins, deep doorway, empty staircase, arch under a bridge or rotting warehouse by the river.

Life, such as it was, pivoted around that magical 4d. A single bed, not double, where they could be cocooned from reality for a few undisturbed hours.

Money. But how to get it? Woman's work was scrubbing, sweatshop tailoring, hop picking, sack or matchbox making. Wages often included the cost of materials. Women were lucky if paid tenpence for seventeen hours' sweated labour.

Prostitution paid better wages. Three-

Suspect No. 2
GEORGE CHAPMAN

Suspect No. 1
DR. NEILL CREAM

pence, twopence or a loaf of stale bread. Whitechapel had twelve hundred prostitutes. London had eighty thousand.

Nichols, Chapman, Stride and Eddowes. Basically, hard-working respectable women. Failures with children, husbands and money. Drink was their escape. None of them young, even good-looking. Nichols was forty-two years old, brown hair turning grey and five front teeth missing. Chapman was forty-five, two front teeth missing, stout, with brown wavy hair. Stride was forty-five, with dark curly hair; roof of mouth missing as well as front teeth. Claimed mouth had been injured in steamboat disaster when husband and children had been drowned.

Eddowes was forty-three years old. Everything she possessed she wore. (As did the others.) Black jacket with imitation fur collar. Dark green dress with pattern of Michaelmas daisies and gold lilies. White vest, drab linsey skirt, old dark green petticoat, white chemise, brown ribbed stockings mended with white cotton, black straw bonnet, men's lace-up boots with steel tips and heels. In her pockets: clay pipes, cigarette case, five pieces of soap, handkerchiefs, comb, and tin containing tea and sugar.

Each had been married. Each had escaped domestic pressures. Each had taken to drink. Each had abandoned families or husbands. Each had since taken up with someone else.

Nichols had been married twenty-two years before the final break-up. Several attempts made at reconciliation. Utterly useless. Left her husband immediately after birth of fifth child. He had custody and care of the five children. No apparent ill-will. For two years he allowed her 5s a week from his carpenter's wages. Stopped it immediately when he learned she was earning money as a prostitute. Her drinking, chief reason for the break-up, he could forgive. She was drunk and staggering when last seen alive, 31st August, 2:30 A.M. She boasted, "I've had my lodging money three times today and I've spent it." She was confident that she could quickly get the extra 4d. She had on a new hat.

"See what a jolly bonnet I've got now."

The black straw bonnet was by her body when it was found, cut and disembowelled, just over an hour later.

Annie Chapman had been separated four years. Her coachman husband had kept their two children, one of them a cripple, with him at Windsor. He allowed her ten shillings a week

Suspect No. 3
THE DUKE OF CLARENCE

Suspect No. 4
JAMES K. STEPHEN

Suspect No. 5
MONTAGUE J. DRUITT

From The Complete Jack The Ripper by Donald Rumbelow, published by New York Graphics Society

from his wages; this stopped with his death eighteen months before. Chapman was an intelligent woman, clever with a needle when sober. Drink stimulated her natural pugnacity. Several days before she died, having lost a lodging house fight, she was creeping around like a sick cat, nursing a black eye and bruised chest. No money for a bed, she was turned out of a lodging house kitchen at 2:30 A.M. on 8th September. Three hours later, she went with Jack the Ripper into the backyard of 29 Hanbury Street, in daylight. Someone heard her cry out as she was seized and fell against the fence. He was too indifferent to look.

Minutes later she was found, her body sprawled obscenely against the steps, throat cut, stomach torn, clothes pushed up around her neck.

Double event, 30th September. No time to linger over Stride. Pony and trap turned into gateway moments after she had been gripped from behind and the throat cut. She lay in the gateway in Berner Street, in her left hand still, a paper tissue of cachous. Her common-law husband for the past three years thought she was at home.

No time to waste. On to Mitre Square in the City of London. Catherine Eddowes had been celebrating. She had been going to see her daughter Annie in Bermondsey. She was arrested dead drunk in Aldgate. She sobered up in the cells and was let out at 1 A.M.

"Night, old cock," she said to the gaoler.

Thirty minutes later she was dead. Throat cut, disembowelled, and the Ripper walking away wiping his bloodstained knife on a piece of her apron.

Mary Kelly breaks the pattern. Time to toy with that sharp little knife, time to gloat, time to linger.

Room 13 Miller's Court, 9th November.

Mary or Marie Jeanette Kelly. Twenty years younger, fresh-looking, pregnant, and walking the streets for the past three years. Before that, a short time in France and a fashionable house in the West End. On 9th November, at 12:30 A.M., singing heard in her room. Later a cry of "murder." So common was it that the listener turned over and went back to sleep.

The Ripper lingered over his work, piling flesh on the table by her bed. Breasts, kidneys, heart, nose, liver.

With this final obscenity the murders stopped.

Since then the theories have grown.

Butcher, baker, policeman, midwife, mad doctor, abortionist, shohet, magician, heir to the throne of England. Jack the Ripper? Nobody knows.

Ironically, as the Ripper moves up the social scale, as he has done with the passing years, so too have his victims; the higher he goes, the higher they must be upgraded. From twopenny whores they have become witnesses to a Royal marriage, the guardians of a State secret.

They have acquired a respectability, a pedigree, an importance which they never had in life.

They have become desirable.

Donald Rumbelow is the author of The Complete Jack the Ripper.

The original of this message from The Ripper is in the Black Museum at New Scotland Yard. Currently, it is not on display.

THE EDINBURGH PILLOW
Hugh Douglas

She must go, I told myself. If only there were a perfect murder method.

I don't think I said it aloud, but it was at that moment the figure appeared at my side, laughing in a rippling kind of way, like a musical scale. He was a small waif-like creature, dressed in an old blue coat which hung open, and tattered moleskin trousers. A cap almost hid his dancing eyes.

"Would ye be after the perfect murder, sur?" he asked. The word "murder" was pronounced *morther* in an Irish way.

"There is no perfect murder method," I answered.

"Sure there is, sur, let me tell you about it. It's called burking after me, William Burke, native of Orrey in County Tyrone, Ireland, but lately a residenter in Edinburgh — a lovely city to be sure but the old town where I lived was a bit run-down, forsaken by the nobility and dilapidated, you might say.

"I lived there in a lodging house wi' my woman, not my wife exactly, because her husband McDougal was still to the fore, and not pretty — no, not at all pretty — but Nelly and I suited one another. Our landlord was a bad pill if ever ye met one — William Hare, and as villainous in temper as he was in looks. They called his wife Lucky because she had been fortunate enough to inherit the lodging house from her late husband. But her luck ran out when she met up wi' that scoundrel."

Burke laughed more drily than the last time, I thought.

"Well, there was another lodger at the house in the autumn of 1827, an old man named Donald — sure I never heard his other name — who died owing Hare four pounds. Hare was beside himself at the loss of the money and he came to me. Sure, I thought, the doctors at the anatomy schools of Edinburgh buy corpses for their students to dissect. A man Paterson, who worked at Dr. Knox's school, once told me they paid as much as ten pounds for a body, so we took Donald there at dead of night and they gave us seven pounds and ten shillings for him. I think they saw we were new to the game for Donald was worth more, but anyway, Hare had his four pounds and I had more nor I could earn in a month, so we were both satisfied.

"Then another lodger took sick wi' the fever, and that's bad for business in a lodging house, so we just slipped a pillow over his face and smothered him, neat as ninepence. And we got ten pounds for him — it was better than work any day."

Burke sang a little tune and danced a jig before he continued.

"Och, but the money didn't last and soon we were in need of more. We just kept our eyes open and it was amazing how many folk we found walking the streets of Edinburgh — it was a heartless place to be poor in — and they were glad to come and take a drink wi' us. Then when they were asleep we just put a pillow over their faces, and helped them on to a lasting peace. And Dr. Knox's boys were glad to buy their bodies off us at the going rate.

"We saw sixteen of them off before Hallowe'en of 1828: old Effie, the pedlar; Daft Jamie; bonnie Mary Paterson, the prostitute; a relative of Nelly; and one of my own countrywomen, Mrs. Docherty. She was the last.

An evening with Burke and Hare.

"Folk thought we were grave robbers — resurrectionists, they called us — so nobody was surprised at our comings and goings to Surgeons' Square. They paid us well, and it was a grand life, better by far than mending shoes or working on farms all summer.

"Our corpses were always prize specimens. They looked as if they had died in their sleep, peaceful as you like, and not a mark on them to suggest violence. Sure, it wasn't really violent: I told the police that."

"The police?" I asked. "How did they come into it? I thought yours was the perfect murder method."

Burke scratched his chin. "So it was, and we'd never have been caught but for the fact that we got careless and Nelly's cousin, Ann Gray, and her man found old Mrs. Docherty's body. They wouldn't be shut up and went to the police."

He smiled. "Aye, even then the police could prove nothing, our murder method was perfect — perfect except that it involved that vile betrayer Hare. He did a nasty deal with the law in return for a promise that they'd let him off Scot free." Burke's voice turned bitter. "Hare and Lucky got away because they told a pack of lies and half-truths about Nelly and me. Aye, but Nelly still got off. I'm glad of that for she wasn't a bad soul — dour and Scottish, but not bad."

"And you?"

He drew a hand across his throat. "I paid the penalty on the gibbet at Edinburgh market cross. A nasty experience that; I thought the mob would get me before the hangman, but they didn't. The others suffered longer: Nelly had to go to Australia and Lucky — lucky to the last — was a nursemaid to a fine family in Paris. Hare got his desserts; blinded in a limepit and left to beg in the streets of London.

"And our perfect murder method of suffocation went into the dictionary as burking. Fancy that, William Burke gave a word to the English language."

"Excuse me, Mr. Burke," I said, "but asphyxiation — I mean, burking — isn't a perfect murder method any more. Thanks to all the dissection of bodies people like you supplied, doctors can tell nowadays whether a body was smothered or not."

"Do you tell me that," he answered. "Now is that not a pity."

He began to hum:

Up the close and down the stair,
Ben the house wi' Burke and Hare.
Burke's the butcher, Hare's the thief,
And Knox the boy that buys the beef.

I turned to speak to him but he was gone.

Hugh Douglas is the author of Burke and Hare — The True Story.

THE DAY I RIPPED OFF LIZZIE'S HOUSE

Ellen Stern

FALL RIVER HISTORICAL SOCIETY

Who, me? I was the daughter who snuck out every Mother's Day in the dewy, dewy dawn to gather a bouquet of violets for pre-breakfast presentation. The daughter who could hear the car coming from six blocks away and streaked upstairs to get Daddy's slippers so they'd be at his favorite chair before he was. I sneezed at cats because she did, scorned his relatives because he did, hummed along with the Whiffenpoofs because she did, guttled raw clams because he did.

So what's a nice girl like me doing with an obsession like this? Why, when there are all sorts of disasters to choose from, does the case of Lizzie Borden absolutely rivet me?

Truly, we have little in common. Lizzie was a dour spinster who loathed her porky step-mother and persisted in calling her Mrs. Borden. She was no more cuddly with her gangly old father, and she yearned for his money. She took none of her meals with the parents, shared no secrets, smiled rarely, and avoided them as much as possible . . . which couldn't have been easy in their narrow little house in Fall River. The tension must have been terrific.

On the muggy morning of August 4, 1892, Lizzie had had all she was going to take. She picked up a hatchet, and hacked. It was a crime convenient to commit. Bridget the maid was out back washing windows; Emma the sister was out of town; Uncle John was out on a walk. The deed done, Lizzie buried her weapon in a bed of ashes in the cellar, washed her hands, changed her clothes, and was in fine spirits when the cops came. She had two different alibis — both perfectly silly, both totally accepted by the neighbors and authorities. A couple of days later, she took the dress spattered with her parents' blood, tossed it into the kitchen stove, and nobody stopped her. And, because the Bordens were a prominent family, and Lizzie a woman (and a churchgoing woman to boot), she got away with murder. I do *not* admire her.

Nonetheless, on a muggy August morning nearly seventy-five years later, I found myself on Lizzie's front step. We were on our way to Cape Cod, a blond chap named Chuck and I, when I located Fall River on the map. Aha! I thought, and casually asked if we might take a slight detour to drive through the town. He said if it wasn't too much out of the way. I said it didn't seem to be.

It was. But by the time this was clear, we were fairly well entangled in Fall River's dusty streets. Chuck's face was blotchy with anger. His foot jerked at the gas pedal.

"What street is it we're looking for?" he raged. By this time, it was evident that we were not here merely to drive through town. We needed The House.

"In 1892, it was Second Street," I answered. "I think it still is."

"You *think* it still is?"

It still was. But the numbers were no longer the same. In 1892, Lizzie did her stuff in a wooden house with a two-gated picket fence in front and a barn in back. The address was 92 Second Street. On my August day, the house looked just like its photographs, but the picket fence was gone and a printing plant had replaced the barn. The number had been changed to 230.

"Stop!" I cried, any compassion for Chuck now turned to frenzy. "That's it!"

"That's *it*?"

He looked with absolute wonder. I couldn't blame him. Who but a devotee would cherish such a site? Such a plain little house. Behind those doors such horrors had happened? From there came legend and a jingle? There?

"I know this sounds crazy," I said, sounding crazy, "but I have to do something."

Chuck sat very still.

"This'll just take a second."

I threw open the car door, leapt into the steaming potholes of Second Street, swirled to the sidewalk, and stood, in awe, before the house. The heat was intense and my hands were shaking (surely more than Lizzie's ever did). What to do now? Knock at the door? Pose as an Avon lady? Order some envelopes from the printer who now inhabited the place? No. I wanted a *souvenir*. But what?

A piece of house.

I needed something that had been there on That Day. So, knowing that beneath the ghastly gray paint, and beneath the coat under that, and beneath the coat under that, etc., etc., was truly The-Paint-From-The-House-That-

Court photograph of Mrs. Borden, in the second-floor bedroom.

> Lizzie Borden took an axe
> And gave her Mother forty whacks.
> When she saw what she had done,
> She gave her Father forty-one.

Court photograph of Mr. Borden, in the living room, on the couch.

FALL RIVER HISTORICAL SOCIETY

She-Lived-In-When-It-Occurred, I reached over and snapped off a chip for myself. A relic is a relic.

When I returned to New York — with my chip and without my Chuck — I had the prize laminated in a Broadway arcade. For years, I carried it with me, displaying it as proudly as a Schliemann his Trojan shard. And then, in some move or other, I lost it.

Every summer, as August looms, I am thrown again into a Lizzie tizzy. And I am bereft.

Ellen Stern is an editor at New York *magazine.*

Chapter 6
MODUS OPERANDI

PARAPHERNALIA
Making Use of What's Available

Jeanine Larmoth

Murders cannot be committed haphazardly. They must be planned. Paraphernalia laid in. Not weapons: paraphernalia. Clocks, mirrors, blotters, telephones, candlesticks, decanters — no object too ordinary. Clocks and telephones help establish times. In the ABC's of murder, B is for "blotter," which soaks up the message in reverse. The mirror can read it. Mirrors also let a witness overlook the flicking of a little arsenic that the murderer did not intend to be seen, the forging of a will, or a delicious embrace in the garden below which, unfortunately, involves the murderer's best friend and his wife. Glasses hold sleeping-draughts; decanters are for poisoned port. In case of need, paraphernalia may be converted so that the least suspicious object, tape measure to flowerpot, turns into lethal weapon, thus giving a familiar object exciting potential and titillating us with the prospect of an outbreak in our own flowerpots.

The telephone, with its connections to telephone exchange, operator, call box and neighbours, is a fine example of paraphernalia. Lonely country houses become infinitely lonelier infinitely faster when lines go down in a storm, or under the killer's wire cutters. Isolation makes the breath come shallow with fear when there's a dead phone in hand; a desperate sense of impotence follows the announcement that the phone is out of order.

Telephone calls work with almost as much efficiency for alibis as timetables. Making such calls from a call box has obvious advantages. A call box in a residential section is an excellent observation post. Tucked behind its little glass windowpanes, one can appear to be making a telephone call indefinitely, meanwhile keeping a certain house under surveillance. Furthermore, a call placed from a call box cannot be traced or overheard by the operator; it may remain anonymous. To be even surer that it does, the wise murderer goes to the call box supplied with another good piece of paraphernalia: a silk scarf to disguise his voice, or for use should it be necessary to strangle a customer already in the box. This action is not the offspring of irritation at having to wait. No, with that same uncanny sense of the time it takes a coin to drop in the box, the murderer knows that a witness has just this minute put two and two together, and is going to make someone else, probably the police, privy to her calculations. That, of course, won't do. Her three minutes are up. Were the same disguised-voice call to be made from home, another member of the household might remark the purple silk scarf stuffed in the murderer's mouth to distort his voice, cackle with laughter at an accent he is affecting, or ask embarrassing questions afterwards, such as, "Why did you say you'd lost your gun when it's just where you left it hidden in the metal box under the rosebush?" Undesirable heckling is avoided in call boxes.

The principal purpose of a car in a mystery is to have it break down. If on a country road, it should break down near a good inn, with a jolly, loquacious landlord ready for pumping, or within easy walking distance of the home of friends, where the driver of the deliberately disabled vehicle wants to do some snooping, at around lunch or dinner time. Lunch is more considerate as it is less formal. It is not a bad idea to understand how a car is put together to know which part, when removed, will stall it.

Following a murder on a train, investigation reveals a plethora of paraphernalia peculiar to the setting, as well as the usual clues. The blood-stained handkerchiefs and knives may be found in a sponge-bag hanging on a locked door between compartments. No worthy Englishwoman goes to sleep without arranging her sponge-bag; it is as imperative as saying one's prayers. Sponge-bags are as properly hung on doorknobs as May baskets to be handy for murderers who mysteriously open the locked door and slip the bloody knife inside. Only the English could call a container for their washing apparatus a sponge-bag. It is clearly a bag of lumpish aspect with drawstrings, fading flowered fabric, and a lining of yellowing rubber. It is never dry, but in a permanent state of fug. A bloody knife won't make it worse.

A murder in almost any location is likely to uncover the tooth-glass with its dregs of sleeping-draught. The tooth-glass is placed on a shelf beneath the mirror and over the washstand. One can, in lieu of sleeping-draughts, drink poison or whisky from it, with somewhat differing results.

Of importance equal to paraphernalia is the murderer's costume. The murderer must be dressed to kill. He should check out his closet and his tailor to be sure he is properly kitted out. Old clothes are best because they blend in better with the scenery, and because they may need getting rid of. A man who sets out to do murder in a jaunty new outfit has only himself to blame. Besides, it is common. If, on the other hand, he chooses loud checks and a cigar, he may find himself the victim instead. Similarly, a too-perfect ensemble is better avoided — shining buttons, yachting cap, that kind of thing. Definitely un-English, therefore

No worthy Englishwoman goes to sleep without arranging her sponge-bag.

unsympathetic. Ease, the ultimate attribute, is better expressed in shabbiness. A murderer may well get away with it if he is properly dressed. He should, however, be sure everything he wears is in good repair. No loose threads left hanging. There is bound to be a thorny rosebush on his path waiting for a strand of tweed to tell it to the police.

One basic is the old raincoat. Apart from being commonplace and disposable, it has pockets. Not for guns alone: that's obvious. Pockets are for gnur. Without a flourishing collection of gnur, where will the police be when they try to analyze the murderer's origins and whereabouts for the last ten years? "Ah, that morsel of yellow dust can only be from a highland estuary of the Upper Ganges!" "He was eating whelks by the London docks just two days ago." "See this fragment of paper? Only used by the War Office to notify heroes that they've received the Victorian Cross." The murderer will, of course, show the same tact in removing the label from his coat as from his victim's.

A cap is handy. It is very easy to fool people by switching caps. They are firmer over steaming cups of tea than false moustaches, and quicker to put on. But if a murderer should decide to wear a cap, he is honorbound to step over to the train station. There is nothing that provides the locals with more innocent entertainment on a dull afternoon than to watch a man in a peaked cap nipping in at one side of a railway carriage and, having climbed out the other side, a few seconds later walking down the platform affecting unconcern and a bowler.

Of course, a murderer must never wear his own shoes. Bigger is better; there's no point being uncomfortable. He'll soon be in a tight-enough squeeze. Also, he can fill the empty space at the toes with weights, for if he doesn't, sure as shooting (or poisoning), his footprints won't sink deep enough for their size, and we know where that leads. Straight to the jailhouse. Plimsolls are worth packing, if only to stuff up the chimney. They needn't even be worn, if the ritual is observed. If they are not

My favorite fiction writers are Victor Hugo, Dostoevsky and O. Henry . . . . Today, the only kind of fiction that I read for pleasure (as distinguished from reading for information) is popular fiction, specifically mystery stories . . . . The incomparably best writer of mysteries is Agatha Christie. She has written dozens of novels, and — with the exception of a few, particularly her last ones — they are brilliantly ingenious, intriguing and suspenseful. My favorites are: Death on the Nile, And Then There Were None, The A.B.C. Murders *and, above all,* The Mysterious Mr. Quin. *(This last is a collection of short stories, and is the best-written of Agatha Christie's books.)*

The Objectivist Calendar, April 1977
AYN RAND

worn, however, they should be smeared with a bit of mud and grass that could grow only in one spot — beneath the victim's window. It is only fair to the police. But as most murders involve a surprising amount of athleticism, it never hurts to have a pair. In fact, a few warm-up exercises won't be amiss. A little light running in the morning or quite late at night not only helps the muscle tone, it helps in establishing alibis. If the murderer can appear at one end of the village five minutes before the murder occurs at the opposite end, a powerful sprint will have stood him in good stead. Or, if he can leap off a train, dash across a meadow, fire a well-aimed shot *en passant*, hop a stile and walk smoothly through the French doors for tea before the train arrives in the village, he is that much ahead.

To put the final touch to a murder, an old suitcase is essential for stuffing things in: the leftover murdering costume, a batch of incriminating papers picked up from the victim's safe, a cachet of jewels to be collected twenty years later from Left Luggage. The suitcase should be cheap and look like everyone else's. Nothing fancy, French, decorated with labels from the Ritz, or otherwise recognizable. It can, naturally, be hurled from a fast-moving train in the midst of a forest, but Left Luggage is better. Then, if the murderer yearns for an evening of nostalgia years later, he can take the ticket, fetch the case out again, and have a round of reminiscences among his souvenirs. He might even have put the flowerpot, slightly used tape measure, or other weapon in there, as well as a flower picked near the scene of the crime.

Success lies in ordinariness. Paraphernalia or costume. "Whoever-would-have-thought" objects, "whoever-would-have-thought" people in the dreariest possible clothes. If a murderer is, as boringly usual, the middle. A murderer should be like everyone else; no one will bother him. The best murderers are the dullest, the sort that have spent a lifetime smouldering in the woodwork. Which also fuels one of murder's stongest motives: the need to do just one thing with panache.

Jeanine Larmoth is the coauthor of Murder on the Menu.

LAUNDERING MONEY
Numbered Accounts and Other Tax Shelters

Stanley H. Brown

MATTHEW SEAMAN

Consider this a cautionary tale for every decent citizen who fantasizes The One Big Caper followed by a life of carefree luxury. I don't know your particular vision of the perfect crime against property but a history professor once planned the theft and disposal of an invaluable ancient coin collection; a machinist used to case the movements of an armored car at a big shopping mall every Christmas season; a social worker dreamed of stamping out urban evil by robbing the take of a big-time heroin dealer. If the score was big enough to markedly change the way they live, they now know that along with whatever guilt and fear goes with their illegal acts, there are new problems to be faced. First, storage; second, using the money without attracting the attention of the authorities, especially the folks at the Internal Revenue Service.

If you figure that all you'd have to do is shove your attaché case full of money under the bed and then reach in every morning for walking-around money, you'd be very wrong. The housekeeper might accidentally find the cache and dip into it as well. So, maybe you decide to clean the house yourself and not let anyone in when you're not there. But you'll bleed a little until you can be sure the satchel is secure.

Safe-deposit boxes run a couple of risks. If you go to the box infrequently, you'll have to carry too much cash around with you. And if you go too often, your attendance record, duly recorded on your file card, may attract attention. Besides, if law enforcement people suspect you of a crime, they can get a court order and have a look.

Put the money in your checking account, and you encounter a different kind of problem. Anytime you show up with more than $10,000 in cash, federal law requires your bank to file a report to the Treasury Department, unless you're in a business where such quantities of cash are normal. But don't think you can avoid that problem simply by depositing a little less, because that will come under the category of an unusual transaction. Your bank may not report you, but a record will wind up somewhere readily accessible to the tax people. Of course, if your loot is relatively small and your dreams of luxury are modest, you probably can risk spending a few thousand a year without attracting any attention. But that's small-time stuff,

The attraction of crime fiction has always been a mystery to me.

JOHN KENNETH GALBRAITH

The cover of an early song sheet which extolled the virtues of "Counterfeit Bill," the operative word being Bill. Research proves women would rather marry men with that name than with any other.

nothing like the fruit of your really big score.

What you're up against is the need to launder your money. Most regular-type people never heard of "laundering" until the aftermath of the Watergate burglary and all those revelations about improper payments by Gulf Oil, 3M, and much of the cream of American corporate enterprise. But don't look to Watergate for instruction in this process.

Strictly speaking, Dahlberg's $25,000 campaign contribution and the money that went from Gulf to Senator Hugh Scott involved the opposite of laundering. In these cases, clean money was dirtied. What they do have in common with traditional laundering is that the origins of the money were concealed in the process. What they also demonstrate is that the President of the United States and the chiefs of some of the best-run enterprises in the world, with access to the finest money handling and accounting services available, got caught.

The lesson here is that if your scheme involves a lot of people, somebody will talk or a record of some part of the transaction will turn up in the wrong hands. The Treasury has made relatively little use of bank reports showing unusually large cash transactions. Nevertheless, banks represent a real danger as corroborating evidence of the existence of untaxed money. In other words, if you mess around with a legitimate bank, you'll leave tracks.

If there is a technical definition of "laundering," it probably goes something like this: the rerouting, or conversion in any way, of hot untaxed money or other assets into untraceable or apparently legitimate cash or assets. Needless to say, there are no textbooks on laundering; nor do bankers, lawyers or others connected with money and its movements want to talk for the record on who does it or how.

What is known about the process comes pretty much from the few instances in which the authorities have managed to get people into court or before congressional committees. A small-time hustler named Jerry Zelmanowitz spent some time a few years ago testifying before a Senate subcommittee on how he turned stolen securities into clean cash for the Mob. Until he came along (he would have us believe), your typical thief would keep the money, jewelry and other disposable assets but throw away whatever securities were stolen. Zelmanowitz says he changed all that by taking the securities to Europe, where he set up accounts in various banks, transferred money around by Telex to establish a pattern of legitimate transactions, then introduced his stolen stocks and

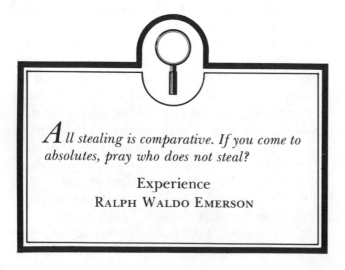

*A*ll stealing is comparative. If you come to absolutes, pray who does not steal?

Experience
RALPH WALDO EMERSON

bonds into the system he had set up. Typically, the stolen paper would be used as collateral for loans, the proceeds of which could then be invested for legitimate purposes. As long as the loans were outstanding, nobody paid any attention to the collateral sitting in the bank vaults. Meanwhile, Zelmanowitz had created a nice pool of usable capital for his clients. They could repay or keep refinancing their debt, or they could even default on the loans and let the bank dispose of the collateral.

The trouble with this method is that some bank clerk might decide to check the numbers on the securities against lists of stolen property. One operative, in what seems to be a kind of underworld banking system, worked out a neat method for getting around that. He found somebody in a bank that held about $10 billion in securities for customers and made him a confederate in exchanging his own hot securities for legitimate ones of the same issue. As long as nobody at the bank checked the serial numbers, there was no problem.

A couple of years ago Chemical Bank in New York discovered its facilities were being used for another kind of laundering. Employees of the bank were routinely changing the small, dirty bills that are the retail currency of the heroin trade. The $1 and $5 bills that come out of your wallet, or some old lady's snatched purse, are cumbersome to deal with. You can't fly down to Mexico with laundry bags full of money to buy more dope. You certainly wouldn't want to walk into a bank in Switzerland with huge loads of street money. It's undignified, and it attracts a lot of attention. So the dealers simply found themselves some bank employees who would exchange the small stuff for $50 and $100 bills. The bank lost nothing in the process, though the employees, against federal regulations in effect since 1974, failed to report the $10,000-plus transactions. What they also neglected was declaring as income the bribes they received from the dealers — about 1 percent of the money they laundered. The U.S. Attorney's office in New York figures that more than $8 million in dirty cash was handled through Chemical Bank.

Any legitimate business that takes in a lot of cash provides a way to clean up dirty money.

The Swiss Credit Bank, Zurich. "Mrs. Helga Hughes" cashed checks here in the amount of $650,000.

One thief used some of his money to buy a diner. He would relieve the cashier, then put some cash in the till and ring up some phony sales. He gradually increased the amount of cash he would process, so as not to attract attention. When he wasn't satisfied with the rate of flow, he bought a second and then a third restaurant. Now he had a business big enough to allow him to travel lavishly on an expense account, ostensibly to scout out locations for other restaurants around the world.

The Internal Revenue Service can be dealt with rather easily. All they want is for you to report your income properly and pay the taxes due the government. Your income is "earned" the moment you complete your crime and take the bonds or coins in hand, not when you get the money from the fence. It's tempting to think of the tax collector as a menacing beast who will be rendered harmless by your paying maybe 60 percent of your loot. But all you can be sure of then is that you won't have federal tax problems. If the revenue people think you got the money by committing a federal offense (you aren't required to state on your return where you get your money), they'll tell the FBI. And if they have reason to believe that you committed a felony under state law, they'll notify state and local authorities. Mostly, they just want their money. But again, by paying up, you attract attention.

There are ways to pay taxes and not attract attention, but you must first put the money somewhere safe while you finish up your laun-

dering. Burying it or banking it has serious drawbacks. Traveler's checks don't. Traveler's checks are secure, easy to buy, to use, and even to recover if lost, stolen or burned. Especially burned.

In any large city in the United States you can buy at least five different kinds of traveler's checks. And within a half-mile of Park Avenue in New York, you can buy them at seventeen different places, then walk over to Fifth Avenue and buy them in another dozen places. The reason you want so many places is that issuing agencies must keep special records on all purchases of checks exceeding $5,000. That means it will take you a couple of days to buy about $150,000 worth of traveler's checks in a way that won't be noticed. If you buy only $1,000 denominations, you'll wind up with a hefty wad; $100 checks will require an attaché case. But your storage problem can be eliminated by one simple act: take your checks home and burn them, then flush the ashes down the toilet. Needless to say, you'll take good care of the receipt showing the numbers on the checks.

What you've done is create disembodied but readily reconstituted cash. If you decide to take off for Abu Dubai, you'll be able to pass through U.S. Customs with no concern about the requirement that you report exports of more than $5,000 in cash — a requirement that in any case has barely been enforced. But it's on the books and you don't want to violate it, because Congress seems on the point of leaning on the Treasury to try harder to close down the laundries. They aren't after you; they're look-

---

LISTENING TO MONEY TALK

The Billion Dollar Sure Thing: Paul E. Erdman
Canceled Accounts: Harris Greene
Going Public: David Westheimer
Not a Penny More, Not a Penny Less: Jeffrey Archer
The Silver Bears: Paul E. Erdman
The Swiss Account: Leslie Waller

SCOTLAND YARD

Among Scotland Yard's trophies are these burglary tools which were left behind after an unsuccessful raid on a bank vault. Paraphernalia included acetylene torches, hack saws, drop cloths and pressure gauges.

ing for all that Mob money we keep hearing about, which, along with petro-dollars, is taking over civilization. But even if they're looking for somebody else's family, they might just stumble into yours.

When you get to where you're going, all you have to do is show up at the appropriate bank and report that your checks have been destroyed. Pretty soon, you'll get replacements that you can spend, or bank, or invest.

The spending is simple. Nobody is looking for you, nobody knows you've done anything wrong. But our tax people have offices over there. Again, they're not out for you; it's the large corporate hustlers they want. Still, they're there, and they might see you throw around more than the average tourist.

You didn't break the law and risk ruin just to blow it all on a big holiday. You want to invest and take your time finding the good life. So you bring your reconstituted traveler's checks to a bank, and despite the recent embarrassment of the Crédit Suisse over the scandal in its branch in Chiasso, Switzerland is still one of the better havens for laundering. The problem here is that the Swiss don't like to be thought of as a haven for laundering dirty money from Third World tyrants and the Mafia, and some of their banks have lately requested that U.S. nationals sign a form releasing the bank from the provisions of the Swiss bank secrecy laws. This enables them to report your activities to U.S. authorities if they're asked. There are, however, plenty of banks in Switzerland that will happily open an account for you when you lay your nest egg on the desk.

Once you have the account, you can instruct the bank to invest or transfer the money. One thing to do with dirty money is to buy Eurobonds. These are bearer securities, so they don't have your name on them. They earn a decent rate of interest. They're safe. And they're easily marketable and redeemable in just about every Western European currency.

But now you've just bought yourself another count of fraud. When you file your tax return, you'll probably answer "no" to the question about whether you have a foreign bank account. A lot of Americans who travel and do business abroad have them for legitimate reasons, so if you've elected to report the income from your caper and pay the taxes up front, you may also want to tell the feds that you have a Swiss account. This may not attract any attention, but it will put your name in a different file and that's not what you need.

Maybe you want the money earning a little interest or dividends. You ought to pay taxes on those earnings at least, because this may simplify your next problem — getting the money back into the States when you're ready to live full-time on your loot. The longer the money sits abroad, the less likely it is to attract attention when it starts coming back into your life.

The Mob (we are led to believe) has all kinds of ways of passing hot cash through otherwise legit enterprises. Any business or profession that routinely takes in a lot of cash offers opportunities for laundering: gambling casinos, restaurants, medical practices — all

have been used effectively.

Even an evangelist was used for a time by a big Midwestern operation. When the tent show hit town, a messenger would arrive with a bag of cash which was dropped into collection boxes as they were passed among the faithful. That money was then counted along with the rest. It got back to its original owners, less a contribution to the greater glory of the Lord, in the form of overpayments for chartered buses, construction of churches and schools, and even legal fees.

Transferring your problem to somebody else can be useful. One thief bought a beach house at a bargain price. What didn't show on anybody's books was that the seller also took a lot of unmentioned cash in payment. The buyer had transferred his problem to the seller.

Every method of laundering has endless variations. Many involve banks and corporate entities in such places as the island of Jersey and the Duchy of Liechtenstein. False but convincing identities abound — so much so that the U.S. Passport Office has been considering the tightening of the passport-issuing process. After all, you have only to get the real birth certificate of someone of your sex and age who is dead. One traveling representative of a crime syndicate had more than twenty U.S. passports that he used as identification for opening foreign bank and securities accounts. He reasoned that since many billions of dollars move by Telex every day through the money markets of the world, no one bank would ever be able to sort out the honest from the crooked money.

Thus money can have a life of its own, irrespective of its origins. The purpose of laundering is to create that new identity. The most important element in the success of such operations seems to be patience. But that is also the trap, because if you've scarred your conscience by committing a heavy crime, you've already lost your patience with the straight and narrow. And once that happens, you're going to leave tracks. And they're going to get you.

Stanley H. Brown's most recent book is the biography of H.L. Hunt.

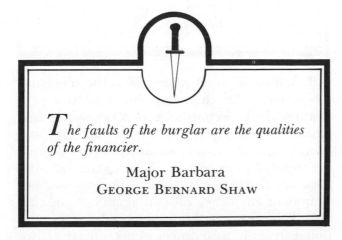

The faults of the burglar are the qualities of the financier.

Major Barbara
GEORGE BERNARD SHAW

SMUGGLING PITFALLS
Letitia Twyffert

Customs agents can spot a chiseler in two seconds flat. What they look for are obvious discrepancies: a seemingly fat person with a thin person's wardrobe; a beehive hairdo on an otherwise chic woman; an adult carrying a stuffed teddy bear; a middle-aged guitar player; perspiration on one's upper lip in the middle of January. Any one of these is apt to get the would-be smuggler a trip to the disrobing room, and if contraband is bared — along with everything else — in will come a medical type, with rubber gloves, who will investigate all of the body's more interesting nooks and crannies.

Intuition is what makes a good customs agent, but unfortunately for the smuggler there are backup systems should the agent's intuition be taking a day off. There is, for example, the Canine Corps: specially trained German shepherds and golden retrievers who sniff up luggage, then yap their muzzles off if they detect marijuana, cocaine, heroin or even plastic explosives. Then there is a little item called the TECS, short for the Treasury Enforcement Communications System — a computer built into the luggage conveyor belt at most major entry points. Your declaration slip is fed into it, and it discreetly signals the agent if you have any sort of record on file with the Department — in which case he whips out his jeweler's loupe to determine if your tiara is Woolworth paste or Harry Winston carbon. Then there are the x-ray machines, the Indian trackers, the frogmen, the closed-circuit TV, the intrusion detector system, the airborne infrared system and the anonymous phone callers. Of course, some informants would

---

SMUGGLER'S SYNDICATE

"A Chemical Detective," the last story in Thomas W. Knox's *The Talking Handkerchief and Other Stories* (1893), concerns a brandy-smuggling ring operating out of the Port of New York.

There's a dead smuggler (and his missing cache of gems) in Erle Stanley Gardner's *Bird in the Hand.*

There's a seafaring smuggler named Captain Gault in a short story collection by William Hope Hodgson called *Captain Gault: Being the Exceedingly Private Log of a Sea-Captain* (1917).

There's Kek Huuygens, indisputably successful smuggler in one novel (*The Hochman Miniatures*) and several short stories by Robert L. Fish.

There's drug smuggling from one end of Spain to the other in Julian Rathbone's *Bloody Marvelous.*

---

rather identify themselves since the Treasury Department has this charming incentive program called "Awards and Compensations" which thrusts up to $50,000 into grasping hands. (Don't worry about the feds having enough bucks to pay up. Next to the IRS, the Customs Department pulls in more money per year than any other federal agency — roughly $5 billion. And it costs them only 3¢ on the dollar to get it. Said one customs official: "If we

An attempt to defraud the Paris custom-house. Modern smugglers hide valuables in their afro hair-dos. A few years back, the bouffant and beehive styles were used with equally unsuccessful results.

sold stock, we'd be a terrific buy; we're a spectacular moneymaking operation. In fact, we do sell stock — U.S. Treasury Bonds.")

Fictional smugglers, say the feds, are either too corny or too eccentric. They'd be caught, zip-zip. Any story in which a smuggler tries to get past customs by means of a false pregnancy, a mislabeled shipping container, a hollowed-out book, a false-bottomed suitcase, a double-diapered baby, a stuffed D cup, a painted-over Rembrandt, a recently implanted back molar inlay, a tricky platform shoe heel or a doll tummied with valuables is a bad account. The customs museum is crammed with just such relics. What's more, the customs people have big mouths; they pass on interesting tidbits such as these to the 135 member nations of the International Customs Council.

And, as they are quick to remind you, don't think for a minute that just because you got past them at the checkpoint, you're home free.

They have five years to catch up with you before the statute of limitations runs out. And that's a long time for thieves *not* to fall out.

Letitia Twyffert once smuggled a box of Oreo cookies into a Weight Watchers meeting.

ITEMS THAT NEVER MADE IT THROUGH CUSTOMS

1. 138 braided dog leashes. Value: $100
2. 420 small bars soap w/ cases bearing legend "Restaurant Laurent, N.Y." Value: $35
3. 2,500 peat pots. Value: $30
4. 822 single rubber disposable gloves. Value: $44
5. 298 basketball nets Value: $220
6. 6 doz. moustache steins. Value: $36
7. 8 sm. boxes Shabbat candles. Value: $16
8. 72 dice sets. Value: $144
9. 65 handsaws. Value: $65
10. 40 lbs. bright common nails. Value: $20
11. 3 pkgs. *Two Gentlemen Sharing*: 9460 ft. comp. pos. 35 mm color safety stock. Good condition English version *Wedding Night*: 9295 ft. comp. pos. 35 mm color safety stock, complete. NO RIGHTS. Value: $1312
12. 2 cans *The Scarecrow in a Garden of Cucumbers*: 7095 ft. 35 mm comp. pos. color safety stock. Good condition English version complete. NO RIGHTS. Value: $497
13. 1 carton 57 paperback books: *The Cooler*. Value: $18

WIRETAPPING
A Session with a Debugger

Thomas Seligson

There are those who say, with the walls so thin, why even bother wiretapping? But they miss the point. Wiretapping to some of us smacks of Bond and brethren. It goes hand-in-cloak-and-dagger with winging to Beirut under an assumed name, putting one's resources for survival regularly to the test, outwitting the Blofelds, vanquishing the Oddjobs and winning the affections of the Pussy Galores. It goes with the .25 Beretta automatics, the Aston-Martins outfitted with oil-slick dispensers. It is part of the standard equipage of the fictional spy. Does a red-blooded American boy deserve less?

Frankly, I've always wanted to plant an ice-cube bug in a Russian general's martini, and I've always wanted to be given the anti-bugging devices that would protect me from his agents doing the same. I've long been riveted to the toys of espionage, and nothing so mundane as thin walls is going to take them away from me.

You needn't even be a bona fide spy to play with these toys anymore. Judging from recent ads in the *Wall Street Journal* and the Sunday *Times* ("Is your phone tapped? We can check it out for you!"), bugging — both in and out of government — is now widespread. Husbands bug wives; corporations bug competitors; presidents bug themselves. It's getting so poor Harry Palmer's going to have to stand on line to get his bugs. Seems the whole world is as enamored of this spy stuff as I am.

In the guise of a Mafia racketeer feeling the heat, I got one of these "bug" companies on the phone. They invited me over to visit and carefully staying within the law said they were not buggers but, in fact, debuggers. The difference is more semantic than practical.

A vice-president escorted me down the hall to his plush corner office. A compact, bearded man, he lived up to my expectations: strong, angular face; dark, deep-set eyes; a long scar on his cheek that looked like it was left by a knife. I would not have wanted to run into him in a back alley of Prague.

There was a large television console beside his desk. Six separate screens with six separate views of the premises.

"That's so I can see who's out front. Saw you on the way in. You don't realize it, but you're being photographed right this second. Tape-recorded as well. I like to keep a record of everyone who comes to see me."

Not an unimpressive opener, I thought, a bit unnerved at the idea of a hidden camera pointed in my direction and a microphone concealed a few inches from my nose. Perhaps more understandable in the Pentagon than in a private company, but certainly amenable to my fantasies.

Then the V.P. explained his company.

"The average businessman doesn't give a damn that the U.S. Embassy is threatened by the Russians. He doesn't care about lasers. He's concerned about his competition, that's all. Sixty percent of our clients are businessmen trying to keep the competition from snooping

Contrary to appearances, this wiretapper is not bugging the wall. He is merely holding up the device he used to intercept a telephone call. The conversation was recorded and used in court, to the detriment of the caller.

at their marketing reports. We get a lot of advertising companies, shipping lines, fashion companies."

So much for my double agents and racketeers. But maybe he himself was a reformed agent? (I have intractable fantasies. They die a slow, malingering death.)

The V.P. leaned back, lit up a pipe and looked for all the world like "M" grown old and crusty. But it turned out his background was engineering and his specialty in school was the design of surveillance equipment. Much too straightforward to be a cover story. He even hinted that he had indeed once worked as a professional bugger and wiretapper. More confessions were halted when his secretary's phone rang and he pressed a button which let him listen in. Now he reminded me of Gene Hackman in *The Conversation* — a security specialist so obsessed by his work that he no longer had even the slightest regard for privacy. I began to get a little uneasy.

"At one time we bugged and we debugged," he said, "but the Crime Control Act of 1968 made electronic eavesdropping by private individuals illegal. At the same time it also made it easier for the police to do legal eavesdropping under certain conditions."

"I imagine the bill must have hurt your business," I said, figuring it probably affected buggers the way détente hurt spies.

My V.P. smiled. "Not exactly. Sixty-eight turned out to be an interesting year. Prior to June 18 everybody who manufactured and sold bugging equipment did so openly. You knew who they were. Once the law came in, all open operations ceased. The major electronics manufacturers — Lafayette Radio, Radio Shack, Allied Radio — knew there was still a market, but it had to be approached differently. So they put out the same kinds of equipment and called them 'baby-sitters' and 'wireless intercom' and 'telephone monitor' and even 'fun toy.' Anything but 'bugging equipment.'

"So you see we had the demise of an official bugging business and the birth of the electronic toy business. And now, since they were produced by large chains, the 'toys' sold for much less than before. Telephone bugging devices used to be in the three-hundred-dollar range. After 1968, Lafayette Radio came out with a 'telephone monitor' for about fifteen dol-

The Spectrum Analyzer. It locates bugs, permits operator to tune in to any RF signal, has a resolution of 3,000 to 30,000 cycles. It is advertised as foolproof and fail-safe.

lars. Consequently, although the purpose of the law was to restrict illegal bugging, its ultimate effect was to make the equipment more readily available to the man in the street.

"Hell, at fifteen dollars a throw, if I want to know what's going on in your office, I can afford to plant a whole line of bugs there. I can even afford to put one where you'll be sure to find it. Once you see that one, you'll think that's all there is and speak freely everywhere but in front of it. So one of my other bugs is bound to pick you up."

The V.P. said the most common way to get hold of bugging equipment was to contact a private investigator. A survey done in the D.C. area showed that twenty-five out of thirty P.I.'s, when called, offered products for bugging. They got their equipment from the electronic stores.

Businessmen. Corporations. Company distributorships. Lafayette Radio. The real world of eavesdropping was hardly turning out to be exotic. In fact, my V.P. made snooping so commonplace, he was taking all the fun out of

it. But what about a bug? That still had a nice sinister aura to it.

Until my V.P. got hold of it. He led me into a large room filled with more machinery than IBM and Xerox make. He pointed at what looked like a combined oscilloscope and FM receiver. Turned out to be a Spectrum Analyzer, a highly sensitive receiver that picks up all the electronic signals in a room — including FM bands and TV stations. When a radio in the room is turned on, it produces squealing noises in the transmitter receiver because of feedback, and one can home in on the location of the bug by then walking around the room with the antenna. The closer one gets, the louder the squeal.

Sometimes, instead of a radio, one can use a small tape recorder with a whistle recorded on it. If the whistle gets picked up, that means someone is transmitting in the room. The transmitters were more my style than the Analyzer. They could be concealed in a desk stapler, pens, lighters, rugs, windows and air vents. I just couldn't see Bond checking into a Teheran hotel with the Analyzer. He probably couldn't even lift it.

The V.P. then got down to the case of taps on the telephone line. "There are thirty differ-

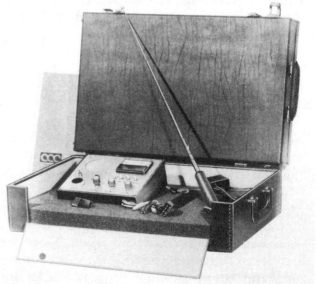

The Telephone "Bug" Detector. It uncovers such eavesdropping devices as: series-type tape recorder starters; parallel-type tape recorder starters; series transmitters; parallel transmitters; audio frequency triggered switches (Infinity transmitters and Harmonica bugs); hot-wired microphones; resistance or capacitance defeated switch hooks; resonant telephone ringers (bells).

ent ways that can be employed to tap a telephone," he said. His all-purpose detector was built into an attaché case. It was not hard, squinting a little, to imagine it being used against Hugo Drax. It not only found the tap but told you the distance from the phone to the tap itself. For example, it could give a reading that showed a tap fifty feet away on the line. Since telephone wires circle around, that could mean the tap was only a few feet away from the phone.

Still thinking of enemy agent type clients, I asked what would happen if a client's phone turned out to have been tapped by the good guys, namely, the cops.

"If the tap is out on the open line," said my V.P., "then whoever put it there — including the police — is violating the law. If a law enforcement agency wants to tap you, they have to do it by legal process, involving a court order from a judge. The order entitles them to go to the telephone company and have your line piped into their office, where it will be hooked up to a recording device. That, by the way, our equipment won't detect. It's put in behind the walls of the phone company's central office, and we can't penetrate it."

If my V.P. and his chums found a tap on a line, they either removed it or suggested a way for the client to make it backfire. This they did with a little gizmo called a wiretap defeat system. If someone is listening on your phone, its light goes on and its needle jumps like crazy. Now that you're on red alert, so to speak, you're in control. You can throw a switch, keep talking, but convey only false information; then

---

PSSST

If you wish to have a private conversation but suspect someone is eavesdropping through the wall, an ex-spy suggests you redecorate. Cover the walls, ceiling and floor with chicken wire. The chicken wire plays hell with sound waves and distorts any conversation. If you are concerned with aesthetics, you could plaster over the chicken wire.

---

you release a switch and it fades out your unwanted listener. At which point, since he suddenly, magically, can't hear you, you give your secret information. Your bugger doesn't know why he can't hear you; he just can't.

The V.P. next proceeded to show me, in no particular order, a telephone decoder, a bomb decoder and a bug alert that could be carried in one's pocket like a package of cigarettes. Here at last was something I could definitely identify with. It seemed tailor-made for Bond's three-piece suit. Fact and fiction were finally coming together.

COMMUNICATION CONTROL SYSTEMS INC.

The Room Sweeper. It emits an ungodly bleep when in the presence of a room bug. The little gizmo on the top also turns bright red (as well it should at some of the language it hears).

By now, however, I was numbed by sheer bulk of equipment. And talk of impedance tests, capacitance switch hooks and integrated circuits went clear over my head. My V.P.'s cool, scientific detachment, not to mention expertise, was also working quicker than knockout drops. I had thought it might be fun to play with spy tools. But seeing them in handsome walnut cases, with two-year warranties, and picturing housewives and advertising executives queuing up for them, took away their romance.

I left not much wiser in wiretapping and thankful for thin walls.

Thomas Seligson was the entertainment editor for Mystery Monthly *magazine.*

THE RULES OF POISON PENMANSHIP

The Stationery

Do not use monogrammed notepaper.
Burn all first drafts.
Use plain, white, #10 legal envelopes — they come in packets of 20 so you can include an extra one for the money, if you like.
Never fold a ransom note — an important word can get lost in the crease.
Unlined paper looks more professional.
Best choice: Eaton's Corrasable Typewriter paper — it's very hard to trace, but more important, is easy to erase, should you decide at the last minute to up the ransom price.
Whatever you do, do *not* keep a carbon.

Hand-Lettering

Follow the Palmer method, exactly.
Or, use one of those alphabet stencils, filling in the appropriate letters.

Note left by The Bat in Mary Roberts Rinehart's book The Bat.

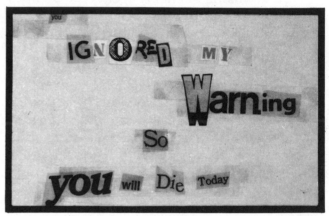

Letter to a bride in Ellery Queen's Eve of the Wedding.

Misspell at least one word per ransom note — somehow, that always looks more threatening, which in this case is good.
Always write in purple ink, if you use a fountain pen.
Resist the urge to dot your *i* triangularly, double-cross your t-bar, or decorate the border with graffiti.
Actually, the most handsome blackmail notes are done with a Crayola.
Death should always be spelled in red, money in green.

Cutting Out Letters

Take your time.
Invest in a good pair of scissors, a giant-size jar of library paste (no Scotch tape, please!), a tweezer to hold the cutouts.
Clip letters from widely read magazines and newspapers, such as *TV Guide* and *The National Enquirer*.
Never clip out letters from such esoterica as the *Merck Manual* or *Gray's Anatomy*. (Nobody likes a wise guy.)

In gluing the letters, make sure you do not include any lint from the rug, cigar ash or cat hairs.

When you're done clipping the magazines, return them to the dentist's office.

Delivery

Never trust the U.S. Mail: hand-deliver. (Doors were created to insinuate things under and egg cups were made to prop up messages.)

Best not to be around when the letter is discovered: You may be an excellent poison-penner but a lousy actor.

The Message

Pretend it's Western Union and you have a ten-word limit.

Be direct — this is no time for subtlety.

Always demand the ransom in U.S. currency.

Like the *Times*, write so anyone with an eighth-grade education can understand you.

Always sign your message with a bloody fingerprint — not yours, however, your victim's.

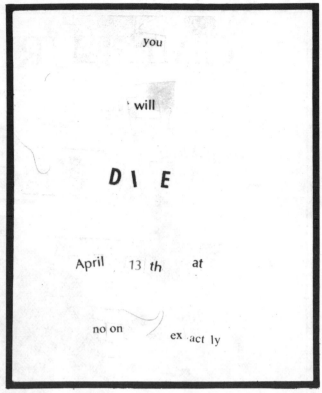

Message received, none too happily, in C. Daly King's Obelists Fly High.

Nutnb. 11794.

The London Gazette.

From **Tuesday** August 5, to **Saturday** August 9, 1777.

St. James's, August 5, 1776.

Whereas it has been humbly represented to the King, That an anonymous Threatening Letter was received from the General Post-Office at Bristol, on Thursday the 24th Day of April last past, by Mr. John Barrett, Collector of Excise there, of which the following is a Copy:

Sir,
You may tell Lilytrap Lovelas Martin and Unferies that if they have a mind to save their Lives they do remove from Bristol for Dam me if we dont put an end to them Umferies and Maish narrowly miss it other Day

And Elton and Barry and you had best alter your Proceedings in incouraging those Villains otherwise your Houses will be made a Dunghil of and your Carcises sent to the Devil for a Firebrand advise Elton and Barry to fine no more Warrants, for we are 50 of us ready to put this our Define in Execution.

Kingswood
April 1776

to stand the Pillory.

AVERAGE PRICES of CORN,
From July 28, to August 2, 1777.
By the Standard WINCHESTER Bushel of Eight Gallons.

	Wheat.		Rye.		Barley.		Oats.		Beans.	
	s.	d.	s.	d.	s.	d.	s.	d.	s.	d.
London,	5	4	3	0	2	4	2	0	3	4
COUNTIES INLAND.										
Middlesex,	6	4			2	5	2	2	3	5
Surry,	6	0					2	4	4	8
Hertford,	6	4			3	4	2	2	3	5
Bedford,	6	11	3	2			1	10	3	9
Cambridge,	5	11	3	2	2	10	1	11	3	4
Huntingdon,	6	3			3	0	2	4	3	10
Northampton,	6	3			3	10	2	2		
Rutland,	6	7			3	10			4	3
Leicester,	6	8	3	6	2	11	2	6	4	4
Nottingham,	6	8	4	0	3	3	2	11	4	7
Derby,	6	9					2	6	4	9
Stafford,	6	4	4	5	2	9	2	2	4	2
Salop,	6	4	4	4	2	9	2	5		
Hereford,	6	9					2	10	4	1
Worcester,	6	5	3	0			2	9	3	11
Warwick,	6	6			2	9	2	4	3	9
Gloucester,	6	10					3	2	3	9
Wilts,	6	1			2	5	2	3	3	4

CAT BURGLAR'S KIT

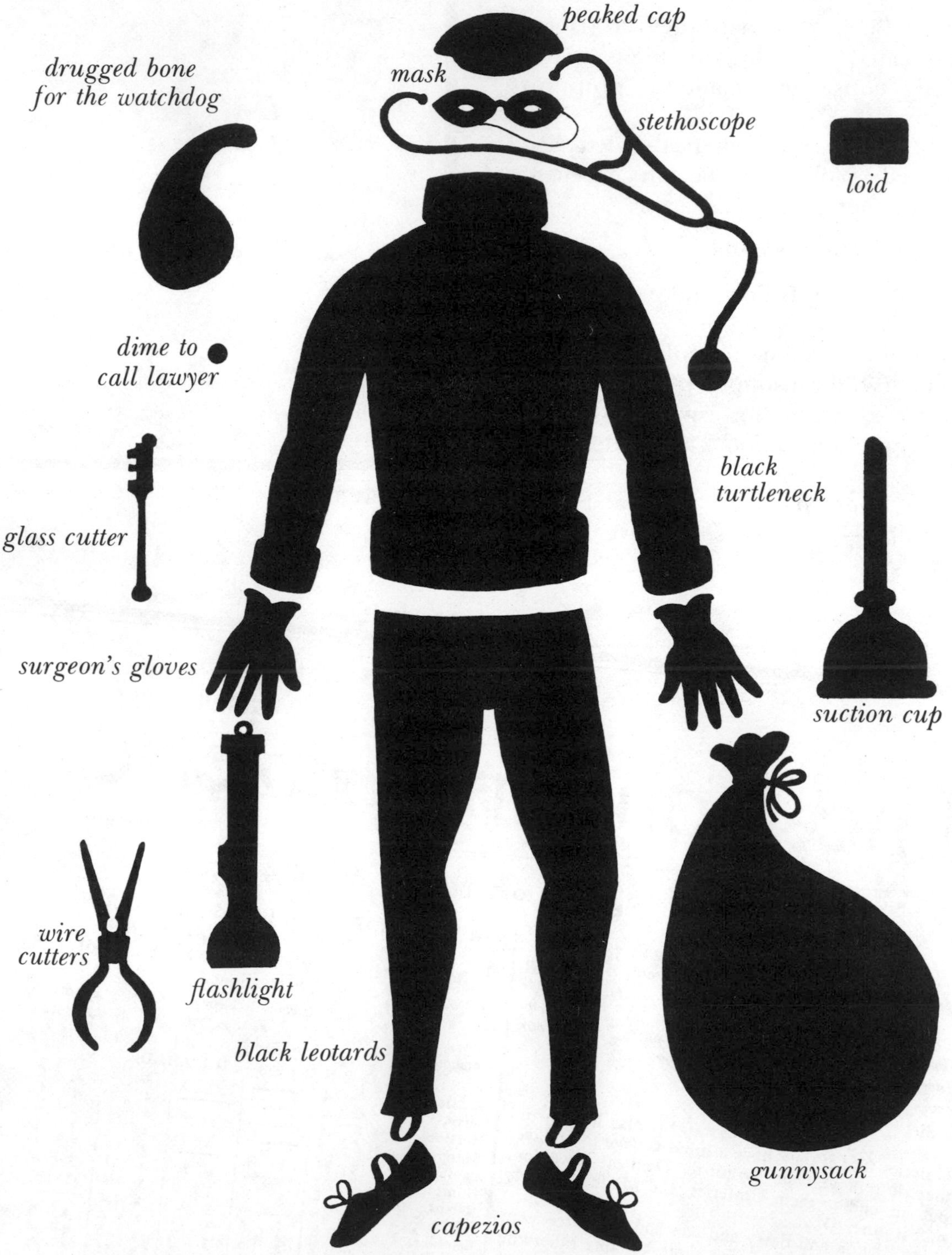

peaked cap
mask
drugged bone
for the watchdog
stethoscope
loid
dime to
call lawyer
black
turtleneck
glass cutter
surgeon's gloves
suction cup
wire
cutters
flashlight
black leotards
gunnysack
capezios

MARTY NORMAN

THE GETAWAY CAR
Step on the Pedal and Go

Warren Weith

Ralph Nader, the man who tried to convince us that the motorcar was the villain, had it all wrong. The automobile may turn people into villains, and it may attract villains, but alone and unattended it's just a collection of bits and pieces waiting to be thrust into furious action by a fool, knave or — if you will — villain.

There's no doubt in which category to place the author of this brief note to Henry Ford:

Hello Old Pal:
Arrived here at 10 A.M. today. Would like to drop in and see you. You have a wonderful car. Been driving it for three weeks. It's a treat to drive one.
Your slogan should be: Drive a Ford and watch the other cars fall behind you. I can make any other car take a Ford's dust.

Bye-bye
John Dillinger

John Dillinger's use of the car as a tool to help him make quick withdrawals from various banks has become part of our folklore. Little known is how Dillinger learned the art of the fast remove. The technique was the brainchild of an ex-Prussian army officer named Herman K. Lamm.

Herr Lamm was caught cheating at cards and drummed out of the regiment shortly before World War I. Thereafter, he drifted to Utah and thence — there being no military defense establishment in those days to offer gainful employment to former army officers — into the life of a holdup man. This path in turn led, in 1917, to Utah State Prison. For Lamm, as for most criminals, a year in the can afforded time to reflect and to refine his technique. When he got out, he had developed a system for removing the uncertainties from bank robbing. It was a three-step plan. Only step three, detailing the getaway, is of interest here. The first requirement for the getaway was a car. Not just any car, but one that had to satisfy two contradictory rules: it had to be high-powered, yet nondescript to the point of disappearing into the cityscape. Next came the driver: best of all was a racing driver who had fallen from grace; at the very least, an ex-truck hijacker would do. Never just someone who was a "good" driver. Pasted up on the headliner over the windshield was a chart of the getaway route. This was more than a map because it indicated turns in miles that had been registered beforehand on the car's odometer and clocked, down to the second, by the driver under different weather conditions. It was a good plan and it worked for almost thirteen years.

It stopped working on December 16, 1930 in Clinton, Indiana. Lamm and three friends were calmly walking out of the Citizens State Bank in that town with $15,567 in a paper shopping bag and several typewriter covers when they were approached by the local barber. He had a suspicious look on his face and was carrying an Ithaca pump gun. Across the street, the getaway driver didn't like the way

COURTESY FBI

The getaway car that didn't get away — due to the driver's sudden illness, which was caused by a barrage of bullets through the windshield.

things were shaping up and tried to help out by making a screeching U-turn in order to bring the Buick closer to the four gentlemen who needed to get away and, at the same time, put it between them and the suspicious barber. All of this would have been very smooth except that the driver, an ex-rumrunner possibly more adept with speedy boats than speedy cars, let things get out of hand and slammed the Buick into the curb with such force that it blew a tire. The five bank robbers limped away in the Buick with double-O buckshot clanking around their ears. Then came the next bad move. Instead of stopping and changing the tire on the car with proven getaway potential, they elected to steal the next machine that hove into view. At this point, the Fates didn't smile — they laughed like hell. The next parked car they saw became, in about five seconds flat, the getaway car. But what they didn't know going in, and learned

during the first mile, was that it was a car equipped with a governor by its owner to prevent his elderly father from speeding. Its top speed was 35 miles an hour. Just fast enough to get the fearless five a bit further out of town and within robbing range of a truck. This worthy vehicle was a bit faster but proved to have very little water in its radiator. It did serve to get them over the state line into Illinois — and into another car. This equipage had one little flaw. There was only one gallon of gas in the tank.

And there it all ended, under the blazing guns of a 200-man posse. Lamm and the driver were killed, and one member of the little band committed suicide. The other two were captured and sent to Michigan City Prison for life. There they taught a young con named John Dillinger all they knew about this almost trouble-free system of robbing banks. Herman

K. Lamm, the master of the fast getaway, is little known among people who use withdrawal slips but nonetheless lives on in our speech. Think of him the next time you hear a TV bad guy growl, "I'm gonna take it on the lam."

John Dillinger, like any good apprentice, added a few personal touches to the master's blueprint. On leaving a bank, he would drape a frieze of hostages along the running boards to silence the guns of any law officers who might be on the scene. While a neat touch, this did have a few drawbacks. A 1930's Terraplane or Essex really wasn't able to cope with four or five bandits and upwards of six hostages. Thus a getaway, which should be performed to a disco beat, turned into a slow waltz out of town. The forces of law and order soon got wise. They would follow at a discreet distance, knowing that sooner or later Bad John would have to drop the hostages off on some country road. At that point, the real getaway and chase would begin. But then another Dillinger touch would come into play — large-headed roofing nails liberally spread in the road. Simple, but effective. What made all this work, though, was the fact that most local law enforcement agencies were woefully ill-equipped. Many of them required that individual officers provide their own transportation. What a $5,000-a-year sheriff could afford to drive was simply no match for the wheels a successful team of bank robbers could — and did — buy.

At about the same time, the French police had somewhat the same problem, although theirs was one particular car rather than a variety. It was the first front-wheel-drive Citroën introduced in the middle Thirties. So much quicker and more agile than anything the flics drove, it made a joke of pursuit. Once out of the bank and into the Citroën, French freebooters couldn't have been any safer if they'd been in their mother's arms. Finally, it got so bad, the Paris newspapers began calling them the front-wheel-drive gangsters. The French, being a logical race, solved their problem quickly by issuing even faster Citroëns to the good guys. (An attempt at a cure for the fast-getaway bandit in this country consisted of FBI men in twelve-cylinder Lincolns.)

Gaelic bank robbers lean toward a shy de-

NOW YOU SEE IT, NOW YOU DON'T

Changing the appearance of a car is a problem that's never really been solved. Anything that can be done quickly — water paint, as used on a bus in a recent movie — only makes the vehicle look unusual, which is not the desired effect. A regular paint job could take more than an hour, and then up to a week to dry really hard. Much easier to just switch to another, "clean" car. The difficulty here is in making the "hot" car disappear completely, because once it turns up, the other car is no longer "clean." Making a car disappear quickly is not as simple as it sounds. Those giant car-crushing machines — like the type that rumor says made Jimmy Hoffa disappear — would be a good bet. Trouble is, there aren't many of them in the country. It is interesting, though, that most of them seem to be owned by gentlemen with Latin-sounding names.

W.W.

parture in a beat-up panel truck — preferably from the mouth of a tunnel that surfaces blocks away from the bank. Here the hot-shoe artist is still with us, though his technique leaves a lot to be desired. An example from a few years ago will serve to illustrate. Admittedly, it was a rather complicated jewel robbery in which a double handful of gems had been stolen and then hidden on the site. The getaway would take place after the swag had been literally crowbarred from its hiding place. The car would be stolen and driven to the scene by one of the break-in team. There he was to change places with the actual driver. All of this took place smoothly enough on the appointed day.

FITTING THE CAR TO THE CRIME

Harrods Heist

Take, for example, a rather exotic job in London. You and your mates have evolved a beautifully orchestrated job of waltzing a whole rack of furs through Harrods Department Store, past all the customers and in the general direction of the back door. Somewhere during this journey the furs are stuffed into a wheeled dustbin. The dustbin is then rolled out onto the sidewalk. No sooner does it hit the sidewalk than a small Bedford dump truck pulls up alongside. The dustbin is almost filled with bits of wire lathe, plasterboard, all the things one usually equates with department store remodeling. Up it goes, down it goes — empty — and off goes the little Bedford . . . and Bob's your uncle. Sound farfetched? Well, the same job, move for move, was pulled in a big department store on New York's Fifth Avenue not many years ago. But notice the getaway vehicle. Work-stained, dented, it fit the part like Sir Laurence once fit Hamlet.

Cartier's Caper

A beautifully groomed matron had an even simpler approach. This consummate actress strolled into Cartier's and asked — in the best Larchmont lockjaw — to see some diamond rings. For an hour she fussed over her decision, or, as it turned out, set the scene. Her choice finally narrowed down to two. The lady then asked if she could see them in the daylight. It being Cartier's, the clerk said, "Of course." The lady was last seen entering a waiting Checker cab. Neat, but not gaudy.

Ponte Vecchio Purge

Gaudy, but equally effective, was the big jewel robbery in Florence. The goldsmiths and jewelers, at least the ones worth robbing, are all on the Ponte Vecchio. One bright Saturday two young gentlemen roared onto the bridge astride an MV Augusta racing motorcycle. The lad on the back got off, strolled into the nearest shop, reached over the counter and calmly scooped up over $80,000 worth of baubles. He then strolled outside and got back on the bike. The daring duo then took off and with a wave to the tourists quit the bridge for parts unknown. The lovely part about all this is the choice of getaway vehicle. Only an Italian would choose a racing motorcycle with open exhausts for such a job. I think the point here is that most of the population were on their side during the escape because of the Italian love for anything fast and loud. Proof of this can be found in the nickname the newspapers gave them: the Con Brio Bandits.

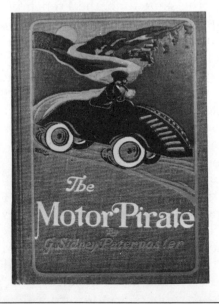

The Motor Pirate
By G. Sidney Paternoster

W.W.

Out ran the jolly swagmen, followed by various and sundry guards and office help. They jumped into the car screaming for the driver to take off. His first attempt ended with a stalled engine. So did his second and third. It was a manual-shift car, and he could only drive an automatic. This farsighted group are still, in 1977, guests of the state. Of course, they were not professionals at the time, but no doubt they will be when they hit the streets.

A nice clean getaway is the mark of a professional, and a professional keeps in tune with the times. In most of the recent successful heists in urban centers, he's used public transport. Under the circumstances, it's quicker and safer than a car. In suburbia the trend seems to be toward a two-year-old, well-dented Ford station wagon with a woman driver. They disappear before they even leave the parking lot. The CB radio, helicopter, and a lack of style on the part of perpetrators have rung down the curtain on the classic car chase. What's left is fiction — the fiction of the shimmering tube or the twenty-fifth pocketbook reprint of an ageless mystery story.

Most people think James Bond was the first man of action to have a car as his co-hero. Not so. Strictly speaking, it was Tom Swift in a slim little volume entitled *Tom Swift and His Electric Runabout*. But if we're talking about a car powered by an internal combustion engine, then Simon Templar, alias The Saint, is a likely candidate. His Hirondel — a make beautifully built only in author Leslie Charteris' imagination — was a magnificent motorcar of staggering performance. Its makers modestly alluded to it as the king of the road, and in Charteris' England of the 1930's that's just what it was. This is what its creator had to say about it as it bore The Saint to a lonely country house in which his fiancée, Patricia Holm, was being held prisoner:

> *If this had been a superstitious age, those who saw it would have crossed themselves and sworn that it was no car at all they saw that night, but a snarling silver fiend that roared through London on the wings of an unearthly wind.*

Makes Mr. Bond's Aston sound like a rental from Hertz.

James Bond was first in one respect, though. He was the first hero driver to have a car equipped with gadgets whose sole function was to kill people. I'm thinking specifically of the twin forward-firing machine guns, hub-mounted scythes, and passenger ejection seat that turned his beautiful silver-gray DB 5 Aston-Martin into a death machine. Needless to say, all were used to great gory effect in one of the first James Bond pictures.

A more skillful approach to the same end, and interestingly enough more exciting, was that taken by the detective character played by Steve McQueen in *Bullet*. He simply outdrove the villains and in the process forced them into a long sweeping bend at an insane rate of speed. The end result was both fatal and suitably spectacular, in a wide-screen sense. *Bullet* was the start of yet another trend — the use of a car that didn't really look the part. McQueen's Mustang, while it was a Mach I fastback, was also hubcapless with a dull black paint job that looked like it had been applied with a whisk broom. It was, in effect, the automotive counterpart of the hero. No glitter, but all guts. The end of this trend was in sight when Peter Falk's Columbo drove into view in a Peugeot 403 convertible so spavined, it had trouble making it across the small expanse of a TV screen. Popeye Doyle — alias Gene Hackman — put the capper on it in *The French Connection* when he completely destroyed a departmental vehicle while chasing a dope pusher. To understand the point being made in this film you would have to have some knowledge of the type of car New York City detectives work in. They don't just work in the car, they live in it, for days at a time. As one member of the force so neatly put it, "They all smell like they'd been used to haul the horse cops to a riot, and they all have the optional dirt floor." And that was the kind of car Popeye Doyle drove, right down to the flurry of empty coffee containers — a long way from The Saint's immaculate Hirondel bellowing through London's fashionable West End en route to rescuing a fair damsel held prisoner in an even more fashionable country house in Surrey. Sadder still, The Saint is reduced to a mere Volvo P 1800 for his rescue missions on TV. So much for a producer who doesn't have the class to commission the construction of at

LICENSE PLATES

Changing license plates inflight, as it were, has always been a subject dear to the hearts of that segment of the motoring public pictured most frequently on post office walls. One ploy that went to the bank once too often was the mud-daubed plate used by a splinter group from the Detroit Purple Gang. Like all good tricks it was simple and depended for its effect on the perverseness of human nature. Going to the bank, the plates on the getaway car were streaked with mud. At the first chance, after the job, the plates were wiped clean. Dumb as it may sound, human nature did the rest. If you're looking for a car with license plate MUD, it just can't be one with license plate KG 7459 — or whatever was under the mud. Simple-minded? No, just simple.

Equally simple, and even more effective, were three or four plates stacked together and wired on. It was only the work of a minute or so to stop, take off the top plate and expose the one underneath. Remembering, of course, not to leave the discarded plate face up in the road. But then again, if a bank robber remembered everything he'd probably wind up a banker.

W.W.

JUDITH WRIGHT

least one magnificent Hirondel.

Where the getaway car is today — in fact or fiction — would be hard to say. But consider this: A national religious organization holds week-long meetings of the faithful in big sports stadiums around the country. Its supporters are not wealthy people and the contributions are in nickels, dimes and crumpled dollar bills. Almost a million dollars' worth of nickels, dimes and crumpled dollar bills. To haul the take to the banks without giving the bad guys — or the faithful — an idea of its size was a problem that was solved very neatly by the elders with a fleet of Cadillac limousines. Very special limousines. Ones with false bottoms. The coinage, hot from the hands of the frenzied believers, is bagged and thrown into the double bottoms and whisked off to a local bank. All day long the PA system pans the mother lode while the Caddies make spring-bending shuttle runs to the vaults. They're getaway cars, jet-age style — to the banks instead of away from them. So far, no free-lancers have tried to derail this silver rush express, but if they do, it might make the *Guinness Book of World Records* as the first getaway car hijacking. Then too, if a rival religion does the job, it could be the start of a religious war and the raw material for yet another disaster movie.

No, Ralph Nader was wrong. The car is not a villain. The only automobile that ever came near to being a murderer was a Type 57 Bugatti. Being a French car, it was only natural that it was a crime of passion. The story in a few words: A young French girl was madly in love with a local layabout who was really in love with a Type 57, which he couldn't come close to affording. The girl's father had a mattress stuffed with money. She killed her father, took the money and bought her lover his love — the Bugatti. He and his love took off in a screech of tires for the South of France. She was left at the curb to stand trial for her crime. It being the middle Thirties, and France, the duped young lady served only one year of a two-year sentence. He killed himself in his Type 57. End of story.

Warren Weith is an editor of Car and Driver *magazine. He drives a '59 Alfa sedan.*

THE DIP
A Dance in 4/4 Time

Choreographer Solomon Hastings was jostled so hard on the dance floor, his wallet fell out of his pocket. Thus inspired, he created the newest dance craze — The Dip — which is part Hustle and part Outright Thievery. He is currently planning a new step called The Stake-Out, in which The Dip is escorted off the floor, directly to jail.

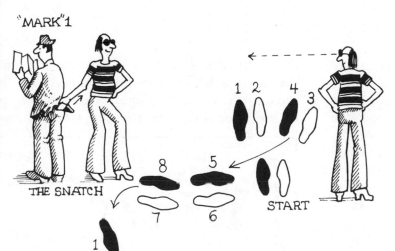

"MARK" 1

THE SNATCH

START

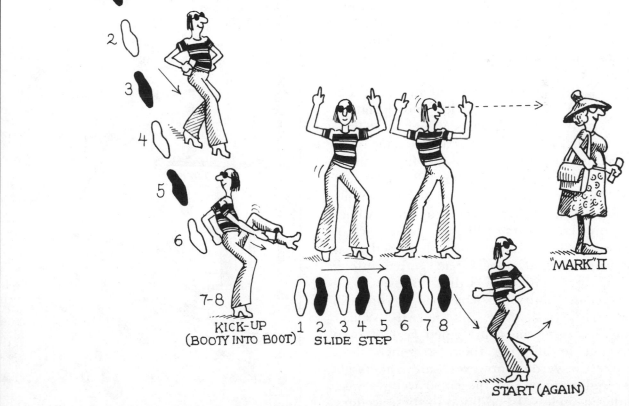

KICK-UP
(BOOTY INTO BOOT)

SLIDE STEP

"MARK" II

START (AGAIN)

DIFFICULTIES OF THE SAFE-CRACKER

R.J. Pilgrim

In many of the mediaeval cathedrals of Europe, in museums, in stately homes and the like, can be found massive wooden chests, hundreds of years old, elaborately carved and with locking mechanisms which appear complex.

These were the safes of their day, made with the best materials and tools available.

It is difficult, therefore, to know where to begin when talking of the history of safes. While we now tend to think of them as massive steel boxes, no doubt the wealthy mediaeval merchant thought of his box as his safe and was quite happy with the protection it provided.

The first patent for a safe, as the term is understood today, was taken out in 1801 by one Richard Scott. This was followed by William Marr in 1834, Charles Chubb in 1835, Edward Tann in 1835, Charles and Jeremiah Chubb in 1839 and Thomas Milner in 1840.

Initially, safes were promoted as a means of protecting one's property against fire damage. This all changed with the Cornhill Robbery of 1865. Walker, who had a shop at 63 Cornhill, London, brought an action against Milner and Son, the makers of his safe, for breach of warranty, since Milner's had described it as "thief-proof" and thieves had gotten into it with wedges. The thieves did, however, have twenty-four hours in which to accomplish their nasty task and this led to Walker losing his case: the court ruled *he* had been negligent in allowing them so much time. Despite the verdict, however, safe makers got busy redesigning and the small wedges were rendered useless. In addition to these wedges, nineteenth-century rogues tried attacks by gunpowder, blow-lamps, diamond drills and

acids. By the end of the century the main threats to safes came from explosives (at first nitroglycerine, then gelignite) and the oxygen cutter. Special devices and alloys were created

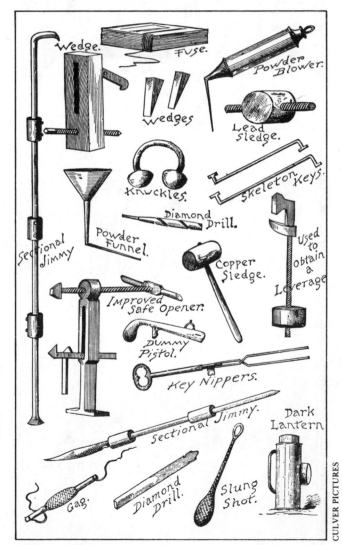

A bank burglar's outfit (excluding sack to carry away the money).

CULVER PICTURES

Gentleman: Having a very obstreperous wife, I require an Iron Safe to keep her in. Please will you forward a price for same. Professor De Crabbs. (Letter sent to Chubb.) There is no record of their reply to the beleaguered De Crabbs.

weighs the chance of success.

Of the weapons used in the battle, the thermic lance is one which illustrates this point most readily. The lance is a heat cutting weapon, used extensively in its early days for the destruction of the massive concrete fortifications of the European coast in World War II. It generates a temperature higher than the melting point of most common materials, so on the face of it there would seem to be no effective counter to its use as a safe-breaking weapon. Yet in the thirty years or so since its development, it has been used relatively little and with only mixed success. The reason is that the sheer bulk of contemporary safes forces the thief to bring to the scene of the attack literally tons of oxygen bottles and steel lances, and the cutting process generates so much heat and smoke that it is virtually impossible to operate clandestinely; ergo, the risk of arrest is high. The logistic difficulties have obviously been enough to dissuade the thief from more extensive use of the thermic lance as a weapon. Yet it will demolish any safe. In the abstract.

There are, of course, some forms of attack which do not present a thief with all these problems, but before discussing these it is useful to look at how a safe is constructed.

The body and door are made as a kind of sandwich, with outer and inner layers of steel enclosing a thick mass which forms the main barrier against the thief. (What the barrier is made of determines the quality, and the price, of the safe.) Good-quality concrete is a barrier possibility, as is a material such as copper, which has high thermal conductivity. The problem arises in that no one barrier is impervious to all attacks.

to counteract them, so the difficulties of the safe-cracker increased as he penetrated inward. Crane hinges, for one, prevented nitro from being inserted round the edges of safe doors.

With the arrival of oxyacetylene welding, around 1900, it was possible to construct stronger safes. Of course, the techniques and the tools available for legitimate industry very soon came into the hands of the thief. What is useful in making a safe can also be useful in destroying it. The romantic conception of the master cracksman pitting his wits against a wily safe becomes a much more prosaic affair of one engineer trying to destroy the work of another, and the battle becomes a matter of the safe maker forcing the safe breaker to make so much noise, use so much material and take so long in his attacks, the risk of arrest far out-

CHAMPION CRACKSMEN

Blackshirt: Bruce Graeme
Boston Blackie: Jack Boyle
Hamilton Cleek: Thomas W. Hanshew
The Lone Wolf; Bourke: Louis Joseph Vance
Raffles: E.W. Hornung
Jimmy Valentine: O. Henry

THE SCHOOL OF THE BELLS

In Ecuador, if you have the right connections, you can enroll in a very special school: all its graduates are professional pickpockets.

To teach a student the light touch, the "teachers" sew little bells onto a dummy — the same little bells that usually grace the throats of stuffed animals. The student is then told to approach the dummy, in the dark, and go for the breast-pocket wallet. If he jostles any part of the dummy en route to the wallet, the little bells tinkle and he must begin again. No student "graduates" until he can successfully steal an object from any part of the dummy without making a sound, and he must be able to do this consistently. Ten times out of ten.

Because of this training, the New York Police Department considers the Ecuadorian pickpockets the best in the world. They seem to travel in groups, possibly as a class on a field expedition, and tend to make the trip to the States twice a year: in time for the Christmas crowds and the summer tourists. They are almost uncatchable.

MARTY NORMAN

Hardness and resistance to drilling go with brittleness, so a material which affords good drill protection might succumb to something more primitive. Like a hammer and chisel. Some of the materials which offer good resistance to heat cutting are relatively soft and can thus be easily drilled.

The selection of the barrier becomes a matter of compromise — of finding reasonable protection at an affordable price. The materials most often employed are concrete, white iron, aluminum reinforced with hard inserts, copper (similarly reinforced) and certain forms of carbon. These materials offer varying degrees of protection against physical violence, drilling and heat cutting.

Protection against explosives requires something extra.

Safe and vault doors are usually kept closed by heavy bolts which in turn are kept in position by the action of the lock. Early explosive attacks were aimed at blowing away the lock by inserting an explosive through the keyhole. With the inhibiting action of the lock removed, the bolts could then be withdrawn and the door opened.

Safes were made, if you remember, to resist this type of attack in the mid-nineteenth century. They called themselves "powder-proof safes" and the method was simple. Underneath the keyway in the lock was drilled a hole, so that gunpowder pushed into the keyhole would fall out again and never reach sufficient concentration in the vital area of the lock to create an effective explosion.

Modern plastic explosives stopped all that, and protection now consists of additional locking devices which come into play when the lock is actually under explosive attack. These added locking devices keep the bolts closed even if the original lock is destroyed.

I once had the delightful experience of acting as advisor to Winston Graham, prior to his novel *The Walking Stick,* on the fascinating subject of explosive attacks. The exact point at issue was whether it was possible for a skilled thief to act so quickly — in the split second after an explosion — that he could prevent the anti-explosive relocking mechanisms from operating. The answer given to Mr. Graham, and subsequently noted in his book, was that with earlier forms of the relocking device, it was just possible. But with modern safes, no.

There is another subject dear to the heart of the crime novelist — combination locks, and the thief who can open them.

Alas, once again, life is more prosaic. In a lifetime's experience in the safe-making industry, I have yet to hear of a good-quality combination lock — of the type found on safe and vault doors — that could be opened by thieves unless they had prior knowledge of the numbers to which the lock was set. Considerable ingenuity has been used to get that information, including telescope observation of the owners fidgeting with the dials and long-range telescopic lens photography to study the numbers. But starting from scratch, with no previous knowledge, a thief would have no success.

These locks operate on four numbers, each between 0 and 100, so there are 100,000,000 groups of numbers to choose from. Trying one a minute, working an eight-hour day and taking statutory holidays, it would take over 800 years to try all the possibilities. So trial and error is not an effective method. Violence is quicker, and experience shows that the thief seems to agree.

The combination lock has many advantages. Changing the numbers to which it is set is easy, and can be done three times a day, if needed. It can be changed for each new staff shift, or if there is even the slightest suspicion that some unauthorized person has found out even one of the numbers. The lock becomes completely individual to the user, with no keys

*O*ld burglars never die, they just steal away.

Chicago *Sun-Times*
GLEN GILBREATH
on facing his thirteenth robbery charge

to carry or lose. Of course, the selection of lock-up numbers is important, and it is vital that the thief not be able to deduce what they are. Birthdays and telephone numbers are bad choices. The safest thing to do is to memorize some entirely random number — but make a note of it and lodge that information at the bank. People can be very stupid about combination locks. I once came across an office at an electric supply company where the safe lock numbers were written on an adjacent wall!

It should be obvious by now that a safe's strength comes from its layers of material and their thicknesses. But there is a limit to the thickness one can incorporate into a safe that must fit a wall opening or recess in a private apartment. Thus such a safe must be treated with discretion, and not entrusted with the protection of high-value jewelry.

Finally, a safe gives the impression of permanence and many people are lulled into a fool's paradise, thinking the old safe, which still looks brand-new, is invincible. The techniques of safe making and safe breaking change constantly, and a safe made thirty years ago may be no match for the modern safe breaker — no matter how sturdy it appears.

Almost all successful safe breakings are against out-of-date safes, which fall victim to attacks they were never designed to withstand. The lesson is obvious: There must be constant updating of security equipment to keep pace with modern technology.

R.J. Pilgrim is the managing director of Chubb Security Services Ltd.

Chubbs safes, en route.

CHUBB SECURITY SERVICES, LTD.

VERSES FOR HEARSES

Isaac Asimov

MARTY NORMAN

Curare

When you've picked out your pitiful quarry
And have dosed him with toxic curare
   Take care what you do
   For once you are through
It's too late to decide that you're sorry.

Belladonna

Deadly nightshade (or else belladonna)
Might be used to avenge one's lost honor
   So if offered a drink
   By a cuckold, I think
You should carefully say, "I don't wanna."

Potassium Cyanide

If you've slipped your rich uncle some cyanide
You might live on his testament, high and wide.
   But if they get after you,
   You'll have no time for laughter, you
Must quickly get ready to try and hide.

Phosgene

In arranging a whiff of phosgene
You'll be pleased, for it's silent and clean.
   But remember, you dope,
   If you're caught, it's the rope,
Or in France, "Êtes-vous pris? Guillotine!"

Arsenic

The classic's a compound arsenial
For murder and that are congenial.
   Yet it's hard on your smile
   For it takes quite a while
And the crime, if you're caught, isn't venial.

Botulism

Potted meat, rich in B. botulinus,
Looks like accident. How's that for slyness?
   Though its onset is slow
   It is quite comme il faut
For an end to an enemy's spryness.

Snake Venom

In your foe's bed you may plant a rattler
It's venom's killed many a battler
   But if you've had aide
   In this snaky charade
Just make sure that your aide's not a tattler.

Arrow Poison

It may be the racing shell's cox'n
You've decided you must be outfoxin'.
   Let him taste that delectable,
   Very strange, undetectable
East African native-dart toxin.

Isaac Asimov is a delightfully mad scientist and author of Tales of the Black Widowers.

THE ASSASSIN'S ARSENAL
David Penn

The pen may be mightier than the sword, but all too frequently it is a damn sight more inaccurate than the pistols it portrays.

In the whodunit, it is only rarely that the correct portrayal of the murder firearm is crucial to the mechanics of the plot, since the emphasis is on logic and the pleasure is intellectual. It matters little to the reader that the author has played safe with an anonymous "pistol," or has invented an exotic "Münslich eight-millimetre flat butt," or has chosen a real ".38 Special Colt Cobra revolver," unless the type and performance of the firearm form a significant part of the deductive process. Such plots are understandably rare, since sufficient technical knowledge for correct interpretation is unusual among readers and practically unheard of among mystery writers. Exceptions do occur, of course, for instance in the well-known naturalist Colin Willock's *Death in Covert,* a classic mystery based on a detailed and accurate knowledge of shotguns and game shooting in England, or in John F. Adams' *Two Plus Two Equals Minus Seven,* not so much a whodunit as a where-did-I-go-wrong. This is narrated by a too-clever-by-half pistolero whose perfect murder goes awry, and who suffers the indignity of being framed for a crime involving a cheap and aesthetically unpleasing Saturday Night Special with which he would never have soiled his hands.

If, however, a firearm is to be the Means to an End in a mystery, I do believe that its role should not strain too far the bounds of logical probability. One eminent English mystery writer managed to contrive a story around the ability of a loaded automatic pistol to fire itself by the contraction of its working parts after it had been left lying around in freezing conditions. Such an occurrence may not, in absolute terms, be impossible. Indeed, there is a known case of a shotgun capable of discharging itself without an intervening human agency by means of the effect of climatic change on its stock. Yet the design of an automatic pistol makes the chances of such an accident highly improbable, since the violence of its operation requires substantial bearing surfaces in the firing mechanism, and the degree of contraction of the metal, which would be compensated for in some degree by spring pressure keeping the parts in proper relationship, would not suffice to disengage them on even the coldest English day. On this occasion our illustrious author followed Sherlock Holmes's dictum that "when you have eliminated the impossible whatever remains, however improbable, must be the truth" beyond the bounds of improbability and into the realms of incredibility.

CULVER PICTURES

Italian 9 mm Beretta automatic pistol. It loads seven rounds but has a short range due to the shortness of its barrel.

When the focus of our attention moves an inch or so from the cerebral world of the Country House to the private-eye or the thick-ear thriller, the *mise en scène* is all. Technical inaccuracy or infelicity of language can puncture the illusion of a hero who is, with certain humorous exceptions, always tough, worldly-wise and competent, whether he be the rumpled sardonic romantic of Chandler or Gavin Lyall, or the sophisticated psychopath of an Ian Fleming. There is a school of thriller, epitomised by

German 9 mm standard pistol, called the Luger *in England and America. Known as the* Parabellum *in Germany.*

the spy stories of the Sixties and by Frederick Forsyth and Sam Gulliver in the Seventies, in which a bravura display of arcane technical knowledge plays a major part in the book's appeal. The police procedural genre is equally dependent on the author's ability to visualise a gritty reality through blood-boltered spectacles.

Some writers in these fields, such as Donald Hamilton or Richard Sale (author of the amazing extravaganza *The Man Who Raised Hell*), are familiar with firearms and incorporate them easily into their plots. Others manage to disguise their ignorance or error by a display of straight-faced confidence that convinces all but the true *amateur des armes* of their veracity. In *The Day of the Jackal*, Forsyth arms his assassin with bullets specially loaded with a mercury blob in a cavity, alleged to have a wondrously mind-blowing effect upon their victim. Far out, but no way would they work. Len Deighton is a past-master at the convincing memorandum and bolstered up *The Ipcress File* with such a wealth of apparently genuine detail that some

alarmist souls voiced concern about undesirable security leaks. All I can say is, if the "Extract from Handling unfamiliar pistols, Document 237.HGF, 1960" is for real, heaven help our secret servants. The anonymous hero of *The Ipcress File* is armed with "a hammerless Smith and Wesson, safety catch built into grip, six chambers crowded with bullets. . . . in an accompanying box were twenty-five rounds, two spare chambers (greased to hold the shells in tight)." Impressive. Except that no hammerless Smith and Wesson is six-shot — it's only five and the safety mechanism does not in strict terms incorporate a "catch," since it does not intercept the motion of an already cocked mechanism but rather prevents an uncocked mechanism from being moved. Deighton means "two spare cylinders," not "chambers." Smith and Wesson has never supplied additional cylinders for the purpose of rapid reloading, since on all models, hinged-frame or side-swing, they take a few moments to remove. With the exception of a little-known Spanish revolver, spare-loaded cylinders went out of fashion when percussion muzzle-loading revolvers became obsolete. Greasing the chambers of the cylinder has a number of highly undesirable possible side effects which I consider would outweigh any benefits.

In some curious way, many thriller readers feel that an author who displays technical ignorance in his writing has somehow betrayed

German Mauser *self-loading automatic pistol. Guaranteed at 10 yards to shoot in a two inch circle; at 25 yards, in a six inch circle. .25 caliber and .32 caliber.*

CULVER PICTURES

Special agents (now retired, some permanently) in firearms practice at the Federal Bureau of Investigation range, U.S. Department of Justice building, Washington, D.C.

his hero by undermining their confidence in his ability to cope with the worst a hostile world can throw at him. A glossy idol cannot withstand a crack, and even a scruffy mat-finish anti-hero can only afford clay on the outside of his boots. This disenchantment is reflected in letters of protest by technology buffs from Bangor to Bangkok. Whether or not such a reaction is a little immature is beside the point, since if that is the audience for whom the author has aimed, he should at least make an effort to deliver the goods. Dick Francis never subjects his fictional jockeys to experiences which he could not himself survive, and writers from the sublime

A member of the New York Bomb Squad waiting for a bomb to deactivate. All suspicious packages are dumped into a bomb tank (shown) filled with oil.

Gavin Lyall to the prolific J.T. Edson go to some lengths to find out whether the gunfights they chronicle are within the bounds of probability.

Perhaps the best-known target of the armchair experts was Ian Fleming. Fleming's fortes were pace and an ability to convey the risqué glamour of an affluent consumer society beginning to glitter after twenty grey years of austerity. Despite his Intelligence background, however, Fleming's knowledge of firearms was sketchy. The .25 Beretta of his early books was at least concealable, and deadly enough if the brain or spine was hit, but it had been subjected to some dubious modifications. To file the firing pin to a point was to invite a punctured primer, an escape of gas and perhaps a lightly grilled shooting hand. The taped skeleton butt would present no improvement in concealability over the standard skinny stocks and would invite all sorts of sticky trouble, such as a difficulty in removing the magazine. Fleming was eventually taken firmly in hand by a Scottish firearms expert, Geoffrey Boothroyd, who is characterised as the Armourer in *Dr. No.* Boothroyd suggested that Bond be armed either with a .32 Walther PPK automatic or a Smith and Wesson .38 "Centennial" revolver.

While both were an improvement over the Beretta, they were themselves idiosyncratic choices, since Boothroyd must have been well aware that the PPK, introduced in 1931 and perhaps still the best pocket automatic made, was available in the significantly more effective .380 ACP calibre as well as the decidedly anaemic .32. The "Centennial" is a compact, well-made and powerful .38 Special snub-nosed revolver, but a concealed hammer weapon capable of double-action fire only and fitted with an unnecessary complexity in the form of a grip safety. Why Boothroyd selected this revolver when the equally compact and powerful but more versatile Smith and Wesson "Chiefs Special" and "Bodyguard" revolvers were available has always mystified me.

The Fleming/Boothroyd axis also demonstrates the danger of trying to graft on someone else's expertise, since Boothroyd suggested that the "Centennial" be carried in a split-front Berns-Martin holster, an advanced design for the day that could be used either as a belt holster or a shoulder holster and allowed a very quick draw with good security against accidental loss. Fleming loved the idea and duly sent Bond forth equipped with a PPK automatic and a Berns-Martin holster, to a chorus of anguished groans from the shooting fraternity since the Berns-Martin was made only for revolvers, not for automatics. As a crowning irony, in recognition of his care in references to firearms in his James Bond stories, Ian Fleming was presented in 1964 with a "Python" .357 Magnum revolver by Colt's, a company whose products had appeared almost entirely in the hands of the bad guys in his books.

Stern injunctions against loquacity preclude turning this chapter into a gunman's *vade mecum*, but having bitten the hands of many authors whose works have given me endless hours of pleasure, I feel obliged to turn pundit for a page or two.

I do not wish to probe too deeply into the gory business of wound ballistics, but it is wise to bear in mind that the projectile fired from a gun is a simple means of transmitting energy to the target. This energy is wasted, and becomes a potential hazard to innocent bystanders, if the projectile either misses or passes right through the victim. The purpose of this release of energy may be to kill, if the shooter is an assassin or a humane hunter, or to cause the recipient to cease and desist from whatever action he happens to be engaged in. Where the police and military are concerned, it is this "stopping" effect that is essential and any subsequent fatality is an undesirable side effect. There is little correlation between the ability of a weapon to kill and its ability to administer an instant and staggering shock. As an analogy, if a bag of oats is stood on its end, and a rapier is thrust right into it, the sharp slim blade will slide through and transmit little shock, but an identical thrust with a blunt walking stick will not penetrate and will knock the sack over. This analogy holds good for pistol bullets, where bigger and blunter is better, but is not entirely valid for modern high-velocity rifle bullets, working at velocities in excess of 2,500 feet per second, where other criteria obtain and the most wounding effect is caused by cavitation. As a rule of thumb, .22, .25 and .32 pistols and revolvers are thoroughly capable of killing if they hit a vital organ, but they do not transmit enough energy to provide reliable stopping power; .38 and 9 mm pistols are effective about 50 percent of the time, and modern .41, .44 and .45 cartiridges are effec-

*I*nfirm of purpose!
Give me the daggers.

LADY MACBETH

tive about 95 percent of the time. In practise, the effect does not seem to be cumulative, so two .38's do not carry the same clout as one .45. All shotguns can be considered effective and messy up to forty or fifty yards, and all modern high-velocity rifles are also reliable one-shot stoppers.

In *Open Season,* David Osborn writes:

> *The rare, British-manufactured seven milli meter H & H magnum twin barrelled breech-loading rifle has, at 300 yards, a velocity of 2,450 feet per second and a striking impact of 1,660 pounds, enough to kill a charging elephant instantly or knock a ¾-ton bull moose not just to his knees but completely off his feet. . . .*

Now, David Osborn has clearly done a lot of hard research into firearms, but he has perpetuated an all-too-common and erroneous assumption that, because a bullet generates an impressive striking energy, it is capable of physically knocking the victim off his feet. Newton's second law remains on the statute books, and this says that if the bullet can knock the victim over, the firearm will knock the shooter over. The armchair theorist fails to take into account the effects of inertia. I know it happens in the movies, but the effect is created by a brisk and timely heave on a piano wire attached to the hapless actor's belt. The real effect is a shock to the nervous system causing sudden loss of control and co-ordination, resulting in collapse, somewhat akin to a marionette when the puppeteer releases the strings.

Robert Churchill, one of the foremost Eng-

ANN LIMONGELLO

Mrs. Raffles by John Kendrick Bangs. Like her predecessor, Raffles, a champion cracksman.

THE KNIFE DRAWER

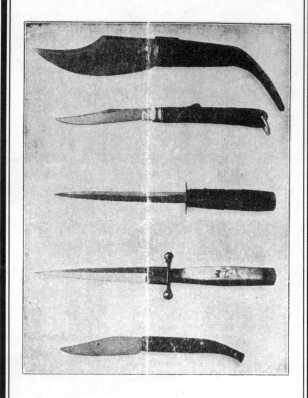

Top: one-hundred-year-old "grosso coltello."
Next: vicious spring-back.
Next: typical stiletto.
Next: "La Pugnale," the "official" weapon of the Malviventi.
Bottom: homemade weapon.

Knives shown were redeemed from Italian criminals and are approximately one-third actual size.

lish forensic ballisticians between the wars, wrote:

> *It is a paradox that in the great majority of offences involving a pistol the people concerned knew next to nothing about the mechanism or potentialities of the weapon. In many cases the fatal shot is the first and last they fire in their lives. Crime guns are usually ill-kept, often mechanically faulty, and commonly loaded with unsuitable or improvised ammunition.*

As a basic standard of competence, an untrained person in a stressful state and shooting a pistol can miss a stationary figure at seven yards and a running one at seven feet. A skilled pistol shot in control of his emotions can reliably hit a stationary figure at a hundred yards and a moving one at twenty-five.

A pistol may give the same sort of comfort as a teddy bear on a cold dark night, but its virtues are light weight and compactness. It is a defensive arm that can be carried along or concealed when a rifle would be a hindrance or an embarrassment. Its virtues become positive disadvantages when the weapon actually has to be fired. A riot gun or sawn-off shotgun is a much more effective weapon favoured by both sides of the law when trouble is expected.

Machine guns, submachine guns and full-size rifles find little favour with the criminal classes since they are large, expensive to acquire and feed, and distinctly unhandy to get in and out of motorcars. In America, overenthusiastic use of machine guns also tends to attract the unwelcome attentions of the FBI, while the trusty shotgun remains a local problem. Criminals are as cost-conscious as any other laissez-faire capitalist and see no need to invest money in fancy hardware when any old 12-bore will do perfectly. Terrorists, who have a different image of themselves and may expect to have to do some serious fighting if things go wrong, are entirely another matter.

While on the subject of criminals and motorcars, it is well to remember that firing pistols at the tyres of moving cars is a pointless exercise, since they are difficult to hit and very hard to deflate. Thanks to Ralph Nader, the laminated steeply raked windscreens of modern American cars have an amazing ability to withstand pistol bullets and shotgun slugs, although the firm of KTW has marketed Teflon-coated steel bullets to combat this problem.

Criminals rarely use holsters. It is easy to drop a pistol down the nearest storm drain but thoroughly embarrassing to have to disengage a holster from a belt or beneath the armpit while attempting to outstretch the long arm of the law.

GUN LORE

The British Empire in its heyday contributed three immortal phrases to the vocabulary of the crime writer: cordite," the "dumdum" bullet and the "automatic revolver." Thanks, I suspect, to Raymond Chandler's education at Dulwich College, an English public school whose Cadet Force would have been issued with cordite-loaded cartridges, he always used this term when referring to any smokeless powder, and it has passed into the English language as a generic term for nitro propellents. True cordite bears a remarkable resemblance to whole-meal spaghetti, was given widespread use in small arms only by Britain and her Empire, and is now obsolete. "Dumdum" derives from Dum-Dum, an arsenal in India where early experiments in expanding rifle bullets took place. Its name took the fancy of the British Press and has symbolised inhumane projectiles ever since. Many a journalist and novelist has been castigated unfairly by so-called firearms experts for employing the phrase "automatic revolver." Such apparent contradictions in terms have existed, the British Webley-Fosbery being the best known, but the Spanish "Zulaika" and the American "Union" were also produced in tiny numbers, and the phrase was widely used by American advertisers to enhance the appeal of conventional self-extracting revolvers.

D.P.

The "secret weapon" is by no means confined to the realms of spy fiction. The SOE and OSS developed a plethora of highly specialised weapons during the last war, including lapel daggers, tyre-slashing knives, and pistols that fired automatically when the arms were raised in surrender (and presumably also when one was waving goodbye to one's loved ones). A fully equipped agent must have weighed about 800 pounds and have been subjected to permanent metal fatigue. The silencer was especially beloved of these clandestine organisations, and the best of them, the .45 ACP De Lisle carbine and the Welrod .32 pistol, are very, very quiet indeed. "Silencer" is, however, a misnomer, the British term "sound moderator" being a more accurate description of the device, its main function being to keep a firearm from sounding like a firearm by muffling noise. The principle of operation is identical to a motorcar silencer, and the Maxim design is indeed still used on tractors. Points to watch are that silencers work well only with subsonic bullets, since supersonic projectiles make a loud "crack" as they pass through the air; that a revolver cannot be silenced effectively by conventional means because the gap between cylinder and barrel allows gas to escape rapidly, thus creating noise; and that, to be effective, a silencer must have a large volume. The two-inch tube stuffed onto the end of a snub-nosed revolver by the movie hit-man would be singularly inefficient. Satisfactory silencers for .45 and 9 mm weapons are about 18–24 inches long and about 2½ inches in diameter. Someone has even invented a "silent grenade," which resembles a suit of armour for an octopus since several silenced barrels radiate from a central sphere. Each barrel is loaded, Roman candle fashion, with multiple charges. When the infernal machine is set into motion, it hops around like a laryngitic crackerjack broadcasting its bullets among the duly astonished multitude.

Having highlighted a few pitfalls in the field of firearms, and left many more still unilluminated, I had better close with the wise words of the old Western gunslinger: "Speed's fine, pardner, but accuracy's final."

David Penn is Keeper of the Department of Exhibits and Firearms at the Imperial War Museum, London, and Secretary of the Historical Breechloading Small-arms Association.

THE CORRECT USE OF THE BLUNT INSTRUMENT

Jennifer Louise Montrechant inherited the Montrechant squint, the Montrechant whine and the Montrechant rubies. Her husband hocked the rubies. Unable to convince her that keeping two out of three wasn't bad, he suffered a shortness of life when she used his shaving mug to recede his awesome buckteeth.

Julian Stuart liked his steak well done. Mrs. Stuart, being of perverse disposition, always served it rare. Meekly he ate it. "How was the steak, dear?" she smirked. "Oh, well done, well done," he replied, then wielding the bone as a conductor's baton, beat her tartare.

Giboney Grace Hartsdale, a dowager of no appreciable income, upended one of Mrs. Smythe's teacups to see if it was Spode and worth pinching. Mrs. Smythe, returning with the lemon wedges, was so outraged, she took the Spode and upended Giboney Grace.

Twenty housewives out of twenty have admitted they have been tempted to bang a few husbandly heads with a frying pan.

Roald Dahl created the most famous of the fictional blunt instruments: a frozen leg of lamb. The second most famous, Ngaio Marsh's magnum of champagne.

Alfredo Fettucine, sneaking up the stairs to tryst with the Lady Emilia, was surprised at the newel post by Helga, the upstairs maid, who knew nothing of the assignation, presumed he was a burglar and promptly dispatched him with a deft toss of a loose finial.

Mrs. T. Edward Poindexter III arrived home from Harrods at the precise moment her husband was informed by his solicitor that he was reduced to living off his principal. Mr. Poindexter picked up Mrs. Poindexter's parcel and pummeled her with it. Harrods refused to credit the account since the merchandise was damaged.

Lefty, Tiger and Mitch decided not to split the proceeds of the bank heist with Cookie, so they started the getaway without him. He had a precarious foothold on the running board of their '48 Packard when they dislodged him with a few swipes of a tire iron. He fell directly in the path of a No. 7 bus. Talk about overkill.

Cynthia Sue Janifer, belle of the Outback, flirted with every man but one. She thought he was too young. He wasn't. He tried her, *in absentia*, in a kangaroo court, found her guilty and caught her just below the sternum with his boomerang. She always did wear her dresses too low.

Amanada Tillinghast decided she would be an heiress and her brother would be mulch. "Come, darling, and look at the roses," she said. He came but brought his shovel with him. "The thorns have snagged your frock," he said, and when she bent to disengage it, he whacked her a good one. He now has the most verdant, albeit lumpy garden in all of Lincolnshire.

Miss Harriet Stearne returned to her classroom to find that nasty Reynolds child drawing a rude caricature of her on the blackboard. Miss Stearne applied ruler to rib cage. The Reynolds child was given an "A" posthumously by Miss Florinda Gentian, Instructress in Art, Miss Dorset's School for Young Ladies, Oxfordshire.

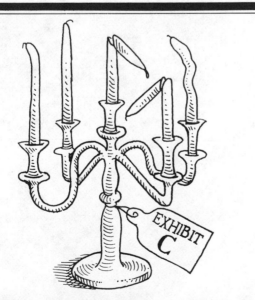

The corniest blunt instrument of them all is the candelabra. (Better for arsonists than bludgeoners.)

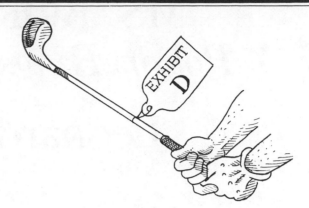

The interlocking grip is preferred by most coshers with a sense of sportsmanship. The overlapping pinkie is necessary to maintain one's steadiness.

Colonel Algernon Pemberton, while looking upward at a speckled field thrush in flight, was coshed from behind by Mrs. Pemberton, who always did think he was for the birds.

Alexander Higgenbottom, ambushed by thugs, rued he'd never learned jujitsu. They tore off his coat, his tie and then — alas for them — his shoe. He swung once at a forehead, once at an Adam's apple, once at the biggest nose since Cyrano. Down they went, home he went, limping slightly from loss of a shoe lift.

Having lost nine games in a row, Penelope Trumbull forgot about good sportsmanship. She heaved the checkerboard — with its full complement of checkers — at her partner, who keeled over under the barrage. It finished any intention he might have had of proposing.

Purity and Chastity hated Sigmund, their brother. "Wanna go skating?" they dimpled. "Lost my skates," he reminded them, whereupon they returned them to him, aiming straight at his head. Their mother, a widow, decided the girls were now old enough to learn how Daddy really died.

Quentin Carstairs was a well-known plagiarist. One hundred sixteen impoverished authors detested him. They elected G.W. Sutherland, from whom he'd pirated 4,073 pages, to chair the Infraction Inquiry. G.W. Sutherland threw both the chair and the rule book at him. The end.

MS. BORGIA & CO.
Poison Rings, Murder Rings

Leonard R. Harris

My father was a gentle man, a man who blushed at his own profanity when he called Hitler a "rat," a sentimental craftsman of poetic wedding rings fashioned of precious metals and glowing gems, an artist in pale watercolors who was profoundly influenced by Charles Gibson's fastidious maidens, a magician who entertained kids in hospital wards, a pianist whose favorite work was "Two Little Honey Bees" . . . yes, a gentle man.

Ah, but when he "fondled the poison rings and murder rings in his collection, a happy light shone in his eyes."

That description is on record in the newspaper of record, the *New York Times;* and it was put there by Meyer Berger, considered by many to have been the greatest reporter of all time, and therefore it must be believed. Berger also reported that my father "tenderly, lovingly" held those rings that had dealt death to dozens. And yes, it's true; I saw it.

Berger might also have described the curious gleam in the eyes of Charles B. Harris, my father, when, between thumb and index finger, he slowly rotated Lucrezia Borgia's poison ring so that the light refracted boldly from a pale emerald and two fiery rubies.

"Lucrezia Borgia was beautiful, but she was *not* a nice woman," my father explained when he showed the ring to me and my brother Bill. "She was married three times," he said, pausing, groping for the gentle way to describe Lucrezia. "And before and even while she was married, she had many . . . uh . . . many other

JUDITH WRIGHT

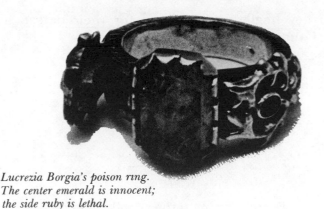

Lucrezia Borgia's poison ring. The center emerald is innocent; the side ruby is lethal.

friends. I'm afraid that she helped many of them on their way to Heaven . . . or, uh, to the other place. I'll show you how she did it . . ."

But first he felt he had to excuse Lucrezia's little quirks. "Rome in the sixteenth century was *not* a very nice place. Not like New York City at all, you understand. And her father, although he did become a Pope, was really . . . well, a rat. Kill, kill, kill! It was probably in her blood."

My brother and I wanted no history lessons. Several years older than I, Bill even knew about Lucrezia's infamous incestuous orgies, although for Dad's sake he pretended ignorance.

The ring *is* stunning. Heavy gold, the emerald centered between the rubies. Carefully lift one hinged ruby — and below is a shallow well, flowing into a hollow tube in the ring itself. Into the well Lucrezia poured a vegetable poison, not unlike curare. "But a slower poison," my father told us. "She didn't like people to die right in front of her. It might have made others suspicious. Just the right delayed-action mixture of poison and alcohol. They died later, after the org . . . uh, parties."

Then my father showed us the ingenious mechanism. He touched a golden flower nestled against the other ruby. One could imagine Lucrezia modestly covering one hand with the other. At her gentle, artless touch, a tiny, piercingly sharp needle emerged from the palm side of the ring. I could imagine Lucrezia tenderly clasping the hand of a "friend," or perhaps fondly placing her hand on his neck. The needle was wet with the deadly juice of St. Ignatius seeds, and the friend was on his (or her) way to The Other Place.

"Poor thing," my father said. "Lucrezia was only thirty-nine when she died. I've often wondered how it happened. Imagine if she'd touched the flower and triggered the needle to get ready to dispatch a friend — and then, without thinking, had slapped a Florentine mosquito that landed on her arm!"

"How did we get the ring?" my brother asked. His "we," even at thirteen, was prescient, since he followed our father into the family jewelry store.

"After Lucrezia died," my father said, "the ring found its way to the de' Medici family. And if you think the Borgias were bad — well, the de' Medicis were worse." He paused. "Real skunks!"

It was a descendant of those de' skunks who sold the ring to my grandfather, then a jeweler in London. *His* family had been jewelers to the Czar at the summer place in Petrograd, specializing in jeweled pistol grips — a glamorous-sounding form of serfdom from which they fled as soon as they could liberate enough gem chips to finance their journey to freedom.

In any event, my grandfather quite naturally distrusted nobility, and kept the ring only because of its gem value. Not until my father became one of the "sons" in B. Harris & Sons, the New York jewelry store founded by

*"I*n that case, Dr. Shorthouse" . . . "how do you account for the fact that in the dregs of Mr. Cayley's lemonade was found strychnine enough to suggest that the full glass contained very much more than was in your prescription?"

Poison in the Garden Suburb
G.D.H. & M. COLE

An antique Venetian poison ring. The stone is hinged and swings open so the pellet may be dropped into the wineglass.

they finally won revenge for their defeat at Cannae:

> Nor swords, nor spears, nor
>   stones from engines hurled,
> Will quell the man whose form
>   alarmed the world.
> The vengeance due to Cannae's
>   frightful field
> Flooded by human gore — a
>   ring shall yield.

Bernard Harris, his father, did one ring into a collection grow.

"The Mexican murder ring was the next I acquired," my father told us happily. "I got it from a Mexican, but I'm sure *he* didn't use it. I didn't bargain with him, though."

The Mexican ring is a plain gold band, rather like a demure wedding band. My father flicked it expertly, and the central section of the ring rose to become a curved semicircular knife, painfully sharp. "Sharp enough to slice a hair," my father said with a curious gleam in his eye. And while I tremulously held a hair, he sliced it with a quick chop. And he quoted from a radio series that he loathed and my brother and I guiltily loved. "Who knows what evil lurks in the hearts of men?" my gentle father intoned. I quaked; the top of the knife had a curious red stain.

A third ring, Venetian, has a hinged stone that covers a depression in which a pellet of poison can be concealed before being dropped into wine. "Breathe on it," my father instructed us. When we did, the gold concealing the hinge became ever so slightly paler than the gold of the band. "Now, if those people of the court had just learned a little bit about the art of the goldsmith," he lectured us, "they might have lived longer lives. A soldered hinge almost always turns color." Then he paused. "I wish I could prove that's how the whole practice of kissing the ruler's ring began." If there's an afterlife, my dad is still researching that theory with some of the victims.

My father loved poetry, and quoted from Juvenal to demonstrate that poison rings were used in even earlier days. The proud Hannibal of Carthage committed suicide (183 B.C.) rather than face capture by the Romans when in battle

Eventually my father's collection embraced memorial rings, made from the hair of a dearly departed; temple rings; magicians' rings; gamblers' rings used to mark cards or concealing a mirror that reveals what cards are dealt; and a variety of enchanting wedding rings. When my brother shows the rings to visitors, though, I notice a curious gleam in his eyes when he tenderly fondles the poison rings. Maybe it's "in the blood."

One November afternoon, eleven years ago, I was in San Francisco and came upon a young craftsman who had duplicated our Venetian pellet ring in Mexican silver. The next day was my daughter's ninth birthday, and I wanted a special surprise for Elizabeth and her party guests. Telling myself it would be a fine way for her and those other dear kids to carry their One-A-Day vitamins to school, I bought the lot.

"Ah!" Liz said when they were distributed at the party — and there *was* a curious gleam in her eyes. "Poison rings!"

And I found myself intoning, "Who knows what evil lurks in the hearts of men?"

Leonard R. Harris is Director of Planning and Development for the New York Times.

A Mexican wedding ring. This simple gold band has a curved center section which can be flicked open to reveal a curved knife.

Chapter 7

SCENES OF THE CRIME

WALKING TOUR OF LONDON

Margaret Boe Birns

Let us go then, you and I, to the Bottle Street Police Station, off Piccadilly. A dirty yellow portal on the left side of the building leads to the dark at the top of the stairs. The darkness continues to descend as we climb until suddenly — a carved oak door upon which there is a small brass plaque, neatly engraved with the simple lettering: ALBERT CAMPION, MERCHANT GOODS DEPT.

But *we* know better, don't we? Inside the flat are some delightful old pieces of furniture, a Rembrandt etching, a Steinlen cat, a lovely little Girton — and a number of trophies from Albert Campion's true line of work, including the infamous Black Dudley dagger.

As befits one rumoured to be of royal blood, Campion's rooms are luxuriously furnished. But for a look at something that will seem truly rare and unattainable, let us stroll over to 110A Piccadilly. It is directly opposite Green Park, in a block of new, perfect and expensive flats. Some say this address was chosen by the famous sleuth who resides within since it divides by two the 221B number of the notable Baker Street address. Second floor: here we are. Is it not like a colourful and gilded paradise in a mediaeval painting? Let us feast our eyes on this whimsical paradise done in black and primrose, with a wood fire leaping on a wide old-fashioned hearth, a Chesterfield sofa suggesting the embraces of the houris, walls lined with rare editions, Sèvres vases filled with red and gold chrysanthemums, a fine old decanter of Napoleon brandy — and over at the black baby grand piano, attacking a Scarlatti

sonata like a man possessed, is Lord Peter Wimsey. He is moody at the moment. Just back from Harley Street, his manservant Bunter tells us, where he's undergone a most unpleasant interview with a Dr. Julian Freke. Something about a body in a bathtub.

As the strains of Scarlatti fade away behind us, let us move on to the beautifully appointed Albany. The thick pile carpet, the air of unhurried splendour — it is the perfect ambience for elegant A.J. Raffles, gentleman and thief. Perhaps we can purchase some Sullivan cigarettes here at the desk, then take a turn into the heart of Mayfair to view the home of the Honorable Richard Rolliston, alias "The Toff." And while in the district, we must visit Whitehaven Mansions. That little Belgian gentleman with the famous moustaches used to live with his friend Captain Hastings at 14 Farraway, but back in the Thirties he moved to this modern block of flats whose geometrical appearance and proportions indulged his passion for order and method. His efficient secretary, Miss Felicity Lemon, and his faithful manservant, Georges, looked after the old gentleman quite well, but — alas — after a recent imbroglio at Styles this illustrious detective with the highly developed "little grey cells" has passed away. Is it possible that the local Elephant-and-Castle will have retained a bit of his favourite *sirop de cassis*? Perhaps we can stop in and raise our glasses to the memory of the late Hercule Poirot.

These are indeed the great good places of London. But there are other London dwellings

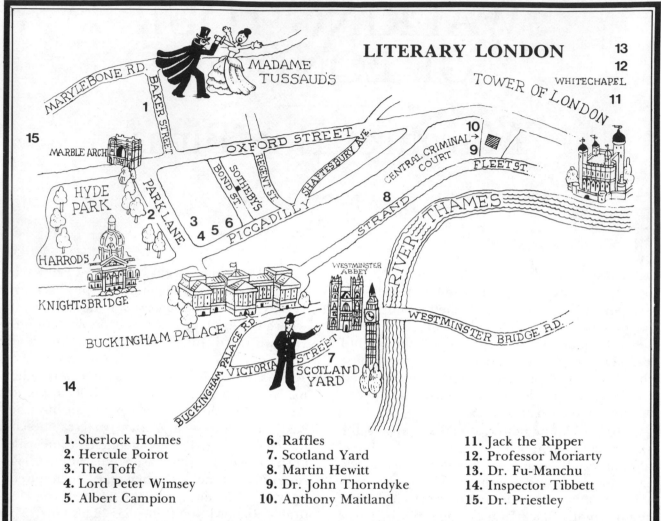

LITERARY LONDON

1. Sherlock Holmes
2. Hercule Poirot
3. The Toff
4. Lord Peter Wimsey
5. Albert Campion
6. Raffles
7. Scotland Yard
8. Martin Hewitt
9. Dr. John Thorndyke
10. Anthony Maitland
11. Jack the Ripper
12. Professor Moriarty
13. Dr. Fu-Manchu
14. Inspector Tibbett
15. Dr. Priestley

MARTY NORMAN

of interest to us. Let us move, then, out of the posh Mayfair district over to The Strand. In an old building near The Strand we can find a plain ground-glass door on which appears the single word HEWITT. It is, of course, the private detective agency of the amiable Martin Hewitt. Stout fellow, Hewitt. For an even stouter fellow let us turn just below The Strand and above the Victoria Embankment to I Adelphi Terrace, where we can find the roly-poly Gideon Fell. There he is, with a pint of bitter next to him. Seems to be indulging in one of his favourite pastimes — reading a mystery story.

And now let's move over to The Temple, nearby. Here we are: 5A King's Bench Walk. One floor up is a massive outer oak door with a name upon it in white letters. This door opens to disclose a baize-covered inner door. Beyond this is a spacious wood-paneled living room with a broad hearth flanked by two wing chairs. In the fireplace is a gas ring, on which a kettle of water boils for tea. On the floor above is a laboratory and workshop, the walls covered with shelves and tool racks bearing all manner of strange instruments. There is also a cupel furnace, occasionally used as a grill for cutlets by the noble manservant Polton. At a table in the laboratory, a tall and very handsome man appears to be making a study of the characteristics of methylene blue on cellulose and oxycellulose. You recognise him? Yes, of course: it is Dr. John Thorndyke.

And while we are in the area, over at the Inner Temple are Sir Nicholas Harding's chambers, which he shares with that English barrister who is the very soul of London urbanity — Antony Maitland.

The fog thickens. It begins to close around us like a shroud as we walk outside the city gates and into the East End. The fog is brown and vile here in Whitechapel Road, among the one-night cheap hotels and sawdust restaurants; menace seems to permeate the very brick and stone itself. Later, in one of these dark, echoing side streets, Jack the Ripper may pay one of his nocturnal visits. Even now, people and objects seem to retreat into the dirty brown mist as we walk the promenade from Whitechapel to Mile End. It is behind the shuttered windows of one of these dingy buildings that we would very likely find the headquarters of a certain Dr. Moriarty, organiser of half that is evil and nearly all that is undetected in this great city.

Limehouse. The smoke-laden vapors of the lower Thames have taken on the aroma of incense. I think that now you may begin to sense the presence of something. If you turn, you will see what you have already somehow sensed — magnetic cat-green eyes, glittering below a dome-shaped forehead. A brow like Shakespeare's, a face like Satan's. Long tapering fingers with sharp taloned nails fold together in front of a black robe embroidered with a silver peacock. The mist closes again, but we know that we have felt a force of malignancy we had never supposed could radiate from any human being, that we have seen a sight we will never forget: the devil-doctor himself — Fu Manchu!

We hear the low whistle of his henchmen, the Burmese dacoits. Quickly, to Scotland Yard, and a consultation with Sir Denis Nayland Smith. How safe it feels here in Whitehall! Now that we have dispatched Sir Nayland Smith to the East End, let us greet Inspector Lestrade. He is on his way to 3 Lauriston Gardens, off the Brixton Road. If we accompanied him, we would see scrawled in blood-red letters the mysterious inscription "Rache." A veritable study in scarlet, as it were.

Let us follow along the corridor to Colonel March at the Department of Queer Complaints. Best walk carefully: there are peppermint cream wrappers on the floor here — Inspector Gently must be about. Ah now, here

are the Dead Ends. Inspector Rason, of course, presides here, with a great deal more success than he had with Fidelity Dove! And speaking of influential ladies, let us peek in on Mrs. Palmyra Pym, the Assistant Commissioner of Criminal Investigation — the highest-ranking woman in the Yard.

That there, over at his desk, is Inspector Wilfred Dover. Unfortunately, he appears to have nodded off to sleep. He is snoring over the papers on his desk and has spilled the remains of his tea on what appears to have been a suspect's signed confession. And there is Commander George Gideon. His nose seems a bit out of joint. Evidently he was presented with a traffic ticket this morning. Best to be off.

Now, for a quick nip over to Chelsea. On the ground floor of that shabby yet genteel Victorian house resides Chief Inspector Henry Tibbett and his devoted, albeit pleasingly plump wife, Emily. And if we just step over to the Fulham Road we can pass Harrington Street and the digs of Commander Gideon.

Let us cross Hyde Park now and enter the Bayswater section of London. Here we are at Westbourne Terrace, home of the brilliant Dr. Priestley. Note how even his house bears the unmistakable stamp of the English aristocrat!

Before we proceed to our final destination, I must inform you of a little side excursion you might, one day, wish to take. Over at Paddington Station Mrs. McGillicuddy is willing to accompany interested bystanders, or available witnesses, on the 4:50 train.

As night falls on the great city, the lamps are lit and we walk past 221B Baker Street. Inside we may expect to find those familiar rooms, the velvet-lined armchair, the array of fine pipes — and smell the aroma of strong tobacco. Even now, the strains of violin music reach us through the sulphurous yellow mist. But wait — out of the night looms a large, totally bald man with a lollipop in his hand. He is about to enter 221B Baker Street. Something about a "stake-out." Something about drugs. Something about a "Baker Street Connection . . ."

Margaret Boe Birns teaches "The Detective Novel" at New York University.

WAYLAID IN LONELY PLACES

The rock quarry . . .

The east parlour . . .

The detour . . .

ST. MARY MEAD AND OTHER TROUBLED VILLAGES

Margaret Yorke

Miss Marple no longer lives in St. Mary Mead, but the village crime novel is still vigorous. Like rural life, however, it has changed and broadened. In the old-style whodunit an ingenious puzzle was constructed among somewhat stereotyped characters. There was the butler, who sometimes found the body and whose short sight might provide a clue; the grey-haired retired colonel; the doctor who happened to be an expert on obscure poisons; the cycling vicar, trusty witness to people's movements. Then there was the small cast of suspects, few of whom worked for a living, though sometimes the local solicitor was the villain. Supporting roles were played by various servants, none of whom, convention decreed, might be the murderer. There would be an eccentric extra charater, to add atmosphere. The sleuth was often an amateur, in the area by chance or summoned by a worried suspect, though sometimes he was a policeman of acumen, if not urbanity. Motives for murder were mainly avaricious, involving blackmail or inheritance. Sex might be implicit, not overt.

Village life was never, in fact, quite like that.

The detective novel's form restricts the number of characters that may appear, but the slice of life shown by contemporary writers using the village setting shows a truer aspect of their chosen section of the scene.

Country villages are dwellings often centred round a manor house, with a church, an inn or two, and usually at least one shop which also does duty as a post office. Motorways have extended the commuter range, and some industries have moved to rural areas, so that many villages have rapidly enlarged. Expansion beyond the village bounds is not allowed, and new houses have sprung up, often mushroom-like in clumps, in what were once paddocks or

---

ST. MARY MEAD

First mentioned in *The Murder at the Vicarage* (1930), St. Mary Mead is described as a "quiet, one-horse village," with no "picture house." Miss Marple's nephew regarded it as "a stagnant pool." It has several small shops, The Blue Boar and a path leading to Old Hall. The train goes up to London, and on Thursdays one can get a cheap ticket. On Sundays one can visit the church with its "rather fine old stained glass." A map of St. Mary Mead is included in the book and according to it, Miss Marple's front gate is catty-corner to that of the vicarage.

The village never really lived.

Deep in the mystery writer's imagination is situated the village. It has a High Street (which is so named because it is high, overlooking the surrounding area), a cycling vicar, a pub, a post office where the residents read each other's mail and an adorable tea shoppe.

large gardens. The result is a denser population and the creation of new tensions.

Some less conveniently situated villages are dying, for mechanised farms employ fewer humans. Cottages which might otherwise become derelict are bought as weekend retreats by city dwellers who arrive on Friday nights and spend their leisure hours cultivating vegetables or knocking down walls to expose all possible beams, and perhaps a fictional corpse. By Monday morning, deserted again, these villages are perfect spots for villains on the run to hide in or hold people hostage, to inter victims in the fresh-dug bean trench or pop them in the freezer.

In the growing villages, social mores are complex. Those who live in picturesque old houses may be envied by others in the more mortgage-worthy new ones, with their tiny gardens which allow no privacy. Newcomers, keen to become part of the community, sometimes fling themselves into drama groups and festivals with an enthusiasm offensive to older inhabitants who resent the changes round them and may, by a neighbour's sale of land for building, have lost their own seclusion.

Existing shops are rarely adequate for the increased population, and there is constant traffic on narrow roads. The once peaceful country air is rent by the car engines of the work force and the shoppers, and borne upon the wind may be the sound of farm tractors, combine harvesters and the whine of the circular saw. Lawn mowers, electric hedge clippers and bonfire smoke may irritate and, by planned timing, induce a state of war.

THE TROUBLED VILLAGE

For those who like a cosy little village setting, and have read most of Mrs. Christie's output, you might turn to the work of Catherine Aird, Elizabeth Lemarchand, W.J. Burley, Elizabeth Ferrars, Margaret Yorke (particularly *No Medals for the Major*), Peter Dickinson (*A Pride of Heroes*), Reginald Hill (*Ruling Passion*), P.D. James (*The Dark Tower, Cover Her Face*), Jessica Mann (*Mrs. Knox's Profession*). Similar in type but spanning out from the village are the works of Anne Morice, Margaret Erskine, Colin Watson and, with more than a touch of kinkiness, Ruth Rendell.

Villages no longer have their own policeman. There may be a constable living in a police house, but he will patrol a wide district by car and may lack time to build up an intimate local knowledge. Vicars, now, are sometimes trendy and introduce rock hymns which enrage traditionalists enough to provoke hostile letters, if not actual murder. A growing sport is campanology: not the mere Sunday summons, but matches played by touring teams sampling rival sets of bells in peals that may last four hours; an incensed listener, forced to endure the assault upon his ears, might well feel tempted to hang a ringer with his own rope.

Mansions, if historically interesting, are often open to the public and fresh tourist bait is constantly added, like tigers in the deer park. A fictional corpse is as likely to be found nowadays in the lion pound as stabbed in the rose garden. Some large houses are divided into flats or become institutions or government establishments; a few may be privately owned by pop stars or financiers, and here there may, indeed, be found a butler, though he is more likely to be a Filipino than a Jeeves.

There is scope now to introduce any type of character and to devise sophisticated crimes: art thefts, kidnappings, industrial or even international espionage. Country crafts flourish: gems or drugs in products from the local pottery? Road improvements may threaten to obliterate historic sites and anger archaeologists who delve to rescue what they can before the approaching bulldozer, while nature lovers seek to protect beauty spots from the same fate. Foul means for their own cause might well be used by either the planners for the future or the saviours of the past.

Some village pubs are little changed, with "snug" bars and dart boards, but also, now, a fruit machine. Others provide excellent bar meals at reasonable cost and are filled at midday with businessmen from nearby towns. The do-gooding village spinster is almost extinct; her emancipated modern sister, and working wives who earn good salaries, may be in the pubs, too. Young mothers, though, are sometimes lonely, tied by the need to drive children back and forth to play group and school in the intervals of stocking up the freezer and operating machines which undertake domestic chores, since human aid has almost disappeared. A few older women will "help out," to "oblige," often because they would otherwise be alone all day themselves. There is an occasional housekeeper to be found: sweet, sinister or seductive, probably widowed or divorced and employed by some lone man; either, in fact or fiction, may have more than mere domestic designs upon the other, and if they haven't, few will believe them.

Human nature alters little, although the scene may change, and the seven deadly sins will never cease to flourish. Today's writer has freedom to explore any or all of them, and plots often arise now from some sort of personal threat or conflict. The psychological or suspense novel with a village setting exists beside the classic detective story. Crimes are usually solved by efficient police detectives backed up by the resources of science, though an occasional amateur still appears. The lure of the mystery novel lies in the reader's knowledge that though the real world is full of horrors, this time it didn't really happen.

Margaret Yorke is the author of the contemporary village mystery, No Medals for the Major.

NOBODY LEAVE THE ROOM!

E. R. Emmet

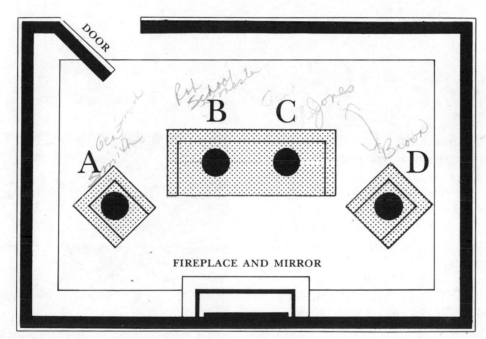

Bilks the bookmaker has just been found dead in the diningroom of the club. Poison in his wine.

Four men seated as above on a sofa and two armchairs round the fireplace in the lounge are discussing the murder. Their names are Smith, Brown, Jones and Robinson. They are, not necessarily respectively, a General, a Schoolmaster, an Admiral and a Doctor.

i. The waiter has just poured out a glass of whisky for Jones and of beer for Brown.

ii. The General looks up and in the mirror over the fireplace sees the door close behind the waiter. He then turns to Robinson, who is next to him, and starts talking.

iii. Neither Smith nor Brown have got any sisters.

iv. The Schoolmaster is a teetotaller.

v. Smith, who is sitting in one of the armchairs, is the Admiral's brother-in-law. The Schoolmaster is next to him on his left.

vi. Suddenly a hand is seen stealthily putting something in Jones's whisky. It is the murderer again. No one has left his seat; nobody else is in the room.

Who is the murderer?
What is the profession of each man, and where is he sitting?

E. R. Emmet is a retired schoolmaster. From Brain Puzzler's Delight, *copyright © 1967, 1970 by E. R. Emmet. Reprinted by permission of Emerson Books, Inc.*

MAYBE YOU BETTER NOT LOCK THE DOOR

Gordon Bean

Dagger in hand, the murderer advances toward his victim. Escape lies just two strides away, through the room's sole door — but the killer darts there first, throwing the bolt. His quarry lunges for a window — too late! His assailant has locked that, too. There is a scuffle. A chair overturned. A lamp dropped to the floor. A corner of the carpet set askew. But there is no place to turn, to hide. A knife jerks up and down repeatedly. A loud thump. And then: a corpse sprawled in front of the fireplace's flickering glow.

Some hours later, the police crash through the window (having failed to breach the door) and find: a bloody dagger; a messy room; a mutilated body. But no murderer. How did he get out? It is quite obvious no one could have left the room. Seemingly, the police must take on a villain who can melt through locked windows and doors like Houdini's ghost. But, of course, the police detective will ultimately expose the "miracle" as trickery and will explain just how the illusion was created.

That, in a nutshell, is the archetypal plot of the locked-room mystery, a subgenre which has puzzled readers since Poe first invented it with *Murders in the Rue Morgue.* Chesterton, Carr, Queen — all have played off this classic theme and have inspired others to tackle it. It is the strictest form of the "impossible crime."

Why the intense, continuing interest in it? Because the locked-room gambit evokes the ul-

The archetypal locked room is a jail cell. This one houses Zeus, who is waiting for Divine Inspiration on how to get out.

COURTESY/BRITISH TOURIST AUTHORITY

timate mystery — the mystery of magic.

Reading a locked-room mystery, you enter a world reminiscent of a fantastic magic show: Men walk through walls, slither through keyholes and vanish like pricked soap bubbles. And not only do you experience magical effects, you are fooled by magical methods as well. Not trapdoors, secret wires, mirrors — these are just gimmicks. Rather, I am speaking of suggestion and misdirection, psychological devices the magician — along with his literary equivalent, the locked-room writer — uses to coax your mind down a prescribed path of "logic" which ends in paradox.

Through suggestion, the author leads you to a false assumption. For example, he can create merely the illusion of murder, causing you to assume — falsely — a murderer's presence. How? The victim could stab himself with an icicle, whose absence (after melting) would suggest the killer has absconded and taken the murder weapon with him.

Important as suggestion is, to fully deceive it needs its counterpart: misdirection. With misdirection, the author does not suggest some-thing false; he hides something true — namely, an illusion-puncturing clue. Such as: the damp spot next to the "icicled" corpse.

But the locked-room mystery's appeal, like that of the magic show, rests mainly in the fantasy it conjures up — not in its puzzle. A good one temporarily suspends logic, filling us with childlike awe. When a simple explanation destroys that awe, we realize how easily we are fooled — a knowledge which provides rare perspective on the intellect's deficiency.

So find (and that's not easy — you could probably get out of a locked room quicker) a copy of Israel Zangwill's *The Big Bow Mystery*, Carter Dickson's *He Wouldn't Kill Patience* or Clayton Rawson's *Death from a Top Hat* and pay attention. See if you can tell how they sealed off the room, now that you know they're out to mislead you. But don't expect any icicles. A real murderer stalks these three rooms. Contrary to popular advice, given the nature of the locked-room novel, I would suggest you don't sit down to read until you've *unlocked* the door.

Gordon Bean is a magician, a student at Brown University, and was the youngest participant on the first Mystery Readers' Tour of Great Britain.

SOLUTION TO "NOBODY LEAVE THE ROOM" PUZZLE

	General	Schoolmaster	Admiral	Doctor
Smith				
Brown		X		
Jones		X		
Robinson	X			

1. From (i) and (iv) Schoolmaster not Jones or Brown (mark in diagram as shown).

2. From (ii) General not Robinson (mark in diagram). And General must be C or D (see diagram) to see door in mirror. Robinson not A.

3. From (v) Smith not Admiral or Schoolmaster. ∴ by elimination *Robinson is Schoolmaster.*

4. Also from (v) *Smith sitting at A; Schoolmaster at B.*

5. Since General next to Robinson (ii) and sitting at C or D. ∴ *General at C.* ∴ General not Smith. ∴ by elimination *Smith is the doctor.* ∴ by elimination *Admiral sitting at D.*

6. Since Smith is Admiral's brother-in-law and neither Smith nor Brown has got any sisters, ∴ Admiral not Brown. ∴ *Brown is General,* and *Jones is Admiral.*

A, Dr. Smith; B, Schoolmaster Robinson; C, General Brown; D, Admiral Jones.

The hand putting something into Jones's whisky must belong to *General Brown.*

OXFORD VS. CAMBRIDGE
The Dark Blues Have the Most
Margaret Yorke

More mystery stories are set in Oxford than in Cambridge. More fictional sleuths are Oxford than Cambridge men. More crime writers live near Oxford than Cambridge. Why?

First, is it true? Yes. Dorothy L. Sayers and Peter Wimsey, Edmund Crispin and Gervase Fen, Michael Innes and his quotation-capping Appleby score instantly for Oxford, whose sporting teams are distinguished from the light blue of Cambridge by their dark blue colours. Then come J.C. Masterman with *An Oxford Tragedy* and *The Case of the Four Friends*, Katherine Farrar with *Gownsman's Gallows* and *The Missing Link* and Robert Robinson with *Landscape with Dead Dons*. James McClure lives in Oxford; Elizabeth Ferrars lived there for five years; three of Gwendolyn Butler's books have Oxford settings. John Le Carré and Geoffrey Household both went there. G.D.H. Cole, a Fellow of All Souls, wrote many detective novels in partnership with his wife Margaret, but she went to Cambridge; Anthony Price went to Ox-

---

OXFORD MYSTERIES

Jeffrey Archer: *Not a Penny More, Not a Penny Less*

Adam Broome: *The Oxford Murders*

Gwendolyn Butler: *Coffin in Oxford; A Coffin for Pandora; Dine and Be Dead*

G.D.H. and M.I. Cole: *Off with Her Head*

Edmund Crispin: *Obsequies at Oxford; Dead and Dumb; The Moving Toyshop*

Colin Dexter: *Last Bus to Woodstock*

Katherine Farrar: *Gownsman's Gallows; The Missing Link; At Odds with Morning*

Michael Innes: *Operation Pax; Seven Suspects; Hare Sitting Up*

J.C. Masterman: *An Oxford Tragedy; The Case of the Four Friends*

Dermot Morrah: *The Mummy Case Mystery*

Raymond Postgate: *Ledger Is Kept*

Robert Robinson: *Landscape with Dead Dons*

J. Maclaren Ross: *Until the Day She Dies*

Dorothy L. Sayers: *Gaudy Night*

Margaret Yorke: *Cast for death; Grave Matters*

GEORGE HALCROW

The Bridge of Sighs, Oxford. In Oxford, the rivers run around, not through the city, and few colleges are alongside them. College bridges, therefore, cross streets, not water.

ford, and lives nearby, but sent his Dr. Audley to Cambridge: two half-hits for the Light Blues here?

So what about "the other place," which is what Oxford persons call Cambridge? P.D. James lived there, her poetry-writing Commander Adam Dalgliesh was certainly at Cambridge, and her *An Unsuitable Job for a Woman* has a Cambridge setting. To support her, there is Glyn Daniel and his sleuth Sir Richard Sherrington. V.C. Clinton-Baddeley's Dr. Davie is a Cambridge don; Margery Allingham's Campion went to Cambridge. Peter Dickinson,

---

CAMBRIDGE MYSTERIES

V.C. Clinton-Baddeley: *Death's Bright Dart*
Adam Broome: *The Cambridge Murders*
Robert Charles: *Dead Before Midnight*
Brian Cooper: *The Path to the Bridge*
Dilwyn Rees: *The Cambridge Murders*
P.D. James: *An Unsuitable Job for a Woman*
R. Lait: *Switched Out*

Robert Charles and Brian Cooper all went to Cambridge. So did J.B. Priestley, whose comprehensive works include a detective novel, *Salt Is Leaving*.

Scenes-of-crime investigation is important when solving mysteries. Let's examine these. Oxford is centrally placed in England, the hub of road and railway lines radiating in all directions on the way to many other places. Cambridge is out on a limb, long ago a port but now an end in itself. Oxford has varied, hilly countryside around the city. Cambridge lies amid flat fenland exposed to cobweb-dispersing winds. Oxford is a grey city, its buildings stone, though the refaced colleges now gleam palely golden as when they were first built in the days before polluted air blackened their façades. Cambridge is a city of colour; many of the colleges are built of mellow brick, and old frontages in the town have been preserved by planners who have hidden modern blocks away from immediate view.

But the biggest difference lies in what is central to each city. In Oxford, the colleges border busy streets: most of those at Cambridge lie along the banks of the tranquil river, each linked by its own bridge to the verdant parkland and gardens on the farther side. In Oxford, the rivers run around, not through the

The Bridge of Sighs, Cambridge. Most of the Cambridge colleges lie along the banks of the tranquil river and punting is a favourite student avocation.

city, and few colleges are alongside them. Both cities have Bridges of Sighs: Oxford's crosses a street; Cambridge's crosses water. But at Oxford, over all, looms the monster motor industry that grew from a cycle repair shop. Cambridge has no comparable industrial complex.

Both universities have much the same student population, but Oxford has more colleges than Cambridge and some are small, tucked away in dark corners. Cambridge colleges are generally large; the eye is led ever upwards and one is aware, always, of the sky. The heavens are not conspicuous above Oxford, where the climate is prone to fog and the atmosphere induces introspection.

Oxford's lead in the crime fiction stakes notwithstanding, Cambridge has a Chair in Criminology while Oxford has only a small research institute. Nigel Fisher, however, Professor of Criminology at Cambridge, was himself at Christ Church, Oxford, and was a Fellow of Nuffield College before he went to Cambridge. Colin Dexter, though, went the other way: he left Cambridge for Oxford, where he sets his mysteries. Nicholas Blake (C. Day Lewis, later Poet Laureate) was at Oxford, then became Clark Lecturer at Trinity College, Cambridge, and later Professor of Poetry at Oxford. Is this movement evidence or a red herring?

Cambridge, strong on science, deals with criminological facts whereas our subject here is crime in fantasy. To invent it, you may have to leave Cambridge. (P.D. James lives in London.) It cannot be coincidence that eight writing members of the Crime Writers' Association live within fifteen miles of the centre of Oxford and only two live as close to Cambridge. On this evidence the verdict must be that Cambridge persons, living beside tranquil water under the wide sky, need no escape into a world of fantasy: where is their Tolkien or Lewis Carroll? Oxford persons, pressured amid their busy streets under darker, lowering skies, suffer from more blues.

Margaret Yorke lives fourteen miles from Oxford, has worked in the libraries of two Oxford colleges and has a sleuth who is an Oxford don, Dr. Patrick Grant.

HARVARD HAS A HOMICIDE, TOO

Timothy Fuller: *Harvard Has a Homicide*

THE GOTHIC HOUSE
Peter Blake

As a modern architect, and as an occasional critic of modern architecture, I am pleased to report that nobody ever gets done in in a modern house. In fact, modern houses tend to be so antiseptic as to rule out almost all passions. In his first and possibly his best novel, *Decline and Fall,* the late Evelyn Waugh described an (almost) fictitious avant-garde architect whom he named Otto Friedrich Silenus and who was commissioned by one Mrs. Margot Beste-Chetwynde to design and build a house of ferroconcrete, aluminum and "vita-glass" (whatever that was supposed to be). Professor Silenus obliged and, a few pages down the line, described his client (who had since proposed marriage to him) as follows: "If you compare her with other women of her age you will see that the particulars in which she differs from them are infinitesimal compared with the points of similarity. A few millimeters here and a few millimeters there, such variations are inevitable in the human reproductive system . . . ." In short, no passions aroused, and certainly none requited.

Indeed, a remarkable number of modern houses designed by myself and by my architect friends have caused the owners to seek divorce almost instantly after the issuance of a certificate of occupancy. Passions had not merely cooled — they had plummeted right through the polar icecap! To the best of my knowledge, there is no record of either party having ever asked for custody of the guilty house.

But people certainly do and did and will again get passionately murdered and otherwise discomfited in so-called "Gothic" houses. Actually, most of the "Gothic" houses that people get murdered in are not, strictly speaking, Gothic at all; they are just about any recognizable or unrecognizable style: Greek Revival, Romanesque Revival, Colonial Revival, Plantation, Stanford White (every town and village in the East has at least one attributed to White — who died of gunshot wounds himself, of course — and most of these attributions are incorrect) and, most dependably, the style best known as "Charles Addams."

I don't recall a single place in which I have ever lived in the U.S. that did not have at least one Charles Addams house: it was usually two stories in height (plus mansard roof); most windows were broken and/or boarded up; its front porch was in a state of collapse, barely able to support the cobwebs strung between its slender (and partly splintered) pillars; its siding was termite-infested; and the paint was peeling throughout. The steps leading up to the porch had long rotted away; the foundation walls (if any) had settled in the general direction of China; and at night shutters (usually dangling from a single hinge) would swing and bang mournfully. Whenever there was a thunderstorm (and even whenever there was not), lightning would be sure to strike the mansard roof, like a sword of fire.

There used to be a Charles Addams house at the end of Long Island, between Bridgehampton and Sagaponack. Everybody *knew* that someone had been murdered inside that terrible wreck. The story went that she (the victim) had been all alone, that there had been no will, and that no one had been able to locate any next of kin. Hence the title to the disaster area was clouded, and the property could not

The worst of a modern stylish mansion is, that it has no place for ghosts.

The Poet at the Breakfast Table
OLIVER WENDELL HOLMES, SR.

be sold. (That's a ridiculous scenario to anyone who knows what's what; the next of kin obviously had to have been at least marginally involved in the bloodbath.)

The house was leaning at an angle the Tower of Pisa would have envied when I decided one day to trespass on the premises (bodyguarded by my then eight-year-old son and a team of killer dogs). The exterior had been posted liberally with NO TRESPASSING signs; the floorboards on the entrance porch gave way with a crash; the front door screeched; and the walls and ceilings sighed. Rats scuttled, bats whizzed by, and so did ghosts. We looked for black widow spiders and original copies of the Federalist Papers.

However, by the time we reached the stairs to the attic (where those priceless Federalist Papers were sure to have been stashed away), we had giant butterflies in our stomachs and the killer dogs were in a state of shock. There seemed to be a great many bleached bones scattered about this Haunted Mansion (they turned out to be droppings left by Colonel Sanders' army), and there seemed to be an awful silence — made more awful by occasional whimpering sounds (my own).

It was in the middle of a sunny summer day, but inside that Haunted Mansion it was very dim and very cold and clammy. We never made it to the attic, where the most telling clues were undoubtedly on display.

My son and I went back a year later, and the Charles Addams house had simply vanished. It had not merely been struck down by one final bolt of lightning, leaving a burned-out cadaver; it had literally dropped out of sight, like a whodunit clue left too long unobserved.

There was absolutely nothing but a great thicket of poison ivy.

Except . . . except that late one night, after a long party in Sagaponack, I drove back heading west on Sag Road, toward Bridgehampton, and suddenly there was this bolt of lightning, to my right, crashing into the now-vacant lot, and I caught sight of it in my rear-view mirror. And there, in this flash of lightning, stood the old "Gothic" house in all its glory, as if entirely new, long before it had been touched by Charles Addams' brush. And on the porch I saw the figure of a lady clad in gossamer cobwebs, and the figure of a brutish man, and something clearly against the felony statutes was about to be done to her, with an ax. So I quickly stepped on the gas and made it to my own, dispassionate modern house in record time.

In their recent book on Gothic architecture in America, Calder Toth and Julius Trousdale Sadler, Jr. (the latter, obviously, a prime suspect by the sound of his name alone) discuss at great length what they have called "The Only Proper Style." Their book is fascinating, an unbroken record of increasingly bizarre disasters: a Gothic church in Buffalo is reported to have burned down "as the result of a rocket alighting on the bell tower during the course of the Glorious Fourth celebrations of 1868" (a likely story!); another is reported to have vanished; Oscar Wilde is quoted as having snarled at a Gothic structure in Chicago, calling it "a castellated monstrosity with pepper boxes stuck all over it"; and the architects of Gothic houses are reported to have died rather precipitously. In summing up, Messrs. Toth and Sadler, Jr., say that, in neo-Gothic times in America, "a man could be born in a Gothic bed, receive baptism in a Gothic church, attend a Gothic school, live in a Gothic house, and at last be buried in a Gothic cemetery from a Gothic mortuary chapel."

Quite so — almost: not only "a man," but also a woman or a child; and not only "live in a Gothic house," but also die in one.

Peter Blake is chairman of the School of Architecture, Boston Architectural Center, and author of Form Follows Fiasco: Why Modern Architecture Hasn't Worked.

STEP TO THE
REAR OF THE BOOK

Frederic F. Van de Water's novel concerns a button snapped from an épée, a half-completed letter, a leather knife sheath.

Lange Lewis' work involves a silver vial, five cigarette butts, an iron dumbbell and a 5" x 7" notebook.

The first Dell Mapback was *Death in the Library* by Phillip Ketchum. It was issued in January 1942. Today that little paperback and the 800 or so others which followed it in the series are much sought-after by collectors, who will pay up to $10 for them. (They were originally priced at 25¢.) The Mapbacks had three outstanding features: the scene of the crime depicted on the back cover; the capsule character descriptions preceding Chapter One, which were often more vividly written than the books themselves; the teaser, which enticed you into reading further by dropping more red herrings in less space than had ever been done before (or since).

"COVE CREST"
Scene of Murder in "DEATH OVER SUNDAY"
Bonfire
Sound
Garages
a-hoo
2nd Murder
Rear Entrance
Woods
Bench
Drive
Side Porch
A DELL BOOK

1-Murdered Man
2-Light Switch
3-Stairway to Hall
4-Stairway to 3rd Fl.
5-Paul McCarron
6-Linda Shaw
7-Nick Damatos
8-Playroom
9-Mike Powel
10-Mr.+Mrs. Harper
11-Sam Stanton
12-Sandra Kennedy

17TH FLOOR ROOF GARDEN
ELEVATORS
TO SERVICE ROOM
16TH FLOOR BALCONY
PARSON'S SUITE 1512
DRYDEN WINSLOW 1510
15TH FL. BALCONIES
608 TERRACE
DONCASTER HOUSE
SCENE OF MURDERS IN "THE WHISTLING HANGMAN"

James Francis Bonnell's story mystifies with some sharp, slim arrows, dark spots on the hall carpet and a bonfire on the beach.

Baynard Kendrick's book employs a blue silk negligee cord, a Gideon Bible, a hotel passkey and 300,000 pounds sterling.

THE UNITED STATES BULLION DEPOSITORY

The Depository was completed in December 1936, at a cost of $560,000. The first gold was moved to the Depository by railroad in January 1937.

The two-story building with basement and attic, is constructed of granite, steel and concrete; exterior dimensions measure 105 by 121 feet. Its height is 42 feet above the first-floor level. Over the marble entrance at the front of the building is the inscription UNITED STATES DEPOSITORY along with the seal of the Treasury Department in gold. Offices of the Captain of the Guard and the Officer in Charge open upon the entrance lobby. At the rear is another entrance for the reception of bullion and supplies.

The building houses a two-level steel-and-concrete vault, divided into compartments. The vault door weighs nearly 30 tons. No one person is entrusted with the combination; various members of the Depository staff must dial separately combinations known only to them. The vault casing is constructed of steel plates, steel I-beams and steel cylinders laced with hoop bands and encased in concrete. The vault roof is of similar construction and is independent of the Depository roof.

Inside the vault are standard mint bars of almost pure gold and coin gold bars resulting from the melting of gold coin. The bars are somewhat smaller than an ordinary building brick, the approximate dimensions being 7 x 3⅝ x 1¾ inches. They contain approximately 400 troy ounces of gold, with an avoirdupois weight of about 27½ pounds, and are stored without wrappings in the vault compartments.

Between the corridor encircling the vault and the outer wall of the building is space utilized for offices, storerooms and the like. In the basement is a pistol range. The Depository has its own emergency power plant, water sys-

HOW TO GET INTO FORT KNOX

Fort Knox was named in honor of Major General Henry Knox, who was Secretary of War from 1785 to 1795. During World War I, the facility served as an artillery training center and school. At that time it was half as large as it is today. Following the war and until 1931, it was used only during the summer months for training civilian components. In 1932, having been reactivated for the mechanzation of army units, Fort Knox became a permanent post. It was here, in July 1940, that the Armored Force — U.S. Armor, as it is known today — was born.

Fort Knox is located on U.S. Highway 31W, approximately thirty-five miles south of Louisville and eighteen miles north of Elizabethtown, Kentucky. The main entrance to the post at the Chaffee Avenue intersection is prominently marked with signs. Once inside, go directly to Bullion Boulevard.

tem and other facilities.

The outer wall itself is of granite, lined with concrete. The materials used in construction comprised 16,500 cubic feet of granite, 4,200 cubic yards of concrete, 750 tons of reinforcing steel and 670 tons of structural steel.

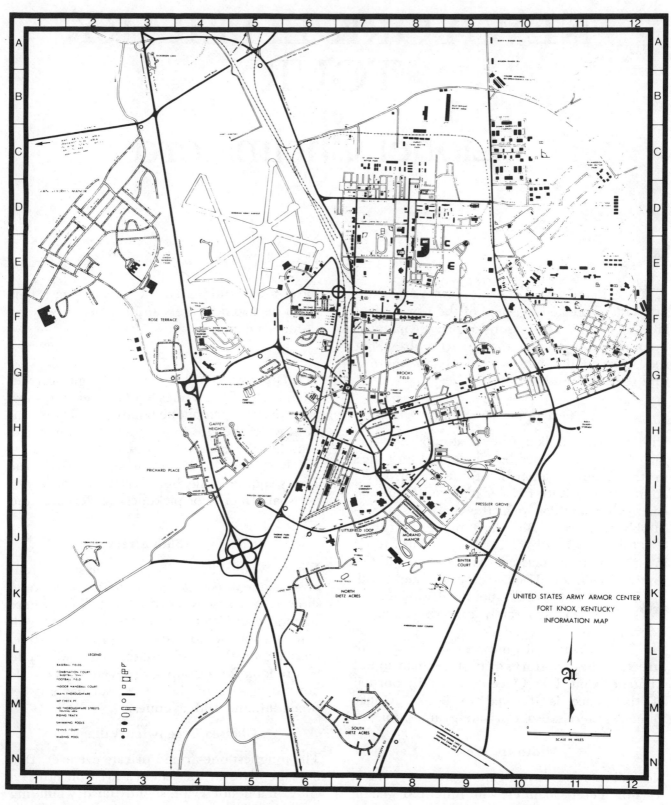

LEGEND

BASEBALL FIELDS
COMBINATION COURT
BASKETBALL - TENNIS
FOOTBALL FIELD
INDOOR HANDBALL COURT
MAIN THOROUGHFARE
MP CHECK PT
NO THOROUGHFARE STREETS
HOUSING AREA
RIDING TRACK
SWIMMING POOLS
TENNIS COURT
WADING POOL

UNITED STATES ARMY ARMOR CENTER
FORT KNOX, KENTUCKY
INFORMATION MAP

SCALE IN MILES

The Depository is equipped with the most modern protective devices and can rely upon additional protection from the nearby Army Post. At each corner of the structure, on the outside but connected to it, are four guard boxes. Sentry boxes, similar to the guard boxes, are located at the entrance gate. A driveway encircles the building and a steel fence marks the boundaries of the site.

No visitors are permitted.

NEW YORK LITERARY TOUR

Lionel Chelmsford

What do you mean, New York's unsafe? It's protected by some of the world's best literary sleuths. For reasons of privacy many of them refuse to divulge their exact address, but they drop enough hints so you'll know where to find them. Should the need arise:

The Upper West Side

Although it's unlikely they'll attend the same faculty meetings since he's a chemist and she's in the English department, Professor Craig Kennedy and Kate Fansler may yet bump into each other as they roam the corridors of Columbia University. Both have offices there.

Ellery Queen lives further downtown, on West 87th Street, between Amsterdam and Columbus avenues. Look for a well-kept, old-fashioned brownstone, about halfway up the block, with an elaborately carved, oak front door; it's probably Queen's.

Still further downtown, on West 70th Street, is the five-story, gray stone mansion of Thatcher Colt. Like Queen's, a goodly portion of the space is devoted to books. Unlike Queen's, there's also a private gymnasium.

Midtown, West

Not all private investigators live in genteel squalor. Peter Chalmer, who inherited wealth, lives in a sumptuous, millionaire's penthouse on Central Park South.

Matthew Scudder, by contrast, lives in a tacky hotel on 57th Street and 8th Avenue, above a bar and across the street from a bar. From his room, he gets an unimpeded view of all-night neon signs.

Times Square

The Great Merlini has a small magic store in the middle of the Times Square area. One suspects there's a telephone booth directly in front of it, which he zips in and out of trying to accomplish the great disappearing trick.

Bart Hardin never moves far from the Times Square locale, but his is the Broadway of newspapermen, not pickpockets, derelicts and pimps.

West 35th Street

Nero Wolfe lives in the most famous brownstone in New York. An aerial view would show it has a glass-covered top floor where Theodore and Wolfe tend to their orchids. William Baring-Gould lists six different street numbers for the Wolfe house, so one would do best to look for a stoop with seven steps on the downtown side of the street, somewhere between 9th and 10th avenues.

Chelsea/Greenwich Village

The toughest one-armed private eye ever, Dan Fortune, lives in the Chelsea area on 8th Avenue, in a nondescript, slightly tawdry building that's seen better days.

Pam and Jerry North, on the other hand, have comfortable and tasteful quarters in the Village, overlooking the Park. Their home is

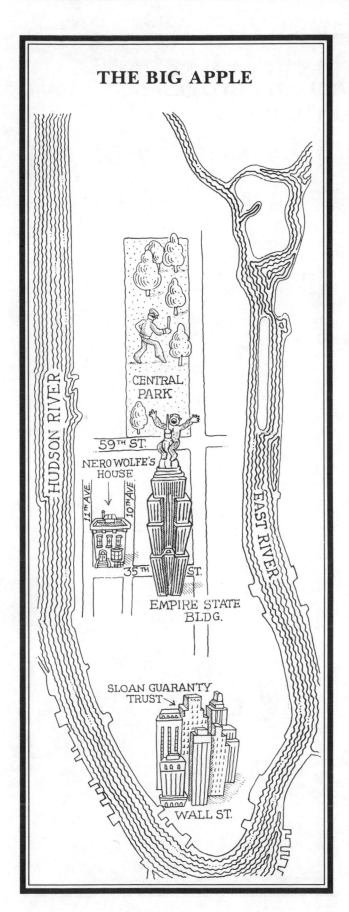

THE BIG APPLE

overrun by cats, but none of the neighbors has ever complained about the smell of kitty litter. So one can conclude they spend much of their day changing it.

Lower Broadway/Wall Street

Reginald DePuyster, who could afford better, being the richest of all literary characters (heir to a $20 million fortune), has offices in the O'Day Detective Agency on Lower Broadway.

Lawyer Arthur Tutt also has offices on Lower Broadway, but they are more in keeping with his background — quiet, unassuming and mannerly.

J.P. Thatcher does not live in the city, but his office is located in the Sloan Guaranty Trust Company building, near enough to Fraunces Tavern to lunch there frequently.

Gramercy Park Area

Philo Vance lives on East 38th Street, in a well-appointed old mansion, the top two (penthouse) floors.

The Upper East Side

Window-shopping in the Upper Sixties, one could expect to come upon Roman Grey's antique store and, a bit further along, the antique store where Emily and Henry Bryce do their furniture refinishing. The Hotel Beaumont, where Pierre Chambrun is the manager, is also in this general area, although possibly closer to Fifth Avenue.

Within walking distance of 59th Street is Henry Gamadge's private house. It's between Park and Lexington avenues, and has a connecting gate between Gamadge's backyard and the rear of his private club. The house is easily recognized by its cleanly painted white front steps.

Norah (and Joe) Mulcahaney lived on East 68th Street, in a remodeled townhouse, when they were first married, but recently they've moved on to bigger quarters no longer in the center of town.

Harlem

Coffin Ed and Gravedigger Jones work Harlem Homicide.

Lionel Chelmsford is lost somewhere in Staten Island.

THE MURDER OF TWO MEN BY A YOUNG KID
WEARING LEMON-COLORED GLOVES
KENNETH PATCHEN

Wait.

                                                            Wait.

                                    Wait.

                        Wait. Wait.

        Wait.

                                          Wait.

                            Wait.

            Wait.

                                Wait.

                                      Wait.

                  Wait.

                                    Wait.

        Wait.

            NOW.

THE SUITCASE CAPER

Harriet Grollier

Each year there are so many new mysteries published, you could put one on every seat in a jumbo jet and not repeat a single title. In fact, you'd have enough left over to fill several flight bags. If a passenger read one a day, it would take him well over a year to finish them all.

What's surprising about this statistic is that mystery readers are always complaining about not having enough to read. They are on an eternal quest for the author who can write them as fast as they can read them.

Most mystery readers would consider the loss of their "light reading" only slightly less serious than the loss of their passport. The problem of replacing the books is a difficult one. Unless you're in England, which, more or less, shares a common language. Or in Scan-

I don't read mystery stories, but I don't know why. I don't suppose I have time. I read Richard Condon and John D. MacDonald on long plane flights, but I don't think they count.

JOHN CHEEVER

dinavia, which publishes a good many mysteries in English. Or in Rome, near the American Express Office by the Spanish Steps. Here, tucked

WHEN YOU'RE ON THE COAST, DON'T FORGET TO CALL:

San Francisco

Pat & Jean Abbot
Boston Blackie
Walter Brackett
The Continental Op
The guys at D.K.A.
Frank Hastings
Sam Spade

Berkeley

Todd McKinnon

Los Angeles

Jacob Asch
David Brandstetter
Bertha Cool and Donald Lam
Philip Marlowe
Perry Mason
Luis Mendoza
Sister Mary Ursula
Moses Wine

Hollywood

Ivor Maddox

Long Beach

Honey West

Pasadena

Virgil Tibbs

Del Mar

Max Roper

Santa Barbara

Lew Archer
Cutter & Bone

San Diego

Max Thursday

away down a long, dark corridor, is the world's best secondhand bookstore — shelf after shelf, stack after stack of mystery books turned in by other travelers. The shop even lets you swap yours for theirs.

Which mysteries are the best to pack? Depends where you're traveling. Many readers use their mysteries as a guide to the country they're visiting. Helen MacInnes' *Decision at Delphi* is an excellent approach to Greece; Arthur Upfield's *Bony* books capture the Australian Outback; James McClure's Kramer & Zondi series pinpoints South Africa; William Marshall's zany procedurals help you find your way in Hong Kong. For the Caribbean, there's A.H.Z. Carr's *Finding Maubee;* for Haiti there's Graham Greene; for Glasgow there's Bill Knox and his fishery stories; for California there's Newton Thornburg's *To Die in California.* For New Zealand there's Ngaio Marsh; for New Guinea there's Charlotte Jay; for Bombay, there's H.R.F. Keating's Inspector Ghote series. And then, of course, for world travelers, the most peripatetic books of all are the international spy stories, which cross borders quicker than you can say false passport.

Naturally, the book to pack is the paperback. It's the best thing to happen to traveling since Banlon. Light, small, bendable, the paperback conveniently fills up the hole between your left shoe and your shampoo bottle. To avoid crimping edges, however, paperbacks are best packed as the bottom layer, before the clothes go in. The average suitcase, 15″ x 25″, holds one paperback in reading position (vertical) and three paperbacks at a 30° angle (horizontal) per row. Multiply by three rows and you have enough material to get you through two weeks (a fortnight if you're in Great Britian). In addition to this dozen, one is advised to stow two in one's hand luggage: one for you; one for the pest the airlines has put next to you. Mysteries may also be tucked into your hatband, jammed into your raincoat pocket, jammed into your other raincoat pocket, slipped into your flight bag, dropped inside your umbrella. Putting one between your shirt and your belt buckle is also good. But ticklish.

Harriet Grollier is the author of The Peripatetic Valise. *She suffers jet-lag.*

Chapter 8
RED HERRINGS

FRED WINKOWSKI

WHODUNIT
A Guide to the Obvious

Matthew J. Mahler

I once knew a man who thought he could outsmart John Dickson Carr. He was reading *The Skeleton in the Clock,* and along about page 56 he decided he knew who done it. In fact, he was absolutely convinced of it. He was all wrong, of course, his thinking detoured by one of the most devious minds in the business. Several years later, the same man picked up the same book and decided to reread it. He wouldn't make the same mistake twice, he said, not him. He'd forgotten everything about the book except whom he'd chosen as the murderer the first time round, so, carefully ignoring that person, he went on to finger someone else and, as you've probably guessed, missed again.

John Dickson Carr, in the words of the people at Vita, was a (red) herring maven. He was expert at creating them. His two closest rivals, according to an informal poll taken by my duped friend, would have to be Agatha Christie and Dorothy L. Sayers, which brings us to an interesting equation: Take *Ten Little Indians,* divide by *Four False Weapons,* and you're left with *Five Red Herrings.* Not to mention the feeling that you've been had by the best.

Any respectable mystery will have at least one red herring in it. Now, a red herring comes in two forms: human and inanimate (in which case it's called a clue; sometimes, an alibi). Human red herrings are easy to recognize. They are usually anybody with a deep dark secret in his past. The deep dark secret is that he is a red herring. In books with more than one murder, the second murder is a red herring.

RED HERRINGS

They are, of course, false clues meant to distract one from the real villain. The term originated in England, and there are instances of its use as far back as the seventeenth century. It seems some people were distressed at the idea of a fox being hunted to its death by a pack of snarling dogs and a party of upper-class riders. To throw the dogs off the track, these anti-hunt people would go to the fish market, buy herrings, take them home and smoke them — which gave them a reddish color — then drag them through the woods and fields. The pungent odor of the fish would cover up the scent of the fox and confuse the dogs, allowing the fox to escape. Thus did red herrings become synonymous with attempts to deceive.

That body, poor thing, died for no other reason than to distract you from the killer's motive for committing the first crime. Other likely red herrings are: a business partner, particularly if

OVERUSED CLUES

Half a pair of scissors
An heirloom brooch
A birthmark
An accent that slips
Cigarette ashes
Lipstick-stained cup
Ravelings from a sleeve
Glass with fingerprints
Torn diary
Pawn ticket
Laundry stub
Address book
Stopped clock
Dogs that don't bark
Whispered telephone conversations

he's disgruntled (too obvious); a woman suffering from amnesia (whereas a man so afflicted is almost always the culprit); at least three of the heirs present at the reading of the will. This last is tricky. How do you know which are red herrings and which, in combination, have sent Grandfather off to their eternal reward? Well, years of study have revealed that any heir who has not yet reached his majority is a red herring, ditto an heir who receives the bulk of the estate (providing the will was not drawn up within a fortnight of the funeral). Any heir who refuses to cry is a red herring; only a red herring would be that unsympathetic.

Mysterious telephone callers, gentlemen with foreign accents who ask a lot of questions in the pub, poison-pen writers and neighbors who own large barking dogs are also red herrings, but that doesn't mean they're guiltless. Usually, though, they're responsible for a sec-

ondary crime, such as extortion, rather than the primary one of murder. You can't discount them, but you'd be wrong to put the blame for everything on them; they're simply not smart enough to handle all that.

There are two other candidates for red herringdom: the least likely suspect and the most likely suspect. Ever since Mrs. Christie conned us in *The Murder of Roger Ackroyd*, we've become extremely wary of ruling out the least likely. It's gotten so we trust no one, not even the victim, who we're convinced — sometimes correctly — is shamming. The tipoff here is how much the least likely talks and if he has a first name. If he seems awfully helpful and full of gossip, and has both a first name and a surname, he's no red herring. If he's quiet, thoughtful and always referred to as Mr. So-and-So, he *is* a red herring. If the cards seem stacked against one character right from the beginning, that person is a red herring. The real killer will appear three pages from the end of the book. (And the author ought to be strung up by his typewriter ribbon; it's a terrible thing to do.)

Clues and alibis also function as red herrings. Clues to disregard are those that come in pairs, such as an earring with a bloody fingerprint on it. That strains coincidence just a bit too much and is an obvious plant. Red herring alibis are those which are airtight. Nobody lives that tidy a life.

Red herrings were spawned years ago. I suppose one would have to credit Mr. Poe (remember those two voices overheard in that upstairs room in the Rue Morgue? Red herrings, if ever there were ones). They proliferated in the Twenties and Thirties, but now with the advent of the police procedural, they're becoming extinct. As the whodunit fades and the whydunit and howtheydunit become more popular, a reader is forced to turn to the older authors to find them.

I don't know what you're planning on reading next, but a friend of mine is taking a third crack at *The Skeleton in the Clock*. This time, he swears he'll get it right.

Matthew J. Mahler is chairman of the Save the Red Herring Movement.

WATSONS
Frederick Arnold

It's a toss-up whether the hero's best friend is a red herring or an albatross.

If there's a clear footprint, he walks across it.

If there's an equally clear fingerprint, he invariably smudges it.

If there's a vital phone message, he forgets to relay it, and if there's a handwriting specimen, he misidentifies it.

In short, if there's a wrong conclusion to jump to, he swings into it with the enthusiasm of Tarzan on the vine.

A Watson (who needn't be a male) is chronically inept, possibly genetically so. He is also the biggest troublemaker since Cain. As he blunders from room to room (pocketing clues as he goes), he keeps up a steady barrage of questions so inane, it's a wonder his chum even bothers answering.

Every now and then, a scholar (with more than a dollop of Watson in his soul) will suggest the hero's friend is a stand-in for the reader. He is supposed to say all the things we would, if we were in his place. His insights are our insights, so the theory goes, and his confusion is our confusion. Perhaps the reader ought to sue for character defamation.

Actually, Watsons exist because, without them, who would lay down the trail of red herrings?

If there is one thing Watsons excel at, it's pointing the way to the fork on the left when the killer has blithely gone on his way to the right. A confirmed mystery addict will recognize this duplicity for what it is, and not be bothered with it. The novice often traipses down the wrong path with him.

To qualify as a Watson, a character must have more faith in the hero than Rockefeller has dimes. And that faith must be absolutely unshakable. Example: The hero picks up a book of Serbo-Croat poetry (not in translation). To the best of a Watson's knowledge, his friend has never been in Serbia or Croatia, has never read a word of the language before. Nevertheless, when he remarks that there's an amusing grammatical error in the third stanza, a Watson not only believes him, but maligns the author for his slipshoddiness.

The best Watsons (i.e., the ones who most frequently succor the enemy under the misapprehension that they are abetting the innocent) are never the same age as their heroes. It doesn't matter if they're older or younger; they simply must not be on a par with the hero on any level, even a chronological one. Besides, if they're older, the hero gets to twit them for being forgetful, and if they're younger, he gets to tease them for still having a lot to learn. (Books with Watsons in them pass this off as witty dialogue.)

Watsons are also good for establishing alibis. For the killer. They are the ones most apt to remark, "Why, Lord Z and I were on that train together. He never left my sight for a moment," thereby confounding the Hero Detective until he reminds his pal of his penchant for dozing off without realizing it.

The red herring-est aspect of a Watson is, of course, his total inability to solve a case on his own. (Think of the Old Man in the Corner's Polly and the Thinking Machine's Hutchinson Hatch.) He has an uncanny ability to do all the legwork and have all the pertinent information

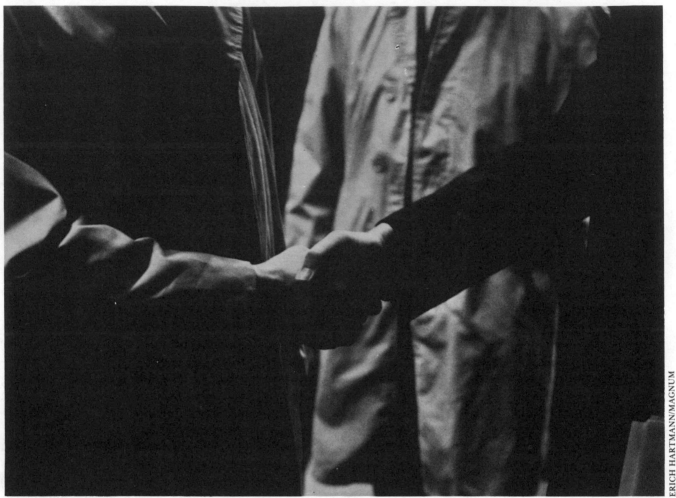

ERICH HARTMANN/MAGNUM

The handshake, universal symbol of friendship, was disdained by most Watsons, who scrupulously avoided touching their chums; in fact, they were under direct orders to keep hands off. Nero Wolfe had a positive fetish about it, and Archie indulged him by never presenting his hand (although he often shook those of perfect strangers).

in front of him (including a few things he really doesn't think matter — such as that old love letter he retrieved from the trash basket which he's shown to no one) yet not be able to see the solution. He must present his findings to the Great Detective, who will then carefully explain to him what it all means. Left to his own devices, a Watson would march even further down that left-handed path. And this *despite* the evidence.

Unlike other red herrings, Watsons never lie. But they have an unfortunate tendency to repeat anything they hear, so killers frequently whisper lies in their ears which they then naïvely perpetuate. This is what trips up the new mystery reader. He assumes trusty Watson would not be gulling him, when, in fact, albeit unwittingly, he is.

Although we're calling this specific breed of red herring a Watson, after the most famous of them all, it really ought to have another name, reflecting the first character who represented the type. The problem here is, the first one was so dim-witted he neglected to tell us his name. You probably remember him, though, as a chronicler of Dupin's tales. Yes, Edgar Allan Poe, originator of most whodunit conventions, also gave us the friend of minus intellectuality. Why he entrusted this oaf with the task of narrating the stories is beyond our comprehension, but others have followed, and it's a safe bet if the narrator isn't the killer, he's the hero's best friend, the red herring *par excellence.*

Frederick Arnold says that since he has two first names, he is his own best friend.

SLEUTHS AND SIDEKICKS
Betsy Lang

*Take one from the left column and one from
the right column and match them up.*

Sleuths

1. Sexton Blake
2. Dr. Daniel Coffee
3. Sir Denis Nayland Smith
4. Albert Campion
5. Lamont Cranston
6. Capt. Jose da Silva
7. Insp. Wilfred Dover
8. John J. Malone
9. Dr. Thorndyke
10. Sherlock Holmes
11. Col. March
12. Perry Mason
13. Mr. and Mrs. North
14. Joseph Rouletabille
15. Judge Dee
16. Rabbi David Small
17. Lord Peter Wimsey
18. Henri Bencolin
19. Modesty Blaise
20. Bertha Cool
21. Insp. Purbright
22. Insp. Gabriel Hanaud
23. Grace Latham
24. Insp. McGee
25. Nick and Nora Charles
26. Nero Wolfe
27. Henry Gamadge
28. Roderick Alleyn
29. Max Carrados
30. Evan Pinkerton
31. Harley Quin
32. Nick Carter
33. Nigel Strangeways
34. Hercule Poirot

Sidekicks

a. Chick & Patsy
b. Mr. Ricardo
c. Insp. Roberts
d. Henry Satterthwaite
e. Bunter
f. Dr. Motial Mookerji
g. Harold Bantz
h. Dr. Petrie
i. Sgt. Love
j. Jeff Marle
k. Magersfontein Lugg
l. Dr. Watson
m. Tinker
n. Capt. Hastings
o. Archie Goodwin
p. Louis Calling
q. Sgt. Bull
r. Insp. Todhunter
s. Hugh Lanigan
t. Insp. Fox
u. Harry Vincent
v. Col. Primrose
w. Martini
x. Christopher Jervis
y. Sainclair
z. Hoong Liang
aa. Maggie Cassidy
bb. Insp. Blount
cc. Willie Garvin
dd. Sgt. MacGregor
ee. Asta
ff. Paul Drake
gg. Donald Lam
hh. Wilson

Answers:
1-m; 2-f; 3-h; 4-k; 5-u; 6-hh; 7-dd; 8-aa; 9-x; 10-l; 11-c; 12-ff; 13-w;
14-y; 15-z; 16-s; 17-e; 18-j; 19-cc; 20-gg; 21-i; 22-b; 23-v; 24-r; 25-ee; 26-o;
27-g; 28-t; 29-p; 30-q; 31-d; 32-a; 33-bb; 34-n.

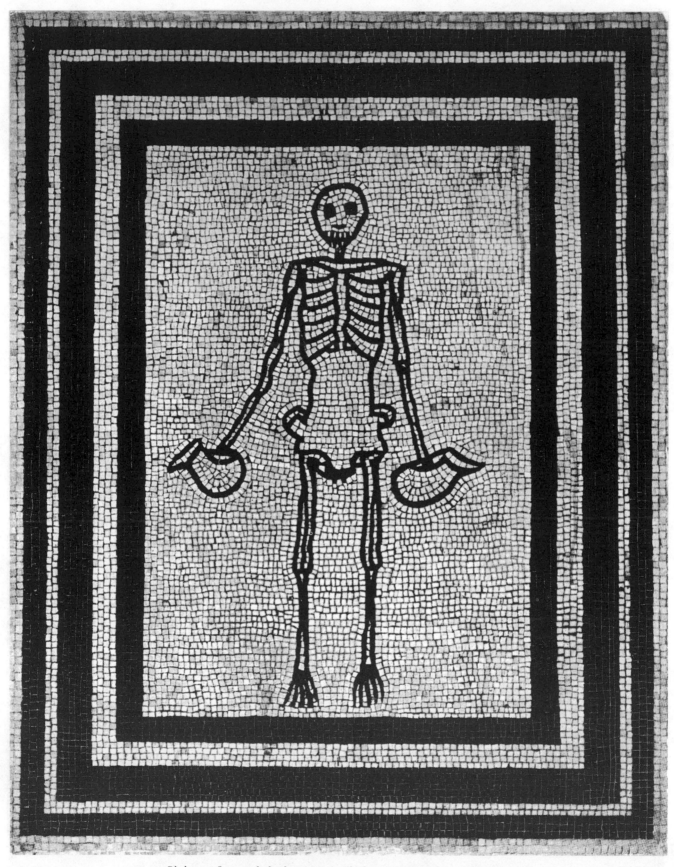

Skeleton of an early butler. Mosaic tile found in the ruins of Pompeii.

THE BUTLER

Dilys Winn

"Madam," said the voice on the other end of the telephone, "this is Mills. How may I be of service to you?"

Right then I knew that I was outclassed. I have always been vaguely uncomfortable around an English accent, particularly if it's been bred in Mayfair, and this one sounded like it was being ladled out on a Georgian spoon, with all the appropriate hallmarks.

"Er, ya see," I Brooklyned, "I wanna know if the butler did it. In real life, I mean. In mysteries he was such a terrific suspect. He knew all the dirt and where the bodies were buried and which shelf in the pantry had the bloodstained gardening trowel, and he was always popping up right behind you to announce dinner in such a way, you knew it would be your last meal on earth. Are you really like that, or what?"

Mills — that is, Mr. John Mills, a government butler formerly in private service, now working regularly for the Chancellor of the Exchequer at No. 11 — agreed to meet at my hotel to discuss the matter.

"We'll have a drink," I added, then bit down hard on my tongue. What had I done! Bunter would never have joined Lord Peter at the table.

Mills, however, ordered a gin.

I was simultaneously relieved I hadn't offended his sense of propriety and disappointed I was so far removed from being a Your Ladyship that he'd drink with me.

My polyester travel-knit took one look at his made-to-measure jacket, with its cuff buttons that actually unbuttoned, and immediately shrank two sizes, desperately trying to hide itself behind the cocktail napkin. I shredded a matchbook cover and upended the peanut dish.

I tried to think of a subtle way to ask Mills about his background.

"How'd ya become a butler, Mills?" I said.

He gave the wrong answer.

Anyone who's read a mystery knows the typical butler served with His Lordship during the Great War and followed after him ever after. Mills, on the other hand, changed Lordships every six months or so. When he thought he'd absorbed enough information, he moved on to another stately home — and a boost in salary.

"Aha, Mills!" I exclaimed, in the manner of Holmes accosting Moriarty. "And you used that information for nefarious purposes, didn't you? A bit of blackmail you presented His Lordship on your silver tray, was it?"

It was nothing of the kind.

Given the household hierarchy, Mills said, if you stayed in service in just one place, you'd be old and gray before it was your turn to play butler. You'd have to work your way up from fourth to third to second to first footman. Then you'd have to put in a spell in the kitchen, first as general helper, then as vegetable cook and next as roast cook. When you finished that up, you got to be hallboy, which included carrying coals wherever they were needed, emptying chamber pots, polishing shoes (including the butler's) and ironing the butler's clothes (you had to prove yourself on them before they let you tackle the family's). Being hallboy also demanded you do the washing up in the servants'

His Lordship, secure in the confines of his study; he occupies himself with the Times *while waiting for his butler to bring the port.*

hall after the other servants had finished eating and that you helped out in the pantry when that was through. Then, if you'd learned to do all these things properly, you were ready to be trained as a valet, which included sessions with a London clothier so you knew which clothes to lay out for His Lordship every morning; sessions with the wine merchants so you could distinguish between a good hock and an inferior port; sessions with a Scottish gun expert so you knew how to load up for a weekend shoot. After all that, if there was a vacancy, you got to be butler.

Mills was too impatient to wait for something to happen to the second footman so he could move up a station. Ergo, when he'd mastered the third footman's job, he'd skip off to another stately home. His shortcuts worked out very well. When he was just twenty-one, he became butler to the Marquis of Bewley, a descendant of Robert the Bruce.

"Hmmmmm," I said, "I never read about a *young* butler. There was Currie, who worked for Philo Vance, but he was no chicken; neither was that prototype of all butlers, the one in *The Moonstone* who was always quoting Robinson Crusoe. You were hardly old enough to read it,

never mind cite it. And what about loyalty, Mills? All my mystery butlers, no matter how suspicious they looked, were loyal."

"Well," said Mills, "I was loyal when I was there, I suppose, but, you see, going back to my younger days — this was in the Thirties — the thing about the position was its security. You never got paid much, but you did get three meals a day, and I did get my own little suite of rooms. If I'd been married, I probably would have gotten my own little cottage on the grounds. And I did have my own valet, which quite spoiled me."

"But, Mills, mystery butlers never had all that. If they did, where would they have gotten a motive? Didn't they overwork you at least?" I was unwilling to let my fantasies die.

"Actually, you're confusing the butler with the valet," he replied. "The valet did the really hard work. For example, Lord Bewley would tell me to arrange a shooting party. I would go down our guest list and ring up the people I thought were suitable, and then show His Lordship the arrangement. But the valet, he had to travel to the shoot with them. He had to get up at five to ready the guns; he had to stand there and load them; he had to carry the game

MARTY NORMAN

His Lordship, a little less secure in his study, which appears to be booby-trapped. (Herbert Adams rigged up a trapdoor in The Dean's Daughter, *A. A. Milne devised a secret passageway in* The Red House Mystery, *Mary Roberts Rinehart created trick paneling in* The Circular Staircase — *to cite just three examples of mysterious exits and entrances.)*

back and oversee its cooking. I stayed home and arranged to pick them up at the train."

"It's a wonder the valet never killed you," I snarled. "Now, Mills, tell me what you did do, tell me how you crept up behind everyone and scared them half to death when they weren't expecting you. Tell me how you went from the library to the master bedroom without anyone noticing."

"Oh, do you mean the secret passageways?" he asked politely. "I worked in several houses that had them. Priest's holes, actually, from Reformation days. They fit behind the bookshelves, but no one used them much. Certainly not me. In one house there was a secret staircase behind the paneling. I suppose one could have stayed back in there for several days. I do know of several communicating rooms. Do you know about them? There was a secret door between them which you had to press just so. A gentleman in one room would often use it to visit an unmarried lady staying in the other. I could always tell if the door had been opened at night. There was dust on the floor, and you could see foot marks, and certain

things were moved a bit, like a chair. It's difficult to explain, but one just knew if the connection had been fiddled with."

"How about your accent, Mills?" I interrogated. "Isn't that a clear giveaway you were impersonating a butler, just like in the books?"

"I was fortunate," he said. "I went to a fairly decent school, the oldest one in the City of London, actually — King Edward School, founded by Edward VI after the dissolution of the monasteries by Henry VIII. Sometimes, as butler, I'd have to discharge a lad who didn't speak correctly. Oh, you'd try to take him aside and help him with it, but if it didn't take, there was nothing else to be done but let him go. It was a reflection on the house, wasn't it?"

I wasn't done yet. I'd saved my heavy artillery for the last. "Tell me, Mills, if you were so blameless, how come when the public goes to a movie and sees a butler in it, if they read a book and a butler's in it, they always cry, 'He did it, the butler did it!' "

Mills shot a hand-turned cuff. "Oh, I expect that's because we did everything else," he said. "Natural assumption."

THE PUB

Hadrian Schwartz

There's a certain type of mystery in which the author strolls you up the High Street, past the post office, past the doctor's surgery, past the old Bermondsey place with its dishevelled lawn, and deposits you in The Bunch of Grapes.

There, the Squire stands you to a lager and you reciprocate. When he leaves, you have a friendly game of dominoes with a North Country lorry driver. Just as you're finishing up, a stranger with a peculiar stain on his waistcoat asks to be directed to the loo. You oblige. As you're settling your bill with Teddy, he suggests you bring in your own tankard and put it there, third peg from the left, over the counter. Before you can answer, Daft Willie intrudes. He offers you his peanut brittle tin. You decline. He cries. You accept, carefully wiping the dirt off the candy before pretending to eat it.

It's all very companionable, very low-key, and you have a thorough good time of it. Until the author invites you to leave.

If you've read as many mysteries as I have, you know you're now in for big trouble — which will hound you throughout the book.

On the walk home, a little the worse for lager, you take a wrong turning, and instead of manoeuvring the High Street you're skirting Miller's Pond. Oops. You slip, of course. As you right yourself, you see it. A silver kilt pin. The Squire's?

Hurrying now, you cut 'cross the gully. Two shadows. Whispers. A snatch of North Country accent?

Exhausted, you arrive at Lady Sarah's. She ushers you into the game room and sits you east; opposite, calmly shuffling, a gentleman with a stain on his waistcoat.

And then to bed, where you fret the night away dreaming of clay-covered peanut brittle tins and empty tankards swooshing left, right, left.

It helps at this point to get a pen and neatly xxxxx out The Bunch of Grapes. Like every other pub in every other village mystery, the name is a pseudonym. This time, it's The Grapes. Next time, The British Queen, or The Three Tuns or The Cheshire Cheese. But actually, though the author can't admit it or he'd spoil his plot, the pub's real name is The Red Herring.

Here, more alibis are created, more suspects congregate, more clues are uncovered, than anyplace else in the whole book. Undoubtedly, you will be suckered in by every single one of them. Who could mistrust something he sees or hears in a place that goes back at least two hundred years?

The typical Red Herring Pub was built in the time of Cromwell. Its sides bulge as though distended by gas. Its door lists in a permanent curtsey to the street. Its exterior, as well as many a patron, needs a nice coat of whitewash. Inside are two small rooms. The left has the dartboard, the dominoes, the walk-in fireplace, the regulars' tankards and the slew of red herrings. The right has the wives. (It's usually empty.) Both have sagging floors and tiny paned windows with the original glass still intact. Shapes are barely recognisable through them.

The publican lives upstairs. In fact, he was born there. He is one of the three men in town who make a decent living, the other two being the butcher and the turf accountant. He has calluses on his palm from pulling pints, an end-

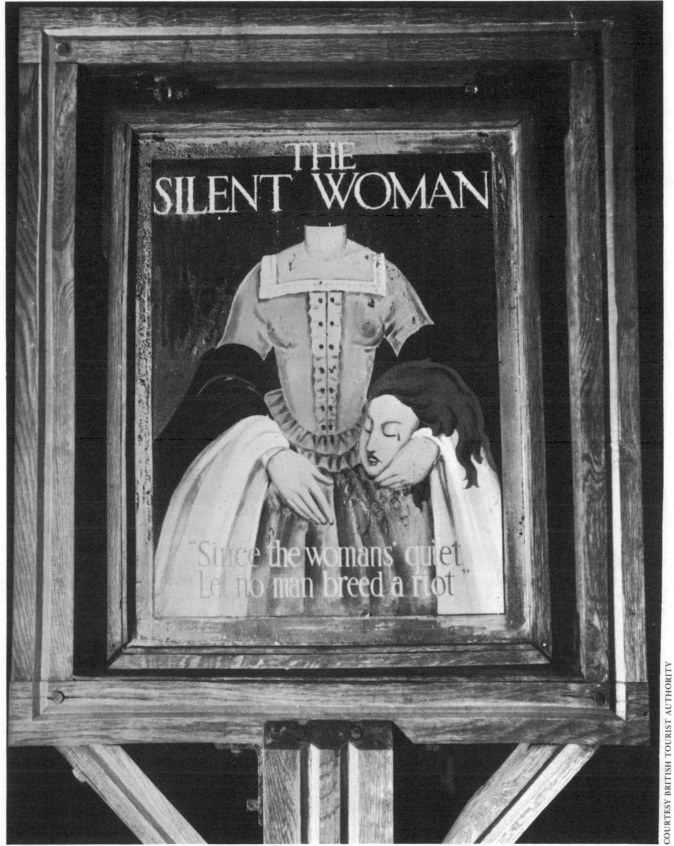

A typical pub sign, painted on wood and hung from a high post.

CORNELL CAPA/MAGNUM

The regulars, having a round on the publican.

less supply of not-quite-clean aprons, and he arbitrates all arguments by calling Time and closing the bar.

He also sets up more red herring situations than anyone else in the story. It is he who picks up a discarded matchbook and remarks, "Fancy that, the Savoy Grille. Someone just been to London, eh?"; who warns Simon he's had a bit of enough and sends him on his way, alone, with a step unsteady and a mind besotted by gin; who loans Colin the weed-killer and Derek the van.

It is he who serves the Inspector a half-and-half and a passel of half-truths, which he repeats as gossip.

The publican himself is not a red herring. He is obviously too busy tending to Rodney's shandy to step across the way, filch Mrs. Greer's locket, hide it and establish an alibi. He hasn't the time to stiletto the Duke, cycle to the dump and heave the knife, and be back for Opening. But as sure as his shandy is a half-pint beer to a half-pint cider, his pub is a red-herring breeding ground.

Think about it. An author can't always be arranging house parties to introduce his suspects. What's more logical than having them stop by the Local for a quick one?

An author can't always rely on conversations being heard outside the French windows. Where better to plant them than in the adjoining booth at the neighbourhood free house?

An author can't always expect the parlour maid to discover and return the button (cigarette lighter, woolly scarf, initial handkerchief, loose key). Who better to notice it than the publican?

There's no such thing as an innocent conversation in a mystery pub. What seems harmless at the time will evolve, two chapters later, into a clue. Similarly, no one who goes to a pub is entirely innocent. A page or so further on, one learns the sociable drinker needed an alibi. That these clues and these alibis have little to do

THE FIVE ALLS

| I FIGHT FOR ALL | I PRAY FOR ALL | I RULE ALL | I PLEAD FOR ALL | I PAY FOR ALL |

An early pub sign with a sardonic message.

with the actual solution of the case should by now be second nature to us. But it's not. We grab hold to the bitter end, staunch in our conviction that what transpired in the pub is of utmost importance. And so it is, or we'd have solved the mystery in the very first chapter and hated the author ever after.

Real pubs are markedly similar to fictional ones. There's the same whimsical choice of names, the same Cromwellian architecture, the same hard-working publican (only usually it's two publicans, a husband and wife). Darts are played; so are dominoes. (Stakes, however, are low. ½p forfeit if you can't go.) Lager outsells gin, gin outsells whisky and lemon squash is more popular than Coke. Tankards are hung over the bar, but they're often bawdy — not like those in mysteries — with naked females forming their handles. Visitors use one room, the regulars the other (and that would play havoc with a mystery plot).

The biggest point of difference is that pub-licans rarely own their pubs. They belong to Whitbread's or Watney's. The free house has almost disappeared, and today publicans are managers rather than owners. Still, the décor is their own and so is the atmosphere.

A recent three-day swing through six London pubs disclosed no red herrings, either. Nobody in them, including me, had found a long-lost glove or noticed a bloodstain on a lorry trunk. A constable had not checked in, and no one had seen a tattersalled Continental asking directions. Mugs were rinsed without a thought to saving them for prints, and plowman's lunches were downed without a single instance of ptomaine, never mind arsenic.

In real life, The Bunch of Grapes is no Red Herring. But I've yet to close the file on Ye Olde Tea Shoppe.

Hadrian Schwartz is a regular at The Blubbering Whale.

DAMES
Allison Wentworth

MATTHEW SEAMAN

Pink is not their color, and they've never developed a fondness for true blue, either. It's blood red that tips their nails and jet black that swathes their bodies, usually in a sweep of taffeta that crackles like crisp new hundred-dollar bills.

Dames have been around since the Thirties, but they hit their prime in the Forties and Fifties. They seduced Spade and Marlowe and Spillane and Archer, and from there on it was downhill all the way. Lately, they've been hectoring Bond, even Parker — and dumber than that, they just don't come.

Dames have one recurring fantasy: a little house with twenty-seven rooms in it, a mink in every closet and a white telephone by the poolside. Every morning, if they had their way, a six-foot gent would exit their bed and on his way out drop some bills on the dresser (nothing smaller than a fifty). Then they'd spend the day boozing it away, gambling it away beside a short fat old man who'd pat them on the fanny every time they rolled a seven, or giving it away to a cast of characters ranging from a kid brother just out of the pen to a well-muscled chauffeur with the odd bullet scar to a wise guy with a scheme so full of holes that the bunco squad could march right through it.

Books about dames appeal primarily to men. They never see what the broads are up to till it's too late and they have no recourse but to black-and-blue their jaw or ventilate their belly.

Men, be they the private-eye hero or the private-eye reader, are tripped up by dark seams stretching up impossibly long legs. A waft of gardenia perfume goes direct to their brain and numbs their thinking. Their eyes get clouded by a toss of hair that's whiter than any pillow cover.

It's not uncommon for such men to think of these dames as red herrings. "Poor kid," they say about a gal who'd sell her mother, "she needs a break." They know she's not quite on the up and up, but they'd rather not face it. It's easier for them to make her a ruse, to treat her as a diversion instead of the instigator.

So the hard-boiled dame functions as a red herring. Unless, as sometimes happens, a woman is reading the book. Women know all the dame's tricks. They know only a female with a yen for black taffeta could arrive at the murder scene in time to commit it, not to be

It ain't no sin if you crack a few laws now and then, just so long as you don't break any.

Every Day's a Holiday
MAE WEST

PERFUMES NOT TO WEAR WHEN COMMITTING A CRIME

Bal à Versailles
Chloë
Émeraude
Je Reviens
Joy
Muguet
Norell
Shalimar
White Shoulders
Youth Dew

framed by it. They know it's no accident the blackmailer was iced once her letters were returned to her. They know if there's any confusion she's at the bottom of it, if there's any death she probably committed it.

Still, the dame is an ersatz red herring. The sentimental will think her guilty — but not really. The cynic will spot her for what she is — a two-timing broad.

When they're not in the swing of things themselves, dames are champion red-herring droppers. Who put one of Saul's cigars in the dead man's ashtray? Who gave Lewis the ticket to a performance that was canceled? Who told Herman to take her car and drive it past the bank — she'd be ready at eleven sharp? Who indeed.

The old-fashioned peroxided dames, with earrings that got lost and diaries that got stolen, are quickly vanishing from the crime writer's lexicon. But they're being replaced by hippie dames, twenty-year-olds who never wear bras and never forget their dexies. These women are not so different in anything but dress. Their morals can be likened to the Easter bunny's, their language smacks of the Fifties truckdriver's. But deep down there is about them a lingering scent of gardenia, a glimpse of a seam going clear to the thigh. They, too, are seemingly vulnerable; they, too, find a susceptible

ASSOCIATED PRESS

Dese dames were all related to Clyde Barrow (the infamous Clyde of Parker and Barrow). Like dames in mysteries, they favored tight curls, tight skirts and tight (buttoned) lips.

private eye to do their dirty work. They don't usually die at the end of the book, but they get sent home to their parents — and to their mind that's tantamount to death.

How did women get started in the role of red herring? I suspect they had all that free time on their hands in which to scatter clues (women almost never work in mysteries, unless it's as a governess in a Gothic) and so they became targets of opportunity.

The next time you read of a woman waiting in a private eye's office, and he opens the door to find her sitting there on the edge of his desk, a long leg beating time against his chair, pay attention. The dame aint there for his health.

Wickedness is a myth invented by good people to account for the curious attractiveness of others.

Phrases and Philosophies for the Use of the Young
OSCAR WILDE

Allison Wentworth is a feminist.

STOOLIES
Christopher Rutledge

His grammar is atrocious. Every sentence out of his mouth begins "I aint" and follows with one of four possibilities:

"I aint done nothin' wrong."

"I aint gonna tell ya."

"I aint a squealer."

"I aint heard nothin' yet."

His words are wheezed past an adenoidal blockage, propelled through the air on a thin, high, unsteady whistle. Sometimes he stutters. Often his words are pulled to the side, turned down, where they must cross the hurdle of a curled lower lip.

Clearly, this stoolie is in need of Professor Higgins, but he will never find him. Like the mystery stoolie, who is almost always American, from big-city fringes, George (not his real name, of course) never ventures far from Chicago's South Side.

Again like his counterpart, George has attached himself to a gang. He is not a full-participation member; in fact, he is not so much one of "the boys" as one of the boys' gofers. It is George who goes for the take-out eggplant parmigiana, then stands around while the boys eat it. It is George who goes for the ten copies of the *News*, who goes for Miss Lalia and tells her Sam wants to see her.

George has one friend, who just happens to be on the Chicago Police Force. It's his cousin, actually, and they have breakfast at 7 A.M. every single day. George likes to talk to him; the kid knows nothing about horses and George is educating him.

George thinks of himself as a double agent. "I aint got no one boss," he says. "I got two, and I control them. But they're so dumb they don't know it. I can tell them what I like, when I want to, and then me and my money are off to the ponies."

Stoolies are usually addressed in the diminutive: Georgie for George; Sammy for Samuel; Louie for Louis. This is done not out of friendship or respect, but to connote their inferior standing in the gang, their childishness.

THE BETTMANN ARCHIVE, INC.

What George doesn't understand is that nobody has much faith in him. According to his cousin, he's like the tipster at the track: It's not that you think he knows better than you do; it's just that he's available, so you check in to see what he's got to say.

In mysteries, the stoolie is used as a red herring. The mob boss gives him a message, a dime to phone it in with and instructions to be back within the hour and report on what happened. Or he'll be allowed to overhear the plans for a caper so he can relay them to the fuzz, thus ensuring a wild-goose chase over to

"*Geez. Everybody knows he was framed. Why don't you put the screws on Big Joe? I don't know anything. And even if I did — I ain't no canary, and I don't sing, see?*"

"*Carozzo's dead.*"

"*The hell you say! Well — all right. I told him I'd croak him. Go on. Ask me something. But you ain't going to railroad me.*"

The Broadway Murders:
A Nightclub Mystery
EDWARD J. DOHERTY

the Loop when the gang's real attack is being staged in Kenilworth. George is too idiosyncratic, too independent. He just might tell more than they bargained for. Besides, George isn't in deep enough for that. All his facts come to him through, well, osmosis, just what he gets from hanging around. He can't recall ever being specifically told to deliver any tidbit to anyone. "I aint gonna do that," he says. "They want a delivery boy, call Western Union. I say what I want to say."

In *Brighton Rock* Graham Greene had

Pinkie send an informer over the banister when he suspected the man had ratted. Oliver Bleeck put a stoolie in an coin-operated drier when he could no longer control him. In mysteries, stoolies are red herrings with the shortest life spans. But in real life it's a little easier. "I aint heard nothing about that yet," says George. "Those guys and the ones you read about in the paper, they weren't like me. I aint gonna die like that. I mind my business. Nobody's gonna do that to me."

On the other hand, George is as poorly dressed as any mystery stoolie who ever crossed the page. Sartorially, he bears a striking resemblance to Dustin Hoffman in *Midnight Cowboy*. His coat came from Goodwill, donated by some soul about 11 inches taller, 75 pounds fatter. Georgie is a little man — no more than 5'2", roughly 120 pounds. And few of those pounds have seen a bathtub with any regularity. If he were a restaurant, the Board of Health would close him down.

It is impossible to estimate George's age. He could be fifty; he could be twenty-five. All he'll say is that he's old enough to vote. Stoolies in mysteries rarely top thirty: their situation is too precarious for longevity.

George has been pulled in only once, Christmas, two years ago. He hated it. "I aint a crook now and I wasn't one then," he says. Exactly what he did do, he won't mention, but it got him thirty days and "some terrific cupsacoffee."

To say George is likable would be stretching it, but there is something awfully appealing about meeting a man who likes his life as it is. The one thing he would like to happen that hasn't, so far, is to meet a cop socially. He once read an article that said if you put a cop and a criminal in the same room at a party they'd gravitate toward each other, even if they didn't know what the other one did for a living. He would like to see if that happened.

Christopher Rutledge is a former reporter for a large Illinois newspaper. He is the recipient of the Malcolm R. Fenway award for excellence: he has a red herring for breakfast every morning.

Chapter 9
COPS AND BOBBIES

CARELLA OF THE 87TH

James McClure

High above rope barriers and waiting nets, a pretty young girl threatens suicide on a twelfth-story window ledge:

> The police and the fire department had gone through the whole bit — they had seen this particular little drama a thousand times in the movies and on television. If there was anything that bored civil service employees, it was a real-life enactment of the entertainment cliché.

So begins Ed McBain's *Like Love*, a tour de force in his 87th Precinct series that says it all. It proclaims the man's genius for honesty, empathy and gentle humour. It explains why his Stephen Louis Carella has become one of the greatest "real" detectives in fiction, and the series itself among the most satisfying. We smell truth here and we are not bored.

The essence of the matter is simple enough. "A truism," Lord Samuel once remarked, "is on that account none the less true" — a sentiment to be echoed wistfully by anyone who has ever used the cliché "I love you." And an obvious truism is that nothing's so trite, nor so engaging, as a real human crisis, the very stuff of police work.

However, hacks excepted, most writers panic when plunged into what one could call cop corn. Some strike out on their own, eyes tightly shut, determined to impose a personal "reality" on the situation — scything down the clichés with meaningful pseudo-insights or building themselves cosy wee nests in the middle of hunt-the-needle haystacks so suffocating that only their imagined policemen, each as endearing as a field mouse, could hope to survive in them. Others climb out and get on the fence, where they often assume a radical stance while painting a picture more terrible, in its way, than Van Gogh's final canvas; the corn writhes, the

carrion crows descend, and God help the pig who gets caught in this glaring light.

McBain, on the other hand, accepts things as they are; if the field that engrosses him is knee-high in clichés, so be it. In he goes, as eager and uncompromising as a child, to grasp the thistle that grows between the rows.

"Great narrative," observed Eric Bentley, "is not the opposite of cheap narrative: it is soap opera *plus*."

"Plus" there certainly is in McBain's writing; not even his most severe critics have been able to deny that, although they occasionally hint dark things about potboilers stretching back twenty-one years or so.

On the evidence, however, that is hardly likely to offend McBain. No pot that ever boiled has contained a more zealous missionary, expounding to the end on the gospel truth of police procedures, while producing platitudes, parables and homilies, with an urgent, often jovial intensity closely linked to an awareness of the underlying nature of things. Provoking behaviour, admittedly, for those who attend the pot, their bellies rumbling again so soon after a light meal of lesser novelists, and who have now

---

LEIU

The Law Enforcement Intelligence Unit is a private organization whose members are all sworn police officers. It's very hush-hush, very low-profile. And that's all we're going to say about it. Except to mention that the Western States Intelligence Conference is up to the same kind of stuff. And it's scary.

to wait until the talk finally stops.

With the directness, then, of one unafraid to get down to essentials at the cost of spurious originality, McBain invariably begins to create the world of Steve Carella by discussing the weather — everyone's favourite banality when confronting strangers. He also, almost invariably, manages to score his first plus this way, as indicated by these opening lines from *The Pusher* (1956):

> *Winter came in like an anarchist with a bomb.*
>
> *Wild-eyed, shrieking, puffing hard, it caught the city in cold, froze the marrow and froze the heart.*

God/the novelist speaking. The section ends with a public consensus, lacking in flair but not in the same foreboding:

> *Winter was going to be a bitch that year.*

A space and then, flatfooted and phlegmatic:

> *The patrolman's name was Dick Genero, and he was cold. He didn't like the winter, and that was that.*

Gone is the novelist, to return only when he has something pertinent to say, and in his place is a policeman writing with the skills of one and the authority of the other.

Most often that policeman is Steve Carella, although his part in any story is not necessarily more important than it would be in an investigation carried out by a squad of detectives. Significantly, when he makes his first appearance on a murder scene in *Cop Hater* (1956), he rates no more than a cursory glance from the homicide double-act already there. What he's wearing is automatically noted, that's all, and it's an utterly conventional neat suit, clasped tie and shirt. It takes a member of the public to reflect: *He was not a frightening man, but when you opened the door to find him on your front step, you knew for certain he wasn't there to sell insurance* — a description which Carella might himself have difficulty in accepting, being more at home with the six-foot-nothing, downward-slanting eyes and brown hair stuff.

The narrator *seems* to be Carella — even when it's not — for two reasons. The first is that McBain has admitted to basing Carella on him-

self, so naturally some blurring is bound to occur. And the second is an extension of that, inasmuch as Carella is our chief source of information about the 87th Precinct and thereby blurs his personal experience with our own.

The reader is shown what Carella sees, however "unseen" it may have become to him through over-familiarity, and learns what he knows, however "second nature" this may have become, too. In other words, the cop corn is ground fine and then baked to fill a larder of goodies to which one returns again and again, even when a plot itself falls flat as in, ironically, *Bread* (1974), that singularly unleavened loaf.

What could be more mundane in mystery writing than a fingerprint? Yet once it has been through the mill, so to speak, there can be no denying its filling properties.

> *There are sweat pores on the fingertips, and the stuff they secrete contains 98.5 percent water and 0.5 to 1.5 percent solid material. This solid material breaks down to about one-third of inorganic matter — mainly salt — and two-thirds of organic substances like urea, albumin and formic, butyric and acetic acids. Dust, dirt, grease cling to the secretion. . . .*

Not that one is likely to remember this — or would even want to — any more than Carella remembers it from the police academy; it's having it made a part of oneself as well, however subliminally absorbed, that makes the difference. Much the same goes for the chunks of city ordinances which are to be found in the text: they, too, provide a taste of life as a police officer that no amount of description alone could achieve.

Just as a description of the books themselves is unlikely to convey their flavour with any accuracy. But a glance along the larder shelves, picking out other odds and ends at random, would at least provide some idea of what is on offer.

Lovely sandwiches of ideas, for a start. In *Cop Hater*, Carella calls on the heavily sensual widow of a murdered colleague and wishes "she were not wearing black."

> *He knew this was absurd. When a woman's husband is dead, the woman wears black.*
>
> *But Hank and he had talked a lot in the quiet hours of the midnight tour, and Hank had*

MIRANDA WARNINGS

You are under arrest. Before we ask you any questions, you must understand what your rights are.

You have the right to remain silent.

You are not required to say anything to us at any time or to answer any questions. Anything you say can be used against you in court.

You have the right to talk to a lawyer for advice before we question you and to have him with you during questioning.

If you cannot afford a lawyer and want one, a lawyer will be provided for you.

If you want to answer questions now without a lawyer present, you will still have the right to stop answering at any time. You also have the right to stop answering at any time until you talk to a lawyer.

MIRANDA WAIVER

1. Have you read or had read to you the warnings as to your rights? ...

2. Do you understand these rights? ..

3. Do you wish to answer any questions? ....

4. Are you willing to answer questions without having an attorney present? ....

5. Signature of defendant ....

6. Time .... Date ....

7. Signature of officer ....

8. Signature of witness ....

many times described Alice in the black night gowns she wore to bed. And try as he might, Carella could not dissociate the separate concepts of black: black as a sheer and frothy raiment of seduction, black as the ashy garment of mourning.

And to follow that section through to its conclusion, for a glimpse of what makes Carella so real:

He left the apartment and walked down to the street. It was very hot in the street.

Curiously, he felt like going to bed with somebody.

Anybody.

Then there are the other people one meets. The cartoonist's gag writer, for instance, in *Ten Plus One*, who features briefly as a suspect. A morose man, he nonetheless obligingly explains the genesis of the funnies in most magazines and shows the detectives the slips he sends out, each carrying a description of the drawing and supplying the caption, if there is one. Four of these slips are reproduced in facsimile — one of McBain's most effective techniques for giving one the "feel" of being right there. Elsewhere one is shown reporter's copy, police forms, timetables, letters, signwriting and, in *Doll* (1965), some photographs. There is something enormously gratifying in seeing something for oneself, particularly if, as in certain cases, it's possible to pounce on a clue before the men of the 87th get to it.

Ten Plus One also features one of McBain's many unforgettable incidental characters, a grouchy token seller called Stan Quentin who has never heard of Alcatraz and doesn't see why the detectives should be so amused. Now, that's so corny one wouldn't dare use it in fiction, whereas it works perfectly for four pages of McBain. Culminating with:

"You know those guys at Alcatraz?"

"We know lots of guys at Alcatraz," Carella said.

"Tell them to take my name off it, you hear?"

"We will," Carella said.

"Damn right," Quentin said.

Long exchanges of dialogue are a characteristic also to be enjoyed, both for the tension they create and for the authentic ring which the conventions of television make impossible. Humour, used to counterpoint harsh realities, is also much in evidence, as in *Cop Hater* when the father-figure of the squad room cuts short an introduction without malice aforethought: "It was simply Miscolo was a heavy sweater, and he didn't like the armpits of his uniform ruined by unnecessary talk." Other times it can be used to steady a flight of fancy: "Detectives are not poets; there is no iambic pentameter in a broken head."

And all this is to say nothing of Meyer Meyer (victim of his father's Jewish sense of humour; nobody could call that a Christian name, for a start), Cotton Hawes, Bert Kling or the odious Andy Parker, who between them handle the work load with varied degrees of success. In one story, largely because the right hand doesn't get to know what the left is doing, they all goof off, including Carella, and an arrest is made — only *after* a catastrophic crime is committed — by a distant patrolman in search, not of fame, but of ice cream.

Such is life. Such is what McBain re-creates by giving his policemen far too much to do (seldom are they ever concerned with one case at a time); a sky over their heads that can, in a heat wave, befuddle them while investigating a shoot-out in a liquor store filled with smashed bottles; and a world as real as Isola's model of New York is real, not a sugary sphere on the end of a lollipop stick.

Sometimes, however, he seems to go too far having fun, and smart-asses who rely on hindsight — what else? — have suggested that he may regret certain parts of the framework he laid down for himself in *Cop Hater*, little suspecting he'd have to live with them through almost a generation. They cite Teddy Franklin, the lovely, lamentably deaf and literally dumb girl whom Carella courted and married in that first book of the series, and quote Philip Norman's interview with the writer, in which it was said she "came from some heartless, fatuous notion of the ideal woman: beautiful and speechless." Fine for a one-off story, just as most jokes will take a single airing, but surely. . .

Nonsense. The very essence of McBain is that he embraces his clichés with the same loving enthusiasm Carella has been known to direct toward his missus — and, with possibly as little thought for the consequences, although

St. Michael the patron saint of all police forces, is depicted in the painting entitled "Restrictions." The painting hangs in the Police Academy museum, New York City.

COURTESY ALFRED J. YOUNG COLLECTION

he has himself so far avoided twins.

If this means he has become, in effect, the Norman Rockwell of the police procedural, that is surely no bad thing — not when he's also Evan Hunter, author of such celebrated works as *The Blackboard Jungle* and *Buddwing*, which must provide him with literary kudos.

Ah, say our literary-minded friends, why didn't you disclose this at the beginning? Hunter is bound to have an influence on McBain at times but plainly indulges in him the excesses of a trained mind allowed to slip its leash, to scamper cute as a spaniel in a public park — sometimes upright, mostly with a strong leaning toward grass-roots kitsch in exuberant figure eights which, despite sudden switches of direction, neatly tie up the ends.

Well, mainly because addicts of the 87th Precinct don't put this about much. Some are simply ignorant of the fact, and possibly much happier that way, being intimidated by "real" novelists, whereas "Ed McBain" is such a reassuring cliché of a name in itself, exactly right for a cop-lover. Others are confident that their emperor isn't going about in the buff (he, too, wears neat suits) — and that it's rare enough even to catch him with his pants down (although this does occur, forgivably, during moments of extreme sentiment).

James McClure won the Crime Writers' Association Silver Dagger for his political thriller, Rogue Eagle.

THE WELL-DRESSED COP

A New York City policeman's uniform, including gun, costs between $400 and $450. (The guns are purchased wholesale for $75. They must be either Smith and Wesson, Colt or Dan Wesson revolvers with a 4″ barrel.) Each police officer is given a yearly uniform allowance of $265.

His baton. *This turn-of-the-century rosewood baton was carried by officers on regular tours of duty.*

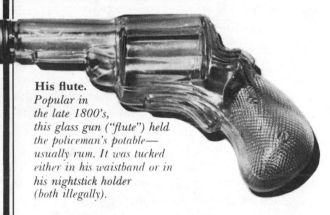

His flute. *Popular in the late 1800's, this glass gun ("flute") held the policeman's potable—usually rum. It was tucked either in his waistband or in his nightstick holder (both illegally).*

His shield. *The first badge was issued in 1845. It was made of copper, hence the term "cop" to denote a policeman. There have been seven style changes in the badge, the most recent in 1902.*

His uniform. *The first offical police uniform was designed in 1853 and over the years has been modified many times. (The gray felt helmet was discontinued in 1906; the frock coat, in 1912.)*

His nippers.
A restraining device, commonly used by police in 1885. Nippers were wrapped around the suspect's wrists, pressure was applied and the alleged perpetrator was unable to move his hands.

His belt and frog. *This leather belt was worn over his jacket and clasped in front with a police department insignia. The "frog" held his nightstick.*

His thumb cuffs.
Made of wood, these cuffs served the same purpose as the more traditional handcuffs. A suspect's thumbs were screwed in place, behind his back.

His leg holster. *This advertisement appeared in a spring issue of* Law and Order *magazine just last year. The magazine is available only to police officers.*

HOW MANY TIMES!!
HAVE YOU WANTED TO KEEP THAT GUN REALLY OUT OF SIGHT??

Put that sloppy shirt and baggy sweater away for good!!

The LEGSTER™ - leg holster puts off-duty and back-up guns comfortably out of sight offering new freedom in choice of clothing.

The LEGSTER™ is designed to hold the pistol in place through the most vigorous exercise. It was designed by a policeman for policemen and has been used in law enforcement for the past four years.

Available at your local law enforcement dealer.

The LEGSTER™ is a product of:

Milwaukee Holster Company
P.O. Box 559
Milwaukee, Wisconsin 53201

Inquiries invited.

PAT. PEND.

COURTESY ALFRED J. YOUNG COLLECTION

SATURDAY NIGHT WITH THE 26TH

Thomas Seligson

It is six o'clock on a Saturday night. I am riding in a patrol car. The back seat. I am not a cop and I am not guilty. Then what am I doing there?

I'm a Civilian Observer.

The Civilian Observer Program is open to block captains, community leaders, law students and journalists like myself. For six hours they let you go everywhere with your assigned cops; they let you get the feel of being a cop, but minus the badge and gun. I chose to observe from the 26th Precinct. It's a mixed neighborhood — part academic (Columbia University) and part war zone (West Harlem).

As I said, it's a Saturday. The day after the arrival of welfare checks. It's warm. There's a full moon. Officers Hess and Ford lock me into the back seat of their patrol car, and off we go.

6:09 P.M. Broadway and 125th St.: Hess hands me a chart listing the code signals I'll hear over the car radio.

"That's so you'll know what's going on," he says. "We're 26-A. If you hear that, we're in business."

"How can you remember all this?" I ask, scanning the chart.

"What do you think I keep it out for? Five years on the job, I still sometimes forget."

"There's only one that's really important." Ford smiles into the rear-view mirror. "10-63."

I look it up. It means "Out of Service (Meal)."

"That's where we're going now," Ford says.

"Hess has to feed his tapeworm. Guy's always hungry."

6:14 P.M. Broadway and 116th St.: Columbia and Barnard students crowd the car. Hess and Ford joke with them. I'm introduced as a "Peeping Tom" they're taking downtown. I keep my hands behind my back as though they're cuffed. There's a dance at Barnard later that night. "Eddie" and "Bob" are invited by the girls.

"Only if you promise me a dance," says Hess. He smiles. "A slow one."

6:16 P.M. Broadway and 114th St.: We stop in front of Hungry Mac's. Hess asks if I want anything inside.

"Maybe a coffee," I say.

"You'll regret it," says Ford. "It's terrible here. Wait'll the next stop."

I take his advice. He lights a True Blue. I bum one.

6:22 P.M. Broadway and 112th St.: We stop in front of Twin Donuts.

"How do you want your coffee?" asks Hess.

"Light and sweet. And a marble doughnut." I reach for my wallet.

"Forget it. It's on me."

While Hess is gone, Ford explains that their sector runs from 116th to 110th streets, Riverside Drive to Morningside. "That's where we cruise, 'less we're needed elsewhere." He says he averages eighteen miles a tour. Of course, it all depends on the number of stops.

Hess returns with doughnuts and coffee for two. "You forgot the cigarettes," says Ford.

FRISKING AND THE STRIP SEARCH

Just in case the suspect is a dirty fighter, or gets to his shiv before you find it, it's better to have two people doing the frisking. That way, you — not the suspect — remain in control.

1. Suspect is told to place his hands on the wall, supporting the full weight of his body on his hands.
2. Suspect is told to drop his head forward.
3. Suspect is told to stretch his legs out as far as they will go. This puts the upper half of his torso almost horizontal to the lower half, and keeps him off balance.
4. Suspect is told to use only toes to maintain contact with the floor. This, again, keeps him off balance.
5. The person doing the frisking then begins from top to bottom, and runs his hands over every part of the suspect's body.
6. Suspect is handcuffed at conclusion of the frisk, but while still in the frisk position.

An alternate method is to have suspect clasp his hands on top of his head, Japanese-prisoner style. The frisker then places his hand over the prisoner's hands and leans his body into the prisoner's, forcing him against the wall. His partner then does the actual frisking.

The frisker's foot is placed in front of the suspect's to restrain him.

A more thorough way of frisking is the strip search, in which the suspect is told to remove his shoes and socks, pull his pants down and take his shirt off. The searchers then go over his clothing carefully for hidden items, such as burglary tools. Prime targets for search: the collar band, the pants fly, inside the neck band and the belt, and under the tie. Suspects also tend, if they have long, bushy hair, to hide picks there. Suspects have been known to fake heart attacks just so they can reach inside their shirt and pull out a knife. Women usually hide weapons in their pocketbooks or in their boots.

"We'll get 'em at the next stop. They're cheaper."

6:28 P.M. Broadway and 110th St.: We stop in front of a twenty-four-hour vegetable and grocery store. Ford gets out so that Hess can now eat. Hess tells me he's twenty-eight, Ford ten years older. Both married, with kids. He doesn't want to be a cop forever. He's taking business courses and hopes one day to run his own.

What's keeping Ford? Hess gets out to check. A minute later he waves me into the store. I join the two of them in the back.

The owner has caught an eleven-year-old black boy rummaging through his open safe. The boy claims he was looking for the bathroom.

"In an open safe?" says Ford. "Don't tell me they look the same. Kid, you got problems."

The owner of the store doesn't want to bother pressing charges. It would mean a day downtown, a day lost from work. Hess and Ford fully understand. They take the kid to the car.

On the way to the station house the kid says I was once his substitute teacher. He says he remembers my boots. His name is Troy. I vaguely remember him.

"Forgive me for saying it," says Hess. "But you didn't teach him very well. Kid's got a lot to learn."

6:52 P.M. Station house: Hess and Ford fill out a Juvenile Delinquency form on Troy. He still denies looking in the safe. They decide to teach him a lesson. Scare him into staying out of trouble. They say they're taking him to Spofford Detention Center. First, however, they'll take him home.

"So you can say goodbye to your mother," says Hess.

7:35 A.M. Somewhere in West Harlem: Troy's sister, jumping rope on the sidewalk, sees him in the back of the patrol car. She runs upstairs to get Grandma. Troy is embarrassed, starts to cry. Grandma thanks Hess and Ford for bringing him home. She promises him a "whupping" soon as he gets upstairs.

7:55 P.M. West Harlem: We drive around the decaying neighborhood. Hess and Ford point out the abandoned buildings which junkies use for "shooting galleries," and the cars from New Jersey, filled with whites come to buy drugs. Ford phones in the license numbers of a few suspicious cars, i.e., those that are very expensive or have a rental number on the plate.

"You get a feeling about some cars you see," says Hess. "It's like a sixth sense."

Headquarters tells us that none of the cars is hot.

8:15 P.M. West Harlem: A call for 26-A

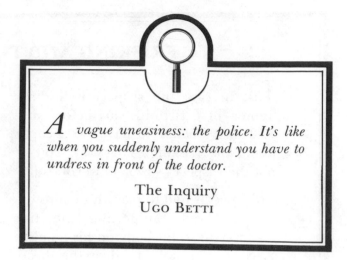

A vague uneasiness: the police. It's like when you suddenly understand you have to undress in front of the doctor.

The Inquiry
UGO BETTI

comes over the air. 10-31 — Burglary in Progress. Broadway Presbyterian Church. 114th Street. Hess, now driving, flips the switches for the siren and flashing red light. The siren doesn't work. He sits on the horn. Screeching tires. High-speed turns. Just like in the movies.

8:18 P.M. Broadway Presbyterian Church: Four people are standing in front. One of them jumps into the car.

"If we hurry up, we can catch 'em," he says. "Two black guys. They broke into the church. I followed 'em, and they pulled a knife on me."

"What'd they look like?" asks Ford, as Hess speeds down to Riverside Drive.

"They had leather jackets and dark pants."

Our complainant is about thirty-five, Italian, with short, graying blond hair. He says his name is Jerry, he lives in the neighborhood, and he spent the day washing cars at the church fair. He spied the burglars while out for a walk.

"I like them people at the church," he says. "Don't want to see 'em get ripped off."

8:25 P.M. Claremont Ave.: Near the back entrance to Riverside Church. "Turn around," says Ford.

Two men meeting Jerry's description have just entered the church. We turn around, park the car and go inside. We're followed by officers from two other patrol cars who've heard about the "attempted burglary." It's a slow period, and they've come to join the chase.

8:45 P.M. Riverside Church: The church is a beehive of activity — a teenage dance, a meeting of several hundred Asian-Americans, and a modern dance concert with an audience of at least 250. Suspects have been seen buying tickets to the concert and are now in the darkened auditorium. Six uniformed officers, myself and Jerry, the complainant, mingle outside with a growing crowd of curious onlookers and tense church officials. One cop suggests stopping the performance, turning on the lights and searching the hall. Hess and Ford prefer waiting for the show to end. Jerry reassures us he'll be able to identify his attackers.

A sergeant arrives on the scene. He immediately senses the potential for an ugly incident. He also doubts that the suspects in question are the "perpetrators."

"No one's gonna burglarize a church, then walk up to another church six blocks away and buy tickets to a dance concert. We're tying up three cars over this. Resume your tour."

9:15 P.M. Broadway Presbyterian Church: Hess, Ford, Jerry and I return to the scene of the crime. Glass door to the minister's office is smashed. A portable television set has been moved. A cookie tin filled with receipts from the day's fair has been opened.

The rector doesn't believe Jerry's story. "How could they have gotten away? You need a key to get out the door. I think you made up the story when we caught you in the office."

It appears that our complainant may, in fact, be our suspect. Hess and Ford go into action. Ford plays nice guy, reassuring Jerry everything is fine, while Hess interviews the rector and his assistants in another room. They claim they never saw Jerry before, that he

showed up to wash cars and was seen wandering around the building.

"Obviously casing the joint," says Hess, smiling at his B-movie dialogue.

The rector thinks Jerry may have hidden in the building after the fair. Hess picks up the phone and calls Ford in the next room. They agree that Jerry is probably their man.

"We'll know for sure when the boys from Forensics check out the cookie tin for prints," says Hess. "In any case, we got enough to take him in."

Hess plays the bad guy. "Jerry, you're under arrest."

He reads him his rights. Jerry starts to cry. I look away.

10:00 P.M. Station house: Ford takes Jerry's prints; Hess types out the lengthy arrest report. I compliment him on his speedy two-finger typing.

"I get lots of practice," he says.

Jerry admits to previous arrests for burglary. He's a methadone addict, and he wants his shot.

11:05 P.M. Broadway and 112th St.: West End Bar. Hess has taken Jerry to a methadone clinic. I go with Ford on another 10-63. Bologna sandwiches, cokes and packs of cigarettes. One of each for Jerry.

"I'm sure he's hungry," says Ford.

11:45 P.M. Station house: Jerry thanks us for the food. He leaves with Hess for the overnight lockup. Hess will work overtime tomorrow, accompanying Jerry to court. Ford, now out of uniform, wearing jeans and a shirt, jokes with the other cops in civilian dress. Some of them look about sixteen.

12:00 A.M. Broadway and 113th St.: Ford, off-duty and on his way home, drops me off at a bar.

'What'd you think?" he asks. Before I get a word out, he answers himself. "You should come with us again in summer. Midnight-to-eight tour. Now *that's* what I call an interesting one."

12:07 A.M. Local bar: I sip my beer. They've got a *Kojak* rerun on. I decide I prefer *Adam-12*.

Thomas Seligson wants to be a cop when he grows up.

OFFBEAT MUSIC

Detective Alfred J. Young, curator of the NYPD Museum, has one of the largest collections of police-inspired sheet music in America — well over 200 sheets. Many of these were written prior to World War I; some, such as Victor Herbert's "The Finest March," were written expressly for the Police Band. Unfortunately, the Department disbanded the 156-instrument group in 1953.

THE NYPD GLOSSARY

Lynn Strong

"In the bag." In uniform.

Blotter. (formerly) A large green book used for logging precinct members' daily movements and any unusual occurrences. One desk sergeant, well-known to the Force, used it for banging heads when he lost patience with the procedure.

Booking. Recording an arrest.

"Brain." Detective. The term is used by non-detectives.

"Catching." Taking on an assignment. ("Henry's catching today.")

"Chamber of Horrors." The trial room at Headquarters.

"Collar." Arrest.

Command. Any unit, such as a precinct, with a commanding officer. ("Call your command.")

"Cooping" ("In the heave"). Time out for lunch, a quick nap, etc. Local funeral parlors and garages are well-suited for this purpose. Mounted police have special problems: one horse, parked in a boxcar, was halfway upstate when his rider returned from lunch.

Detail. A temporary assignment to another command. (See FLYING)

"Downtown." Headquarters.

"Family man." A clean-living member of the Force.

"Flaking." Depositing incriminating evidence on or near the suspect to facilitate arrest.

"Floater." A body dragged from the river.

"Flute." A whiskey-filled pop bottle in plain brown wrapper, donated to the SH by a grateful civilian.

"Flying." Temporarily assigned to another command. ("I flew to the eight-seven last night.")

"Gentleman." A superior respected for his fairness.

"In grays." Probationary; not yet graduated from the Academy.

"Gun run." A response to a report of person seen with a gun.

"Hat." The sum of $5 used by a civilian as an attempted bribe. ("Here, buy yourself a hat.")

"Heater." (*obsolete*) Gun.

"Jug day." A celebration for promotion or retirement. ("Tomorrow is Kelly's jug day.")

"Jumper." A potential or actual suicide victim.

"Kite." A complaint received through the mail.

Line-up. Five persons (suspect plus four others of similar physical description) on view for purpose of identifying suspect. Civilian

NYPD ABBREVIATIONS

ACU Anti-Crime Unit
ADA Assistant District Attorney
AKA (a.k.a.) Also Known As
APB All Points Bulletin
CCRB Civilian Complaint Review Board
CD Chief of Detectives
CO Commanding Officer
DA District Attorney
DET Detective
DOA Dead On Arrival
HQ Headquarters
IAD Internal Affairs Department
INS Inspector
LT Lieutenant

MPU Missing Persons Unit
NYPD New York Police Department
PA Police Academy
PCO Police Commissioner's Office
PCT Precinct
PI Private Investigator
PIU Precinct Investigators Unit
PO Police Officer
POF Police Officer, Female
POM Police Officer, Male
PP&C Pickpocket and Confidence Squad
RMP Radio Motor Patrol (car)
SGT Sergeant
SH Station House

non-suspects are paid $5. Now closed to the public, line-ups were once a source of neighborhood entertainment.

"Loid." (from *celluloid*) Small stiff piece of paper, as a credit card, used to open locks on doors. (See PICK MAN)

"Murphy man." Con man.

Observation. Watch kept on a stationary object, as a house, bar, etc. (See SURVEILLANCE)

Operator. The driver of an RMP. (See RECEIVER)

"Pick man." A professional lock-picker, equipped with special tools (unlike counterpart LOID man).

Post. The area of a PRECINCT covered by a patrolman (synonymous with "beat" in other cities). A "one-armed" post includes only one side of the street.

"Potsie." Shield.

Precinct. Geographical area whose boundaries are determined by population and police hazards.

"Rabbi" ("Hook"). An influential friend, either on or off the Force.

Receiver. The officer in an RMP who handles communications. (See OPERATOR)

"Ripper." A safe-cracker, usually employing a torch.

"Round robin." A comprehensive check-out preceding transfer, promotion, etc.

Sector. The area of a PRECINCT covered by a patrol car, (equivalent of POST).

Shield. A badge worn or carried to designate rank. "Working with the white shield" describes a PO assigned to detective's duties. A "gold shield" is another name for a detective. (*Note:* The word "badge" is not used by NYPD members.)

"Squeal." Complaint. ("Who's catching the squeal?")

Surveillance. Watch kept on a moving object, as a person, car, etc. (See OBSERVATION)

Ten-thirteen. Assist police officer.

"Tin." Shield.

"On the tin." Free; without being asked to pay. ("I got this at Louie's on the tin.")

"Torch." Arsonist.

"Undesirables" ("Germs"). Pimps, prostitutes, junkies, etc., as a group. ("Hey, there's a bunch of undesirables in front of Bickford's.")

"Yellow sheet." Record of previous arrests (now a white computer print-out).

Lynn Strong is an editor and current informer and former friend of the NYPD.

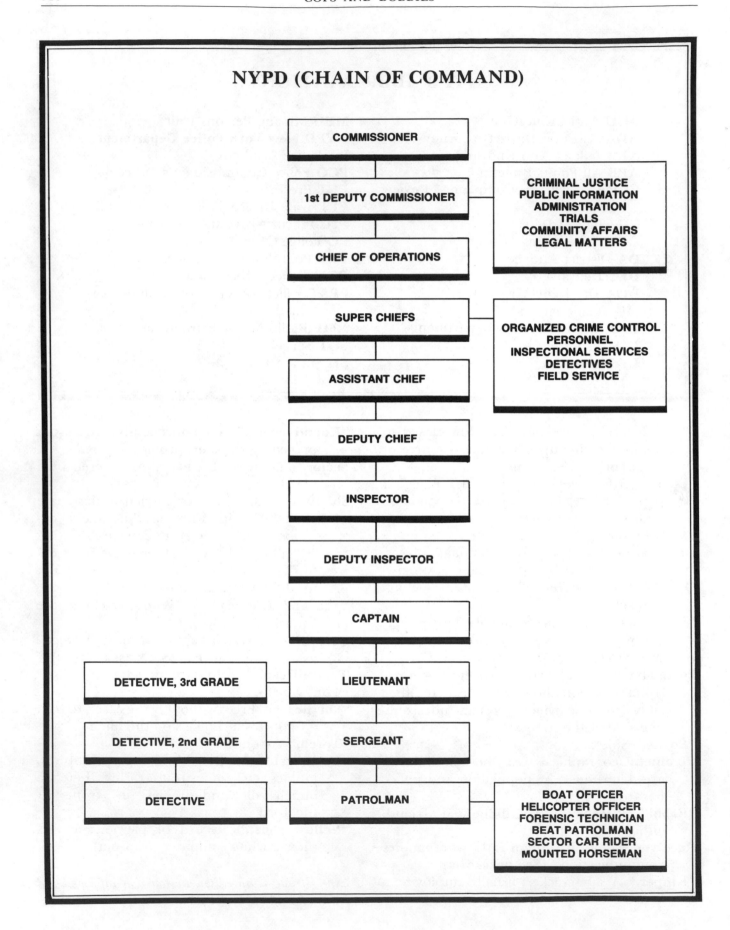

NYPD (CHAIN OF COMMAND)

COMMISSIONER

1st DEPUTY COMMISSIONER

CRIMINAL JUSTICE
PUBLIC INFORMATION
ADMINISTRATION
TRIALS
COMMUNITY AFFAIRS
LEGAL MATTERS

CHIEF OF OPERATIONS

SUPER CHIEFS

ORGANIZED CRIME CONTROL
PERSONNEL
INSPECTIONAL SERVICES
DETECTIVES
FIELD SERVICE

ASSISTANT CHIEF

DEPUTY CHIEF

INSPECTOR

DEPUTY INSPECTOR

CAPTAIN

DETECTIVE, 3rd GRADE — LIEUTENANT

DETECTIVE, 2nd GRADE — SERGEANT

DETECTIVE — PATROLMAN

BOAT OFFICER
HELICOPTER OFFICER
FORENSIC TECHNICIAN
BEAT PATROLMAN
SECTOR CAR RIDER
MOUNTED HORSEMAN

THE HISTORY OF THE ENGLISH POLICE

Peter N. Walker

The name Bow is pronounced as in "bow and arrow." Bow Street still exists in London and contains a very busy magistrates' court.

The first magistrate of Bow Street was Thomas de Veil, who was appointed in 1740. He was described as a courageous man, unafraid to expose himself to the criminals and mobs who terrorised London at that time. There was no police system to counteract their activities, other than the incompetent local watchmen; furthermore, criminals could bribe the justices to overlook their crimes.

Henry Fielding succeeded Veil and became a magistrate at Bow Street in 1748. He was a noted author (*Tom Jones*) and vigorously campaigned against the widespread corruption among the justices. His brother, John, who was almost blind, assisted him, and together they made a register of all crimes committed in London. The numbers horrified the brothers, so in 1750 Henry recruited six "thief-takers" to arrest the wrongdoers.

Top-hatted English bobbies, c. 1860.

SCOTLAND YARD

These were ordinary householders "actuated by a truly public spirit against thieves." They were ready at a moment's notice to perform their duty but were unpaid. Their task was to pursue all villains and bring them to justice; their reward came from the "blood-money" paid upon the arrest of a villain or upon the recovery of stolen goods. Fielding was their leader, a task he shared with a man called Saunders-Welch, who was High Constable of Holborn. The "thief-taker" wore no uniform and carried only the staff of a parish constable.

But they did achieve success; in addition to arresting thieves, they managed to break up gangs, and far-sighted people began to ask for a paid police force.

Fielding's men became known as Bow Street Runners about 1785 and at one time boasted two horse patrols. Fielding also published a news-sheet of criminal activities, listing known rogues and their crimes, but gained little official support from the government. His small band of men, as low as four in some cases, remained until the formation of the Metropolitan Police in 1829. Sadly, the Runners were unfit for recruitment into the regular police, but their memory lives on.

Sir Robert Peel

Sir Robert Peel, founder of the modern English police force, was born on 5th February 1788 near Bury in Lancashire, England. His grandfather, also called Robert, was a calico printer who progressed to the spinning-jenny after he spun himself a fortune out of cotton. Peel's father, another Robert, was the third son of this self-made man; he became a Member of Parliament for Tamworth and was awarded a baronetcy in 1800.

Our Robert was educated at Harrow and Oxford, where he was a friend of Byron, the poet. He took first-class degrees in Classics and Mathematics, and in 1809, at the age of twenty-one, he, too, became a Member of Parliament. A dedicated Tory, he was an outstanding speaker and acquired a deep knowledge of Parliamentary procedures. Only three years later, he became Secretary for Ireland, and there he instituted the Irish Constabulary in an

TIPSTAVES, TIPSTAFFS AND TRUNCHEONS

Today, recognising an English policeman isn't difficult. He wears a uniform and carries a warrant card. But before 1829 his sole symbol of office, of authority, was his tipstave, his tipstaff or his painted truncheon.

The tipstaves, being short, were either put in one's pocket or stuffed in one's waistcoat. They usually had a brass handle and a crown on the other end. Some of the crowns unscrewed and warrants were rolled up inside.

The tipstaffs, being very long, were used for ceremonial occasions, usually for parades and fancy processionals.

In 1829, the advent of the first officially recognised police uniform — blue coat, blue trousers, top hat — eliminated the need for the tipstave and the tipstaff. However, the truncheon was still carried and was still regarded as a symbol of authority. Often, it had to be produced by a plain-clothes detective when he questioned a suspect. The painted truncheon had a crown motif on top, with the Royal Coat of Arms or the Burgh Coat of Arms below it. Gradually, the elaborately decorated truncheons disappeared, until in the 1870's it was virtually extinct. It was still produced for ceremonial purposes, however, as late as the 1920's.

D.R.

attempt to preserve life and property. This body of men became known as "Peelers."

In 1820, he married the daughter of General Sir John Floyd. She was named Julie, and they had five sons and two daughters. His family life was said to have been very happy.

In 1825, Robert Peel began his famous reform of criminal law in England, resulting in the birth of London's Metropolitan Police in 1829. It took four hard years to overcome the prejudice of his government, who saw the police as a threat to personal liberty. They failed to see that unchecked crime was a greater threat.

Peel, who was Home Secretary at the time, did not want his policemen to look like soldiers, so he dressed them as civilians in black top hats

Sir Robert Peel (the first bobby).

SCOTLAND YARD

THE POLICE BLOTTER

Every English police station maintains a record of daily occurrences. In America, this is known as the Police Blotter but in England it is variously called the Occurrence Book, the Message Log and the Daily Log. In some areas it is known simply by the relevant form number; for example, if the messages are printed on a Form 24, the blotter itself is called Form 24.

Whatever its name, its function is simple. It is a record of every message that comes into a police station, and of every incident, together with the action taken by the police. It includes messages from whatever source: personal callers, telephone, radio, Telex, computer — or even internal police instructions. Every policeman should read it before the start of his tour of duty, or it should be read out to him.

It will include, for example, in time sequence, every item of lost-and-found property, arrests, holes in the road, reports of traffic accidents, air crashes, rapes, burglaries, missing people or dogs, sudden deaths, wanted persons, escaped mental patients or budgerigars, emergency calls, murder, mayhem and suicide. And more besides!

P.N.W.

and blue tailed coats. They were unarmed. Political disturbances in 1832 brought them into rapid conflict with the general public, who looked upon them as a political tool of the government. They hated the police and called them "Peel's Bloody Gang" or "Blue Lobsters." It took thirty years for them to become acceptable, and during that period, crime diminished and public order was restored.

Once they had become accepted by the public, the police became known as "bobbies" in honour of their founder, Bobby Peel. The English policeman is still affectionately known by this name.

Robert Peel, who has been described as one of the hardest workers and greatest intellectuals England has known, was thrown from his horse on Constitutional Hill, London, on 29th June 1850, and died on 2nd July that same year.

Peter N. Walker is a police inspector in the North Yorkshire Police. He is also the author of over thirty crime books.

THE BOBBY GLOSSARY
Peter N. Walker

Antecedents. A criminal's history, including his education, work, family record. ("What are the accused's antecedents?")

Bat phone. A police officer's personal radio. (slang)

Book on/Book off. To report on/off duty. ("I'm booking on at 2 P.M.")

Break. (a) A breakthrough in a major enquiry. ("I've got a marvellous break in the murder enquiry.") Or:
(b) A crime where property, like houses or shops, is broken into, e.g., burglary. ("I've got a few breaks to deal with today.")

Brothel creepers. Boots with very soft soles.

Charge room. A room in a police station where criminals are processed, i.e., searched after arrest and charged with their crimes.

Chief. The Chief Constable. ("Have you seen the Chief lately?")

Climber. A burglar with an ability to climb drainpipes, walls, etc. A cat burglar.

Collator. An officer who keeps local records of suspected and/or convicted criminals, their movements, friends, haunts, etc.

Divisional sleuth. A detective. (slang)

Fence. A person who disposes of stolen goods. ("Jack is the best fence in this area.")

Flasher. A man who indecently exposes himself. ("There's a flasher in the park.")

Gong. A medal of any type.

Going equipped. Being in possession of instruments or tools for use in crime. ("I arrested Fred for going equipped.")

Handler. (a) A police dog handler.
(b) A receiver of stolen goods; a fence.

Horror comics. Police circulars, crime bulletins, information sheets, etc. (slang)

Heaven. The Chief Constable's office. (slang)

Juveniles. Persons under 17 years of age.

Knock-off. An arrest. ("I got a good knock-off last night.")

Lock-ups. Arrested persons placed in custody. ("I had seven lock-ups last night.")

Lab. A forensic science laboratory.

Metro. The London Metropolitan Police.

Manor. A police officer's area of responsibility, e.g., streets in one part of a city. (slang) Also, a criminal's area of operation. ("I'm going for a trip around my manor.")

Motor patrol. The Police Traffic Department; police officers who specialise in patrolling main roads to deal with vehicular traffic matters. Sometimes known as Traffic Section.

Mug shot. Photograph of a prisoner. (slang)

Nick. The police station ("Take him to the nick.")

Nicked. Arrested, or reported for a minor offence. ("I got nicked for a parking offence.")

Noddy bikes. Small police motorcycles. (slang)

Panda car. Small car used for local beat patrol duties; named "Panda" because the originals were two colours, e.g., blue and white.

Nutters. People of unsound mind.

Prints. Fingerprints.

Previous. A criminal's previous convictions. ("Has he any previous?")

Queen bee. A senior woman police officer. (slang)

Rings. Phone calls to the police station to see if anything has arisen which requires attention. ("I make my rings on the hour.")

ABBREVIATIONS

A.B.H. Actual Bodily Harm: a serious assault

A.C.C. Assistant Chief Constable

B.O.P. Breach of the Peace: a disturbance

C.C. Chief Constable

C.I.D. (a) Criminal Investigation Department
(b) Coppers in Disguise (slang)

C.O.P. Chief of Police

C.R.O. Criminal Record Office

D.C. Detective Constable

D.C.C. Deputy Chief Constable

D.C.I. Detective Chief Inspector

D.H.Q. Divisional Headquarters

D.I. Detective Inspector

D.S. Detective Sergeant

D. Supt. Detective Superintendent

F.A. Found Abandoned (applicable to cars illegally borrowed and dumped after use)

G.B.H. Grievous Bodily Harm: a serious assault

G.P. Car. General Purpose Car: a police vehicle with no specific duties; it deals with any incident that might arise

H.Q. Headquarters

ID Parade. Identification Parade

INSP. Inspector

M.P.D. Metropolitan Police District: the area policed by the London Metropolitan Police

N.F.A. No Fixed Abode

P.C. Police Constable

P.N.C. Police National Computer (All English and Welsh forces are linked to the P.N.C.)

R.T. (a) Road Traffic
(b) Radio Transmitter

Sgt. Sergeant

SOCO. Scenes of Crime Officer (spoken as "Socco"): police or civilians who visit scenes of crimes to photograph them or to undertake other scientific investigations

Supt. Superintendent

T.W.O.C. Taking Without Owner's Consent (spoken as "twock"): unlawfully borrowing a motor vehicle ("I arrested two men for T.W.O.C.")

T.I.C. Taken into Consideration: a term used when a criminal on trial for a crime asks a court to punish him for other offences he has committed in the past; this "cleans his slate." ("He asked for eight other burglaries to be T.I.C.")

U.B.P. Unit Beat Policing: a system of patrolling with five officers and a "Panda" car; the officers are made responsible for a given area which they patrol, so they become well acquainted with the residents

U.S.I. Unlawful Sexual Intercourse with a girl under sixteen years of age
P.N.W.

Station. A police station.

Sussed. Suspected; to realise a person is guilty. ("I sussed him the moment he opened his mouth.")

Scene. The scene of a crime. ("Make sure the scene is protected and cordoned off.")

Tonsil varnish. Tea or coffee served in police canteens. (slang)

Verbal. An oral confession.

Voluntary. A statement, freely given, in which guilt is admitted. ("He has given a good voluntary.")

Wopsie. A woman police constable (from the initials WPC). Today, women are not distinguished in this manner; since 1975 they have had equal rights with male officers and a woman is known simply as "Police Constable X."

Working a beat. Patrolling on duty, in a specified area, either on foot or in a car.

Whiz kid. A rapidly promoted officer. (slang)

The Yard. Scotland Yard.

Yellow perils. Traffic wardens. (slang)

Yobs. Thugs, vandals, trouble-makers. (slang)

THE BLACK MUSEUM OF SCOTLAND YARD

Laurence Henderson

All police forces have a museum in which they locate relics of exceptional cases. The first of these, and still the most famous, is the criminal museum at Scotland Yard. The original intention was not to collect mementos for their curiosity value but as a detective training aid. Any officer undergoing a senior detective course, will, as part of his training, make a tour of the museum in order to learn that there is nothing new under the sun — that the tricks of present-day criminals are only variations on those of the past — and to see how his predecessors fared in grappling with them.

The museum is divided into a number of sections. The historical section contains the declaration signed by George III which brought into existence the first official police force. Here also is an original police uniform from those early days, curios such as the skeleton keys of Charlie Peace and the knighthood regalia of Sir Roger Casement, and a collection of death masks taken from prisoners hanged at Newgate Prison in the early nineteenth century. (The only recent death mask is that of Heinrich Himmler, which was taken by the Army Special Investigation Branch as proof that the body they held was indisputably that of the Nazi Chief of Police; it had served its pur-

appropriate place to record the end of the greatest mass murderer in history.)

The main sections of the museum cover burglary, drugs, abortion, fraudulent gaming devices, forgery, murder, terrorism and kidnapping, with a final section for sexual perver-

sion. All of the sections are constantly updated, but each new exhibit has to win its place either because it is startling in degree or because it is original in its criminal inventiveness: the device, for example, invented by a jewel thief specialising in the Mayfair area which, based upon the principle of a geared cork remover, is capable of winding out a spring lock from the street side of the door; a walking stick, built of interlocking tubes, which can be extended into a hook-ended ladder almost twenty feet long; the shaved dividers of a rigged roulette wheel; two-way radios built into hearing aids for the heavy poker game; and, in the forgery section, examples of outstanding artistic ability in bank notes drawn freehand, totaliser betting tickets altered within minutes of the end of a race to show a winning combination, and postal orders altered to a higher value — again free-hand — by a single hair dipped in watered ink.

Since forgery of bank notes has become a matter of photogravure processing, it no longer requires the high skills of the criminal engraver, who now operates in the high-risk field of fraudulent bonds and share certificates. The most active area of forgery has nothing to do with bank notes or share coupons: It is apparently easier and less risky to forge airline ticket blanks and Social Security frankings, which are sold to crooked travel agents, accountants and company secretaries. An area not usually thought of in connection with forgery is that of consumer goods: the label and wrappings of an expensive perfume, for example, which has a ready sale to buyers who believe they are cheaply acquiring stolen goods.

The most fascinating exhibit in this section is that of a coiner rather than of a forger. Coining is generally regarded as a dead criminal activity but it does still continue in the field of gold coins. One particular character was in operation from the mid-1940's until the beginning of the 1960's. Well aware that most fake gold sovereigns are detected by either a weight or chemical test, his technique was to take a small cross section of half-inch copper piping and place it between dies, first spooning into the hollow centre a carefully measured quantity of mercury. He would then trap the mercury within the copper by exerting pressure on the dies with a gallows device powered by a pneumatic jack. The result was a coin the approximate weight of a genuine sovereign, which he coated in gold obtained by melting down stolen cigarette cases and old watches. (*In*

WHY "SCOTLAND YARD"?

London's first police office was situated at No. 4, Whitehall Place, London. The rear entrance was along a narrow lane called Scotland Yard.

From that time, the name has been given to all subsequent buildings which have accommodated the headquarters of London's Metropolitan Police.

New Scotland Yard is in Victoria Street. It is *not* the headquarters of *Britain's* police; it is the headquarters only of the Metropolitan Police.

The fifty or so police forces of England, Wales, Scotland and Ireland each have their own policemen with their own chief constable and their own police headquarters. All are complete units, and between them they service the entire British Isles outside London.

There is no national police force in England, although the Home Secretary is responsible to the government for law and order, and in this capacity issues guidance to all police forces.

P.N.W.

THE BETTMANN ARCHIVE, INC.

First came Scotland Yard, then came New Scotland Yard, then came another Scotland Yard which by rights should be called New New Scotland Yard but, like its predecessor, bears the name New Scotland Yard. Pictured here: New Scotland Yard and New Scotland Yard (Version Two).

extremis, he would purchase commercial gold leaf.)

During the fourteen years or so of his career, he made and sold thousands of his fake sovereigns to coin dealers, tourists, smugglers and others who think it smarter to keep money in gold rather than bank notes. The police have an amused regard for him. What I find entertaining is that, when he was eventually arrested, it was not on a charge of coining at all, but for receiving stolen copper piping.

The largest section of the museum is devoted to murder, with various sub-sections allotted to terrorist murder, murder associated with kidnapping and the murder of policemen. From the point of detection techniques, however, the more interesting murders are those committed by individuals for personal ends. The two obvious cases in this sense are those of Neville Heath, who savaged his victims with whips, knives and teeth solely for his sexual satisfaction, and of Christie, who murdered in order to supply himself with dead bodies, since he obtained no satisfaction in connecting himself with live ones.

The section on perversion does not collect dirty photographs or films for their own sake,

NO, IT DOESN'T SELL POST CARDS

The Black Museum is not called that by its curator. The term "black" was coined by a reporter who liked the negative emotionalism of it.

The museum is open by special arrangement. Visitors are met at the reception desk on the ground floor by a Yard official who escorts them to the door of the museum. The curator lets them in, then locks the door behind them. No one is allowed to wander the building at his leisure.

A tour takes approximately one and a half hours, at which time the visitor is released from the locked room and escorted downstairs and out the door.

although there are certainly plenty of both, but rather as unique examples of their own very special kind. It is sobering to consider that whatever the human mind can envisage in its wildest moments of madness, sickness or aberration — the worst, most disgusting, utterly vile thing — not only has already been thought of but has already been brought to actuality. However experienced a police officer, he must surely be taken aback, at least momentarily, by the life-size crucifix with its barbed-wire attachments, or the case in which a man was truly crucified by nails driven through the hands and feet; the leather collar with the inward-pointing nails, the macabre surgical trolley and the other, quite ordinary objects, like the wind-up Gramophone, which have, with fiendish ingenuity, been transformed into instruments of pain and perversion.

It is with mixed emotions that one leaves the Black Museum. When I was asked which exhibit had struck me the most, it was not any of the objects of refined sexual torture or aids to perversion; it was not even the photographs that record the handiwork of the sadist Heath or the necrophiliac Christie.

In 1945 a girl, living in Southampton, sat opening the gifts she had received for her nineteenth birthday. One of the parcels that came through the mail contained a pair of binoculars and a card that said she would be surprised "how closely it brings things." She put the binoculars to one side while she opened the rest of the gifts, and it was her father who picked them up and casually touched the central focusing screw, whereupon needle-sharp spikes sprang from either eyepiece.

The binoculars had been painstakingly carved from solid wood, the spikes fitted inside on a rachet, powered by a coiled steel spring, and then the whole thing disguised with black rexine and enamel paint. The workmanship is incredible, the cunning intelligence of its execution is frightening and the monumental hatred behind its creation is demoniac. It is also an unsolved crime.

Laurence Henderson is the author of Major Enquiry.

SCHEMATIC OF THE POLICE SYSTEM OF ENGLAND AND WALES

Peter N. Walker

In England and Wales, a person (man or woman) may join the regular police service as a constable at eighteen and a half years of age. After an initial course of ten weeks at a police training centre, the recruit is posted to a police station. There he/she spends almost two years undergoing further training on a practical basis, under close supervision. This is known as the "probationary" period of service.

After two years, he/she may take an examination to qualify for promotion to the rank of sergeant, and successful candidates are promoted to that rank if and when suitable vacancies arise. Not everyone who passes the examination will be promoted. After passing the qualifying examination to sergeant, a candidate may sit the examination for further promotion to inspector. Promotion to inspector and the higher ranks is by selection, and no further examinations are required.

Detectives are selected from the uniformed members of the service. After serving in uniform for the first two years of service, a police officer can be selected for training as a detective because of his/her aptitude for this work. He/she attends a course at a detective training school and may then become a detective police constable, working in civilian clothes. To qualify for promotion, the detective must pass the same examinations as his uniformed colleagues, and it is quite common for detectives to return to uniform duty for a short period be-fore being promoted within the Criminal Investigation Department.

For example, a detective inspector may have progressed from a uniformed constable to a detective constable, then from a uniform sergeant to a detective sergeant before winning his promotion to detective inspector (see chart on the next page). This system provides valuable experience in all departments.

Peter N. Walker is the author of The MacIntyre Plot.

MILEAGE ON THE BEAT

A constable on foot patrol covers perhaps only 10 miles per day. Before cars became so widely used, he would walk his beat for 7¼ hours, taking ¾ hour for a meal break. A reasonable walking speed is 3 miles per hour, which means he could cover up to 20 miles during every tour of duty. It is of interest to know that, for this reason, until 1975 most English bobbies received a boot allowance!

"Panda" cars travel about 40 miles per gallon of petrol. Cars work three tours of duty each day, so it is possible to cover 600 miles per day.

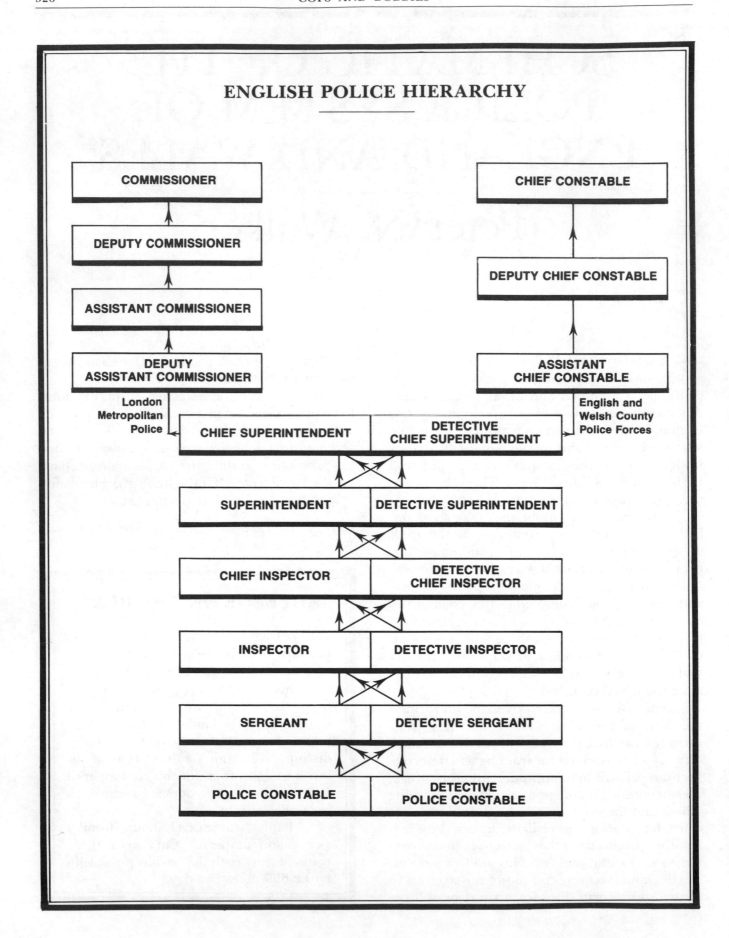

ENGLISH POLICE HIERARCHY

FICTIONAL CHARACTERS IN THE HIERARCHY

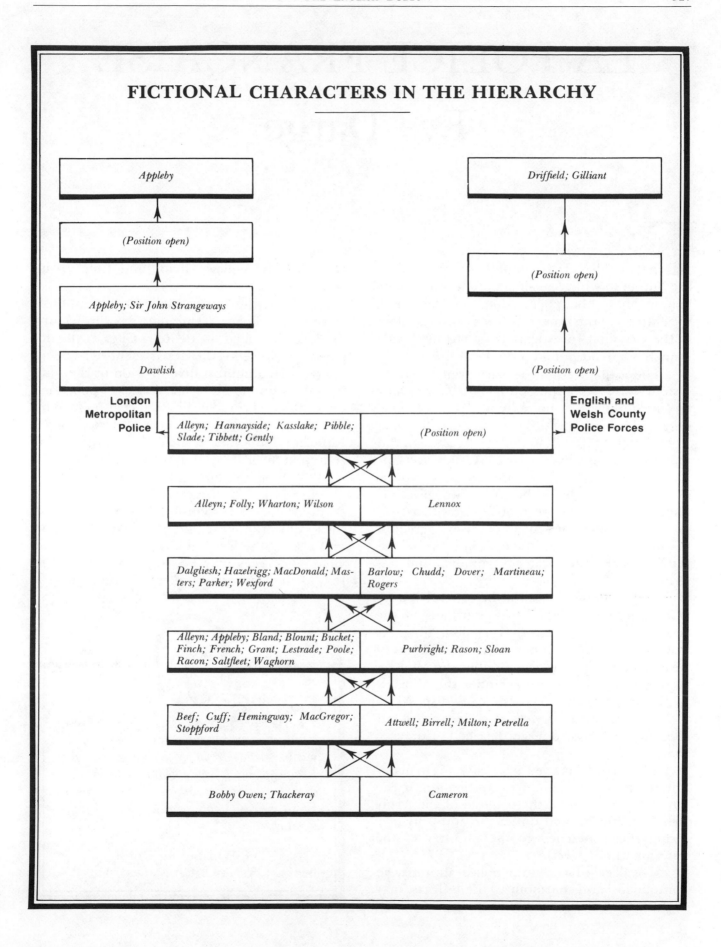

LA POLICE FRANÇAISE

Eve Darge

First of all, let us remind the reader that the Sûreté to which outsiders often refer when talking about the police, does not represent the entirety of the French Police. It applies solely to the Criminal Investigation Department with branches spread out all over the country.

The organization of the French police system — its establishment, its attributions and its functioning — is not easy to define. To understand it (very few do) is even more difficult.

Why is it difficult to define? Because of the many parties involved in a confusing overlapping of responsibilities of the multiple groups of police under the authority of two different ministries (we really mean different with a capital D here, since they may not always agree on the means to maintain the order or ensure the public peace), the local governments and the Army.

The National Police (or the general police), "Gardiens de la Paix," the guardians of the peace, in time of war or turbulent times, is under the jurisdiction of the Army, whereas in peacetime it is just as much under the Ministry of the National Defense as under the Ministry of the Interior that has also at its disposal an infinite number of services of police spread out in large cities according to the need of the moment.

The "gendarmerie," whose duty is to maintain the order and conduct investigations in the rural areas, is also at the disposal of the Army (being part of it) and under the authority of a local official attached to the Ministry of the Interior (the Prefect).

The lack of a central police authority to consolidate and harmonize the efforts may symbolize the policy "Divide and Rule" at its best.

In Paris, the general police is the responsibility of the Police Headquarters, "Préfecture de Police," located on Île de la Cité. At the departmental level — the department here being a territorial administrative division of the state (ninety-four in total) — all services of police are under the authority of the Prefect appointed by the Ministry of the Interior. Not elected. Since Napoleon (1800), he is the official government representative, the Administrator, the former royal "Intendant" during the Monarchy.

Even though the services of the police are theoretically his responsibility, they belong on the technical and disciplinary side to the Region and also to the Central Office in Paris, whose views and ideas may be quite different from that of the local government. (In their surveil-

Write, or cable me care of the Sûreté, Paris, the exact location *of that nick in the missing left ear of Murgatroyd, as per morgue photo. I have encountered two other nicked ears since leaving New York, one of which is indubitably related to the Murgatroyd case.*

The Whispering Ghost
STEPHEN CHALMERS

lance of the personalities, for instance, they also check on the Prefect and report to the Central Office.)

Each police precinct (commissariat) is headed by a police officer, the commissioner, whose rank theoretically corresponds to that of a colonel in the Army. His commanding officers of the guardians of the peace rank from first lieutenant to lieutenant colonel, according to the importance of the city. Police officers, in plain clothes or uniformed, are non-commissioned officers.

The officers come out of the National Police Academy, which admits candidates with prior master's degrees from universities and who have passed with highest scores a competitive entry examination. Exceptionally gifted candidates with lower degrees and, in rare cases, directly from the ranks, might also be enrolled.

Paradoxically, the head of the Paris prefecture and his immediate subordinates are civilian high officials appointed by the government. (Their knowledge of criminology, according to the whispers of some real pros, is no more than what can be rapidly acquired through a police novel.)

The gendarmerie officers, ranking from lieutenant to colonel, come out of the Military Academy of St. Cyr and the Military School at St. Maixent. Some may also have risen from the ranks after a probationary stage in a "gendarmerie school."

In the capital and larger cities, the police

M. Gondureau, Chef de Sûreté, appeared in Balzac's Le Père Goriot; *Inspector Hanaud, in A.E.W. Mason's* At the Villa Rose. *John Dickson Carr's Henri Bencolin was* juge d'instruction *in* It Walks by Night. *None of them ever directed traffic.*

Vidocq, founder of the Police de Sûreté (pictured above), wrote about his more scandalous escapades in the four-volume Mémoires *(1828–29). Rumor has it, they were ghost-written.*

are now to a large degree highly motorized. That entails motorbikes (Vespas) as well as automobiles. Because of the many narrow streets and traffic circles, only the little Renault is used, often referred to as "pie" (pronounced *pee*), the French for the magpie bird, because of its striking color resemblance — black and white.

France is proud of its police, which in spite of all is sophisticated, resourceful, efficient and effective. The fact that so many people are involved — so many personalities from the Prefect to the Ministers, who in no circumstances must be embarrassed — may very well keep the police on its toes and force it to outdo itself.

The French police have been criticized and often accused of treating as an "enemy" anyone not conforming. To remedy this, special courses on human relationships have been conducted during recent years among the various services.

For the tourist visiting Paris for the first time, it is worthwhile mentioning that the policeman they meet is not a "gendarme." The gendarme is, as we have said, the rural police dressed in navy blue uniforms slightly different from the policeman's dark blue. The guardian of the peace is addressed with the words "Monsieur l'Agent" (the *t*, at the end, not pronounced).

Under unusual circumstances — namely, in case of civil unrest — a different policeman, and wearing a khaki uniform, is called in as a reinforcement to the capital. He is the C.R.S., a member of the "Compagnie Républicaine de Sécurité," a paramilitary organization comparable to American state troopers. He happens to be the least popular among the masses because of the symbol of force he represents and the stringent measures he is likely to use.

Parking tickets are handed out by an auxiliary unit consisting of females, nicknamed "Aubergines" (eggplants) because of the particular uniform color they wear. In the same vein, let us mention that the police are referred to as "les Flics" (but never, never to their faces!).

Eve Darge is an executive supervisor for Air France.

VIDOCQ

Peter N. Walker

François Eugene Vidocq was a criminal who became chief of the Paris police.

Born in 1775 at Arras, he had an overpowering weakness for women. When he was only fifteen, he disguised himself as the sister of a willing serving maid so that he could accompany the lady of his desires on holiday. He had a fortnight's bliss without the lady's husband ever suspecting his wife had a lover.

His parents thought he would be best employed in the army, but there he continued his amorous exploits. Out of the army, he was an acrobat, forger, swindler, thief and highwayman, and his capacity for trouble brought him eight years' hard labour on the galleys at Brest. He escaped twice and was recaptured; upon his third escape he lived among the thieves and criminals of Paris, learning their ways. Armed with this knowledge, he offered himself in 1809 as a spy to the Paris police, and his energetic work eventually led to his becoming head of the reorganised detective department. He worked with a body of ex-convicts under his command and was known for his genius for catching crooks.

It was in 1811 that he hit upon the idea of the Sûreté, crime fighters who had no boundary limits. In 1817, his small group made 811 arrests, among which were 15 assassins, 341 receivers of stolen goods and 14 escaped prisoners. He started a card index of criminals, but his success did not please the orthodox police of Paris. They suggested that Vidocq arranged the crimes he successfully solved.

Vidocq's strong point was his extrovert personality. He was a master of disguise, a brilliant speaker and a humorist; on the debit side, he was always in trouble and constantly chasing women, especially actresses. He liked duelling, stalking the night life of Paris in disguise, raiding criminals' lairs or defending himself in court with his customary eloquence.

His disguises ranged from coalmen to women (he once escaped from prison disguised as a woman), but an example of his skill is shown in his efforts to disguise himself as an escaped prisoner called Germaine.

To discover Germaine's hiding place, he needed to fool the escapee's acquaintances. He studied pictures of Germaine and made himself up to look like him. He blistered his feet and faked the marks of the fetters about his ankles. He obtained some shoes and a shirt marked GAL, indicating service in the galleys. Next, he stained his shirt with walnut juice and let his beard grow. He caked his nostrils with gum and coffee grounds to give himself Germaine's nasal intonations, and finally he even obtained some lice to place upon his shirt. After all this, his disguise failed because someone revealed his true identity.

In 1827, Vidocq retired and started a paper mill, staffed with ex-convicts, but it was a failure. He tried to re-join the police and in 1832 succeeded by being allocated political duties. But Vidocq wanted only to return to detective duties, and it is said he organised a daring theft, one which he could solve in order to prove his worth. Once his real part became known, he was dismissed from the service.

It is also said he died in poverty, a broken man, although some accounts deny this. Some say he continued to work privately as a detective into ripe old age, still chasing the women, and that he lived in reasonable luxury until his death in 1857.

MAIGRET INTERVIEWED

Eve Darge

My assignment takes me to the very heart of Paris, "Île de la Cité." I glance at the Towers of Notre Dame watching over the city since the twelfth century. Turning to the left of the Cathedral I arrive at the Conciergerie, the former palace of the city's superintendent where memories of the French Revolution still linger. Marie Antoinette spent her last days here. It houses now the Palace of Justice, the Court House, the Police Headquarters. The place I am to visit, the right wing, was added by Napoleon the Third.

My taxi has dropped me at the entrance, Quai des Orfêvres.

"Right wing, second floor, Room 202," the guard says.

This is where the Homicide Squad operates.

"The Commissioner wants you to wait for him in his office," conveys young detective Janvier.

I have arrived just in time to avoid the gusty winds and the torrential rain falling now heavily on the city.

Heavy footsteps down the corridor. The solid, well-known silhouette appears at the door. His other detective — Lucas, I believe — helps him take off his drenched overcoat and hat. I stand up.

"Please remain seated." He exchanges his flooded pipe for a fresh one. "So, they send me women now! I have nothing against that . . . I've always had a preference for them. I get along better with them."

E.D.: Commissioner . . . how does one address you?

MAIGRET: Call me Maigret, you're a civilian!

E.D.: Monsieur Maigret, I should perhaps come back . . . this bad weather . . .

MAIGRET: No. It's your work. Bad weather has never interfered with mine.

E.D.: This weather reminds me of home . . . Lorraine, at the Belgian border.

MAIGRET: It's true. Always starts in England. The English try to unload it on us through the Belgians, who get it twenty-four hours earlier. Excuse me while I change my shoes. My feet are soaked.

E.D.: You should have had rubbers.

MAIGRET: I hate them! I also seem to have a certain allergy for raincoats and umbrellas. Besides, I used to lose them regularly.

E. D.: Monsieur Maigret, you just completed an investigation — what is your feeling when the murderer has been arrested?

MAIGRET: The satisfaction of the work done, the duty accomplished. The satisfaction of knowing that the perpetrator of a crime will not commit another one, as it sometimes happens, to cover the first.

E.D.: What are the most common motives you have encountered in your investigations?

MAIGRET: At the source, you'll always find the capital sins. Envy is the motive of the murderer who kills to get the property of others without working. Uncontrolled anger, a sort of temporary insanity, may also transform a man into a killer. Jealousy, of course, which is nothing other than a violent rejection of abandonment. The killer in that case will not admit to having his love or security usurped.

E.D.: You have not mentioned lust, or gluttony.

MAIGRET: Lust rarely generates murders. It does not generate anything. It degenerates, rather . . . gluttony, ah, that is my weakness. I have a strong appetite. Nothing moves me like good country cooking odors. In my time, we never counted calories and as a result people were much more level-headed. Particularly women!

E.D.: Do you imply that the modern woman lost some of her equilibrium when she lost her . . . excessive roundness?

MAIGRET: I have always preferred them pleasantly plump.

E.D.: Monsieur Maigret, you seem to know them very well. Women of all walks of life. It is even said that you know the prostitutes particularly well. That you have for them a certain fondness, a bias.

MAIGRET: No. Not a bias. But I do not condemn them. I try to understand the reason that brought them there. In general, they are not malefactors . . . but the victims.

E.D.: Coming back, Monsieur Maigret, to the confessions you obtain. It is rumored that you dissect souls. That people do not confess their crimes, but rather confide in you.

MAIGRET: I don't know if I dissect the souls. But I think I am able to put people at ease. I get their trust. The criminal is perhaps the human being who suffers the most. The one who has never been understood. Faced with someone who is able to discover what he is really like, to expose him to himself, he soon softens up. The weight of his guilt was becoming unbearable. This is the only way for him to feel some relief.

E.D.: In the course of an investigation, do you immediately recognize the guilty?

MAIGRET: No. But I recognize instinctively the non-guilty. I proceed by elimination. In difficult cases, I investigate the antecedents. Their childhood tells me more than their adult lives, which they might have been able to keep partly hidden.

E.D.: That makes you a disciple of Freud. I noticed while waiting for you that your library counts as many Treatises on Psychoanalysis as Manuals on Criminology.

MAIGRET: I believe everything is related to childhood.

E.D.: Beside the murder act, which are in your opinion the most hideous crimes?

MAIGRET: Without any doubt, blackmail and breach of confidence. Many years ago, while in Vichy, I became involved in the investigation of the murder of a woman. She had had, in her youth, a brief relationship with a man in Paris, and had moved away. Under the false pretext that he was the father to a son, she made him pay fantastic sums of money for more than twenty years — with the promise that they could come together when the boy would be of age. The man, being married and childless, waited patiently, and when finally faced with the truth that no child ever existed, in a fit of anger strangled her. For me, the real victim was the murderer . . . I had wished that he would be acquitted. And there is a justice . . . he was.

E.D.: You seem to be well liked by your associates. They call you "Patron" and "Boss" with reverence. Your former detectives assigned in different parts of France continue calling you "Boss".

MAIGRET: Well . . . they're a fine bunch. But the real boss is the French taxpayer. This is why we must do our job even better. We must protect him.

E.D.: What sort of private life do you lead, Monsieur Maigret?

MAIGRET: A very quiet life, between my wife and my office. I should say between my wife's dinner table and my office . . . I am not much for formal affairs. I hate wearing a tuxedo. Tuxedos should be worn only by men that look like Prince Philip.

E.D.: What do you do for leisure?

MAIGRET: Not much. I love to take walks along the Seine River looking at the simple people, along with my wife, my understanding wife. We get along so well, we don't even have to talk. I don't have much time for novels. But to really relax, I read Simenon. Even though he comes from the other side of the border, we seem to have a lot in common. You see . . . before all . . . he is human.

Eve Darge is a French poet living in New York.

POLIS! POLIS!

K. Arne Blom

In Sweden, the police procedural focuses on man's relationship to society. In Britain, its emphasis is on the struggle between good men (the police) and bad men (the criminals). In America, the police novel is most concerned with the interaction of characters with each other, not with the police; the policeman here is the dispassionate observer, the detective who unravels the story but does not get involved.

Most Americans think the Swedish police procedural begins and ends with Maj Sjöwall and Per Wahlöö. True, they wrote the first Swedish police novel (*Roseanna*, 1965), and one should not underestimate their influence. They showed that police procedurals were the perfect format for, in their words, "psychological balance, realism, sociological analysis and social consciousness."

But it would be a mistake to think they were an immediate success. It took four books before the Swedish critics appreciated them. One reviewer called *Roseanna* an "entertainment for unreflecting readers." It was not until the Mystery Writers of America bestowed the Edgar Award on *The Laughing Policeman* that the Swedish critics and general public took notice of Martin Beck & Co.

Their work divides into three categories. In the first three novels, they show the influence of Simenon. Beck is much like Maigret in that he reflects on the criminals' motives and tries to understand their actions in relation to society. In the next four, there are strong overtones of Ed McBain's 87th Precinct. Here, the emphasis is on the team and each member's response to the criminal. In the last three, Sjöwall and Wahlöö follow no one but themselves. These books are more political, more meditative, and have found an audience outside of "mere" mystery readers. In all ten novels, there is a strong Marxist orientation and the tendency found in many fictional works to exaggerate, to reveal some unpleasant truths — in this case, about Sweden.

The first Swedish writer to follow in their footsteps was Jacob Palme. He has written five procedurals. His books are ambitious, perhaps a bit naive, but the plots are interesting as is his attempt to explain human reactions to hopeless situations.

Olle Hogstrand wrote his first book in 1971. He is an exceptional writer, able to combine the action of the political thriller with the classic requirements of the police procedural. He, too, is concerned with the psychopathy of crime; why it was committed.

Olov Svedelid has written five procedurals, each concerned with the growing violence in society, the struggle between bad and evil. His series character is much the lone wolf, the solitary avenger. He has said that his sole purpose is to entertain the reader, and his books do qualify as a "fast read" — a bit sloppy, perhaps, but nonetheless effective.

Kjell E. Genberg is a comparative newcomer, having written just two novels. Both tackle organized crime and show the tendency of the police to catch the little guy and not the professional big shot.

I, too, write procedurals, but not because I regard them as superior — morally and aesthetically — to any other kind of mystery. They tell us about our society and about that subject of unfailing interest to us: ourselves. It was not the work of Sjöwall and Wahlöö which most influenced me, but that of American author

Hilary Waugh. Like him, I employ the "iceberg" method: at the tip, the crime; underneath, the weaknesses that caused it. I write of people whose dreams have crashed, who cannot handle their alienation, who strike back in the most desperate ways. Violence creating violence in a never-ending circle — that is my leitmotif.

In Sweden, the most popular current writer in the police genre is Ed McBain. There is a veritable McBain fever. Actually, he was the first American police writer published in Sweden (*Cop Hater,* 1957). The translation was incredibly bad; the cover, a nightmare. Not too surprisingly, the book was a failure. When McBain was reissued in 1962, he was accorded better treatment from the publishers, but critics were still unimpressed. One wrote that he could not understand why a decent Swedish publisher would undertake to reprint such violent rubbish. He claimed they were not good mysteries — not much better, in fact, than the Cardby books by Hume.

In addition to Waugh and McBain, Swedish mystery lovers thrive on Lillian O'Donnell and Dorothy Uhnak. No, they're not done in translation but are published in the original. In Sweden, most people are able to read English.

A typical Swedish cop in uniform.

Although police procedurals did not really become popular until the Sixties (in America and Britain as well as Sweden), their history, of course, can be traced much further back. I suppose one could say the first police procedural was born in 1931 with the arrival of *Dick Tracy.* Soon afterwards came *Radio Patrol* and then, in 1943, the best of the comic-strip lot: *Terry Drake.* It is reasonable, therefore, to claim that the childhood of the police novel was spent in the comics.

It was an American who wrote the book credited with beginning the genre, *V as in Victim* by Lawrence Treat (1954). I once asked Mr. Treat why he wrote that particular book, and he told me he had wanted to write about realistic policemen solving crimes. No, he said, he had not been influenced by the comic strips.

Although Treat's book was the first in the field, it did not really start the trend toward police procedurals. That fell to Sidney Kingsley's play *Detective Story* (1949). It has been said that this opened the mystery writers' eyes to the possibilities inherent in the police situation. I think it difficult to claim that any one work is the single decisive factor in starting a trend. My belief is that after World War II, readers, as well as writers, found it hard to escape reality. They wanted to read about it in order to better understand their own lives and their own conditions.

Regardless of why, the police novel prospered. In 1952, Hilary Waugh published *Last Seen Wearing;* then came the Gordons, Ben Benson, Thomas Walsh and countless others. Not to mention the TV staples: *Dragnet* and *Line-Up.* In the Sixties, Elizabeth Linington appeared and, fast on her heels, Robert Fish. The Seventies have seen the debut of Rex Burns, whose *Alvarez Journal* proves one can take the police format and turn it inside out, yet at the same time, keep it procedural.

Small wonder, then, that police procedurals have maintained their popularity. Action. Excitement. Psychology. Methodology. What more could one ask for?

K. Arne Blom is the author of The Moment of Truth, *which won Sweden's Sherlock Award as the best suspense novel of the year (1974).*

INTERPOL

UNITED PRESS INTERNATIONAL

The International Criminal Police Organization (Interpol) is really nothing more than a seven-story file cabinet stashed away in Saint-Cloud, a suburb of Paris.

It has no police force of its own, no detectives, no multi-aliased spies, no agents of any kind. It does not actually catch criminals at all. Rather, it alerts local authorities and lets them do the dirty work.

What Interpol does have is a well-crammed computer and about 100 staff members who are good at pushing its buttons. This computer houses approximately 700,000 cross-indexed names of criminals, along with their description, fingerprints and photographs. It also has access to about 2 million file cards containing, among other things, experts who may be called upon in a pinch. For example, a forensic specialist in New York may have a card on file at Interpol headquarters. Should a case come up that warrants his particular expertise, Interpol's computers would spit out his data and then pass the information on to the appropriate source.

Typically, Interpol is used by its 100-odd member nations to keep tabs on drug traffickers, art thieves, counterfeiters, and bad guys who skip one country to settle in another that doesn't believe in extradition.

The first International Criminal Police Commission was established in Vienna in 1923 and stayed operative until 1938 when the Nazis overran Austria. After World War II Interpol again surfaced as the central clearing house for information on international criminals and their capers.

To commemorate Interpol's fiftieth birthday Nicaragua issued a series of Interpol stamps in 1973, each bearing the picture of a famous fictional sleuth. *Ellery Queen's Mystery Magazine* was asked to decide which sleuths should be used. The magazine conducted a poll amongst its readers, leading mystery writers and critics, and the top runners were those chosen for the honor.

Chapter 10

THE LAB

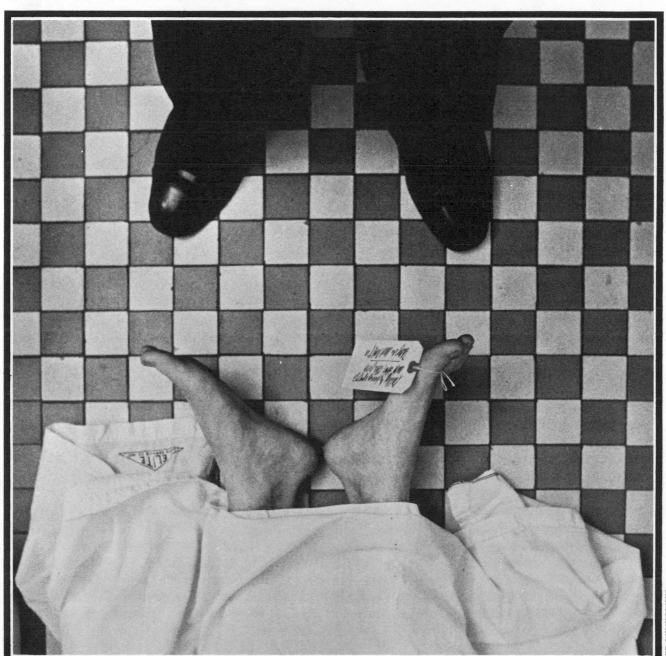

A FICTIONAL PROGNOSIS
P.D. James

It must be a minority of mysteries in which a doctor doesn't make at least a brief appearance. In any civilised country, following a suspicious death, a medical man is invariably called in to examine the body and pronounce life extinct, and later a forensic pathologist will perform an autopsy. The descriptions of some of these medical experts is often as superficial as their appearance in the story is brief. They perform their necessary functions with varying degrees of efficiency and depart leaving the detective, amateur or professional to carry on with the investigation. But occasionally doctors and nurses play a more important role — suspect, detective or even murderer — while a number of mystery writers have chosen a medical setting for their stories — a hospital, clinic or nursing home.

It is easy to understand the attraction of a doctor as suspect or villain. He has the means of death readily at hand; he has knowledge of poisons, their symptoms and effects; his intimate acquaintance with his patients and their private lives gives him particular opportunity; he has professional dexterity and skill, and — particularly if he is a surgeon — he has nerve. Occasionally, too, he has the hubris with which most murderers are afflicted. If all power corrupts, then a doctor, who literally holds life and death in his hands, must be at particular risk. Sir Julian Freke, one of Dorothy L. Sayers' two medical murderers, is an example of the arrogance of the fictional brilliant surgeon who regards himself as above morality and law. It is interesting that of Sayers' eleven full-length murder mysteries, two have medical murderers, both eminent specialists, while a third has an ex-nurse who kills by the doubtfully feasible method of injecting air into the patient's vein. But perhaps the nastiest of all the medical murderers is Dr. Grimesby Roylott of Conan Doyle's *The Speckled Band.* As his author says:

> *When a doctor goes wrong he is the first of villains. He has nerve and he has knowledge.*

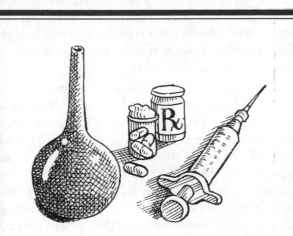

IS THERE A DOCTOR IN THE BOOK?

You can stake your life on it (and sometimes have to). Some famous fictional doctors are: Max Brand's James Kildare, August Derleth's Lyndon Parker, Arthur Conan Doyle's Watson, R. Austin Freeman's Christopher Jervis and John Evelyn Thorndyke, Matthew Head's Mary Finney, Seabury Quinn's Dr. Throwbridge, and Sax Rohmer's Dr. Petrie.

MARTY NORMAN

Palmer and Pritchard were among the heads of that profession.

It is perhaps surprising that a medical setting is comparatively rare in detective fiction, considering its attractions. Here we have the closed community beloved of detective writers for the neat containment of victim, suspect and murderer; a strongly hierarchical community with its own esoteric rules and conventions; a mysterious but fascinating world of men and women performing a great variety of necessary jobs from consultant surgeon to ward cleaner, where the reader, like the patient, feels vulnerable, apprehensive and alien. To write convincingly about hospitals usually requires special knowledge, and those who have done it best, in whose books the smell of disinfectant seems literally to rise from the page, have usually had a medical or nursing background. Josephine Bell (*Murder in Hospital; Death at the Medical Board*) is herself a doctor, and Christianna Brand uses her experience as a voluntary nurse during World War II in what I still consider one of the best detective novels with a medical setting — *Green for Danger.*

The peculiar advantages of special knowledge, professional skill and insight into character which are enjoyed by the doctor as villain also apply to the doctor as detective. The list of medical fictional detectives is varied and impressive, including such very different characters as Josephine Bell's Dr. David Winteringham, H.C. Bailey's amiable, hedonistic but deeply compassionate Dr. Reginald Fortune and R. Austin Freeman's Dr. Thorndyke — perhaps the greatest medical legal detective in fiction. Dr. Thorndyke is essentially a forensic scientist rather than a medical doctor and, in addition to exceptional intellectual powers, has a profound knowledge of such diverse subjects as anatomy, ophthalmology, botany, archaeology and Egyptology. He is also exceptionally handsome. Freeman writes:

His distinguished appearance is not merely a concession to my personal taste but also a protest against the monsters of ugliness whom other detective writers have evolved. These are quite opposed to natural truth. In real life, a first-class man of any kind usually tends to be a good-looking man.

HOSPITABLE CHARACTERS

The most famous nurse in mystery lore is Sarah Keate in Mignon G. Eberhart's *The Patient in Room 18* and *While the Patient Slept.* Nurses and doctors are on call in P.D. James' *Shroud for a Nightingale,* and doctors are busy killing and curing in Josephine Bell's *Murder in Hospital* and *Death at the Medical Board,* Christiana Brand's *Green for Danger,* Agatha Christie's *The Murder of Roger Ackroyd* and E. Spence DePuy's *The Long Knife.*

If you need a good G.P., there's Margaret Carpenter's Huntingdon Bailey, Theodora DuBois' Jeffrey McNeil, Rufus King's Colin Starr and Jonathan Stagge's Hugh Westlake.

Should you need a specialist in pulmonary diseases, contact John Creasey's Stanislaus Palfrey, and if surgery is indicated drop by the infirmary of H.C. Bailey's Reggie Fortune.

It is not surprising that a number of the most successful medical detectives are psychiatrists. As Helen McCloy's Dr. Basil Willing says: "Every criminal leaves psychic fingerprints and he can't wear gloves to hide them. . . . Lies like blunders are psychological facts." The appro-

A public drugstore in Chicago c. 1904. Then, as now, customers often purchased powders for uses their manufacturers never intended.

priately named Dr. Paul Prye, the tall whimsical psychiatrist who features in Margaret Millar's first three books, would no doubt have agreed, as would the very different philosopher and psychologist Prof. Henry Poggioli, who features in the only mystery novel written by T.S. Stribling — *Clues of the Caribbees*.

Some medical detectives are general practitioners and have the advantage of that intimate knowledge of the local community and the day-to-day lives of their patients, their families and backgrounds which is so important to successful detection. Rufus King's Dr. Colin Starr is a G.P. working in a fictional small town in Ohio who, in *Diagnosis: Murder*, suspects that a number of the apparently natural deaths in the community are actually murders and is able to prove it. Jonathan Stagg's G.P. detective, Dr. Hugh Westlake, also works in a small town,

but here the stories, although they have a medical background, also contain a strong atmosphere of terror and the supernatural *(The Stars Spell Death; Turn of the Table; The Yellow Taxi)*.

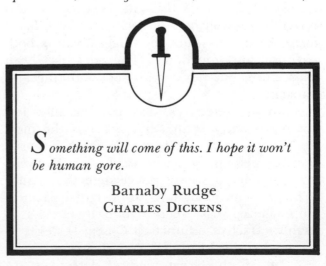

*S*omething will come of this. I hope it won't be human gore.

Barnaby Rudge
CHARLES DICKENS

THE FIFTY-MINUTE CRIME

Need a psychiatrist to help you solve a problem? Contact Gene Goldsmith's Dan Damon, Kyle Hunt's Emmanuel Cellini, Helen McCloy's Basil Willing, Hugh McLeave's Gregor MacLean, Lynn Meyer's Sarah Chayse, Margaret Millar's Paul Prye, Gladys Mitchell's Beatrice Bradley, Hugh Pentecost's John Smith or Patrick Quentin's Dr. Lenz.

If you'd prefer a psychoanalyst, try Henry Kuttner's Michael Gray.

If you'd rather visit a psychologist, try Edwin Balmer and William Mac-Harg's Luther Trant or T.S. Stribling's Henry Poggioli.

Still another specialist you might try is the one who makes a career out of nervous disorders — Anthony Wynne's Eustace Hailey.

Finally, you might consider contacting Lucy Freeman, who not only has created a series psychiatrist sleuth in *The Dream* but has coauthored many psychology books with leading (real) doctors in the field.

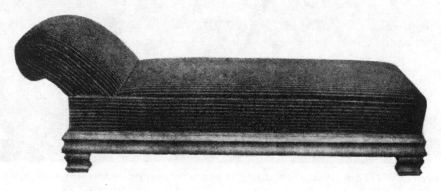

A superb book about a psychiatrist: Amanda Cross' In the Last Analysis.

But one of the best-known general practitioners in crime writing must be the narrator of Agatha Christie's brilliant but controversial novel first published in 1926, *The Murder of Roger Ackroyd,* in which the village doctor is both narrator and murderer. The trick has been used since, but never with such cunning and panache.

Nurse detectives are considerably less common than doctors, but perhaps the most well known is M.G. Eberhart's Sarah Keate, a middle-aged spinster who works in a Midwestern city with a young police detective, Lance O'Leary — an intriguing and original partnership where Miss Keate's inquisitiveness is a highly effective adjunct to O'Leary's "eyes in the back of his head and ears all around."

But all the great medical detectives are from the past. Although in England Gladys Mitchell, after fifty books, is still writing admirably about her eccentric and formidable psychiatrist, Dame Beatrice Lestrange Bradley, there has been a definite move, at least in the orthodox detective novel, toward a professional police hero. Apart from Dame Beatrice, it is difficult to recall a modern medical detective, and it may be, in an age of increasing specialisation, that the heyday of the brilliant omniscient amateur like Dr. Thorndyke, whether medical or lay, is temporarily over.

P.D. James won a Crime Writers' Association Silver Dagger for The Black Tower. *Her most recent novel,* Death of an Expert Witness, *features a forensic laboratory.*

THE MYSTERY READER'S PHARMACOPOEIA

Rodger J. Winn, M.D.

There's no accounting for taste. Some mystery writers/readers prefer the archfiend having his way with a completely irreversible drug, while others favor the super-sleuth with an antidote in the nick of time. Some like the culprit to be a gardener, calmly purchasing his weapon from the local hardware store, and some fancy a demented arachnidologist, importing a South American *Loxosceles laeta*. Some like a convulsive screaming death; others, a long-drawn-out deterioration.

THE WRITER'S NIGHTMARE

There have been instances of fact following fiction — when a case reached the newspapers which almost exactly duplicated a novelist's method. One such case involved Agatha Christie's *The Pale Horse*. A mass murderer, released from an asylum, attempted another murder, this time using Christie's suggestions. This same book, however, in 1977, was responsible for saving a life. A nurse was reading it and noticed the similarities between a patient's condition and that described in the book. She told the doctors her suspicions and they proved correct. Without her help, and Miss Christie's, the doctors are not sure they would have been able to effect a cure in time.

Whichever your favorite diabolical twist, a basic knowledge of poison pharmacology is as essential to the mystery writer/reader as familiarity with the floor plan of a Tudor mansion or the infrastructure of a foreign intelligence service.

To guide you through the toxicologic data, we offer the following scenarios and their appropriate poisons.

The classic poison: arsenic. Often called "inheritance powder" because of the tendency of family members to use it on each other, this white, odorless, tasteless powder is readily available in ant pastes and weed killers, and provides a broad range of acute and chronic clinical spectra. For the get-it-done-in-a-hurry job, a dose of about 1 gram is more than enough. Within 3–4 hours the victim lies deathly ill with vomiting and diarrhea, followed in 24–72 hours by death from circulatory collapse. A super-sleuth may be able to make a diagnosis on the basis of the characteristic garlic breath of the victim and will confirm his suspicions with a single urine specimen. If the diagnosis is made after death, analysis will utilize the victim's hair and nails for testing arsenic levels. For a slower death, a pinch of arsenic a day will lead to the victim's progressive weakness, baldness, development of roughened skin and characteristic white ridges of the nails (Aldrich-Mees lines). Eventually, the poor imbiber begins to suffer multiple nerve paralyses, hoarseness and a hacking cough. At first, he will feel sensations of cold and numbness in his limbs, and these can progress to permanent

paralysis over a matter of years. The intriguing aspect of chronic arsenic poisoning as a homicidal modus operandi is that the poisoner may build up his own tolerance to arsenic by taking tiny amounts over a long period (Careful, too much leads to death not to tolerance.) Thus he may serve sumptuous suppers liberally spiked with arsenic and, unlike his victim, emerge horse-healthy. One should be warned, however, that arsenic does not always work. The historical example of this is Rasputin's refusal to react to the poison.

The horrible demise: strychnine. Within 15 minutes a fiend can relish the sight of his quarry racked by convulsions that lift him off the floor but still leave him fully conscious to suffer the excruciating pains of the powerful spasms. The lightest stimulation — the shining of a light or the gentle nudge of a foot — can set off another round of the bone-breaking contortions. Strychnine is for the victim you wish to torture before you kill. A most seriously unpleasant death.

Please pass the mushrooms: Amanita phalloides. The use of this deadly poison in a delectable package allows the poisoner to be well on his (or her) way to the hinterlands by the time the victim succumbs. Even the most sophisticated gourmet will not notice the tiny white gills and wartlike scales that differentiate the deadly *Amanita phalloides* from *Agaricus campestris*, the common, edible mushroom. Since cooking does not remove the toxins, a hot meal can be prepared without diminishing the deleterious effects. All is well and good for 12 hours before the onset of nausea, vomiting and diarrhea, which initially is not too severe so that it may be another 24 hours before intensive medical care is administered. By this time the patient may go into circulatory collapse. If he is lucky enough to escape thus far, he has still not really escaped, for in 3–4 days he will begin to turn yellow as his liver decays. A bonus to the poisoner is that unless the history of the mushroom meal is elicited — a nicety easily overlooked by the critically ill — tracing the poison source is very difficult.

The poison in the fake tooth: cyanide. Every spy worth his alias knows instant death is preferable to the tortures from his sadistic enemies. He bites down, and the convenient cyanide pellet embedded in his bridgework acts in a matter of seconds. This is due to cyanide's ability to bind the body's internal breathing apparatus. Found in nature in bitter almonds, and peach and apricot pits, the tip-off to cyanide's presence is the intense smell of bitter almonds on the victim's breath. Because the body cannot use the blood's oxygen, the skin of the individual turns a violent pink — this despite his difficulty in breathing. However, the combination of almond breath and bright pinkness can lead to an early diagnosis, and a quick-witted hero can rescue the incipient corpse with an amyl nitrite pearl.

The blowpipe poison: curare. Curare is isolated from *Chondrodendron tomentosum* and blocks the spread of impulses from the nerve to the muscle, thereby paralyzing the victim. (And anyway, what was he doing at a South American tennis camp staffed by Orinoco Indians?) Minutes after the injection (usually by a curare-dipped dart, since curare is not effective if eaten) there is a flushing of the face and a soft cough. The muscle paralyses start in the head so that the poisonee may have drooping of the eyelids, double vision because of weak eye muscles, difficulty swallowing due to secondary throat-muscle paralyses and, finally, respiratory failure due to his inability to move the muscles of the ribs and diaphragm. Though almost impossible to trace after death, the effects of curare are instantaneously reversible by the intravenous injection of one ampule of prostigmin.

Come into my parlor: the black widow. This petite little lady, about half an inch long with an hourglass on her belly, spends much of her

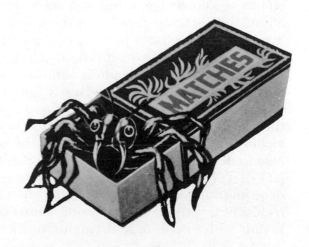

time in unsavory places (privies) and so genitals and buttocks are favorite attack sites. The sharp bite is similar to the slight tingling of a needle and may possibly go unnoticed. The pain begins in one half hour as the poison affects the nerve endings. There is an ascending cramplike sensation starting in the legs or abdomen and, eventually, severe spasms; if touched, the victim's abdomen has a boardlike rigidity. This mimics closely the clinical picture of a perforated ulcer and medical evaluation may go totally down the wrong path. The patient is anxious, in a panic, and appears acutely ill since he is bathed in a cold sweat and has a thready pulse. The severe spasms last a day, then slowly subside over the next 48 hours. Death is rare, however, from one bite. Perhaps it would be best to have several of these venomous females on hand.

Another troublemaker is the South American brown spider, recognized by the violin markings on its back. The bites of this Latin import are very painful and become agonizing after 8 hours, leaving a large, swollen, black-and-blue area. The venom attacks the blood cells in about 36 hours, rupturing them so that the victim passes urine dark with the breakdown products of his hemoglobin. He progresses to a state of jaundice, kidney failure and shock.

Vapors through the vent: carbon monoxide and nerve gas. Carbon monoxide has the advantage of accessibility for our would-be assassin. This odorless, tasteless gas is formed from the incomplete combustion of carbon products such as coke or charcoal, and it does not take much technical knowledge to hook a tube from an automobile exhaust pipe into a room vent or to leave a low-lit hibachi in a room for heat, enabling the gas to do its insidious job. Carbon monoxide has a tremendous affinity for the body's hemoglobin, binding closely and tightly to it so there is no room for the blood to carry the life-supporting oxygen. Thus, although the victim actually gets enough oxygen, he is unable to deliver it to his tissues and he dies from lack of it. The victim goes through two stages of deterioration. The first is characterized by headaches, giddiness, increasing shortness of breath with exertion, and ringing in the ears.

BOOKS FAVORING POISON

Behold, Here's Poison: Georgette Heyer
Murder to Go: Emma Lathen
Nursey, Tea and Poison: Anne Morice
The Poisoned Chocolates Case: Anthony Berkeley
Strong Poison: Dorothy L. Sayers

This progresses to a drunken condition, with agitation and confusion, during which time there is a noticeable impairment of judgment; even though the victim knows something is wrong, he does not attempt to leave the noxious environment. (Even nicer for the would-be assassin is the fact that if the victim recovers, he generally has complete amnesia and can offer no incriminating evidence.) In the second stage the skin turns a shade of pink known as cherry red and breathing becomes more labored, occasionally exhibiting a Cheyne-Stokes pattern: periods of 30 seconds of no breathing followed by 6–8 rapidly increasing deep breaths, then again the absence of breathing. Eventually, the victim begins to twitch, convulse, and then slip into unconsciousness and probably death, just prior to which his body temperature may rise to 108°. Death usually comes in the first 2 days after massive exposures but may be delayed as long as 3–8 days. Even if the victim recovers, his troubles are not over: late-occurring sequelae include severe psychological reactions, i.e., overtly psychotic behavior.

Nerve gas is indicated for the more deadly *coup de grace.* Killers with names such as Tabun, Sarin or T-46, Soman, DFP or DCP, all work in the same manner. They prevent the breakdown of the substance (acetylcholine) which transmits impulses from the nerves to the muscles, thus leading to the hyperexcitability of the victim. These substances are colorless, basically odorless, and can be inhaled or absorbed by skin. The initial symptoms are runny nose, wheezing and chest tightness, followed by excessive salivation, the inability to tolerate light and, finally, paralysis and death. Old gases may take 20 minutes to work, but newer improvements have cut down the time, making the administration of the antidote — atropine — almost impossible. A particularly sadistic scenario may find the victim in possession of a syringe filled with the antidote but too paralyzed to squeeze the plunger and save himself.

The gardener's caper: rat poisoning. As any sly weekend gardener knows, rat poison offers the convenience of the nearest hardware store and a believable alibi — one needed it to tend the weeds and the rodents, didn't one? For human as well as furry fare-thee-wells there are two effective poisons: thallium, currently one of the leading homicidal agents in the world, and the warfarin drugs.

Thallium has been removed from U.S. markets since 1965 because of its lethality, but it is readily available in European settings. Odorless and tasteless, the chemical blends superbly with sugared grain, making a delectable feast for rodents and a tasty tidbit for those humans with a sweet tooth. The action is slow, first declaring itself with diffuse pain and severe constipation 3–4 days after consumption. Supersleuth can make a diagnosis of it at this early stage by detecting a peculiar dark pigmentation around the roots of the hair. During this period

The wittiest place to bury a corpse: a hemlock forest.

the victim is often thought to be hysterical or psychologically disturbed, rather than poisoned. In the second or third week after ingestion the victim begins losing his hair, not only on his head but also on his body — except for the middle third of his eyebrows and his pubic hair. The skin appears dry and scaly, the heart beats rapidly and various nerves become paralyzed so that the eyelids may droop, the feet drag, blindness ensue. Ultimately, death occurs with pneumonia and congestion of the lungs. Like arsenic, thallium can be added in small dabs and the homicide accomplished over a period of months for subtlety.

In the United States rat poison has been replaced mainly by warfarin, which interferes with the blood-clotting system. Thus the victim gets signs of increasing bleeding such as nosebleed (epistaxis), gum bleeding (gingival hemorrhages), black-and-blue marks (ecchymosis), bloody urine (hematuria), bloody vomit (hematemsis) and bloody bowel movements (melena and hematochezia). A disadvantage to the evildoer is that this poison affects humans only slightly, so that large amounts are needed. The potion does mix well with corn porridge, and a series of good hearty breakfasts can do the job. The antidote would be large doses of vitamin K.

Come slither: poisonous snakes. The silent, relentless undulation of a snake, replete with glittering fangs, is a surefire candidate for arousing terror. Poisonous snakes can cause two kinds of death, depending on whether their venom is a neurotoxin (attacks the nerves) or a hemotoxin (attacks the blood cells). In the first type the victim has very little reaction at the bite site but in 1–2 hours becomes progressively paralyzed. Typical snakes causing such a condition are the U.S. coral snake and the sinister Asian cobra. The blood attackers cause tremendous pain, swelling and bleeding at the site of the fang marks, and in one hour there is the onset of shock as the blood breaks down and the clotting mechanisms disintegrate. For exotic variety there is also the horned viper of the eastern Sahara, which burrows in the sand and lunges at its victim, and the deadly fer-de-lance, which can leap several feet off the ground to strike with its venomous fangs.

The O.D.: heroin. Since heroin is normally cut or diluted many times with quinine and sugars, an injection of the pure substance will be many times more powerful than even the most hardened addict can tolerate. If the victim is a junkie who has cut back on his intake, he can no longer handle the same amounts of heroin as before and giving him his previous dosage will cause an overdose. Unconsciousness stemming from an overdose can be almost instantaneous; the victim may be found with the syringe still in his arm. The drug victim lies in coma with slowly decreasing respiration, to the point where he may be breathing only 2–3 times per minute. The pupils of the eye are initially pinpoint, but as the blood pressure falls and shock with its cold clammy skin intervenes, the blood supply to the brain diminishes and the pupils may grow large as death approaches.

The Doctor's black bag: a poison potpourri. The tireless, faithful family practitioner is a walking arsenal. Should he switch from healing to homicide, he has only to dip into his ubiquitous black bag to use:

Insulin — to drive down the blood sugar, causing convulsions and death.

Potassium — to slow the heartbeat and eventually cause it to stop.

Calcium — to send the victim into kidney failure and coma.

Barbiturates — to fatally slow the metabolism.

Amphetamines — to irrevocably speed up the metabolism.

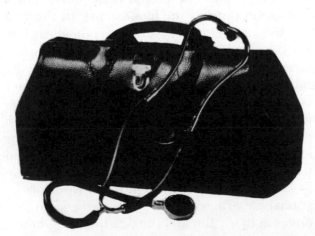

If the doctor comes to kill, not cure, should one pay him for a house call?

*I*t's the immutable law — the characteristics are both mixed up with each other somehow in the same chromosome, don't you see? — it's the only instance in which color blindness ever goes into a woman, and then only from a six-fingered parent. . . .

The Matilda Hunter Murder
Harry Stephen Keeler

Oxygen — to remove the drive to breathe in a victim with emphysema of the lungs, resulting in a condition known as carbon dioxide narcosis.

Not quite in the little black bag is the *air bubble,* but who knows better how to inject it than the physician?

All these agents are part of every doctor's armamentarium against disease, but all can be abused.

The Mad Scientist at work: recombinant DNA. If the mystery reader/writer demands novel ways of committing mayhem, he might well consider the new field of molecular biology called recombinant DNA experimentation. Purely in the hypothetical stage, of course, this involves splicing together the genetic material (DNA) of two species so that the resultant creation has some of the characteristics and properties of each. One could conjecture creating a bacterium which is resistant to all known antibodies or achieving a germ that is normally at peace in the human body but now excretes deadly botulinum toxin. Even more macabre might be the creation of a mosquito that injects a deadly poison or a tumor-causing virus. The possibilities are limitless, and the evil, cackling genius can manipulate all the forces of nature for his demented purposes. Dr. Frankenstein revisited, if you will.

Rodger J. Winn is a practicing physician in New Jersey.

THE BUSIEST MORGUE IN THE WORLD

William DeAndrea

The building on the corner of First Avenue and 30th Street is not a very impressive one. Transport it to a college campus and it would look like any other mid-Fifties dormitory; move it to a medium-size town and it would pass for a solid, respectable insurance company. But the large aluminum letters on its exterior do not say STUDENTS HALL or METROPOLITAN LIFE; rather, they spell out NEW YORK CITY MEDICAL EXAMINER'S OFFICE — commonly called the morgue.

Approximately 8,500 autopsies are performed here every year, roughly twenty to twenty-five per day. Yours will be one of them if your death is considered unnatural: if, say, you die under violent circumstances; if there's a hint of foul play; if you keel over unexpectedly with no previous record of medical difficulties. Your case will be handled by Dr. Dominic Di-Maio, chief medical examiner, and his staff of three to four deputy medical examiners, four to eight assisting doctors and four to eight dieners (helpers). They will be concerned not with *who* did you in, but with *what* did you in. Method, not motive, is what interests the forensic pathologist, who tends to view each autopsy as a learning experience, a fact borne out by a Latin inscription in the lobby of the morgue: *Taceant colloquis effugiat risus. Hic locus est ubi mors caudet succurere vitae.* (Loosely translated: Let conversation stop, let laughter cease. This is the place where death delights in helping the living.)

Upon entering the morgue, one steps into a blue-tiled lobby with large house plants framing picture windows and a row of chairs backed

---

SUICIDE? OR MURDER?

There are fashions in the means of suicide; the current vogue is jumping from high places.

Myopic jumpers invariably remove their eyeglasses and put them in a pocket before jumping. The Medical Examiner's Office considers traces of prescription glass in a suicide's face a sure tip-off that it was a murder.

Similarly, stabbing suicides never stab themselves through their clothes, and most of them prefer to do their stabbing in the bathroom, facing the mirror.

Characteristically, a woman will strip to the waist (sometimes leaving on her bra), then stab herself in the abdomen 25–30 times with a small knife until she passes out from loss of blood. Death from exsanguination follows.

A man, on the other hand, pulls back his shirt, or removes it, then kills himself with a single thrust to the heart with a long-bladed knife.

Variations from these two methods will make the medical examiner think closely about murder rather than suicide.

W.D.

up against a wall. Not very ominous, but not very inviting, either.

Death waits downstairs.

It rests in a gray-and-white tiled room, and the minute you step in it the smell hits. The detective story cliché about the "unmistakable smell of death" turns out to be a simple statement of fact. The smell *is* unmistakable, even to those who have never smelled it before. It is also unforgettable and indescribable, and maybe from some primal survival instinct it makes you want to run away.

This body-storage room is a rectangle within a rectangle. The inner rectangle is a stainless-steel refrigerated chamber, kept at 38° F. The bodies are inside it, each on a sliding slab, each behind its own numbered door. There are 130 of these little square doors, and they look not unlike the lockers at airport and bus terminals. Most of the morgue's cadavers, except the badly decomposed and the children, are kept inside them. They each have their own room and own set of compartments on either side of the larger rectangle.

The day I visited the morgue, Jean Pierre Lahary, a forensic reconstructionist, was my guide. He wasted no time in opening one of the little doors. There was a grating sound and, I thought, an impossibly loud noise. Having read for years about the staring eyes of a corpse, I braced myself to meet them. I needn't have bothered. The slab held the headless, handless body of a young black woman. Mr. Lahary ran a finger over the characteristic marks made by a saw as it cut its way through bone. He picked up one of the severed hands, which had been found some months after the rest of her, and gestured with it to illustrate a point. I wasn't really paying attention.

I had told myself I wouldn't react, but for a moment my stomach did calisthenics, my eyes fogged over and I broke out in a cold sweat. When that passed, however, I found I could then observe with almost professional detachment. Almost. I was still revolted by the smell. (Later, in talking to other people who had been to the morgue, I learned that they, too, after an initial adjustment, found they could "take" it. A not-uncommon fantasy for morgue visitors is to imagine themselves as medical students. This

THE REMAINS

The Signs of Somatic Death

Algor mortis (cooling of the body)

It takes approximately 40 hours for the body to cool to the environmental temperature. For the first few hours the body cools at the rate of 3–3½°F per hour; it then cools at 1°F until it reaches the environmental temperature. To estimate how long a body's been dead, take the normal body temperature minus the rectal temperature of the corpse and divide this figure by 1.5.

Rigor mortis (muscular rigidity)

This stiffening is caused by the precipitation of protein and occurs 4–10 hours after death, passing off in 3–4 days. It starts in the muscles around the head and neck, with jaws and eyelids stiffening first.

Livor mortis (post-mortem staining)

This is an irregular reddish discoloration of dependent parts of the body due to gravitational sinking of the blood. It causes a splotchy appearance at all points not in contact with external supports (the floor, a chair, etc.), which aids in detecting whether the body has been tampered with (e.g., turned over) after death occurred. The process stops after 10–12 hours.

Putrefaction

This occurs 24–48 hours after death and is due to bacteria eating away at the body. The body turns green, bloats with gas, smells. The degree to which this occurs depends on the climate, whether the body is immersed in water, etc.

depersonalization keeps them on their feet.)

Lahary then escorted me into the autopsy room, separated from the adjacent storage rectangles by two sets of swinging doors. There are seven tables, and the day I was there three of them were in use. On one, a body was being hosed off. (The surface of each table is a metal grating, and below it is a shallow tub with constantly running water to flush away the blood.) At another table a doctor was using a circular saw (electric) to open a skull. When he finished, he lifted off the top portion of the head, rather like halving a cantaloupe, scooped out the brain and weighed it. The cadaver's face was then pulled down so the forehead practically reached the chin. (Imagine peeling an orange halfway, then reversing the peel over the intact part. Same procedure.) At the third table a doctor had just made the famous Y-shaped incision on a fifteen-year-old girl who had been found the day before floating in the bathtub. The Y opened her in such a way that her chest could be flapped back to cover her face and her abdomen could be turned back to either side to reveal her internal organs. I was surprised to learn that human fat tissue is a rich yellow, like chicken fat, and that human flesh on the inside resembles the cheaper cuts of pork.

The doctor explained that this young woman may have been raped: There was a bruise above her knee and a fingernail mark in her vagina. She may also have been murdered, he added, indicating bruises on her neck and shoulders which might have been caused by someone trying to hold her underwater.

I stayed long enough to see the woman stitched up. The needle was enormous and so were the stitches.

Mr. Lahary moved my tour upstairs to his office, where we were joined by deputy medical examiner, Dr. Michael Baden. The two imparted the following:

The first thing that's done to a body upon its arrival is to give it a bath.

The corpse is then put into its compartment, feet first, with an identifying tag knotted around its right big toe.

In usual cases bodies are kept at the morgue between fifteen days and one month, but parts of bodies — legs, arms, etc. — are kept up

---

THE PATHOLOGIST'S REPORT

Dr. David Wintringham, pathologist, appears in Josephine Bell's *Fallover Cliff* and *Death at the Medical Board*.

Dr. Daniel Webster Coffee, pathologist, appears in Lawrence G. Blochman's *Diagnosis: Homicide; Recipe for Homicide; Clues for Dr. Coffee*.

Dr. Grace Severance, pathologist and professor of medicine, appears in Margaret Scherf's *The Banker's Bones*.

Dr. Paul Standish, city medical examiner, appears in George Harmon Coxe's *The Ring of Truth*.

Dr. Samuel Prouty, assistant medical examiner, appears in books by Ellery Queen, and Dr. Emanuel Doremus, medical examiner, appears in the works of S.S. Van Dine.

The City of the Dead by Herbert Leiberman deals with the Office of the Chief Medical Examiner, New York City, and the Office's fictional occupants greatly resemble the real ones.

---

to six months in hopes of finding the rest.

A corpse left in a dry air draft will not decompose normally but will, instead, dehydrate and mummify.

As the blood settles in the corpse, it causes large discolorations, like obscene black-and-blue marks.

Each morning a deputy medical examiner makes "rounds." He is accompanied by a medical stenographer who records such data as the condition of the corpse and the physical condition, and this becomes part of the permanent autopsy record.

New York is one of the few places in the country to use the medical examiner system. Most places have a coroner, a politically chosen official who doesn't (necessarily) have any special medical or legal expertise.

Mr. Lahary then took me up to the top floor of the morgue to the museum, which

DO THEY STILL USE TOE TAGS AT THE MORGUE?

Toe tags are available in white or blue. No one knows why those colors were chosen.

Yes.

The tags, however, are slipped on the toes *before* they arrive at the morgue, either by hospital personnel or by the local police.

The tags are made of reasonably sturdy manila, with a string looped through one end. They are similar to the tags one puts on packages or luggage. Nothing very fancy, nothing very special.

The tags do have a tendency to slip off, but nobody makes a fuss; they're merely slipped back on again.

documents — with photographs, souvenirs, organs and body parts preserved in formaldehyde — the lessons learned from the dead. Lahary, when he is not performing his other morgue duties or acting as special consultant to Interpol, acts as the museum's curator. Most of the specimen museum's visitors are forensic scientists or police officers, although now and then a special-interest group is admitted.

One more thing that must be mentioned: the attitude of the people who work at the morgue. According to Dr. Baden, doctors in general and pathologists in particular are prone to alcoholism because of the occupational stress. They are also, I can attest, living exponents of gallows humor. Their conversation is positively gleeful. Of course, it takes a bit before one becomes accustomed to what they consider amusing. Dr. Baden, for example, related an anecdote about an aquarium shark regurgitating a human arm. And yes, strange though it may seem, I laughed.

William DeAndrea is the author of Killed in the Ratings.

THE FORENSIC ODONTOLOGIST

Lowell J. Levine, D.D.S.

The role of the dentist as detective has been sadly neglected by mystery writers. Despite their attempts to explain this away on the grounds of mere ignorance, I suspect a more valid reason: Most mystery writers I've met have terrible teeth and have obviously suffered at the hands of my colleagues; ignoring us, they're exacting subconscious revenge. My purpose, then, is to make the consumer, the mystery reader, aware of the part we forensic odontologists play in homicide investigations. Hopefully, the reader will force the mystery writer to cast his prejudices aside and acknowledge a branch of the field of dentistry well known to the real professionals in law enforcement: the dental detective!

The forensic odontologist works in a number of areas. Most familiar to the layman is the identification, from teeth, jaws and oral structures, of skeletonized, burned, fragmented, decomposed or otherwise unidentifiable human remains. Much useful information can be gathered from visual and x-ray examinations of the homicide victim. From the types of dental restorations present, we can tell the relative economic status of the person, and areas of the country or world where the fillings, caps or bridges might have been done. We can determine habits, occupations and diseases: the heavy stain of the pipe smoker; the wear of the carpenter from clenching nails; the yellowed mottling of certain Texans from regions with too much fluoride in the water.

We can determine the relative age of a child victim within a few months; the adult, within a five-year span.

We can positively identify from written dental records or from a single dental x-ray of one small part of the jaw. The combinations of teeth present or absent, various filling materials, types of caps or bridges, portions of the tooth having filling materials, all make a dentition unique to an individual. The pattern of the bony architecture which shows in an x-ray, along with tooth shape, root shape, anatomic landmarks and the like, give us literally dozens of areas of comparison in a single x-ray even if no fillings have ever been done.

Of course, it is possible to be too sophisticated. Early in my career, I examined a decomposed body fished from New York Harbour and proclaimed it to be that of an eastern European, probably a seaman who had fallen overboard. Nevertheless, it was later identified by fingerprints as that of an American who had never even left the country. Further investigation showed that all the work on his teeth had been done by a dentist practicing in Newark . . . but trained in Poland.

Identification of the victim is usually the first step in the successful homicide investigation, for only when the victim becomes known do the motives for his murder arise and suspects become known to the police. Proving identity is also essential for the prosecution of the case.

Recognition of dental evidence at the murder scene can lead to a rapid solution. To illustrate: Across the room from a victim found shot to death at an after-hours club, a detective noticed a small pool of blood with some whitish fragments in it. He collected all the fragments and brought them to the Medical Examiner's Office. When the fragments were assembled, they proved to be the crown of an upper left first molar. A subsequent x-ray showed numerous tiny pieces of metal, probably bullet fragments, on the reconstructed crown. Examination of the victim revealed an intact upper first molar, so the fragments had to belong to either the perpetrator or a witness. Detectives began a canvas of local hospitals, and the first one they went to had had an admission that morning with a gunshot wound of the left cheek. He was not the perpetrator but a witness, who supplied the name of the murderer.

Examination of injuries to the face, teeth and jaws is another area in which the forensic odontologist works. A young woman complained to the police of an attempted rape. She said she had received numerous kicks and blows to her face and jaw that had knocked out two teeth. In fact, she had had two front caps knocked out, but there was no evidence of any injuries to the lips, cheeks, face or soft tissues of the mouth. According to the suspect, an acci-

---

SOMETHING TO SINK YOUR TEETH INTO

Michael Baden, M.D.,
Chief Medical Examiner of the City of New York

I first got interested in Dracula when they mounted the expedition to exhume his body. It's hard to find exhumations of 500-year-old bodies. (I once worked on a 2,000-year-old mummy, though. You'd be surprised what I learned from that. Could even type its blood.)

Anyway, all the Dracula expedition found was animal bones. They looked at these bones and thought they'd been duped, that there was no Dracula, so they packed up and came home. By the time they found out there was a Middle European tradition of burying animal bones on top of human remains — it was done to fool graverobbers, the idea being if they saw the animal carcass they'd think that was all there was and the body underneath would remain undisturbed — it was too late to do anything about it. I don't know if they ever got another expedition going, but it's something I'm considering. I'd love to lead it.

You see, we're becoming more fully aware of exhumation as a teaching aid. Burial is really long-term storage. The body is there for you. With cremations you don't get a second chance to see what happened.

From time to time at the Morgue we see deaths by impalement, and this comes direct from Dracula. He popularized the method by using it as a way of dealing with recalcitrant Turks.

I don't think Stoker's prose warrants a reading. That's hardly what makes *Dracula* a good book. In fact, I never quite understood how this postal clerk — Bram Stoker — had the creativity to incorporate these Rumanian vampire myths with the real life of Dracula. But he did manage an intriguing study of his age's concept of death. Both Dracula and Frankenstein are very effective dramatizations of popular fears about death. When I was a kid, I was terrified by these stories. Now my daughter watches them on television and laughs. Too much knowledge. It takes away the mystery.

In my bookcase at home I have a first edition of *Dracula*. I keep it right alongside my first edition of *Gray's Anatomy*.

THE FIRST FORENSIC DENTIST

None other than Paul Revere.

Most people think of him riding about the countryside with a lantern. If they stretch their memories they may recall he was a silversmith. He was also a dentist and in at least one instance was called upon to identify a gentleman from that gentleman's remains — which included a rather handsome set of teeth. These were teeth Revere had worked on — filling, polishing,

FROM PAUL REVERE AND THE WORLD HE LIVED IN BY ESTHER FORBES. PUBLISHED BY HOUGHTON MIFFLIN CO. COPYRIGHT RENEWED 1969 BY LINWOOD M. ERKSKINE, JR.

pulling, and so forth. He was able to establish, to his satisfaction, that the teeth belonged to his former patient.

COURTESY MUSEUM OF FINE ARTS, BOSTON
(GIFT OF BUCKMINSTER BROWN)

General Joseph Warren's skull, showing the artificial teeth (at least some of them) made for him by Paul Revere. The portrait of Warren, in considerably better shape, is by J.S. Copley, 1738–1815.

dental fall had knocked out the caps. His story was much more consistent with the medical and dental evidence, and the grand jury to whom the case was presented refused to indict.

The most fascinating area of forensic dentistry for the layman seems to be the examination of bite mark patterns in the skin of either homicide victims or perpetrators. Since every person's teeth are unique in respect to spacing, twisting, turning, shapes, tipping toward the tongue or lip, wear patterns, breakage, fillings, caps, loss and the like, all of which occur in limitless combinations, it is possible for them to leave a pattern which for identification purposes is as good as a fingerprint. These varying combinations reproduce themselves in skin to different degrees. No healing occurs after death, so we have found fixed bite marks even on victims who have been dead for as long as a

month. We have also found five-day-old bite marks on living persons that were useful for comparisons. By taking small biopsies we can tell whether the bite marks on a victim were made before death, around the time of death, or after death. This is often useful in establishing time frames for a murder.

This type of evidence is found almost exclusively on two types of murder victim: the child homicide victim, most often a "battered child," and the victim who has been involved in sexual activity around the time of death. The sexual activity can be either forcible or voluntary, and we find bite marks in both heterosexual and homosexual killings. In the heterosexual cases the bite marks are most often found on the breasts or thighs; homosexuals most often have them on the upper back or shoulders.

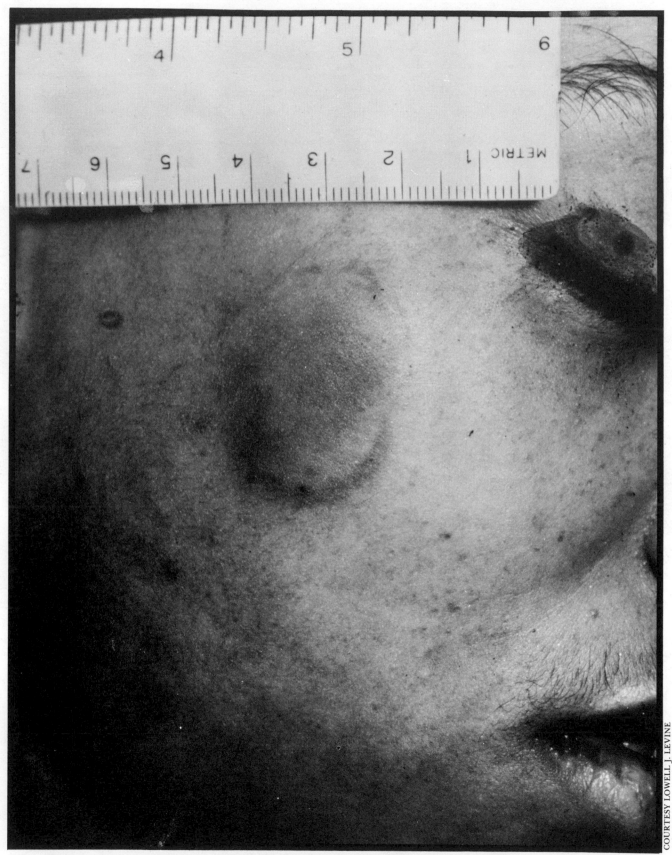

Bite mark with pronounced suck mark on cheek of rape homicide victim.

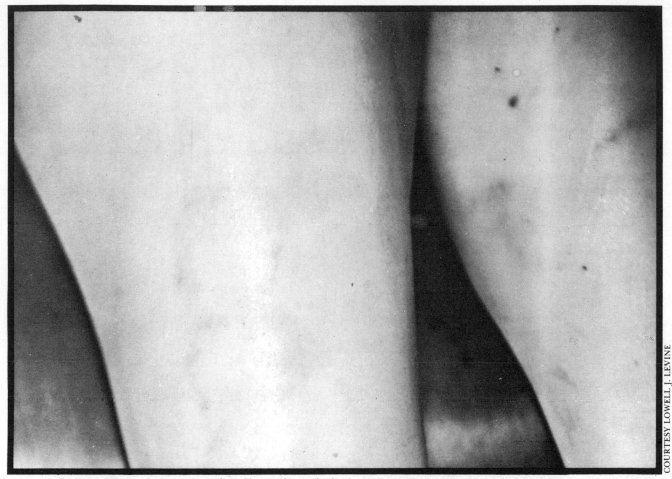

COURTESY LOWELL J. LEVINE

Three bite marks on thigh of rape homicide victim.

The bite marks left during sexual activity are quite characteristic, usually exhibiting clarity of detail and a central suck mark. In addition, they usually have linear abrasions radiating out in a "sunburst" pattern. They have been left slowly and sadistically. Those left during attack or defense situations show a rapid, random distribution over the body, distortion caused by the motion of the scuffling, and no central suck mark.

The saliva left during the infliction of the bite can be grouped similarly to blood, semen, sweat, vaginal secretions, tears and other body fluids.

Police officers responding to a call of a fight in an apartment at 4 A.M. stopped a young man who was walking out the door. In the apartment they found the nude body of another man who had been beaten to death. The young man told the officers he had met the victim in a bar and was invited to the apartment

for a drink. Once in the apartment, the victim made homosexual advances. The young man tried to leave and a fight ensued. The killing appeared to be in self-defense. Examination of the victim, however, showed that he had bite marks on his upper back and shoulders which proved to have been inflicted by the young man. They were quite typical of sexually inflicted bite marks and not of the attack or defense variety, and ultimately the young man pled guilty to murder.

This short essay is meant only to whet the appetite of the mystery reader. Hopefully, one day the mystery writer will serve up a gourmet dinner of this most subtle science, forensic odontology.

Lowell J. Levine teaches Forensic Dentistry at the medical and dental schools of New York University and since 1969 has been consultant to the Office of the Chief Medical Examiner, New York City.

THE FORENSIC ANTHROPOLOGIST

Clyde Collins Snow, Ph.D.

Murderers often hide the bodies of their victims in woods, thickets, marshes, caves and other isolated places. Months or years later, the victim, now a skeleton, may be discovered by hunters, bird watchers, lovers or small boys who visit such out-of-the-way spots on more innocent errands. Naturally, such finds arouse the curiosity of the police and the local coroner. Curiosity, however, may quickly turn to frustration, as skeletons are notoriously uncommunicative under routine methods of interrogation. After a month or two, the bones, by now collected in a neatly labeled plastic bag, are banished to one of the darker shelves of an evidence locker. From my experience, I suspect there are enough unidentified human skeletons gathering dust in sheriffs' offices, police stations and crime laboratories throughout the country to populate a good-sized cemetery. For each skeleton there is a murderer smug in the knowledge that he got away with his crime.

Such cases are becoming rarer, however, as police forces and medical examiners are gaining increasing awareness of the talents of a small but growing number of specialists known as forensic anthropologists. The latter are physical anthropologists who, at least temporarily, are willing to turn away from their studies of our fossil ancestors in order to help in the identification of more recent skeletons. Currently, there are about two dozen forensic anthropologists in the United States.

When examining an unknown skeleton, the forensic anthropologist first attempts to establish the time of death. This estimate is gen-

erally based on the degree of preservation of the soft tissues still adhering to the bone. The time required for a body to be reduced to a skeleton is extremely variable and is controlled by many factors. In the South, a body lying exposed during the summer may be completely skeletonized within one or two months. In colder climates, total disappearance of soft tis-

ANN LIMONGELLO

VITAL POINTS OF THE BODY

Study these structural weaknesses of the human body carefully and use extra caution in an attack on those areas which are vulnerable, for a moderate blow can cause serious injury and even death. The average man is usually unaware of the full potential of his strength, and in the heat of combat he does not always use full discretion.

Temple. A very susceptible vital spot. If struck with sufficient force may cause unconsciousness or death.

Ears. May be attacked by clapping the open hands against them. This method is very effective for breaking holds from the front.

Eyes. Avoid direct contact, especially with clubs.

Nasion. The summit of the nose. May cause unconsciousness. If struck with sufficient force may cause death.

Philtrum. The spot under the nose at the top of the upper lip. Attack to this area may also cause unconsciousness or death.

Jaw. Vulnerable at the point where the jaw hinges.

Throat. The Adam's apple is a most vulnerable and sensitive spot.

Clavicle. The collarbone.

Solar Plexus. If struck with sufficient force may cause death.

Lower Abdomen. Spot just below the navel. May be attacked with fist or kicking technique.

Testes. May be attacked with fist or kicking technique. Causes strongly focused pain. The attacked may fall into shock, resulting in death.

Knee Joint. May be attacked with the side of the foot to break opponent's balance or dislocate the joint.

Shin. A sensitive area, effectively attacked with a club or by kicking.

Instep. May be attacked by stamping technique; the attack is very effective in breaking a hold.

Base of the Cerebellum. At the nape of the neck. A severe blow may lead to unconsciousness, even death.

Mastoid Process. Just behind the ear. Pressure applied with knuckles of fingers or thumbs is very effective in rousing drunks.

Upper Back. Specifically, a spot directly between the shoulder blades. Very effective area for attack to break holds.

Kidney. May be attacked with the edge of the hand, hammer fist or kicking technique.

Coccyx. The tail bone. When struck with sufficient force, the blow may cause death.

Achilles Tendon. The back of the heel.

Pulsation (Inner) Side of the Wrist. Very effective area for attack against armed opponents.

Elbow Joint. An extremely sensitive point.

Back of the Hand. A sharp blow or strong pressure applied to this area is effective in releasing holds or to open the hand.

As a general rule avoid striking the area of the mouth. If a blow is struck with a club, excessive damage to the attacked's teeth may result; a barehanded blow is quite likely to cause incapacitating injury to the attacker's hand.

Reprinted from Clubs in Self Defense and Mob Control *with permission from Monadnock Lifetime Products, Inc.*

"Portrait Parle" class, Paris, in which students absorbed the Cyrano lecture on characteristic nose shapes. Advanced classes discussed ear symmetry. Though doctors attend similar seminars today, their attire is less refined.

sues may require a year or two. Other factors affecting decomposition rates include the accessibility of the body to insect and animal scavengers, humidity, and whether or not the body was buried and, if so, the depth of burial. All of these conditions must be taken into account in estimating the time of death, and for this reason the forensic anthropologist generally needs to visit the scene — preferably before the skeleton is moved.

When the soft tissues have completely disappeared, the bones themselves may offer some clues to the time of death. Exposure to sunlight, extremely hot or cold weather, and soil chemicals all affect the surface texture and composition of bone. From these features it is sometimes possible to determine within five or ten years how long a skeleton has been exposed. While not as precise as we would like them to be, such estimates at least broadly bracket a time span that can helpfully limit the search for missing persons.

Usually the next step in examining an unknown skeleton is a determination of the individual's age at death. Fortunately, the bones offer many clues to age. In infants and very

young children, the bones are incompletely calcified. At certain ages — different for each bone — centers of calcification appear within the cartilaginous precursors of the bone. In teenagers, the bones are more or less completely calcified but are still separated into several parts by thin plates of cartilage. These plates persist until growth ceases (usually somewhere between age twenty and twenty-five). By comparing the state of skeletal development with standards for normal children, the age of a child or adolescent can usually be estimated within a couple of years.

In adults, age determination is more difficult. Oddly enough, one of the most reliable indicators is the pubic symphysis — the joint formed by the two hipbones in the front of the pelvis. The joint surfaces of the symphysis undergo some fairly regular changes throughout adult life. Thus, by examining the symphysis, the forensic anthropologist can usually tell a skeleton's age within three to five years. Another reliable method depends on the microscopic restructuring changes that occur with age in the long bones of the limbs. Broader age estimates are sometimes provided by pathological changes that occur with age around certain joints. For example, arthritic lipping of the joint margins seldom becomes evident until after age thirty-five or forty.

Sex can be determined from the skeleton with great reliability. The most striking differences occur in the pelvis. The female pelvis, adapted to its reproductive functions, differs strongly in shape from that of the male. In females, the pelvis is shallow and broad — cradle-like — compared to that of males, which is narrow and steep-walled. The birth canal, the bony ring through which the infant must pass during childbirth, is wide and ovoid in females, constricted and angular in males. There are also some strong differences in the skulls of males and females. Typically, the male skull is larger and more robust; that of the female, small and delicately modeled.

The diagnosis of race from the bones is more difficult. However, it is usually possible to assign a skeleton to one of the three major racial groups — Negro, White and Mongoloid — with a fair degree of confidence. Here the forensic anthropologist relies primarily on the skull. Many of the skeletal features of race are also reflected in the living. For example, the nasal aperture of the skull tends to be broader in Negroes and Mongoloids than it is in Whites. Mongoloids (a category which includes American Indians as well as most Asiatics) have flatter facial skeletons and broader, more prominent cheekbones than either Whites or Negroes. These and perhaps a score of other bony traits allow us to correctly diagnose race in about 80 percent of skeletons examined.

Stature is another trait useful in identification. In this country, the height of most missing individuals can be obtained from their police, medical or military records containing their physical descriptions. To match these with the height of an unknown skeleton is a fairly simple procedure, since the lengths of the bones of the arms and legs are usually proportional to stature. This relationship can be expressed by mathematical equations so that if we know, for example, the length of the thighbone, we can calculate the living individual's stature within an inch or two.

After age, sex, race and stature have been determined, the forensic anthropologist turns his attention to other skeletal traits which, singly or in combination, may further characterize the individual. For example, each bone is examined for signs of old fractures or other injuries which might be recorded in the medical record of a missing person. Many diseases such as syphilis, tuberculosis and a wide variety of hormonal and nutritional disturbances may also leave a characteristic imprint on the bone. Finally, such unique features as an unusual gait or postural habits may be reflected in the bones.

At this point, the forensic anthropologist is usually able to provide the police or medical examiner with a fairly detailed description of the living person now represented by a skeleton. The next step generally involves a search of police records to find one or more missing persons who match the description. When these are collected, a more extensive review of their medical and dental records is begun. Here the forensic anthropologist works closely with his colleague, the forensic dentist — especially in cases where the skeleton has extensive dental work. Hopefully, a detailed comparison will enable them to find a single individual whose description matches that of the skeleton in sufficient detail to establish positive identification.

Once the police know who the victim is, they have come a long way toward finding his murderer.

Clyde Snow, Ph.D. is a forensic anthropologist for the Civil Aeromedical Institute.

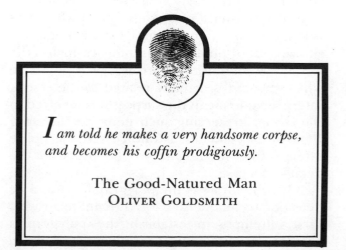

I am told he makes a very handsome corpse, and becomes his coffin prodigiously.

The Good-Natured Man
OLIVER GOLDSMITH

THE PINOCCHIO MACHINES

George O'Toole

A person given a polygraph test sits in a chair in a quiet room with the polygraph examiner. A corrugated rubber tube is stretched across his chest to measure his respiration, his arm is encircled by an inflatable blood-pressure cuff and a pair of electrodes attached to his fingers read the electrical resistance of his skin. The output from these three "sensors" is recorded by three electrically operated pens on a moving chart in view of the examiner but hidden from the gaze of the subject.

The polygraph, then, is not a "lie detector" at all, but merely a very sensitive instrument for observing certain body responses. The true "lie detector" is the person operating the polygraph, and his task is to compare the subject's polygraph responses to a series of questions.

Prior to the actual test, the examiner will interview the subject and review the questions he plans to ask. There are a variety of polygraph interrogation techniques, but most include control questions designed to measure the level of response to touchy issues ("Have you ever in your life stolen anything?"), irrelevant questions intended to measure the subject's general level of anxiety ("Are you wearing a white shirt?") and relevant questions relating directly to the matter under investigation ("Did you hold up the store?"). The examiner asks his questions in a fixed sequence, pausing ten or fifteen seconds after each response to watch the changes on the moving chart. The subject is instructed to answer simply yes or no, and must sit motionless during the entire process to avoid making extraneous changes on the polygraph chart. The test is based on the principle that the liar will show a significantly stronger polygraph response to the relevant questions than he will to either the irrelevant or the control questions. Exactly why this happens is not completely understood, but it involves anxiety (the fear of being found out) as well as the increased intellectual labor required to support a lie — the weaving of a tangled web.

The Peak of Tension Test

Another type of polygraph examination tests for guilty knowledge rather than lies. The Peak of Tension test is designed to show whether a suspect knows some detail of a crime that has not been released to the news media. For example, a suspect in a stabbing case might be shown a series of weapons (a knife, a screwdriver, an ice pick), only one of which was actually used in the crime. Or he might be shown a set of photographs, one of which is the victim. A significantly stronger response to whatever item is actually related to the case is interpreted to mean the suspect was involved in the crime. Preserving such items for use in a Peak of Tension test is one reason the police often refuse to disclose to the press all the details of a case.

How accurate is the polygraph test as a lie detection technique? That is difficult to answer. First, attempts to establish the polygraph's accuracy in the laboratory involve "simulated lies," in which an experimental subject will attempt to "lie" about some trivial matter, such as which card or number he picked. Obviously, the heightened blood pressure, pulse or respiration caused by the anxiety of a suspect in a criminal case will not be present. Second, attempts to measure the polygraph's accuracy in the field are frustrated by the absence of the neat, controlled conditions of the laboratory. Finally, there is a large element of subjective judgment in conducting polygraph tests, and there are such great differences in the skill of individual polygraph examiners that it is almost meaningless to talk of the accuracy of the polygraph test in the abstract. But for whatever they may be worth, studies of polygraph test accuracy have come up with figures ranging from 73 to 97 percent.

Can someone "beat" the polygraph? Maybe. The polygraph itself is simply a measuring instrument and cannot in any sense be beaten. But the polygraph examiner is human and therefore fallible; it is possible, at least in theory, for a suspect to outwit him during the test. When someone sits down to take a polygraph test with the intention of lying and getting away with it, he enters into a game of wits in which the odds are stacked heavily in favor of the polygraph examiner. Clifford Irving, author of the bogus biography of Howard Hughes, seems to have played this game and won; his publishers had him take a polygraph test to check his truthfulness, and the examiner failed to discover he was lying. Still, most people who try to beat the polygraph test will fail unless they have received some special training, such as the courses in "polygraph countermeasures" taught at the U.S. Army Intelligence School at Ft. Holabird, Maryland. Attempts by amateurs to beat the test will usually be obvious to an experienced polygraph examiner and will only serve to make his job easier.

OSWALD AND THE PSE

I ran a check of Oswald's voice tapes on the PSE, and the results showed he was telling the truth — he didn't assassinate Kennedy.

So I showed the results to the PSE experts: the inventors of the machine; the man who taught the course in how to use it; the Maryland policemen who had field-tested it.

I didn't tell them details. I merely said, "Look, here are the charts of a young man, in a police station, who has been accused of killing an executive."

And their response to that was "Why bother us with this problem? When you have a difficult case, come to us and we'll help you read the charts, but if you can't interpret these, there's something wrong with you. This is a clear-cut case of a man telling the truth." Then I told them who the voice belonged to.

They didn't want to believe it. Everyone said, "What! You must have done something wrong! Run the tape wrong. Or been fooling with it."

I gave them another tape to judge by. Same results.

But nobody wants to believe it.

G.O.T.

Narcoanalysis

The polygraph is not the only lie detection technique in use. Another widely misunderstood interrogation aid is so-called "truth serum." Contrary to popular belief, there is no drug that will magically force someone to babble the truth. However, there are chemicals that can be used to weaken a subject's determination to lie or conceal information. Scopolamine has been used for this purpose since the early 1920's. More recently, barbiturates such as sodium amytal and sodium Pentothal have been used.

The correct name for the technique is narcoanalysis. Typically, the drug is injected into the subject in amounts that keep him on the thin edge between sleep and wakefulness, a psychological state in which he has least resistance to interrogation. While such medication may cause a subject to reveal what he has previously concealed, the highly suggestible state of mind produced by the drug may cause him to confess to wholly imaginary crimes. Narcoanalysis can be used to help a witness suffering from amnesia, but it is rarely used for lie detection purposes in criminal investigations. In addition to being unreliable and still poorly understood, the technique requires a physician to administer the drug, making it impractical for routine investigative use by law enforcement agencies.

The Psychological Stress Evaluator

The most recent development in lie detection is the discovery that psychological stress is registered in the voice as well as in those body variables measured by the polygraph. The stress changes in the voice are not audible, but they can be detected by specially designed electronic circuitry. The Psychological Stress Evaluator (PSE) was invented for this purpose by three former Army intelligence officers, Allen Bell, Jr., Charles McQuiston and Wilson Ford.

The PSE performs the same function as the polygraph, without putting the subject in the uncomfortable embrace of breathing tubes, blood-pressure cuffs and skin electrodes. The new instrument works through the simple medium of the tape recording: the subject's answers are recorded during interrogation, then later played back through the PSE, producing a chart showing the level of stress on each reply. Like the polygraph test, lie detection with the PSE is accomplished through the comparison of stress levels on the subject's replies to different questions. While developing the new instrument, the PSE's inventors tested it on broadcasts of the popular television panel show *To Tell the Truth*. Seated before their television sets, they were able to identify correctly the bogus contestants 95 percent of the time.

Many polygraph examiners have raised objections to the new instrument for all the reasons any group resists technological change. However, the PSE is easier to use than the polygraph, has superior accuracy and is now in widespread use, having been adopted by more than 100 law enforcement agencies across the United States.

There's a popular misconception that the results of lie detection tests cannot be admitted as evidence in a court of law. It's true that federal courts reject lie detection evidence; however, in many state and local courts lie detection evidence has been admitted for years under what is termed "stipulation." This means both the prosecution and defense agree beforehand that the defendant will be given a lie detection test and the results will be admitted as evidence, regardless of the outcome. They also agree on the kind of test and the examiner who will give it. Both the polygraph and the PSE have been admitted into court on this basis.

Perhaps the defense should always be permitted to introduce lie detection evidence when eyewitness testimony has been introduced by the prosecution. Still, even lie detection is not without some hazard to the accused. Three years ago a Virginia jury could not decide on the guilt or innocence of a man accused of armed robbery, even though several defense witnesses testified the defendant was elsewhere when the crime took place. Before a new trial was scheduled, the accused requested a polygraph test and asked that the results be admitted as evidence. In his letter to the judge, the man wrote, "It is the only way to show my innocence without any doubt and to get to the truth of the matter."

The defendant got his wish, but he flunked the test. When he tried to have the test result kept out of his new trial, the judge refused.

"You're trying to have your cake and eat it too," the magistrate told him. "Fair play is fair play. If the result had been favorable, you would have insisted on your rights to introduce the test into evidence."

The accused man forgot the most important thing to remember about the polygraph: It's something less than 100 percent accurate.

George O'Toole is a former employee of the Central Intelligence Agency and author of The Agent on the Other Side.

THE ASTROLOGICAL IMPERATIVE

Peter Bull (Sebastian Seer)

Any idiot could have seen immediately by looking at the birth charts of Miss Bonnie Parker and Mr. Clyde Barrow that they were up to absolutely no good at all.

Clyde's Moon, for example, was in Taurus (trine Mars and Uranus, also trine Jupiter in Virgo). To astrologers this is as clear a bit of incriminating evidence as a blood-stained knife, for such a combination will produce acute need for dangerous living. His Sun Sign shows that with Saturn in Aries the poor chap (well, *fairly* poor chap) yearns for an immediate feeling of power and is fed by an intense ruthlessness in obtaining it.

Bonnie's chart is almost completely complementary to her chum's. She had an important configuration composed of the Moon, Uranus and Jupiter. There was also a conjunction of Venus with the Moon, and the Venus aspect pointed to terrific romantic overtones. She was a Libran and, in consequence, felt a compulsion to help the man with whom she was inexorably linked. This, with the effects of Neptune in her chart, indicated a penchant for the "glamorous" aspects of her adventures. Another riveting parallel with her lover's chart is that her Sun, like his, is completely unaspected except for a Mars conjunction and an injunction to Saturn. This indicated a probable and immediate response to a certain type of egotism and aggressive assertion which requires a tremendously close liaison with another being in order to fulfil itself.

Astrologers know that since the Sun in a woman's chart gives a vivid indication of the men in her life, and the Moon in a man's does ditto, a survey of these relative positions makes their attraction for one another quite obvious.

Of course, it is very dangerous to lay down any fixed laws about any astrological fact. But Cornell says Moon conjunct Saturn in Scorpio denotes a killer, and these are Mr. "Legs" Diamond's combinations, if you know what I mean. Mr. Cornell, by the way, is the gent who wrote *The Encyclopedia of Medical Astrology,* so presumably he knows what he's talking about. He also adds an extremely specialised observation which I, in my detective capacity, would have used when following the nefarious career of Mr. D.: He has the 19th degree of Sun on Fixed Star Castor, which indicates danger of becoming a murderer or being murdered (chart, page 369.)

In many ways, the chart of Laurel Crawford, (born August 18-19, 1898: midnight) mass murderer, is similar to that of "Legs" Diamond. Pluto is in the First House. On the other

I'm trying to figure out the greatest of all mysteries — Life and Death!

GLORIA SWANSON

hand, every portent is below the horizon, which usually indicates a dark life. Again there is the vital need to impress others — if necessary, in a ruthless and destructive way. Pluto is conjunct with Fixed Star Rigel, which supposes an excellent brain but a life ending in disaster. The late Czarina of Russia had her Sun on Rigel, and poor Caryl Chessman had his Mars on the same Fixed Star.

With Crawford, for starters, there were three murderous planets in the First House, square Moon and Mercury in the Fourth and Fifth Houses, which indicate dangerous loss of self-control. In particular, Mercury as Moon Ruler, in exact square to Mars, "provides the impulse to murder." (Cornell) The tragedy is that, if the aspected chart were slightly different, all the energies might have been channelled into artistic creation. But, in fact, Crawford found himself trying to prove his cleverness at hoodwinking the public. Add to this Mars conjunct Neptune, and it is my guess that he was probably both intellectually and sexually stimulated by the thought of murder, though this combination frequently prophesies spells of actual madness.

William Hickman started his murderous life (February 1, 1908: 4:45 A.M.) with a very badly aspected Mars, and the ruler Jupiter in a "perversion" degree in the House of Scorpio (Eighth) makes him the reverse of Diamond: a hot-blooded murderer who kills where others make love, for transient physical satisfaction.

Hickman's chart shows an extraordinarily complicated arrangement of tendencies. Sagittarius Rising gave him the feeling he could rely on luck, and with Jupiter in the "Death" House he probably could. But the gentle, loving Venus in Pisces was hardened and chilled by conjunction with Saturn, and there was probably some tragic accident in his family which gave him the notion that death-dealing was a way of life. He had a grudge against humanity, thinking he was denied a living (Jupiter opposition to Second House). It is highly probable that Hickman was a victim of extreme cruelty in a former life.

In all criminal episodes it is never wise, when death is involved, to ignore the possibility of suicide, and Charles Carter in *The Astrology of Accidents* has been a tremendous help to me in solving some of my trickier assignments. Of course, the facts he discloses are not always new to me. I know that not only, as an Arian, am I clumsy and accident-prone, but hitting my head on something has become a hideous habit. All Fire Signs are impetuous, and it seems more likely that they would be involved in violent and/or sudden deaths.

Mr. Carter draws the following conclu-

THE MURDERER'S THUMB

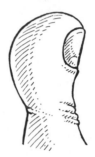

The Clubbed Thumb is the best-known giveaway in both fictional and factual detection. It is so called because it is as thick as a club. In Cheiro's book *Palmistry for All* the author asserts that people having this class of thumb belong to the Elementary type as far as will is concerned. They are brutal and like animals in their unreasonable stubbornness. If opposed, they fly into blind rages and anything may happen. They have no control over themselves and can go to extremes, culminating in any crime in the book. This defect has also been called "The Murderer's Thumb," since so many convicted of homicide are found to possess this physical characteristic. The possessor could not, however, plan or premeditate a crime, for he would not have the determined will or power of reason to think it out. The shorter the thumb, the nearer the possessor is to The Brute and his probable lack of control.

P.B.

sions:

• In cases of Asphyxiation by Suicide, Pluto and Saturn are deeply involved.

• He took several examples of drowning or narrow escapes from the water, including the bandmaster of the *Titanic,* a young lady drowned in the same ship, and others, and there were contacts between Mercury and Saturn. I need hardly tell you that Neptune is bound to come into this form of death, although not as strongly as Saturn. There is also a frequent occurrence of Sagittarius as an ascending sign.

• He examined a lot of international shooting incidents, and they show, beyond dispute, that bullet-wounds and probably all violent blows on small areas of the body, in the shape of cuts and stabs and so forth, relate to about six degrees of Aries or Libra. This combination occurs again in cases of accidental wounds. A death, reported in the *British Journal of Astrology,* didn't have quite similar indications, but as the person concerned swallowed a knitting needle which penetrated the throat, this sort of thing cannot be treated as a test case. Or can it?

• With vehicular accidents, the signs are all over the place, as might be expected. Afflictions to the mutable planets, Mercury and Jupiter, are almost always present, the former being more in evidence in cycling accidents and those arising in the course of routine journeys. Saturn afflictions tend to broken bones; Uranus, to shock. Afflictions in mutables and especially in Gemini-Sagittarius are common.

In accidents caused by skids, stresses are heavily Saturnian. Surprise! In railway disasters there is always a distinctly Uranian flavour to the casualty list.

• Death by accidental poisoning is, happily, not very common, but in any supposed murder case the possibility cannot be ruled out entirely. Out of ten analysed incidents Mr. Carter found that Jupiter occupied Aquarius in six of them. And in two others it was square to bodies in that sign. There appears no reason for this, and a layman might expect that this phenomenon would appear in drowning cases, but as has been shown this doesn't work out. I don't want to alarm Sagittarians, but it must be admitted that their sign has a high accident-ratio and a marked suicidal propensity.

At the risk of blowing my own trumpet, I must end this documentary brouhaha on a piece of information which may be news to some of you. Quite simply, at the time of the Great Hatchet Murders, I was having a mild affair with a well-known lady palmist of the day called Georgina. Acting on certain information supplied by her, I was able to apprehend Miss L. Borden, though for some extraordinary reason she escaped her deserts, and she and her Murderer's Thumb ended their days peacefully — which is more than can be said for her parents.

THE ILL-FATED

Utterly Useless Bits of Astrological Accident Information: (1) In two severe cases of stings from insects, there were afflictions in the radix between Uranus and the Sun and both victims were Gemini. (2) The sign of Taurus has absolutely no connection with bullfight accidents, though Scorpio pops up frequently in the combatants.

Peter Bull (Aries) is an international film star and co-owner (with Don Busby, Leo) of Zodiac, *the Astrological Emporium, in London.*
Their astrological advisor is Joyce Sanderson (Cancer).

THE LEGS DIAMOND CONFIGURATION

Joyce Sanderson

♋ ☉ , trine ☽ , ♅ and ♄ in ♏ : obviously not the maternal, nourishing and cherishing aspect of ♋ , but concern for the Crab shell, the appearance (dress, hair style, manner). ♋ and ♏ both "deadpan" signs: no emotion on the face and high capability of hiding all outward manifestation of inner turmoil.

19th degree ☉ on Fixed Star Castor: "danger of becoming a murderer" or "being murdered." (Cornell)

♇ in 1st: vital need to impress one's own personality and views on others; inscrutable, adventurous, courageous, self-sufficient and skeptical.

♆ in 1st in dual sign: before-and-after personality, up and down moods, e.g., whole personality change upon hearing a piece of music; strong imagination but shallow emotions.

Fixed Star Aldebaran exactly on the Ascendant: fame or notoriety, resulting in periods of great stress.

☽ conjunct ♄ in ♏ , which denotes a murderer. (Cornell) Here also ♂ ♅ — sudden violent acts — and all □ ☽ 's nodes — likely to ride roughshod over conventional morality. ♄ □ ☽ nodes: isolated by society. All trine ☉ and ☿ , so both nature and mentality put to work to intensify these trends.

Very much a ☿ -ruled chart: ☿ ♂ ☉ , ♊ asc, ♇ and ♆ in ♊ in 1st, ♃ and ♂ in ♍ in 4th, ♋ 's natural house. Therefore a "cold-blooded" murderer; ♂ weak and □ ♀ , so not prone to impulsive, violent ♂ acts of murder.

♇ in 1st □ ♃ and ♂ , ♂ ♆ : ruthless, destructive (Plutonic, ♏ , "tearing down" aspect); fanatical. ♂ ♆ : dangerous delusions. ♇ -ruled ☽ and two other planets in ♏ : in 6th, employment and servants; something to do with death! ♇ is ☽ significator and □ ♂ (danger of killing someone). ♅ ♂ ♄ is said to show moral lapses. Asc also □ ♂ and ♃ .

July 10, 1897: 2 a.m.

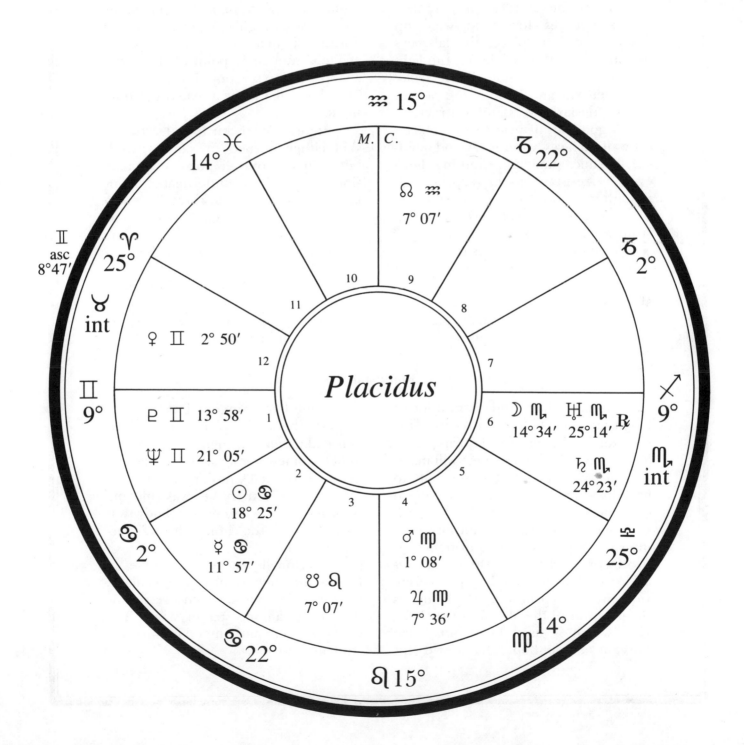

INCRIMINATING EVIDENCE

Fingerprints

Fingerprints *do* get left at crime scenes — often enough to put over 10,000 individual prints in the FBI files. Even the craftiest of perpetrators sometimes forget to wipe up everywhere. The places the lab boys dust first are: the doorknob; the light switches; the underside of the table; the toilet seat and handle; the picture frames, desk drawers and ashtrays.

A good set of prints can be taken off wall surfaces, windows, wood molding, Formica paneling. Clothing, however, is resistant to fingerprints, although right now they are working on a process which will recover prints from woolen fibers.

Most everyone realizes that no two people have identical prints, even if they are identical twins. Each individual's prints are specific to him.

Fingerprints are actually a combination of four shapes: arches, loops, whorls and composites. The most common configuration appearing on a finger is the loop (60 percent). Composites and whorls make up 35 percent and arches roughly 5 percent. Identification is made by matching prints at a minimum of 16 points. (Obviously, a loop is a loop is a loop. It is the breaks in its lines that allow a match-up to be made.)

Bodies have been found with the skin either burned or sandpapered, but prints were still possible to take since the ridges underneath maintained the original markings. This also makes it possible to take a set of prints from a decomposed corpse. The epidermis is not necessary in the matter of fingerprinting.

The sole of the foot and the palm of the hand also have distinctive markings which yield good prints and aid the police in identification.

Bloodstains

The size, shape and distribution of bloodstains are helpful in reconstructing exactly what occurred during an alleged crime. Often a suspect will maintain he acted in self-defense, only to have his story disproved by the pattern of blood spill.

One of the principal authorities in interpreting bloodstain evidence is Professor Herbert MacDonell, who is also well-known for his pioneering work in fingerprinting. (MacDonell is the inventor of the MAGNA Brush device, which is used by identification bureaus throughout the world for processing latent fingerprints.)

On the basis of bloodstain evidence alone, MacDonell has been able to determine whether a victim was in a defensive or attack position at the time of death; whether he was moving or stationary; whether his body was moved after the homicide was accomplished.

MacDonell teaches a course in bloodstain evidence at Elmira College, Corning, New York, which stresses the differences among spatter stains. The course is a seminar, limited to thirty-six students.

Chapter 11
MOUTHPIECES

HOW TO PICK A GOOD LAWYER

Washington C. Beenson

Make an appointment with Perry Mason. Mason has tried eighty-five cases, and we know for sure of only one he's lost. Some others are dubious, but his record is far and away the best of all practicing attorneys. If he thinks the situation warrants it, he just might handle your case minus a retainer, and it's hard to find a lawyer more altruistic than that. In the courtroom his interrogation techniques are second in force to . . . Torquemada. It's the rare man who can look him straight in the eye, lie and get away with it. Yes, definitely pick Perry if you want to be acquitted. On the other hand, to have Hamilton Burger on your side is tantamount to having the word "guilty" stamped on your forehead. In indelible ink. Avoid Burger at all costs.

The lawyer you pick, of course, depends on what you've gotten yourself involved in. If it's a crime concerning the government, either ours or theirs, you might ask to see David St. John's Peter Ward. Ward's not only a lawyer, he's an undercover agent for the CIA as well. (And St. John should know all about that; his other name is E. Howard Hunt.)

In New York, Harold Q. Masur's Scott Jordan seems honest and upright, a man with few discernible bad habits. But if you prefer someone with more experience there's Arthur Train's Mr. Tutt, born July 4, 1869. Mr. Tutt, according to those who know him, ought to be nominated for sainthood. It's doubtful there's a sweeter, wiser, more eloquent lawyer in or out of fiction.

In London, there's Sara Wood's Anthony Maitland, who specializes in lurid homicides (although he himself lives a quiet domestic life). Or, you could ring up Gideon Fell and ask for Patrick Butler's phone number, particularly if you're locked in a room and can't extricate yourself.

Should you find yourself transported to China in a Wellsian time machine, Judge Dee is your man — but only if your case is exceedingly difficult and borders on the sadistic.

Shyster Lawyers

Heading the list of lawyers to avoid would be Melville Davisson Post's Randolph Mason, whose strange schemes at the turn of the century turned the letter of the law against itself — in fact, inside out. (Rumor has it Perry Mason stole his last name from Randolph; in-

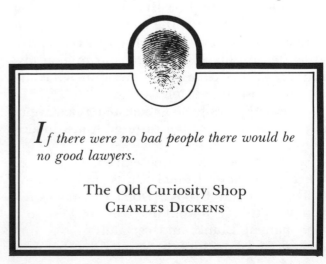

If there were no bad people there would be no good lawyers.

The Old Curiosity Shop
CHARLES DICKENS

A FOOL FOR A CLIENT

If you think you might like to conduct your own defense, the following books may serve as a primer:

Delano Ames: *She Shall Have Murder*

Mel Arrighi: *Freak Out*

H.C. Bailey: *The Garston Murder Case*

James Francis Bonnell: *Death over Sunday*

Henry Cecil: *Brother in Law; Daughters in Law; Fathers in Law*

August Derleth: *Murder Stalks the Wakely Family*

D.M. Devine: *My Brother's Killer*

Warwick Downing: *The Mountains West of Town*

Lesley Egan: *A Case for Appeal*

Sydney Fowler: *The Murder in Bethnal Square*

Erle Stanley Gardner: *The Case of the . . . .*(series, 85 titles); *The D.A. Holds a Candle*

Anthony Gilbert: *A Case for Mr. Crook; After the Verdict*

Michael Gilbert: *Smallbone Deceased*

Edward Grierson: *The Second Man*

Richard Himmel: *I Have Gloria Kirby*

Roderic Jeffries: *Dead Against the Lawyers*

Frederic Arnold Kummer: *The Clue of the Twisted Face*

Hugh McCutcheon: *And the Moon Was Full*

Ross Macdonald: *The Ferguson Affair*

Harold Q. Masur: *Bury Me Deep*

Margaret Millar: *Ask for Me Tomorrow*

Hugh Pentecost: *Around Dark Corners*

Frank G. Presnell: *Too Hot to Handle*

Craig Rice: *Trial by Fury*

David St. John: *Return from Vorkuta*

Michael Underwood: *Murder Made Absolute*

Sara Woods: *Let's Choose Executors*

---

deed, some have wondered if he is not related to him in much the manner of Wolfe to Holmes — the wrong side of the bar, so to speak.)

Shyster may be too strong a term for them, but one should think twice before letting A.A. Fair's Donald Lam or John Robert's Jigger Moran defend you: Both men have been disbarred.

Others you might wish to bypass are: Craig Rice's John J. Malone (he consumes an inordinate amount of rye); Cyril Hare's Frank Pettigrew (before his marriage he was in a steady, unsuccessful decline); Mel Arrighi's Harrington (he's lost his last ten cases).

Leslie Egan's Jesse Falkenstein is a marginal proposition. He's not dishonest, just indecisive.

Two Londoners to be extremely chary of are H.C. Bailey's Joshua Clunk and Anthony Gilbert's Arthur Crook. (Don't the names tell you something? I wouldn't trust my life to a man named Clunk, and certainly not to one named Crook.) Clunk is detested by the Yard contingent, although it's moot whether this is because he solves their cases or because he (the hypocrite) quotes scripture at them. Crook is another schemer, a sharpy who will undoubtedly get you off, then just as undoubtedly run you into a lamppost with his wretched little car. He'll try to revive you with one of his omnipresent beers, but be careful — that leads straight to a charge of drunken driving.

The Author-Attorney

Amongst a certain coterie you might find your problems brilliantly solved, only to reappear again between the pages of a book. Author-attorneys include Henry Cecil, Erle Stanley Gardner (who passed the bar without going to law school), Michael Gilbert, Cyril Hare, Joe L. Hensley, Roderic Jeffries, C.H.B. Kitchin, Edgar Lustgarten, Harold Q. Masur, Francis M. Nevins, Melville Davisson Post, Arthur Train, Miles Tripp and Michael Underwood.

Washington C. Beenson is a jailhouse lawyer.

HOW TO MAKE A WILL

"Now read me the part again where I disinherit everybody."

A will should not be written on ordinary stationery, as the paper is too inflammable. H. Rider Haggard found the perfect nonperishable substance: human skin. In *Mr. Meeson's Will* he had the will tattooed on a woman's back. The court upheld it.

A good will must be written under duress. In Patricia Wentworth's *The Fingerprint* it came about as a response to an anonymous letter. Needless to add, the note sender recommended that he be remembered in the new will.

A will must inconvenience the heirs. In Margery Allingham's *Death of a Ghost* it was stipulated that the heirs reconvene once a year. On the eighth reunion, when he least expected it, one of the heirs was dispatched.

A will should promise much and deliver little. In Charles Dickens' *Bleak House* the inheritance shenanigans dragged on for years; by the time the will was settled, there was no inheritance—it had all gone to pay legal fees.

One final note: When you hear of a death, immediately suspect the heirs. Even if you happen to be one of them.

BOOKS BY CROOKS

Milt Machlin

In my eighteen years as editor of *Argosy*, I had considerable contact with jailed would-be authors, especially as *Argosy* was the home of the Court Of Last Resort. In particular, I remember one John D. Matthews, who persistently tried to con me into a highly improbable meeting with Joe Adonis and Virginia Hill — both made famous in the McClellan crime hearings in the Fifties. "Chesty" Matthews, as he liked to be called, had a long record as a burglar and holdup man. When he got out of prison twenty-odd years ago, he found he could make a passable living by bicycling his story around to various magazine editors in New York, peddling — or pedaling — his criminal expertise in the form of fables, fantasies and even a few fact-based anecdotes. His greatest triumph, however, was to sell the same ghostwritten book to three paperback publishers. Every week he delivered a different chapter to each one — carbons to the second two, with the explanation that the original had been damaged, mutilated or lost — and in this way managed to acquire three separate advances, an achievement to be admired by any writer. (Later, Chesty Matthews overcalculated his hype when he tried to shake down a Jersey City slot machine entrepreneur who happened to be the son of one of the mob's top leaders, himself a star in the McClellan hearings. In some manner never clearly established, Chesty ended up with a bullet between his eyes, dead as an out-of-print novel, and the slot man was let off with a plea of self-defense.)

In any case, since the book had been ghostwritten by Jeffrey Roche, a crime reporter for the now-defunct New york *Journal-American*, I hardly feel that Chesty Matthews would qualify for a place in the Books by Crooks Hall of Fame.

Malcom Braly certainly qualifies for the top of the American list of Books by Crooks. After he made his criminal start by stealing a classmate's coat and getting caught at it (and *in* it) at the age of fourteen, Braly, as he says himself, "served more time for a handful of inept burglaries than most men have served for having killed a police officer." His first major novel, *On the Yard,* which Kurt Vonnegut, Jr. called "the great American prison novel." was published in 1967. His most recent book, *False Starts,* was released to mass critical applause last year and, the last I heard, was being readied as a major Hollywood film.

Probably the most successful, financially, of the ex-con writers would be Paul Erdmann, whose third novel, *The Crash of '79,* has been bought by Paramount for a movie, and has been read avidly by corporate leaders and government executives. In 1970 Erdman was sent to jail when several officers in a Swiss bank of which he was president illegally used $40 million of depositors' funds to speculate in commodity futures. Ten months later he posted bail and left Switzerland, where he was subsequently tried *in absentia* and given an eight-year sentence. But Erdmann is tapping away at his home overlooking San Francisco Bay, and at his ranch in Sonoma, on his fourth novel, about "international corporate bribery."

Perhaps one could say that making a living by writing is the next best thing to stealing.

Milt Machlin coauthored French Connection II.

THE BEST DEFENSE

Paul Chevigny

While the law of murder in the United States varies in detail as to place, in its broad outlines it has changed little from the common law and similar themes are treated in a similar way from state to state. I am going to discuss murder — with a look at a couple of the more dramatic problems of evidence that come up in murder cases — in California, New York and Illinois. I like to think that it is the flavor of the milieu, rather than the actual viciousness of the environment, that so often causes our novelists to place their stories in Los Angeles, New York City and Chicago. But who knows, the tastiest milieus may yet be proved to be the most vicious . . .

The threshold problem, no matter where the killing has been committed, is to establish that there has in fact been a homicide. It is here that the hoary phrase "corpus delicti" usually appears. Breathes there a reader who yet believes that the words refer to the corpse of the dead person? If such reader no longer breathes, many murderers must still believe it since they go to such lengths to destroy all traces of the body. In a recent "bluebeard" murder case in New York, the defendant, a preacher, burned the bodies in gasoline; unfortunately, he did so with the assistance of at least one other, who testified against him. The term "corpus delicti" in fact refers to the "body of the crime" — the proof that the victim is dead, and that caused by a criminal agency. When there is a witness, then, the corpus delicti can be established without a corpse. It continues to be true, however, that where there is no corpse and no witness, it is extremely difficult to establish the existence of a murder.

The ancient judge-made law recognized no degrees of murder. Murder was simply homicide "with malice aforethought," a concept which was not the same as the modern "premeditation" or "lying in wait." It referred instead to a general malicious intent — "the mental state," as *Wharton's*, the leading treatise, has it, "of a person voluntarily doing an act which ordinarily will cause serious injury or death to another without excuse or justification." It included both the "felony murder" rule, which made one guilty for any killing committed in the course of a dangerous felony, even if the killing was not intentional, as well as a great many other violent acts which might not involve a specific intent to kill but simply show a reckless disregard for life. Murders resulting from wantonly firing a gun into a lighted house or a moving passenger train are the classic examples.

In the nineteenth century, murder was broken into degrees — usually First Degree, which was typically the premeditated variety, and Second Degree, which was murder with plain old vague malice aforethought. Right there is where we still find California's law of murder, not changed in more than a hundred years. In California all homicides with malice aforethought are murders, and murders committed with premeditation or in the course of particularly violent felonies like robbery and rape are first-degree murders.

Manslaughter in California also follows an old-fashioned pattern. It is divided into voluntary manslaughter, which is killing "upon a sudden quarrel or heat of passion." Shooting the spouse's lover, surprised in the act of adultery, is the typical case. Involuntary manslaughter is a killing in the commission of an unlawful act and without intent. The famous illustration here is the case of punching the nose of a hemophiliac, who bleeds to death on the spot.

It is easy to see that both juries and judges would have had a great deal of trouble distinguishing between "malice aforethought" and "heat of passion," at least in the cases where the killer might have been acting recklessly and without premeditation. They did and do have such difficulties all the time, and in an attempt to simplify the problem New York and Illinois have scrapped the distinctions that appear in California law. They now essentially define murder as homicide with intent to kill or do great bodily harm, or with the knowledge that there is a strong probability of death or great bodily harm, or in the course of a forcible felony. In a way, this change is a throwback to ideas even older than the nineteenth century, although the magic incantation of malice aforethought has finally been abandoned. Voluntary manslaughter is still defined in terms similar to those of older law, covering a killing "under a sudden and intense passion." Involuntary manslaughter makes a little more sense in New York and Illinois than it used to, being limited now to a killing in the course of a crime which would have been expected to create serious bodily harm, such as a really violent assault or a hazing.

New York and Illinois are both very proud of their streamlined murder laws, but in fact all three states continue to have very similar problems when they get away from the case where there is premeditated intent to kill. When juries and lawyers deal with the "reckless" act (an alias for "the strong probability of great bodily harm") or with the killing in the course of a felony, they still have to crack the same old chestnuts.

The felony murder rule has given rise to curious cases. In New York and California the death of the victim in the course of a felony is enough to make everyone involved guilty of murder, even when there is no shared intent to kill. If several people pull an armed robbery, and one of them surprises all the others by unexpectedly shooting the storekeeper, all are guilty of murder. In Illinois, when a policeman accidentally killed a third party in the course of pursuing some burglars, the burglars were still found guilty of murder.

The "reckless act" type of murder leads to even more puzzling cases, one of which reached the U.S. Supreme Court in 1977. On a very cold winter night in upstate New York, two men in a bar left with a third man, who was extremely drunk. Once in their car and on the highway, the two men robbed the drunk, forcing him to lower his trousers to see if he had money concealed and taking his glasses. They then put him out beside the highway, across and down the road from the nearest lighted building. When the drunk tried to struggle across the road, he was struck by another car and killed. The two were charged with murder. This was not thought to be a felony murder, because the death did not occur in the course of the robbery, but instead the reckless sort of act in which the two should have foreseen the result either of the man freezing to death or being struck by a car. The conviction has ultimately been affirmed.

The tough problem for the law of murder, no matter where the crime is committed, and no matter what magic phrases — "malice aforethought" or "intent to kill" — are used, is still that of the intent of the killer. And even when a "lying in wait" or a killing in the course of a violent felony is proved, the question of intent is not always at an end. Because, as the saying goes, you don't have to be crazy to kill someone but it helps. Killers frequently have some history of mental disturbance (like practically everyone else on the streets of the big cities), and the judge and jury often come to grips with the question of whether the killer is so bonkers that he is not responsible for his acts.

The classic English rule, from McNaghten's case, was that an insane person was not guilty of crime (in the usual sense) if he or she could not distinguish between right and wrong or could not understand "the nature and quality of the act," that is, could not understand what was happening. This rule would work passably well for a literally delusional state in which the killer thought he was, say, a sacrificial priest cutting the victim's heart out in an Aztec rite or in which he did not believe he was killing the victim at all. But for most cases of insanity,

---

ALIBIS WE NEVER WANT TO HEAR AGAIN

1. At an all-night poker game. Ask Fingers or Louie.
2. I was taking a walk. Alone. No, of course I saw no one. Wait, wait a minute — there was someone — a woman in a red dress. At the bus stop. I remember thinking how odd she'd be out alone at that time of night.
3. Here are my theater stubs.
4. Check with the hospital if you like. I was on call all night.
5. I sat with Mother until she dozed off. About ten o'clock, wasn't it, Mum?
6. Randolph, you're not going to like this, but I was in bed with your wife.
7. Right outside the door, just like I was supposed to be, Sarge.
8. The Governor and I were lunching at the Club.
9. Don't you remember — I rang up just past nine — you had trouble hearing me because the church bells were striking.
10. The last thing I saw was a hand, then there was this dreadful smell, and then I'm afraid, everything went black.
11. Awful tie-up on the Al.
12. I refuse to drag an innocent woman's name into this, Inspector. If you can't take the word of a gentleman . . . well, then, so be it.
13. Miss Pettigrew asked me to stay and help with the blackboards. Wasn't that all right, Mommy?

---

where the killer is aware of what he or she is doing, it has mostly been a source of grief for the psychiatrists who have to testify as well as for juries who have to listen to them.

Despite the grief, New York and California have resisted change from the McNaghten rule, fearing that any reduction in the standard of personal responsibility would simply give free reign to a gang of hoodlums who are already admitted to have a tolerably poor grasp of the difference between right and wrong — in killing as in everything else. Illinois, however, has adopted a new formulation which affords a defense if as a result of mental disease the killer "has no substantial capacity either to appreciate the criminality of his conduct or to conform his conduct to the requirements of the law." This common-sense formula probably expresses what sensible juries have always done, under any rule and in any state, with the poor devils who are uncontrollably psychotic.

In any state, killers sometimes botch the job, leaving the victim with a chance to say a few words before he dies. If he names his killer, the police and the D.A. have the problem of getting his statement before the jury, even though any report of it is rank hearsay and the speaker is not alive to be questioned. Centuries of law have grown up to protect the victim's right effectively to identify his killer in a "dying declaration." The court reasoned that the expectation of death and the possibility of hellfire would prevent the victim from telling an untruth. Accordingly, the dying declaration is admissible before the jury *only* if the victim knows he is dying and has no hope of recovery. This famous rule gives rise to the dramatic set-piece where the tough-but-professional detective rasps to the victim: "Listen, you're dying. You haven't got a chance. You understand that?" The face, gray against the white pillow, turns toward the other man. The paper-white lips part in a whisper: "I know. The doc told me." "Do you believe you can recover?" the detective continues mercilessly, fearing death at any moment. A pause, the paper lips say no. And then, of course, he doesn't tell you who did it; he utters three Delphic words which require seventy-five thousand more to elucidate.

Paul Chevigny is the author of Criminal Mischief.

THAT "BASTARD VERDICT"

Avon Curry

The Scots, as any Scott will tell you, are an exceptional race. They remain distinctively themselves although linked geographically and historically to a richer nation to the south, and in no area of life are they more "separate" than in their system of law. Although Scottish law has many of the costumes and settings of English law, the actors have different names — the terminology is different.

It may surprise you to learn, for instance, that the Sheriff plays an important part in Scotland — but he would die of the shock to his dignity if he were asked to wear a star and a six-gun. There is also an important official called the Procurator Fiscal, a term which alarms Americans because they feel it has something to do with tax prosecutions. Nothing of the kind. He fulfils a role something like the French *juge d'instruction*, looks into suspected crime and, in the case of an unexplained death, is the equivalent of the English coroner.

And speaking of the unexplained death, we come to murder and the part of Scottish law that probably interests crime fans most — the famous verdict of Not Proven.

Not Proven can be brought in for any accusation, but it takes on its utmost importance in a murder trial. For here the accused has a two-out-of-three chance of walking out free, whereas in the rest of the world, in general, there are only two verdicts: Guilty and Not Guilty. The Scots would say that as usual they are ahead of everyone else in providing an alternative to the Not Guilty verdict — Not Proven.

This is a very cool way of looking at evidence; it goes back in history to a time when Scottish juries were asked to condemn prisoners accused of a breach of the laws concerning religion. Unwilling to do so, they were instructed by the Lord Advocate that they must examine the facts and not the opinions in the case; if the facts proved the offence, they must so declare. They took him at his word: If the prosecution did not satisfy their minute examination of the facts, they brought in the verdict Not Proven, and it has remained.

One of those involved in the Burke and Hare case (1829) was a woman called Helen McDougal, who was accused of taking part in the murders whereby these grave-robbers provided corpses for the students of anatomy at Edinburgh University; she was set free by a Not Proven verdict. Mary Elder (or Smith) was charged with poisoning her maidservant in a strange and scandalous case the previous year; she received the benefit of the Not Proven verdict. Sir Walter Scott, who was at the Mary Elder trial, thought she was undoubtedly guilty, and it was he who coined a phrase for the result which is often used by those who disapprove of it — "that bastard verdict."

The case which most crime fans recognise at the mere mention of the name is that of Madeleine Smith. Her trial (1857) has all the ingredients of a great novel and has in fact been the basis for many books, both fact and fiction, and at least two plays. There's no doubt the story attracts attention because Madeleine was young and pretty, and the turns and twists of

THE CERTAIN RESULTS OF STEALING.

To What the First Step in Crime Ultimately Leads.

First Theft and Robbery—Then Murder.

From Jail to Execution.

THE steps from house-breaking to murder are but few. Too often, from the effects of evil associations in childhood, our worst thieves and burglars are young men in their teens, and almost as frequently we find them taking life in order to gain money.

PROPERTY and life must be protected against dangerous criminals. When it is discovered that a boy or man is disposed to take for his own the property or life of another, the time has arrived when it becomes necessary to visit upon him the severest penalties.

Appropriating the Money of the Bank and the Final Consequences.

The Dishonest Confidential Clerk.

Sentenced to Imprisonment for Ten Years.

A YOUNG man, lacking moral principle and possessing ambitious desires, is entrusted by his employer to handle large sums of money. He sees his opportunity to speculate and make money, and cannot resist the temptation to steal. Too late he finds that he is ensnared.

ONLY a little time has elapsed since he stole his employer's money, yet he has been detected, tried, convicted and sentenced to imprisonment at hard labor. Reputation gone —prospects blasted—degraded to hardship and prison fare for ten long years—How sad the story !

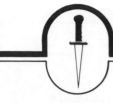

If once a man indulges himself in murder, very soon he comes to think little of robbing; and from robbing he comes next to drinking and Sabbath-breaking, and from that to incivility and procrastination.

On Murder Considered as One of the Fine Arts
THOMAS DE QUINCEY

the evidence unfolded a passionate, year-long yet secret romance.

Pierre Emile L'Angelier died of arsenic poisoning. The prosecution claimed Madeleine had murdered him rather than let him expose their shameful affair to her tyrannical father. Three of Scotland's most eminent lawyers handled the prosecution. For the defence appeared the Dean of the Faculty of Advocates, John Inglis, later to become Lord President of the Bench. With him were George Young, later Lord Young, and Alexander Moncrieff. The Ayrshire *Express* said Madeleine entered the court with the air of a belle entering a ballroom.

There were three charges: two of administering arsenic, one of murder. When the chancellor (foreman) of the jury announced the verdicts, they were: Not Guilty, Not Proven, Not Proven. It's said that Madeleine hoped for a complete acquittal, but there were too many extraordinary coincidences and oddities in the evidence for that — even though there was no proof that she actually did give Pierre the poison she had bought.

One could say that here the "bastard verdict" proved legitimate. Alas, almost exactly seventy years later it freed an equally young accused, John Donald Merrett, whose mother had died of a gunshot wound to the head. Mrs. Merrett had taken a fortnight to die after the injury and during that time was either unable or unwilling to explain how she received it.

Donald insisted she had shot herself — and this was just possible, as she had money troubles.

It says much for the pleading of his defence and the uprightness of the jury that, despite the strong feeling against Donald, he was allowed to escape the death penalty through the Not Proven verdict. He was taken off to prison to serve a sentence for forging cheques, on completion of which he embarked on a life just as strange as its beginning.

He defrauded shopkeepers, married the daughter of a woman who claimed a title to which she had no right, became a smuggler and gun-runner during the Spanish Civil War and changed his name to Ronald John Chesney. He served in the Navy during World War II and acquitted himself well. In 1946 he was involved in the black market in Germany, became known to prison officials in various European countries and collected several mistresses.

At last, in 1954, he decided to get rid of his wife so as to marry his current girl friend and made a special trip from Germany to London. Later, his wife was found drowned in the bath and his mother-in-law, who seems to have been unlucky enough to have met him on the stairs, battered and strangled to death. The case against him mounted, and once it became known that Ronald John Chesney and John Donald Merrett were the same man, it seemed the police need only lay hands on him to bring the matter to a close.

But Merrett-Chesney settled the debt to society himself. He put his Colt revolver in his mouth and pulled the trigger. Thus ended a career which perhaps should have been cut off in the High Court of Justiciary in Edinburgh twenty-six years earlier.

The usual view of the Scottish verdict is: "We couldn't prove it this time, so you can go away. But don't do it again." In the case of Madeleine Smith, it worked. She lived on to a ripe old age in America, unheard of. In the case of John Donald Merrett, the accused didn't take the implied advice. In all other Not Proven murder cases, the advice has been heeded.

At least, so far as we *know* . . .

Avon Curry is a past chairman of the Crime Writers' Association.

HOW IT FEELS WHEN THE BAD GUY GETS OFF

Lee Fowler

New York is one of the toughest cities in the world, and those who know it well will agree the toughest part is the South Bronx: block after block of burnt-out buildings and empty lots; broken glass and tin cans; boarded-up windows and stray dogs. But the worst rubble is the humanity that lives there. Pimps. Pushers. Murderers. Junkies. Men who rape little kids. Kids who murder old ladies. "Animals," Ed Hayes calls them, and he should know. He was Assistant District Attorney, Bronx Homicide Division, for close on to five years.

Hayes earned a reputation as the A.D.A. who would take the worst cases, the ones no one else would touch because the crimes were so vicious and the "smoking guns" so scarce. He won them anyway. In 1976 he put more murderers in jail than anyone else in the city — more than sixty, twelve of them for life. "I executed them on behalf of the state," he says. "I figured, he hurt somebody, he deserved it. Sometimes I felt like an avenging angel."

Hayes talks tough, and until he quit, his was a tough world, with characters straight out of mystery books. There was the macho Italian cop who wouldn't walk through a blood-soaked room because he didn't want to get his white patent-leather shoes dirty; the defense lawyer who had a grudge against Hayes from a former case; the call girl who wanted to sleep with him in lieu of a fee; the girl who covered for her boyfriend after he'd raped and stabbed to death a seven-year-old.

In books, the bad guys always get caught, but Hayes saw it a little differently. Take his first homicide case. Two boys, eighteen and seventeen, beat an old man to a pulp, then strangled him in the back of his restaurant, took his money and left. Hayes was prosecuting the eighteen-year-old, who had been in and out of juvenile court on charges ranging from sodomy to rape to robbery.

"He was a real animal," says Hayes, "and we knew he'd done it. There was a witness, the kid they'd asked to be lookout. They'd told him they were going to have to kill the guy to do the job. But the jury didn't believe the witness be-

Manhattan's Supreme Court House, October 1937. The case being tried: a lurid divorce action. The women comprising the distaff half of the first mixed jury to ever serve repaired their make-up during recess.

cause by the time the case came to trial, he was doing time for blasting some guy's brains out with a shotgun. How could the jury believe him?

"Anyway, I did this real dramatic thing. The night before my summation, I got hold of the defendant's stepmother, who hated his guts, and who'd seen him at the scene of the crime a few minutes before it happened. I had her flown in from California, and I put guards on her 'cause she was getting threats. It was like a scene from a movie. I brought her in the last day of the trial, guarded by this mean-looking cop who'd killed so many guys, he didn't care any more. And the cop had his hand in his coat, resting on his gun, and he was looking from side to side, just waiting for somebody to make a move. But the jury didn't want to believe her either, because she was a heroin addict and a prostitute. It was a case where the jury didn't know who to believe, so they acquitted him. After the trial, the guy comes up to me and says, 'Hayes, I told you I was gonna beat it, and I beat it,' and I said, 'Yeah, pal. *You* beat it.' You want to know how I felt after that? I went out for a big Italian dinner at this place in Brooklyn, and when I got home I spent all night vomiting it up."

There's another way real life isn't much like books. "There's too much magic in them," according to Hayes. "In real life you win cases because you do everything you're supposed to do, every time you're supposed to do it, and then the percentages work in your favor. Plodding, slow, lots of detail. That's why I like the Sjöwal and Wahlöö stories, because they're real

---

THE DEFENSE ATTORNEY'S CREED

If you don't have the law, bang the facts.

If you don't have the facts, bang the law.

If you don't have the law or the facts, bang the table.

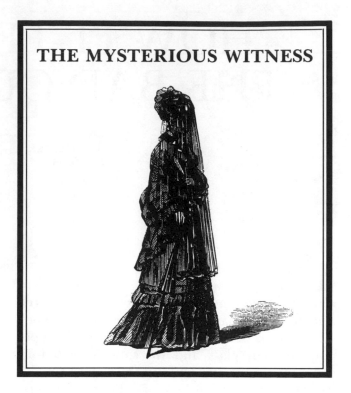

THE MYSTERIOUS WITNESS

---

life. You work your ass off checking everything out, and then, maybe, you get a break. The greatest compliment I ever got, someone said, 'If that f——— guy had to throw himself in front of a train to do something for a client, he'd do it.' "

Even hard work doesn't always work. "Another real animal," says Hayes, "we knew he was guilty from the lie detector test. He asked what it was, and when they told him it would tell if he were guilty or innocent, he didn't want to take it. But his lawyer stressed it could be used to show he was innocent. Well, he took it. And it showed he was guilty.

"All I had was circumstantial evidence, but I presented every bit of it. I was unbelievably well-prepared. And then we got a hung jury. I went crazy. Everybody knew the guy. He'd done time for rape and robbery, and now he'd thrown a little kid out of a window. The cop who picked him up told me later if he had known what that guy had done when he'd picked him up, he'd never have taken that m———f——— alive. I know just how he felt.

"It never would have happened to Perry Mason. That guy gets all the breaks. Witnesses are always breaking down on the stand for him. His clients are always innocent. How are you going to beat that? I feel sorry for Hamilton Burger. Lew Archer I like because he's tired, and you're always tired. Tired of finding out things aren't what they seem, tired of seeing here's another bad guy." Which, in part, is why Hayes left the D.A.'s office. "No matter how many times you put guys away, you still couldn't bring people back. I felt terrible for those poor people."

He still reads thrillers for relaxation, however, but not the ones with bodies strewn all over the place. "There aren't that many murders in real life," he explains. "Murder is cathartic. One guy gets mad at another and kills him, but then he's done for the day. Except in mob warfare, when they're killing guys left and right, and all you can do is stand back and watch.

"I like to read George Higgins; he's got the dialogue down pat, the treachery that's a normal part of criminal behavior. I like Robert Parker because he understands cops. In one of his books he had three or four cops talking about putting lead in a guy, and that's just the way cops do talk, only they don't do it. I also like him because his hero is a real physical fitness freak and likes gourmet food, and that describes me."

Hayes, in fact, has all the attributes of a good fictional hero: he's tall, lean, blond, good-looking, and meets one woman for dinner and another for the late shift. He also has a fondness for hand-tailored suits and handmade shoes.

He's also not above a little courtroom his-

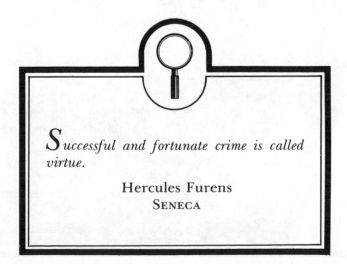

*S*uccessful and fortunate crime is called virtue.

Hercules Furens
SENECA

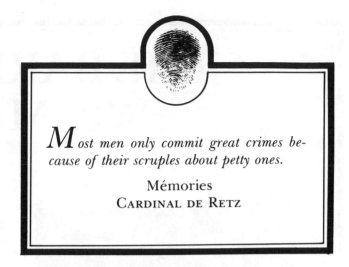

*M*ost men only commit great crimes because of their scruples about petty ones.

Mémories
CARDINAL DE RETZ

trionics. He modeled one summation after the famous Dreyfus case *J'accuse.* "I started soft. 'Nothing I can say can equal the loss of this man to his family. Nothing I can say can describe the horror of his death. The only thing you can say is guilty.'"

He came close to tears during that summation. "I was believing everything I was saying. I kept thinking how terrible it was. And I can tell you exactly how I felt when that guy got off. I felt like shit."

Perhaps this is why Hayes identifies with Marlowe. "He knows most people are dishonorable. He knows you can't win every time. But at least you can try."

Once Hayes actually started to write his own thriller. There were three heroes: an old street-wise black detective; a young Irish cop who'd been brought up in the tradition of old Irish cops and wasn't quite at home in the new police department; a young Spanish detective who really believed in the system. In Hayes' story, the detectives were on the trail of some pushers who were being ripped off by a group of narcs, and somewhere in the middle of it all, the Irish cop's girl friend got killed because she was an A.D.A. and was getting onto the narcs. In the last scene, there was a big showdown — narcs, pushers, detectives. Only the detectives lived.

In Hayes' book, the bad guys don't get off.

Lee Fowler is a New York-based writer who dotes on crimes of passion.

THE BARRISTERS' WIGMAKER

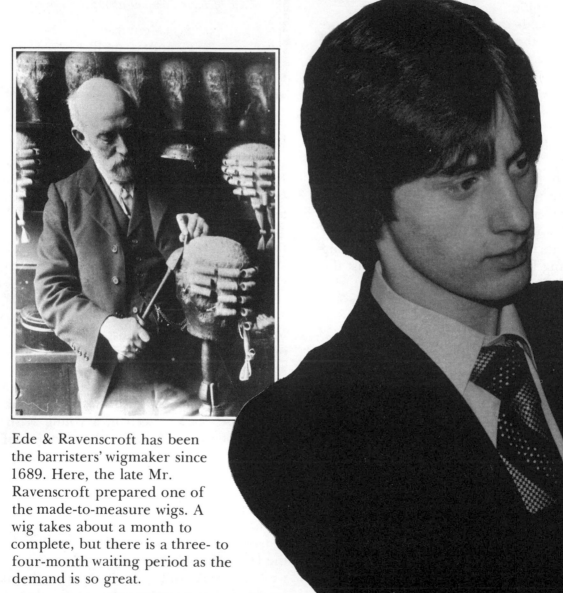

Ede & Ravenscroft has been the barristers' wigmaker since 1689. Here, the late Mr. Ravenscroft prepared one of the made-to-measure wigs. A wig takes about a month to complete, but there is a three- to four-month waiting period as the demand is so great.

Young Mr. Clifford, an apprentice, prepares a wig. Like all barristers' wigs, it has two pigtails and four rows of little curls. (The judges' wigs do not.) It is made of bleached horsehair and costs £88.50 from the London headquarters of Ede & Ravenscroft.

Mrs. Kathleen Clifford, head of the Wig Room, stands in the Bar Room, to which the barristers retire for a fitting. She is holding a judges' shoe. Also available: judge's britches. On the table are the famous black and gold Ede & Ravenscroft carrying cases — the oval circuit box (for exporting wigs), the tray case (for everyday bench wigs), the full-bottomed circuit box (for judges' wigs).

To make a wig, five separate head measurements must be taken. These are done at one fitting. Then the wig is shaped on various sized wig blocks. The darker grey the wig, the more it is regarded as a "status" symbol.

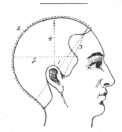
COURTESY COLIN R. MACER

THE OLD BAILEY

The Old Bailey is one of the most familiar court buildings in the world, standing as it does in the centre of London. It is surmounted by a copper dome and a fifteen-foot gilded statue of the figure of Justice. One hand of the figure holds the traditional scales of justice, and the other the symbolic sword. This particular statue is unique in that it is not blindfolded. Over the door of the building are carved the words: "Defend the children of the poor and punish the wrongdoer."

The site of the Old Bailey had a long criminal history as Newgate Prison. Standing next to Newgate was a building known as the Justice House, or, alternatively, the Sessions House. This was erected in 1550 "over against Flete Lane in the old bayley." The latter referred to the street it was built on, and the building soon acquired that nickname. John Stow, a writer in Shakespeare's time, believed the name came from the word "ballium," used to describe an open space in front of the old wall of the Sessions House to allow guards and watchmen a better view. The ballium in front of the original Newgate Prison was on ground rising from what is now Ludgate Hill. Londoners called it Old Ballium, which has been corrupted into Old Bailey.

A new Sessions House was built in 1774, and this also became known as the Old Bailey; it was extended in 1824 and again in 1834, but it was always too small for the increasing court work of London.

In 1902, the old Newgate Prison and the Sessions House were demolished to make way for the Central Criminal Court, which would accom-

The figure of Justice atop the Old Bailey is unique in that it lacks the traditional blindfold.

modate all the criminal work of London and the surrounding area. In 1907, it was opened by King Edward VII, but it immediately assumed its old nickname and again became the Old Bailey.

During the opening ceremony, the King said, "The barbarous penal code which was deemed necessary one hundred years ago, has been gradually replaced in the progress towards a higher civilisation, by laws breathing a more humane spirit and aiming at a nobler purpose."

The Old Bailey is purely a criminal court and has no civil jurisdiction. It is now a crown court and continues to provide the location for some of England's most famous trials.

P.N.W.

THE DIFFERENCE BETWEEN A BARRISTER AND A SOLICITOR

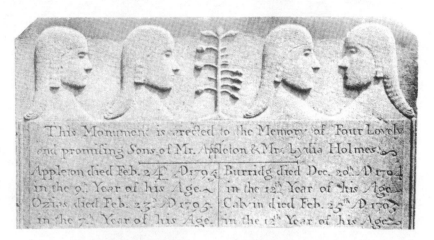

The solicitor is the general practitioner of the law, but the law is so vast that no general practitioner can give you detailed advice on every part of it. Therefore, a solicitor has to have specialists to go to — in exactly the same way that doctors have specialists to turn to. That is the primary role of the barrister in England. He is a specialist in his own branch of the law — tax, patents, whatever it may be. It has nothing to do with wearing wigs in court.

In Italy I found that one firm of *avvocati* would freely consult another firm who happened to have a reputation for knowing more about a particular branch of the law. In England this rarely happens. Solicitors in difficulty consult barristers.

Barristers also have a secondary role. They hold a monopoly on the conduct of pleading in certain courts. The parameters are getting narrower, but at the moment the barristers' monopoly is total in the High Court, in the Court of Appeals and in the House of Lords. However, there are many other courts — crown courts, police courts, magistrate courts and tribunals, quasi-judicial bodies that are springing up everywhere — and in all of these a solicitor is allowed to stand on his feet and plead. (If he doesn't want to, of course, he can hire a barrister to do it for him.)

This is not dissimilar, I understand, to what takes place in the United States, where in large firms some do court work and others do desk work. The difference is that they're not called by separate names, and they are all in the same firm.

One geographical restriction on barristers is that they have to retain office space in one of the four Inns of Court (Grays Inn, Lincoln's Inn, Inner Temple or Middle Temple). Unfortunately, there are many more barristers than there are rooms. Two barristers of my acquaintance (both now very successful) started by sharing a mantelpiece.

Michael Gilbert is a lawyer and one of the twelve founding members of the Crime Writers' Association.

PRISONS
Getting In — Getting Out
Thomas M. McDade

COURTESY METRO-GOLDWYN-MAYER

So you want to visit a prison . . . just to see what it's like. Well, in the first place, nothing you see will give you an inkling of prison life as it affects the inmate. I have been in many, I won't say the good and the bad, as there are no good prisons. Let us say the better and the worse — Leavenworth, Joliet, Green Haven, Riaford, Alcatraz, Huntsville, Sing Sing, Raleigh. All I have learned is a smattering of customs, rules, schedules and argot. Only the man who has done time is qualified to say what prisons are really like.

For the non-inmate, getting in is harder than getting out. For example, at the gate you must clear the electronic metal detector. How often, having emptied my pockets of change and keys, the machine kept clicking and I had to remove my belt (metal buckle) and even my shoes (because of the steel arches). And this at a prison I had been visiting for years, where I was known to the guards!

Don't carry pills or a pocketknife with you when you visit; you would have to leave them at the entrance gate. But you can bring food, clothing or reading matter. Such things are left at the gate for examination and passed to the inmate later. Money may be left for credit to his account; inmates may not have money in their possession.

The visiting rooms have changed in recent years. Formerly, you were separated from the inmate by a metal grille or glass shield. Direct contact with the inmate was forbidden, and in many cases you had to speak to him on a telephone. Now you generally sit opposite him and talk over an open counter in a large room where fifty visitors may be seeing inmates at the same time. Before the inmate arrives at the visiting room he is frisked by a simple pat-down; when he leaves to return to his quarters, he must be strip-searched to ensure that no contraband was slipped to him.

No tour of the prison will include a look at the punishment cells. Officially known as Segregation, the area has some innocuous name like C Block or Block 14, but to all the inmates it is known as "The Hole." In the old days it literally was a hole — often an underground cell with no light. Inmates might sleep on a stone floor in a freezing cell, often without clothing and toilet facilities. Sadistic guards have been known to hose down inmates with cold water. Those who want details can find them in the decisions of the federal courts. A case in point is Wright v. McMann 387 F2d 519.

The courts, the riots and the activities of a number of agencies have forced the authorities to provide a minimum of the necessities: a toilet, blankets, light and a reasonable amount of food. Now in the modern prisons Segregation is hardly different from the remainder of the facility. Recently, visiting an inmate in "The Hole" of a state prison, I was escorted by a guard down a lengthy corridor to a distant steel door. He rang a bell, another guard eyed us through a peephole and finally we were let in. Through two more steel doors we came to a block of cells, in one of which sat my client. He was the only inmate in the block, his cell door was open and he had the run of the area, which resounded with the noise of his radio. The latter amenity is optional depending on the reason for the segregation. In some cases inmates are put in "The Hole" for their own protection.

You might think it odd to have to make an appointment to see a prisoner; after all, you would hardly expect him to be "*not* in." At a women's prison I called to see an inmate then in the fifteenth year of a life sentence for murder. I went on a Saturday, and when I told her I had thought of waiting until Monday, as inmates are often occupied on weekends, she said, "Oh, I wouldn't have been here then."

"Where would you have been?" I asked.

"I have a job at IBM; I go there weekdays."

It seems that after the day's work as a punch card operator she would go by bus to a community college where she was studying, then about 9:30 P.M. take a train to a station where a prison car would pick her up. So today, with furloughs, work release programs, college courses and often court appearances, you do have to make an appointment to catch the inmate "at home."

A typical prison day starts at 6:30 A.M. with a bell ringing in the cell block. Inmates have an hour to rise, wash and dress. The cell doors open at 7:30 A.M. with the completion of the first head count. Release from the cell tiers is staggered so that all the inmates will not be moving to the mess hall at the same time. By 8 A.M. they are on their way to their jobs in laundries, workshops, hospitals and kitchens. At 11:30 A.M. they return to the mess hall and by 12:15 P.M. are back in their cells for a lock-in head count. From 1 P.M. to 3 P.M. they are at work again, after which there is yard recreation till 4:15 P.M. in winter or 7:30 P.M. in summer.

Good jobs are as hard to come by in prison as they are outside. Best pay is for those with a skill: carpenters, electricians, painters and top clerks are in Grade IV and earn $1 to $1.15 per day, often with double pay for overtime. The lowest grade of common labor runs from 35¢ to 50¢ per day. If the institution has no job to assign, the inmate gets 25¢ per day as unemployed. If he is offered a job and refuses it, he can be classified "idle," for which he will get no pay and, in addition, may have to spend all his time in his cell.

If a prisoner has a highly rated job, he will have a "runner's" pass which permits him to move about freely on the inside. The law clerks in the law library are in this favorable category. Other inmates get a special pass as required which permits them to move from one area to another. What the visitor soon realizes is that most of the day inmates are visible in large numbers all over the institution while guards are few and far between.

As I recall it, one of the great scenes from *The Big House*, an early prison picture, took place in the dining hall, where hundreds of cons banged their cups on the tables and chanted in time . . . a sort of mess hall strike. Eating today in some prisons is different.

"I haven't been in the mess hall in six months," was the surprising answer one of the inmates gave to my question about the quality of the food. How did he eat? "Oh, I make my own arrangements." It was then I learned about the commissary and the dozens of private "kitchens" hidden about the institution in workshops, art classes, gymnasiums, chapels and paint shops.

Remember the army PX? Well, prisons have them, too, except they are called commissaries. Prices are generally lower than in

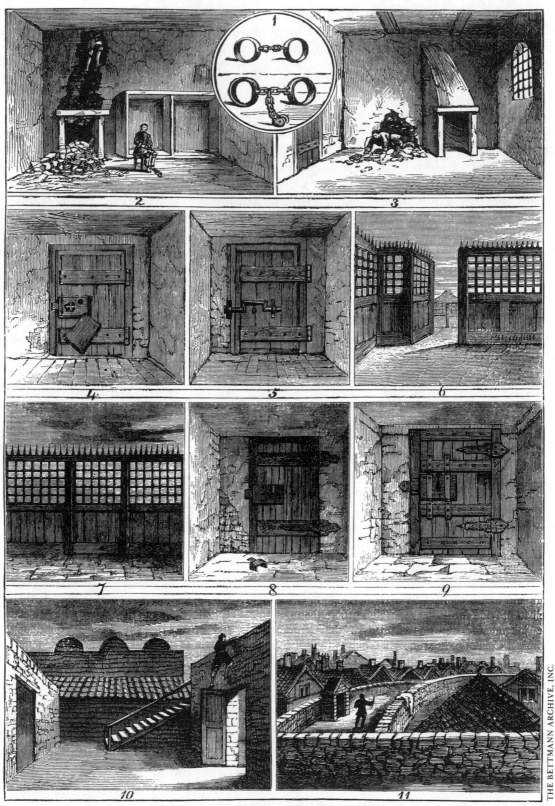

JACK SHEPPARD'S ESCAPES.

1. Handcuffs and Feetlocks, and Padlock to Ground.   2. Cell over the Castle, Jack Sheppard fastened to the floor. Climbing up the Chimney, where he found a bar of iron.   3. Red Room over the Castle, into which he got out of the Chimney.   4. Door of the Red Room, the lock of which he put back.   5. Door of the Entry between the Red Room and the Chapel.   6. Door going into the Chapel, which he burst open.   7. Door going out of the Chapel towards the Leads.   8. Door with a Spring Lock, which he opened.   9. Door over the same Passage.   10. The Lower Leads.   11. The Higher Leads, the walls of which he got over, and descended by the staircase off the roof of a turner's house into the street.

your supermarket and the more than 300 items listed, with regular stock numbers, include garlic powder, red clam sauce and Fig Newtons — this last being, at one time, the basic unit of exchange in an economy in which money is banned.

Maximum-security prisons are not quite so casual, but even they have their "courts" where wood stoves improvised from steel drums dot the yard and cons may prepare their evening meal and dine as one might in one's own club.

The visitor may be surprised at the variety of clothing worn by the prisoners. In New York the inmate must wear the regulation green trousers; all other items of clothing are optional.

The question of beards and haircuts is still not fully resolved. Can you conceal a weapon in an afro? Some prisons are fairly liberal on the question of hair styling; others claim that long hair and beards disguise identity and, therefore, seriously limit them. But generally the arbitrariness of prisons is easing. Mail censorship is limited to a cursory check of articles to prevent dangerous contraband; when writing letters out, the inmate seals them himself and in most places there is no restriction on the number of letters he may write. Books and magazines of almost any kind are now admissible, and where once periodicals could only be received from the publisher, the source is no longer a matter of interest.

When an inmate is discharged, he is given "gate" money ($40 in New York, along with a railroad ticket to his home) and a suit of clothes. The suits were once made in the prisons; now they are purchased. Few of those being discharged take the pair of shoes offered them. They are Navy-type brogues and, in the street world, a sure sign that he has just been released.

Charlie Scaffa, one of the great private detectives, told me some years ago of a man who visited his office.

"Look at me," the caller said, "prison suit, prison shoes. I just got out. I can't let my friends see me like this."

He wanted Charlie to lend him some money to get some new clothes. Charlie, who had never seen him before, asked him what he

had been sent up for and who he knew. In the language of the street he was a "heavy" — a gunman. On the strength of his criminal connections Charlie gave him $150 and thought that would be the last he would see of him. A month later he saw the man drive by in a big new car. Not long after that his phone rang.

"Charlie", asked the con, "are you interested in that load of furs they took last night?"

"Yes, I am," said Charlie. "I'm handling the case for the insurance company. Do you know anything?"

"You can find the load in a warehouse on Degraw Street" was the reply.

That afternoon, with the police, Charlie recovered $50,000 worth of hijacked furs — all for his investment of $150 in an ex-con's wardrobe.

Seeing the inmates moving freely about the corridors and rooms, strolling in the yard in sportswear, you almost forget you're in a prison. Then one scene can quickly bring you back to reality. Arriving early one day, I noticed some buses waiting at the main gate. When I was passed in by the guard, I was asked to wait in a sitting room near the entrance. An unusual shuffling sound made me look up. A line of prisoners was moving through the room. Were they ill or injured? Their steps seemed faltering and slow. Each prisoner had a pair of leg irons around his ankles; a long chain ran the whole length of the line, linked to each pair of irons. Yet it was strangely silent. There was no clank of metal, only the scuffling sound of their shoes. Each marcher was holding the end of a cord in his right hand, the other end of which was fastened to the long chain so it could be kept from dragging on the floor. The line moved through in slow motion, out the door and into the waiting buses. The men were being transferred to another prison.

Thomas M. McDade was an FBI agent and supervisor back in the Thirties. He has served as legal counselor to the inmates of two prisons. In 1961 he received an Edgar from the Mystery Writers of America for his bibliography of American murder trials, The Annals of Murder.

INTERVIEW WITH A WARDEN

William Gard doesn't call himself a warden; he calls himself a superintendent. But then, he doesn't call it Sing Sing, either; he calls it the Ossining Correctional Facility.

Regardless of the wishes of Gard and the New York State Department of Correctional Services, the old names persist. A sign facing the metal detector at the prison's entrance lists "Sing Sing" protocol and a retiring guard who stopped by Gard's office to say good-bye kept referring to him as "Warden."

Gard has spent thirty-one years in the prison system, beginning as a machine-shop instructor at Auburn in 1945. In 1950 he took the Civil Service examination, passed it and became a guard. Another exam in 1960 made him a sergeant and another in 1967 made him a lieutenant. In 1970 he made captain, in 1972 he was appointed deputy superintendent and finally in 1975 he was named superintendent.

His large office has a spectacular view of the Hudson, if you don't mind viewing it from behind bars. Says Mr. Gard, "I don't even see the bars. I suppose it's the same in any occupation; after a while, you just don't notice things. I'm sure the engineer doesn't see the grease on the floor, either. It's a way of life."

He's not the only one not to notice things. The old death chamber where Julius and Ethel Rosenberg were electrocuted is now a changing room for prisoners. They barely comment on it as they put their civilian clothes into lockers on returning from their community work placements.

Mr. Gard, and 360 other officials, watch over a prison population of 800, most of whom are in transit to other correctional facilities. Sing Sing has become a "processing" depot in recent years, rather than a permanent Big House. The Department wisely preferred to locate prisoners elsewhere when they realized Sing Sing was the only prison in the country with a major railroad running straight through the middle of it.

But back in the good old days the likes of Willie Sutton were guests here. Mr. Sutton didn't much like the accommodations and broke out, a remarkable feat when one considers that Sing Sing was built along the lines of Cheops' pyramid, with massive walls and floor-to-ceiling bars at every major corridor junction.

Mr. Gard is a low-key, soft-spoken man when he talks about himself, but turn him to the subject of what makes a criminal a criminal and he bursts with the emotionalism of the revivalist preacher. "He's the victim of the society you and I continue to tolerate, and if we return him to that environment, you and I are guilty," he shouts. "Clean up those damn ghettos out there. Reduce unemployment so he can find a job when he gets out of here. It's a fact of life these people never had a chance, and right now society is still not provid-

The warden's office at Sing Sing before remodeling. One table and two panels are all that remain.

NEW YORK STATE DEPARTMENT OF CORRECTIONAL SERVICES

ing them with one."

Well, what retraining is actually done at Sing Sing, then? "Look," says Gard, "you can learn every aspect of the business here. If a man wants to spend his whole sentence learning how to hijack a liquor truck, he can probably get very professional training in that in here. On the other hand, he can also earn a college degree. That's available, too."

License plates are no longer the main outlet for keeping prisoners' idle fingers busy, it seems.

Still, the prison librarian and one of the guards seemed to think a prisoner was more apt to learn to be a moonshiner than anything else. Not a week goes by that the authorities aren't dismantling an illegal still somewhere on the premises.

One thing that's not a problem at Sing Sing is stool pigeons. Says Gard, "They don't approach me very often. It's known that I don't like them. They compare with the employee in a business who's always buttering up the boss, and it's always done for personal gain. An ego trip. They try to reverse their role: to assume the role of employee rather than inmate."

Gard's daily routine consists of touring the grounds and doing the usual amount of Civil Service paper work. He also, on occasion, sees prisoners who have some complaint. Now and then, there's a major crisis, such as the escape of two prisoners in 1976. Vacations? Mr. Gard gets four weeks off a year, but he can't remember the last time he used the full time. "I get bored," he explains.

ACCOMMODATIONS
AT SING SING

A turn around the exercise
yard in the early 1900's.

This doorway led to an old cell
block housing the more
recalcitrant inmates. Note
thickness of wall.

When Sing Sing was a permanent
facility, its inmates walked two by two,
in formation, around the exercise
yard.

For some prisoners the only way
out was feet first. Sing Sing had
its own burial grounds
overlooking the Hudson.

NEW YORK STATE DEPARTMENT OF CORRECTIONAL SERVICES

The first execution at Sing
Sing took place on
July 7, 1891.

The condemned cells. A side door
led to the execution chamber and
the "last mile," actually a walk of
about fifteen feet.

Sing Sing is the only U.S. correctional
facility bisected by a railroad. Two
prisoners escaped in 1976.

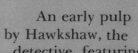

An early pulp
by Hawkshaw, the
detective, featuring the prison.

NEWGATE PRISON

Newgate's history is virtually inseparable from that of the Old Bailey; for over 1,000 years, criminals have been brought to Newgate Prison, London, for trial, imprisonment or even execution. The true origins of the prison have been lost in the passage of time, but it is known that the Romans built lock-ups here for their criminals.

It was the Britons who named the site New Gate. Henry I built a large prison here, calling it Heynouse Gaol of Newgate. The name Heynouse meant "hateful gaol." At that time, thieves were hanged without trial, and conditions in this gaol were appalling, even by mediaeval standards. Nonetheless, that prison lasted over 300 years, after which time the walls began to crumble and it became grossly neglected. Even so, it continued to be used.

Prison Yard, Newgate, shortly before demolition in 1902.

When London's famous Lord Mayor, Sir Richard (Dick) Whittington, died in 1419, he left considerable sums of money which were used to re-build London's main prison, which was Newgate. Four years later, it received its first entry of new prisoners and became known as "Whit's Palace" in honour of Whittington.

The prison survived the Great Fire of London in 1666 and endured for some 350 years until London architect, George Dance, designed a bigger gaol. This one took eight years to construct and was completed in 1778. Unfortunately, it survived only two years: it was destroyed by the Gordon Rioters in 1780. Another Newgate Gaol arose on the site in 1783 and remained until 1902, when it was demolished to make room for the Central Criminal Court, which we all know as the Old Bailey.

Newgate Prison was always notorious for its cruelties and appalling conditions. For example, in Cromwell's time, a prisoner who refused to plead when standing trial by jury was pressed with heavy weights in an effort to make him plead. Without pleading, he could not be tried and condemned, and the object of the weights was to compel him to plead so the trial could continue. Many prisoners nevertheless continued in their refusal and so suffered an agonising death. Known as *peine forte et dure,* the procedure was carried out in a specially prepared chamber called the Press Room.

Another grisly tale about Newgate

is that when the prisoners left their cells for their last journey to a place of execution, the bells of nearby St. Sepulchre's Church would begin to toll. They tolled for the entire journey to Tyburn, three miles away. The custom was started in the seventeenth century by Robert Dow, who asked the sexton to call upon the accused to make his peace with God. The sound of the bell gave rise to the term "hang-ing march." This practice ended in 1890.

P.N.W.

Exterior view of Old Newgate Prison, 1902.

THE BETTMAN ARCHIVE, INC.

1833 broadside listing the results of trials the week of February 23 and February 27.

SENTENCES OF THE
PRISONERS,

IN NEWCASTLE and MORPETH who have taken their Trials at the assizes Feb. 23, 1833, before the Honourable Sir EDWARD HALL ALDERSON, Knight, and the Honourable Sir JOHN GURNEY, Knight, also a CALENDAR of the PRISONERS in DURHAM GAOL, who have to take their Trials at the Assizes, Feb. 27, 1833, before the aforesaid Knights.

NEWCASTLE GAOL.

CHARLOTTE CHARLTON, aged 21, charged with having assaulted Thomasin Errington, and stole 14s. 9d., one woman's pocket, and two thimbles.— *Death, recorded.*

JOHN TURNBULL, 20. charged with stealing a silver watch.— *7 years Transp.*

JAMES MACCAULER, aged 35, charged with having in his possession, nine false and counterfeit shillings, with intent to utter the same.— *6 months imprisonment.*

HINDMARSH THOMPSON, aged 49, charged with having stolen one silk umbrella, value ten shillings, and one cloak, value twenty shillings.— *6 months ̶I̶m̶p̶r̶i̶s̶o̶n̶m̶e̶n̶t̶*

ANN HOYLE, aged 41, charged with having stolen one harden sheet, one iron spoon, and one knife and fork, belonging Newcastle Infirmary.— *6 months imprisonment.*

GRACE NEILSON, 27, charged with stealing 8 sovs.— *14 years Transportation.*

GUISEPPE SIDOLI, 29, charged with killing H. Ross.— *7 years Transportation*

MORPETH GAOL.

JAMES GIBBESON, charged with burglary in his master's house. *Transported for life*

ANDREW BOHILLS, charged with stealing a metal roller— *4 months imprisoned*

JAMES COOK, charged with stealing a gold ring.— *Six months hard labour.*

THOMAS JEWITT, charged with cutting and wounding John Elliott, with intent to murder him.— *Transported for life.*

THOMAS ELLISON charged with maiming Mary Walker, at Hazlerigg.— *Transported for Life.*

WILLIAM GREY, charged with maiming Job Davies, at Hazlerigg.— *Acquitted.*

GEORGE MORDUE, Joseph Peel, and Henry Temple, charged with riot and assault at Hazlerigg.— *To be tried next Assizes—out on bail.*

THE HANGMAN'S STORY

Laurence Henderson

Teutonic hanging (multiple)

The last man to die on the scaffold in England was hanged in 1965, and when a few months later the capital penalty for murder was abolished, it ended a carefully calculated ritual of execution that had been followed for almost a hundred years. The code had arisen out of the rough-and-ready methods that had been used in the previous eight hundred years and, as finally adopted, had some claim to being the most efficient as well as the most humane method of state execution ever operated.

The man under sentence would be brought back to the prison in which he had been held during his trial, then taken not to his previous cell in the remand wing of the prison, but to a special cell that completely isolated him from the rest of the prisoners.

This cell contained a prison cot, table, chairs and an alcove with washbasin and toilet, and from the moment he entered the cell until the moment he finally left it two warders were constantly with him. Six warders were allocated to this special duty, rotating in pairs at eight-hour intervals. While in the cell, they not only watched the man but also engaged him in conversation, helped him to write letters if he was illiterate, played cards or other table games and generally kept him company. They also reported every word that the man uttered, and any reference to his crime was immediately forwarded to the Home Office official who was dealing with the case papers.

Three clear Sundays had to elapse between the passing of the sentence and its execution, a period originally laid down so that the man could reflect upon his crime, express remorse and make peace with his God. In practise this period was used by the defence lawyers to appeal against the sentence or, if there were no legal ground of appeal, then to petition for mercy. Also during this time the government official who was responsible for the case papers would be studying the case and collecting all relevant information, including an opinion on the man's sanity if this had not been an issue in the court hearing, and would then make a final

THE LAST COG IN THE LAW MACHINE

Anne Worboys

"That man," said somebody at the party, " is Albert Pierpoint."

Albert Pierpoint, the public hangman, not halfway across the room from where I was standing.

He was of smallish stature, his thinning hair cut short, back and sides. He had a broadish face with ruddy cheeks and pointed chin. He wore a navy blue suit and gaily striped tie. A Yorkshireman, they said, with a Yorkshireman's ability to speak his mind. (They don't call a spade a spade up there; they call it a bloody shovel.) He looked amiable enough to me.

"Do you want to meet him?" (They told me afterwards my eyes were sticking out like organ stops.)

"Give me a moment," I said.

What did I want to ask him? For a start, I wanted to know if he had ever had a grudge against society. A mental hang-up, with no pun intended. Then, how did he feel when pulling the switch/turning the handle/jerking the rope? And what did the Act of Parliament abolishing the death penalty mean to him, the man whose job it had been to destroy other men fairly consistently? More pertinently, what had he looked for since, to take the place of those high-tension days?

"Okay," I said, "let's go."

At closer range I saw he had the twinkliest eyes in the room. He seemed amused at the sight of this startled-looking woman approaching him.

He inherited the job, he said straightforwardly. His uncle had been the hangman before him and his father had been the hangman before his uncle. He simply followed on. I felt he was going to say, "Why not?" but he didn't.

He didn't feel anything, he explained. He didn't think about it. After all, he added, if he'd thought about it, he'd have gone mad, wouldn't he?

He said they would ask him to come at a certain time, and he would get on the train and go, do the job for which he was paid, then turn round and come home again.

What did he do after retiring as public hangman? He kept a pub.

Anne Worboys won the 1977 Romantic Novelists Association award for her suspense novel Every Man a King.

report to the Home Secretary. It was this minister who had the final decision on whether the sentence should be confirmed or commuted to life imprisonment.

During this time the man wore ordinary prison clothing except that the jacket and trousers were held together not by zips and buttons, but by tie-tapes, and that instead of shoes he would be given felt slippers. His food came from the prison kitchens, but the doctor could authorise any diet and in most cases the man could choose his own meals. He would also be allowed a daily amount of beer or liquor and, if a smoker, would be supplied with cigarettes or tobacco. He could choose any books that he wished from the lists of the prison library and he could read newspapers, so long as any reference to his own case had been deleted. He could write or receive any number of letters, but they first had to be read by the chief officer of the prison. Each day he would be visited by the prison governor, doctor and chaplain.

If the man had visitors, he would be taken from the cell to see them in a nearby interview room. Such visits were limited to thirty minutes unless otherwise sanctioned by the prison governor, who usually did so only if the visitor was the man's legal advisor. The man could also leave the cell to attend religious services in the prison chapel or to take exercise. This exercise was always taken alone, at a time when the other prisoners were either locked in their cells or at recreation.

The governor had to make a daily report on the man's health and demeanour, and it was also his task to tell the man when the sentence had been confirmed by the Home Secretary and that there was no longer any possibility of reprieve.

Once this decision had been taken, a long, japanned box was delivered to the prison and carefully locked away until it could be handed over to the hangman, who would arrive at the prison with his assistant sometime during the afternoon of the day before that set for the execution. Once inside the prison, he would be unable to leave again until the execution had taken place: a relic of the times when the hangman was inclined to arrive at the scaffold reeling from the gin shop.

This gibbet was typical of those erected in France in the sixteenth century. It was suitable for hanging up to twenty-four persons. The gentleman in the foreground is swatting away the low-flying buzzards.

The hangman adjusts the noose.

The hangman would open the execution box and thoroughly examine its contents before signing that he was satisfied with the equipment provided. In the box were two six-foot lengths of inch-thick hemp rope, one end of each rope spliced around a two-inch brass-faced eyelet and the other lashed around a thick brass disc with a bolt hole drilled through its centre. The rope would be doubled back through the brass eyelet and for the first eighteen inches would be faced with chamois leather. Both ropes were precisely the same, but one was absolutely new and the other a rope that had already been used in an execution. It was the hangman's option as to which should be used. Also in the box was a white linen bag with tapes for putting over the man's head, a broad leather belt with attachment straps for his arms and a second belt to pinion his legs.

The hangman would be given details of the man's age, height and weight, as well as an opportunity to see the man without being observed so that he could form a judgement as to the man's general build and likely muscular strength. He would then sit down and make his calculation, take all factors into consideration and decide the length of drop that was required.

During that final evening, while the man was seeing a visitor or being exercised for the last time, the hangman and his assistant would enter the execution chamber, which itself was an extension of the condemned cell. The trap, measuring eight feet by five, was split along its centre, the two halves being hinged along the sides. At the end of the trap was a lever, held locked by a cotter pin, which, when operated, retracted the central bolts and allowed the two halves of the trap to drop away.

The trap was spanned some nine feet above by a heavy beam from which hung a number of chains, one of which was selected and bolted into position over the centre of the trap, its length being either taken up or extended according to the drop decided upon by the hangman. The selected rope was attached to the final link of the chain by a U-bar and bolt through the brass disc at the end of the rope. A bag of sand the same weight as the man would then be put into the running noose and the trap operated. If this worked to the hangman's satisfaction, the bag of sand would be drawn up, the trap reset and the bolts and lever reoiled. If the man was still out of his cell and time permitted, the hangman would finalise his arrangements by setting two hand ropes on the beam to hang on either side of the noose and putting two planks across the length of the trap below the hand ropes.

The hangman could also, if there was time,

set the noose by taking it up to the approximate head height of the man, coiling the slack above the noose and then tying it in position with a piece of thread. If the man was expected to return to his cell, these final preparations would be made in the very early morning, if possible while the man was asleep, the important consideration always being that the man should hear nothing of the preparations that were being made on the other side of the thin, movable partition. On the morning of the execution the hangman and his assistant would enter the execution chamber, make a final check, and then, ready with the restraining harness, wait for the false wall to be moved aside.

In the cell the man would be with the prison chaplain, either seated at the table or, possibly, kneeling in prayer. The door of the cell would be opened by the chief officer, who would lead in the prison governor, doctor and either the Under Sheriff or some other representative of the Lord Lieutenant of the County in which the execution was taking place. As the man rose to face the group entering the cell,

The Execution of "Tipperary Bill" in the Yard of the County Jail, June 10, 1859. The curious well-to-do were allowed to watch, but other prisoners destined for a similar ending were barred from the proceedings.

When a man is hanged, the rope is jerked with such force it not only breaks his neck but leaves a severe rope burn. These markings are clearly shown on death casts, a collection of which are on display in the Black Musuem at New Scotland Yard. (The Wood Street Police Station Museum also has them.) These sketches appeared in a London newspaper on February 15, 1873. The rope marks are most obvious at the base of the neck and up behind one ear, where the rope lifted as the body dropped. Capital punishment is no longer practiced in Great Britain, although many law enforcement officials feel it will be reinstated within the next ten years. The last hangman was Albert Pierpoint, who followed his father and his uncle in the job. Mr. Pierpoint recently published his memoirs. Invited to the United States during World War II to act as consultant, he found American procedures not only antiquated but inhumane.

one of the warders slid aside the false wall for the hangman and his assistant to come forward.

The first awareness the man had of their presence was the restriction on his arms as they were brought into the harness. It was as the hangman turned him that he saw, for the first time, that the scaffold was only a few feet from the bed in which he had been sleeping for the past three weeks. While the hangman tightened the strap around the man's body, the two warders would take him by the elbows and walk him to the scaffold, keeping him between them as they stepped onto the planks and grasped the hand ropes with their free hands.

The hangman set the noose over the man's head while his assistant placed the final strap around the legs. The noose was then placed around the man's neck, and the hangman immediately stepped from the trap and pulled the lever; the doors of the trap crashed open and the condemned man disappeared between the two warders. The broken fragments of thread drifted slowly past a rope that hung as straight as an arrow, showing barely a shudder of movement from the tension placed upon it.

The time taken from the moment the chief officer opened the door of the cell until the man fell through the doors of the trap would have been less than twenty seconds.

The hangman and his assistant would descend to below the scaffold, erect a ladder and take the man from the rope. The doctor would examine the body and confirm that death had occurred. Since under English law all unnatural deaths have to be inquired into, a local coroner and his jury would be waiting. The inevitable medical evidence would be that death had resulted from a fracture dislocation of the 2/3 cervical which had severed the cord. The coroner would then record the jury's verdict that death had resulted from judicial hanging and the body would be released for burial. This always took place immediately and within the precincts of the prison; the position and identity of the grave would be carefully recorded on a plan of the prison grounds, but the grave itself would be unmarked.

Laurence Henderson is the author of four crime novels. The most recent is Major Enquiry.

Chapter 12
CAUGHT IN THE ACT

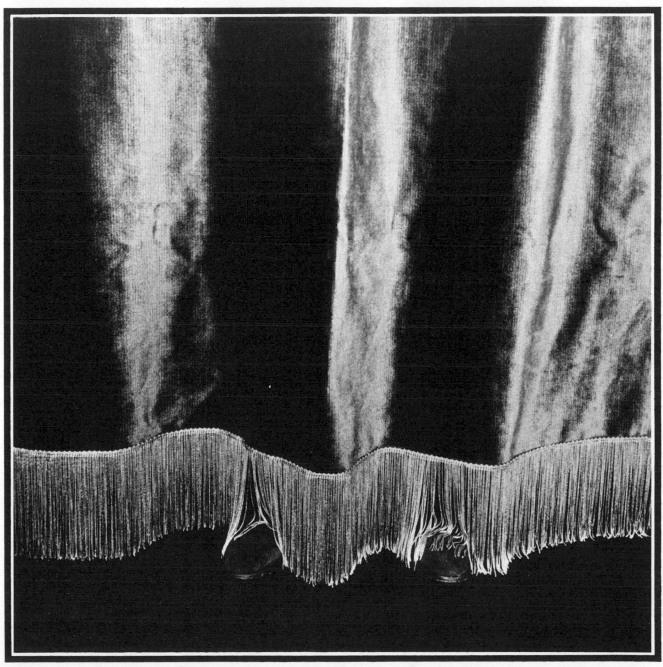

EXEUNT DYING

R.M. Whyte

Back in the old days (circa 1600) the primary charm of the crime play was its gore. The "sanguifulminous stage" was held by Shakespeare's *Macbeth,* Marlowe's *Edward the Second* and domestic tragedies such as *Arden of Faversham,* described on its title page as the tale of a man who "was most wickedlye murdered, by the meanes of his disloyall and wanton wyfe, who for the love she bare to one Mosbie, hyred two desperat ruffins, Blackwill and Shakbag."

This passion for they-done-its and this-is-how-they-done-its lasted until late in the nineteenth century. A constant parade of notorious felons was plucked from real life and thrust upon the stage to become the sensational rage. One drama even advertised that its central props (knife, pitcher of poisoned punch, bed, chair and bloodstained furniture) came direct from the victim's house. The audience was enthralled.

In 1899 William Gillette put Sherlock Holmes onstage and kept him there, virtually without pause, until 1931. Conan Doyle was so disinterested in the fate of Holmes he gave Gillette carte blanche to alter the character as he saw fit. Gillette threw him into the arms of a woman at play's end, which alarmed nobody at the time but greatly unnerved audiences when the play was recently revived by the Royal Shakespeare Company.

In 1912 the archetypal mystery melodrama was produced — *Within the Law* by Bayard Vellier. In it, Mary Turner, working girl, was railroaded into the slammer. When she was released she formed a gang of blackmailers and exacted her revenge by marrying the son of the man responsible for her imprisonment. Her immortal second-act curtain line, delivered to her enemy, Gilder Edward: "Four years ago you took away my name and gave me a number. Now — now I've given up that number and I've got *your* name!"

Within the Law also boasted the first stage appearance of the Maxim revolver silencer. Said the thug to the cops, "Some class that, eh? Them things cost sixty dollars and they're worth the money, too. They'll remember me as the first to spring one of them, won't they?"

Awful dialogue was the mainstay of the mystery play for years. Take this bit of dialogue from *The Bat* (1920): "Miz Cornelia, I've stood by you through thick and thin — I stood by you when you were a vegetarian, a Theosophist, and I seen you through socialism, Fletcherism and rheumatism — but when it comes to carrying on with ghosts . . .!"

THE EVER-RUNNING MOUSETRAP

It opened in London in 1952 and it's still one of the hottest tickets in town. New Yorkers, however, disliked it. It had a short Off-Broadway run, also in 1952, and closed quickly and quietly. Ironically, Londoners say it is the American tourists who keep it going in the West End.

The play is based on Christie's novelette *Three Blind Mice,* and the original London cast included Richard Attenborough and Sheila Sim, directed by Peter Cotes.

The last big hit in this melodramatic vein was John Willard's *The Cat and the Canary* (1922), which had a plethora of sliding panels, creaky stairs, clutching hands and, of course, victims. When the play reached London, it had a jingle attached to it: "If you like this play, please tell your friends; But pray don't tell them how it ends." Years later, as a student at the Yale School of Drama, I saw a New Haven tryout of a play which concluded with the star taking an ill-deserved bow (the moosehead on the wall in the first act was far the better actor) and asking the audience to observe that old 1922 jingle. (He didn't credit it, of course.) I was happy to oblige. A play can have an ending too bad, as well as too good, to reveal.

With the arrival of Agatha Christie's *Alibi* (1928), featuring Charles Laughton as Hercule Poirot, the mystery play became more sensible. It's been reported that Mrs. Christie felt Laughton was "utterly unlike Poirot, but a wonderful actor."

BROADWAY, BLOODY BROADWAY

1896 *Secret Service,* by William Gillette
1899 *Sherlock Holmes,* by William Gillette
1912 *Within the Law,* by Bayard Veiller
1913 *Seven Keys to Baldpate,* George M. Cohan
1914 *On Trial,* Elmer Rice
1920 *The Bat,* Mary Roberts Rinehart and Avery Hopwood
1920 *Trifles,* a one-act play by Susan Glaspell
1922 *The Cat and the Canary,* by John Willard
1926 *Broadway,* Philip Dunning and George Abbott
1928 *Diamond Lil,* by Mae West
1931 *Mourning Becomes Electra,* murder melodrama by Eugene O'Neill
1933 *Night of January 16th,* by Ayn Rand
1936 *Night Must Fall,* by Emlyn Williams
1939 *Angel Street,* by Patrick Hamilton
1940 *Ladies in Retirement,* by Edward Percy and Reginald Denham
1941 *Arsenic and Old Lace,* by Joseph Kesserling
1944 *Ten Little Indians,* by Agatha Christie
1948 *Murder on the Nile,* by Agatha Christie

1949 *Detective Story,* by Sydney Kingsley
1950 *The Innocents,* by William Archibald
1952 *The Mousetrap,* by Agatha Christie
1952 *Dial M for Murder,* by Frederick Knott
1953 *The Caine Mutiny Court Martial,* by Herman Wouk
1954 *Witness for the Prosecution,* by Agatha Christie
1956 *Towards Zero,* by Agatha Christie
1961 *Write Me a Murder,* by Frederick Knott
1962 *Rule of Three,* by Agatha Christie
1964 *Hostile Witness,* by Jack Roffey
1965 *The Desperate Hours,* by Joseph Hayes
1966 *Wait Until Dark,* by Frederick Knott
1966 *Loot,* by Joe Orton
1968 *The Real Inspector Hound,* by Tom Stoppard
1970 *Sleuth,* by Anthony Shaffer
1970 *Child's Play,* by Robert Marasco
1972 *Are You Now or Have You Ever Been,* by Eric Bentley
1976 *Something's Afoot,* by McDonald, Vos and Gerlach
1977 *Dracula,* production designed by Edward Gorey

That, however, was in London. In America 1926 ushered in *Broadway,* the *ne plus ultra* backstage–New York-night-club–show-biz–chorus-girl–Chicago-gunman–whoop-it-up, resolved by a corn-fed young detective named Dan McCorn. Which wasn't such a strange name, considering the other monikers involved: Ruby, Mazie, Grace, Porky, Joe, Lil and Scar Edwards. This play will long be remembered for its closing moments, when a character grabs his ukelele and admonishes the chorus: "Remember — you're all artists! Here we go — here we go!"

From downright silliness to an outright gimmick is not such a giant step, and Ayn Rand took it with *Night of January 16th* (1933). It was a courtroom drama whose proceedings were held up every night until a jury was selected from the audience. The play was written with two endings, and the cast inserted the appropriate one — depending on the jury's decision.

The psychopathic killer came trouping onstage in the character of Dan, the sinister bellboy of Emlyn Williams' *Night Must Fall* (1935). Williams wrote the play for himself to star in, and he had a laudable run of 435 performances. (Williams also tried his hand at the Rand trick ending with *A Murder Is Announced.*)

The first London psychological thriller was called *Ladies in Retirement,* set in an 1885 pre-Tudor farmhouse situated in Thames-side marshes, predictably near a somber convent. The play is still dusted off and given an airing by every middle-aged actress with any clout in a little-theater group. *Ladies* was a smash hit in New York, with Richard Watts, Jr., of the *Herald Tribune,* enthusing: "Just the sort of good, sound murder play that the dramatic season has been so insistently demanding!"

But 1941 brought an even bigger hit, *Arsenic and Old Lace,* a play which holds the stage the way gum sticks to the bottom of a theater seat. Helen Hayes has said, "I have played it twice and enjoyed every minute of it."

Relentlessly naturalistic dramas took over for a while, and these included *Detective Story* and *Dial M for Murder.* (Publishers guesstimate there are 350 amateur productions of *Dial M* a year, with another fifty or so stock-company presentations.) But the days of the mystery play

THE ROLE I WANT MOST

Jerry Stiller's Views

A man like Watson enthralls me. Why? Because he dabbles in crime, and what better way to deal with crime than to dabble in it?

I'd love to play Watson. Nigel Bruce, of course, was the embodiment of Watson, but that wouldn't stop me. With Bruce you could almost see the man stopping off at Fortnum & Mason's for some jams; you felt, all the time, how he catered to Holmes. Rathbone, as Holmes, accepted this. It was a case of two idiosyncratic men complementing each other.

My Watson would have a different relationship with his Holmes. I never thought of Watson as dumb; I always suspected he was well aware of what was going on, more aware than he let on. He humored Holmes at least as much as Holmes humored him, and that's what I'd like to bring out. After all, he always did manage to be where he was supposed to be — right in the middle of things — at the scene of the crime.

The Holmes I'd feel most comfortable with would be Richard Harris. I think we could show the two men as the deep friends they were, how they balanced each other.

No, I don't consider myself similar to Watson. We are far removed in character and style. But that's what makes playing him so appealing to me. In fact, I'm waiting for someone to ask me. Anyone. I'd do Watson anywhere, even in a community theater. But they'd have to get Harris, too.

on Broadway were numbered; the obsession for plot itself as the primary subject matter would soon go out of fashion. The last grand gasp of the traditional mystery was Christie's *Witness for the Prosecution* (1954), which won the New York Drama Critics' Circle Award as the year's best foreign play — the only mystery play ever to do so. This was Christie's second and last Broadway success. (*The Mousetrap* flopped.)

Recently, it's been bleak for mystery theater. *Sleuth* and *The Real Inspector Hound* are the only two productions to achieve any kind of audience acceptance, and there were those who considered them a put-on — a sort of intellectual hogwash. The mystery musical has fared even worse: *Baker Street* and *Something's Afoot* were scandalously inept. Only the revival of *Angel Street* (nee *Gaslight*) had any charm, and the critics were even unimpressed with that.

Broadway, however, is not the world. What won't play on the Great White Way *will* play in Paducah. Across America, in 30,000 high schools, 3,000 colleges and countless rep and stock companies, the mystery play — albeit an old one — is alive and well.

Charles Baker, co-head of the Macmillan Performing Arts Division, tried to explain this phenomenon: "Most mystery plays just don't look like blockbuster productions. If you pay $20 to see a play, you want to see every penny of it up on that stage. And it better be something you can't see on TV, or at the movies."

Christopher Sergel, of the Dramatic Play Service, had a few opinions as to why mysteries do so well regionally: "First, a large cast, with every role having a few good 'bits' in it. Next, the leads tip toward female characters, and

---

STAGE STRUCK: MYSTERIES WITH THEATRICAL THEMES

Dancers in Mourning: Margery Allingham

Exit Charlie: Alex Atkinson

Curtain Call for a Corpse: Josephine Bell

The Case of the Solid Key: Anthony Boucher

Death Steals the Show: John Bude

Panic in Box C: John Dickson Carr

Murder in Three Acts: Agatha Christie

The Backstage Mystery: Octavus Roy Cohen

Obsequies at Oxford: Edmund Crispin

The Candles Are All Out: Nigel Fitzgerald

Blood on the Boards: William Campbell Gault

Hamlet, Revenge: Michael Innes

Murder Off-Broadway: Henry Klinger

The G-String Murders; Mother Finds a Body: Gypsy Rose Lee

Death on the Aisle; Death Take a Bow: The Lockridges

Abracadaver: Peter Lovesey

They Can't Hang Me: Jacqueline Mallet

Enter a Murderer; Final Curtain; Killer Dolphin; Night at the Vulcan; Vintage Murder: Ngaio Marsh

Cue for Murder: Helen McCloy

Walking Shadow: Lenore Glen Offord

The Roman Hat Mystery; Face to Face: Ellery Queen

Puzzle for Players: Patrick Quentin

This Rough Magic: Mary Stewart

A VISIT WITH ONE OF THE SNOOP SISTERS

Mildred Natwick

In the late 1930's I was in a mystery play called *Night in the House,* based on a Hugh Walpole novel. It was a terrible flop, ran only three weeks. We were supposed to be three little old ladies living in a flat. One was a gypsy, I think. I owned a rare piece of amber that one of the other ladies wanted. So she murdered me for it. I was strangled, I believe. How did I play dead? I just lay there gasping for breath. And then slid off the bed onto the floor. The critics were not kind.

THE CRUMPLED TUTU AND THE SOURED NOTE: TWO CHECK LISTS

Opera productions just love to strew bodies across the stage. The soprano kills the tenor, the bass strangles the contralto and the chorus often does them all in. As for the ballet — well, have you ever known the swan to live? Obviously, these two stage disciplines hold great promise for the mystery writer. Below, a sampling of some of the better mysteries with ballet and opera themes.

THE CRUMPLED TUTU

Death in the Fifth Position: Edgar Box
A Bullet in the Ballet; Murder at La Stragonoff: Caryl Brahms and S.J. Simon
The Bali Ballet Murders: Cornelius Conyn and Jon C. Martin
Corpse de Ballet: Lucy Cores
Two If by Sea (Came the Dawn): Andrew Garve

THE SOURED NOTE

The Savage Salome: Carter Brown

Serenade: James M. Cain
The Bohème Combination: Robin Close
Dead and Dumb (Swan Song): Edmund Crispin
Ghost Song: Dorothy Daniels
The Photogenic Soprano: Dorothy Dunnett
Take My Wife: Winston Graham
Murder at the Met: Fred G. Jarvis
Death of a Fat God: H.R.F. Keating
The Blue Harpsichord: David Keith
The Phantom of the Opera: Gaston Leroux
Murder in the Opera House; Murder Meets Mephisto; Death Drops Delilah: Queena Mario
Murder Ends the Song: Alfred Meyers
Death at the Opera: Gladys Mitchell
Funeral of Figaro: Ellis Peters
The Fidelio Score: Gerald Sinstadt
Murder Plays an Ugly Scene: L.A.G. Strong
The Metropolitan Opera Murders: Helen Traubel
The Assassination of Mozart: David Weiss

drama departments usually have more women than men. The untricky set is easy to reproduce."

Stanley Richards, doyen of drama anthologists, is optimistic about the mystery play's future: "There aren't many right now, I know. Out of every two or three hundred plays I read, maybe twenty-five will be mysteries. Most of them come from England or Australia, because they still produce mystery plays on a professional level. We used to, but now there's a whole generation of American playwrights who haven't been exposed to quality, top-flight productions. It'll about-face, I'm sure. I know a truly wonderful short gothic mystery just coming out by avant-garde playwright Rochelle Owens. That's a good sign."

For the lover of mystery plays, this leaves only one option: play scripts. They, unfortunately, are a non–art form unto themselves. However, people do learn to cope with subtitled films. Stage directions, with a little practice, can be just as easily ignored.

Meanwhile, what's next for Broadway? Two of the more talented men around have set their sights on a mysterious Broadway. Edward Gorey has designed the sets and costumes for a production of *Dracula* and Stephen Sondheim is readying *Sweeney Todd, the Demon Barber of Fleet Street* as a musical.

But there is one harbinger of doom. Stanley Richards believes "our theater audiences have gotten out of just being entertained. They aren't prepared for mystery plays any more."

R.M. Whyte is the Soho Weekly News *book editor.*

THE FIRST SUCCESSFUL MYSTERY MOVIE

Richard Townsend

MEMO: To Studio Chief Fred Fellsberg
FROM: Richard Townsend
RE: My screenplay for Big Bread-Making mystery movie

Persuant to our confab at the World Trade Center last Tuesday. You're absolutely on target, F.F. The time is ripe for a moola mystery. It's très clear this genre hasn't been making it on the big screen because of the intrinsic difference between hard covers and hard core. The literary mystery is a study in the intellectual process of unwinding the layers of death, deceit and destruction that dwell deep within our domes. But movies mean *action*. Direct, devastating, de-lovely. So I've come up with a sure-fire dazzler that'll keep the people flocking to the box office and leave them starved for a sequel. The idea is to bring together in one flick everything the public wants. It'll be expensive and time-consuming, but what does that mean when the fate of our beloved studio is at stake. *Gone with the Godfather,* an interplanetary love story with music, has got *IT*!

Our hero, a New York Jewish Intellectual, is played against type by Woody Allen, who starts the action by returning to his Fifth Avenue duplex to discover the nude, mutilated and expiring body of Sissy Spacek. Dangling from Sissy's hand is a large glass key, unfortunately broken in two but with the name Liza written across it. Just as Woody wonders whoever Liza could be, his phone rings and his ex-girl friend Diane Keaton is calling from Hollywood to ask for his help with a few quick jokes, since her best girl friend Liza Minnelli has appeared at her Malibu shack, hysterical with rage and fury at having been sadistically beaten by her lover, Art Carney. Woody calms down the two women and casually asks Liza if she's the owner of the other end of a glass key. Choking on her hot chocolate, Liza screams and goes into a coma, forcing Woody to grab the next flight for L.A. On his arrival at the hospital Diane has mysteriously disappeared, leaving only a mute Liza to respond to Woody's questions with a slight quaver of her eyelids. As Woody leans over Liza, he is hit over the head.

Upon awakening, he finds himself in a large blimp flying over Shea Stadium. Although he is deeply drugged, he dimly recognizes a white-haired, white-uniformed

JOSEPH PAPIN

dwarf, played by Marlon Brando, who appears to be cutting at him with scissors and forceps. When fully awake, he finds he is now played by Robert Redford, as total plastic surgery has been necessitated by the knowledge he possesses but cannot interpret. Marlon the Magician explains that a less obvious face like that of the blond bombshell Bob will render him unnoticeable, especially to women. As Woody-Bob is digesting this info, the blimp careens down into the stadium, dropping poison pellets in the form of free hot dogs, which arc lapped up by an ignorant populace. "They're all Communists," says the grinning Marlon, who parachutes out a tunnel of the crazily cavorting blimp speeding our hero into outer space.

Landing on the freezing planet of Oz, Woody-Bob is welcomed by its Queen, Ozetta, a gospel singer, winningly played by Barbra Streisand, who sings the title song, "Gone with the Godfather." It seems that after losing the role of Scarlett in the *Gone with the Wind* remake, Ozetta has taken her rock band, and a fan following of 80 million people, and started a new world in which she'll have no competition. Craftily, she inquires about Liza's stroke, and Woody-Bob knows there's something afoot. Before he can answer, Barbra has him tied and nailed to a huge microphone, and as she seals a permanent Steve McQueen mask across his face and almost naked body, she tells him she must have him as her singing co-star for her remake of *Ben-Hur*. So Woody-Bob has now turned into Woody-Bob-Steve, who's sexier and more expensive than anybody.

When Barbra's back is turned, a little waif played by Tatum O'Neal appears to spirit Woody-Bob-Steve off to the remote estate of her Godfather, Charles Bronson, who needs a good ring-kisser fast. Jumping into Tatum's Toyota, the twosome zip across a bloody desert, strewn with the hands and limbs of folk who didn't recognize Godfather Charles as the top banana. Fade into Big Charlie's plantation, where he's having a porno romance with his moll Farrah Fawcett-Majors. When Farrah sees Steve, a scene of hot, sultry passion ensues, climaxed by her throwing him on the bed and promising to make him an angel. Just as Steve's wings are about to sprout, Big Bronson turns up with his henchmen James Caan and Michael York. Jimmy and Mike are about to gun down Steve when the disgusted Charles tells them to take Farrah instead and do with her whatever they want. Following is a scene of horrifying torture as Farrah clings to the pant legs of the reluctant gunmen who *refuse* to rape her. In retaliation she shoots them with her ray-bra, turning them into instant sex maniacs, but alas it's too late for them.

Farrah has returned to Charlie's digs, and not wanting to be his angel any more, she drops a capped tooth into his drink just as he's about to sign Steve to a lifetime contract as a live-in Godson. Farrah and Steve grab the nearest Concorde and whiz back to Earth, immune to the blandishments of Barbra's siren song (a repeat of our gold-record musical theme).

On terra firma Farrah stops to change bras

at the apartment of her chums, a jaunty married couple played by Robert Shaw and Lily Tomlin. Though he's a professional shark hunter and she teaches Esperanto, they like to solve crimes on the side under the names of Nick and Nora Charlie-O. But first the frolicky four have to list all the crimes. Remembering them is tough. The most important seem to be: Who killed Sissy Spacek? Who poisoned Liza Minnelli? What made Marlon Brando shrink? And, who really did Streisand out of *GWTW*? The group decide that the same person who abducted Diane Keaton is probably responsible for all the misfortunes pummeling Woody-Bob-Steve. For a quick answer Lily consults her telephone directory and finds the name of a crystal-gazer in the yellow pages.

Entering the dark domicile of mystic Glenda Jackson, the group is instructed to peer into her glowing glass. There they see that it's now Diane Keaton who's being beaten by the versatile Art Carney. Speeding to Art's place, they find Art and Diane making out but feel too embarrassed to stay. As the heartbroken and disillusioned Woody leaves, Diane manages to slip him the other part of the glass key. It says "Doolittle" on it! Woody realizes that the key never belonged to Liza Minnelli at all, but is the property of Eliza Doolittle, heroine of *My Fair Lady*. Since both Julie Andrews (who portrayed Eliza on stage) and Audrey Hepburn (the screen version) are in town making comebacks, the group invites the two stars to an after-interview supper. The sweet-and-lovelies arrive and insist they know nothing, but Audrey puts in a call to her more

political sisters Shirley MacLaine and Jane Fonda, who arrive with their campaign manager Bob De Niro. Here we interpolate a little musical bit as Shirley dances, Jane makes a speech and Bob does a saxophone solo. As they swing into the second chorus, the entire group is gunned down by a mysterious stranger garbed in black. It's Greta Garbo, who removes her facial mask to reveal the long-dead Sissy Spacek, who has managed to spare only Woody-Bob-Steve so that he can be her three top leading men and she will become the only female star left alive.

Just as she's showing our hero how she brilliantly enacted her own death, Sissy is knifed by Glenda Jackson, who delivers an Oscar-acceptance speech and descends into total madness by forming a sister act with the evergreen Barbra Streisand, who appears just in time to sing the title song again, under the closing credits. Which girl gets Woody-Bob-Steve? We'll leave that for the sequel, *The Continuation of Gone with the Godfather*.

Well, F.F., I hope you loved the treatment. Please forgive this simplistic version, which I will expand upon after my rewrite of *A Star Is Born* for Mason Reese. Although why I'm doing that one is a mystery to me.

Sincerely,

Richard

Richard Townsend is a novelist, playwright, screen writer and journalist who has interviewed many of the celebrities cast in this scenario.

STARRING IN A HORROR

Roy Scheider

COURTESY
METRO-GOLDWYN MAYER

The first motion picture I ever did was called *Curse of the Living Corpse*. I was an actor at the Arena Stage, and the producer came up to me with the idea of filming a horror mystery on the estate of Gutzon Borglum, the guy who did the sculptures on Mount Rushmore. You have to understand that when they started this film, they went to the film library in New York, picked out all the titles of horror movies that had made big money and from this list put together the three most popular words — "corpse," "living" and "curse." First they wrote the title, then they wrote the script.

Anyway, as an actor who'd never done a movie, I couldn't pass it up. Not only that, but the script was the most outrageous thing I'd ever read in my life.

I played the drunken-sot-weakling-brother in a family that were all after the father's inheritance and wouldn't get it if they committed any of the standard unspeakable acts. In this film I got the opportunity to: burn my mother in her bed; cut off my brother's head; strangle my wife; kill three servants; slip through secret passages behind the library bookcases; wear an outfit that looked like something out of *The Shadow;* move around the house for an entire hour and a half with the audience unaware that I was the villain. At the end, when I'm found out, there's a tremendous battle in a quicksand bog, and I sink in it, and die.

Every fantasy, every dream, every kind of horror story that I ever imagined as a young man, I got to act out in one movie.

This film has become a minor classic in that it plays on network television, in almost every major city in America, on Halloween — usually about two o'clock in the morning. I've had friends call me up from San Francisco, New Orleans, Mexico City, and say, "Oh, Roy, what I'm watching on my TV set! It's just terrific! And look at how young you look, how strange!"

This turkey has haunted me for fifteen years.

WALTON'S WHEELS
Readying the Orient Express

Solomon Hastings

The murder weapon, a small gaudy dagger purchased at a bazaar in Istanbul, lies forgotten in the prop room at Elstree Studios outside London. Some of the authentic fittings, doors and washbasins, have been incorporated into a research museum opened in London by film producer Richard Goodwin. But Hercule Poirot's monogrammed cane is now in the Manhattan apartment of Tony Walton, production and costume designer for the 1974 film version of Agatha Christie's *Murder on the Orient Express.*

When director Sidney Lumet initially approached Walton, he asked, "How would you like to have a holiday?" He gave the impression, says Walton, that the producers Goodwin and John Brabourne were planning "a small, Ealing comedy — a *Lavender Hill Mob* kind of film, with Alec Guinness, perhaps, as Poirot." Only later did Lumet decide that since they were handling a bit of "high-class fluff," they should pull out all the stops and create a really glamorous Thirties epic with the Betelgeuses of the film world.

Walton, who usually takes about a year to complete his work on a major film, was amused upon release of the film to find that most people assumed he had simply used the real train for the interiors. In fact, with Lumet and Goodwin, he had extensively researched the project in train museums and warehouses in Paris, Ostend and Istanbul, then created the interiors, with much heightened detail, on the Elstree Studio stages.

Using the original metric plans and elevations loaned to him by the Wagon-Lits company, Walton combined existing panels from the Ostend train graveyard with much freshly constructed material to create the exaggerated aura of "movie" glamour demanded by Lumet.

Lalique panels and cast-iron luggage racks were borrowed and copied. Improper but evocative varieties of upholstery were selected and installed. Floral motifs and splendid glass lamps were added in the interests of glamour rather than accuracy. A studio signwriter, who had painted many variations on Thirties travel posters for the film, was assigned the task of painting minutely detailed wood inlays all along the newly built train corridor panels.

This interest in fanciful detail was carried

As for an authentic villain, the real thing, the absolute, the artist, one rarely meets him even once in a lifetime. The ordinary bad hat is always in part a decent fellow.

The South of France
COLETTE

through to such items as a bullet ring for Poirot. Because Poirot's limp is an integral part of his make-up, Walton created the brass ring with, supposedly, the shell of the bullet which had lamed the great detective. Such curios were indeed popular during the period, and Albert Finney, Poirot's portrayer, gamely wore it despite continually having to clean a creeping green stain from his finger.

According to Walton, location shooting involved one day of filming exteriors at a ferry in Istanbul (the ferry interior was constructed in the Elstree Studio). Prior to that, the production crew had gone to Pont d'Arles on the Swiss border to shoot the scene where the train gets stuck in the snow. Although the film company had been assured there was always snow in that area at that time of year, there was none when they arrived. Indeed, there had been no snow for weeks. In one of those rare moments that make one feel God must love the movies, there was a record blizzard the night before the scene was to be shot.

The Istanbul Hotel dining room was recreated in the Finsbury Park Cinema tea room in London because it had appropriately Hollywood-Moorish-Deco architecture in which the film company's golden palm trees and "fountain" railings looked at home. The Istanbul station was built in an engine shed outside Paris — as the proper engine could not be brought to England because of the difference between English and Continental rail gauges.

All other interiors were shot at Elstree, where snowscape panoramas were painted on enormous translucent rear-projection screens to simulate the specific type of glaring light that one would get if one were stuck in a snowbank.

Designing the costumes in London created problems because of fabric shortages. One piece of silk for actress Jacqueline Bisset's gown — the one worn in the film's climactic scene — was promised daily by the French manufacturer, but he, unlike God, failed to deliver. Miss Bisset ended up wearing what was in actuality the pattern for the proposed dress, stenciled with a design from Walton's scarf to look as presentable as possible.

At the London Royal Gala premiere of the film, Dame Agatha, by this time in poor health, put aside her wheelchair and stood in line for the formal presentation to the Royal Family. The producer's mother, the dowager Lady Brabourne, herself a ramrod-erect octogenarian, was unimpressed by Dame Agatha's royal curtsy: "Not a very good eighty, is she?"

Solomon Hastings is the pseudonym of a shy, wealthy, busy theatrical costume designer.

"THE KING OF TRAINS AND THE TRAIN OF KINGS"

The Orient Express ran for the last time on May 17, 1977.

It ran for the first time on June 1, 1889.

The train from Paris to Istanbul (the former Constantinople) took three days and passed through Vienna, Budapest, Belgrade and Sofia. In 1906 a new rail tunnel between Switzerland and Italy shortened the trip by twelve hours, but the train no longer stopped at Vienna and Budapest.

During World War I and World War II the train did not run, no matter how many spy stories would have you believe the contrary.

In March of 1953 day coaches were added to the train.

According to the Associated Press, the final journey took two and one-half days and a first-class sleeper ticket for one person cost $375.

If everybody who swore they'd ridden on the train actually had, the train probably would not have had to shut down.

Wagon-Lits ashtray from the Orient Express in which the burnt paper clue was discovered.

GREENSTREET AND LORRE

Could you love a man who's grossly overweight, who walks like a finicky water buffalo, or another one who quivers in a perpetual state of terror, whose eyes resemble two soulful fried eggs? Yes, of course. Indeed, Sidney Greenstreet and Peter Lorre were (and remain) the world's favorite Terrible Twosome. Most famous as Joel Cairo (Lorre) and Max Gutman (Greenstreet) in *The Maltese Falcon*, the Twosome represented consummate villainy, deceit, double-dealing and danger to generations of moviegoers.

Traveling companions. Greenstreet reads Pearls of Wisdom *while Lorre questions him on it in* The Mask of Dimitrios.

A rueful Lorre and an elegant (even in death) Greenstreet in The Mask of Dimitrios.

THE MACGUFFIN MAN

Peter J. Schuyten

The door opened. I fancied I could hear the strains of Gounod's *Funeral March of a Marionette*. I would not have been surprised if the first words out of his mouth had been, "Good evening, ladies and gentlemen. Tonight's program . . . "

Instead, he offered a simple, almost shy, "Hello, how are you?"

Actually, I was fine, considering I was in the presence of the man who in less than a minute of filmmaking had kept me out of the shower for the better part of a month. I was all right, considering I was in the same room with the man Truffaut called "an artist of anxiety" and placed on a par with Dostoevsky, Kafka and Edgar Allan Poe.

Alfred Hitchcock has probably terrified more people, more artistically, than anyone else in the history of movies. And he has done it, as Hitchcock aficionados well know, without showing any violence on screen. "I made *Psycho* in black and white for one reason," he said. "So I wouldn't have to show blood. It would have been repulsive to show that girl being stabbed in the bath with all that blood running down the drain. In fact, you never did see the knife touch Janet Leigh's body. It was all impressionistic. There were seventy-eight cuts in that forty-five-second scene, and each one was sketched out in advance. The blood, by the way, was Hershey's chocolate syrup."

Another technique he uses to horrify moviegoers is called by Hitchcock "the subjective." "Take the car-out-of-control scene in *Family Plot*. Most people don't realize that most chase scenes are shown objectively. In other words, the audience is on the sidewalk. Cars may race, bash against each other, jackknife and collide, but it's all shown from the distance. Not in *Family Plot*. The first two or three shots show the girl saying to George, 'Slow down, will you. Slow down.' I showed her viewpoint which included the windshield and the dashboard. But as the car's speed increased, I went from her face to her viewpoint again — this time without the windshield and dashboard — because if you were experiencing the same thing, you wouldn't be looking at them, either. You wouldn't even see the hood. All you would be looking at would be the road ahead. I put the audience in the character's place, or what I call the 'subjective.' The best subjective picture I ever made was *Rear Window*. There you had a man, James Stewart, looking out the window. The camera showed what he saw, then cut back to him for his reaction. That doesn't happen in the theater, and an author can only try to describe it in a book, but the screen is the way true

---

MR. HITCHCOCK, WHAT'S A MACGUFFIN?

A MacGuffin is a demented red herring. It has no significance whatsoever, except to the characters chasing after it — who are convinced it's terribly important. A MacGuffin can be a sack of jewels, a scheme to take over the world, a piece of paper with writing on it that nobody's ever seen. It is a device that moves a Hitchcock plot along and is not to be taken seriously by anybody but the people who are acting in the movie. And they must have absolute belief in its existence. We, however, know better. Don't we?

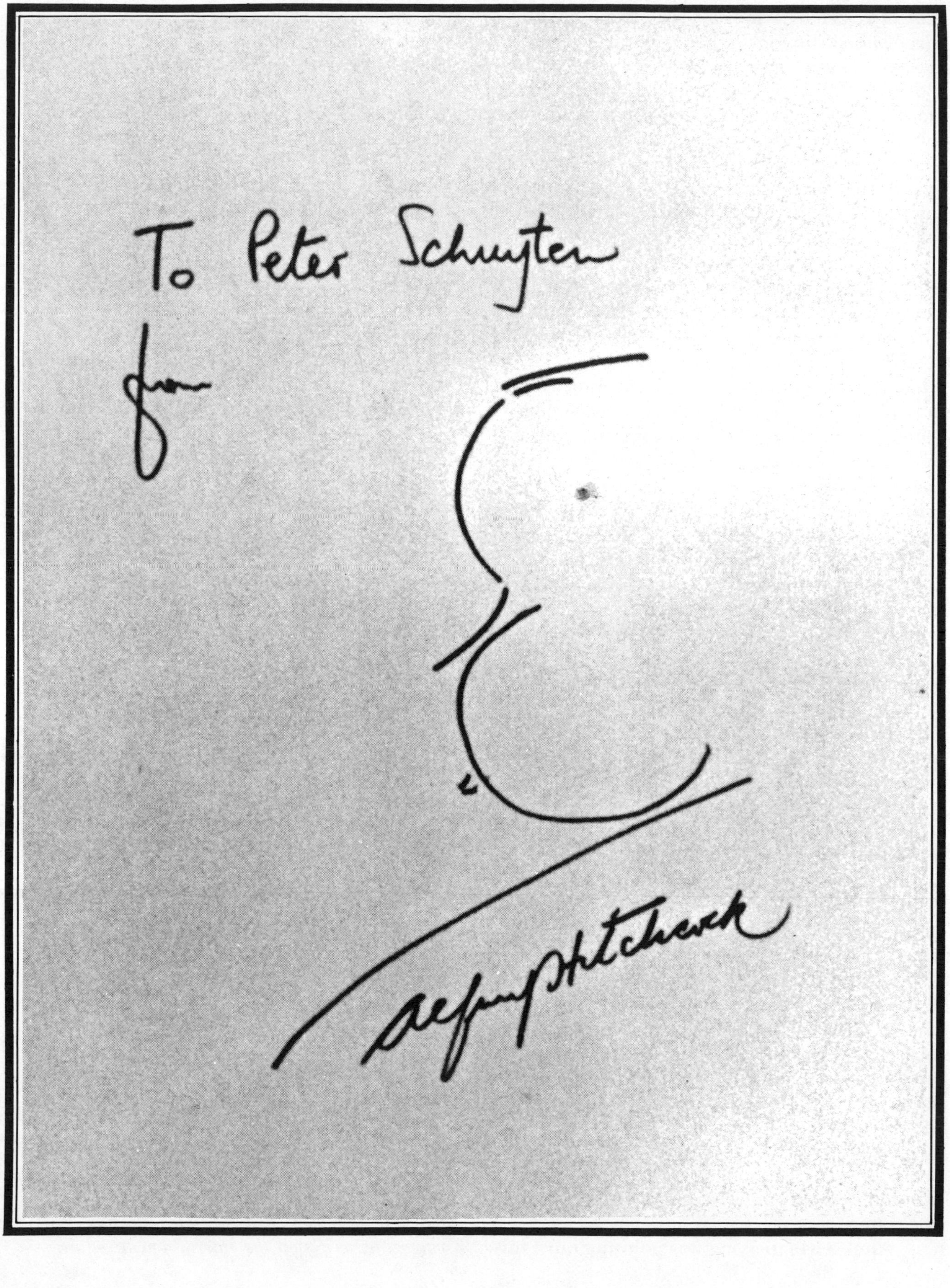

To Peter Schuyten
from

Alfred Hitchcock

subjective can be achieved. It's a combination of three shots: the look; what he sees; how he reacts. *That's* pure cinema."

Hitchcock also specializes in what he calls "journeying" pictures. "They are picaresque jobs. You choose a journey, find out what is on that journey, where it takes you, how you get there and, more importantly, what is interesting on the way. In adventure chase stories you're always building up to something, but I have some very specific rules as to how to do it. For example, Cary Grant in *North by Northwest* gets trapped in an auction room. He can't get out because there are men in front of him and men behind him. The only way out is to do what you'd do in an auction room. Bid. He bid crazily and got himself thrown out. Similarly, when he was chased by a crop duster, he ran and hid in a cornfield. There was one thing that crop duster could do — dust some crops. That drove him out. Using the costume ball in *To Catch a Thief* was much the same idea. I don't believe in going into an unusual setting and not using it dramatically."

One scene Hitchcock wanted to use, he couldn't. It was meant for *North by Northwest.* "I had it all worked out that Cary Grant would slide down Lincoln's nose when he was on Mount Rushmore, then hide in Lincoln's nostril, then have a sneezing fit which gave his position away to his pursuers. It's a shame I was never allowed to do it. The Department of the Interior said that if I used Mount Rushmore, any chase or fight scene had to take place between the heads, not on them. Why? I was told it was a shrine of democracy."

Hitchcock considers *Shadow of a Doubt* his most nearly perfect picture. "I've always said that if you devise a picture on paper, you have achieved 100 percent. In fact, after a script is finished and I have run the whole film in my mind, I wish I didn't have to go and make it, because by the time you finish shooting it you end up with only 60 percent. There are so many complications. Casting is not perfect. You don't always get the right setting. With *Shadow of a Doubt,* however, I had everything. Character. The original small-town setting. There was no compromise anywhere. And that was very satisfying."

Almost as satisfying was pointing out a mis-take to a man who made life difficult for him when he first came to the States back in the Thirties. Says Hitchcock, "I once ran into a very funny situation when Selznick [David O. Selznick, former head of MGM Studios], with great pride, showed me the big scene from *Gone with the Wind.* It was the scene with all the soldiers lying in the station yard and there was this high pull-back showing Vivien Leigh looking for her man. She was wearing a pale violet dress and you could hardly see her. I said, 'David, why didn't you put a red dress on her? When the camera finally reached the high point, all you would have seen was this little red dot.' That shook him. He had never thought of it. Ridiculous not to think of a thing like that. He missed the whole point of the scene entirely. And wouldn't that have made some retake?"

Hitchcock is the consummate detail man. Overseeing everything from red dresses to sneezing noses to Hershey's syrup. Lest you think that leaves him little time to be concerned about people's feelings, let me tell you one more story. A few weeks after our interview, when I was back in New York, I received a large manila envelope in the mail. Postmarked Universal City. Somewhat puzzled, I opened it. As I looked at the drawing, I could again almost hear the strains of Gounod's *Funeral March of a Marionette.* Hitchcock had sent me *his* caricature of the famous Hitchcock caricature. He had drawn it, signed it and inscribed it to me. A very thoughtful man is Mr. Hitchcock. And although I resist the term, I shall always be his fan.

HITCHCOCK UNSURPASSED

The Thirty-Nine Steps (based on the 1915 John Buchan novel).
The Trouble with Harry (based on a 1950 John Trevor Story novel).
Suspicion (based on the 1932 Francis Iles novel *Before the Fact*).

Peter J. Schuyten, an associate editor at Fortune *magazine, writes on the entertainment industry.*

COSMETICS TO MAKE YOU LOOK WORSE

The Make-Up Man's Art

Solomon Hastings

He laughed, recalling how Sidney Lumet came up to him with James Coburn during the filming of *The Last of the Mobile Hot Shots* and barked, "I want him to bleed *here*," indicating the actor's mouth, "*here*," his ears, "and *here*," his nose. "All at once. Can you do it?"

"Sure."

"How?"

"Beat the shit out of him."

He didn't, of course, because Vincent Callahan has been a professional make-up man for twenty-four years, working stage, TV and film, and he has become expert at creating cosmetic mayhem.

In effect, Callahan was supposed to simulate an internal hemorrhage for Coburn. Nothing to it. He ordered spaghetti-sized plastic tubing from a medical supply house, carefully laid it on the actor's face and disguised it with facial hair. The tubing was attached to a squeeze bulb in Coburn's hand. On cue, Coburn squeezed and Callahan's fake blood gushed up, first from the mouth, next from the nose and finally from the ears. Authentic for such a hemorrhage. Ever the perfectionist, Callahan even arranged for a special deep dark blood — the kind that indicates internal bleeding.

How does one go about concocting blood? There are several commercial fake bloods on the market. One called Nextel is manufactured by 3M. But Vince prefers to mix his own. He mushes karo syrup and food coloring together, feeling that he can get a truer color and consis-

I'll go to any mystery movie, or watch practically any detective thriller on the tube, but I never read detective novels. I don't know why that is. Maybe it's a mystery in itself.

My wife reads them though, and so I often buy them for her.

About thirty-five or maybe more years ago Emlyn Williams wrote, directed (I think) and acted in (a dual role) my favorite whodunit flick, The Norwich Mystery. *I have since then never met a soul who's ever heard of it, let alone seen it. It has vanished utterly into the void. You've never heard of it, either. Leaving me a cult of one.*

PETER DE VRIES

tency that way. It also, so he says, wipes off more easily.

Curious about how gunshot wounds are rigged for the camera for such bloodbath scenes as those in *Bonnie and Clyde* and *The Godfather*? Vince's technique entails placing metal plates on the actor's body in the appropriate spots. On each plate, as a sort of sandwich filling, sits a sack of blood which is topped off with an explosive charge of squib. Electrical

HOW TO LOSE A MOVIE FIGHT

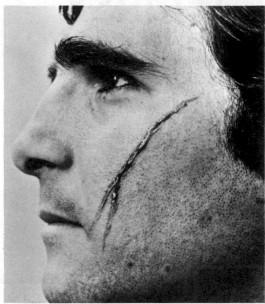

A scar. Drawn with a brown eyebrow pencil, puckered with a thin line of Nuplast, which is then covered with blue-gray eyeshadow, blood, ochre eyeshadow and pancake make-up. Finally, a touch of Gordon Moore's Ruby Red toothpaste, imported from London.

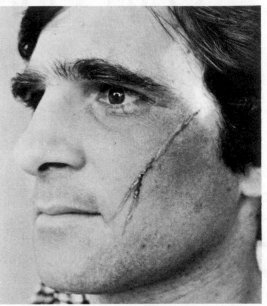

A bad bruise. Sponged on with blue-gray and ochre eyeshadow, highlighted with dark gray pencil. Then, a dab of blood and vibrant peony lipstick.

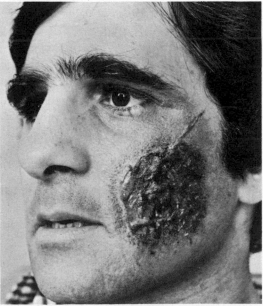

A burn mark. Created by applying Nuplast with a brush, then picking bits away before it hardens completely. Scorch marks added with dark brown shadow. Vaseline added for oozing effect.

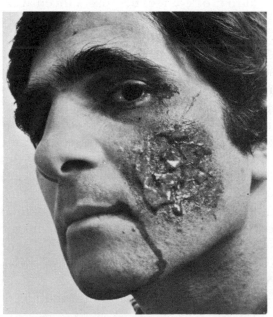

A bloody lip. Karo syrup mixed with food coloring is dribbled from the corner of the mouth. There are several commercial "bloods" on the market, including Nextel from 3M.

wires are attached to the explosive and run down the actor's body, under his costume. They stretch out to a point off camera where, under Callahan's tutelage, they are detonated. Instant carnage.

For *Shamus* one character had to have the back of his head blasted off from close range. A specially shaped plate was constructed that followed the contours of the actor's head. It was camouflaged with a toupee.

When the shooting occurred, the force of the charge was so strong, it threw the actor forward several feet and spattered blood on the lens of the camera. Studio audiences thought the effect was sensational.

Callahan's talent extends far beyond bullets and blood, however. If the wound is to be deeper, such as from an ax sunk into a character's head, Callahan is equal to it. He is fiendishly deft in making a matched dummy which is inserted just before impact. If a body part is to be amputated, he makes a full prosthesis, usually out of plastic, meat and bone. Since there is little or no action required of the victim (except to lie there and be hacked away), it is fairly simple for Callahan to strap the actor's real limb to his body, or bury it in trick holes in the furniture, then secure the prosthesis, cover the join with latex, foam rubber and make-up, and let the villain have a go at it.

For a face that only a gorgon's mother could admire, replete with dewlaps, warts, bashed-in chins and shattered cheekbones, Callahan first makes a cast and then, from that cast, creates a new plastic face for the actor to slip into. Until recently, such casts were made by coating the actor with plaster of Paris, but the heaviness of the plaster usually distorted the actor's features. Callahan now favors a lighter, quicker-drying substance called Monlage. Callahan can't recall any actor looking at himself in one of these horror faces and being appalled, but he did get a violent reaction from an actor who sat for a face cast and discovered in the process he had rampant claustrophobia.

What about burns, bruises, scars? Child's play. A dab of latex, a smear of liquid plastic such as collodium or Tuplast, a soupçon of ordinary face make-up — albeit in Halloween colors — and the actor looks ready for the

SPILLING ONE'S GUTS

Contemplating hara-kiri? Then you'll need a lateral abdominal. Need any other slices, slashes and gashes? Then you must hie yourself to Woodstock, New York, and call upon the Simulaids Company. They are the Michaelangelo of artificial wounds, which they construct to order, to go, out of latex with tubes attached for distributing the blood at the requisite spots. According to Kevin M. Sweeney, the company was founded in 1963 to create visual aids for first-aid instructors. But now and then an order creeps in for a ruptured appendix or a yard or so of perforated intestinal tract from someone other than an educator. Frankly, we did not inquire who he or she might be. And we'd just as soon you didn't tell us.

S.H.

intensive care unit. The trick, Callahan insists, is in observing actual wounds and in mixing make-up colors to conform to reality. New York provides more of a challenge to his imagination than Hollywood, because in New York he must create from scratch while in Hollywood the studios maintain permanent laboratories to crank out cosmetic disasters.

Callahan's life is not totally comprised of making people look like thugs and Frankenstein's progeny. His plushest job was that of East Coast head of make-up and hair for *The Great Gatsby,* and his most satisfying was anything at all that involved George C. Scott. Callahan has worked regularly with Scott for the past fifteen years. His wife, too, is involved in the business, as a hairdresser.

What's the most difficult thing he's ever done? Not blood. Not guts. Not wounds. Not warts. But glamorous make-up for women that will look natural in daylight.

Soloman Hastings is the pseudonym of a famous cosmetic consultant.

TO WALK AMONG SHADOWS

George Baker

Chief Inspector Alleyn looked at the *poinsettia, its top-most flower well above his head, and said "I am amazed." "Dear Br'er Fox" he thought "if you could see the wonders of New Zealand. Palms grow over cool streams, streams cool enough for trout. Can you imagine trout fishing in the blazing sun, standing in the shade of a palm. There are more things in heaven and earth, Br'er Fox."*

The very English Chief Inspector Roderick Alleyn, Scotland Yard, is the creation of Dame Ngaio Marsh, a New Zealander and one of the world's foremost detective story writers.

I was wandering around my house in London wishing a part would be offered that would interest me and stretch me as an actor, and as a bonus take me abroad for a week or two. The phone rang so close upon the wish that I laughed when my agent said, "Would you like to go to New Zealand and play Inspector Alleyn in four television films? Of course, the producer wants the answer yesterday!"

"Say yes," I said.

"Don't you want to read the script?"

"As a formality," I answered.

"Or know what the money is?"

"Naturally."

I couldn't tell her I was quite unable to refuse the part, as it had all the qualifications with which I had endowed my wish. It was Friday afternoon, and we agreed that the scripts should be sent to me by taxi so that I could read them over the weekend and return my answer by Sunday night or Monday morning.

I took *Died in the Wool,* the first book to be filmed, from the shelf and started to reread it. The other titles for filming were *Vintage Murder, Opening Night* and *Colour Scheme.*

I was delighted with Inspector Alleyn and his faithful subordinate, Inspector Fox. Unfortunately, Fox does not appear in these particular books, but Alleyn often speaks to him in thoughtful soliloquy.

"And St. John Acroyd," he says in *Vintage Murder.* "There, my dear old Inspector Foxy, a subject fit for you and me. A stock comedian, a funny man with a funny face, and unless I am much mistaken, a mean disposition." And with those few words Alleyn sets up another suspect and the reader has another clue for the Dame's crime puzzle.

Now, how to play him? How to play him would by *my* puzzle. What were my clues?

A product of Eton and Balliol, Alleyn entered the Foreign Office before transferring to Scotland Yard. These were the clues to his background. So I deduced that he was a well-bred Englishman of some social standing who had followed a conventional pattern through to his thirties. He broke away from these conventions when he transferred to Scotland Yard. It was Dame Ngaio's genius to create a professional policeman who also carried the mores of his amateur rivals Lord Peter Wimsey and Father Brown — breeding and education. Inspector Alleyn married an exceptional and gifted wife, Troy. And in that, too, he broke with convention. I had a glimpse of a man whose mind and interests were at variance with his social upbringing.

I carefully dressed him in the tweeds and brogues of the period. If anything, I made the clothes more severe and reserved than they need have been in order to give myself the opportunity to contrast the exterior and the interior man. Now, what was I going to use to aid me in bringing out Roderick Alleyn's humour?

Through her extraordinary gift of drawing character, the Dame lets the reader catch glimpses of Roderick Alleyn's humour. For an actor, thoughts are communicated through the mind and through the eye. I invented a pair of half-spectacles for Alleyn to frame that humour which would not be spoken.

It was all very well for me to have these thoughts, but I hadn't yet met the producer and was by no means yet on my way to New Zealand to appear as Chief Inspector Roderick Alleyn.

My agent set up a meeting with John McRea, the producer. We agreed to lunch at the Cumberland Hotel, London, on Monday morning. Since my wife and I were then rehearsing a recital I had compiled of scenes from Shakespeare, the interview had to be snappy so that I could get back to the rehearsals in good time. I parked my bicycle with the porter of the hotel and went in. John McRea introduced himself and offered me a pre-lunch drink. After being served, I said, "If you're offering the part, I'd like to play it."

"I'm offering the part."

"Right," I said, "when do we start?"

"I want you to be ready to fly out in two weeks' time."

Our recital was scheduled for eight performances on a ten-day tour. That would leave four days for putting together the year's accounts and making all the arrangements for a trip of five months' duration. Well, why not? I agreed to do it.

On 14th March I flew to Auckland, New Zealand, via Singapore. Inspector Alleyn grew on me more and more as I travelled the 13,000 miles to play him. I re-read *Opening Night* and *Vintage Murder,* and became more and more convinced that the Inspector's humour was going to be the most pleasurable factor in the part and the most difficult to convey.

THE MURDER GAME

Roderick Alleyn debuted in 1934 in *A Man Lay Dead.* The Chief Inspector was called in to investigate a murder that occurred during a weekend house party. Sir Hubert's guests were gathered in the parlour to play "The Murder Game." The lights were turned off while the game was in progress. When snapped back on they revealed a very dead gamesman, his back skewered by a jewelled dagger. Alleyn solved the case. To the best of anyone's knowledge, no one at Sir H.'s ever played the game again.

On arrival at Auckland I was met by John McRea, who took me to the studios to meet the two directors. From the beginning we got on well. Our discussions were pointed with laughter and relaxation. When the costume designer joined us, I realised that we were all on the same wavelength. The feeling of rightness I had had in London was still with me.

So Roderick Alleyn began to prepare himself to step out of the books he had made famous for his creator and make his debut on the screen.

"Dear old Foxkin, the New Zealand countryside is quite breathtaking and the locations found for the four stories are so like the places of imagination our dear author describes, I believe she may have taken a peep or two at reality when she put us into the settings we share. It's all shrewd observation, Foxkin, and knowing human nature. You will forgive me if I go now. The smell of the frangipani wafting past me on the night air as I stand on the verandah makes me suspect foul play in the woolshed . . . indeed Flossie Rubrick may have *Died in the Wool.* I might investigate."

George Baker, in addition to an acting career, has written for the BBC and his The Trial and Execution of Charles I *was performed by the Royal Shakespeare Company.*

AN EERIE RADIO QUIZ

Chris Steinbrunner

All together now, what was it that The Shadow knew? The evil which lurked in the hearts of men, *that's* what he knew. Here are twenty questions on some of the great mystery radio shows of old: programs you may have listened to under the bedcovers so your parents wouldn't hear; programs that (what vanished art!) needed your own imagination to swirl up the atmosphere accompanying those sinister peals of filtered laughter and organ chords; programs that are now like vanished civilizations overrun by jungle, like lands now lost in the mists. Score 5 points for each correct answer and *don't look back* — not until you're finished, that is.

1. *Suspense* in its twenty-year radio life was certainly, as the narrator reminded us each week, "radio's outstanding theater of thrills." For the first few years that narrator had a name — or at least a description. What was it?

2. John Dickson Carr wrote a memorable but short-lived radio series narrated by a ship's doctor about strange crimes in foreign ports of call, actually a spin-off from a celebrated drama he wrote for *Suspense*, a show that was repeated often and called by the same title. What was it?

3. The Shadow is really Lamont Cranston, and only his close friend Margot — that's the official way they spelled it in the scripts — Lane knew to whom the voice of the invisible Shadow belonged. Who was the irascible police official — a continuing character 'in the series — whose mind Lamont often clouded?

4. Carleton E. Morse's *I Love a Mystery* was the greatest radio adventure series of all time, and its trio of heroes — Jack, Doc and Reggie — have joined the immortals. Give the

"Who knows what evil lurks in the hearts of men? The Shadow knows." So began the weekly radio series based on Maxwell Grant's elusive character, who learned how to cloud men's minds while in the mysterious East. Orson Welles was the original radio program narrator.

last names of at least two of the three.

5. Basil Rathbone, who played the role on radio for seven years, *was* Sherlock Holmes. Name at least *two* other actors who have played him before the microphone.

6. What was the relationship between The Lone Ranger and The Green Hornet?

7. The semi-documentary *Gangbusters* was the creation of what famous radio producer (who made a career of fact crime)?

8. Among the earliest spook shows on network radio were *Inner Sanctum*, in which host Raymond swung on the creaking door, and *The Witch's Tale*, featuring blood-chillers told by "Old Nancy, the witch of Salem." What was the name of her wise old cat?

9. *Charlie Wild, Private Eye* succeeded for a time the *Sam Spade* radio slot. How did this detective get his name?

10. *The Man Called X*, perhaps radio's most urbane detective (he was played by Herbert Marshall), hung out in places like Cairo and had sidekicks named, not Mike or Spud, but Pagan Zeldschmidt! If you weren't calling him X, what *would* you call *The Man Called X* . . . his real name, please.

11. For years Jack Armstrong adventured with his adoring Uncle Jim and cousins Betty and Billy. Then, falling under the influence of a reformed criminal turned scientific investigator named Vic Hardy, the all-American boy became an agent of an organization remarkably like the FBI. Name the agency.

12. *Big Town* was a newspaper drama — and a good one. Name the paper which supplied the screamed-out headlines for the show, as well as its crusading editor (first played by Edward G. Robinson).

13. An easy one. Agnes Moorehead appeared on *Suspense* in 1943 in a one-woman show so chilling it became a landmark in radio terror. What was the story (written by Lucille Fletcher)?

14. Remember Nick Carter? A wild rapping on the door . . . a woman's anxious voice: "What is it? What's the matter?" . . . the reply: *Another case for Nick Carter, Master Detective!* Who, then, was *Chick* Carter?

15. Out of the fog, out of the night and into his American adventures stepped which famed British hero making a most unlikely transatlantic transition?

16. *Tired of the everyday world? Ever dream of a life of romantic adventure?* Thus opened a thriller-series that was the best of its kind, bringing us such classic settings as a lighthouse swarming with rats and a department store where mannequins came to life at night. What was the show's one-word name?

17. Jack Webb is best known as police sergeant Joe Friday of *Dragnet*. But Webb was the hero of several other crime shows. Name at least one.

18. *The Whistler* was always giving you a little tune while he told you the most grotesque stories, and on *Lights Out* the weird narrator was always ordering you into darkness. But where were you always running into *The Mysterious Traveler* as he kept telling you those really queasy reminiscences?

19. Just by sending in a label from the sponsor's product you got Captain Midnight's decoder and other crime-fighting devices. These allowed you to personally assist in the Captain's struggle against the international menace of superspy Ivan Shark and become a member of "The Secret Squadron." What was the well-known product?

20. *Yours Truly, Johnny Dollar*, the adventures of an insurance investigator, was the last continuing-hero mystery series to leave radio. What weekly activity on Johnny's part formed the basis for each show?

Those are the questions. There are more which come to mind . . . for instance, who answered the desperately troubled souls who wrote to *Box 13*? (Alan Ladd); who played Ellery Queen on radio, stopping just before the solution to allow guest armchair detectives to guess? (Hugh Marlowe, Larry Dobkin, Carleton Young, among others); Basil Rathbone hosted and starred in a mystery series for which cigarette sponsor? (*Tales of Fatima*) But that's for another quiz. Here are the answers to this one, and if you get a fair amount right — nobody can remember *everything* — you get a diploma from the College of Radio Knowledge. . . .

1. He called himself The Man in Black.

2. *Cabin B-13*.

3. Commissioner Weston, played grumpily for many years by Santos Ortega.

4. Jack Packard, Doc Long, Reggie Yorke. Bless all three of 'em!

5. Orson Welles, William Gillette, Tom Conway, Richard Gordon, Louis Hector, Ben Wright, John Stanley, John Gielgud — take your pick.

6. The Green Hornet was The Lone Ranger's grandnephew.

7. Phillips H. Lord.

8. She called her cat Satan.

9. His name was a creative reworking of the sponsor's jingle: "Get Wildroot Creme Oil, Charlie."

10. X signed his name "Ken Thurston." He was a detective.

11. The S.B.I. (Scientific Bureau of Investigation).

12. Hard-hitting Steve Wilson was editor of *The Illustrated Press*.

13. *Sorry, Wrong Number.*

14. Chick was Nick's adopted son, who had a weekday afternoon series all his own in which he *never* talked to his dad.

15. Bulldog Drummond, who on American radio was very un-Sapperish.

16. *Escape*. The two stories mentioned, "Three Skeleton Keys" (the lighthouse) and "Evening Primrose" (John Collier's department store), were oft-repeated favorites.

17. Jack Webb was also the star of a great private-eye series, *Pat Novak for Hire*, as well as such mystery shows as *Jeff Regan* and *Johnny Modero, Pier 23*.

18. On a commuter train. ("Oh? You have to get off here? What a pity. . . .")

19. Chocolate-flavored Ovaltine.

20. Itemizing his expense account, the detailed explanation of each expenditure unfolding the story. And when all the expenses were totaled, it was "End of report . . . yours truly, Johnny Dollar."

Chris Steinbrunner, while still in high school, sold a radio script to The Shadow.

Sorry, Wrong Number, *which starred Agnes Moorehead in a virtuoso solo performance, was based on the novel of the same name by Lucille Fletcher.*

COURTESY RCA

FOGHORNS, FOOTSTEPS, GUNSHOTS, A SCREAM

The Noisy Memories of a Radio Effects Man

Chris Steinbrunner

The radio sound effects man is as archaic as the blacksmith. But Barney Beck remembers when. In a wildly pioneering past he was, for nearly every radio show you can think of, the man of a million sounds — a master of sound effects. And for radio in its heyday, that was *it* . . . no one was more important, more needed, more creative. *He* was the one who set the stage, painted the scenery, built the mood and provided the leitmotif: the creaking door of *Inner Sanctum;* the mournful train whistle ushering in *I Love a Mystery;* the foghorn and footsteps which were *Bulldog Drummond;* the pounding on the door which started each new case for *Nick Carter.* Actors were often interchangeable, but a sound effects genius was the cornerstone of the radio mystery show. Did not Agnes Moorehead hold hands with her sound man on *Suspense* just before the start of her (and his) classic performance in *Sorry, Wrong Number* — not *during* the show because a sound man on duty needs at least eight hands, all of them free — and did not the same expert, for the same series, spend three weeks researching the sound of a severed cerebrum for *Donovan's Brain?*

Barney Beck did nearly all the classic programs originating in New York (*and* the repeats staged four hours later for the benefit of the West Coast before the advent of nation-wide hookups): *Ellery Queen, Inner Sanctum, Perry Mason, Casey Crime Photographer* (with its obligatory jazz piano bar music as Casey explained the caper), *The Shadow, Nick Carter, Charlie Chan, True Detective, Official Detective* and countless others. Today, Barney frequently lectures about radio sound at schools and clubs, bringing his effects table and gear with him, simulating once more the 1,000-plus gunshots, fistfights and footfalls which decades ago colored and enriched his art.

According to Barney the first sound effects people to bear the name were a husband-and-wife team asked to set up a department for sound at the old Mutual studios. The husband had been a drummer, and it seemed a logical extention for an expert at drum rolls to provide the mood and effects noise for early radio. Much of what came after was trial and error. In the days of "live" programming, error was often a factor. At the end of a *Shadow* episode, just as Lamont Cranston was summing up, a nervous sound man hit an auto horn by mistake. The quick-witted actor playing Lamont covered the *beep* nicely: "Our friends downstairs are waiting, Margot, but before we go, let me tell you how I figured out this case . . ."

Gunshots, too, presented problems, says Barney. Recorded shots were not favored, as one could always detect the scratch sounds of

SHHH... LISTEN TO THE CORNSTARCH

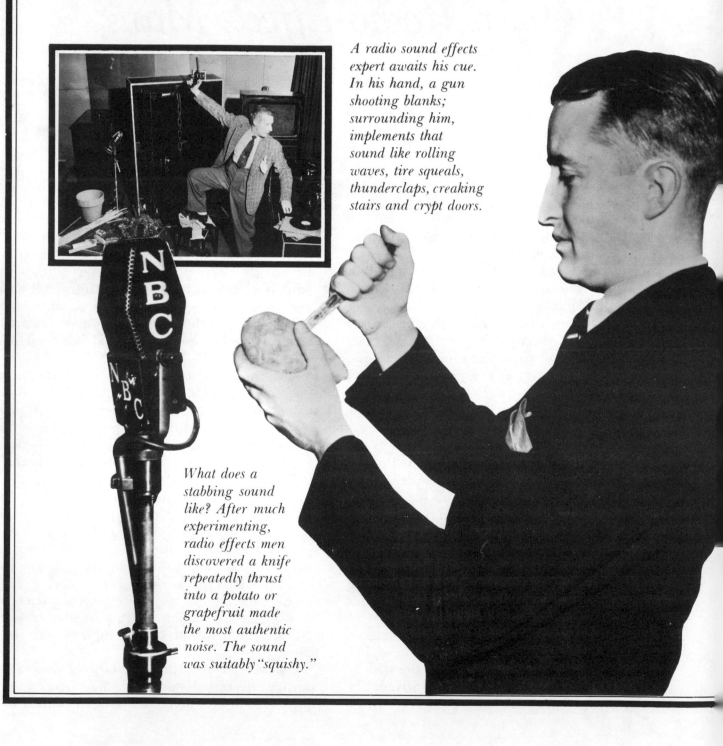

A radio sound effects expert awaits his cue. In his hand, a gun shooting blanks; surrounding him, implements that sound like rolling waves, tire squeals, thunderclaps, creaking stairs and crypt doors.

What does a stabbing sound like? After much experimenting, radio effects men discovered a knife repeatedly thrust into a potato or grapefruit made the most authentic noise. The sound was suitably "squishy."

Whacking an ordinary household sponge duplicated a good right to the jaw, a left to the chin.

When a script called for a cold night wind to whistle through the undergrowth as the murderer slunk past, the effects man reached for his wheat stalks and shook vigorously. Thousands of radio listeners became too terrified by this ominous rustling sound to switch stations.

If the program was set on a snowy February night and the victim had to go outside to check if the telephone wires had been cut, it was the sound man's job to create his footsteps. The crunch was nothing more than a squeeze of cornstarch.

the grooves and the shots could never seem to be cued up properly. So the sound effects man stood by, a gun loaded with blanks in each hand — just in case the first revolver would not go off. (There have been cases on record where neither gun functioned. The nimble actor who switched murder weapons — "Lucky I had this *knife*" — is definitely not aprocryphal.) During an opulent special production of the life of Lincoln, the gun jammed during the fatal scene at Ford's Theater. The fast-thinking sound man dashed to the studio orchestra — it was a *big* show — and struck the timpani, which gave off a reverberating sound like a shot and then some. "That's the first time," the director hissed at him afterward, "Lincoln was assassinated by cannon!"

To prevent malfunctions of this nature, sound effects men in radio's Golden Age generally worked in pairs, but on such lesser-budget shows as *Nick Carter* or *Bulldog Drummond* one man — namely, Barney — did all, and he was generally *very* busy. He learned by experience. And innovated. One show called for the steady drip of a Chinese water torture: actual water just didn't sound right; pebbles dropped on a piece of cloth were better. To simulate the police breaking down a door, Barney twisted and crushed a fruit basket. How was *Inner Sanctum*'s squeaking door — the most classic of all radio mystery sounds — achieved? By Barney's slowly pressing on the back of a noisy swivel chair. Week after week. Honest.

Sound effects men were sometimes carried away by their work. Fistfights, a radio crime show staple, were orchestrated by sound men punching the palms of their hands in unison with the actors' grunts. Barney remembers one director whose sense of realism was so strong he wasn't satisfied unless the sound effects men *winced* as they hit themselves. An actor was "stabbed" on mike by a knife thrust into a grapefruit; one overenthusiastic sound man managed to stab his own hand. It is to his credit that he did not cry out until the show was over.

The *Shadow* program, endlessly macabre, inspired effects men to some of their proudest achievements. (One of the few perimeters dictated by sound effects was that The Shadow could never talk on the telephone — the electronic filter used for voices on the other end

of the line was also used to suggest The Shadow's invisibility.) Once, Barney was asked to create a complete mad scientist's laboratory. For a bubbling effect, he blew down a straw into a glass of water. More bubbling was gotten by cooking oatmeal on mike — surprisingly grim and loathsome. At one point, Lamont and Margot were to explore a quicksand-filled cellar under the lab. For this, Barney stomped plumbers' suction cups over masses of wet paper towels. The result made the listener think of feet being sucked into oozing mud — a truly grisly effect and, for Barney, a wet one; by the end of the show, he was sopping.

Although it was Barney's mandate to fill the air with sound, he knew how to use silence. Leonard Bass, a director of *Gangbusters*, once told him: "There's nothing more exciting than dead air." An exaggeration, perhaps, but a pause was sometimes as effective as rapid-fire noise. As John Cole, who directed *The Shadow* during the program's Blue Coal zenith, kept telling his casts: "We all know it's pulp. Now let's treat it as if it were a *masterpiece*."

Toward the end of radio drama, an invention came to Barney's attention: a huge sound effects console, incorporating hundreds of tape loops featuring every imaginable noise, to be played like a grand organ. Could push-button technology be grafted to creativity? There was little chance to find out. With the advent of television, drama deserted the radio airwaves.

Of course, there is always a need for special skills, and Barney is kept busy supplying sound for the mini-dramas of radio commercials. And the mystery seems to be making something of a comeback — programs like *The Radio Mystery Theater* are heard cross-country seven days a week. Radio, the great theater of the imagination, can yet provide an alternative to much of television's vapid programming. For sound man Barney Beck, who believes dramatic radio is not dead, just resting, the eerily squeaking door may swing out again. And guess whose hand will be pushing it!

Chris Steinbrunner is co-editor of The Encyclopedia of Mystery and Detection, *winner of a 1976 Mystery Writers of America Edgar.*

Chapter 13
ACCESSORIES AFTER THE FACT

MYSTERY FANS AND THE PROBLEM OF "POTENTIAL MURDERERS"

Edmund Bergler, M.D.

In the course of a psychoanalytic appointment with an attorney, the necessity arose in connection with the interpretation of a dream to trace back his activities during the preceding day. Said the patient ironically: "Oh, yes, I forgot to mention that last evening I was with 800 potential murderers. I saw a gruesome detective story in the movies." "How many murders were involved?" I asked. "Only one," replied the patient. "I don't mean the picture; I am referring to the fascinated spectators." "Why do you call the spectators potential murderers? Aren't you stretching the point, calling every movie fan of detective stories a potential murderer?" I objected. "Of course not. I am completely serious," he replied. "In my humble opinion every fan of movie detective stories, mystery thrillers, and gangster intrigues, and every passionate reader of detective stories, is an inhibited or potential murderer." "And what about you?" was my next objection. "Why did you go to that picture?" The reply was a little irritated: "Because of my psychological interest in the reactions of the spectators. You know it's my profession — I'm a criminal lawyer." He clung to that justification, could not be moved at the moment to analyze his own reactions. This was understandable from the standpoint of his resistance. His whole analysis centered around his inner passivity, and further investigation into his interest in gruesome detective stories

would have brought forth the fact that he used them unconsciously as a pseudo-aggressive defense mechanism against his inner passivity.

His analysis so far had proven that he was inwardly passive and had a strong unconscious feminine identification; he unconsciously warded off the passive tendencies in his defensive fantasy that he was aggressive. There was even the probability that his choice of profession was influenced by such a defense: inner identification with the criminal's miserable situation under the disguise, "I am different and above such nonsense."

A deep impression had been made upon him by the reluctance of one of his clients, a confessed and convicted murderer, to sign a petition for commutation of his sentence from capital punishment to life imprisonment. His client had not been at all grateful for the commutation which my patient had secured for him. He had described another incident in which, during the First World War, a deserter was tried for running away from the hospital. During the court proceedings it was discovered that this was the man's third desertion. From a relatively harmless offense, a capital trial resulted, since in the patient's country a third desertion near (not directly at) the front was punishable by death. The prosecutor tried to "simplify matters" by asking the defendant if he had any objections to the trial. The presiding judge explained to the defendant the significance of the question, and before my patient, the defendant's attorney, could intervene, the defendant waived objections to the trial. Only with great difficulty could my patient force the jury to postpone the trial for the purpose of fact-finding, while his client continued to insist on "getting it over with in a hurry." The patient dwelt upon these and similar cases in his practice continually, stressing the "queerness" of criminals. Having learned about psychic masochism in analysis, he called all of his clients "potential death seekers." Amusingly enough, his understanding did not for a long time stretch to include himself.

The decisive objection to my patient's assumption that detective fans were potential murderers was the analytic knowledge that what appears on the psychic surface, in consciousness, is *never* the unconscious wish, but rather the defense against that wish. All of these clinical and theoretical considerations pointed to the assumption of a basic conflict of passivity in such fans.

Typical Rationalizations

Since the clinical experience described above, I have paid attention to the problem, noting what type of books my patients read, what type of movies they prefer, and to what radio stories they tune in.

1. In nearly all persons interested in "detective stuff," as one patient put it, I could observe a queer objection to love stories. These were declared to be boring. Some patients could not even bear the typical love admixture in detective novels. Because of some schematization, the detective almost invariably falls in love with a girl involved in the murder in some way. The patients had the inner necessity of proving to themselves that they had outgrown the romantic form of love, acknowledging sex only as transitory pleasure and rejecting tenderness in love as unmanly.

2. Every detective story contains open aggression and irony directed against the officials conducting the investigation. The outsider — the private detective — outsmarts the officials. It is likely that unconsciously this aggression also represents the repetition of the child-father situation in reverse: the weak child outsmarts the powerful father. In other words, a childlike fantasy is involved. Rex Stout, the well-known writer of detective fiction, referring to this aggression toward the official police, once stated in a radio discussion that the detective story is a typical product only of democracies, since in authoritarian countries the citizen must respect authority. He corroborated his statement by pointing out the well-known fact that the United States, England, France, and the Scandinavian countries have contributed 90 percent of writers of detective fiction. Stout's assumption is undoubtedly correct. The question remains unanswered, of course, as to why this aggression toward authority is necessary, what it inwardly implies, and why it is so generally enjoyed by detective fans.

The forehead of a quarrelsome and murderous man, according to Phinella and seconded by Spontini. These experts could read the face for ominous personality traits as easily as you read the morning paper.

3. Some of my patients declared that their interest in detective stories was based on their desire to test their ability in drawing correct conclusions. The writer of the thriller gives a few hints or clues, tries to sidetrack suspicion, confuses the issue. Every reader knows that the least suspected and most harmless person in the story has a 95 percent chance of being proven the malefactor, whereas the initially suspected has the same chance of being cleared of suspicion. In other cases the most likely person is the malefactor.

After reading a few hundred books of this sort and concentrating attention on small clues, nearly every reader is capable of solving the majority of cases correctly. Interestingly enough, my patients were often surprised, after the dénouement, at the number of clues they had overlooked. One could not escape the conclusion that *not* arriving at the correct solution was part of the game they unconsciously played with themselves. What the game signified was of course unintelligible from the point of view of their rationalizations.

4. Another rationalization which I encountered claimed that the interest in detective stories centered in the peculiarities of the detective types.[1] The progress of the detective story brought into play different types of detective, constructed with more or less skill. Well, the salad dressing does not make the salad. We will note that point, which is basically without major importance, simply for the sake of being complete.

5. Some patients denied interest in detective fiction specifically, admitting, however, their interest in "thrills" in general. One patient admitted: "I like adventure, spy stories, murder cases, in short, thrill in general. Life is so boring and monotonous, why not imagine that one lives in a wider world, where one can do as one pleases?" He answered my objection that the detective or adventurer could not always do as he pleased with the argument that the *clever* detective or adventurer was practically omnipotent through his cleverness. The reader of the thriller could thus imagine that he was as clever as the hero.

6. The most intelligent rationalization was offered by a young girl patient, who said, "I like mysteries because they are a continuation or substitution of the gruesome fairy tales told me in my childhood. Then I was thrilled and frightened. Today in the movies I am still thrilled but not frightened, consciously at least, since I know it's all a fake. I even make fun of the thrill sometimes by an ironic exclamation during the performance. Perhaps the whole atmosphere of the movies — darkness and seeing something strange — has something to do with it."

We note that all of these rationalizations stress an aggressive or at least teasing element, *none* the passive one.

A Triad of Unconscious Motivations

If, in a mystery thriller, a man commits a murder and a clever detective hunts the killer, there are theoretically two possibilities for the reader: He can identify *temporarily* with the hunted or with the hunter. In terms of rationalization, his "interest" centers in one of them. Behind that "interest" a temporary identification is hidden.

What determines the choice of this identification? Always the *inner need* to express in a roundabout way repressed wishes and defense mechanisms. Of course, we cannot expect the individual to guess correctly the reason for his interest. On the contrary, he must of necessity guess incorrectly, as a part of his defense mechanism. For instance, the criminal lawyer, with whose remarks the article opens, was of the opinion that his interest in detective stories was purely theoretical and psychological — misinterpretation No. 1. He was furthermore of the opinion that all of the spectators were potential murderers — misin-

---

[1]The problem of the different "Watsons," the detective's companion, has been repeatedly discussed. Interesting material is gathered in *Murder for Pleasure* by Howard Haycraft. The first Watson was anonymous; Dupin's companion in Poe's *Murders in the Rue Morgue*, the first detective story, had not even a name of his own. There are historical and technical reasons for keeping alive the detective's "alter ego" in detective fiction, which Haycraft enumerates. Rex Stout believes, for instance, that Conan Doyle's Watson psychologically represents Mrs. Holmes. This may be so. I personally assume that the respective Watsons represent a projected part of the detective's unconscious personality and, in other instances, the reversal of the child-father situation. It is the father now pushed into the role of the admirer. Watson's famous "Excellent" and Holmes' condescending reply, "Elementary, Watson," point in that direction. On the other hand, many variations of the Watson problem have

been introduced; for instance, the ironic Watson representing unconsciously the ironic superego doubting the child's ability. Basically, every detective story contains the father-son conflict, symbolized, perpetuated, and projected ad infinitum. This is visible in the problem itself (". . . the detective story is at bottom one thing only: a conflict of wits between criminal and sleuth" — Haycraft, *loc. cit.*), furthermore in the aggression toward the official police and, last but not least, in the respective Watsons. On different levels the old fight stemming from childhood is perpetuated; the child is victorious — hence the detective outsmarts the criminal and the official police.

The unconscious reasons leading to that superficial triple "aggression" cannot be discussed here without discussing the psychology of writers' unconscious in general. (See my paper, *A Clinical Approach to the Psychoanalysis of Writers. Psychoan. Rev.*, 1944)

THE MURDER INK OPINION POLL

Mystery readers on average are between twenty-five and thirty-five years old, claim to have a college degree and are employed as (in order of frequency) lawyers, copywriters, schoolteachers, librarians, and homemakers.

They read three books per week, although this number swells during the summer, the Christmas season and vacation periods, and diminishes during March, April and September.

They consider Penguin the best mystery book publisher.

Their favorite English author is Dorothy L. Sayers.

Their favorite American author is Raymond Chandler, with Rex Stout running a close second.

Those subscribing to *Ellery Queen's Mystery Magazine* also subscribe to a mystery book club.

Given the opportunity to invent a code name for themselves, the women overwhelmingly picked Irene Adler and the men chose Old Bailey. No one picked 007.

According to them, a cat burglar's kit should include: a loid; a gunnysack; skeleton keys; a flashlight; a black leotard; glass cutters; suction cups; a rope ladder; a lawyer's telephone number; fur balls.

They described a police blotter as having: Trixie's address and phone and measurements in the upper left-hand corner; pizza and beer stains; attempts to solve the *Daily News* puzzle; drawings of a particularly lewd nature; the best graffiti in town.

Most admitted they had been duped into buying duplicates because of title changes, but cover changes did not seem to bother them.

Authors' names they had the most difficulty in pronouncing: Sjöwall and Wahlöö, Ngaio Marsh, Julian Symons, Dashiell Hammett (in that order).

Without exception they preferred books with a continuing character. The reason most often cited was, it saved the reader the trouble of getting to know new people. Also mentioned: They like to watch the character mature, to grow up with them.

They felt the murderer usually turned out to be: the least likely suspect; the doctor.

Their favorite fictional blunt instrument was a frozen leg of lamb.

Their favorite fantasy blunt instrument was: a train; a toeshoe; a hanging plant; a frying pan; a small bronze statue; a candlestick; a wedgie; a croquet mallet; a typewriter; a magnum of champagne.

As fit punishments for those who reveal the endings of mysteries, they suggested: forcing them to read science fiction; forcing them to reread Agatha Christie; forcing them to read mysteries whose last three pages had been torn out. They were also partial to death by misadventure and adhesive tape across the mouth.

Over half of the respondents had tried to write a mystery themselves or were planning to.

Method of polling: One thousand questionnaires were randomly distributed to customers of the Murder Ink Bookstore during March, April and May of 1977. Seven hundred twenty-one responses were either left in the store or mailed in to the editor of *Murder Ink*, who tabulated the results by a highly unscientific method she will reveal to no one.

terpretation No. 2. Forced to admit that he was as much involved in the thrillers via identification as the persons he would observe, he confessed to a "streak of cruelty" in his make-up — misinterpretation No. 3. The idea that he and the other spectators identified with the victim, that they unconsciously enjoyed psychic masochistic pleasure of passivity and being overwhelmed, never occurred to him. It was difficult, not only to convince him of his own passivity, but to make him understand that his "potential murderers" were also using *pseudo*-aggression only as a defense.

This passivity explains all of the aggressive conscious rationalizations. It has already been stressed that the six previously mentioned rationalizations had one common denominator — aggression. The problem is only whether this aggression was genuine or an unconscious defense against the opposite tendency, namely, passivity. I am of the opinion, gained from clinical experience, that the latter was the case.

Our conclusion so far is that the mystery fan unconsciously enjoys passivity and appeases his inner conscience with pseudo-aggression. He enjoys, via unconscious identification, not the killing but the being mistreated or killed, on the condition that even his pseudo-aggression be only a game.

This inner passivity explains, by the way, why the reader or spectator of mysteries is so often fooled. He does not connect the clues because he wants to be overwhelmed. Intellectual solution of the riddle would diminish his unconscious pleasure, so he gladly sacrifices logical thinking.

Is *unconscious enjoyment of passivity* the only element which makes up the mystery fan? Of course not. There are two other elements of prime importance: *enjoyment of uncanniness* and *voyeuristic enjoyment of the forbidden*. These three elements of the forbidden are a triad producing the mystery fan. The last two elements need some explanation.

Freud pointed out in his paper "The Uncanny" that the feeling of uncanniness is of two types. One is that produced when an impression revives repressed infantile complexes; the other, when the primitive beliefs we

The forehead of a man destined to die a violent death. If someone of your acquaintance has a similarly shaped forehead, be kind. Someone's going to get him.

have surmounted seem once more to be confirmed. Says Freud:

> Let us take the uncanny in connection with the omnipotence of thoughts, instantaneous wish-fulfilment, secret power to harm, and the return of the dead. The condition by means of which the feeling of uncanniness arises here is unmistakable. We – or our primitive forefathers – once believed in the possibility of these things. . . As soon as something actually happens in our lives which seems to support the old discarded beliefs, we get a feeling of the uncanny; and it is as though we were making a judgment something like this: 'So, after all, it is true that one can kill a person by merely desiring his death!' or, 'Then the dead do continue to live and appear before our eyes on the scene of their former activities!'

In continuation of Freud's paper, which appeared in 1919, and in application of his newer formulations on anxiety in his book *The Problem of Anxiety*, I could show in *The Psychoanalysis of the Uncanny*[2] that we are dealing in the specific case of uncanniness with an anxiety-signal, warning the subject of some inner danger. That danger is experienced when the feeling of omnipotence of infancy seems to have returned. But at first glance it is not obvious why the dearest belief of our childhood — our own omnipotence — should

[2] Int. J. Psychoan. (London), 1934, XV, pp. 215-244.

suddenly have become terrifying upon its reappearance. The explanation is this. The original sense of omnipotence was "knocked out" of the child, in the last resort, by his dread of castration. With the recrudescence of the old omnipotence-wishes the old castration anxiety is also revived. The sense of the uncanny represents a saving in anxiety and psychic work. In my opinion, this anxiety signal at the approach of inner danger from the aggressive instinct is a characteristic of the uncanny. The danger apprehended is condensed within the infantile ideas of grandeur. What we observe clinically in uncanniness is, however, *not* the aggression, but the sexualization of the aggression turned like a boomerang against the person himself because of guilt — *psychic masochism.*

If we apply the results of such studies to the mystery fan, we find that he enjoys uncanniness with all of its masochistic consequences. In other words, he resuscitates childlike megalomania via identification with the "omnipotent and omniscient" detective, criminal, or adventurer. But it is only *historically* correct to speak of identification with the murderer because of resuscitation of one's own omnipotence. What *actually* happens is only enjoyment of masochistic-passive drives, even

A woman's forehead marked with lines of adultery and mendacity. If she becomes a victim, you won't have to ask why; it's as plain as the forehead on her face.

in the feeling of uncanniness. Were real aggression enjoyed by the mystery fan, he *would never experience the feeling of uncanniness,* which is the secondary and masochistic elaboration. Since the feeling of uncanniness is typical in the reading of thrillers, no real aggression can be involved.

Another very justifiable objection might be raised. Do not people have enough real and original aggressions? Why could not an aggressive reader identify with the murderer because of his aggressive deed? The answer depends on an understanding of the criminal psyche. I believe that the criminal is not at all the embodiment of aggression, but uses a *pseudo*-aggressive defense mechanism. He represents a specific case of failure to overcome the oral disappointment, and one unique in its specific "solution." The feelings of pre-oedipal disappointment in the mother and helplessness to take revenge for this disappointment force the criminal into his herostratic act. His situation is that of a dwarf fighting a giant who refuses to take cognizance of his fight. The only way he can show his intention to take revenge is, so to speak, by using dynamite. That tendency to take revenge, projected upon society, is coupled with self-intended punishment; only unconscious anticipation of punishment makes crime possible for the criminal, since it appeases his inner conscience. In every criminal action two factors are involved, a constant one and a variable one. The *constant* factor ("mechanism of criminosis") explains the motor act, the real conundrum in crime. It is based on the masochistic attempt to overcome the feeling of helplessness stemming from pre-oedipal orality, mentioned above. The *variable* factor pertains to the psychologic contents of the specific crime; it must be determined in every specific case, and is as multitudinous as human motivations in general. In my opinion, the social factors in crime play a relatively subordinate role. In the majority of cases they are rationalizations for hidden unconscious motives or the hitching point for masochistic repetition of injustices experienced in reality or fantasy in the child-mother-father relationship, afterward projected and perpetuated masochistically

The forehead of a man destined to be wounded in the head. (Phinella does not indicate whether by blunt instrument, dumdum bullet or quick flick of a knife.)

upon society or the social order in general.

At this point an interesting fallacy must be looked into. Since, genetically, crime has its roots in deepest pre-oedipal passivity and the enjoyment of mystery thrillers also seems to indicate unconscious passivity, what is the distinction between the criminal and the crime reader? It would seem that the pessimistic criminal lawyer was on the right track after all. The fallacy of this reasoning is easily made apparent. These two types of passivity are genetically completely dissimilar. The *pre-oedipal* (oral) passivity of the criminal and the passivity of the mystery fan are different from each other. The *phenomonology* in itself — passivity — does not automatically give any clue to the *genetic* basis. That and that only is the pivotal point. The idea that seeing or reading a mystery thriller induces murder is *not* based on genetic facts. True, it is sometimes given as a rationalization by a murderer. It results from a misunderstanding of crime in general and of the power of the mystery thriller in particular, giving the latter an enhancement it by no means deserves.

The third decisive element of the triad is the voyeuristic enjoyment of the forbidden. We recall the statement of the young girl, which refers to two facts. First, even as a child she enjoyed gruesome fantasies of being over-whelmed; second, she identified the "mystery" in the thrillers with other mysteries which she wanted to solve as a child. Then the mysteries were in connection with sex; she wanted to know what her parents were doing during the night. (It is not by chance that mystery and night are unconsciously associated.) The fact that later in the life of mystery fans the mysteries pertain in general to murder can be explained by the sadistic misconceptions children have about sex and, furthermore, by the creation of a defense alibi in which aggression is substituted for sexual wishes. In other words, the interest in sex is shifted and masked; the sex problem is replaced by an aggressive conundrum. I have had the opportunity to check on this assumption; clinical experience has proved its validity.

The criminal lawyer mentioned previously was of the opinion that all of these facts proved that every human being was a potential murderer, who enjoyed his murderous tendencies in disguise via the gangster or detective thriller. Such a view seems pure nonsense. It is based on a misunderstanding of the genetic reasons for crime in general. What these facts do prove is the *enormous amount of inner passivity in people.* Since, in seeing or reading a thriller, this inner passivity can be enjoyed with two face-saving alibis ("I am aggressive" and "The whole thing is only a game"), the attraction is irresistible to some, especially since it is coupled with enjoyment of childlike megalomania resuscitated by the appearance of the uncanny.

These millions of mystery fans do not represent the reservoir of "potential murderers" but are, criminologically speaking, harmless. These people get temporary release of their tension vicariously. Of course, the whole process is unconscious.

The late Edmund Bergler, M.D., was a psychoanalyst in New York and the author of twenty-five books and more than 300 professional papers. This article appeared in The Selected Papers of Edmund Bergler, M.D. *and in* The American Journal of Orthopsychiatry. *Abridged and reprinted by permission of the Edmund and Marianne Bergler Psychiatric Foundation.*

SIMENON, APOLLO AND DIONYSUS
A Jungian Approach to the Mystery

John Boe, Ph.D.

At night, before going to bed, Carl Jung liked to read mystery stories. The great psychologist explained this habit rather simply: The stories were absorbing enough to keep him from thinking too deeply and losing sleep, yet not so fascinating that he was unable to turn them aside after a few pages. And like so many of us, he loved to read about *other* people's problems. He was especially fond of Georges Simenon's mysteries ("C.G. Jung's Library," by M.L. von Franz in *Spring* 1970).

By considering Simenon we can gain a deeper understanding of Jung and the mystery. Simenon's first detective novel was *Maigret and the Enigmatic Lett*. It is here that he first defined his central character, Inspector Maigret. Maigret triumphs not through intellect or courage, but through a psychological understanding of the criminal, built out of sympathetic feeling and, above all, intuition. Simenon emphasizes the "kind of intimacy" that always grows up between detective and criminal, who for weeks and months concentrate almost entirely upon each other. Maigret finally solves this mystery (which involves a schizophrenic twin) by studying old photographs and finding out childhood secrets. He solves the case by looking for the *human* factor that shows through the criminal. In this case Maigret reminds us of a psychoanalyst searching for the childhood secrets of a schizophrenic. And when

Maigret finds the key to the mystery, he doesn't bring the criminal before the law but allows him the dignity of suicide.

In *Maigret's First Case*, Maigret reveals his own childhood secret: he used to imagine a sort of combination doctor and priest who, "because he was able to live the lives of every sort of man, to put himself inside everybody's mind," is able to be a sort of "repairer of destinies." Then, later in life, Maigret is forced to abandon his medical studies and finds himself, almost by accident, becoming a policeman.

Jung (like a detective or novelist) was himself a sort of combination doctor and priest, working with others' destinies, using his capacity to put himself inside another's mind

The study of crime begins with the knowledge of oneself.

The Soul of Anaesthesia
The Air-Conditioned Nightmare
HENRY MILLER

Sigmund Freud, age eight, with his father. Prof. Dr. Freud enjoyed a good mystery, particularly those written by Dorothy L. Sayers. (Jung preferred the work of Simenon.)

more than his superior intelligence. Thus, between patient and doctor as between detective and criminal, there can occur a "participation mystique," an unconscious bond. This involves what Jung calls relativization of the ego: If the ego can abandon its claim to absolute power, the psyche can open up to the unconscious within and the unconscious without (in the form of other people's psyches). In *Maigret and the Hundred Gibbets*, Maigret can address the assembled suspects and not need to finish his sentences. They know what he means even when he doesn't speak: "It was as if they could hear what he was thinking." Insofar as Maigret and Jung rely upon their unconscious, upon their intuition, they act without specific theory or technique. Jung denied being a Jungian, and Maigret is almost embarrassed when younger policemen want to observe his "methods."

Like a detached analyst, Inspector Maigret doesn't judge, he only unveils. Once the detective has unmasked the guilty party, he has de-

cidedly little interest in punishing him; this is also the case in many of the books of Dorothy L. Sayers (Freud's favorite mystery writer). While sometimes the guilty party is not formally punished, it often seems that the murderer brings punishment upon himself. In one case Maigret allows the statute of limitations to run out on a group of men since it is plain that they have already been punished for their parts in a murder (and, just as important, they have children).

Jung was also acquainted with the psychological fact that murder can exert its own punishment. In his autobiography, *Memories, Dreams, Reflections,* he recounts an early psychiatric experience. A woman came to him for a consultation, to share an unbearable secret. She had killed her friend in order to marry the friend's husband. She got her man, but shortly thereafter he died and all of life soon turned sour for her. She was condemned to a lonely life; even dogs and horses seemed to sense her guilt. As Jung commented, the murderer had already sentenced herself, for one who commits such a crime destroys her own soul.

It is easy to understand why Jung was attracted to the psychological detective stories of Simenon, to the introverted, intuitive Inspector Maigret. But we should also consider the archetypal impulses behind the detective story, and a good place to begin is Greek mythology. Perhaps the most famous detective story involves the infant Hermes' theft of Apollo's cattle. At first, Apollo is mystified; Hermes has diguised the tracks so that it looks as if a giant led something *into* the pasture. Apollo first asks an eyewitness, an old man who seems to remember seeing a small child. He then uses his godly intuition: when an eagle flies by, he divines that the thief is a son of Zeus (since eagles are the birds associated with Zeus). According to some versions, he uses operatives to find where Hermes is hidden.

Apollo looks for clues, interviews eyewitnesses, uses his intuition and employs operatives. He is the archetypal detective. While Apollo as God of Divination and Prophecy does have a special relation to intuition, he is also the God of Law, with a special interest in murder. It was Apollo's province to exact blood for

> *As a semi-reformed mystery addict with catholic tastes (including Father Brown) I avoid mysteries; no time. Am liable to be hooked by any author who can lure me past the first three pages. I slip every so often without remorse. What are this year's best? —please do not reply to that.*
>
> HUMPHRY OSMOND

blood; it was his rule that a murderer must be purified (through punishment). Thus, instead of personal revenge (the central event of so many tragedies), the state (representing Apollo) avenges. And thus the detective, the impersonal avenger, is Apollo's agent.

If Apollo represents the detective, it is his traditional opposite, Dionysus, who represents the murderer. While Apollo inspires wisdom and was equated by Jung (in *Psychological Types*) with introverted intuition, Dionysus inspires madness and was equated (by Jung) with extroverted sensation. To Dionysus belong the ecstasies and excesses of drunkenness and passion. And as Inspector Maigret asserts in *Maigret Stonewalled*, at the bottom of the criminal mind one always finds "some devouring passion." Dionysus in his madness committed many murders. This behavior is perhaps explained by a childhood trauma: as a child Dionysus was murdered. (This is perhaps true of mortal murderers as well; they are metaphorically murdered in childhood.) The Titans tore the infant Dionysus to pieces, but Zeus (or Rhea) helped him to be reborn. According to Orphic myth, the Titans ate most of Dionysus before Zeus destroyed them with a thunderbolt. From their ashes rose humanity. Thus, in a central Dionysian mystery, the initiate tore a bull (a symbol of Dionysus) to pieces with his bare hands and ate of his flesh, reenacting (in this murder mystery) the murder and incorpo-

ration of the divinity. Dionysus is therefore the god who is murdered and the god who murders; he is the god of murderers and victims alike. We can thus understand how Dionysus was sometimes equated with Hades, Lord of the Dead.

But if the detective often uses Apollonian reason or intuition, he is also deeply involved in a Dionysian mystery. His full attention is focused upon murder and murderer. And while Inspector Maigret does withdraw into introverted spells of intuition, he usually accompanies them with the Dionysian aids of beer and wine. (Remember how many other detectives abuse alcohol and drugs.) The central event of the mystery plot is usually a mysterious (and often passionate) murder, but the plot itself is usually reasonable, fair and intricate. And the representative of that great and reasonable thing — the law — is often possessed by a spirit of the dead, the living image of the murdered. Thus Maigret often catches the criminal by getting to know the victim. In *Inspector Maigret and the Dead Girl*, he befuddles the murderer by telling him he would have swallowed his story if he hadn't known the dead girl. His totally pragmatic and reasonable subordinate believes the false story because "no training course teaches policemen how to put themselves in the place of a girl brought up in Nice by a half-crazy mother."

Insofar as the detective identifies with the evil murderer and his dead victim, he identifies Apollo with Dionysus. (That Apollo and Dionysus were one and the same god was a paradox of the later Orphic mysteries.) In Jungian terms we could talk about the ego assimilating the shadow side. Assimilation of the shadow results in a darkening and deepening of the whole personality; a proximity with evil can lead, paradoxically, to a moral improvement. The detective is conscious of the evil he partakes in; he doesn't gloat in his moral superiority. Carl Jung, like Inspector Maigret (and Philip Marlowe and countless other detectives) saw in the whole person both good and evil, passion and reason, Dionysus and Apollo.

John Boe has never (to his knowledge) committed murder.

CROSSWORDS AND WHODUNITS
A Correlation Between Addicts?

Colin Dexter

I noticed with vague disquiet a recent report in the *British Medical Journal* asserting a significant correlation between eating cornflakes for breakfast and the onset of the dreaded Crohn's disease. Yet correlations are notoriously cock-eyed, and it was some consolation for me to recall that the annual number of iron ingots shipped from Pennsylvania to California was once significantly correlated with the number of registered prostitutes in Buenos Aires. With such wildly improbable findings to encourage us, may we please tentatively assume that there is likely to be a positive correlation of sorts between those who enjoy crosswords and those who enjoy detective stories? At the very least, I think there *ought* to be one. Why is this?

Let us begin in familiar surroundings: a murder and a conveniently small circle of suspects, one of whom is the murderer. As in the cryptic[1] crossword, *clues* bestrew the scene; but they will be read correctly only by our hero, who, if not exactly a roaring genius, is an investigator of alpha-plus acumen. Between times the writer will dangle each of the suspects in front of our noses in such a way that we shall fail to recognise the murderer until the surprise

dénouement. Such is the stuff of the classic sleight-of-hand whodunit; and clearly there is much in common between this genre of detective fiction (though much less so between the broader "crime" story or the "thriller") and the cryptic crossword. Each is a puzzle for which clues are cunningly laid, and to which there is a final, unambiguous solution.

In the actual process of clue-ing, both the whodunit writer and the crossword composer (not "compiler," please!) have a duty to be fair. They need not necessarily say what they mean, *but they must mean what they say:* it is fair to mislead, but not to mislead by deliberate falsification. Let us take an example from the great crossword composer Ximenes: "An item in fuel is somewhat fluctuating supply" (6). "In" means "contained within," and the six letters of the answer are contained, consecutively, within the next three words (no padding). Fair enough. But where is the definition of LISSOM? For any composer worth the name will include a definition. Well, we have been deceived. We see the words "fuel" and "supply," and the misleading connection is immediately forged in the mind: "misleading," because the second word is not "sup*ply*" but "*supply*"—the adverb from the adjective "supple"—and LISSOM means "fluctuating *supply*." That is the way of it, and instances abound of such ambivalent words, frequently to be found in combination. "A number

---

[1] A "cryptic" clue is, loosely speaking, one which is not merely a straight definition but which also leads to an answer by disguised means, usually by allusion to individual letters or parts of that answer.

of members," for example, may refer not only to a local golf club but also to a local anaesthetic; for it is the way *we* look at these words which determines their significance—the words themselves remain the same.

Similarly, the whodunit writer must seek to be fair, or at least not deliberately unfair. The match-stick found on the scene of the crime may have been used either to light the assailant's cigar or to pick his teeth—but it must always remain a *match-stick*. So, too, with the other clues. If, in the first chapter of a book, we are invited to survey a blood-bedrenched boudoir, we shall feel cheated if, in the last, we are informed that the putative victim had an incurable bedtime passion for the taste of tomato sauce. No. Clues must form a basis for logical deduction — a process as much at the heart of detective fiction as of crosswords.

But deception may, of course, begin from the start. Ximenes once published a puzzle (on April 1st!) wherein the clue to 1 across provided two quite legitimate answers: MAHOGANY and RAMBUTAN. Each clue thereafter provided a similar pair of answers, and all fitted into one another perfectly — with the exception of one space. Only by working from RAMBUTAN could the puzzle be finally completed. Such cumulative deception is also practised by the whodunit writer. In *The Greek Coffin Mystery,* for example, Ellery Queen can arrive at a convincing solution halfway through the book, only for the reader to discover that one key problem remains unresolved. Back to square one! And in *The Murder of Roger Ackroyd* (the most famous deception of all) Agatha Christie throws the reader onto the wrong track from the very first sentence.

So much for clues. When it comes to *solutions,* it has been said that the whodunit reader doesn't really *care* who committed the crime, but that he has to *know;* and such a situation is familiar to the crossword addict. Ideally, the solution, in each case, is one where the bewildered victim can kick himself for not having guessed it before. Let me illustrate. There is little satisfaction in crossword solving if an inordinately obscure clue leads to a dialectal word, now obsolete, in Lowland Scots. But how different when the word is perfectly well

known, when only minimal demands are made upon outside knowledge! Consider "What the Jumblies kept in the sieve" (6). Most of us know that the Jumblies went to sea in a sieve. But which of their (doubtless) quaint possessions did they *keep* in the wretched thing? We are tempted to say: "If only I could remember the whole poem!" Or, "What object *could* they have kept in a sieve, anyway?" But no. The simple answer is AFLOAT, and we knew it all the time. Excellent!

Some few practitioners in each genre have raised their work to the level of a minor art, and it is perhaps the very limitations of this art which make it so enjoyable to so many. What are these limitations? Well, whodunits are games, really; games played to a set of rules, however loosely applied. With the emphasis upon coherent deduction, there is little room for characterisation in depth, and death itself is no "fell sergeant," but merely a convenient point of departure — the messier the better. Crosswords, too, are played to rules — or at least the best ones are, as those who have read *Ximenes on the Art of the Crossword* will know. (And what a pity it is that the Americans, sticking for the most part to their rather tedious definition clues, have given themselves so little chance of producing an Afrit, a Torquemada, a Ximenes, or an Azed.[2] After all, it was the New York *Sunday World* which was the first in the field.) In each genre we learn the rules and we

[2]*Afrit:* the late Prebendary A.F. Ritchie, of *The Listener.* His pseudonym is formed from the two Christian-name initials and the first three letters of his surname. Appropriately, the word "afrit" = "an evil demon in Arabian mythology."

Torquemada: the late Edward Powys Mathers, of *The Observer.* His pseudonym derives from the Dominican Tomás de Torquemada, the Grand Inquisitor appointed in Spain by Pope Sixtus IV in the reign of Ferdinand and Isabella. He was a great pioneer in the art of the crossword, loved by addicts and feared by the uninitiated.

Ximenes: from 1942 to his death in 1971, D.S. MacNutt concealed himself behind the pseudonym "Ximenes" — François Ximenés de Cisneros, Cardinal, Archevêque de Tolède, Grandinquisiteur, et Régent d'Espagne. The standards set by Ximenes in his famous *Observer* puzzles have achieved world-wide renown, and in the opinion of many (including me) he ranks as the greatest of the crossword composers.

Azed: the pseudonym of Jonathan Crowther, also of *The Observer,* a composer of bold ingenuity. The name "Azed," apart from its comprehensively alphabetical connotation (a–z), maintains (by a reversal of its letters) a continuity with its two predecessors, for Don Diego de *Deza* was Spanish Grand Inquisitor from 1498 to 1507, between Torquemada and Ximenes; and a particularly beastly fellow he was, by all accounts, who burned 2,592 heretics alive.

MURDER INK
Eugene T. Maleska

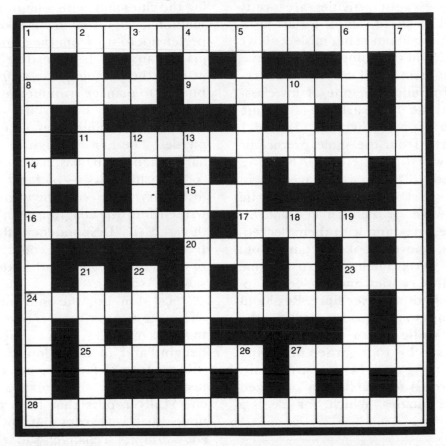

Across

1. *Watch on the Rhine* scriptwriter
8. Apply blunt instrument to skull
9. Gave the third degree
11. Criminal's style
14. Polygraph peak
15. Roscoe
16. Prey of Venus's-flytrap
17. What ratiocination is
20. Capet was one
23. Thing, to Perry Mason
24. D16 agent
25. Sluggishness
27. Red herring
28. 1955 Edgar winner

Down

1. Legal verdict
2. Hard-boiled houses
3. Poison pen necessity
4. Campion's valet, Wimsey style
5. _____ objects open locked doors
6. Part of story in which sleuth solves crime
7. Manhattan, Kansas sibling
10. Harriet's husband's title
12. Easily crushed spinal pad
13. Like some pills, but unlike horror stories
18. _____ Reaper
19. Gothic locale
21. Something strange
22. aka A.A.
26. Clue for a gumshoe
27. Sing Sing

Solution on page 450.

Eugene T. Maleska is the crossword puzzle editor of the New York Times.

play the game, and in so doing we escape for a while from the harsh world: there is little or no emotional involvement.

Clearly, then, the reasons for the popularity of these two escapist activities are pretty similar: we revel in mystification; we are curiously uncomplaining about being misled; above all, we enjoy the final dropping of the penny.

My own first memory of crosswords? I recall my deep admiration for one of my classmates who solved the unremarkable (and quite unscientific) clue "Ena cut herself" (7); and I was soon to learn, from the same precocious youth, the answer to the riddle "Nothing squared is cubed" (3). (Do you have *Oxo* in America?) My first acquaintances in the whodunit field were Dr. Gideon Fell and Sir Henry Merrivale, wrestling with their "locked-room" mysteries: uneven books, certainly—but what a joy they were! Then, in a rush, came most of the Christie classics, and I've been happily hooked on whodunits ever since. Rex Stout particularly springs to mind as I write, since the oversized Nero Wolfe, when not tending his oversized orchids in his roof-garden or solving a case without stirring from his oversized chair, was wont (so I read) to exercise his oversized brain on *Ximenes* puzzles. Which, for me, is a

happy illustration. To be truthful, I've always wanted to be a supersleuth; and when I tackle a new crossword I'm childish enough to see myself as the great detective magisterially surveying the clues and, with a bit of luck, finding the solution — all on my own. Like Wolfe, too, I'd prefer not to stir from the armchair, since I am just as anxious for the detective to manage without the pathology lab as for the crossword puzzler to manage without the dictionary. Fancifully, I wonder how Wolfe would have fared with the following clues taken from *Ximenes* puzzles. The first he might have found a little hard (might even, alas, have needed to look up "od" in Chambers' — by far the best crossword dictionary); the second he would probably have written into the diagram with only a second's thought. (i) "Despondency, Reichenbach's effect, unsolved crime . . . could have led Holmes to *this*" (10); (ii) Eyes had I, and unfortunately saw not" (6).[3]

To sum up, the glorious thing for me about the two activities is that each is engaged in for its own sake, with a simple sense of fresh delight; and to those long-faced counsellors who are forever ferreting out some pretentious justification for all human activities, we can cheerfully report that here there is *none* — none, that is, except our own pleasure. *Ars gratia artis*, for a change. And why on earth not?

Monsignour Ronald Knox (himself no mean writer of detective stories) was one day sitting in a train with the *Times* crossword on his knee. For several minutes he stared earnestly at the diagram but filled in not a single letter. When a young man sitting beside him suggested a possible answer to 1 across, Knox smiled serenely and handed him the crossword: "Here you are. I've just finished."

So have I.

SOLUTION TO MURDER INK

[3](i) HYPODERMIC (hyp - od + anag. of "crime" & lit.)
(ii) WATSON (anag. & lit.)

[Any reader who is still puzzled by "number of members" should be reminded of the verb "to numb." Poor Ena (who cut herself) - bled.]

Colin Dexter is the author of The Silent World of Nicholas Quinn *and was three times national champion in the Ximenes clue-writing competition.*

A SLIGHT DEBATE
A Hard-Boiled Fan and a Country-House Fan Discuss the Genre

Marilyn Stasio
and
Richard Hummler

SCENE: *A breakfast nook in an upper-middle-class suburban American home. A married couple, Mike and Margery, face each other across a glass breakfast table.*

MARGERY

Christie.

MIKE

Chandler.

MARGERY

Marsh.

MIKE

Who?

MARGERY

Ngaio.

MIKE

Oh, right . . . the New Zealander.
(*Sucks in gut.*)
Spillane. (*Pause. Lasciviously.*) Mickey.

MARGERY

I'm simply not going on with this if you won't behave decently.
(*Pause. They glare at each other.*)

MIKE

Ross Macdonald.

MARGERY

That's better . . . Margery Allingham.

MIKE

(*Unbuttons his shirt collar and wrenches his tie away from his neck. Grins.*)
Walker.

MARGERY

(*Looks away from him nervously as she straightens the tea cosy.*)
Who?

MIKE

Francis X. Walker, sweetheart. Detroit. His detective is Mickey Reilly.

MARGERY

Hardly in the premier rank, I'd say. *(Pause)* Michael Innes. No — make that P.D. James. *(Pause)* I'm saving Innes.

MIKE

Gores.

MARGERY

(Pause) Are you making yours up?

MIKE

(Rolls up his shirt sleeves and slams his elbows on the table.)
Joe Gores. Nobody you'd know, baby. Just one of the greatest detective novelists in American crime fiction.

(Margery rattles her teacup ominously.)

MIKE

Don't gimme that, Maggie. Just because Gores writes about *real* people killing other *real* people for *real* reasons, instead of effete Oxford dons knocking each other off with African blowguns, doesn't mean you have to turn your nose up.

MARGERY

You've dribbled egg on your chin. *(Sniffs.)* Maybe I should have cooked it *hard-boiled*. *(Opens her newspaper — the London* Observer *— and screams.)*

MIKE

(Slams down the Daily News.*)*
What the —

MARGERY

John Dickson Carr died.

MIKE

(Pause) Who?

MARGERY

You must be joking. He is *the* master mystery craftsman of the century. His books are the *ne plus ultra* of the locked-room genre.

MIKE

(Lights a cigarette, blows the smoke in her eyes.)
Figures.

MARGERY

And what is *that* supposed to mean?

MIKE

Only broad I know gets so worked up when some academic pedant kicks off.

MARGERY

(Picks up her knitting and begins to work the long needles savagely.)
And when Mickey Spillane dies, I suppose you won't disappear into some bar for a week of sodden grieving.

MIKE

(Crumples his empty Lucky Strike pack and tosses it into a plate of cold kippers.)
Listen, sweetheart — maybe guys like Parker and Stark have never seen the inside of a cathedral close, but they tell it like it is, not like it *was*.

MARGERY

Name me one who writes with the literary erudition of Nicholas Blake. Or the wit of Edmund Crispin.

MIKE

(Sullenly.) Raymond Chandler.

MARGERY

(A hoot of contempt.) And I suppose that John D. MacDonald is a better writer than Michael Innes.

MIKE

Okay, so that's how you want to fight?
(Pause. He spikes his orange juice with a shot of Jack Daniel's. She winces.)
MacDonald at least tells a good story. Those English biddies you read — you can't even follow the plot if you don't have a Ph.D. in Etruscan funerary statuary.

MARGERY

(Smiles grimly over her knitting.)
Any intellectual demand beyond the size of a woman's bra cup is utterly beyond the mental capacities of your heroes.

MIKE

(Stands up, grabs his coat.)
Let me put it this way, Maggie. SHUT UP!

MARGERY

Why is it, every time we have this discussion, you retreat into macho petulance? *(Pause)* Are you really going to wear that filthy trench coat to the office, Michael?

MIKE

Now, don't go giving me that macho stuff again. A little normal sex is healthier than all those repressed vicars and inbred toffs sitting around doing crosswords in the drawing room.
(Lurches over to her. Grabs her knitting.)
And when you stop wearing riding tweeds and those damned English brogues, then you can start telling *me* how to dress . . . *sweet*heart.

MARGERY

(Nervously.) The sense of societal . . . uh . . . communality does get a bit thick with some of the older writers, I admit . . .
(Fortifies herself with another sip of tea.)
But the familial social structure has a distinct advantage, I should say, over the blatant fascism of your lone-wolf avengers. *(Pause)* More tea?

MIKE

(Mumbling to himself.) Buncha chinless snobs . . .
(Pause) Coffee.

MARGERY

(Sweetly.) I don't suppose you've ever analyzed the latent misogyny of the blood-and-guts brigade?

MIKE

(Gives his coffee a blast of Jack Daniel's.)
Don't get sarcastic with me or I'll shut a drawer on your fingers.

MARGERY

George V. Higgins, I believe. *(Pause)* And I suppose Travis McGee isn't a closet queen?

MIKE

(Mumbling.) Buncha chinless snob *faggots!*

MARGERY

(Furiously butters a scone.)
Adolescent mentalities attempting to compensate for their own impotence.

MIKE

(Getting more incoherent.)

Lester Dent . . . Henry Kane . . .
(Reaches for the bourbon bottle; knocks it over.)

MARGERY

Sexual sadists!

MIKE

(Draws himself up.)
I'm warning you, baby . . .

MARGERY

(Wildly shreds watercress.)
You want to destroy it all — the puzzle, the pace, the atmosphere, the literary clues. *(Pause. Sobs.)* The compound-complex sentence.

MIKE

(Draws a gun from his trench coat pocket.)
No jury would convict me.

MARGERY

Do you smell that soufflé in the oven? *(Pause)* It's your first edition of *The Big Sleep!*

MIKE

That does it sweetheart.
(He shoots. She falls across the table, scattering the watercress.)

MIKE

Thirty-eight-caliber automatic. Makes a nice clean hole. Not too much blood. *(Pause)* She never did like blood.
(He grabs his throat. Chokes. Slumps back in his chair.)

MARGERY

(Weakly.) Potassium cyanide. Two grains. Chemical symbol: KCN. Crystalline salt with the following properties: colorless, soluble, poisonous. *(Pause)* Used in electroplating.
(She dies.)

MIKE

I won't play the sap for you, angel.
(He dies.)

— THE END —

Marilyn Stasio and Richard Hummler are a husband and wife team working in the theater. She is drama critic for Cue *magazine and* Penthouse. *He is a former* Variety *reporter now working for producer Alexander H. Cohen.*

THE BEST BOOK I NEVER WROTE

Judith Crist

We also serve who only sit and read. Let the uninitiate think we Mystery Readers serve the writers by our purchase and consumption of books and magazines and by our devotion, blind or very wise, to the masters of the craft and their creatures. We aficionados know that our greatest service has been our refusal to put down on paper, let alone publish, The Great American Detective Story that each of us carries around in his head. After all, we can devote a lifetime to perfecting plot and personnel as we consume the goodies the "public" writers provide and we grow fat on their creations. But we grow cautious, too, and taste humility from time to time as we encounter a more cunning crime, a cannier deduction, a tauter twist and better breath-bater than ever we dreamed of. And so the revisions go on and on as standards are set higher and higher. We Mystery Readers remain closet mystery writers.

I have spent my adult life in that closet, deposited therein by a parental attitude that designated moviegoing and detective story reading as prime time-wasters. Even so, it was on the family bookshelves that I found Sherlock Holmes and then a host of others in a ten-volume set of *The World's Greatest Detective Stories* that the Literary Digest had apparently foisted on the household as a subscription bonus. And it was at the Saturday movie matinées that I encountered Warner Oland's Fu Manchu, Warren William's Perry Mason, Edward Arnold's Nero Wolfe, William Powell's Philo Vance, Ronald Coleman's Bulldog Drummond, Edna May Oliver's Hildegarde Withers, Peter Lorre's Mr. Moto, and Warner Oland again as Charlie Chan. These introductions at least fulfilled Hollywood's educational pretension: they led me to read the books — all of them — and keep on reading.

But though in my adolescence as an aspiring writer I had no hesitation about attempting Dickensian sagas, Hemingwayesque stories and Thomas Wolfean *Weltschmerz*, I didn't attempt an unwritten mystery until graduate school. It came upon me suddenly — "Murder Cum

I stopped wasting money on new mystery novels years ago. Those I tried, stank. Except I do look on the stands for any new Lew Archer paperback. Hence my mystery reading is limited to re-reading: Simenon, who helps keep my French in condition; Rex Stout, since Archie Goodwin is always delightful; Matthew Head, whom I read between the lines as a personal diary. Dashiell Hammett and Raymond Chandler have been re-read so often that I no longer go back to them.

JOHN CANADAY
(MATTHEW HEAD)

JERRY DARVIN

Laude" — a bitterly satiric view of academe, wherein a variety of scholars met their doom and a beautiful, slim and brilliant graduate student helped a charming, couth and educated cop (a novelty in those days, I assure you) determine whether it was the Shakespeare scholar, the doctoral candidate or the janitor who did it. A couple of years went by as I devised cleverly academic methods of murder, all of which had to go by the boards (college, of course) when I switched my professional interests to journalism and "Murder Makes News" got into my head. This was to be a bitterly satiric view of newspapering, wherein a variety of columnists met their doom and a beautiful, slim and brilliant reporter helped a charming, uncouth and semi-educated cop (I had learned the facts of life) determine whether it was the publisher, the aspiring columnist or the copyboy who did it. My real-life reporting experiences with crime — most memorably a murder on the Columbia campus, suspicious deaths among wealthy elderly patients of a Connecticut doctor, the slaughter of a family with an eight-year-old survivor the possible killer — made me worry a lot about methodology; encounters with a couple of corpses and discovering the reality of "the stench of death" took some of the fun out of the murders.

But I soon found that my domestic interests superseded my professional life and had put "Marriage for Murder" into my mind. This was to be a bitterly satiric view of matrimony, wherein a variety of young couples met their doom and a beautiful, slim and brilliant wife helped her charming, couth and educated cop husband (it was no more than the gal deserved) decide whether it was the bachelor, the playgirl or the butcher who did it. While I was concentrating on avoiding any Northian taint to a martini-drinking Manhattan-couple tale, I found myself replacing it with "The Lying-In Murders," a bitterly satiric view of a maternity ward, wherein a variety of young mothers met their doom at the hands of the obstetrician, pediatrician or hospital trustee. In no time at all, or so it seemed, this had given way to "The Sandbox Slayings," wherein a variety of abominable toddlers were done away with by a mommy, a nanny or another toddler.

When my professional life, now that of

They're logical up to a point, murderous, of course, but that makes them familiar if one is at all observant of business and family life. They give me a world somewhat between the real one and that of the serious novel with its fragmented consciousness. A good mystery provides a suspense which is lulling for me because it is polite and formal. That's why the good ones work as a soporific for me.

HAROLD BRODKEY

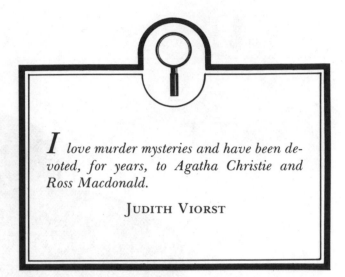

I love murder mysteries and have been devoted, for years, to Agatha Christie and Ross Macdonald.

JUDITH VIORST

theater and film critic, expanded to include television, however, domestic matters yielded to "Murder for Today," wherein a variety of morning-show guests were knocked off, on camera yet, and the heroine, no longer my vicarious alter ego but the attractive, sharp interviewer on the show, determined on her own whether it was the anchorman, the producer or everybody's researcher-mistress who did it. For a while this one shared headroom with "The Critic Killer," wherein a drama critic was murdered in mid-review (multiple murders were becoming a bit too taxing) and his beautiful, slim and brilliant associate (reenter the dream alter ego) determined whether it was the producer, director or star of the show he was covering who did it. These two, in recent years, were replaced by "The Film Festival Murders," with an international cast, of course, and endless possibilities for doing away with the unbeloveds of my medium. I'm staying with it. On the other hand, a recent campus weekend with my son has started "The Cambridge Killings" buzzing in my brain . . .

But have no fear, you darlings of my noncinematic hours. We closet mystery concocters know that those who can, do; we, who like to think that we could if we would, are smart enough not to. Not yet. Meanwhile, we also serve. We sit and read.

Judith Crist, film critic for the New York Post *and* TV Guide, *was named Mystery Reader of the Year (1971) by the Mystery Writers of America.*

CHRISTMAS GIFTS FOR MYSTERY FANS

Carol Brener

What happens if he's read all the Wolfes and she's read all the Wimseys?

What happens if they haven't read them all, but you don't know which they've missed?

Happily, crime characters have charming eccentricities and some prompt terrific gifts. Here, then, an imaginative assortment of Christmas presents for the true mystery addict.

For *spy thriller* readers: Used army trench coats (who wants to look like a *new* spy?) from Weiss & Mahoney, Inc. (142 Fifth Ave., New York, N.Y. 10011). From $5.95. Or, a total immersion course in Russian at Berlitz School of Languages (40 West 51st Street, New York, N.Y. 10019). $5,150. The cost is the same for Chinese.

For *private eye* buffs: A day of a private eye's services. Rates in the New York area start at $20 per hour for one operative, $40 per hour for two.

For *English village* fans: A subscription to *The Garden Book* by Amos Pettigill of White Flower Farm, Litchfield 676, Conn. 06759. $4 annually.

For *police procedural* fans: From the company that supplies the police, a fingerprint kit and fingerprint chart. Faurot, Inc. (299 Broadway, New York, N.Y. 10007). Kit, $31 (#638A); chart, $4.50.

For the *I-love-them-all* fan: A custom-made collage, 10″ × 10″. Will incorporate names, titles, quotations, pictures, clues, whatever. $75 from The Stonehand (245 Centre St., New York, N.Y. 10013). Allow three weeks.

For the *Lizzie Borden* specialist: The "Hudson Bay Kindling Axe," #6111J in the L.L. Bean, Inc. catalog. (Write c/o L.L. Bean, Freeport, Me. 04033.) You can carve something appropriate — like the name of a good lawyer — on the 18″ hickory handle.

For the *Lew Archer* fan: A room at the spiffiest place in Santa Barbara — The Ambassador by the Sea Motor Hotel (202 West Cabrillo Blvd., Santa Barbara, Calif. 93101). $26.32, double occupancy, in high season.

For the *James Bond* fan: The closest thing to a Turkish-Balkan blend — Sobranies' non-filtered cigarettes from Lane Ltd. (122 East 42nd St., New York, N.Y. 10016). Pack of ten, $1.10.

For the *Bony* fan: A cake as big as the Outback — in the shape of Australia! If you supply the locales, the icing will mark the spot where Bony's cases occurred. $35 from Creative Cakes (400 East 74th St., New York, N.Y. 10021). Allow two weeks.

For the *Charlie Chan* fan: A number one son, if you can manage it. If not, dinner for two at the House of Chan (7th Ave. and 52nd

St., New York, N.Y. 10019). Allow $12.50 per person.

For the *Dick Francis* fan: Membership in the National Steeplechase Association (Box 308, Elmont, N.Y. 11003) provides entry to all hunt races and steeplechases in the U.S. and U.K., including the Grand National at Aintree and the Colonial Cup at Camden, S.C. $40 for one year.

For the *Inspector French* fan: Turn-of-the-century railroad watches — most are gold-filled, all work — from William Scolnik (1001 Second Ave., New York, N.Y. 10022). From $140.

For the *Sherlock Holmes* fan: A gasogene, the "classic syphon" from Hammacher Schlemmer (147 East 57th St., New York, N.Y. 10022). $35.95. Or, a deerstalker from Worth & Worth, Ltd. (331 Madison Ave., New York, N.Y. 10017). $11.95.

For the *Maigret* fan: A gourmet lunch at home with you, every day for a week. Followed by an early evening walk, holding hands. Followed by a glass of Calvados.

For the *Philip Marlowe* fan: A private showing of *Murder My Sweet* starring Dick Powell. Available from Films, Inc. (440 Park Ave. South, New York, N.Y. 10016). $85 for a one-day rental, and they'll even tell you where to rent a 16mm projector.

SPRINGER/BETTMAN FILM ARCHIVE

For the *Miss Marple* fan: A hand-knit shawl, if you've the talent, or a one-ounce jar of "Mr. Lord's Potpourri," redolent of roses. From Caswell-Massey (518 Lexington Ave.,

New York, N.Y. 10017). $6.50

For the *Poirot* fan: A mock-tortoise moustache comb, $2.50; Gelle Frères stick moustache wax, $3.00; Pinaud moustache wax in a tube, in a range of colors including glossy black, $2.00 the bottle or $3.50 the jar. All from Caswell-Massey (mail-order department, 320 West 13th St., New York, N.Y. 10014). Or, a good selection of ready-made moustaches from Barris & Zervoulei (982 Second Ave., New York, N.Y. 10022). $10.

For the *Roger Sheringham* fan: A chocolate greeting card with the words "these are not poisoned chocolates." 6″ × 8″ card of milk or semi-sweet chocolate, $15. Double-size card, $30. From Kron Chocolatier (764 Madison Ave., New York, N.Y. 10021). Shipped in wooden crate ($2.50, small; $3.50, large). No summer shipping.

For the *Sam Spade* fan: A replica of the infamous Maltese Falcon. So convincing it could fool Greenstreet, Lorre, Astor, even Bogey. Perch it on your desk, sweetheart. From Get Plastered (2964 N. Lincoln Ave. Chicago, Ill. 60657). $20.

For the *Philo Vance* fan: The opulence of Beluga caviar. When available, about $160 the pound from William Poll (1051 Lexington Ave., New York, N.Y. 10017). They will deliver, and will also mail.

For the *Lord Peter Wimsey* fan: A frameless monocle with a serrated edge and a tiny hole for the chain or ribbon, from $20; gold-rimmed monocles from $35. Both from the Ultimate Spectacle (1032 Third Ave, New York, N.Y. 10022). Or, membership in the Dorothy L. Sayers Society, $3.00 annually. Contact Sister Mary Durkin, 7900 West Division St., River Forest, Ill. 60305, for further information.

For the *Nero Wolfe* fan: Yellow silk pajamas may be custom-ordered from A. Sulka & Co. (711 Fifth Ave., New York, N.Y. 10022). $160. With piping, $170. "Nero" in script on pocket, $9.00; initials, $6.00. Or a variety of orchids, such as cattleyas in bloom, from $25. From Plantworks (8 Waverly Pl., New York, N.Y. 10003).

Carol Brener is author of The Underground Collector *and proprietor of* Murder Ink, *the mystery bookstore.*

TEA WITH ELLERY QUEEN

Dilys Winn

Before Murder Ink was a book, it was a bookstore and I wanted everything about it to relate to the mystery, including its location. As I saw it, I had two choices: Either open it on West 35th Street, where Nero Wolfe lived, or open it on West 87th Street, where Ellery Queen lived. I opted for uptown. (Need I add the city was New York? I'd have had a hard time putting it in either place if the city had been Chicago or L.A.)

Eventually, Murder Ink got customers, and sooner or later they'd say, "Say, did you know in *The French Powder Mystery* it mentions that Ellery Queen lived on this street? Nearer the park, mind you, but still . . ." Well, of course I knew it; I'd planned it.

Fittingly, the first letter the store ever received was from Fred Dannay, the surviving member of the Ellery Queen writing partnership. He wished the store well and asked to be kept posted on how it was doing. He also included a return address. My God! Ellery Queen expected *me* to write to *him!* For months afterward I wrote thank you notes to him in my head. That's as far as I got. Now you must understand, I am not a particularly humble person. I do not speak softly, nor do I fear to tread almost anywhere. But Ellery Queen — that was different. To me, he was more than a mystery writer; he was The Mystery Story. And I was only a reader. Sure fools may look upon kings. (Queens?) But speak to them? Don't be absurd.

Once, I was introduced to him at an MWA Edgar Allan Poe dinner. Torn between kissing

---

THE DOUBLE CROSS

Most people put only one line through their Q's. But most people aren't as inventive as Fred Dannay, who uses two strokes. The second stroke is to indicate that Ellery Queen encompasses two men, himself and Manfred B. Lee. If you're fortunate enough to own an inscribed Queen novel, take a look at the signature. The Q will be double-crossed.

"Ellery Queen"

---

his ring and curtsying, I merely stood there and gaped, which was all the opportunity the hordes needed. They stepped on, over and around me to get at him. Intimidated, I backed away.

It took me close on to five years to actually talk to Ellery Queen and that only happened because I finally did write him a letter. To say it was outrageous is to understate the case. I wanted to include him in *Murder Ink* — the book, not the store — and Eleanor Sullivan suggested if I wrote down a few questions, he'd be glad to answer them.

Do you consider two pages, single-spaced, no margins, elite type, a few questions? What happened was, I kept rereading the questions and thinking, God that's dumb, better ask another. I thought he'd look at them, correct the grammar and then refuse to have me as a fan. Awe attacks some people in the knees; me, it gets in the syntax.

Presumably because he thought it would take less time to be interviewed than to synopsize his lifework — which is about what my questions demanded — Fred Dannay rang me up and invited me to tea. Little did he know I'd be more addled in person. Remember, it took me the better part of five years just to finish a letter. How long did he think it would take me to drink a cup of tea?

Actually, six hours. In fact, I parlayed it into dinner and was working my way up to asking to be adopted when common sense took over and I asked to be excused instead.

What did we talk about? Why had there not been a recent Queen novel? The last one appeared in 1971. The answer surprised and saddened me. It began with an explanation of the time absorbed in editing a monthly mystery magazine and then softly, reasonably, continued to this: A writer has to know when to stop. Mr. Dannay also suggested he might ultimately be better known for the magazine than for his coauthorship of Ellery Queen. He suffers, I think, from rampant humility. Let me be immodest for him: The man who thinks his work as a writer will eventually be eclipsed is the man who has won five Edgar awards, a special Raven award, and has sold more than one hundred fifty million books worldwide. The conclusion is obvious: Never ask an author to judge his own work.

Mr. Dannay is not easy to interview. He has been through it all so many times before, you see, that the answer is ready before the question is asked. And frankly, my questions were no more original than anybody else's.

I did learn, however, why he turns down speaking engagements. Seems he used to do them and was terrified by them, so much so that he spent the entire night before them being ill. On the other hand, teaching is something he enjoyed. He believes only in laboratory courses in which the student writes and the teacher criticizes. He recalled once discussing a single sentence for a whole session and there was a look on his face as if he remembered it as time well spent.

He seemed puzzled that his most often an-

AUTOGRAPH PARTY ETIQUETTE

Very rarely are mystery writers tendered an autograph party. Bookstore owners have discovered they are poor draws in comparison with, say, sports figures and movie personalities. They have been known to loiter by their books for two and even three hours and promote no more than ten sales.

A terribly nice author, who had written a rather risqué mystery — in fact, it was downright tawdry — once sat patiently for an hour, waiting to sign a purchase. The store owner prodded a sweet young thing over to him. The author smiled, introduced himself and discreetly proffered his book. She glanced at it, returned it, smiled equally sweetly and said, "Can you tell me where they keep the Dorothy Sayers?"

It is considered bad form to tell the author that you will wait for the book to come out in paperback; that you thought it miraculous he got his last book published; that you guessed whodunit on page 12; that you only browse in bookstores and get all your books from the library; that you're writing a book yourself and could he tell you the name of his agent. Equally gauche is to swipe his pen.

If you have been specially invited to an autograph party, do not go unless you plan on buying the book. Anything else is freeloading.

thologized piece was a short description of how he came to read Conan Doyle and first met Sherlock Holmes and that it could prompt the likes of Dale Carnegie to read it and say, "Now I know why my wife loves you."

He seemed unhappy with many current reviewers, excepting Anatole Broyard, whom he liked. He warmed to the idea of an American Mystery Museum or Mystery Hall of Fame, had, in fact, proposed it to MWA years ago, and even has a few artifacts to contribute — some of Jacques Futrelle's things given to him by Mrs. Futrelle, including a pocket notebook containing plot ideas for *The Thinking Machine*.

He was silent on how he and Manfred B. Lee actually did their collaborating, except to say Mr. Lee always wanted it to be a secret and he felt he should keep that confidence. But he was absolutely voluble on two counts: designing jacket covers and conveying dying messages. Mr. Dannay was once, long ago, an advertising art director and whipped off a rough drawing for the cover of Queen's first book, *The Roman Hat Mystery* (1929). Somehow or other the publisher never got around to having the artwork rendered and his first sketch became the final product. He is an inveterate tinkerer with

*L*ife's too short — I can't read 10 percent of the good *science fiction now published,* let alone anything else. . . . But I'm proud of the fact that the only *crime story I ever* wrote ("Trouble with Time" in Tales of Ten Worlds) *was published by* Ellery Queen *(as "Crime on Mars").*

ARTHUR C. CLARKE

EQMM covers and, so I'd heard, with *EQMM* story titles. He said he didn't think he was an incorrigible title changer and I was on the verge of believing him until not five minutes later he said, "About this title of yours, *Murder Ink.* I think. . . ." That critics and readers identify Ellery Queen with the convention of the dying message seems to him a misplacement of emphasis. "It was just a device," he said, "we used in stories for a greater sense of compression and 'fun and games.'" More to his taste was the subtle use of the invisible or negative clue — the clue that ought to be there and isn't. Even more to his taste were his, well, political statements in the Queen novels. The man who is world-renowned for his fair-play ingenuity, for his challenges to the reader, would rather be associated with his attempts to tell society what must be redressed. I don't blame him. And I can't think of anyone who could tell me these things and entertain me at the same time quite as well as Ellery Queen.

Then we got down to the nitty-gritty: gossip. But I can't repeat it. You'll just have to get Fred Dannay to invite you to tea and tell you himself.

When I went to leave, I realized what had been vaguely bothering me all afternoon. How do you tell a man you love him when his wife is sitting right there next to him the whole time?

The first issue of Ellery Queen's Mystery Magazine *appeared in the fall of 1941. It cost a quarter and included stories by Dashiell Hammett, Margery Allingham, T.S. Stribling, Anthony Abbott, Cornell Woolrich and Queen himself. Today, it is considered a collector's item.*

Dilys Winn is the editor of Murder Ink *(the book) and the founder of* Murder Ink *(the bookstore).*

DEAR MR. GARFIELD
An Author Opens His Mail

Brian Garfield

Fan mail. Sometimes it praises; sometimes it condemns. With the exception of the occasional crackpot accusation or obscene vilification, it gratifies a writer because it reassures him that somebody out there is actually reading his work. He knows his publisher's sales figures, but they only tell him people are buying books; for all he knows from that, they may be using them as doorstops. Fan mail to a writer is like applause to an actor. I don't know any writers who don't get a kick out of a fan letter; I don't know any writers who don't answer their mail. Fan mail is too valuable to be ignored.

There are a few problems with it, however. One is the delivery system. Most writers are private people who don't advertise their home addresses on the jacket flaps of their books. To send a letter to a novelist, you must address it in care of his publisher. If, say, you are writing c/o a paperback publisher, then the paperback house must forward the letter to the hardcover publisher who originally published the book. The hardcover publisher in turn forwards it to the author. Often this procedure takes six to ten weeks. By the end of ten weeks the reader may have forgotten the book, the characters in it, and everything else except that he sent a letter to the author and the churl didn't answer him. By the time he receives the author's reply it's too late: the damage has been done; hatred has set in.

Sometimes the first letter a writer gets from a fan is one that begins, "Why didn't you answer my first letter?" Well, publishers' mail rooms lose things. They lose manuscripts, too, but that nightmare is a different story.

One category of fan mail stands by itself: gun mail. I find its implications fascinating.

You can write a book in which a key scene is a European Grand Prix auto race in the late 1930's involving Hispano-Suizas and Duesenbergs and all sorts of tactics and technical detail. Do you get letters from antique-car buffs? No.

You can write a book in which aviation plays a large part in the story; such books may deal with Ford Trimotors or B-17 bombers or C-47 Dakotas or Piper Apaches. Do you get letters from airplane buffs? No.

You can write a book in which horses, equestrian gear, Studebaker wagons and all kinds of nineteenth-century trappings are

Regarding mysteries, I read the first ten pages. Then I write my guess down as to who is the murderer. Then I look at the end of the book, and if my guess is correct I don't bother to read the rest.

REGINE

detailed and employed. Do you get letters from Western-history partisans? No.

You can write books set in the Russian Civil War or World War II or Vietnam or the Indian wars of the American West, in which tactics and the materiel of military ordnance figure as inevitable background. Do you get letters from armchair strategists? No.

Perhaps once a year you'll get a letter from someone who castigates you for confusing palominos with Appaloosas (the former is a color, the latter a breed), or from someone who appreciates the fact that you know they still had third lieutenants in the Russian Army in 1920. But these are rare. They are individual letters and seldom duplicate one another.

Make one trivial mistake about a gun, however, and you will be buried in an avalanche of mail.

I committed the unpardonable error, for example, of arming a gunslinger with a .38-40 revolver. This provoked instant reaction from dozens of letter-writers, all of whom had exactly the same thing to say: A .38-40 is a "ladies' gun," has no stopping power and cannot be compared with a .45 for lethal effectiveness. I learned more about the failings of .38-40's from these letter-writers than I ever wanted to know. At the end of the barrage I was left wondering why the manufacturers had ever bothered to make and sell the things at all, since they evidently aroused such contempt.

I armed the character in *Death Wish* with a .38 revolver. This in itself caused only a small reaction from readers who thought he should have been armed with a cannon. But when the filmmakers armed Charles Bronson with a .32 revolver, I was broadsided once again — as if I were in charge of the prop department. Instantly I was battered from all sides with snarling know-it-all advice about the ineffectiveness of .32 revolvers and the superiority of, and I quote, "a .38 police revolver with hollow-point 158-grain slugs" — a tediously technical description which was followed by a nauseatingly specific account of the anatomical damage that can be inflicted by such a bullet.

After a few hundred such letters it becomes a matter of almost vindictive pride to be able to turn the tables on the babbling gun experts. I was condemned by one reader who found a reference to a .38-56 Winchester rifle; the reader insisted no such rifle existed. I was happy to point out to him I had actually held one in my hand and fired it on a target range; it was manufactured in 1886 and was a fairly popular model for a while. Another reader insisted the Luger automatic pistol had never been manufactured in .45 caliber, and I was gleefully happy to prove him wrong. You do get caught up in this nonsense. For example, the Spencer repeating rifle of U.S. Civil War vintage was mass-produced in *both* .47 and .51 calibers, dear readers, and I don't want to hear any more about that from you. The Colt "Lightning" or "Bird's Head" or "Billy the Kid" revolver was manufactured in *both* .38 and .41 calibers, dear readers, and don't bug me about *that* one, either.

You see, the kicker is, I am somewhat of a gun expert myself, and this always throws the gun-mailers for a loop. They assume anybody effete enough to sit down and write books must be an ivory-tower egghead who can't tell a fulminate-of-mercury percussion cap from a push-type ejector spring. I served an apprenticeship as a gunsmith, boys, and I was eighteen at the time, and I outgrew it, and I no longer swagger around festooned with weapons, but I still remember what it feels like to get shot by mistake with a .45 — it did no permanent damage, but it was not fun — and when I write a gun into a story it is quite often a gun I have held in my hand and dismantled and repaired and test-fired. Over the past twenty-five years I have learned to respect the things and most often to loathe them. The more I write, the less I write about guns. (An exception is a current work-in-progress about an exhibition sharpshooter. But he shoots targets, not people.) This is what I think of as encroaching maturity. But it doesn't seem to be happening to the rest of you, and I am curious.

PRONUNCIATION GUIDE

proe-nun-sea-ay-shun guyed

(f u kn rd ths u kn rd a mstry)

Roderick *Alleyn* *al*-inn
V.C. Clinton-*Baddeley*** *baad*-uh-lee
Modesty *Blaise* blaze
Anthony *Boucher* rhymes with
   "croucher"
Ernest *Bramah* rhymes with "comma"
John Buchan *buck*-in
Max *Carrados* *care*-uh-dose
Auguste **Dupin** awe-*gooset* dew-*pan*
Elizabeth *Ferrars* as in "terrors"
Jacques *Futrelle* zshahk foot-*trell*
Emile *Gaboriau* as in Zsa Zsa + ee-oh
Ganesh **Ghote** ga-nesh *go*-tay
Robert van *Gulik* *goo*-lick
Dashiell **Hammett** *dash*-el
Jack *Iams* *eye*-mz
Michael *Innes* *inn*-iss
Maurice *Le Blanc* luh-*blahn*
John *Le Carré* luh-car-*ray*
Monsieur *Lecoq* luh-*coke*
William *Le Queux* luh-*q*
Gaston **Leroux** gas-*tone* luh-*roo*
Arsene **Lupin** are-*sen* loo-*pan*
Maigret may-*gray*
Ngaio **Marsh** *nye* (as in hi) + oh
Berkely *Mather* *bark*-lee *may*-thurr
Patricia *Moyes* rhymes with "noise"
Hercule **Poirot** heir-*cool* pwah-*row*
Sax **Rohmer** sacks *row*-murr (as in purr)
Joseph *Rouletabille* roo-luh-tah-*bee*-yuh
Georges **Simenon** zshorzsh sea-muh-*no*
Maj **Sjöwall** as in Taj; *show*-vahl
Julian *Symons* as in Crimmins
Josephine *Tey* tay
François **Vidocq** fran-*swah* vee-*duck*
Per **Wahlöö** pair vahl-*oo* (as in boo)
Hilary *Waugh* as in law
Peter *Death Bredon* Wimsey
   as in "teeth"; *bree*-dun
Dilys **Winn** as in "kill us"; rhymes with
   "djinn"

What is it about guns that so fascinates the American reader? It cannot be anything so simple as the tedious Freudian cliché of the phallic power symbol. It is something verbal; otherwise, I would get as many letters from antique-car buffs and airplane types as I get from gun fanatics. Yet the ratio is something like one to fifty. The true antique-car buff is, if anything, more passionate about his obsession than the gun fanatic is; yet he does not write letters to novelists.

The peak of idiocy came a few years ago when I published a novel in which nobody shoots a gun at all — and even on *that* book I got gun mail. Most of it began, "Why didn't you give the character a gun?" My answer was that the character is, like me, the kind of guy who does not feel comfortable lugging a gun around with him; that bullets do not answer any questions; and that guns do not solve problems, they only create new ones. But this didn't seem to make any sense to the gun-mail writers and after a while they gave up on me in disgust on that one.

Both Donald E. Westlake and I received several letters from a deputy sheriff out West who provided us with endless dissertations on guns; at one point, early on in the correspondence, the deputy wrote to Don, "I have read your new book and I am glad to see that Brian Garfield has straightened you out on gun details." Actually, Don and I have better things to do than discuss the trivia of firearms; we had never discussed the subject at all. God knows what led the deputy to his conclusion. But the correspondence was indicative of the painstaking care with which the gun fanatics read novels. They will disregard any implausibility so long as it does not involve ballistics. They cheerfully follow you through holes in your plot that a Boeing 747 could be driven through. But just see what happens if you ever confuse a Colt with a Smith and Wesson.

If I knew why that was the case, I think I'd know everything there is to know about the American character.

Brian Garfield won the Mystery Writers of America Edgar for Hopscotch.

Chapter 14
LOOKING FOR (MORE) TROUBLE

FRED WINKOWSKI

THE DEVOUT
Benefit of Clergy
Catherine Aird

Clergy in the mystery are part of the literary tradition even though they don't go back quite as far as Cain and Abel. This, the first murder of all, certainly began a long connection between religion and crime. Another Biblical link was forged a little later than the Old Testament — in the Apocrypha.

If you remember, it was the Apocrypha that included the two tales about the prophet Daniel which are said to be the original mysteries. The earlier was "The Tale of Susanna and the Elders," in which certain malicious charges were laid against the blameless Susanna; the prophet Daniel proved her innocence in the classical manner — by demonstrating that the evidence given by two separate accusers did not hang together. The second was "Bel and the Dragon," in which the miscreants were confuted by as nice a piece of circumstantial evidence as you'll find outside a crown court.

Daniel's successors in detection have been many and various — and ecumenical. Father Brown, the lovable little priest with the endearing traits of dowdiness, untidiness and a complete lack of pretension, was one of the first. Rabbi David Small is one of the latest. In between have come both Uncle Abner (a religious detective if ever there was one) and a succession of vicars of the Church of England — to say nothing of an archdeacon or two. (Promotion comes late to fictional clergymen engaged in solving mysteries; they have to be satisfied with another sort of preferment.)

But what they have all had in common, these detective clergy, is the ability to reason. If

Drawing by Alain; © 1943, 1971 THE NEW YORKER MAGAZINE, INC.

"Still, did you ever stop to think where you and I would be if it weren't for evil?"

they had faith as well, and I am sure they did and do, all I can say is that it doesn't come into the story the same as their deductions do. It is their logic that we admire. Cogent argument seems to come so easily to these incumbents of the page. Be this a Jesuitical nicety or a rabbinical pilpul, our clerical detectives have us convinced in a couple of paragraphs.

Of course, they have advantages over other amateur sleuths. A thorough grounding in theology, for a start. After all, what is the modern detective story but an extension of the mediaeval morality play? That earlier art form was simpler — the Devil invariably entered from stage left, and you always knew who he was — but it is essentially the same. Our hero now seems able to recognise the Bad'n or the Rotten Apple in the Barrel or the Sinner or the Unfortunate Victim of Circumstance (according to period) with the same sure facility.

Not only do our clerical heroes instinctively know the difference between right and wrong, but they have a professional interest in making sure that Good Triumphs over Bad in the last chapter — if not sooner. Then there's all this experience of the confessional. The Depths of Human Wickedness have already been plumbed by these unshockable men, and this is a great help in the detective story. They have cut their milk teeth on the World, the Flesh and the Devil, so by comparison little foibles like Wine, Women and Song come as very small beer indeed. They've heard it all before.

This isn't the only advantage they have. Besides being well-versed in the ways of the world — at a respectable distance, of course — their occupation leaves them time and energy in which to pursue villains. Evensong never seems to clash with a dénouement when the amiable Archdeacons of Thorp and Garminster, creations of C.A. Arlington, D.D., are solving a gentle mystery. This author, incidentally, was at one time Dean of Durham — a novel combination of Dean and Chapter.

Another real-life clergyman who wrote detective stories — and much else — was Monsignor Ronald A. Knox. It was he who in 1928 laid down the famous "Ten Commandments" (it is quite difficult to get away from the analogy, isn't it?) for the writing of detective stories.

Yet the peculiar situation of all these literary men of the cloth is even more felicitous than their just having ample time between Matins and Compline. Their parochial duties actually give them a good reason for being where the action is. This far from small matter is normally a sore trial to those authors whose detectives are amateur — but it is no problem with the ordained. It might only be collecting for the organ fund: it is more likely to be making arrangements for that uniquely English form of in-fighting known as the parish fete. But somehow it always seems perfectly appropriate for the vicar to be there, whatever the setting.

This goes for where you will find him, too — cottage or castle — for nothing so spans social life as the visiting list of the parish incumbent. Not only is there no one quite so well-placed to appreciate the passion aroused by, say, the church flower-arranging rota, but there is no one better to whom the confession of the murderer in the last-chapter-but-one can be made. A case, you might say, of a good living meeting a bad dying . . .

Then there's the distaff side. There may as yet be few detective nuns (though the play *Bonaventure* by Charlotte Hastings comes very near to this), but the convent has been used more than once as a setting for murder. And we must never forget it is the wool from black sheep which is used to make nun's veiling.

But there: I've nearly left out something important. Most amateur detectives have a love-life that — let's face it — can get in the way. More often than not it comes between the Mountie and his getting his man and, at the very least, distracts the mind from the serious business of crime. Far easier the division of the human species into men, women and clergy. By all means, let the curate cast a flirtatious eye at the leading lady in the choir but leave us with the certainty that, however much our hero may pontificate about being sure that other people's sins will find them out, he hasn't committed any of his own. Unfrocking has no place here: *Clerical Error*, C.E. Vulliamy's nicely named tale about a clergyman, concerns something quite different.

Some detective stories in the canon (if you'll forgive the allusion) go further still and are actually set in the church. Charles Dickens

SOME CLERGY IN THE MYSTERY

C.A. Alington: *Archdeacons Afloat; Gold and Gaiters*

H.C. Bailey: *The Bishop's Crime*

Anthony Boucher: *Nine Times Nine; Rocket to the Morgue*

G.K. Chesterton: *The Innocence (Wisdom, etc.) of Father Brown*

Edmund Crispin: *Holy Disorders*

Antonia Fraser: *Quiet as a Nun*

Dorothy Gilman: *A Nun in the Closet*

Tim Heald: *Unbecoming Habits*

Leonard Holton: *The Saintmaker; Pact with Satan; A Problem in Angels*

Harry Kemelman: Rabbi David Small in all-the-days-of-the-week series

Ralph McInery: *Her Death of Cold*

Thomas Patrick McMahon: *The Issue of the Bishop's Blood*

Alice Scanlon Reach: *The Ordeal of Father Crumlish*

Margaret Scherf: *Gilbert's Last Toothache* (Rev. Martin Buell, Christ Church)

Charles Merrill Smith: *Reverend Randolph and the Wages of Sin*

C.E. Vulliamy: *Tea at the Abbey*

Jack Webb: *The Brass Halo*

David Williams: *Unholy Writ*

began this with his *Mystery of Edwin Drood*. We don't, in fact, know what was to be found in the crypt of Cloisterham Cathedral and now never shall because the author died before finishing the book — but naturally we suspect the worst. Another book centred round a cathedral is Michael Gilbert's neatly titled *Close Quarters*. The town is Melchester, and the setting is what may be aptly called the other sort of precinct: a cathedral close.

Men of the cloth don't always come into the story in a detective capacity. Dorothy L. Sayers, a noted theologian in her own right, left the detection to Lord Peter Wimsey but gave us two affectionate pen portraits of Anglican clergymen. The Reverend Theodore Venables in *The Nine Tailors* and the Reverend Simon Goodacre (Magdalen College, Oxford) in *Busman's Honeymoon* are happy specimens of their kind — and Goodacre is a nice name for a clergyman when you consider that the churchyard is often known as "God's Acre." (Venables isn't far from Venerable, either.)

Emma Lathen, in her customary pithy way, gives us an evocative vignette of a Catholic priest, Father Doyle, taking action after a murder in *Ashes to Ashes*. Josephine Tey in *Brat Farrar* goes further. She allows her rector, George Peck, to destroy evidence which would have spoilt what in a detective story can't very well be called a happy ending.

> "George!" said Bee. "What became of the pen?"
>
> "The stylograph? I lost it."
>
> "George!"
>
> "Someone had to lose it, my dear. Colonel Smollett couldn't: he's a soldier, with a soldier's sense of duty. The police couldn't: they had their self-respect and their duty to the public to consider. But my conscience is between me and my God. I think they were touchingly grateful to me in their tacit way."

And if you like the connection to be vicarious remember that Sir Arthur Conan Doyle's Sherlock Holmes appears at least twice in clerical disguise — in "The Final Problem" and "A Scandal in Bohemia."

So do read on. Preaching and detecting do go hand in hand in an acceptable plurality (even if only a bishop actually gains by translation). Whatever your theological persuasion, you must agree that Satan versus Godliness is the onlie begetter of the detective story . . .

Finally brethren, let me assure you that Caesar's wife has nothing on your detective clergyman. Not only is he above suspicion but, dear reader, there is one thing in this uncertain world of which you can be absolutely sure: The Vicar didn't do it.

Catherine Aird is the author of The Religious Body.

THE EDUCATOR
The Case of the Screaming Spires

Reginald Hill

Every crimiculturalist knows that mayhem breeds best in hot-house conditions. First find your closed community, then drop a mould-warp into the humus.

Jane Austen in her well-known advice to Agatha Christie (among others) says, "Three or four Families in a Country Village is the very thing to work on." As a rural parson's daughter she was clearly aware that the best bestialities took place out of town, and it was a dull week-end when, swollen by house-party guests, Daddy's congregation didn't contain at least one gifted amateur detective to every three homicidal maniacs.

But had Jane Austen lived a century later, when her sex was beginning to be disadvantaged by higher education, she might have modified her advice to include the great centres of learning.

After all, she might have asked, what is a university but a large village? What is a college course but a continuous house-party? And is it not a truth universally acknowledged that students and teachers alike perform short stints of work punctuated by long periods of idleness which can most profitably be filled by crime and its solution?

It might be useful at this point to extend our list of universally acknowledged truths about the world of higher education. So self-evident are they that they need as little statistical support as the basic tenets of other branches of entertainment fiction, *viz* cowboys smell nice and shoot straight, foreigners smell nasty and

spy, spilt blood will out and blue blood will tell.

The following bear the same stamp of authority.

(1) *Students are sex-mad.* When you look at them, it's obvious. When you can't look at them, it's because they've gone to an orgy.

(2) *Students are unbalanced.* Prof. A.E. Houseman, the well-known expert on rustic violence, wasn't joking when he said, "Cambridge has been an asylum to me in every sense of the word." Come exam time, the mental wards install bunk beds.

(3) *Students are dishonest.* They steal food, books, bicycles, lingerie from clothes lines and small change from locker rooms. Also, it is well known that they use the small change they steal to pay for drugs and examination questions other students have stolen.

(4) *Students are revolutionaries.* The only students who are not left-wing anarchists are those who are right-wing terrorists.

As for the teaching staff, suffice it to say that a university lecturer is a student who liked it so much, he didn't want to leave. And a professor is a lecturer who excels.

But to be attractive to the crime novelist, it is not enough for a section of society just to breed potential criminals. The business world, or the Church, can do that quite as well.

It must also breed potential detectives.

And here the crime writer can prove in a flash what educational psychologists have been debating for centuries — the theory of the transfer of training. At its most basic in

CORNELL CAPA/MAGNUM

Does college prepare one for life? Many mystery writers insist it prepares one for death instead. They maintain higher education is synonymous with a higher crime rate.

nineteenth-century England, it asserted that a good classical education inculcated habits of thought and attitudes of mind that fitted a man to administer an Empire. But the claims go beyond the classics and extend to any academic disciplines requiring the application of logic and reason. And how easy it is to point to many influential figures in modern life who have moved freely between the Groves of Academe and the Corridors of Power!

Yet, even with this evidence, many scholars continue to believe in the theory of the transfer of training.

Arthur Conan Doyle realized its implications when, searching his mind for a detective hero, he recalled the diagnostic techniques of his old medical professor. R. Austin Freeman drew similarly upon personal experience in creating his famous forensic scientist, Dr. Thorndyke. And Jacques Futrelle was the first

to give his detective formal academic status when he created, perhaps, the greatest logician of them all — Prof. Augustus S.F.X. Van Dusen, "The Thinking Machine." Futrelle went down with the *Titanic*. Van Dusen, having made such light work of Cell 13, almost certainly escaped.

This early establishment of the suitability of top academic minds for detective work has been followed by the evolution of the student into the state of potential criminality already described. And since World War II, donnish detectives and campus crime novels have abounded. Indeed, for a while it seemed as if all those lecturers who were not filling their long idle periods by committing crime must be writing stories about it.

This brings us to a final point of interest about the academic setting.

Library shelves are full of books set in

countries, cities or social environments which the author has observed only in his mind. Shakespeare never went to Bohemia, Poe never visited Paris. But the academic setting is rarely used except by those who know it personally and often intimately.

Herein lies the difference between the "truth" of the academic mystery and the "truths" of other forms. Those who look closely at such matters must confirm, albeit reluctantly, that six-guns were low on accuracy, cowboys were high out of as well as in the saddle, some foreigners are quite nice, some aristocrats are quite nasty, and most villainy goes undetected.

But few who move and work in our universities and colleges have not at some time been aware that under many a swirling gown lurks the blade of the assassin, and under many a scarlet hood prick the ears of the bat. Words are the grains of sand heaped up against a tide of blood. And if there sometimes seems a shortage of bodies, it may be because in these places the dead keep on walking rather longer than in the world outside.

THE TUTORIAL

Charlotte Armstrong: *Lay On, Mac-Duff*

Francis Bonnamy: *The King Is Dead on Queen Street*

Clyde B. Clason: *The Man from Tibet; Green Shiver*

Edmund Crispin: *The Moving Toyshop*

Amanda Cross: *The James Joyce Murder; Poetic Justice*

James Duff: *Dangerous to Know*

Reginald Hill: *An Advancement of Learning*

Clifford Knight: *The Affair of the Scarlet Crab*

Lee Langley: *Dead Center*

Amanda MacKay: *Death Is Academic*

D.B. Olsen (Dolores Hitchens): *Love Me in Death*

Wirt Van Arsdale: *The Professor Knits a Shroud*

UNDERSTANDING ACADEMIA

O' (Ordinary) Level.

These are exams taken by students who wish to leave school at the age of fifteen. (They must be in attendance until that time.) A student takes a different exam for each of his subjects, so it is not uncommon to hear someone say, "Yes, I got 7 O' levels." This means he passed all 7.

A' (Advanced) Level.

These exams are given to students who have remained in school another two years and wish to qualify for college. They are roughly equivalent to the American College Boards. Again, a student will take them in his major fields of study and 3–4 A' levels are generally acceptable for college entry.

"He read history at Balliol."

At the Oxbridge colleges, a student does not "study" a subject; he "reads" it.

"He was sent down last year."

A student who has been "sent down" has been ejected from his college. This can be for many reasons, ranging from academic difficulty to disciplinary action.

Here, then, for the subtle palate, are soufflés of death and violence served on plates of gold. Taste them in comfort and let who will go down those mean streets, tiptoeing through the cadavers with Chandler and Chase, to whom (among others) Jane Austen said, "How horrible it is to have so many people killed! And what a blessing that one cares for none of them!"

Reginald Hill is the author of An Advancement of Learning, *a crime novel with a professorial touch.*

THE ENVIRONMENTALIST
Storyteller Country

Duncan Kyle

BRUCE DAVIDSON/MAGNUM

There is a kind of novel, one I greatly enjoy reading and try to write, in which there is an extra principal character: the setting. I have no idea who wrote the first, but I think my own first realisation of the importance of *place* came with *Wuthering Heights*, which I read young because I grew up a comfortable morning's walk from the Haworth Moors.

They're story-teller country, these novels, and they're popular because people love tales that take them, as the song says, to faraway places with strange-sounding names. It may be escapism, it may be just armchair travel. But people do enjoy a hero engaged not only with human opponents, but with Nature herself. That, after all, is the history of mankind.

Richard Hannay, handcuffed to the beauteous damsel, dragging her across Scot-tish moors that are at once enemy and friend, provides a good example: it's the moors that make the story sing, not the people; the Forth Bridge, not the villain. Erskine Childers' *Riddle of the Sands*, with one man in a tiny boat confronted not only by Germans but by murderous intricacies of weather and tide, is another. It may even be the best of all.

But there *is* C.S. Forester: not his *African Queen*, though it's a good example, but *Brown on Resolution*, with a lone sailor on a tiny volcanic island pitted against a warship. Sounds unlikely? Begin it, and be convinced. Feel the hazard the island presents, scalpel-sharp rocks, heat to flay off the skin. Mark again the extraordinary demand to endure, which has always been, and is, man's need.

Some people can compose magical settings

and make them real. Lionel Davidson's deep ravine in *Smith's Gazelle* which not only presents problems of survival, but forces bonds to grow between people with cause for enmity, is one of these. Davidson's *The Rose of Tibet,* too (without in any way disparaging Hilton's *Lost Horizon),* is a masterly demonstration of the force of place upon people.

And that, really, is what I'm talking about. But I *do* mean place, not object. Ships don't count: they are too nearly human, anyway. Aircraft, on the other hand, are all too neutral, forcing the attention back toward people and weather and places.

Okay, okay, so where's Hammond Innes? Isn't he the international grandmaster? He is indeed, and I'm coming to him now. He's criticised, sometimes, for failing to create interesting people — which all too often means he doesn't write about the boozy infidelities of antiquarian booksellers. In any bookshop you'll find work by authors who do, but you'll find only one Hammond Innes. Listen. A man is in a small boat on the Atlantic, looking for a difficult and dangerous landfall:

> *An islet loomed in the fog, white with the stain of guano, and as I skirted it, the wind came funnelling down from the hidden heights above, strong enough to flatten the sea; and then the downdraught turned to an updraught, sucking the fog with it, and for an instant I glimpsed rock cliffs . . . they rose stupendous to lose themselves in vapour; dark volcanic masses of gabbro rock, high as the gates of hell.*

Well, you could call it florid, I suppose. You could say there are clichés around. But having said whatever you're going to say, read it again, and *sniff!* Something in your nostrils now — and a picture on the screen of your mind, of place and man and hazard — that tickles something deep inside. We know we're going, once again, to stir up those ancestor-memories. Read on, read on — how on earth could you not?

It is a real place (St. Kilda, if you must know, disguised as Laerg) and recognisable to the place-man. Innes has been there and has the feel of it. With him it's always a real place, and he can show it to you as no one else can.

You become enmeshed in the realities of storm and cold, of animals, of navigation, of mining and geology. It's not just identification: you and the hero seem to merge.

Going there, of course, is all-important. It *is* possible, and indeed has been *done,* to write place novels by careful reading of, for example, the *National Geographic.* But it just isn't the same. I wrote a novel whose finale was played out on a small island and a sea stack in the Shetlands. I'd read about them and seen a lot of photographs. Yet when I got there . . . Nobody had said the great skuas (called Bonxies, locally), which nest there among the grass tussocks in comfortable solitude, would fly at me on five-foot wings, from six directions at once, fast and silent, brushing by close, rough enough to raise welts on my face. Nobody had said the only path ran up beside the high cliffs and the skuas knew all about it and were careful to herd you that way. Nobody had told me what it's like to stand over six hundred sheer feet and watch the gannets fall suddenly, like white darts, after fish.

Go there and material accumulates. The pity is that one can only use so much before the book becomes overloaded. Mine do, anyway. Hammond Innes' unique skill lies in the way he draws in the detail, so that the plot is ultimately composed of small parts of knowledge. Sometimes I turn green, I really do.

But if he's the nonpareil, there are others: Desmond Bagley, conjuring up the Andes in *High Citadel;* Derek Lambert's grim and grinding Moscow in *Angels in the Snow;* Berkely Mather (number two only to Innes), drawing beautiful pictures of the Himalaya lying gigantically in wait to oppress a few lonely, desperate — and desperately *small* — men.

No women? Come now, I did begin with Emily. Yes, there are women. Mary Stewart knows how to use a setting. So does Helen MacInnes. But in general (in *my* experience, that is, and I'll be delighted to widen it) women writers like the people larger than the landscape. No criticism there, or implied, just a matter of approach.

Duncan Kyle is a past chairman of the Crime Writers' Association.

THE HISTORIAN
Once Upon a Crime

Peter Lovesey

Fog, swirling through the streets of London. Footsteps quickening. They stop. A moment of silence, then an agonised scream. Blurred shapes running. The blast of a police whistle. The beam of a bull's-eye lamp directed onto a lifeless form. Another victim.

Meanwhile, the great detective sits in his rooms in Baker Street before a blazing fire, reading the personal column of the *Times*.

For atmosphere, the counterpoise of teacups and terror, cosiness and crime, the Victorian mystery is supreme. The architects of the

---

HISTORICAL MYSTERIES

Gwendoline Butler: *A Coffin for Pandora*

John Dickson Carr: *The Bride of Newgate; The Devil in Velvet; Captain Cut-Throat; Fire, Burn!; Scandal at High Chimneys; The Witch of the Low-Tide; The Demoniacs; Most Secret; Papa Là-Bas; The Ghosts' High Noon; Deadly Hall; The Hungry Goblin; The Murder of Sir Edmund Godfrey*

Agatha Christie: *Death Comes as the End*

Carter Dickson: *Fear Is the Same*

Doris Miles Disney: *Who Rides a Tiger*

Mignon G. Eberhart: *Family Fortune*

Richard Falkirk: *Blackstone; Blackstone's Fancy*

Joan Fleming: *Screams from a Penny Dreadful*

John Gardner: *The Return of Moriarty; The Revenge of Moriarty*

William Irish: *Waltz into Darkness*

Peter Lovesey: *Wobble to Death; The Detective Wore Silk Drawers; Abracadaver; Mad Hatter's Holiday; The Tick of Death; A Case of Spirits; Swing, Swing Together*

Victor Luhrs: *The Longbow Murder*

Theodore Mathieson: *The Devil and Ben Franklin*

Anthony Price: *Other Paths to Glory; War Game*

Ellery Queen: *A Study in Terror*

Francis Selwyn: *Sergeant Venits and the Imperial Diamond*

Jean Stubbs: *Dear Laura*

Josephine Tey: *The Daughter of Time*

P.W. Wilson: *Bride's Castle; Black Tarn; The Old Mill*

VOID of all grace, &, for fake of the money,
The cruel Boatfwain the fame did complete:
As they were on the deck lovingly walking,
He fuddenly tumbled him into the deep.

HELP! MVRTHER!

popular detective story — Poe, Dickens, Wilkie Collins and Conan Doyle — built citadels of suspense that still dominate the scene. Any modern author setting a story in the Victorian period starts with the knowledge that hansom cabs and London fogs are redolent of Holmes and Watson.

And how productive the nineteenth century was of motives for murder! The need to achieve security by inheritance, or life insurance, or marriage; the risk of losing it when scandal threatened; the equating of sex with sin; the stigma of insanity; the things that went unsaid. Our world of social welfare and easier divorce and psychiatric care has removed many of the bad old reasons for murder. How unin-

spiring, too, by contrast with times past, are the modern weapons — the gun with telescopic sights, the car-bomb and the hypodermic syringe. Give me Jack the Ripper's knife or Neill Cream's bag of poisons or Lizzie Borden's ace!

Of course, the historical mystery has reached back beyond the nineteenth century, millenniums before the first police officers appeared on the streets. Ancient Egypt of 4000 B.C. (*Death Comes as the End*), Tang China (*The Chinese Bell Murders*) and Alexander's Greece (*The Great Detectives*) have all been used as settings, while characters as various as Machiavelli, Richard III and Ben Franklin have been featured. Treatments range from documentary novels researched from actual cases, such as Michael Gilbert's *The Claimant* and John Cashman's *The Gentleman from Chicago*, through brilliant pastiches like Lillian de la Torre's *Dr. Sam: Johnson, Detector* to extravaganzas like Anthony Price's *Our Man in Camelot*, in which the CIA becomes involved with King Arthur. The trend is toward more fantastic plots, more dazzling tricks, with a strong infusion of humour. All we ask of the historical mystery is that it tell a story consistent with known facts and that those facts arise naturally from the plot. If we want a history lecture, we can go to college.

The fascination of a mystery set in the remote past is easily explained: it provides an escape from modern life. But we are not at the mercy of a science-fiction writer's fantasizing. The world we enter is real and under control. There is a framework of fact. Even the most extravagant plots conform to historical truth. Yes, the CIA does become entangled with King Arthur. Read it and see!

And the greatest of all fictional detectives has tangled with the worst of criminals (*Sherlock Holmes Versus Jack the Ripper*) and discussed psychology with Sigmund Freud (*The Seven Per-Cent Solution*), while his old adversary is launched on a whole new career of crime (*The Return of Moriarty*). Thank heavens Holmes is alive and well and reading the *Times* in London!

Peter Lovesey won the Panther-Macmillan prize for his first historical mystery, Wobble to Death.

GARDENING
Thou Bleeding Piece of Earth

Avon Curry

Gardeners and crime writers have quite a lot in common, not least that they are both fond of a good plot. Writers, like horticulturists, have to labour at improving the groundwork: you can start off with a good idea but it's the way you tend it that produces a good crop — either of blossoms or of saleable words.

Gardening is particularly basic to the British. You know, it's said that if you give a quarter of an acre to a Frenchman, he'll plant a vine and invite a pretty girl to share the vintage; a Japanese will grow enough rice to feed a family of ten; an Englishman will lay out a lawn and sit on it to drink tea.

A crime writer will at once see a quarter-of-an-acre garden as the answer to one of the three great problems in plotting a mystery — how to get rid of the body. The perceptive reader would be well advised to look out for a passing remark about how well the roses are growing compared with those next-door, because it's under that rose bed that the deceased is sleeping. If you allow your garden to run wild, undergrowth is a useful camouflage for the quickly hidden corpse and provides good descriptive stuff when you begin talking about the heavy boots peeping out among the bluebells, or the tangle of blond tresses among the brambles.

Gardeners often burn their rubbish. If you take the trouble to establish the character ("plant the idea," as we significantly say when chatting about plotting) as a thoroughgoing efficient husbandman, you can justify the big incinerator in which bodies can be reduced to ash. I recall a garden incinerator proved very handy to that well-known "husbandman" M. Verdoux. The drawback in Britain is that the weather's seldom dry long enough to keep the bonfire going for the requisite time — so that brings us to the compost heap.

Compost is very "big" in British gardening at the moment. There was a time when to talk about it branded you as a crank, but now you're an ecologist. Foolhardy would be the policeman who dared open up a keen gardener's compost heap without the very best possible evidence that a corpse was providing a large part of its

---

GARDENING

Herbert Adams: *The Crime in Dutch Garden*
Agatha Christie: *The Mirror Cracked*
Wilkie Collins: *The Moonstone*
J.J. Connington: *Murder in the Maze*
Elizabeth Daly: *Any Shape or Form*
Richard Forrest: *The Wizard of Death*
Richard Hull: *The Murder of My Aunt*
Veronica Parker Johns: *Servant's Problem*
Rex Stout: *Some Buried Caesar; Black Orchids; In the Best Families*
Jack Webb: *The Brass Halo*

bulk. Moreover, compost heaps are messy things. Smelly, too, the uninitiated believe. Policemen are more than likely to leave them alone so that the corpse is left in peace where the convocation of politic worms can keep busy.

Gardens are a good excuse for collecting the tools of death. You have only to look at the names of chemicals sold to garden-lovers — "tox" on the end of the word means, of course, that the mixture is extremely toxic; words that include the consonance "kil" or the straightforward "slay" or "bane" speak for themselves. One might almost say that in many garden-lovers there lurks a hater of other life forms — and a murderer is after all a person with enough hate to want to kill another human being.

Modern gardening chemicals are extremely dangerous. If you read the instructions — and I strongly recommend it both as a piece of academic research and as a practical life-saving exercise — you'll see you're to wash at once if a spot lands on your skin, that you're not to inhale the spray, that children mustn't get at it, or even pets. In the early days of DDT, puppies and kittens died from licking flea-killing powders from their coats. DDT has gone, but worse things have replaced it. Bear in mind, too, that the effect of these poisons is irreversible; the poison builds up with every tiny drop.

J. CRAWHALL

Venus's-flytrap. Not shown: the boringly harmless flowers which grow at the end of the stalk.

FAMOUS HORTICULTURISTS

Sergeant Cuff
Senator Wentworth
Webster Flagg
Nero Wolfe
Jane Marple
Father Bredder

So the easiest way to get rid of your enemy is to rent the house upwind of him, and spray your roses every time there's a strong breeze. It may take a while, but by and by he ought to get very sick if he will insist on sitting on that lawn of his.

For the knowledgeable gardener, poison need not come out of a bottle. There are deadly plants all around us, in every lovesome plot, God wot. The most innocent products can provide the most efficacious alternative to the bare bodkin. The potato, for example. Good to eat, unless you allow the tubers to become green through exposure to light, in which case the skin becomes very harmful. The leaf of the rhubarb plant (*Rheum rhaponticum*) is very toxic, although the stalk is used in pies and preserves. Ivy is poisonous. So is laburnum — remember *My Cousin Rachel?*

Nor need you actually grow the plant yourself. Once you have weeded your own garden, it dawns on you that hedgerows and wastelands are teeming with lethal growth. The datura is a member of the same family as the harmless tomato and potato. Deadly nightshade. Hemlock . . . there's a historic aid to death: Socrates drank a brew of hemlock at the behest of the Athenian rulers. Mushrooms . . . perhaps you don't want your victim dead, only out of his head: a handbook on fungi will soon tell you which to offer him, as in *The Documents in the Case.*

I can hear male readers saying that although gardening opens up endless varieties of poison, this is a very tricky and feminine form of murder. Those who like action-murder might prefer to deliver a hearty clout with a

The more unscrupulous the gardener, the more likely he is to engineer a maze — into which he will entice his victim and leave him stranded. Shown: Hampton Court Maze, which may yet be used with such aplomb.

spade or shrivel the opposition with a weed flame-gun. The motor-mower or the mini-cultivator might run amok at the psychological moment — but you need a big garden to justify big equipment. Your small-scale gardener, your patio-gardener, must rely on having the victim trip up and hit his head on the Alpine rockery; or perhaps he could fall face down among the water-lilies in the decorative pond (*Nymphaea capensis* is a good bright blue variety, recommended for contrast to the drowned features when he is fished out).

There's nothing like a little knowledge of horticulture to make you aware that life is precarious, that the prize at the Flower Show is only gained by eternal vigilance against enemies natural and unnatural. The crime-writing gardener is acutely aware of an under-meaning in the famous lines from the *Rubáiyát:*

> *How oft hereafter rising shall she look*
> *Through this same garden after me—in*
> *vain!*

But the crime writer who sets his murder in a garden wants you to look in vain — until at least the end of the book. He has a splendid chance of mystifying you, because it's standard practice for a garden-lover to direct your attention to the good things and distract you from the spindly growths or the rogue intruders. You must have heard the excuse: "The rhododendrons aren't at their best now — you should have been here last week."

Indeed you should. That was when he was suffocating his victim with the plastic bag in which the fertiliser was delivered.

Avon Curry is a member of the Royal Horticulture Society.

Something Between a Sport and a Religion

HOBBIES OF THE FAMOUS

The Old Man in the Corner sits at a back table in a London tea shop, tying and untying knots in a single piece of string.

In The Singing Sands *Alan Grant corrects his doctor, who calls trout fishing a hobby. Says Grant, it's "something between a sport and a religion."*

Gideon Fell's chubby fingers are surprisingly graceful when it comes to making elaborate houses out of a deck of cards.

Lyon Wentworth relaxes by rising above it all. He has the most unusual hobby of the lot — ballooning.

MARTY NORMAN

Characters in crime fiction tend to take their hobbies as seriously as their homicides. One suspects if the Almighty Himself paid a call on Nero Wolfe during orchid-growing hours, even He would be asked to wait. If you're in the market for a new hobby yourself, you might consider that Charlie Chan likes swimming and chess, Sgt. Beef is adept at darts, Gervase Fen goes on long drives, Holmes practices the violin, the Norths cuddle up to a cat, Evan Pinkerton is a devoted moviegoer, J.G. Reeder is a chronic patience player, Dr. Davie adores the opera, Ellery Queen collects rare books, Max Carrados collects rare coins, Travis McGee loves his boat the *Busted Flush*, and Sister Ursula, Sgt. Ivor Maddox and D.A. Douglas Selby are addicted to reading mysteries.

Prepared by Anne N. Nixon.

Says Sergeant Cuff, "I haven't much time to be fond of anything, but when I have a moment's kindness to bestow, most times, the roses get it."

Captain Duncan Maclain assembles huge jigsaw puzzles, sensitively fitting together pieces he will never see. (Maclain was blinded in the war.)

Mitch Tobin, like Churchill, is soothed by constructing a wall, brick by brick.

Hildegarde Withers is passionate about only two things: murder investigations and her collection of tropical fish.

COMMUTING
An Unscheduled Stop at an Isolated Junction

Hugh Douglas

I*t was five o'clock on a winter's morning in Syria. Alongside the platform at Aleppo stood the train grandly designated in railway guides as the Taurus Express. It consisted of a kitchen and dining-car, a sleeping-car and two local coaches.*

Thus Agatha Christie starts her classic whodunit *Murder on the Orient Express.*

Two local coaches, a sleeping-car and a kitchen and dining-car hardly add up to romance, but we know that the route lies through half of Asia Minor to Istanbul, where the great train waits to carry readers on across Europe for three days to Paris. It is a journey which most will make only on the pages of a book — a journey into a web of murder they'd never expect to encounter in reality.

The famous train is as unrelated to their lives as is the murder they await, and just as romantic!

Trains of every kind, named expresses, night mails and smelly little local puffers, have been a favourite setting for crime writers and their readers since the crime novel was born. They have inspired authors to make the wheels of fear spin in their readers' minds as no other mode of transport could.

What's so special about the railroad that ships, airplanes or automobiles don't have? Why does *Mystery of the Blue Train* capture attention on the bookstalls while *Mayhem on the Queen Mary* would hardly rate a second glance? What is there about the grinding of iron wheels on iron rails that sets the adrenalin flowing like a rogue oil-well?

Ships and planes have been used successfully by crime writers, of course they have, but as a location they suffer from the disadvantage that they're not really in our world as they travel: their routes don't relate to real life or death, so they are soulless phantoms orbiting beyond man's environment until the moment they touch land. And then, seaports or airports are not at the heart of cities — where people live, love and commit violence against their fellow man. Even the motor car is a capsule sealed off from humanity. Look down on a highway and you see little automated ants rushing to and fro, starting, stopping, and missing one another by a hair's breadth as if directed by some kind of formic radar. And who ever heard of a whodunit about ants, for heaven's sake?

The train is different. It has all the good qualities that other modes of travel offer to the crime novelist, but it has more. Although quite isolated from its environment, the train never ceases to be a part of it. A real world of houses, villages, cities, fields, cows and even people pass by the window. Yet this world is quite out of reach, unable to affect the traveller for good or ill. Reality is just beyond his fantasy world, but quite unattainable. The wheeled thing rolls on, out of the reader's control. There is no escape.

In this enclosed space the tension heightens all the way to journey's end.

The train is a universe of its own. It is confined, remote and comfortable. Whodunit victims always travel first class so their blood soaks into the thick plush cushions, leaving no vulgar mess. Indeed, the whodunit train resembles that other favourite venue of the thriller, the secluded country house, with the compartment as closely confined as a smoking-room. Here must be no vulgarity, no undue ostentation, no overindulgence — just solid comfort.

But unlike the country house the reader's companions on the train are strangers — or so he thinks. Who are they? Who is victim and who villain? Half a dozen people eye one another, reading (or is it lurking?) behind a newspaper, dozing fitfully, or glancing apprehensively from window to fellow passengers and then to the door. The train rushes into a tunnel, and the overhead reading lamp clamps a mask over the face of the man opposite, turning him from a benign Dr. Jekyll to a savage Mr. Hyde. Can he really be as sinister as he looks, or is he one of the red herrings with which the whodunit's track is strewn? And who is that old lady knitting in the other corner? Her eyes are everywhere. Is she waiting for the chance to thrust a No. 10 needle six inches into someone's heart, or is she dear Miss Marple biding her time to unravel the problem?

Truly, travellers are strange bedfellows. Bedfellows? My God, the sleeping car is lethal. Here is the most isolated place in the whole world, a tiny square of space, lonelier than the summit of Everest. And what are all these switches, buttons and bolts for? Does the door lock securely? It is impossible to try it without opening it again. And will the distant clanging of the bell be answered by the steward, or will it bring some sinister caller?

It's bad enough when the train is moving; noise covers up other noises, the scream or gunshot will never be heard over the clickety-clack of the wheels, the roar of the tunnel will shut out the stealthy footstep in the corridor, the engine's strangled whistle will drown the cry of danger in the next sleeping berth. But what happens when the train stops in the middle of nowhere? Trains do. The Orient Express stuck in a snow-filled waste, deep with drifting fear. Help could not reach it; escape was impossible. This prison was as secure as Devil's Island, as well guarded as Sing Sing, but it held the person who had wielded the knife in the night, and he might wield it again.

ONE-WAY TICKETS

Lawrence G. Blochman: *Bombay Mail*
Lynn Brock: *The Slip-Carriage Mystery*
Stephen Chalmers: *The Crime in Car 13*
Agatha Christie: *The Mystery of the Blue Train; Murder on the Orient Express*
John Creasey: *Murder on the Line*
Michael Crichton: *The Great Train Robbery*
Freeman Wills Crofts: *Death of a Train; Double Death; Sir John Magill's Last Journey*
Laine Fisher: *Fare Prey*
Graham Greene: *Orient Express*
Dolores and Bert Hitchins: *End of the Line; F.O.B. Murder; The Grudge; The Man Who Followed Women; One-Way Ticket*
Sebastien Japrisot: *The 10:30 from Marseilles*
Baynard Kendrick: *The Last Express*
Henry Leverage: *The Purple Limited*
Francis Lynde: *Scientific Sprague*
Sue MacVeigh: *Grand Central Murder; Murder Under Construction; Streamlined Murder*
Frederick Nebel: *Sleepers East*
Frank L. Packard: *The Wire Devils*
John Rhode: *Death on the Boat Train*
Mary Roberts Rinehart: *The Man in Lower Ten*
Wilson Tucker: *Last Stop*
Ethel Lina White: *The Lady Vanishes*
Victor L. Whitechurch: *Thrilling Stories of the Railway*

GLOBE PHOTOS

The 11:18 passing through Watford. One of the most famous trains in mystery fiction was Eden Phillpott's "Flying Scotsman."

A wakeful man in a sleeping car is the loneliest man on earth.

Day restores the scene to that comforting, comfortable country house, filled with elegance and peopled with feudal staff. In the dining car the stewards show all the attentiveness of old family retainers, and breakfast is as generous as it would be for a house party in Devon, with only the food-loaded sideboard missing. But in the train there can be no relaxed feeling for long, because murder has been committed and work is in hand to solve the crime. While the innocent hover in fear, the murderer's confidence crumbles. He is as much the victim of the confined space as of the detective's skill.

The train journey has shape, and shape is what the writer is seeking when he plans his novel: within a time-scale the crime will be perpetrated, discovered and solved. Journey's end will reveal all, convict the guilty and release the innocent. It is very tidy.

Of course, not all novelists confine their story to the train — the crime can pursue the traveller home and then his detectives go to work on time-tables, proving the impossible by a mere thirty seconds between trains, for the railway time-table is the train crime writer's *vade mecum*, as essential as his typewriter.

Alas, the heyday of the train was the heyday of the railway whodunit, when trains were drawn by lumbering dinosaurs that left behind them a trail of fire, smoke, steam and mystery. Diesel or electric locomotives are clinically clean and lacking in romance, and it is largely their fault that the train no longer attracts the crime novelist or his reader. But memories are memories. The classics of the genre still are read and reread by those who seek a glimpse into the lush past, taking their crime elegantly and with a whiff of nostalgic smoke.

Hugh Douglas loves trains almost as much as mysteries, as well he should, since he works for British Rail.

COMPETING
The Sporting Blood Syndrome

John L. Powers

Abner Doubleday, an American, may have invented baseball, but I feel confident it will be an Englishman who finally perfects the curve ball — putting an extra spin on it with a spit or so of nitroglycerin. The British seem to have more sporting blood than the rest of us, to see more potential for crime in athletic contests than we do.

To them, a golf bunker is a natural place for a corpse (*An Awkward Lie*, of course) and a cricket match the perfect backdrop for a surprising arrest (*Murder Must Advertise*) and a Chelsea-Arsenal soccer game a good opportunity to catch a glimpse of a suspected murderer (*The Plot Against Roger Ryder*).

Horse racing, tennis, rugby, field and track, skiing, boxing, bullfighting, archery — all have been used as settings by English mystery authors. "Good show, old sport" is as apt to apply to someone using the cricket bat as a blunt instrument as it is to someone maneuvering his hansom cab in a pea-souper.

Not to be outdone, the Americans have, of late, turned their hand to recreational treachery. And being American, they have gone about it bloodier, gorier, bigger and, if not better, certainly bizarrer.

At least two thrillers — *Black Sunday* and *Two-Minute Warning* — have been wrung out of the Super Bowl, probably America's glossiest and most overblown sporting event. And they've barely scratched the event's potential. After all, it's seen by more than 80,000 people, including senators, corporation heads and presidents, and it draws more illegal gambling interest than any other single event in the nation. Can anyone doubt what a fine forum it is for kidnapping or blackmail or what a smorgasbord for a lone killer or terrorist group? What's more, it's always held in a massive stadium in a major city — like the Superdome in New Orleans, the Los Angeles Coliseum or Miami's Orange Bowl — and provides a nice hiding place for escapees from . . . anywhere.

What makes sporting events, with either an English or American accent, so appealing to the crime writer as well as the crime reader? Familiarity.

Most of us know how the game — whatever it may be — is played, and that makes a twist on it all the more chilling. We can imagine all too easily a cleat put in the wrong place, a puck whacked in the middle of the goalie rather than the middle of the cage. And one hardly has to leave the locker room to find a good victim, a good weapon, a good opportunity and a good motive. Consider, for example, a power forward for the Lakers taking a pre-game shot of Novocain for a sore knee — and ending up in a coma — with game seven of the NBA finals only moments away and $4 million of Mob money riding on the 76ers.

There also happens to be a ready supply of suspects. Enough of them, in fact, to fill Madison Square Garden twice over: ambitious understudies; insecure coaches; greedy quar-

BAD SPORTS

Horse Racing

John Creasey: *Death of a Racehorse*

Charles Drummond: *Death at the Furlong Post*

Dick Francis: *Dead Cert; Nerve; Forfeit; Rat Race; Smokescreen*

Frank Gruber: *The Gift Horse*

Stuart Palmer: *The Puzzle of the Red Stallion; The Puzzle of the Happy Hooligan*

Judson Philips: *Murder Clear, Track Fast*

Kin Platt: *The Princess Stakes Murder*

S.S. Van Dine: *The Garden Murder Case*

Edgar Wallace: *The Green Ribbon; The Flying Fifty-Five*

Tennis

John Dickson Carr: *The Problem of the Wire Cage*

Stanley Ellin: *The Valentine Estate*

Frances and Richard Lockridge: *The Judge Is Reversed*

J.J. Marric: *Gideon's Sport*

Brown Meggs: *Saturday Games*

Lillian O'Donnell: *Death on the Grass*

J.B. Priestley: *The Doomsday Men*

Baseball

Robert L. Fish and Henry Rothblatt: *A Handy Death*

Leonard Holton: *The Devil to Play*

Robert B. Parker: *Mortal Stakes*

Robert Wade: *Knave of Eagles*

Basketball

Charles Drummond: *Death and the Leaping Ladies*

Lee Langley: *Dead Center*

Kin Platt: *The Giant Kill*

British Rugby Football

David Craig: *Double Take*

Reginald Hill: *A Clubbable Woman*

Football

Eliot Asinof: *The Name of the Game Is Murder*

George Bagby: *Coffin Corner*

Alan Nixon: *The Gold and Glory Guy*

John Stephen Strange: *Murder on the Ten Yard Line*

Soccer Football

Leonard Gribble: *The Arsenal Stadium Mystery*

---

terbacks; disappointed groupies; crooked trainers; worried gamblers; overly competitive competitors.

If a little privacy is needed in which to commit one's crime, think of the player's tunnel at Oakland–Alameda County Coliseum, or the losers' dressing room an hour after the game. Need a crowd to obscure a villain? How about the members' enclosure at the Henley royal regatta or the ninth tee at St. Andrews mid-tournament? For that matter, someone could turn the bullpen at Tiger Stadium into the prototypical locked room.

Plot ideas? Well, how about a kidnapping with an international flavor? Nothing wrong with an Amsterdam betting syndicate spiriting away the Liverpool goalie a few hours before the European Cup Final against Ajax. Looking for a political assassination in a genteel atmosphere? Why not the gentlemen's final at Wimbledon, with the Queen looking on from the royal box? How about a Minnesota Vikings quarterback murdered by a Denver assistant coach? Or a Czech tennis player blackmailed into being a double agent during a Davis Cup match in Krakow? (There seems,

Peter Handke: *The Goalie's Anxiety at the Penalty Kick*
Maurice Procter: *Rogue Running*
Julian Symons: *The Plot Against Roger Ryder*

Boxing

Richard Falkirk: *Blackstone's Fancy*
William Campbell Gault: *The Canvas Talk Loud*
Ed Lacy: *Lead with Your Left*
Vernon Loder: *Kill in the Ring*

Bullfighting

Patrick Quentin: *Puzzle for Pilgrims*
Julian Rathbone: *Carnival*

Archery

Leo Bruce: *Death at St. Asprey's School*

Ballooning

Richard Forrest: *A Child's Garden of Death; The Wizard of Death*

Track and field events

Peter Lovesey: *Wobble to Death*

Cricket

Adrian Alington: *The Amazing Test Match Crime*
John Creasey: *A Six for the Toff*
Michael Gilbert: *The Crack in the Teacup*

Geoffrey Household: *Fellow Passenger*
J.J. Marric: *Gideon's Sport*
C. St. John Sprigg: *The Corpse with the Sunburned Face*
Clifford Witting: *A Bullet for Rhino*
Barbara Worsley-Gough: *Alibi Innings*

Winter sports

Emma Lathen: *Murder Without Icing*
Hannah Lees: *The Dark Device*
Patricia Moyes: *Dead Men Don't Ski;*
Jeremy Potter: *Foul Play*
Owen Sela: *The Bearer Plot*
Jean-François Vignant: *The Alpine Affair*
Margaret Yorke: *Silent Witness*
Phyllis A. Whitney: *Snowfire*

Golf

Herbert Adams: *The Nineteenth Hole Mystery; The Body in the Bunker*
Miles Burton: *Tragedy at the 13th Hole*
Agatha Christie: *Murder on the Links; The Boomerang Clue*
Michael Innes: *An Awkward Lie*
Owen Fox Jerome: *The Golf Club Murder*
Angus MacVicar: *Murder at the Open*
Rex Stout: *Fer-de-Lance*
Anthony Wynne: *Death of a Golfer*

by the way, to be a natural affinity between tennis players and mystery writers. Both are involved in a game of wits, a one-on-one game: the detective is pitted against the murderer as the No. 1 seed is pitted against No. 2, surely the most competitive situation extant.)

Curiously, not too many sports figures read mysteries. Back in the days when they took trains to get from city to city, game to game, they were more likely to read. Now with the advent of the red-eye plane flight, they seem more interested in sleeping than in reading.

One exception is Tommy Heinsohn, coach of the Boston Celtics. Not only does he read thrillers (such as Ira Levin's *The Boys from Brazil*), but he passes them on. I know, because he gives them to me.

Obviously, sporting blood can be spilled almost anywhere, by anyone. En garde, my friend. It is not a friendly game, after all.

John L. Powers is a sports writer for the Boston Globe. He plays a vicious game of tennis.

HOLIDAYING
The Christmas Mystery Lecture
Bill Vande Water

Let us address ourselves to that curious paradox of detective fiction known as the "Christmas" mystery. The most curious thing about it is that it exists at all. Christmas is supposed to be the time of peace, of joy and love, when Macy and Gimbel shake hands, suddenly repentant Scrooges toss ten-dollar bills in Salvation Army kettles, families are reunited, old friendships rekindled, and children are on their best behavior. Why spoil such warm, nostalgic, tug-at-the-heartstrings scenes with a petty theft, much less a murder?

The cynic will answer with one word: money. Being the high-minded people we are, however, we shall ignore the base suggestion that authors write merely to sell to the Christmas issues of mystery magazines. (Besides, Isaac Asimov's "The Thirteenth Day of Christmas" came out in July.)

Instead, let us consider that Christmas is joined with crime for historical, indeed theological, accuracy. One of the wise men (they figure as detectives in R.L. Steven's "The Three Travellers") brought myrrh, an embalming spice. King Herod celebrated the first Christmas with a mass killing of babies. Even mistletoe has a criminal record: it was the murder weapon used to kill Balder, the most loved of the Norse gods. And the Puritan fathers of Massachusetts made the celebration of Christmas itself a crime, punishable by a five-shilling fine.

It becomes apparent that in real life, then, crimes do occur at Christmas. Good will may increase, but so does the homicide rate. By some strange quirk of human nature, the same season that fills the stores and churches also fills the jails and morgues — and motivates the mystery writer like no other holiday could ever hope to.

We must understand, however, the peculiar distinction between Christmas mystery novels and Christmas mystery stories. The novels, without exception, favor homicide as a leitmotif; in them, a writer may use pine, spruce, holly or even money for his Christmas green, but his Christmas red had better be blood. The stories, on the other hand, are partial to theft and burglary.

The tradition of the nonlethal Christmas detective story goes back to the master himself and his "Adventure of the Blue Carbuncle." This story also started the tradition of stolen and hidden jewels and was followed by G.K. Chesterton's "The Flying Stars," Dorothy L. Sayers' "The Necklace of Pearls," Margery Allingham's "The Snapdragon and the C.I.D.," Ellery Queen's "The Dauphin's Doll," Agatha Christie's "The Adventure of the Christmas Pudding," Georges Simenon's "Maigret's Christmas" and Damon Runyon's "Dancing Dan's Christmas."

Conan Doyle also started the tradition of the "season of forgiveness," in which the criminal, although discovered, is allowed to escape with nothing more than a warning and a good scare.

One of the best of the Christmas short

stories is August Derleth's "The Adventure of the Unique Dickensians." This double pastiche combines elements of Doyle and Dickens and is a true tour de force.

Christmas mystery novels fit into three categories. The first is a Christmas mystery by courtesy only. Christmas is mentioned, but it is really there as an excuse for assembling a group of people who otherwise would not be caught dead together — so that at least one of them may be so caught. The best example of this misuse of the Christmas theme is Agatha Christie's *Murder for Christmas;* the next best (or worst, depending on how strongly you feel

about this type of thing) is Michael Innes' *Comedy of Terrors;* not quite as bad, but reaching, is Georgette Heyer's *Envious Casca.*

The second category of Christmas mystery novel features, more often than not, police procedurals. Private detectives and nosy old ladies may go home for the holidays, but for the police it's just another busy day, what with pickpockets and shoplifters working the Christmas rush. Among the best of these realistic, ironic novels are Ed McBain's *Pusher* and *Sadie When She Died*, Dell Shannon's *No Holiday for Crime* and James McClure's *The Gooseberry Fool.* Not a police procedural, but still

CHRISTMAS AND CRIME

Novels

Agatha Christie: *Murder for Christmas (Holiday for Murder)*
Charles Dickens: *The Mystery of Edwin Drood*
Elizabeth X. Ferrars: *The Small World of Murder*
Cyril Hare: *An English Murder*
Georgette Heyer: *Envious Casca*
John Howlett: *The Christmas Spy*
Michael Innes: *A Comedy of Terrors; Christmas at Candleshoes*
Ed McBain: *Pusher; Sadie When She Died*
James McClure: *The Gooseberry Fool*
Ngaio Marsh: *Tied Up in Tinsel*
Jack Pearl: *Victims*
Ellery Queen: *The Finishing Stroke*
Patrick Ruell: *Red Christmas*
Dell Shannon: *No Holiday for Crime*

Short Stories

Margery Allingham: "The Case of the Man with the Sack"; "The Snapdragon and the C.I.D."
G.K.Chesterton: "The Flying Stars"
Agatha Christie: "The Adventure of the Christmas Pudding" ("The

Theft of the Royal Ruby"); "Christmas Tragedy"
John Collier: "Back for Christmas"
August Derleth: "The Adventure of the Unique Dickensians"
Arthur Conan Doyle: "The Adventure of the Blue Carbuncle"
Stanley Ellin: "Christmas Eve"
O. Henry: "Whistling Dick's Christmas Stocking"
Edward D. Hoch: "Christmas Is for Cops"
Ellery Queen: "The Dauphin's Doll"
Damon Runyon: "Dancing Dan's Christmas"; "Palm Springs Santa Claus"
Dorothy L. Sayers: "The Necklace of Pearls"
Georges Simenon: "Maigret's Christmas"
Rex Stout: "Christmas Party"; "Santa Claus Beat"
Julian Symons: "The Santa Claus Club"; "Twixt the Cup and the Lip"

Nonfiction

A.C. Greene: *The Santa Claus Bank Robbery*

RICHARD KALVAR/MAGNUM

There is a Midwestern state which has made it illegal for women to appear on the street dressed as Santa.

falling within this category, is Ian Fleming's *On Her Majesty's Secret Service,* in which James Bond makes his violent escape from SPECTRE headquarters on Christmas Eve and Christmas Day. In these novels the Christmas background offers a depressing commentary on the kind of world in which peace is so frequently converted to death.

The third and perhaps most effective category of Christmas novel is the one in which the crime, or detection, or both, could take place in no other season. The accouterments of Christmas are necessary to the novel's success. These tend to feature Santa Claus. Burglars, detectives, bank robbers, the police, murderers, victims, even a few (relatively) innocent bystanders — all have made use of this disguise. Nor have Santa's criminal appearances been confined to fiction. A.C. Greene's *The Santa Claus Bank Robbery* concerns a real-life use of the ubiquitous Santa disguise that went dead wrong. (There is, by the way, a Midwestern state which has made it illegal for women to

appear on the street dressed as Santa. Make of that what you will.)

Next to Santa the most popular Christmas motifs, in a novel, are Christmas house parties, reunions, mistletoe, trees, toys and seasonal foods. In *The Finishing Stroke* Ellery Queen even makes special use of a song, "The Twelve Days of Christmas." Be assured, however, that novels in this category do not use Christmas as mere trimming; it is integral to their plots.

In closing, may I remind you that Charles Dickens, creator of that syrupy tale *A Christmas Carol,* eventually tired of all the Christmas niceties. The next time someone tells you he longs for a typically Dickensian Christmas, ask him if he had in mind the kind of Christmas Eve Dickens gave to *Edwin Drood.*

Bah, humbug to all, and to all a good fright.

Bill Vande Water manages the Film and Videotape Library for CBS News Archives.

SINISTER ORIENTALS
Everybody's Favorite Villains

Robin W. Winks

When Goldfinger's Korean body-guard, Oddjob, was given the shock of his life by James Bond, he was simply dying for The Cause, yet one more Sinister Oriental gone to his just reward. After all, as Goldfinger had told Bond, Oddjob was "simple, unrefined clay, capable of limited exploitation." He was above the Chigroes, to be sure, since he was not half-caste (only Dr. No, half Chinese and an obvious if emaciated descendant of Fu Manchu, rose above what Somerset Maugham would have called "The Yellow Streak" in Ian Fleming's work), but not much above, and while wily enough he obviously was created simply to be outwitted by Bond, as Fu Manchu's only purpose seemed to be as a foil to the ultimately victorious Englishman, Sir Denis Nayland Smith.

If one smells a giant rat from Sumatra in all this, one is meant to, for the Mysterious East has been a staple of the entertainment industry ever since hack writers took the sounds but not the sense from Thomas De Quincey's *Confessions of an English Opium Eater* after they appeared in the *London Magazine* in 1822. The rise of the "penny dreadful" to its peak in the 1840's and the success of Wilkie Collins' *The Moonstone* in 1868 were two stages on the path toward a persistent English, and later American, fascination with the Orient, a fascination both pejorative in content — as when Egyptians were dubbed Wogs, for "Westernized Oriental Gentlemen" — and at times highly respectful.

The persistent tone of Western popular interest in the Orient has been one of high ambiguity coupled with creative drift.

The drift has been toward greater respect joined with greater fear, and the appearance of the Sinister Oriental as hero or villain in Western thriller and detective/spy fiction has usually coincided with a period in which China, or latterly Japan, played a role in world affairs. Orientals were sinister because they were inscrutable (or, as the music halls had it, they couldn't get pregnant in the normal way), strange, far away, incredibly hard-working, "able to live off the smell of a greasy rag," and addicted to "half-hatched eggs" — or so the *Westminster Review* told its readers in 1866.

The notion of an inexplicable East bites more deeply than this, however, for the journals of early explorers and voyagers reported upon "strange and wondrous" sights as early as Marco Polo's visit to the Court of the Great Khan. If Magellan's chronicler, Pigafetta, could assert that within the contemporary Philippines there was a race of men with ears so large they curled them under as pillows, then the Victorians might equally well insist that the Chinese, Japanese, Malays and others engaged in incredible sexual practices, devoured birds' nests and were persistently hung over from ubiquitous opium dens. The great Kraken, the gigantic octopus creature which legend placed in the South China Sea (later to transfer it to the Sargasso), was shown with hooded eye and beak, the very caricature of an Oriental. Bamboo splinters under the fingernails, the Chinese water torture, child brides, bound feet — all were indications of a culture that knew better than the West how to construct the exquisite Torture Garden of pornography. Sherlock Holmes might appear to make opium respectable, but even he could not bring himself to reveal the tail of that Giant Rat of Sumatra.

In general, the Sinister Oriental was Far Eastern, not South Asian. There was no lack of thriller literature about India, rampant with *thuggee*, widows' funeral pyres, cobras in the bedcovers, rampaging elephants and cursed jewels. But the Indian never took on the same sinister connotations as did, in particular, the Chinese, and no Indian series figure was sustained in the literature until the clever but hardly sinister Inspector Ghote leapt full-blown from the imagination of H.R.F. Keating in 1964. Those who have read Collins know that he admired the Indians of *The Moonstone* and reserved his harshest judgments for such figures as Godfrey Ablewhite and the retired Anglo-Indian officer John Herncastle. Perhaps the fact that the British came to know the Indians well, as they became part of the empire, removed some of the sense of distance on which mystery thrives. Since Americans had little interest in South Asia, few American thrillers appeared with Indian settings.

East and Southeast Asia were another matter. With the evolution of the energetic and respectable "boys' magazines" out of the penny dreadfuls, Asians became simpler if no less villainous. By the 1870's the "penny packets of poison," as one critic called them, had rolled out the entire inventory of horrors: rape, bloodsucking, burial alive, cannibalism, lingering and exquisite torture, the dissection alive of a victim's face. This was too strong for the boys, so S.O. Beeton's *Boy's Own Magazine* (1855–66) and the Religious Tract Society's *Boy's Own Paper* (1879–1967) set a higher tone. Nonetheless, the Chinese continued to be wily (although deserving respect as well as some tolerant amusement), and in *Boys of England* one read of the heroic battles of upright traders who sailed home from Canton with their costly cargo only to be attacked by "Malay scum . . . Chinese, Japanese, Javans, Papuans, Pintadoes, Mes-

tizoes," and even a few Spaniards and Portuguese. All this was simply a romanticizing of the very real threat posed by sea Dayaks and pirates out of Borneo. So "Christian" a writer as Charles Kingsley, author of the treacly *Water Babies,* could write: "You Malays and Dayaks of Sarawak, you . . . are the enemies of Christ . . . you are beasts, all the more dangerous, because you have a semi-human cunning . . . I will blast you out with grape and rockets."

Four contributions to popular fiction probably did more than all others to promote the notion of the Sinister Oriental. The first of these, oddly, did not depict the Oriental as sinister so much as sinuously enterprising and wickedly clever: E. Harcourt Burrage's Chinese hero, Ching Ching, of the "celestial charm." He too had his own boy's journal, *Ching Ching's Own* (1888–93), and one of the books that were spun off from the magazine, *Daring Ching Ching*, won a substantial readership among adults in England.

The second, and far most important, contribution to the creation of the Sinister Oriental was Sax Rohmer's Dr. Fu Manchu, who sprang into diabolical life during the period when the Yellow Peril was perceived to be at its most insidious. Racism was at its most virulent just before, during and immediately after World War I, when so benign a Canadian writer as Agnes

Laut could warn her fellow countrymen against the "dangers within, not without," of letting down the barriers to "too many Jappy-Chappies, Chinks, and Little Brown Brothers." Rohmer, who had been doing research on the Chinese District of London, created his Devil Doctor to meet a public mood and sent him into the world in *The Mystery of Dr. Fu Manchu* in 1913. Fu Manchu moved onto the silver screen in 1923. (For a full account of Rohmer's crea-tion, see *Master of Villainy: A Biography of Sax Rohmer* by Cay Van Ash and Elizabeth Sax Rohmer.)

A third major contribution to the image of the clever Chinese was Earl Derr Biggers' Charlie Chan, the member of the Honolulu Police Department who works on the side of Good and who coins quasi-Confucian (and sometimes very funny) aphorisms. It may be argued that Chan was an antidote to the notion of the Sinister Oriental, and that *The House Without a Key*, which appeared in 1925, was the first of a series of replies to the yellow-robed evil Doctor, but the Chan of the books — as distinct from the amusing Chan of the films — often casts a chilling shadow over his ratiocinations.

Finally, who can forget the first issue of *Detective Comics*, which appeared early in 1937 and for one thin dime gave the reader a healthy case of the shakes? A malevolent Chinese peered out from the cover, and inside the story of "The Claws of the Red Dragon," by Maj. Malcolm Wheeler-Nicholson and Tom Hickey, carried one into San Francisco's Chinatown and face to face with the Yellow Menace. By 1939 the Orientals of comic book thrillers had taken on an increasingly Japanese look, and through the war they would supplant the Chinese — bestial, red of tooth and claw.

Today the Japanese have recovered their features, and it is once again the Chinese who present a sinister face to us. But we are somewhat more sophisticated now, and certainly more ambivalent in our views of Asian societies. To the true mystery fan, no one did more to correct the balance than the Dutch diplomat and Sinologist Robert van Gulik, who began to reconstruct from actual records the cases of his fictional seventh-century Judge Jen-Djieh Dee. Between *Three Murder Cases Solved by Judge Dee*, first published in Tokyo in 1949, and *Willow Pattern*, published in 1965 (other, less interesting books were to follow), van Gulik provided a chilling, sometimes truly sinister, historically accurate and balanced picture of Chinese justice at work. *The Manchurian Candidate* may have kept the stereotype alive; Judge Dee freed the aficionados.

Robin W. Winks reviews mysteries for The New Republic.

SINISTER MR. RIGHTS

Not all Orientals plead at the bar sinister. Harold Gray, the creator of Little Orphan Annie, influenced by Charles Dickens and Joseph Conrad, introduced the Orient through the Asp — a slim, black-clothed, Far Eastern protector of capitalism, i.e., of Daddy Warbucks — and through Punjab, a turbaned South Asian who frequently appeared to rescue Annie from the sinister West. In the late 1930's Hugh Wiley introduced to *Collier's* magazine a Chinese detective, James Lee Wong, who soon moved on to the silver screen in the person of Boris Karloff and later Keye Luke (who had been Charlie Chan). At the same time, John P. Marquand created an immaculate detective, Mr. I.O. Moto, who appeared in five books within seven years. In 1957 Marquand unsuccessfully revived him for the book *Stopover: Tokyo*. And beginning in 1949 Dutch diplomat Robert van Gulik introduced Western readers to Judge Jen-Djieh Dee, modeled on a seventh-century Chinese magistrate. Wise and always controlled, Judge Dee would contrast sharply with the madcap Hong Kong police of William Marshall's *Yellowthread Street*, and other adventures of the 1970's, proving not only that the left hand knows not what the right does, but that the Orient can produce its Laurel and Hardy, too.

R.W.W.

HOMOSEXUALS IN THE MYSTERY
Victims or Victimizers?
Solomon Hastings

"**R**ather unhealthy" was the way Miss Climpson, one of Lord Peter Wimsey's operatives, described the relationship between two murder suspects in Dorothy L. Sayers' *Unnatural Death,* published in 1927. Such was the typical attitude toward the homosexual in early crime fiction. Obviously, it was a character trait one tried one's best to ignore.

Until recently there was a tendency to allude to homosexuality rather than to talk openly about the "taint." The gay was relegated to the red herring role, sometimes as a minor criminal and occasionally as a victim, as in Ruth Rendell's *From Doon to Death.* Gays were shown as isolated characters, and a bit quirky at that, who lived maladjustedly in a straight world. No one indicated there was any such thing as a gay subculture, not even in the large metropolitan cities.

Eventually, homosexuals were forced to come out of the crime closet — probably because the closet was so full of skeletons to begin with, there just wasn't enough room in there.

One of the first renderings of a true gay environment appeared in Edgar Box's *Death in the Fifth Position* in 1952, when Peter Cutler Sargeant II, straight press agent and amateur sleuth, to gain information, pretended an interest in Louis Giraud, a gay ballet dancer. Sargeant was permitted to go barhopping with the gay. A date, if you will.

But it took a bit more time to show homosexual crimes and characters in homosexual settings. In England they are still having a problem with it. It is curious to note that even today in the classic English-style mystery, the most liberal and sympathetic CID superintendent turns hard-nosed when a "pouf" becomes involved in a case. They compensate, sort of, in that not many really nasty homosexual villains appear. One exception: Valentine Quentin, a six-foot-four blond sadist trafficking in stolen diamonds in James Quartermain's *The Man Who Walked on Diamonds.* Hands down, he wins the-man-you-most-love-to-hate sweepstakes.

In the Sixties in America there began to appear mysteries such as Tucker Coe's *A Jade in Aries,* dealing with the gay milieu. The gay client is honestly dismayed at the murder of his lover and the police department's apathy in finding his killer. (Factually, this is still a problem to the gay community.) Emotionally, the book is sound, but it is not free of stereotyping: apparently, if we are to believe the book, all homosexuals wear brightly flowered ruffled shirts and wave their cigarettes about to a staccato Bette Davis beat (when they're not busy dangling them from incredibly limp wrists).

Dealing with the same problem of police indifference to a gay murder is Richard Hall's excellent *The Butterscotch Prince* (1975). In it, Cord McGreevy, a Manhattan schoolteacher, searches for the killer of his former lover and good friend, and moves through a well-written and honest version of the gay scene in New York.

The first American gay sleuth was Pharaoh Love, a black Manhattan cop who appeared in George Baxt's *A Queer Kind of Death* (1967), reappeared in *Swing Low, Sweet Harriet* and died under extremely odd circumstances in *Topsy and Evil*. The books are rather like a gossip column from *Women's Wear Daily*. They move about glamorous pop-society circles and are enjoyable reading as intentional High Camp.

In *Fadeout* (1970) Joseph Hansen created David Brandstetter, insurance investigator for Medallion Life in Los Angeles. Hansen himself lives in L.A., where he is one of the directors of the Homosexual Information Center. His Brandstetter is the most honestly portrayed gay in crime fiction: a middle-aged man — who happens to be a homosexual — with mundane, everyday problems. Some of his cases involve homosexuals; others do not. He develops romantic relationships, but he does not let his personal life style interfere with his work. It merely adds richness to his character in much the way any ongoing heterosexual relationship deepens anyone else's life. Written in the dry

THE HOMOSEXUAL IN CRIME

Edgar Box: *Death in the Fifth Position*
W.J. Burley: *Three-Toed Pussy*
John Evans: *Halo in Brass*
James Frazer: *A Wreath for Lords and Ladies*
Joseph Hansen: *Death Claims; Troublemaker; Pretty Boy Dead*
John Paul Hudson and Warren Wexler: *Superstar Murder?*
Allen Hunter: *Gently with the Ladies*
Meyer Levin: *Compulsion*
Elizabeth Linington: *Green Mask*
Patricia Moyes: *Season of Snows and Sins*
Ellery Queen: *The Last Woman in His Life*

BLACKMAIL POSSIBILITIES

In real life many lesbians indulge in cross-dressing, or travesty. This means they prefer to present themselves as men, and sometimes it is only after their death that their true gender is disclosed. The most widely publicized travesty was the case of Murray Hall, born Mary Anderson, a prominent politician, member of the General Committee of Tammany Hall and close friend of State Senator "Barney" Miller. She was a shrewd poker player, a good whiskey drinker, and she puffed away on large Havanas. It was only when she died, in 1901, that her true sex was revealed. Billy Smith, a top British jockey at the turn of the century, was also discovered to be a woman upon her death in Australia. Any blackmailer worth his stationery would have had a field day if he'd known the true story of either of these figures. Fictionally, cross-dressing was common in Shakespeare, then went into hiatus and was revived by Leone Hargrave's literate Gothic, *Clara Reeve*, in which a woman was raised from birth as a man in order to qualify for an inheritance forbidden to female offspring. Mystery writers in need of a good plot, please note.

S. H.

style common to all West Coast detective and private eye stories, Hansen's work has found an audience beyond the gay community. Chandler fans, Maling fans, any and all of the MacDonald (John, Ross, Gregory) fans find them satisfactory reads. Which is not too surprising, since with Hansen the homosexual in crime fiction finally achieves three-dimensionality.

Solomon Hastings divides his time between London and New York and reads mysteries in both places.

A FEW (MILLION) WORDS ABOUT MY GOOD FRIEND HOLMES

Otto Penzler

Since 1887, when *A Study in Scarlet* first appeared, there have been over 10,000 novels, short stories, parodies, burlesques, pastiches, critical studies, reviews, essays, appreciations and scholarly examinations devoted to Sherlock Holmes. Virtually all the material is important in that it refers to the world's greatest detective; however, life being short, the Holmesian collector may never be able to possess all of it. This Holmesian shopping list itemizes the 100 indispensibles. To amass them requires only three things: fabulous wealth, infinite patience and divine intervention.

1. 1887 DOYLE, ARTHUR CONAN: "A Study in Scarlet." (Contained in *Beeton's Christmas Annual.* London: Ward, Lock, $7500.) First Book Edition (London: Ward, Lock, 1888, $2000). First American edition (Philadelphia: Lippincott, 1890, $1000).

2. 1890 DOYLE, ARTHUR CONAN: "The Sign of the Four"(contained in *Lippincott's Monthly Magazine* for February 1890, London, Philadelphia, $400). Also of importance is the first book edition (London: Spencer Blackett, 1890, $400; the spine of the earliest issue has Spencer Blackett's name and the later issue has the imprint of Griffith Farran) and the first American edition (New York: Collier's Once a Week Library, 1891, $250).

3. 1892 DOYLE, ARTHUR CONAN: *The Adventures of Sherlock Holmes* (London: Newnes, $300). Also the first American edition (New York: Harper, 1892, $150). The first short-story collection.

4. 1894 DOYLE, ARTHUR CONAN: *The Memoirs of Sherlock Holmes* (London: Newnes, $200). Also first American edition (New York: Harper, 1894, $200). The English edition contains 12 tales; the American, 13.

5. 1894 BARR, ROBERT: *The Face and the Mask* (London: Hutchinson, $50). Contains "The Great Pegram Mystery" — the first parody, originally published as "Detective Stories Gone Wrong: The Adventures of Sherlaw Kombs" by Luke Sharp in *The Idler Magazine*, May 1892.

6. 1897 BANGS, JOHN KENDRICK: *The Pursuit of the House-Boat: Being Some Further Account of the Divers Doings of the Associated Shades, Under the Leadership of Sherlock Holmes, Esq.* (New York: Harper, $15). The first American book containing a Holmes parody.

7. 1901 LEHMANN, R.C.: *The Adventures of Picklock Holes* (London: Bradbury, Agnew, $75). The first Holmes parody cycle.

8. 1902 DOYLE, ARTHUR CONAN: *The Hound of the Baskervilles* (London: Newnes, $200). Also the first American edition (New York: McClure, Phillips, $100). The most famous mystery ever written.

9. 1902 TWAIN, MARK: *A Double Barrelled Detective Story* (New York: Harper, $75). A book-length satire on detective fiction, particularly Holmes.

10. 1902 HARTE, BRET: *Condensed Novels Second Series New Burlesques* (London: Chatto & Windus, $40). Also the first American edition (Boston, New York: Houghton, Mifflin, $40). Contains "The Stolen Cigar Case" about Hemlock Jones. Ellery Queen considers this the best Holmes parody.

11. 1905 DOYLE, ARTHUR CONAN: *The Return of Sherlock Holmes* (London: Newnes, $200). Also the first American edition (New York: McClure, Phillips, $75). The sixth Holmes book.

12. 1907 LEBLANC, MAURICE: *The Exploits of Arsene Lupin* (New York, London: Harper, $75). Translated from the French edition of the same year by Alexander Teixeira de Mattos. Contains "Holmlock Shears Arrives Too Late," the first of several confrontations between Holmes and France's great rogue.

13. 1909 DUNBAR, ROBIN: *The Detective Business* (Chicago: Charles H. Kerr, $75). The first book of mainly nonfiction writings about Holmes.

14. 1911 HENRY, O.: *Sixes and Sevens* (New York: Doubleday, Page, $40.) Contains "The Adventures of Shamrock Jolnes" and "The Sleuths," by America's master of the short story.

15. 1912 DOYLE, ARTHUR CONAN: *The Speckled Band: An Adventure of Sherlock Holmes* (London, New York: Samuel French, $100). (Note that the earliest state has green paper covers; later states have light brown covers.) The first published play.

16. 1912 HOLMES, SHERLOCK: *Practical Handbook of Bee Culture, with Some Observations upon the Segregation of the Queen* (Sussex: Privately printed, $1,000). The author's *magnum opus*.

17. 1913 SAXBY, JESSIE M.E.: *Joseph Bell, M.D., F.R.C.S., J.P., D.L., etc.: An Appreciation by an Old Friend* (Edinburgh and London: Oliphant, Anderson & Ferrier, $60). The first book about the man who was Doyle's professor in medical school.

18. 1913 DOYLE, ARTHUR CONAN: *Sherlock Holmes: The Adventure of the Dying Detective* (New York: Collier, $400). The only Sherlock Holmes story to be printed separately before appearing in a collection.

19. 1915 DOYLE, ARTHUR CONAN: *The Valley of Fear* (London: Smith, Elder, $25). Also the first American edition (New York: Doran, $40). The last Holmes novel, called the best of the four by John Dickson Carr.

20. 1917 DOYLE, ARTHUR CONAN: *His Last Bow* (London: Murray, $50). Also the first American edition (New York: Doran, $30).

21. 1918 THIERRY, JAMES FRANCIS: *The Adventure of the Eleven Cuff Buttons* (New York: Neale, $65). An early book-length parody.

22. 1920 STARRETT, VINCENT: *The Unique Hamlet: A Hitherto Unchronicled Adventure of Mr. Sherlock Holmes* (Chicago: Privately printed, $300). A rare book, issued in a very limited edition of indeterminate number. Although Starrett said 200, and De Waal 33, it is probably 110, of which 100 have the imprint of Walter H. Hill and 10 of Starrett. The best Holmes pastiche.

23. 1920 CLOUSTON, J. STORER: *Carrington's Cases* (Edinburgh: Blackwood, $150). Contains "The Truthful Lady," a parody about Watson.

24. 1922 GILLETTE, WILLIAM: *Sherlock Holmes: A Drama in Four Acts* (London, New York: Samuel French,

$50). Although Arthur Conan Doyle is credited with coauthorship, he had nothing to do with writing the play. The best Holmes play.

25. 1924 LUCAS, E.V. (ed.): *The Book of the Queen's Doll's House Library*, 2 vols. (London: Methuen, $125). Contains "How Watson Learned the Trick," a parody by Arthur Conan Doyle. Limited to 1,500 copies.

26. 1924 DOYLE, ARTHUR CONAN: *Memories and Adventures* (London: Hodder & Stoughton, $50). Contains "The Adventure of the Two Collaborators" by James M. Barrie. In the opinion of Doyle, it is the best of the many burlesques of Holmes.

27. 1927 DOYLE, ARTHUR CONAN: *The Case-Book of Sherlock Holmes* (London:Murray, $40). Also the first American edition (New York: Doran, $25). Last book in the Canon.

28. 1928 KNOX, RONALD A.: *Essays in Satire* (London: Sheed & Ward, $20). Contains "Studies in the Literature of Sherlock Holmes," regarded as the first essay of "higher criticism."

29. 1929 FULLER, WILLIAM O.: *A Night with Sherlock Holmes* (Cambridge, Mass.: Privately printed, $175). A handsomely printed pastiche, limited to 200 copies.

30. 1929 CHRISTIE, AGATHA: *Partners in Crime* (London: Collins, $50). Also the first American edition (New York: Dodd, Mead, $20). Contains "The Case of the Missing Lady," a parody by the first lady of crime.

31. 1930 MORLEY, CHRISTOPHER (ed.): *The Complete Sherlock Holmes*, 2 vols. (New York: Doubleday, Doran, $20). Contains "In Memoriam: Sherlock Holmes," the first printing of the most widely published essay on Holmes. The first complete American edition of the Canon.

32. 1931 ROBERTS, S.C.: *Doctor Watson: Prolegomena to the Study of a Biographical Problem* (London: Faber & Faber, $20). The standard life of Watson.

33. 1932 BLAKENEY, T.S.: *Sherlock Holmes: Fact or Fiction?* (London: Murray, $65). The first book-length biography of Holmes.

34. 1932 BELL, H.W.: *Sherlock Holmes and Dr. Watson: The Chronology of Their Adventures* (London: Constable, $75). The first attempt to date all of Holmes' adventures, recorded and unrecorded. 500 copies.

35. 1933 STARRETT, VINCENT: *The Private Life of Sherlock Holmes* (New York: Macmillan, $65). The standard biography of Holmes.

36. 1934 BELL, H.W. (ed.): *Baker Street Studies* (London: Constable, $65). The first critical anthology devoted to Holmes.

37. 1934 SMITH, HARRY B.: *How Sherlock Holmes Solved the Mystery of Edwin Drood* (Glen Rock, Pa.: Walter Klinefelter, $200). A rare pastiche, limited to 33 copies.

38. 1934 CLENDENING, LOGAN: *The Case of the Missing Patriarchs* (Ysleta, Tex: Privately printed for Edwin B. Hill, $75). With a note by Vincent Starrett. Posthumous adventure of Holmes, limited to 30 copies.

39. 1934 DOYLE, ARTHUR CONAN: *The Field Bazaar* (London: Athenaeum Press, $150). Holmes parody written by Doyle in 1896. 100 copies.

40. 1938 MORLEY, FRANK V.: *A Sherlock Holmes Cross-Word Puzzle* (New York: Privately printed, $250). Often credited to Christopher Morley. The original test for membership in the Baker Street Irregulars. Rare; limited to 38 copies.

41. 1938 SMITH, EDGAR W.: *Appointment in Baker Street* (Maplewood, N.J.: Pamphlet House, $40). Profiles of everyone who had dealings with Holmes. Limited to 250 copies.

42. 1938 HONCE, CHARLES: *A Sherlock Holmes Birthday* (New York: Privately printed, $85). Reminiscences of the

1937 Semicentennial. The first of his Christmas books. 100 copies.

43. 1938 KLINEFELTER, WALTER: *Ex Libris A. Conan Doyle Sherlock Holmes* (Chicago: Black Cat Press, $60). Sherlockian essays. 250 copies.

44. 1940 STARRETT, VINCENT (ed.): *221B: Studies in Sherlock Holmes* (New York: Macmillan, $25). The first American anthology of essays.

45. 1940 SMITH, EDGAR W.: *Baker Street and Beyond* (Maplewood, N.J.: Pamphlet House, $65). The first Sherlockian gazetteer. 300 copies ($35), the first 100 in deluxe binding.

46. 1940 BOUCHER, ANTHONY: *The Case of the Baker Street Irregulars* (New York: Simon & Schuster, $25). A mystery novel involving many Sherlockians.

47. 1941 HEARD, H.F.: *A Taste for Honey* (New York: Vanguard, $25). A detective novel about "Mr. Mycroft," a pseudonymous, reclusive Holmes.

48. 1941 MCKEE, WILBUR K.: *Sherlock Holmes Is Mr. Pickwick* (Brattleboro, Vt.: Privately printed, $50). A whimsical pamphlet. Limited to 300 copies.

49. 1941 WILDE, PERCIVAL: *Design for Murder* (New York: Random House, $30). A detective novel with Sherlockian overtones.

50. 1943 OFFICER, HARVEY: *A Baker Street Song Book* (Maplewood, N.J.: Pamphlet House, $50).

51. 1944 QUEEN, ELLERY (ed.): *The Misadventures of Sherlock Holmes* (Boston: Little, Brown, $100). The best anthology of parodies and pastiches. A special edition of 125 copies was distributed at the 1944 BSI dinner.

52. 1944 SMITH, EDGAR W. (ed.): *Profile by Gaslight* (New York: Simon & Schuster, $25). A large collection about Holmes. A special edition of approximately 125 copies was distributed at the BSI dinner in 1944 ($100).

53. 1945 ROBERTS, S.C.: *The Strange Case of the Megatherium Thefts* (Cambridge: Privately printed, $125). A flavorful pastiche. Limited to 125 copies.

54. 1945 SMITH, EDGAR W.: *Baker Street Inventory* (Summit, N.J.: Pamphlet House, $50). The first bibliography of the Canon and the writings about the writings. A preliminary pamphlet appeared in 1944. Limited to 300 copies.

55. 1945 DERLETH: *"In Re: Sherlock Holmes": The Adventures of Solar Pons* (Sauk City, Wis.: Mycroft & Moran, $50). The first Pons book, with an introduction by Vincent Starrett.

56. 1946 YUHASOVA, HELENE: *A Lauriston Garden of Verses* (Summit, N.J.: Pamphlet House, $40). Attributed to Edgar W. Smith. 250 copies.

57. 1946–49 SMITH, EDGAR W. (ed.): *The Baker Street Journal*. The official publication of the Baker Street Irregulars; 13 issues were published ($130).

58. 1947 CUTTER, ROBERT A. (ed.): *Sherlockian Studies* (Jackson Heights, N.Y.: Baker Street Press, $40). Seven essays, sponsored by The Three Students of Long Island. 200 copies.

59. 1947 WILLIAMSON, J.N., and H.B. WILLIAMS (eds.): *Illustrious Client's Case-Book* (Indianapolis, Ind.: The Illustrious Clients, $40).

60. 1947 KEDDIE, JAMES, JR. (ed.) *The Second Cab* (Boston: Privately printed, $40). Essays, ephemera by The Speckled Band of Boston. 300 copies.

61. 1947 CHRIST, JAY FINLAY: *An Irregular Guide to Sherlock Holmes of Baker Street* (New York: Argus Books. Summit, N.J.: Pamphlet House, $40). A concordance.

62. 1948 BAYER, ROBERT JOHN: *Some Notes on a Meeting at Chisam* (Chicago: Camden House, $75). Father Brown and Holmes. Limited to 60 copies.

63. 1949 CARR, JOHN DICKSON: *The Life of Sir Arthur Conan Doyle* (New York: Harper, $15). The standard life of Watson's agent.

64. 1949 GRAZEBROOK, O.F.: *Studies in Sher-*

lock Holmes, 7 vols. (London: Privately printed, $100).

65. 1950 SMITH, EDGAR W.: *A Baker Street Quartette* (New York: The Baker Street Irregulars, $40). Four Sherlockian tales in verse. 221 copies.

66. 1950–52 DOYLE, ARTHUR CONAN: *Sherlock Holmes,* 8 vols. (New York: Limited Editions Club, $300). The ultimate edition of the Canon, edited by Edgar W. Smith and profusely illustrated. Limited to 1,500 sets.

67. 1951 BREND, GAVIN: *My Dear Holmes* (London: Allen & Unwin, $15).

68. 1951– SMITH, EDGAR W. (followed by JULIAN WOLFF, M.D.) (ed.): *The Baker Street Journal (New Series).* The quarterly publication of the Baker Street Irregulars ($450).

69. 1952– DONEGALL, MARQUESS OF (ed.): *The Sherlock Holmes Journal.* Semiannual publication of the Sherlock Holmes Society of London ($350).

70. 1952 PETERSON, ROBERT STORM, and TAGE LA COUR: *Tobacco Talk in Baker Street* (New York: Baker Street Irregulars, $40). Contains an essay and a burlesque.

71. 1952 WOLFF, JULIAN, M.D.: *The Sherlockian Atlas* (New York: Privately printed, $35). 13 detailed maps of Holmes' world. 400 copies.

72. 1953 SMITH, EDGAR W.: *The Napoleon of Crime* (Summit, N.J.: Pamphlet House, $35). The standard life of Professor Moriarty. Limited to 221 copies.

73. 1953 ZEISLER, ERNEST BLOOMFIELD: *Baker Street Chronology* (Chicago: Alexander J. Isaacs, $100). A new dating of Holmes' adventures. Limited to 200 copies.

74. 1953–71 SIMPSON, A. CARSON: *Simpson's Sherlockian Studies,* 9 vols. (Philadelphia: Privately printed, $100). The first 8 pamphlets limited to 221 copies; the last was reproduced from the unpublished manuscript in 1971.

75. 1954 MONTGOMERY, JAMES: *A Study in Pictures* (Philadelphia: Privately printed, $65). The first guide to the illustrators of Holmes. The most elaborate of the author's 6 Christmas annuals (1950–55). 300 copies.

76. 1954 DOYLE, ADRIAN CONAN, and JOHN DICKSON CARR: *The Exploits of Sherlock Holmes* (New York: Random House, $25). 12 pastiches by the agent's son and a brilliant writer.

77. 1955 GILLETTE, WILLIAM: *The Painful Predicament of Sherlock Holmes: A Fantasy in One Act* (Chicago: Ben Abranson, $20). Introduction by Vincent Starrett. Gillette's *other* Sherlock Holmes play, first performed in 1905. 500 copies.

78. 1955 CLARKE, RICHARD W. (ed.): *The Best of the Pips* (New York: The Five Orange Pips of Westchester County, $30). Called "the most erudite" essays By Edgar W. Smith.

79. 1955 MITCHELL, GLADYS: *Watson's Choice* (London: Michael Joseph, $35). A novel with Sherlockian flavorings.

80. 1957 WOLFF, JULIAN, M.D.: *A Ramble in Bohemia* (New York: U.N. Philatelic Chronicle [*sic*], $45). A report on the commemorative Holmes stamp issued by the Republic of Bohemia in 1988. A stamp accompanies some copies of the pamphlet.

81. 1957 WARRACK, GUY: *Sherlock Holmes and Music* (London: Faber & Faber, $15). The definitive guide to Holmes's life as a musician.

82. 1958 DOYLE, ARTHUR CONAN: *The Crown Diamond: An Evening with Sherlock Holmes. A Play in One Act* (New York: Privately printed, $100). A very short play written just after the turn of the century and published for the first time. With an introduction by Edgar W. Smith. 59 copies.

83. 1958 HARRISON, MICHAEL: *In the Footsteps of Sherlock Holmes* (London: Cassell, $15). An authoritative geographical examination of Holmes' world.

84. 1958 TITUS, EVE: *Basil of Baker Street* (New York: Whittlesey House, $15). The first of the best series of

juveniles for Sherlockians; illustrated by Paul Galdone.

85. 1959 STARR, H.W. (ed.): *Leaves from the Copper Beeches* (Narberth, Pa.: The Sons of the Copper Beeches, $30). Mostly humorous essays. 500 copies.

86. 1959 HOLROYD, JAMES EDWARD: *Baker Street By-Ways* (London: Allen & Unwin, $15). A commentary by the chairman of the Sherlock Holmes Society of London.

87. 1962 BARING-GOULD, WILLIAM S.: *Sherlock Holmes of Baker Street* (New York: Clarkson N. Potter, $15). The most authoritative life of Holmes.

88. 1962 SMITH, EDGAR W.: *Sherlock Holmes: The Writings of John H. Watson, M.D.* (Morristown, N.J.: Baker Street Irregulars, $40). A comprehensive bibliography of Holmes' adventures.

89. 1963 KLINEFELTER, WALTER: *Sherlock Holmes in Portrait and Profile* (Syracuse University Press, $10). Introduction by Vincent Starrett. The definitive study of illustrations.

90. 1964 KAHN, WILLIAM B.: *An Adventure of Oilock Combs: The Succored Beauty* (San Francisco: The Beaune Press, $30). A parody originally published in the October 1905 issue of *The Smart Set Magazine*. The first of the Christmas keepsakes of Dean and Shirley Dickensheet. 222 copies.

91. 1964 KLINEFELTER, WALTER: *A Packet of Sherlockian Bookplates* (Nappanee, Ind.: Privately printed, $75). A compendium of the bookplates of eminent Sherlockians, extensively illustrated in color. 150 copies.

92. 1966 FISH, ROBERT L.: *The Incredible Schlock Homes* (New York: Simon & Schuster, $25). The funniest series of Sherlockian parody-pastiches.

93. 1966 QUEEN, ELLERY: *A Study in Terror* (New York: Lancer, $10). Also the first English edition, and the first in hardcover, retitled *Sherlock Holmes Versus Jack the Ripper* (London: Gol-

lancz, 1967). A novelization of the film, with added material, which records Holmes' encounter with The Harlot Killer.

94. 1967 BARING-GOULD, WILLIAM S.: *The Annotated Sherlock Holmes*, 2 vols. (New York: Clarkson N. Potter, $45). The definitive edition of the Canon, heavily illustrated and annotated by a preeminent scholar.

95. 1968 WINCOR, RICHARD: *Sherlock Holmes in Tibet* (New York: Weybright & Talley, 50¢). Noteworthy as probably the worst book about Holmes.

96. 1974 MEYER, NICHOLAS: *The Seven-Percent Solution* (New York: Dutton, $10). The book largely responsible for a new Sherlockian boom.

97. 1974 GARDNER, JOHN: *The Return of Moriarty* (London: Weidenfeld & Nicholson, $10). The most literate, enthralling and atmospheric pastiche in half a century.

98. 1974 DE WAAL, RONALD BURT: *The World Bibliography of Sherlock Holmes and Dr. Watson* (Boston: New York Graphic Society, $50). A monumental reference book and a prodigious achievement, listing 6,221 items relating to Holmes.

99. 1976 TODD, PETER: *The Adventures of Herlock Sholmes* (New York: The Mysterious Press). With an introduction by Philip Jose Farmer. Contains 18 parodies by Charles Hamilton under the Todd pseudonym. Published orginally in a British periodical in 1915–16, they are the first of the longest Holmes parody cycle (100 stories). Limited to 1250 copies ($10), 250 deluxe ($20).

100. (IN PREPARATION) HOLMES, SHERLOCK: *The Whole Art of Detection*. In preparation for more than fifty years; and will contain everything learned in the preceding fifty years. Priceless.

Otto Penzler wrote The Private Lives of Private Eyes, Spies, Crimefighters and Other Good Guys.

GOOD LITTLE GIRLS AND BOYS

Phyllis A. Whitney

Oh, no! I would never buy a mystery for my granddaughter. I want to give her something *worthwhile*."

This unenlightened remark is often heard by booksellers, and it is fortunate that both booksellers and librarians know better and provide the mystery titles their readers enjoy. And from which (surprise!) they can learn so much.

The mystery for young people should never be confused with the blood-and-violence school, yet it is an interesting comment on writers of juvenile mysteries that they can compete with that strong stuff on television. We know something that Hitchcock learned long ago: it isn't the flying bullets, the number of cars that crash together, the wild chases over fences that build suspense; true suspense is made up of other ingredients.

Suspense is the fear of something unknown just around the corner — the fear of something dreadful about to happen to someone you like, or the fear that something hoped-for won't happen. In either case there is the anticipation of something deliciously scary. Only the danger that *might* happen can really frighten. When this threat is met and defeated at the end of the story, the reader is satisfied. Whereas all that gun-to-gun tackling at the end of the television play gives us no warm sense of satisfaction.

The fear, of course, and the anticipation must be directly connected with characters we care about. Straw men won't do it The writer of juvenile mysteries is particularly skilled in reaching out to the readers and pulling in their sympathy for the story's main character. It doesn't really matter whether the character is a girl or a boy. In my own books the viewpoint character (whether first or third person) is always a girl. Yet these days I receive as many fan letters from boys as I do from girls. It is the characters, the story, the *suspense* that counts. And perhaps mystery writers have learned to build the last two items better than has the "straight" novelist.

With young readers there is another ingredient as important as suspense. It is something I look for even before I discover what the actual mystery is going to be. I want some human situation that can carry a special meaning for my readers and that will perhaps leave them with something to think about — even to use in their own lives.

To give an example: *Secret of the Stone Face* is about a girl whose father has died and who is terribly afraid that her mother is going to remarry. The girl is prejudiced from the beginning against the man who will be her stepfather. Her prejudice is human and natural, yet if she is not to be unhappy and to cause her mother great unhappiness, she must learn in the course of the story that such prejudice is unfair and unfounded. So, as I build a story, the mystery and the human problem become intertwined, and my young heroine, as she solves the mystery, learns something valuable about life — and about herself.

No mystery plot descends from the sky full-blown and complete. It is something built a bit at a time, idea by idea, through months of work before the actual writing begins. It grows from the story background and from the problems and characters of the people in the book. There must be youthful opposition to the purpose that drives a young heroine. Even though the stepfather problem in *Secret of the Stone Face* concerns adults, it is the young people in the story who must be of the greatest importance. Villains are necessary, and they can be either children or adults, or sometimes both, but it is the young people *onstage* who must carry the story.

One rule to hold to through all writing for children: Never put the main character into dangerous situations that will set a bad example for the reader. Characters may do foolish things at times, or be led by others into difficult situations, but they must not take high risks. They must not set off single-handedly to capture a dangerous criminal.

Settings are always important, whether one is writing for adults or for young people. Perhaps because I have lived in so many places,

I have no one locale that I use. I must find a new setting for every story. If I can give a glimpse of another country, or of a part of that country, that will take my readers there in their imagination, this is something worthwhile. Still, a background should never be allowed to remain a static painted scene, like an old-fashioned stage setting. The background is not only something the characters move about in; it affects them and affects the story. One of the things I most enjoy about using new settings is the way in which they furnish unexpected story action and help to mold and change my main character.

That is something else that must happen in a good story of any kind. The main character must change, must learn and grow in the course of the story. A character who stands still never satisfies the reader. We all want to become partisan as we read. We want the character to win, and in order to win there is always some growing to be done.

We must be wary, however, of preaching. No soapboxes! Let the character learn through the action of the story and through interplay with other characters — and never because the author steps in and gives a lecture.

Most important, if the "worthwhile" things are to be accomplished, we must never forget that it is all for fun. If we forget that we are first of all entertainers, we will never make our readers listen and pay attention to what we have to say.

I had a letter recently from a girl in sixth grade in Nazareth, Pennsylvania. In her postscript she says:

"When I feel mad your books get it all away."

That is the nicest thing that has ever been said to me, and I think it speaks for the entire mystery field. The grandmother whom I quoted at the start of this piece should change her approach. When she goes into a bookstore, she must learn to ask the clerk: "What do you have in a good mystery for children?"

Phyllis A. Whitney is equally well known for her adult suspense novels and her mysteries for young people, which have won her two Edgars. Her Writing Juvenile Stories and Novels *is a standard text in the field.*

ENCYCLOPEDIA BROWN

The most popular children's mysteries concern a young man (he's about ten years old) named Encyclopedia Brown. The stories are by Donald Sobel, who has followed the format of the old-time *Minute Mysteries* in creating them.

Master Brown runs his own detective agency, and on tricky cases he consults with his father, a police officer.

The exploits of Brown are so appealing to children (Mr. Sobel has become the Judy Blume of mysterydom) that there is now an Encyclopedia Brown Book Club.

It would be a mistake, however, to assume Brown was the first boy detective. Let's not forget Mark Twain's Tom Sawyer or Ellery Queen's Djuna, who took on seven of Queen's own cases.

ARE GIRLS MORE INHERENTLY EVIL THAN BOYS?

Arnold Madison

Well, of course girls *are* more inherently evil than boys. No knowledgeable person really doubts that today. The real question is why.

Perhaps we ought to go back to the primal state and consider nature. We all know it's the female black widow spider that should be avoided unless one wishes to court illness and possible death. And what about those crepe-paper beehives where a queen bee is carefully bred and faces a royal fight to the death upon emerging from her birth cell? The victor rules the world of the bee and relegates all males to the status of slaves. Part of the answer as to why girls are more evil than boys may be that nature has provided a predilection for evil in the female of the species.

There is also the matter of historical conditioning. Various eras and ages have provided numerous heroes for the average citizen to admire. The stories about young girls' bravery, however, are the most thrilling. Generally, time reveals that the male heroes had feet of clay. But Joan of Arc? Would anyone dare hint that she was not the epitome of heroism? While the boy king was cowering in his chambers, Joan was on the battlefield, leading the fight against the enemy armies.

And of the millions of people who tragically died under Hitler's maniacal reign, who most personified the terrible suffering and cruelty inflicted upon those human beings?

Anne Frank. Her diary touched the heart of anyone who read it.

At first, these examples may seem to be proving that girls are not more evil than boys. But consider why these accounts affect us so deeply. Who do we have among the brave young males? A boy who stuck his finger in a dike and prevented a flood. And that story has sexual connotations. The reason heroines move us emotionally much more than heroes is that most people view girls as pure and far removed from evil. Boys seem more adept at fighting an enemy because we see them as bad themselves, so the battle is more evenly matched.

Even old bearded Plato decided: "A boy is, of all wild beasts, the most difficult to manage." And there is the old English proverb which declares: "One boy is more trouble than a dozen girls." A boy, after all, is puppy dogs' tails. Ah, but girls! They are sugar and spice and all things nice — or so the legend goes. This misconception is very encouraging to Evil.

Evil is a tangible thing. Those gifted persons who can sense another person's aura also have the ability to spot Evil lurking within another individual. Unfortunately, only a select few possess that talent. The rest of us often fail to spot Evil, which knows its best ally is a good disguise. What better cloak for Evil than to wrap about itself the external appearance of a girl?

The innocent, guileless smile. The slight

whimpering voice announcing: "I'll always be Daddy's little girl." The feigned shock when something unpleasant occurs. Now *that's* a disguise. And, like any criminal suspect, Evil has sought and found the perfect red herring. When Evil commits its act, the investigator's attention turns to the male and Evil is left free to create even more damage.

There is another reason a girl is the perfect haven for Evil: society. From an early age girls have learned how to manipulate those around them. They know the performance destined to sway their fans. This makes it easy for Evil to emerge as Insincerity.

Also, from the moment of birth, a girl is treated much like the queen bee of the hive. Her every want is satisfied. Parents try to wrap

---

MYSTERY KIDS

Marjorie Carelton: *The Night of the Good Children*
Anne Chamberlin: *The Tall Dark Man*
Freeman Wills Crofts: *Young Robin Brand, Detective*
Thom Demijohn: *Black Alice*
Thomas B. Dewey: *A Sad Song Singing*
Fielden Farrington: *A Little Game*
Roy Fuller: *With My Little Eye*
Michael Innes: *The Case of the Journeying Boy*
Elizabeth Linington: *No Evil Angel*
Arthur Lyons: *All God's Children*
Ross Macdonald: *The Far Side of the Dollar; The Underground Man*
Quentin Patrick: *A Boy's Will*
Hugh Pentecost: *The Day the Children Vanished*
Ellis Peters: *Death and the Joyful Woman; Flight of a Witch*
Evelyn Piper: *Bunny Lake Is Missing*
Jonathan Stagge: *The Yellow Taxi*
Josephine Tey: *The Franchise Affair*
Hillary Waugh: *The Young Prey*

---

their daughters in a cottony cocoon, protecting them from reality and any unpleasantness. But boys — well, boys have to grow up tough. They're going to know all the sinful things in life, so we might as well harden them as quickly as possible. Coddled and cuddled throughout her early years, a girl matures with every blow softened and every whim granted.

What a receptive home for Evil! This type personality makes it so easy for Evil to assume the guise of Greed. If everyone caters to a child and showers her with gifts, Greed is excited and motivated to seek even more. Greed knows no bounds, but even humans reach a point when they say no to a girl. Now Greed is frustrated and becomes angry. Psychologically, the function of anger or rage is to destroy frustration. If the rage becomes great enough, Evil is transformed into Murder. For someone who has always had every wish fulfilled, the death of a hated individual is simply one more desire — like that for another piece of candy — to be satisfied.

Naturally, eight-year-old Rhoda Penmark in *The Bad Seed* murdered Claude Daigle. After all, he had the penmanship medal that she wanted. And what did Bonnie's big blue eyes reveal in *The Godsend*? Only that what Bonnie desired, Bonnie got, whether it be the death of a baby or a boy's drowning or acceptance by a mother who knew full well that Evil inhabited her daughter's body. And consider Carrie White, the girl who everyone would have voted "the least likely to succeed." Carrie became the queen of Ewen Consolidated High School's prom — a queen who was to wreck more destruction than Lady Macbeth. The school dance literally ended in a blood bath and fiery holocaust: the king was dead; long live the queen.

Yes, fiction is truly a mirror of life. There are those of us who know that Evil finds a girl to be a safe harbor and a base of operations. But what do we do? What *can* we do?

Perhaps this is merely one more accomplishment of Evil.

Arnold Madison is the author of Drugs and You *(1971) which was nominated as one of the best books of the year for children by the* New York Times.

INDEX

WARNING

ANY PERSON CONVEYING OR CAUSING TO BE CONVEYED TO AN INMATE ANY UNAUTHORIZED ARTICLES INCLUDING INTOXICATING LIQUORS, DRUGS, FIREARMS, EXPLOSIVES, OR ANY DEVICE WHICH MAY BE USED IN AN ESCAPE OR ATTEMPTED ESCAPE IS SUBJECT TO IMPRISONMENT FOR NOT MORE THAN FIVE (5) YEARS AND A FINE OF NOT MORE THAN $1,000 OR BOTH.

(SEC. 53-162 (a) CONN. GEN. STATS.)

D

I

N

O

P

R

Z

This book was appropriately set in Baskerville.